Penguin Education

D1324199

Half Way There
Report on the British Comprehensive School Reform
Second Edition

Caroline Benn and Brian Simon

Caroline Benn is the Information Officer for the
Campaign for Comprehensive Education and editor of the
journal *Comprehensive Education*. She is also a member
of the Inner London Education Authority and a
governor of several colleges and schools in London. As
well as being a teacher and writer of many articles and
surveys in education, Mrs Benn is a comprehensive-
school parent.

Brian Simon has taught in both secondary modern and
grammar schools and is now Professor of Education at
Leicester University. He has written and edited many
books on education, including *Intelligence Testing and the
Comprehensive School* (1953), *The Common Secondary
School* (1955), *Intelligence, Psychology and Education*
(1971) and *The Radical Tradition in Education in Britain*
(1972). He is editor of the educational journal *Forum for
the Discussion of New Trends in Education*.

Half Way There

Report on the British Comprehensive School Reform

Second Edition

Caroline Benn and Brian Simon

Penguin Books

Penguin Books Ltd, Harmondsworth,
Middlesex, England
Penguin Books, 625 Madison Avenue,
New York, New York 10022, U.S.A.
Penguin Books Australia Ltd,
Ringwood, Victoria, Australia
Penguin Books Canada Ltd,
41 Steelcase Road West,
Markham, Ontario, Canada
Penguin Books (N.Z.) Ltd,
182–190 Wairau Road,
Auckland 10, New Zealand

First published by McGraw-Hill 1970
Second edition published by Penguin Books 1972
Reprinted 1976
Copyright © Caroline Benn and Brian Simon, 1970, 1972

Made and printed in Great Britain by
Richard Clay (The Chaucer Press) Ltd
Bungay, Suffolk
Set in Monotype Plantin

Contents

Appendices

List of Tables

Acknowledgements

The authors and publishers gratefully acknowledge permission to quote
from the following publications: *London Comprehensive Schools:
A survey of sixteen schools* (1961), and *London Comprehensive Schools
1966* (1967), Inner London Education Authority; *Teaching in
Comprehensive Schools, a second report* (1967), Incorporated Association
of Assistant Masters; *Comprehensive Schools in Coventry and Elsewhere*
(1963), by G. C. Firth (Coventry Education Committee);
The Comprehensive School (revised edition, 1969), by Robin Pedley;
Comprehensive Education in England and Wales (edited by
T. G. Monks, 1968), National Foundation for Educational Research.

Glossary

AASE	Association for the Advancement of State Education
CASE	Confederation of Associations for State Education
CCTV	Closed Circuit Television
CEE	Certificate of Extended Education
CEO	Chief Education Officer
CSC	Comprehensive Schools Committee
CSE	Certificate of Secondary Education
DES	Department of Education and Science
GCE	General Certificate of Education (at O-level and A-level)
HND	Higher National Diploma
IAAM	Incorporated Association of Assistant Masters
ILEA	Inner London Education Authority
LEA	Local Education Authority
NAS	National Association of Schoolmasters
NFER	National Foundation for Educational Research
NUS	National Union of Students
NUT	National Union of Teachers
O and M	Organization and Methods
ONC	Ordinary National Certificate
OND	Ordinary National Diploma
PTA	Parent–Teacher Association
RIBA	Royal Institute of British Architects
ROSLA	Raising of the School Leaving Age
RSA	Royal Society of Arts
SCE	Scottish Certificate of Education (at O-grade and H-grade)
SEA	Socialist Education Association
STEP	Stop The Eleven Plus

Preface

Comprehensive schools are no longer an experiment; they are becoming the standard pattern of secondary education throughout Britain.

Much has already been written about them. Publications range from massive research reports to ephemeral newspaper stories, from accounts by teachers working in one corner of a school to speeches by those who believe in the principle of comprehensive secondary education but may never have studied a school at work. Those few who oppose this principle continue to argue against comprehensive schools; while those who uphold it often press for one particular development as against another.

All this discussion tends to settle into a sediment of information and opinion about comprehensive schools which may bear little relation to what they actually are and do. In addition, data piling and theoretical debate sometimes overwhelm the ordinary teacher or parent or education committee member who merely wants to find out what actual experience in the schools has shown to work or not to work.

Events also move quickly in the comprehensive reform. Sometimes decisions firmly taken are reversed; in other areas radical new departures in practices or organization are introduced with little fanfare, so that those outside the immediate region do not know about them for a long time. Nationally and locally, governments come and go. Policies replace one another with what seems like unseemly haste. For the ordinary student of the comprehensive reform just keeping up with events and decisions becomes an insuperable task.

But despite all the uncertainties and changes the comprehensive reform itself pursues its slow pace. At the time of writing there are about two thousand comprehensive schools in Britain, and their number will continue to grow throughout the next decade and beyond. Their teaching, curriculum and organization have evolved from careful trial. As a result, fundamental new features on the educational landscape have come into being, developments that will profoundly affect the structure and practice of education at all levels. This book is an attempt to chart some of these developments and to illuminate some of this landscape for those who will teach in, send their children to, or have responsibility for the comprehensive schools of the future.

The book was originally intended as a counterpart to James Conant's reports on the American comprehensive high school. While it is in some respects also a report and contains, as did Dr Conant's, recommendations on future developments, it is necessarily of a very different order. This is not only because the British system is unique to Britain, but also because the British comprehensive school in its modern sense is at the beginning of its life – not, as in some other countries, in the middle.

The main body of the book is based on information we have collected from the schools themselves. We have visited many comprehensive schools in all parts of the country, and talked to heads, staff, parents, pupils and administrators. In 1968 we surveyed the whole field of comprehensive schools then in existence in England, Scotland and Wales. The high response rate to that set of questions showed how anxious comprehensive schools were to cooperate with us in making information about comprehensive school practice more widely available. In the same year a smaller sample of schools answered a further set of questions, explaining their practices and giving their opinions in far more detail.

For the second edition we undertook two follow-up sample surveys on particular aspects of the reform in the school year 1971–2. Again we had excellent response rates and once again we are indebted to the schools for taking so much trouble to help us. In addition to the follow-up surveys, we have also visited and revisited schools and many local education authorities. An account of all these surveys and the names of the schools and colleges answering further questions are given in Appendix 1.

As an introduction to the material we have collected, Part One places the present comprehensive reform in its historical and international context, examining the reasons why secondary education for all is now such an urgent item on the agenda of almost all industrialized nations. This section ends with critiques of circulars 10/65 and 10/70 and of the national conduct of the reform. For this second edition we have added a new chapter following up developments under the Conservative government since June 1970 and assessing Labour's overall policy from 1964 to 1970.

Part Two examines the three basic patterns of reorganization that have emerged in Britain, discussing and illustrating the advantages and disadvantages of the various types of comprehensive school. Part Three looks at schools from the inside, at the essential educational tasks of lower, middle, and upper sections of the comprehensive school. It also covers liaison with primary schools and the training of teachers. In Part Four the school as a community is examined: its social organization, and the relationship of pupils, parents, staff and outside agencies in the new partnership of education that is growing out of the comprehensive movement. Part Five looks at the relationship of the comprehensive school to its own community, examining regional and geographical and other differences and discussing the relationship of the comprehensive school to its neighbourhood. A short conclusion draws the threads together and makes recommendations.

As the table of contents indicates, authorship of the separate chapters has been undertaken on an individual basis by the authors. We are both, however, in full agreement on all opinions expressed and all recommendations made throughout the book.

Our first debt is, of course, to the comprehensive schools and colleges themselves: to the head teachers, staff and parents, both those who welcomed us on visits, putting their time and schools at our disposal, and those who answered our postal questionnaires. We are very grateful to the heads and staff answering these detailed questions, especially those whose schools are listed in the Appendix. We would also like to thank the education officers who received us so kindly and helped us so generously.

Outside the schools, James Conant gave us helpful advice on problems involved in a survey of secondary schools. Guy Neave has been a constant help to us in too many ways to name, but particularly in the preparation of the questionnaires for computer analysis. To John S. Hornsby, head of the University Computer Centre at Bangor, and to Ifor Jones, the programmer, we are also in debt. Clyde Chitty gave us valuable assistance in the section on social organization, as did John Chamberlin, Michael Yeadell and Hugh Rhys in summarizing statistical material from various reports, Ian Bell and Don Lawrence in checking the tables, and Stephen Kew in checking references. Geoffrey Dixon, of the Society of Indexers, kindly undertook to prepare the first-edition index at short notice. Members of the Comprehensive Schools Committee were also very helpful, particularly Judy Smith, Helen Peston, Joan Galwey, Dee Lawrence and Jean Standing; and in the many typing tasks and the ferrying of material, Jasmine Ball and David Ball.

Lastly, to the many hundreds – and there have indeed been hundreds – of boys and girls in the comprehensive schools themselves, we owe a debt. They were always ready to give their views on the widest possible range of subjects. The best argument for the reforms, perhaps, is the quality of the help they have always been able to give us.

Part One
Background to the Reform

Chapter 1
The International Context

The question of transforming the selective system of secondary education in Britain into a single system of common, or comprehensive schools, has long been debated. Discussion has been primarily conducted in terms of British conditions and needs, and rightly so. But, as a result, it has not always been recognized that there has been a general movement towards providing a common secondary education for all in many countries of the world. Placed in an international context, recent developments in Britain appear as a special instance of a universal trend which itself is a response to a new scientific and technological revolution.

Radical reconstruction is now being envisaged in countries of Western Europe with long established systems of secondary education in which the key position is held by schools with a strong academic tradition, recruiting pupils by selective methods and in turn closely linked with universities relatively restricted in numbers. In France the *lycée*, in Germany the *gymnasium*, in England the grammar school, are schools of this kind. By contrast the two great world powers of the mid-twentieth century – the United States and the USSR – have the most comprehensive forms of secondary provision. It may be added that another leading industrialized country with a high growth rate, Japan, also has a unified secondary system established since the Second World War, when there was also an unprecedented expansion of universities and places in higher education generally.

There have been many comments on this close association between an open school system at the secondary stage and success in industrial development and growth.[1] Generally speaking, the more backward a nation economically, the more heavily committed it is to a highly segregated secondary system – as might be expected, since opportunities for employment of the educated are few. Within Western Europe, Spain and Greece, for instance, have the lowest standard of living and the most élitist systems of schooling; the same may be said for almost all Latin American countries where educational systems have followed the traditional European model.

In sum, systems of secondary schooling range from the completely 'open', or non-selective, on the one hand, to the highly competitive, or segregated, on the other. The former type of system has only one secondary school, designed to provide education for all the youth of a locality, and so usually including a wide variety of courses and facilities. The second type of system has differentiated schools providing alternative forms of education at the secondary stage. Selective systems vary a great deal, but perhaps the one constant factor is a school providing only for academic studies, geared towards the interests of the small section of pupils who look to enter the universities and professions. It might be said that Britain now stands near the half-way mark of this spectrum, half realizing the need for, but still fearing the consequences of, a radical break with tradition.

Secondary schooling in Western Europe

In the mid-nineteenth century Britain was the leading industrial power but by no means in a leading position as far as education was concerned. Recognition that other major European powers, most notably Germany, were developing efficient systems of education – whereas in England old-established universities and schools were out of touch with new knowledge, if not in a state of disorganization bordering on decay – had a good deal to do with prompting official action. But the educational reorganization undertaken in Victorian England, like other contemporary policies, represented a blending of new elements with the continuation and adaptation of ancient institutions. In the outcome, educational reform – accomplished by the winding route of a succession of royal commissions, whose major recommendations were realized by act of parliament – fell as far short of a new beginning as it fell directly in line with Victorian social philosophy. Education, seen primarily as a means of consolidating the social structure and training each class to take its appointed place in society in relation to occupational status, was planned in a series of well-defined grades.

The first step was to transform a handful of the grammar schools of old foundation, which had at one time or another gained a particular reputation, into new model 'public' schools for the upper class; though these, once brought more up to date, were left to make their way independently, as it were, rather than being subject to the control exercised over other schools. Then smaller grammar schools with old endowments were reorganized, in three grades corresponding to what had been defined as three sections of the middle class, differentiated according to occupational, or social, status. Finally, in 1870, a system of elementary instruction for the working class was organized, a virtually separate system in that it had only the most tenuous of links with secondary schools. The secondary schools took pupils quite young and so, rather than providing for the continued education of children attending elementary school, represented a parallel form of education for sections of the middle class. Far from selective at this time, these schools accorded most of their available places to any boy or girl whose parents could afford to pay the fees. Much the same was true of the universities.

The argument that the highly selective grammar school has for centuries trained the brains of the nation has, therefore, no foundation in fact. It was only after the 1944 Education Act that the grammar schools became highly selective, and this academic form of secondary education provided the only route to the universities at a time when the development of science and technology was the question of key importance. That this outmoded form persisted for so long may be traced back to the establishment of a state system of secondary education in 1902. The policy then was to reinforce the academic direction of the secondary programme – the old 'clerkly' tradition – at a time when the chief need was seen as that of remedying a shortage of clerks in the modern sense, and very little was done to open up the road to secondary schooling for greater numbers going into other professions or minor professional occupations. By the same token, technical education – developed to a high level in Germany, Switzerland and other countries – remained a neglected area in Britain, and the teaching of scientific subjects in secondary schools (both grammar and public) accorded much less importance than was its due.

In most Western European countries, where the academic school continued to predominate, it was the practice to provide for scientific and technological education in separate schools, rather than making any attempt to enlarge the traditional secondary curriculum. When, therefore, there were moves in the post-war years of the 1920s to improve and extend education, the question of widening the outlook of the secondary school and of opening up access to secondary education were linked together. At this period there was a movement in Germany to create a more unified educational system, based on the *Einheitschule*, a common school for all up to the age of twelve, followed by secondary education for all in the form of a variety of courses. But the only outcome – apart from a brief success in Thuringia where there was a revolutionary government for a short period in 1922 – was the institution of scholarships to enable a few more children to pass into the traditional secondary school. Commenting on this, I. L. Kandel, the leading comparative educationist writing in the 1930s, noted that 'a great opportunity was lost' in the face of overpowering opposition from spokesmen of the *gymnasia* and universities who forecast a disastrous fall in standards were any such change made.[2]

In France, again according to Kandel, the fact that secondary education was 'still largely a privilege, not only of a minority, but of a minority drawn from the well-to-do classes, led to widespread criticism and unrest' after the First World War – a time when the French economy was being transformed from an agricultural into a predominantly industrial economy. Here, a more radical programme for the *école unique* had been launched during the war, envisaging a complete reorganization of the educational system to eliminate class distinctions and ensure the utilization of all resources of talent. In 1924 an official commission was set up which proposed an end-on system of schools: a common primary (or elementary) school from six to twelve, lower secondary schools from twelve to sixteen, higher secondary schools from sixteen to nineteen. But, in the event, only a common primary school had been established within the state system by 1939. Even advocates of the *école unique* did not envisage a common secondary education as practicable policy at this time, in a country where elitist conceptions were deeply rooted, not only in the academic world but from the right to the left in political circles. Thus the radical politician Edouard Herriot, when Minister of Public Instruction in 1927, underlined as the main educational task 'constantly to create an elite' and avoid any tendency towards 'levelling downward'. Summarizing the position in 1933, Kandel described French secondary education as 'provided and organized to secure an elite', adding a forecast which, on the whole, proved correct:

Whatever modifications may be introduced with the fuller development of the movement for the *école unique*, they will still be based on the principle that the function of education as it advances upwards is selective . . . the future will see the organization of a system of selection on the basis of more differentiated courses.[3]

In Britain the demand in the 1920s was for 'secondary education for all', not in an academic school but in different schools providing different forms of curriculum; or, as the demand was sometimes framed, in one secondary school providing the whole range of necessary courses – a 'multilateral school'. Here, also, development on the lines of the single school was deflected, in this case by maintaining the division between elementary and secondary school systems, although allowing some movement of pupils at eleven from one to the other. This marked something of a step forward, or would have done had the promise of reorganizing the upper sections of elementary schools into full secondary schools been honoured. But all that in fact happened was that some new senior schools were built for elementary pupils aged eleven to fourteen, while other elementary schools were merely reorganized internally in the same old buildings, the senior schools or departments continuing to be financed as if they were still providing elementary education. So partial, and protracted, was the process of reorganization that by 1939 the aim of providing all children with a secondary schooling still remained well out of reach. Only with the outbreak of another world war was the longstanding demand for secondary education, as an essential stage in the education of all children, conceded in a new Education Act. This was the first major legislation since the Education Act of 1918, which had also been intended to inaugurate a new era in education; its major provisions had, however, been nullified in the 1920s, to give place to the piecemeal readjustment of the 1930s already described.

In France, during and immediately after the Second World War, there were also far-reaching plans for educational reform. Indeed, such plans were an important aspect of schemes for post-war reconstruction in all countries. Not only was there the need to rebuild shattered industries, or to make a smooth transition from an economy geared to war to one geared to new peacetime needs, but the question of re-educating those subjected to fascist indoctrination loomed very large. While from this point of view there was insistence on the humanist aspect of education, the massive scientific and technological breakthrough of the war period clearly heralded a new era when a basic general education for all to a much higher standard than had previously been envisaged would be essential. But, while there was recognition of these trends in some quarters, opposition to any radical reorganization of secondary schooling remained sufficiently strong to prevent the formulation – let alone the implementation – of adequate educational policies in the late 1940s and 1950s. Only from the late 1960s – with the advent of something of a crisis in the academic world in many countries, including student protest against irrelevant forms of education – can it be said that recognition of the need for radical reform became general throughout Europe. One sign of this in Britain was acceptance by the Conservative party of the principle of comprehensive reorganization of secondary education, but this, as we shall see, was short-lived and in any case hedged around by provisos directed to preserving a privileged area, whether in terms of selective schools within the state system or the fee paying 'public' schools for the wealthy.

With this brief outline of trends in education in Western Europe in mind, we may turn to the historical background of secondary education in the United States and the USSR which provide the chief examples of non-selective systems.

Secondary schooling in the United States

After the American revolution, with the transition from colonial to national status, education took an increasingly important place, and the system originally intended for England – the predominantly academic school under the supervision of the Church – was progressively modified.

From at least the 1820s there was growing support for the public school, open to all in the locality and under public control and, with this, for a secondary stage of schooling planned to follow on the elementary stage for all children alike. Henry Barnard, who played a leading part in promoting this conception of the common high school, defined the relevant terms. By a 'public or common high school' is intended a single school 'for the older and more advanced scholars of the community' which the school directly serves, 'in a course of instruction adapted to their age, and intellectual and moral wants, and, to some extent, to their future pursuits in life'. Later, when secretary to the Massachusetts Board of Education, Barnard defined the conception from the point of view of community control:

A *public* school I understand to be a school established by the public – supported chiefly or entirely by the public, controlled by the public, and accessible to the public upon terms of equality, without special charge for tuition.[4]

A series of legislative measures, following on the Civil War, provided a firm legal basis for establishing and financing the common high school with the specifically American feature of decentralization and local control. High schools organized on these lines provided scope, in turn, for the necessary development of education at a time of rapid industrialization – and served also, in due course, to absorb and acclimatize a growing flood of immigrants from the more impoverished areas of Europe. The outcome, by the late nineteenth century, was a secondary system which contrasted sharply with the traditional Western European model. In the United States, wrote Kandel in 1932, 'the problem of the common school with which many European and other countries are struggling at present' had been settled half a century earlier. It had been clearly determined that 'the same school should serve the needs of all pupils, boys and girls, coming from the elementary school' up to the stage of entry to college. The normal pattern then comprised a four-year high school from the age of fourteen, following on an eight-year elementary school from the age of six.

It was clearly accepted that a secondary school, designed to take children of all social backgrounds and vocational aspirations, should provide a wide variety of courses. By 1900, thirty-six recognized courses had emerged – including courses with an industrial and commercial basis – and at this stage what has become a leading characteristic of American education developed, the 'unit' system. Based on the conception that all subjects should be treated as of equivalent value, this system defined as a unit any subject studied during five periods a week over one year. This introduced a flexibility in marked contrast with the rigidity of the traditional curriculum. In European countries, moves to extend the scope of secondary education took the form of providing separate types of school, notably the technical school, leaving the academic school intact. In the United States (with very few exceptions, in terms of a few former academic schools that survived and a few vocational schools in the greater cities) the high school was '*par excellence*, the post-elementary school of all its adolescent population'.[5] This presented the task of transforming the secondary school, previously conceived of only in academic terms, into something new.

The American high schools made up a secondary system sufficiently resilient to meet what became a massive demand for education after the turn of the century. Already by 1910, the high schools were taking in 81 per cent of children aged fourteen, 68 per cent of fifteen year olds, 51 per cent aged sixteen, 35 per cent of seventeen and over. As James Conant was to claim in 1953, 'for nearly half a century the American people have supported public secondary schools that enroll three times as large a fraction of the youth sixteen years of age as *now* attend school in England, Scotland or Australia'.[6]

The rapid expansion in the first thirty years of the century has been ascribed to the great increase in national wealth, the growing desire of parents to open up opportunities for their children, and the increasing complexity of an industry which was by then dispensing with unskilled labour so that there were few jobs with any prospects for those under sixteen. The concomitant of the vast expansion of the public system of education was a marked decline in the proportion educated privately. Whereas in 1900 there had been 519,251 pupils in the public sector and 110,000 in private schools, in 1930 there were 5,212,179 in the public schools by comparison with 309,000 in private schools.

Meanwhile, following on criticism of the original pattern of eight years' primary schooling and four years in high school, a new overall pattern was introduced to cover the great expansion in the older age groups remaining at school. The primary course was reduced to six years, and a junior high (or middle) school with a three-year course introduced, followed by a senior high school course of three years, taking some pupils up to eighteen. By 1930 this pattern was widespread. Free transport had also been made available and, where needed, free dormitories, in an attempt to ensure equality of opportunity in rural areas. The resulting expansion of facilities at the secondary level outstripped that in any other country. But, contrary to a general belief, the *average* roll of high schools was not large, but was only 234 pupils, even when, in the 1930s, over 47 per cent of the fifteen to eighteen age group were in school.

In the United States, as elsewhere, the two world wars focused attention on education and led to some decisive policy decisions and action. In 1918 an official commission reported on the future of secondary schooling under the heading 'Cardinal Principles of Secondary Education'.[7] Underlining the great changes in the number and nature of the secondary-school population since 1900, and stressing the needs of many new immigrants, it recommended that secondary education be directed to developing 'a sense of common interest and social solidarity' among all students in a community – whether academic or vocational, whether full-time or part-time – and that all instruction be provided in the 'comprehensive high schools, and not in the separate continuation school which is the custom in less democratic societies'.[8] This involved the wide extension of courses to which reference has already been made, but it is a mistake to see this development solely in ideological terms, whether in the form of democratic aspirations or the specific influence exercised by such outstanding educationists as John Dewey. As has been noted by James Conant, it was primarily the falling demand for the unskilled juvenile in industrial and other occupations that determined the lengthening of school life and consequent demand for more varied programmes; parents, seeing no opportunities open for their children's employment, were forced to keep them in school and this, 'in turn, forced the school administrators, teachers and educational theoreticians to accommodate high schools to the new order'.[9]

It has been a characteristic feature of the comprehensive high school that, when a new order requires accommodation, it has adjusted to allow for it. Although in the last few years the American school system has been under severe pressure and the subject of much public criticism, it adapted itself rapidly to new demands following the Second World War – particularly after 1957 when the Soviet technological challenge focused attention on the quality of science and mathematics teaching at the secondary stage. Accordingly, there has been an intensification of academic courses at the top of the high school for pupils entering university. Other attempts at adaptations have, however, been less successful, and it is interesting to note that, in most cases, inadequacies can be traced back to the fact that the high school, however long established, has not yet lost the mark of its origin in the traditional academic school imported from seventeenth-century England. Within it, the academic course has been better provided for than the vocational course and – another aspect of the same problem – the white race better provided for than the black, and, more recently, the suburbs favoured by comparison with the city centres. While it has rightly been stressed that the numbers staying on in school are very large, by comparison with other countries, it must also be recognized that the problem of early leavers still remains, especially among low-income families. It is to meet this problem that the idea of having a separate vocational senior high school for the fifteen to eighteen age groups is now being revived – a move that proved unpopular in the 1930s and never achieved any real momentum. This development has given rise, in some quarters, to a belief that America is abandoning the comprehensive high school in favour of reintroducing the selective academic school. But this is not the case. No new academic high school has been built anywhere in the United States for many years, and it is only in the older eastern cities that a few old academic schools remain in being as state high schools. Outside New York City, which is a special case, such schools number only about two dozen in all, out of a total of almost 25,000 schools. On the other hand, a recent tendency (reflecting the 'de-schooling' movement) has been the setting up of so-called 'free schools' sometimes within but sometimes outside the jurisdiction of the elected school boards.

A vigorous programme of providing adequate and relevant vocational (including commercial and technical) education within the comprehensive high school has, however, been under way since the late 1950s. In many areas, according to Conant, the resulting adaptation has been sufficient to meet the problem of early leaving. But there are some areas where schools have not met the challenge, or where the problems are greater than schools can be expected to solve. These are the older parts of the greater cities where schools are often ill-equipped and understaffed and set in districts which it is now common form to describe as ghettoes. Here, too, problems characteristic of a selective system of education arise. For instance, in 1968 a case was brought in Washington DC, before the US District Court of Appeals, on behalf of negroes and poor whites who pleaded that the city school system differentiated courses in the secondary years, by a system of 'tracking', in such a way as to restrict free choice and access. It was argued that the black pupil was deflected into the less esteemed courses while the whites gravitated into the more favoured, or university-oriented, courses. The court found for the plaintiffs, judging that 'tracking' operated to the disadvantage of the poorer, and the coloured, pupils. This indicates that within some comprehensive high schools there has been a disadvantaged sector, just as there is a deprived sector on a national scale in terms of the inhabitants of deteriorating city centres by comparison with the newer, richer, predominantly white, suburbs. It is within these sectors that the perennial problem of early leaving remains in its most acute form.

This said, it must be recalled that early leavers constitute a minority in the United States where 80 per cent remain in school until eighteen, by contrast with, say, Britain where up to 50 per cent leave school at fifteen. In Britain, as in Europe generally, discussion as to the best method of providing for the deprived child tends to centre on the argument on the one hand that a divided system is best, in that it provides an opportunity for a small percentage of working-class children to pass into a favoured academic school, and on the other hand, that selective segregation so discriminates against the working class *as a whole* that comprehensive provision coupled with raising the leaving age is indispensable. In the United States there is, however, no discussion as to whether or not to abandon the comprehensive secondary system. Indeed the most striking recent development has been the establishment of comprehensive junior colleges with open enrolment catering for the eighteen to twenty age group – that is, the extension of the comprehensive principle upwards into higher education. Present arguments, prompted by increasingly acute social problems, are about whether racial desegregation of schools should be attempted or not, whether vocational schools for fifteen-plus teenagers in certain areas would enlarge educational opportunity or further curtail it by reinforcing segregation, and about how to introduce greater flexibility within the comprehensive system itself.

Secondary education in the USSR

While the educational system of the United States has been set on its present course since the 1820s, the Russian education system changed course abruptly in the 1920s, to reach within thirty years a standard which caused a re-examination of educational policies and levels in America, and in other countries as well. It is, in fact, in the matter of the content of education – the course content required of all children in an age group, excepting only the mentally handicapped – that there is the greatest difference between the American and Soviet systems. Both accept the need to provide secondary education for all without selection, but, by contrast with the American 'unit' or 'elective' system, all Soviet pupils follow a common course as defined by the Ministry of Education, which sets specific levels of achievement for each subject in each year of the school.

The first Education Act of the new Soviet government, passed in October 1918, attracted little attention at the time by comparison with measures of the same date in Britain and elsewhere, but was, perhaps, the most significant. A year earlier, four days after the seizure of power in the October revolution, the new People's Commissar for Education, Lunacharsky, had issued a decree 'on Popular Education' which set out the immediate and long-term aims of educational policy. 'In a country where illiteracy and ignorance reign supreme' the achieving of 'universal literacy' was seen as the most urgent task, but it was argued that 'real democracy' could not be brought about by way of 'universal elementary instruction'. The need was 'to organize a uniform secular school of several grades' as a preliminary to working towards 'equal and if possible higher education for all citizens'. Meanwhile, 'transition through all the school grades up to the university ... must depend entirely upon the pupil's aptitude, and not upon the resources of his family'.[10]

Looking back to these initial plans in 1937, Sidney and Beatrice Webb underlined the sharp break with the past and the new scope accorded to education in society. The traditional system had been completely swept away, and, from 1917, the Soviet government was committed to establishing

a universal and classless provision of both 'enlightenment' and training for life in all its fullness and variety, for all ages from infancy to manhood; disregarding practically all ancient scholastic tradition; avowedly based exclusively on the latest science in every branch, and free from every kind of mysticism; devoted to the end of fitting everyone for life in the service of the community; the whole system to be, in principle, gratuitous, secular and universally obligatory.[11]

A central feature of this system was the unified, or common, school. The original plan was for an elementary grade with a five-year course from eight to thirteen, followed by a secondary grade from thirteen to seventeen. This was to constitute what a Soviet educationist described in 1930 as 'one uninterrupted educational ladder', or a system without any blind alleys.[12] The effort necessary to make an advance on these lines was, of course, immeasurably greater in the USSR than it had been in the United States. Starting from a low level even in the Russian Federation of Republics, and a much more basic illiteracy in others, it was only possible to make a four-year elementary education universal by 1939. Nevertheless, the expansion of numbers in school was impressive, including republics where alphabets had to be created or languages committed to writing for the first time, before schools could teach in the native tongue. During the five years between 1929 and 1934, the numbers in elementary schools rose from 11,687,000 to 19,163,000, and in secondary schools from 2,453,000 to 6,674,000.[13] Despite great material difficulties, particularly in providing sufficient school buildings and qualified teachers, this rate of expansion was maintained up to 1941.

An essential aspect of the common school in the Soviet Union was that it was 'unified in its internal programme as well as in its external organization', in the words of Pinkevitch: the intention being to eliminate any form of streaming, or 'tracking', of the kind which – as one American educationist was already arguing in 1922 – acted as an internal system of selection in the comprehensive high school.[14] A system of streaming was introduced in some urban schools in the USSR in the early 1930s, under the influence of psychologists who accepted theories of intelligence current in the West and used corresponding 'intelligence' tests, but the

practice was forbidden in 1936.[15] Before this, various experimental
methods had been tried out, including the Dalton plan which approximates to the elective system, but this approach was also discarded. There
has since been no differentiation, whether of pupils according to ability or
of courses in the general secondary school; all pupils have been placed in
classes in their year group to follow a standard course planned to cover the
basic areas of knowledge – the humanities, science, social science and
technology.

If there has been this basic difference between the common schools of
the USSR and the United States, in another important respect they follow a similar pattern. In both countries the common school recruits pupils
from the immediate locality and is envisaged as a 'neighbourhood school'.
Also common to the two countries is a readiness to adapt schooling to meet
changing economic needs, and, in so doing, to face the problem of modifying the traditional academic approach at the secondary level. In this last
respect, however, the Soviet secondary school has tended to be uniformly,
and unrepentantly, intellectual in emphasis, other forms of activity being
catered for by a wide range of out-of-school activities provided in an
organized way. In addition, vocational education has been provided,
following the European rather than the American pattern, in separate
technical and vocational schools, directly supervised by the ministries
responsible for the relevant sector of the economy rather than the Ministry
of Education. To this extent, there has been a divided system of secondary
education, but at and after the age of fifteen rather than eleven as in
England.

It is during the years since the Second World War that the Soviet
educational system has realized its promise, to reach a standard which
stimulated many other countries to look to their own provision. The
school leaving age has now been raised to seventeen for the vast majority
of pupils while concomitantly a basic reform of the curriculum has been
carried through. This reform, besides bringing subjects up to date,
modifies what has hitherto been a standard curriculum up to the age of
seventeen by allowing for a certain degree of bias in the top two classes of
the general secondary school (ages fifteen and sixteen). In 1968 the proportion of pupils attending general secondary schools in the RSFSR after
the age of fifteen was 67 per cent, those passing to technicums constituted
15 per cent, while 18 per cent went to vocational schools biased towards a
particular industry or to work.[16] As in the United States at an earlier stage,
it was becoming increasingly difficult for young people under sixteen to
find jobs with prospects, and this had contributed towards encouraging
completion of a full secondary education. But, as also in the States, there is
a disadvantaged sector, in this case in the more remote rural areas where

educational facilities are less highly developed, though boarding schools have been established to assist in remedying the situation.

General conclusions

There are various problems to be met in both the USSR and the United States in the next stages of development at the secondary stage, and it would be rash to predict what new solutions may be found. But the point to be made here is that these two great world powers with basically different social and political systems, and a quite different historical background, both have a secondary system adapted to the needs of a scientific and technological age – a system which has been consciously adapted in the past to meet changing economic and social needs and is capable of future change. By contrast, the more traditional Western European systems of secondary education, planned to maintain a certain social pattern and so incorporating barriers to contain the pressure of a rising demand for education, necessarily lack flexibility and have proved incapable of adequate adaptation. That these systems have been retained for so long, despite demands for reform based on recognition of scientific, technological and social changes following the Second World War, means that the countries concerned have fallen badly behind in providing the basic level of education now necessary. As against the claim that the grooming of selected intellects is the best way of meeting the growing need for experts or specialists, it may be argued that experience in the USA and the USSR suggests that raising the general level of education is not only important in itself but the best means of ensuring an adequate scaling of the peaks of achievement. That the traditional academic school is too limited and inflexible in outlook to provide the form of secondary education now needed – even for potential experts – has been sufficiently well illustrated in the last twenty-five years, not least in Britain, by the failure to fill the scientific and technological faculties of expanding universities.

Moreover, so long as the traditional academic school continues to be accepted as the model of what a secondary school should be, so long are other schools at the secondary level seen, as it were, in terms of the reverse side of the medal. This has been particularly apparent in England, where the so-called 'modern schools', for the majority of children, have lacked intellectual content and, for that matter, vocational direction as well. Just as, in the United States of the 1920s and 1930s, parents kept children longer in school because of lack of adequate jobs, and growing aspirations, and accordingly demanded relevant opportunities in school including access to college and university-oriented courses, so a generation or more later English parents have made their wishes felt on similar lines. This has made an important contribution to the breaking down of a selective system of education which has long outlived any justification it may have had, and to an agreement to substitute a comprehensive school at the secondary stage.

Elsewhere the same social and economic realities have prompted a similar change in policy. Already before the Second World War, in 1939, the government of New Zealand decided, in the words of the then Minister of Education, 'to convert a school system, contructed originally on the basis of selection and privilege' to one that could 'cater for the needs of the whole population over as long a period of their lives as is found possible or desirable'. The Swedish government took a similar decision in the late 1940s, as also did the countries of Eastern Europe and Japan. All these now have comprehensive systems in which streaming has been abolished or, at least, modified – in Japan 85 per cent now complete the course in comprehensive schools at eighteen.[17] In China a main aim of the 'cultural revolution' of 1966 was the elimination of continuing inequalities in education; it is now clear that the school system is being opened up in a quite new way.[18] The trend towards unification is also now becoming clearer in countries of Western Europe. In Italy a comprehensive middle school, up to the age of fifteen, has been established; in both France and Western Germany decisive steps are now being taken to develop comprehensive systems of secondary education. The school systems of Latin America are almost always based on a European rather than North American model, but there are now moves to develop more flexible forms of secondary teaching and organization. The movement towards comprehensive education is not, then, peculiar to Britain alone; it is part of a worldwide movement concerned to adapt the structure of secondary education to the new demands of scientific, technological, social, racial and cultural progress.

Notes

1. J. J. Servan-Schreiber, *Le Défi Américain*, pp. 93–4, Paris 1967.
2. I. L. Kandel, *History of Secondary Education*, pp. 263–4 (n.d.); see also his *Studies in Comparative Education*, pp. 727–9, 1933.
3. Kandel, *Studies in Comparative Education*, pp. 683, 703.
4. Kandel, *Comparative Education*, pp. 793–4; *History of Secondary Education*, p. 441.
5. Kandel, *Comparative Education*, pp. 794, 797.
6. James Bryant Conant, *Education and Liberty*, pp. 2, 4–5, 1953; see also his *American High School Today*, p. 7, 1959.
7. *Bulletin No. 35*, Department of the Interior, Bureau of Education, 1918.
8. ibid., p. 31. It was, of course, the chief feature of the English Education Act of 1918 to provide separate day continuation schools for the majority of children leaving school at fourteen, though the policy was never operated.

9. James Bryant Conant, *The Revolutionary Transformation of the American High School,* p. 5, 1959.
10. The decree is printed in full in John Reed, *Ten Days that Shook the World,* pp. 297–9, 1961 edn.
11. S. and B. Webb, *Soviet Communism: A New Civilization,* vol. 2, p. 889, 1941 edn.
12. A. P. Pinkevitch, *The New Education in the Soviet Republic,* p. 155, 1930.
13. Webb, op. cit., pp. 890–91*n.*
14. Pinkevitch, op. cit., p. 156; G. S. Counts, *The Selective Character of American Secondary Education,* 1922.
15. The decree on intelligence testing and streaming of July 1936 is given in full in E. D. Simon, *Moscow in the Making,* pp. 130–35, 1937.
16. Joan Simon, 'Differentiation of secondary education in the USSR', *Forum,* vol. 11, no. 3. Summer 1969.
17. *Guardian,* 28 December 1971, quoting an OECD report.
18. Caroline Benn, *The Times Educational Supplement,* 5 November 1971, 12 November 1971, 19 November 1971.

Chapter 2
Secondary Education for All in Britain: 1945 to 1965

In the context of the general developments that have been briefly outlined, moves in Britain towards creating a unified and open system of secondary education appear slow and indecisive, rather than hurried and doctrinaire as is sometimes asserted. Even today, seven years after the decision to reorganize on comprehensive lines, and twenty-five years after the first such schools pioneered the way, there is little clarity about this policy and what it implies; the actions of the Conservative government since their return to office in 1970 have served only to confuse the issues further.

About the economic and social trends which compel educational change in this direction, there is today a large measure of agreement. A succession of official reports in the immediate post-war years both underlined the need to increase numbers in higher and secondary education in order to meet future demands from the professions, and pointed to the reserve of ability available to profit from such provision.[1] Other influential reports, published in the 1950s, made the same points more generally, notably *Early Leaving* (1954) and the Crowther Report (1959), before the matter was brought fully into the public eye with the Robbins Report (1963). The committees responsible for these last two reports made a specific point of studying the educational systems of other countries. The Crowther Report, giving a telling account of the wastage of ability, stressed that the current technological and scientific revolution demanded a parallel educational revolution in England, and concluded 'it is not only at the top but almost to the bottom of the pyramid that the scientific revolution of our times needs to be reflected in a longer educational process'.[2] That there is both a need for, and a possibility of, educational expansion on a quite new scale is now generally accepted. Indeed, today, when universities, colleges of education and school sixth forms have expanded beyond the limits envisaged even in the Robbins Report – and without reducing standards – there is no alternative.

To accept this is, in effect, to accept the need for an open system of secondary education, a flexible system which can easily adjust to changing needs and one adapted to the education of the whole child population at this stage. But there has been reluctance to adjust policies accordingly, with the result that educational advance has been impeded during the twenty-five years since the Second World War ended. Vocal objections to the unified school have confused the issues. These are not based on any long-term assessment of economic and social trends, nor could they be. They derive directly from present and past practice, making the most of virtues and leaving inherent limitations out of account. Such are arguments which uphold the selective grammar school because it provides for a mixture of classes, and by comparison decry the neighbourhood comprehensive school as one which would (in working-class districts) provide only for a single class; but which omit to mention that the very existence of selective grammar schools presupposes many secondary modern schools which are both single-class and blind-alley schools, the primary cause of wastage of ability.

This is precisely the point at issue, that to provide a full secondary education – and of a predominantly academic kind – only for a selected 25 per cent of the child population is no longer a viable policy. Britain is making a difficult transition from an imperial homeland to a component of Europe with diminishing overseas commitments, with a financial, administrative and industrial structure in need of modernization and more efficient management, with calls for scientific and professional skills at many levels. It is a country that must in future, in a way that it has not had to do in the past, live by its brains. In this situation, the only relevant educational policy is one that both opens up access to, and changes the nature of, a secondary education which evolved in quite other circumstances. What is now needed is a new kind of secondary education for all.

This calls for a fresh educational outlook, a breaking free from the limited views imposed by the selective system – which has presented grammar-school teaching in terms of early specialization for selected intellects, and modern-school teaching in terms of adjustment of curricula to the level of children, including those who may already have suffered intellectual and cultural deprivation. Neither of these represents an *educational* approach. Evidence of a new outlook is to be found in the present reorientation of curricula and teaching methods, in moves to bring the content of subjects up to date, in the search for new techniques of presentation which make use of new technological aids, and in the emphasis laid on facilitating children's learning and motivating their interests. These are to be seen not as approaches suitable for the 'less able' child, while the 'able' child is left to the mercy of the traditional academic approach. Rather they represent the reorientation necessary to enable effective teaching at the secondary stage of what are now rapidly growing and changing bodies of knowledge. This stage is one that all children must now accomplish, and not in highly specialized channels, nor in courses which lead nowhere, but in an all-round way.

Early specialization – no longer an answer to current problems arising from the 'explosion' of knowledge, let alone an educational solution – has been in large part the product of a highly competitive system of secondary and higher education. Grammar schools have been geared to the preparation of the small proportion of their pupils who might gain university places, themselves in very short supply, and this has shaped their whole ethos. But with the expansion of universities, polytechnics and colleges, the beginnings of a modification of degree courses, above all the expansion of post-graduate work, 'higher education' itself begins to look like a stage – rather than the ultimate peak to the system – as it already is in the United States, where intensive specialization belongs chiefly to the post-graduate level.

With these developments, the secondary school can be seen in a new perspective, and the possibility of planning an effective, general education for all children comes within reach. It is to enable a reorientation of this kind, bringing secondary education up to date, to create a form of organization which allows for the progressive adaptation that will be needed in the coming years, that the comprehensive school has been advocated.

As in other countries, the need to open up educational opportunity and the need to transform the content of education have tended to coincide. It is the former that often receives most stress, and it is true that parental pressure for greater opportunities – and advocacy by the Labour movement of equality of opportunity – have been among the chief influences in bringing about a breakdown of the bipartite secondary system established and fostered since 1945. It is within this system that the first comprehensive schools began their work in the late 1940s and that most comprehensive schools still operate, and this has influenced their progress in many ways. But from the outset these schools, established by local authorities, some of which consciously rejected the selective system, have also seen their task as that of breaking new ground in an educational sense. This they have had to do for themselves, without the assistance of any clear directive policy, for so long as the selective system was officially upheld, so long were reports and recommendations framed in these terms. Rather than looking ahead in educational terms, they discussed how to cater for children within the framework of the grammar/modern-school pattern. So insular has the approach been that it has not seemed peculiar to write off 70 per cent of British children as virtually ineducable to a secondary standard, capable of following only a strictly modified curriculum, when other advanced countries take all normal children through a complete secondary education. On the contrary, this conception of the limitation of abilities, derived from past educational practice and a class stratification peculiar to England, has dominated educational thinking as it has also determined the pattern of school organization.

It is important to recall this background, and the resultant directives which have shaped comprehensive schools – at first as lonely 'experimental' outposts, allowed only on sufferance within the selective system. To recall past controversies is also to throw light on still current questions, for most of the arguments used against comprehensive reorganization from the late 1940s can still crop up in only slightly modified form today – although confined to a smaller and smaller group.

The Education Act 1944 and its aftermath: the tripartite system and selection

When a new Education Act was under discussion during the Second World War it was the overt aim to provide a full secondary education for all and end the evils attendant on a highly competitive system. As the official White Paper, issued in 1943 to prepare the way for legislation, put it: 'There is nothing to be said in favour of a system which subjects children at the age of eleven to the strain of a competitive examination on which not only their future schooling but their future career may depend.'[3] This suggested an intention to reorganize the school system in such a way as to avoid early differentiation.

But plans under consideration did not, in fact, envisage any new departure. This soon became evident when the proposals of the Board of Education (as it then was) were published in another document. It was the intention to make all education after the age of eleven 'secondary' in character, with equivalent grants and staffing, but it was also the intention to maintain three different types of secondary school: the former grammar school (unchanged), the modern school (the senior elementary school renamed) and the technical school (the junior technical school upgraded). Here was a clear indication of inability to think ahead, of adherence to the pre-war policy of piecemeal reform within the traditional framework: three grades of secondary school related to vocational direction, or social status, was in fact first proposed by the Schools Inquiry Commission in 1867.

True, recommendations in the 1944 Act were not couched in this form. On the contrary, it was affirmed that all types of secondary school would be of equivalent status. But, as many pointed out at the time, this was an expression of pious hope rather than a likely development, especially as grammar schools were to retain their former place monopolizing the road to higher education. In this context, official explanations of policy became progressively more unreal, as 'educational' arguments were formulated to justify what was, in essence, a social policy. Soon the educational world was peopled with 'modern-school children' with certain supposed educational needs, and 'grammar-school children' whose mental features corresponded precisely to the traditional academic programme offered by grammar schools and whose numbers corresponded precisely to the available desks in existing schools. This exercise in double thinking was first performed by a special official committee chaired by Sir Cyril Norwood, former headmaster of Harrow, which reported in 1943. The wordy circumlocutions of this report – framed to present a picture of children born into the world with either an academic, a 'technical', or a 'modern' cast of mind – were immediately challenged by both psychologists and educationists. But this picture continued to be reproduced – indeed, stated almost as if it were a scientific finding – in successive publications put out by the new Ministry of Education after 1945.

The 1944 Education Act did not, in the end, include a clause defining how secondary schooling should be organized. There had been a great deal of public discussion of the measure, which had centred largely on this point, and opposition to the official view was sufficiently strong to secure a relatively flexible statement of intent. The relevant clause simply stated that secondary education – that is, 'full-time education suited to the needs of senior pupils' – must be provided, offering such variety of instruction and training 'as may be desirable in view of their different ages, abilities and aptitudes'.

As events were to prove, this began a shift of emphasis from 'types of mind' to 'levels of ability' as the decisive factor in allocating children to different secondary schools. The Act also laid down that the necessary reorganization of education should be accomplished by the usual method of cooperation between local authorities and the central authority. Every local authority must submit for approval a development plan, covering the next twenty years, setting out its proposals for providing secondary education in line with the intentions of the Act. But, while this was to adhere to traditional procedure, an important modification had been introduced. With the reconstitution of the old 'Board of Education' as a ministry there went a new definition of the powers of the Minister; in future his task was to be to

promote the education of the people of England and Wales and the progressive development of institutions devoted to that purpose, and to secure the effective execution by local authorities, under his control and direction, of the national policy for providing a varied and comprehensive educational service in every area.

This was the first clause of the Act.

In the outcome it was at this level that official policy was enforced. Whatever may have been the balance of opinion in Parliament and the country about the way secondary education for all should be provided, the Ministry of Education had its own interpretation, and this was the touchstone applied to every local development plan submitted. On this interpretation, to provide an adequate secondary education in accordance with 'age, ability and aptitude', it was necessary to establish separate schools, with differentiated programmes, to which children were recruited at eleven by means of 'selection tests'. If, in very exceptional circumstances, such provision were made in a single school, then that school must be large enough to comprise, as it were, the three separate types of school under one roof.

Here we meet with a characteristic of British political life, that what may be called 'official' policy frequently survives changes in political administration. Before the war Conservative governments had been the rule. In the wartime coalition, the President of the Board of Education was R. A. Butler, an experienced Conservative politician, who piloted through the Education Act. In 1945, a Labour government came to power with a large majority, a reflection of popular readiness for new policies in the post-war world. The Labour party was specifically committed to the common secondary school, by a series of conference resolutions dating from the early 1940s, so that a mandate for development on these lines had been given. But when this government left office in 1951, after six years, there were only a dozen comprehensive schools in being, with some others 'approved'. In other words, official Ministry policy had prevailed to the exclusion of a reorganization of secondary education, since recognized as necessary by many Labour organizations. This alone would seem to exonerate the Labour party from the accusation of precipitate innovation.

That there were some important innovations during these years was due primarily to the influence of a few powerful local authorities, notably the London County Council, that of the West Riding, and the city of Coventry. These established the right to begin providing secondary education in comprehensive schools, if at first gradually and on a small scale. It was difficult to refuse a demand to act on these lines to cities where schools had been destroyed wholesale, as in London and Coventry, so that no question arose of the 'destruction' by absorption of existing grammar schools. But developments were firmly kept within these limits; in Coventry, as in London, new comprehensive schools grew up under an umbrella of selective grammar schools, which kept them firmly to their place as something less than genuinely common schools – and this remains the case. Other authorities which had considered a unified secondary system were discouraged from formulating development plans accordingly, and very few

persisted; Oldham was one, but realization of the plan was held up by lack
of grants for building. Only in isolated, sparsely populated areas, such as
Anglesey and the Isle of Man, was an entirely comprehensive system of
secondary schooling permitted. That the Ministry would block other
moves in this direction was made clear in 1948, in the case of Middlesex.
Here the authority drew up a viable plan for transforming six secondary
schools in one area on a comprehensive pattern using existing buildings –
in somewhat the same way as the county of Leicestershire was to act in
1957. But in the case of Middlesex 11–18 schools for some 850 pupils were
envisaged and these, the Ministry could readily argue, were too small to
provide a viable sixth form. In the outcome, only two of the comprehensive schools planned were established, which quite shortly provided concrete evidence about what comprehensive schools could achieve to set
against statistics drawn from the past practice of grammar schools.

Until such evidence became available it was only possible to expose the
educational bankruptcy of the bipartite policy in general terms. The
development plans of both the LCC and the West Riding gave educational
arguments for rejecting this policy and adopting a unified form of secondary provision. Education, said the LCC, is a matter of 'all-round growth
and development, physical, intellectual, social and spiritual'; it is, then,
'indefensible to categorize schools on the basis of intellect only', rather
than providing an all-round education which can also 'promote a feeling
of social unity among adolescents of all kinds and degrees of ability'. The
West Riding Education Committee was unable to accept the double-think
of the Norwood Report, or the 'suggestions . . . made or implied in various
reports or Ministerial circulars'. These were 'that, at the age of eleven,
children can be classified into three recognized mental types, and should
be allocated to grammar, modern and technical schools accordingly'; that
'the numbers to go to each type of school should be determined by an
arbitrary percentage of an age group'; 'that at the age of eleven children
show certain aptitudes which can be relied upon to indicate the type of
school to which a child should be allocated'. The Committee then quoted
from the report of the Advisory Council on Education in Scotland – a
country with a more democratic educational tradition than England –
a paragraph which 'excellently expressed' their own views:

The whole scheme rests on an assumption which teacher and psychologist alike
must challenge – that children of twelve sort themselves out neatly into three
categories to which these three types of school correspond. It is difficult enough
to assess general ability at that age; how much harder to determine specific bents
and aptitudes with the degree of accuracy that would justify this threefold
classification. Status does not come with the attaching of a name or by a wave of
the administrative wand, and the discussion to date has left the position of the

modern school neither defined nor secure. Indeed, it seems clear to many that the modern school will, in practice, mean little more than what is left, once the grammar and technical types have been housed elsewhere, and that the scheme will end not in tripartite equality but in dualism of academic and technical, plus a permanently depressed element.[4]

This view was amply borne out by events, except for the fact that the technical secondary school never got off the ground in most areas, so that the tripartite system envisaged became in effect a bipartite one – a trend which undermined the Norwood 'ideology'. The Ministry had never been very specific about the proportion of 'technically minded' children in the population, but in practice, in terms of the number of school places provided, it never rose above 5 per cent. Since, on average, grammar-school places were available for some 20 per cent, this left three-quarters of the child population to be directed to modern schools for which the Ministry advocated *ad hoc* courses not designed to lead to any form of qualification – least of all the General Certificate of Education examination which opened the way to university. These schools were at first *specifically forbidden* to enter their pupils for this examination under the age of *seventeen*, a regulation which effectively debarred entry (circular 103, May 1946).

It is opportune to recall at this point how the Ministry defined the common secondary school in 1947, primarily with a view to dissuading authorities from entering on any general development on these lines. First, it defined the 'multilateral' secondary school (the kind of all-in school with varying courses envisaged in the 1920s, as an alternative to the Hadow reorganization which laid the foundations of the bipartite system). A multilateral school is 'one which is intended to cater for *all* the secondary education of *all* the children in a given area, and includes all three elements (grammar, technical and modern) in clearly defined sides'. The Ministry was inclined to accept the occasional school in this image, in sparsely populated areas, and in due course many bilateral schools were to come into being in country areas. As for the comprehensive school, this was negatively defined as 'one which is intended to cater for *all* the secondary education of *all* the children in a given area, without an organization in three sides'.[5] In 1947, this conception seemed as way out to many as undifferentiated (or non-streamed) classes appear to some today. It was, therefore, almost inevitable that, if they avoided a division into 'sides', some early comprehensive schools should fall back on the only other accepted means of internal organization, that is, the grading of children in streams, according to performance on selection tests.

By 1952, however, there were only thirteen comprehensive schools in existence, most of them on offshore islands (Anglesey and the Isle of Man) or in isolated county areas with a scattered population, in which case they were small, like the school at Windermere. However, significant experience in the organization of large secondary schools of a comprehensive type had been gained by the LCC, since it had set up eight 'interim' comprehensive schools by merging selective 'central' with modern schools to make a unit of some 1200 pupils, housed in available buildings. This could not arouse serious objections, since no grammar school was involved, but there was trouble when plans for new, purpose-built schools came to fruition, and the first of these was successfully launched in 1954 only by warding off Ministry interference. Similar schools were opened this same year in Coventry and Glasgow, and this marked the beginning of a new phase of development. By now it was possible to gauge academic achievement in comprehensive schools, and evidence of this kind came to hand at a moment when the selective system was running into growing difficulties. The essential difference between a unified and a bipartite system was underlined when, in the autumn of 1953, all primary-school children in Anglesey passed into the neighbourhood comprehensive schools without any form of examination or selective test – of the kind that was now beginning to arouse protest in many areas.

Selection procedures at eleven plus proved to be the Achilles heel of the bipartite system. Heavy stress was laid on the fact that there was no longer a 'competitive' examination, only an objective process of allocation, but this necessarily implied making large claims for the tests in use. So it was that 'intelligence' tests were generally described as objective measures of a child's inherent intellectual powers, so exact as to permit an accurate forecast of what he would achieve in later school life, and in life itself. This was no new assertion. Precisely this argument had been put in the Spens Report of 1938, which quoted expert psychological advice to this effect and used it to uphold advocacy of the tripartite secondary system. A similar argument had figured earlier in the Hadow Report on the junior school of 1931, which on this basis strongly advocated streaming by ability as the best form of internal organization in the larger primary schools. In the years after 1945, as the selective system was consolidated, rigid streaming increased rapidly in junior schools, some of which concentrated as much attention on getting A-stream pupils into grammar schools, as grammar schools concentrated on getting their A-stream pupils into university. Whereas secondary education for all had been intended to open up opportunities, the system established was chiefly remarkable for closing doors, and parents showed a growing awareness of the contradiction. Indeed, much as in America in an earlier age, changing patterns of employment and social life prompted new educational aspirations; and once parents' demands were loud enough, administrators and experts, psychologists and teachers, were forced to pay attention and turn their minds to reorganizing the school system.

The attempt to perfect selection procedures by authorities concerned to protect their own position as arbitrators of children's destinies, cruelly exposed the limitations of the 'intelligence' test and the falsity of the claims made for it. Whatever may be its uses in psychological research, this instrument was revealed as an altogether unsuitable guide to educational practice. Various developments contributed to this exposure, including the examination successes of children in modern schools where teachers refused to recognize restrictions, and the failure of a significant proportion of the children so carefully selected for grammar schools. But the final blow to the 11-plus examination came in 1957 when a committee, appointed by the British Psychological Society to examine growing criticism of the validity of 'intelligence' tests and the psychological theories supporting them, pronounced against the use of such tests to select children.[6] The report issued supported arguments long advanced by educationists; namely that the process of education itself promotes intellectual development, that it is neither possible nor desirable to predict future intellectual achievement by 'measuring the intelligence' of a child of eleven, still less of seven, that 'intelligence' tests do not in fact measure genetic endowment but rather educational experience. Consequently the practice of streaming in junior schools was also deprecated, on the grounds that this very differentiation, by determining young children's educational environment, set limits to their development in an unwarranted way.

The previous year sociological surveys had been published which brought to light the effect of so highly selective an educational system in a class-stratified society. It was found that the population of secondary modern schools, supposedly for less intelligent children, was predominantly working class; while in maintained grammar schools, intended for intelligent children of all classes, the middle or professional class was over-represented (the more selective direct grant grammar schools were found to be even more heavily weighted with middle-class pupils).[7] This had been the position in the pre-war days of fee paying; it was still the position when careful allocation was made according to the results of 'intelligence' tests. There seemed, therefore, a case for considering whether the 'intelligence' test was an objective measure, or whether it merely reflected academic notions of what 'intelligence' is, which in turn implied a heavy bias towards the middle-class norm. In fact, the 'intelligence' tests used for selection, since they were intended to locate children who could effectively do grammar-school work, tended to equate 'intelligence' with the kind of mental operations required in school subjects presented on traditional lines.

Perhaps the final straw was that the National Foundation for Educational Research, set up by local authorities and the chief source of the innumerable tests they depended on for selection, also began an about turn in 1957. A report issued that year estimated that some 12 per cent of children were allocated to the 'wrong' schools at the age of eleven; and, moreover, that even the most stringent methods of allocation could not reduce the error below 10 per cent of an age group. Any authority which allocated, say, 1000 children a year must in future live with the knowledge that in at least 100 cases they might as well have used straws as an 'intelligence' test.

It was at this stage that the retreat from selection seriously began. Not only could education authorities no longer defend the practice, but politicians were beginning to find that to defend selection was a sure means of losing support. It is important to emphasize, however, that there was a retreat from an exposed position, rather than any clear recognition of the educational implications of rejecting testing as a guide to practice. There have been corresponding consequences both in terms of organization and educational outlook. Once selection proved indefensible, the reorganization of secondary schooling began in an *ad hoc* way and many variations appeared in different areas. Equally there was little rethinking in terms of seeking a new educational approach, and ideas derived from 'intelligence' testing still have considerable force, even within comprehensive schools. It could hardly be otherwise when some authorities 'abolished' selection merely by superseding open testing with hidden testing or by placing the onus of allocating children to a still operative selective system on teachers in junior schools.[8] Much the same could be said of the practice of those comprehensive schools which introduced a rigid system of streaming from the age of eleven.

The defence of the grammar school

Educational reform has always been conceived, at the secondary stage, in terms of providing a certain degree of social mobility from the lower levels of society to the higher. To increase the degree of mobility is, necessarily, to modify social structure to some extent and arouse deep disquiet in those who have previously occupied a position clearly differentiated from those below them. Secondary education has traditionally been the preserve of the middle class. The last major educational reorganization in England, in the period 1850 to 1870, overtly assigned types of secondary school to different sections of the middle class while allocating working-class children to the separate elementary system. Subsequent reforms were concerned to provide a ladder from elementary to secondary school, by way of the 'scholarship examination' at eleven. This examination was, however, a barrier. By retaining this barrier, while at the same time professing to provide secondary education for all, the 1944 reform resulted in a system of 11-plus selection which acted as a grid holding back a rising tide of educational demand. Once that demand, representing the pressures of a scientific and technological revolution as well as of parental aspirations, swept aside the grid, there was no effective barrier to the reorganization of secondary education on comprehensive lines. None, that is, except the vocal objection of particular sectional interests, couched sometimes in social, sometimes in educational, terminology. These objections have not only delayed introduction of comprehensive schools, they have also determined the climate in which comprehensive schools have developed up to now, the demands made upon them, and the terms in which they have been required to provide 'evidence' of their achievements.

The leading advocates of a selective system argued not only that children could be selected early according to intelligence tests, but that the traditional grammar-school curriculum from which they would profit was itself excellent. Eric James, former High Master of Manchester Grammar School and late Vice Chancellor of York University, further argued that 'when our economic stability and . . . social progress demand the fullest use of our intellectual resources', to jeopardize the proved efficiency of grammar schools would be 'irresponsible'. They had recorded an 'astonishing success in facing two tasks of immense social importance'; to supply 'highly trained manpower' and to 'provide opportunities for the child of any class to compete successfully with his more fortunate contemporaries'.[9] As we have already pointed out, the grammar-school sector was failing in precisely these tasks: providing sufficient manpower for certain specific professions and faculties – most notably the scientific, mathematical, and technological (as well as wasting talent in the so-called '11-plus failures'); and secondly, in providing opportunity for working-class children to receive overall the same kind of educational opportunity that middle-class and upper-class children continued to receive. Moreover, it was the very existence of a static selective sector that prevented the expansion that was required on every front.

As for the arguments against the comprehensive school itself, these were effectively met by evidence of the progress of the few existing schools. The headmaster of the first Anglesey comprehensive school, at Holyhead, demonstrated in 1953 that 'the sixth form of the former grammar school' (absorbed into his school) 'has not only increased in numerical strength but has broadened its field of specialist studies'.[10] A survey of this and other schools in 1954, conducted by Robin Pedley, showed that

Every school which has been even partly comprehensive in type for five or more years can give examples of pupils who would have failed to qualify for grammar-school places in that locality, who were on entry graded 'non-academic' and put in a low form, yet who subsequently made remarkable strides and did well in GCE – in some cases at advanced level.[11]

This final point illustrates a weakness on which another opponent of comprehensive schools, William Alexander of the Association of Education Committees, was quick to comment. In so far as a rigid system of grading, or streaming, was adopted within the comprehensive school, the claims of its advocates 'that differentiation at eleven plus will cease, proves to have no foundation'. Indeed, it could be argued, there is more precise differentiation within some comprehensive schools than in the tripartite system, with the corollary that these schools were not overcoming the main problem they were supposed to solve.[12] A reply to this was provided by evidence that some of those originally graded as 'non-academic' in fact could make progress within a comprehensive school, to the extent of taking A-levels; progress of a kind that was much more difficult, if not impossible, within the tripartite system where movement depended on whether local authorities operated an efficient and generous transfer system at the age of thirteen. That comprehensive schools often continued to stream remained true, but this could be seen as an adherence to the pattern which William Alexander, among others, had been at much pains to popularize and promote – to the exclusion of examining alternative educational procedures.

Another argument advanced against comprehensives was that the right of 'parental choice' must be upheld. This argument admirably illustrates the middle-class angle of vision, with its attendant blind spots. The average parent has had no choice of secondary school under the selective system; his child has simply been allocated to the nearest modern school, often a school whose whole tone and prestige has been completely coloured by the fact that it was designed as a place for children to mark time before proceeding to jobs which require no special qualification. That among the 25 per cent or so attending grammar schools are some working-class children, who have broken out of a limited environment, has hardly acted as a solvent of class divisions. On the contrary, as some of the individual children concerned have since testified, what they underwent at grammar school was a process of grooming which prepared them for entry to university and the professions as new recruits to the middle class.[13]

This is but another way of saying that an educational system necessarily reflects the values of the society of which it is a part. Schools alone cannot solve deep-seated social problems, nor obliterate the lines of a stratified society which accentuates class divisions in many ways, whether they be grammar or comprehensive schools. To recognize this led, in some cases, to despair about any positive solution of the controversy over the organization of secondary education. Writing in 1952, H. C. Dent, once an advocate of the unified school, complained that this controversy had been dragging on for at least fifteen years, absorbing 'time and energy that might have been much better occupied'. He himself had come to the conclusion that it was beside the point whether or not the comprehensive school is a good thing. 'I am concerned only to point out, what has become even more obvious, that at present English parents and teachers simply won't have it. And the reason? Because it just isn't in the English tradition.' No theoretical argument was really of any weight when set in the balance against 'long-established and fondly cherished social traditions'.[14]

Seventeen years later, in 1969, the National Union of Teachers passed a resolution at its annual conference calling on the government 'to make the necessary legislative changes to bring about comprehensive education by abolishing selection for secondary education', adding that 'the continued existence of the grammar school completely nullifies all attempts to create a fully comprehensive system' and calling on the Secretary of State 'actively to intervene forthwith and demand that local education authorities present comprehensive schemes of secondary reorganization immediately . . . '.[15] That teachers, a conservative profession, had reached this point was in part the result of parental pressure which grew in volume from at least the middle 1950s. The uncritical, and erroneous, conclusions reached by Dent in 1952 may usefully be compared with the critical approach in 1940 of Fred Clarke who skilfully laid bare the hypocrisy – or double thinking – of so much 'educational' discussion in England.[16] It is, as he pointed out, a characteristic of this discussion that it deals in what sociologists would call 'ideology' rather than making an honest, and objective, examination of the facts. Thus, to invoke 'tradition', as if it were a single and autonomous factor, is to overlook that there have always been at least three 'traditions' in English education. The first of these is the ruling-class tradition of education, the academic tradition invoking the classically orientated 'liberal arts' and closely associated with professions which themselves are conservative in organization. The second is the vigorous tradition reaching back through nonconformity to the Protestant reformation, and forward to the middle-class reformers of the nineteenth century who were concerned to promote the teaching of science and revolutionize traditional education both at secondary school and university. The third is the tradition of instruction for the working class, provided for them by their betters. It is this last, Clarke urged, that must be brought to the surface and transformed, and this also involves a rethinking of current secondary education which remains cast in the academic mould; for there has been no real absorption of scientific attitudes, only the tacking on of scientific courses side by side with the old courses in classics or modern arts subjects. What has been happening in English education since the late 1950s marks the beginnings of an understanding that these are the real problems to be solved.

There was no official encouragement for the development of comprehensive schools after 1951 by the Conservative government which then took office and was to remain in power until 1964. On the contrary, with the plans of the LCC and some other authorities beginning to come to fruition, there was an active intervention to limit further development on these lines. This was first evidenced in 1954 when the Minister of Education vetoed LCC plans for two comprehensive schools, both of which would have embodied grammar schools. In 1955 a new Minister, David Eccles, declared that the government would 'never agree to the assassination of the grammar school', as a prelude to announcing the policy of permitting the establishment of comprehensive schools only on new housing estates and in new towns, where there were no grammar schools in being.[17] Any projects which went further than this – as did plans submitted by Manchester and Swansea – were turned down, on the grounds that they involved 'the extinction of the existing grammar schools, whose traditions are too good and too precious to be endangered'.[18]

Subsequently, in December 1958, this point was underlined in an official statement of policy, *Secondary Education for All, a new Drive*, which advocated, as a means of mitigating the rigidity of the bipartite system, the further development of advanced courses in secondary modern schools; a development previously frowned upon but one to which a number of local authorities had resorted as a means of meeting popular demand for an effective secondary education in these schools. This marked a concession, a recognition of discontent with the bipartite system. This was now increasingly voiced by authorities in county areas, faced with the task of providing separate grammar and modern schools for relatively under-populated areas, with all the attendant inefficiency and expense this incurred. In fact, a year earlier, in 1957, the Leicestershire education committee had launched a plan, initially as an experiment in two areas of the county, to reorganize all local schools on comprehensive lines, in a two-tier pattern. Accordingly, the new official policy now recognized that in some rural areas it might be necessary and desirable to institute comprehensive schools. But it also remained the policy to resist any change in this direction in urban areas and in 1958 plans to develop a comprehensive system in the county borough of Newport, Monmouthshire, were vetoed; in 1959 Darlington also was prevented from initiating a comprehensive school.

Against this background the slow rate of development of comprehensive schools is understandable. Nor was it only a question of lack of speed. An official policy which reluctantly conceded that a common secondary school makes sense – at least from the point of view of efficiency and economy – on new housing estates or in rural areas, but refused to countenance such schools elsewhere, because they altered the former function of a grammar school, was laying the basis for a vast organizational, and theoretical, confusion. No *educational* thinking lay behind this policy, as is evidenced by the terms in which it was promulgated; nothing positive was ever said about the comprehensive school, as an educational unit, nor for that matter about the grammar school – except in rhetorical terms, as 'too precious' a tradition to be endangered.

This confusion was reflected in the main report of this period, the Crowther Report (1959). In some ways the best of the many educational reports issued, one which showed itself aware of the scientific revolution and urged the necessity for a more flexible system of secondary education, this report included a chapter on 'the sixth form' which can only have been written by another hand, for this almost returned to the Norwood ideology with such assertions as 'the more intelligent a child, the more subject-minded he is'. It is on arguments relating to traditional sixth-form teaching, as has been seen, that the case for the grammar school – and with it for the selective system – always ultimately depends. But the case for retaining grammar schools, and selecting pupils for them at eleven, also depended on the viability of existing means of selection. By 1960 the 'intelligence' test had ceased to be an adequate support of the bipartite edifice.

The breakdown of the selective system

In the early 1960s there was apparent the beginnings of a movement to do away with the selective system at the secondary stage, one which represented a reversal of the position established in the late 1940s when the central authority had firmly contained development on these lines. Now it was the central authority that retreated before local authorities, though still uttering some final vetoes as it went, until in 1965 the policy imposed in 1945 – itself one inherited from pre-war days – was jettisoned.

There was a great deal of movement around the country at this time, for many local authorities, which are usually somewhat averse to learning from each other, now sent deputations to areas which could demonstrate functioning comprehensive schools. Urban authorities seeking guidance could go to London which now had many schools in action; to Coventry which had pioneered the house-system in comprehensive schools; to Bristol where new housing estates surrounding the city had been provided with comprehensive schools; to the new towns of Crawley in Sussex, Harlow in Essex, Kirkby in Lancashire, where there were entirely comprehensive systems. Events had also moved rapidly in Scotland; by 1962 Glasgow had twenty-two comprehensive schools. County authorities most frequently made their way to Leicestershire, where the initial experiment had proved successful and been extended; this was of particular interest since it had been planned in such a way as to make use of existing buildings, so ensuring a relatively rapid transition and abolition of the 11-plus. But in Wales, where grammar schools had always provided for a high percentage of children – and had produced in turn many recruits to the teaching profession in England – there was also a general turn to the comprehensive school. Among English counties now planning the transition were Staffordshire and Derbyshire, Oxfordshire and Gloucestershire, Devon and Cornwall.

In 1963 the north of England began to move decisively towards the establishment of an overall system of comprehensive schools. Plans came initially from Liverpool and Manchester, then from the county of Lancashire and other county boroughs – Preston, Rochdale, Blackburn, St Helens, Bolton, Wigan, to add to Oldham which had always had comprehensive plans. In Yorkshire, Bradford education committee advanced a plan for a two-tier system which could be put into action almost immediately, by using existing buildings. Significantly, this was accepted by the Minister of Education, Edward Boyle, so that Bradford became the first English city to abolish selection at eleven plus for its maintained schools. This was in 1964. In that year the Labour party was once again elected to power nationally after thirteen years out of office. The establishment of the comprehensive school and the abolition of selection at eleven plus had been in its electoral programme since 1955. One of the Labour government's first jobs upon taking office therefore was to present its plans for reorganizing secondary education upon comprehensive lines. To the fate and the fortune of these measures we now turn.

Notes

1. For instance, the Barlow Report entitled *Scientific Manpower: a Report of a Committee Appointed by the Lord President of Council*, HMSO 1946 (Cmd 6824).
2. *15 to 18* (Crowther Report), vol. 1, pp. 123–4.
3. *Educational Reconstruction*, 1943 Cmd 6458.
4. *Education*, 15 October 1948; *Secondary Education*, A Report of the Advisory Council on Education in Scotland. Edinburgh, HMSO, 1947, Cmd 7005, p. 31.
5. Circular 144, 16 June 1947.
6. P. E. Vernon, *Secondary School Selection*, 1957.
7. Calculated from DES *Statistics of Education*, 1961, Supplement, Tables 12 and 13.

8. This move from selection based on attainment tests in English and arithmetic to verbal reasoning tests (plus teacher assessment) is described in *Allocation Procedures to Secondary Schools*, NFER, 1969.

9. Eric James's arguments in favour of the selective system of education were presented in *The Content of Education*, 1949, and *Education for Leadership*, 1951. They are summarized in his chapter entitled 'An opposition view', in R. Pedley, *Comprehensive Schools Today; An Interim Survey*, 1955.

10. *The Times Educational Supplement*, 6 February 1953.

11. *Education*, 8 October 1954.

12. W. P. Alexander, 'Principles for action', in Pedley, op. cit., p. 52.

13. Brian Jackson and Dennis Marsden, *Education and the Working Class*, 1962.

14. H. C. Dent, *Change in English Education*, pp. 11–12, 1952.

15. *Teacher*, 18 April 1969.

16. Fred Clarke, *Education and Social Change*, 1940.

17. *Schoolmaster*, 7 January 1955.

18. *The Times Educational Supplement*, 6 January 1956.

Chapter 3
Circular 10/65 and English Empiricism

The famous circular 10/65 – asking local authorities to reorganize on comprehensive lines – was issued in July 1965, nine months after the Labour government was elected in 1964. Most people think of this circular as setting reorganization in motion, but as chapter 2 has shown, the move to reorganization had begun much earlier. The effect of the introduction of the circular was to accelerate rather than to begin – or to complete – a process.

Origins of the six schemes for reorganization

Schemes for secondary education were not new. The 1944 Education Act had also asked for them to be submitted (in 1945) as part of local authority development plans. Although most schools planned at this time were either grammar or modern schools, 5·5 per cent of all schools in these development plans were supposed to have been comprehensive schools by 1965.[1] Had these plans been carried through, 12·5 per cent of secondary pupils would have been in comprehensive schools by 1965. But in fact they were not all carried through. Only 8·5 per cent of secondary pupils were in comprehensive schools by this time,* and it was not until two years after circular 10/65 that the 1945 development plan target was reached.

Enthusiastic government and departmental backing for comprehensives in the 1950s was not conspicuous, as the failure to reach even the modest target figures of the 1945 development plans suggests and as chapter 2 has shown. Where any pioneering was done, it was due to progressive local authorities, both Labour and Conservative controlled. It was to local authority practice then, relayed by the Inspectorate,[2] that the government and the Department of Education and Science (DES) turned when it came to drawing up circular 10/65.† All six of the schemes suggested were either in operation or proposed through local authority initiatives. The 'central guidance' that 10/65 claimed to give in effect amounted to passing around to all authorities what the DES had found in its suggestion box in 1965.

* See Table 5.1, page 102.　　　　　† For Scotland's Circular, see p. 392.

The six schemes, briefly, were these:

1. All-through comprehensive schools for ages eleven to eighteen years.

2. Tiered schools where *all* pupils transfer at thirteen or fourteen from lower tier to upper tier.

3. Parallel tiered schools – where only *some* pupils (a) choose or (b) are selected for transfer to upper tier.

4. Tiered schools where all pupils (a) choose or (b) are selected at thirteen or fourteen between long-course and short-course upper tiers.

5. 11–16 schools followed by (a) a sixth-form college or (b) a junior college; or (c) 11–16 schools coexisting with 11–18, the latter providing the sixth forms.

6. Middle schools straddling the age of eleven, e.g. 8–12 or 9–13, leading on to variants of scheme 2, 4 or 5.

When the Labour government was elected first in 1964, there were 189 comprehensive schools in thirty-nine local authorities.[3] Many were exceptionally successful. Most of these schools, pioneered in London, Anglesey, Bristol and Coventry, were 11–18 schools. It was both the dominant position of the 11–18 at the time and the Labour party's preference for this form of comprehensive that led the framers of circular 10/65 to recommend this as the 'orthodox' method of reorganization. How far local education authorities (LEAs) were pressurized into adopting 11–18s is hard to say. But whether, as 10/65 said, they were always the 'simplest and best solution', is certainly open to argument.

Circular 10/65 was categorical about the merits of the 11–18 schools. By contrast, it was off-putting in its introduction of others. For example: 'At first sight the 11–16 school has few arguments to recommend it'. (11–16 schools were possible in both scheme 3 and scheme 5.) In particular 10/65 seemed to regard scheme 5 – with 11–16 schools and sixth-form centres or colleges – as especially daring, even though it had already been put forward by some authorities, and by individuals, as far back as 1942.[4] Sixth-form colleges themselves were referred to in section 20 as 'experiments' and 10/65 said only a 'limited number' would be allowed. On the subject of rationalizing post-sixteen provision within an authority – in terms of utilizing facilities of further education and technical colleges in reorganization planning – 10/65 had very little to say, even though cooperation between sixth forms and local colleges was already taking place in many areas – and one area (Darlington) had already suggested a sixth-form college reorganization scheme taking this cooperation further.

Circular 10/65 was also contradictory about the subject of entry into sixth forms – the sixteen-plus situation, one might call it. In section 16 it speaks of two kinds of sixth-form college: one, a junior college catering for the needs of all local students in the sixteen to nineteen age group; the other, a college only 'to be entered on certain conditions (e.g. five passes at ordinary level)'. There is a very great deal of difference between a sixth form requiring five GCE (General Certificate of Education) passes and one that anyone can enter. This passage in 10/65 therefore suggests it is permissible for schools or LEAs to decide individually. Later, however, in section 35, when discussing the sixth forms of schools to which *some* pupils could transfer at thirteen or fourteen, it says that pupils who did not transfer at thirteen 'should be able to transfer at sixth-form stage as a matter of right'. Which did 10/65 really mean? Was entry to the sixth form to be a 'matter of right' or 'on certain conditions'? Circular 10/65 apparently says both. This cannot be called 'national policy' or 'central guidance': it is merely a reflection of what was actual practice in different sixth forms at the time.

But sixth-form schemes seem positively encouraged when compared to 10/65's presentation of scheme 6 – or middle-school schemes – where schools straddle the transfer age of eleven. Even though section 1 of the Education Act of 1964 gave the Secretary of State specific power to approve schools of eight to twelve or nine to thirteen, circular 10/65 said that the Secretary 'does not intend to give his statutory approval to more than a very small number of such proposals in the future'. Why? The government and DES presumably assumed the public would object, because, as one observer had written, the break at 'eleven was firmly embedded in the public consciousness'.[5] It is also true that the Plowden Council, having been asked to make recommendations about the best age of transfer from primary to secondary education, was still sitting. There was, therefore, a good deal of pressure from political opponents of the government's policy to 'wait for Plowden'. But those who had advocated, and were planning, this type of rearrangement of schools were well informed – Alec Clegg, the Chief Education officer of the West Riding, was one – and it must have been obvious to anyone surveying the situation that one of the main obstacles to reorganization was the relatively new postwar building that could not be replaced for decades. No new 1000-size schools could be built in many areas. Schools of 300 to 500 would have to be used. Dividing schools up into 11–13 and then 13–18, or 11–14 and 14–18, and preserving the old transfer age of eleven, had snags, as we shall see. The flexibility of middle-school arrangements would add immeasurably to the range of choices open, and in many areas might prove 'simplest and best'. So it was to turn out. Despite the damp discouragement of

10/65, so many areas submitted these schemes that a bare nine months afterwards the Secretary of State had to retreat from this 10/65 position and announce that approval would be given to scheme 6 as to any other.

It is hard to say how many authorities would have gone for middle-school arrangements had encouragement been given them from the start. Certainly some local authority documents state that as circular 10/65 did not 'exactly encourage' middle-school schemes, they therefore would not consider them seriously.* Once again it was entirely local initiative that pressed ahead with middle-school planning, mostly of break-at-thirteen schemes – initiatives that made the Plowden Council's recommendation of transfer at age twelve obsolete long before it was made.

When it came to the two interim schemes, 3 and 4, they were set out in great detail and with relatively few warnings – considering their obvious drawbacks, the most obvious of which was that selection was retained. Scheme 4 was particularly unsatisfactory, with two clear disadvantages: the two-year school from 11–13 and the continued segregation between ex-grammar and ex-modern schools at age thirteen. Bradford, which operated the scheme from 1964, managed to make of it an experiment of immense value. The drawbacks, however, were too great for other areas. Up to 1972 no other authority had operated this scheme.† At the time of 10/65, the DES and government could perhaps by then have concluded that the drawbacks were rather too severe, and that if any type of reorganization was to be 'discouraged' it should be this one rather than middle-school scheme 6. But because it was established local practice in one LEA, it was included as the fourth of the six main methods.

Scheme 2, where there is transfer of *all* pupils at thirteen or fourteen, had been proposed for a few areas by 1965.‡ This was a relatively simple form of reorganization, where ex-secondary modern schools usually become the lower, and grammar schools the upper, tiers. Its drawbacks were threefold: only two years in lower school in one version or two years' run-up to GCE in the other, which most upper schools or ex-grammars considered too short a time. Since so much local authority reorganization planning is dominated by the local grammar lobby and this lobby is primarily concerned about GCE examinations, these schemes have not been widely adopted. Others worried about 14–18 schools for another reason: those who would leave school at fifteen would have only one year in the upper school. On the other hand, this form of reorganization could be introduced relatively quickly, since little major new building was

---

* See, for example, the minutes of Berkshire authority on reorganization, June 1966, p. 74.

† A similar scheme was proposed in County Armagh, Northern Ireland, however.

‡ Great Yarmouth, for example, proposed such a scheme in 1963.

required, and the incentive to stay to sixteen is strong. With the school-leaving age now at sixteen, and the possibility of examination reform at sixteen, the disadvantages are fewer now.

In many ways there is little distinction between circular 10/65's scheme 2 above and the first of the interim schemes set out under 3: where 11–14/15 schools lead to 14–18, the scheme adopted in Leicestershire. It would have been much easier and clearer for LEAs if the two had been considered as one, scheme 3 as a transition stage to scheme 2. But they were separated in 10/65 because they came from two different authorities' practice. This was rather unimaginative.

Scheme 3, which we come to last, was by far the most complicated and controversial of the six schemes. Controversial because it allowed two *types* of comprehensive school and as a result introduced into educational practice the principle of selection by guided parental choice – about which we shall have a great deal to say in this book. And complicated because it put forward under the blanket of one form of reorganization two schemes that were very different. In the first scheme 'choice' was genuine, in the second it was not.

Both versions of scheme 3 have overlapping secondary schools. The lower tiers were either 11–16 or 11–14/15 – that is, with or without GCE and CSE (Certificate of Secondary Education) courses – in itself a rather major point of difference. Upper schools are usually 13–18, but can be 14–18. At eleven all pupils go to the lower school, but at thirteen or fourteen only *some* transfer upwards.

The controversial aspect in scheme 3 (and in scheme 4) was the need to select those who would move up. Here is where the difference in the two versions of the scheme became apparent. In some areas, especially those where the lower schools had no examinations and ended at 14/15 years, choice of transfer was left to parents. Here the upper schools were expected to, and usually did, expand gradually each year, as more and more pupils chose to stay on and to come to them. The upper schools in some cases were lukewarm about receiving the increase, since many pupils were not traditional grammar-school pupils and these upper schools were almost always traditional grammar schools. Some adapted well, others did not. Some adapted quickly, others did not. But the principle of parents choosing was more or less operative.

In the second version of scheme 3, however, the upper schools planned to remain exactly as they had always been, 'grammar' schools offering a grammar course. They had no immediate plans to enlarge. They would not expect pupils to enter who were not prepared to take the full GCE course. Since accommodation was to remain the same, the numbers accepted were fixed. And therefore intake had to be regulated from the first. Here the principle of transfer was also 'choice', but quite obviously the final choosing had to be done by the schools rather than by the parents. This version of scheme 3 had been first put forward by Doncaster. It had also operated in Scotland in those cases where 12–16 schools (with H grade I and II) run parallel with 12–18 schools, *some* pupils making the transfer at fourteen and the rest remaining in the 12–16 school.*

The difference between 'genuine' parental choice in scheme 3, which operated in Leicestershire, and 'guided' parental choice which operates still in parts of Cumberland, Cambridgeshire and Kent, Doncaster and Wakefield, and is planned for Northampton, would seem obvious. But the circular made no distinction and assumes *all* choice would be genuine. True, it warned against parents who may not know what is involved and cautioned they should be informed. But information about what is involved can, and does, lead just as often to guidance *not* to choose as it does to guidance to make the choice, as research since has shown.[6]

Not only was there from the first a very real confusion here between free choice and guided choice, but also confusion about the interim and permanent nature of these types of schemes. Fixing a date for total transfer of all pupils is obviously easier and more likely in free-choice schemes – and in most of these this was settled to come into operation when the school-leaving age was raised. This has meant free-choice schemes could be real transition schemes, the upper school progressively adapting itself to the larger proportions opting to come, as the scheme became established.

But this was not the case with most 'guided' choice type-3 schemes. For in these, the grammar schools were to remain much as they had always been – except that they took in at age thirteen or fourteen rather than at eleven. There was no 'exam' at thirteen, but there was selection all the same. The operation of schemes in these areas proves this beyond a doubt, as do the many leaflets explaining the schemes to parents.† And the question is, could it not have been guessed by the framers of 10/65 that some areas would see this as a way of retaining grammar-school selection? It is true 10/65 recognized the schemes as selective and said they would have to evolve 'eventually', but when was 'eventually'? This was never made clear. It is ironic that 10/65 should have been so unrealistic as to ask all authorities to begin interim plans by September 1967 – a very short time indeed – but never to have defined 'interim', and indeed, never to have given a final date for permanent schemes to have begun or to have been completed.

All the same, it is clear that few areas plan to have scheme 3 on a

* For an explanation of Scotland's various Certificate courses, see part 5, chapter 17, p. 394.
† See, for example, those from Thameside, Kent and Whitehaven, Cumberland.

permanent basis.* Why, then, the fuss? Simply because under the mantle of comprehensive reform in 10/65 the principle of 'guided' parental choice has been introduced into educational practice generally. If it had been used only at age thirteen or fourteen and only in schemes 3 and 4, the problem would have been less serious. But it has been, and is being, used to replace the old 11-plus in many areas. We discuss this new version of 11-plus selection in more detail in chapters 6 and 19, including the growing disquiet among teachers about being given this responsibility for 'deciding' a child's future at eleven or twelve or thirteen. At the very least it would seem an unsatisfactory practice to recommend in a circular advocating comprehensive reform.

Why, then, was it included in 10/65? The answer again is because before 1965 it had been put forward by a particular authority, i.e. Doncaster, and had been suggested by others before that in the late 1940s and early 1950s: Brighton, Ipswich, Surrey and Montgomeryshire.[7] Later advocates were drawn to it because it did away with the notion of 'rejection' implicit in the 11-plus. Grammar school would be entered 'as a result of a choice made by parents and children and not the outcome of some process involving acceptance or rejection at one particular stage in a child's career'.[8] It also appeared to have been accepted by some teachers. The Middlesbrough NUT, for example, agreed to it in 1964 for that area. On the other hand, the Doncaster NUT published a pamphlet in 1964 outlining its objections to scheme 3 and to guided parental choice. It was a very thorough document and the framers of 10/65 could not possibly have been unaware of the arguments it contained. In 1966, the NUT nationally at its annual conference came out against guided choice, and the Teeside NUT (now responsible for Middlesbrough), having watched scheme 3 in action, said in 1968 that it was 'socially divisive'.[9] Although the framers of 10/65 were only reflecting current suggestions in putting forward this scheme, and tried to warn of the pitfalls, it is clear that they did not make any real attempt to assess its likely working. Nor did they look ahead to possible consequences of 'guided' choice schemes that were then operating, or planned, with an eye to what might be desirable in the future rather than merely what had been suggested in the past.

Circular 10/65 was naïve then on the question of selection. Not only with regard to 'guided' parental choice, but also, for example, to middle-school schemes, which it said 'seem to lead naturally to the elimination of selection'. Why? Selection can just as easily be retained when the transfer age is twelve as when it is eleven. Norfolk is a case in point. It decided early that it would adopt a twelve transfer, but would still retain selection.

* See Table 5.3, p. 115.

Direct grant schools

As has been observed since, 10/65 had some 'notable evasions' in it[10] – most notably on voluntary aided schools, that powerful group whose status problems have held up Inner London Reorganization for so many years. But above all, 10/65 failed with direct grant schools. There was no LEA initiative to rely on, of course, and there was the traditional DES reluctance to disturb direct-grant-school arrangements.* Nevertheless 10/65 asked LEAs to ask direct grant schools to 'associate' themselves with LEA plans – what one researcher has said was 'like asking the Athenaeum to consider ways in which it could become a Youth Centre'.[11] 'Association' was never defined in 10/65. No guidance was ever given on status. Later, because so little progress was apparent (only two direct grant schools out of 172 had gone comprehensive even by 1972), the Secretary of State in 1966 delivered the direct grant schools what he called 'a shot across their bows',[12] warning them that he would have to take action if they did not cooperate. They did not cooperate.

Eventually their whole future was handed over to the Public Schools Commission, which reported on these schools and day public schools in the spring of 1970. The report was bracing and did indeed recommend that Atheneums should evolve into Youth Centres – that is, direct grants become comprehensives. It is one of the ironies of the period that one of the clearest and most concise summaries of both the need for, and the support for, comprehensive reform appears in this second Public Schools Commission report. It argued that direct grant grammar schools were little different from maintained grammars, and if it was national policy to reorganize – that is, 'if maintained grammar schools are being reorganized . . . it is indefensible . . . to preserve and support other grammar schools having similar aims and functions'.[13] The majority recommendation was that direct grant schools become maintained and participate in local reorganization schemes. There was no one solution that suited all direct grant schools any more than there was one for all maintained grammars. Indeed one of the most important findings of the Commission was that direct grant schools were not a unique national group, but varied, and different, each individually related to a 'local' school situation. Other interesting findings were that direct grant schools were 'predominantly middle class', as many had long suspected, and that local authorities were not 'saved' any money at all by educating their pupils in direct grant schools rather than in their own schools,[14] which many had not realized.

* For one proof see R. Saran, *Secondary Education Policy and Administration in Middlesex*, unpublished Ph.D. Thesis, University of London, 1968.

The Commission was less positive, however, in its advice about what kind of maintained status direct schools should take. In their inclusion of voluntary-aided-school status as a possibility, it is obvious they had little studied the problems and difficulties already being faced by local authorities trying to integrate voluntary aided grammar schools in reorganization (e.g. Inner London). The Commission was also disappointing in its assessment of the various schemes direct grant schools had already entered into in various authorities in an attempt to 'play a part' in reorganization. True, it said that most of these 'new agreements . . . fall short of the patterns recommended in circular 10/65'[15], but in view of its already near categorical conclusion that 'traditional' grammar schools ' . . . cannot be combined with a comprehensive system of education: we must choose which we want',[16] it is obvious that almost all of the thirty-one arrangements of direct grant school 'cooperation' in reorganization it examined were unacceptable because they left direct grant schools playing their traditional selective role. In many schemes their role was even more selective than before, for the new arrangement involved their agreement to take in *more* selective pupils from comprehensive schools, thus undermining local comprehensive schemes, or 'creaming' them, still further. In chapters 8 and 9 we discuss this creaming problem in detail.

Since so many authorities have already given notice that they regard selection for direct grant schools as incompatible with reorganization and that they will cease to take up places in these schools once their own reorganization is complete, we can expect direct grant schools to be drawn into controversy still more surely in the future. The 'solution' is obviously a local one and must be worked out in respect of each direct grant school in each area. That the framers of 10/65 were unable to think this through, and that the government was unable to take the steps that would make 'association' possible, is another indication of the tentativeness of 10/65 policy. In this field more than any other, perhaps, it was naïve to have expected integration in response to an instrument that had no statutory powers of any kind.

Problems of implementation

That 10/65 had no legal force – as one writer said, had not the 'force of a Royal Command'[17] – was not realized immediately. To judge from the uproar among those opposed to reorganization – in the Commons, the Lords, and on hostile local education committees – it seems to have been taken as mandatory. At least for a while. For all the goodwill the government or the department hoped to gain by choosing to take the reform slowly and by agreement – via circular rather than via legislation – they might as well have introduced a bill in the first place. It was some time, however, before local authorities and opponents of reorganization realized that Circular 10/65 had no real teeth.

Why was a circular chosen rather than legislation? Because the Labour government and the DES chose to pursue reorganization by means of persuasion rather than by means of law. From the beginning they elected to assume that every authority would wish to reorganize – despite much evidence to the contrary. In 1966, for example, a few months before 10/65's requested plans were due from local authorities, when it was widely known that only about 50 per cent of authorities had any plans at all, the Secretary of State said he expected 'very nearly 100 per cent are going to submit plans for going comprehensive by July'.[18] To the government it made more sense to pretend for as long as possible that everyone was in fact reorganizing and that the problem of non-cooperation would be 'absolutely trivial'.[19] This is what one MP called the policy of 'kidology'.[20]

Information about reorganization was therefore always positive. It was mainly confined to irregular announcements of the mounting numbers of authorities which were reorganizing. These announcements divided authorities into those with plans approved for the whole (or most) of their areas and those with plans for only part. Even if an authority was planning only a few schools it was added to the total of those which were reorganizing. Naturally the numbers rose higher and higher at every announcement.

But these announcements were somewhat misleading, as *Education* remarked, tending to make progress 'look a lot more impressive than it has ever been'.[21] Sterner critics have since called those DES statistics relating to the speed of reorganization 'worthless', with 'the rate of change ... artificially inflated by counting authorities rather than the proportion of school pupils involved in schemes'.[22] It was certainly true that the plans receiving DES approval varied widely, and that many had alarming gaps. First, many left out large areas or large numbers of schools from their plans. Second, many had no dates fixed for much of their reorganization – one approved scheme actually included the announcement that for most of its schools it intended to 'take no action' with regard to comprehensive reorganization.[23] Thirdly, many were schemes that were interim only and retained selection.

The Labour government not only tended to gloss over large numbers of authorities which submitted incomplete or unsatisfactory plans, but also constantly played down the extent of the non-responding areas, both those where there was outright defiance and those where there was a lot of talk but little action. These latter areas did not openly defy the government. There was no need to. As the *Guardian* observed some time ago, the best way of defying the Minister 'is practical investigation and endless consultation'.[24]

Yet another problem, and this a much bigger one, was where local councils changed political hands in the middle of planning for reorganization. This began to happen in the usual post-general-election swing towards the party not in national power in 1967 and 1968. Most local authorities did not do an elaborate about-face – this was quite unnecessary; and some who tried it (Darlington) found it did not work. Most, therefore, stalled or quietly altered: Bexley, Halifax, Southend and Reading were a few of many examples.

But the biggest dilemma of all – and the ultimate proof of the impotence of 10/65 in the crunch – came whenever an authority submitted such patently non-comprehensive plans that they had to be returned. Birmingham's 1967 plan is an example. In theory this right of sanction should promote reorganization; in practice, it only reinforced the status quo. For authorities with 'returned' plans were simply left with the 11-plus and with a selective sector intact. But there was yet a last problem: some areas actually went backwards. Parts of Leicestershire and Staffordshire, to name only two, having been reorganized successfully for many years, found that as a result of town boundary extensions, the 11-plus was reintroduced into some of their primary schools and that some flourishing comprehensive schools became creamed.

One cannot escape the conclusion that the decision to effect this major reform by bark rather than bite – by circular rather than legislation – was questionable. At the time it was easy to see why it seemed the sensible course. Reform through cooperation is always preferable to reform through coercion; and 10/65 made cooperation eminently possible. It can perhaps be argued that for the sake of sweet reasonableness, it was worth a try.

But for this policy actually to achieve reform there had to be some grounds for assuming that total cooperation was likely. And in 1965 all signs pointed to this issue as one that was controversial – as indeed are most educational issues in advanced industrial societies. 'Education having become the main avenue to success and power, it cannot avoid its agonizing role at the centre of the power struggle.'[25]

The failure to grasp the nettle in 1965 can be traced in part to political naïvety and under-preparation by the Labour party of the necessary strategy for implementing a comprehensive school policy, but also in part to a departmental naïvety in assuming that education should or could be 'non-controversial' in this day. The department clearly desired to stay 'neutral' in the face of any controversy involving selective schools: grammar or direct grant. This prevented them from an outright commitment to a comprehensive system, a commitment which was, and is, the first essential for effective reorganization.

This non-commitment came out in all sorts of ways. The clearest indication of it was the failure to provide up-to-date and continuous information on the exact progress of reorganization. Another indication was the practice of appointment to working parties, and of sponsoring courses and research, in respect of *future* secondary school development that always included grammar and secondary modern schools – as if they would be carrying on indefinitely. Sometimes representatives of comprehensive schools, or comprehensive schools themselves, were also included, but occasionally they were not.* In any case, it was clear that the department was assuming a permanent state of coexistence. Department-associated bodies, like the National Foundation for Educational Research, continued with research into methods of ability selection at eleven plus. There was no attempt during the years following the issue of circular 10/65 to abandon this kind of investigation and to divert attention to the crucial question of methods of allocation that comprehensive systems would have to employ.

In its forward research, appointments to committees, and working parties on future school curriculum or organization, the department from 1965 to 1970 gave every indication that it expected grammar and modern schools to continue alongside comprehensive schools indefinitely. As we have clearly seen, any policy that continues to underwrite a system of 'two types' of secondary school makes development of a national system of genuine comprehensive schools impossible.

The department's non-commitment was serious not only because it conditions policy inside the department but also because it infects policy in local authorities and in closely allied bodies – for example, the National Foundation for Educational Research. The NFER, because it has been given the major role to play in following through the nation's comprehensive reform with research projects, is vitally important to the reform. Like the DES it is non-committal – its First Report on reorganization laid great stress on the fact that it could not say whether or not comprehensive education was a 'good thing' (p. 81), as if to say that research into a reform could not be reliably carried out by a body committed to the principle of the reform. In its 1969 publication on eleven-plus procedures it seemed mildly surprised to find that twenty-six authorities had abandoned (and 104 would in future abandon) eleven-plus selection, although it added as an afterthought that this was 'not entirely unexpected in view of pressures over the last years to abolish the eleven-plus and the reorganization of secondary education' (*Trends in Allocation Procedures*, 1969, p. 2).

* See C. Benn, 'The timetable problem', *Comprehensive Education*, Summer 1969. DES-sponsored research into the use of computers for timetables for secondary schools of the future did not include any comprehensive schools in its first field trials in 1966 and 1967, which were run in grammar and secondary modern schools only.

This one mention of 'pressures' is the only reference in this document to Circular 10/65. Circular 10/65, of course, was supposed to have been more than 'pressures', it was supposed to have been national policy. This is but one example out of dozens of how little impact 10/65 really made on so many important bodies and how very easy it was for both the NFER and the department and many authorities to carry on planning or researching for the future as if the bipartite system – with comprehensives added – was to remain indefinitely. Had a comprehensive system been completely accepted in 1965 by the government and the DES, all forward research into new methods of 11-plus selection would have been automatically abandoned to concentrate research on the many pressing educational problems that comprehensive reorganization involves. All forward planning by the department would automatically have been in respect of comprehensive schools only. There could have been no value in research into secondary modern schools, for example, with a view to their organization or timetable or their head teachers' tasks in 1980.

Even in very small ways the department's cautiousness comes out. In the excellent bulletin on middle schools, describing how existing schools could be converted for use in 10/65's scheme 6, the architectural possibilities of converting existing junior schools are illustrated at length; but questions on important pedagogical matters are bypassed on the grounds that 'any lengthy and possibly controversial examination of the educational characteristics' of middle schools should not be brought up, 'especially to those confronted with the practical problems involved in planning middle schools'.[26] A moment's reflection will tell us that the practical problems of comprehensive reorganization cannot possibly be solved *without* 'examination of the educational characteristics' of comprehensive schools. To suggest avoiding this – merely because it is 'possibly controversial' – is an indication of the neutrality which the DES tried to preserve over reorganization. In fact, circulars 10/65 and 10/66 were the only total departmental commitments to a comprehensive reform. And they were inadequate because circulars as instruments of reform are inadequate.

Circulars are generally useful as a means of 'guiding' local authorities and have long been in use in the DES. They are, however, generally old-fashioned instruments for modern government, and other government departments (except for housing and health) have gradually curtailed their use. They are certainly inadequate for major reforms. They operate best when the question is non-controversial: for example, on teacher supply. Where matters are controversial – as, for example, on immigrant population in schools, they can be less successful. So too with comprehensive education, which was both a major reform and controversial.

But the circular method of reform was not chosen merely because it might be less controversial. It was chosen because it could continue the impetus to reorganization through local authority initiative rather than through central direction. Although 10/65 claimed to be laying down national policy and giving central guidance, the failure to write the comprehensive principle into law and to coordinate it carefully from the centre meant inevitably that the centre remained without real responsibility for pursuing reorganization and in an exposed position *vis-à-vis* those areas where local impetus was lacking.* This conflict between local authority and central government initiative was nothing new. The 1944 Act gave the Minister the 'duty' to 'secure effective execution of the national policy for a varied and comprehensive service in every area'. But at the same time there was a strong tradition of allowing local authorities autonomy. The DES evidence to the Local Government Commission says 'it is the duty of the Authority to decide the main lines of policy and to lay down the broad pattern on which the service should be developed'.[27]

Two duties then, one national for a national policy and one local for a local policy. What if the two are in conflict? And it is here that we see the weakness of 10/65. For 10/65 gives specific priority to local policy, saying that in 'matters of principle' reorganization is to be left to 'locally elected representatives of the community'. This meant that national policy and principle had to take second place in local authorities where the education committees had a temporary majority ready to vote them down. A national reorganization policy that in effect amounted to permission for local authorities to go their own way could not genuinely be a national policy and it naturally resulted in a piecemeal state of affairs. This problem is compounded by the alternation of local political power between the political parties which has, and will continue, to take place. As A. D. C. Peterson of Oxford wrote of 10/65 early on: 'leaving reorganization so completely to local authorities may well prove to have been mistaken'.[28]

Circular 10/66 – announcing no allocation of building money in future for schools not designed to fit into reorganization plans – retained some of the control at the centre, however. It was an absolutely logical next step in prompting a national policy and 10/65 would have had much less chance of being accepted without the backing of 10/66. There are some who feel that if only 10/66 had been properly enforced, legislation would have been superfluous.[29] But the difficulty here is that some authorities did not need new buildings. Others needed buildings only for new schools (their grammar schools could remain as they were). And a few authorities appear to have been able to obtain allocations for grammar school projects where full

* See 'Behind the Curzon Street curtains', *The Times Educational Supplement*, 2 May 1969. 'There is nothing we can do about local authorities which tell us to mind our own business' (comment of Miss W. Harte of DES on reorganization by circular 10/65).

reorganization in the LEA was not certain.* So this means of effecting reorganization, though in principle sound, was in practice sometimes less so.

The fact that 10/66, like 10/65, was not written into law has also led to a threat of its being challenged in law. Since reform by circular was partly designed to avoid precisely the protracted legal wrangling that took place on at least two separate occasions – with a third always threatened – it can hardly have been said to have been a 'best buy' for either the government or the department if either had really been hoping to avoid legal trouble.

Need for central guidance

But perhaps the most serious consequence of circular rather than legislative reform, with its inbuilt shedding of responsibility for initiating reorganization by the central department (in contrast, say, to Sweden, where the government itself systematically backed and promoted the reorganization reform from the centre), has been that authorities were left without any continuing guidance on procedure, or any continuing information about the progress of reorganization after the issue of circulars 10/65 and 10/66.

This shows up most clearly in local authority documents and in local education committee deliberations on reorganization, where the approach to reorganization has been bewilderingly various from area to area. Some areas started at once with adoption of a particular scheme in principle, details to be worked out later. In other areas, the facts were first collected and a plan evolved eventually – teaching staff in some cases being consulted, in others not. Sometimes one professional body was consulted, in other areas another. Some LEAs went to great trouble collecting information about their schools and especially about likely future trends.† Others appeared to have gathered hardly any information at all about their schools, especially about likely future numbers. Where predictions were made – for example, on the percentages likely to stay for sixth-form education – these differed wildly from area to area, as did the local plans based on them.

In some cases planning went on in secret; in others, in public. Some authorities had excellent public relations and 'consulted' widely. Others, often because the local controversy was so very inflamed, found that any public consultation was impossible and that outline plans had to be arrived at first and presented for discussion – otherwise 'planning' a reorganization scheme simply revolved around the question of 'saving' the local grammar schools, often only a single school. Some authorities

---

* Plymouth, 1968; Sutton, 1969.
† The Preston and Darlington documents are models here.

took decisions on financial grounds, others on pedagogical grounds. Many committees appeared to be dominated by the opinion of the local grammar school heads and staff, or middle-class parents. (An example of this domination is the fact that time after time, the chief subject mentioned in these LEA documents is Latin. A visitor from another planet reading them through would imagine Latin must be the single subject essential for twentieth-century survival.*)

In some cases – like Darlington – the local education officers were influential, in others they were mere background figures. Some committees had working parties, others did not. Some sent for, or went to see, other LEAs and their plans. One – Stoke-on-Trent – even went to the USA. Others merely sat at home with 10/65, hoping to work something out. Some LEAs submitted documents that were detailed and fully explanatory expositions of their plans, running to hundreds of pages; others submitted mere statements, with just the bare outlines of a plan in a few paragraphs, sometimes with important details of the actual scheme still undecided. Examples of schemes of all types were accepted and passed by the DES.

Reading through all the local authority planning, one is struck not only by its piecemeal nature, but also by the lack of method. Time and again an authority would begin its submission by giving long explanations of why it had *not* chosen the rejected alternatives. The impression given was that a few schemes were arrived at by default, rather than by serious investigation of alternatives. In 1965 an independent report on Bristol's reorganization[30] commented on the 'amateur and lackadaisical' fashion in which some LEA schemes seemed to have been planned; also, on the fact that outside offers of help were turned down.† Another report[31] gives a blow-by-blow account of deliberations in a new town area, showing how a few specific interest groups could dominate all planning.

The department generally held aloof from planning, although they were sometimes consulted informally by authorities. A few LEAs constantly consulted them, others appeared to have had almost no contact. A few individual schools and authorities we have questioned praised the guidance and interest of DES officials. Where the DES was most helpful seemed to be in areas where there was least local controversy, particularly where there was no entrenched local grammar-school interest. Where

---

* See, for example, the reorganization documents of Bolton, Barrow and Carmarthenshire; see also accounts of reorganization in Leicestershire, p. 120, and Oxfordshire, p. 176 in Elizabeth Halsall (ed.), *Becoming Comprehensive*, 1970. See also *Scottish Educational Journal*, 4 November 1966, p. 1051, and three following weeks, for a debate on Latin in Scottish Schools.

† Jean Floud, the educational researcher, offered help to the ILEA, for example.

there was, it was sometimes different. The head of one comprehensive school in Wales told us that 'the part played by the Ministry of Education is recognized by all supporters of the scheme to have been deplorable'. His complaint was that the DES had attempted to delay the local plan and to turn the comprehensive into 'a glorified secondary modern'.

Where reorganization was successful, it was once again due to strong local initiative. This meant that there would either have had to be a strong-minded and fair-minded Chief Education officer, whose views were definite and whose judgement was Solomon's, and/or a particularly determined and knowledgeable leader or group on the education committee. They could be Labour or Conservative, although more often they were Labour. When one looks at any two authorities – very often so very much alike – but sees one reorganized, one still not, the difference very often rests in the character and determination of one or two men or women. Accounts of reorganization also make it quite clear that in more than one case the 'progressive' members of either political party have had to overthrow their 'leaders' on reorganization.[32]

In other areas it is the officers who need to be pushed, for during the make-or-break stage 'neutrality' on the comprehensive issue is as impossible at local level as at national. In one area the apparent conversion of the Chief Education Officer to the comprehensive principle was cited as 'the most important development during the three years' of the comprehensive controversy.[33]

Not all authorities' planning was chaos or controversy, however. Not all LEAs turning down alternative reorganization did so without exhaustive investigation. Some authority submissions were models of research, consultation, and patient working out of detail. But enough of these LEA deliberations are chronicled in the pages of the local press and enough of the conclusions are printed in the pages of their official submissions to enable anyone reading through every single one to come to the conclusion that the total approach was uneven and unsystematic and suffered from the lack of any real 'central guidance'. It also suffered from delay. Many authority documents record their distress at the long waits experienced before DES officials could give decisions on plans.* During these years a team was at work inside the DES dealing with comprehensive plans as they came in. But although from the point of view of the reform, plans were coming in far too slowly to achieve reorganization, the team vetting schemes was *over*worked and 'plans were coming in at least as fast' as they could cope with them, the problem being one of a 'limita-

* See, for example, supplement to fourth report of Chief Education Officer, Barnet Authority, October 1968, p. 2, setting out resolution from Barnet Head Teachers' Conference of 2 October.

tion . . . of human and physical resources' inside the DES.[34] This suggests a gross miscalculation about the type and size of the secretariat which would be required to deal with reorganization plans, and is yet another indication of the failure to commit the proper resources of time and manpower towards this major piece of national policy.

But it was not just that this dedicated team inside the DES was overworked, it was also that all around the country local authorities were in need of guidance they never got.

If there ever was a situation where guidance was needed, it was in this field of comprehensive reorganization. Long before 10/65 was issued this need was apparent. In the July 1964 debate on the Education Act, ministers were asked why 'LEAs were not receiving any guidance or help or even information from the Government?'[35] The Minister was asked to 'collate and render readily available information about reorganization of secondary education'. This was not done, nor was it really done when the government changed and 10/65 became official government and departmental policy – with the exception of the periodic 'scoreboard' announcements of 'who is reorganizing', the building bulletins and the large-scale NFER project. The NFER's research project was never due for completion until the early 1970s in any case, so was little likely to be of immediate help. Towards the end of the 1960s the DES published some excellent explanations of middle schools and a book explaining comprehensive schools to parents, all clear and encouraging,* and just the kind of information which many hoped would have been available at the beginning of the reform. Failure to get out information in time was partly the tradition of no central interference in LEA affairs but partly again a fear of controversy. All understandable, perhaps, but, as one MP asked in the earlier debate, 'how do people in schools – administrators and teachers – find out what is going on in other schools in other areas?'[36]

In the event it was to the educational journalists and such publications as *Forum* and *New Society* and the *Teacher* – but particularly to the Comprehensive Schools Committee – that many had to turn for this information. But this assistance was not enough to meet the urgent and widespread needs, especially among education committee members, who, like many members of the general public, had only the vaguest ideas about the difference between various methods of reorganization. When an educational writer spoke of 'The Common Base, the Special High Schools, the Leicestershire Plan, the Nottingham Plan, Comprehensive County Colleges' as possible forms of reorganization,[37] what education committee

* *Towards the Middle School* and *Launching Middle Schools* and Tyrrell Burgess's *Inside Comprehensive Schools.*

members knew the full implication of any of these? To which of 10/65's six schemes did any of these approximate? It was not just that information was lacking; sometimes information assumed was incorrect. For example, Croydon was regularly assumed by educational writers and many local authorities to be proceeding with its 1954 sixth-form college plan many years after it had been abandoned.[38] Then, too, schemes were always being confused. The junior college and the Leicestershire schemes were listed as the *same* scheme in many places, and right up to 1970, in fact.[39] In political debates speakers of all parties often made assumptions about particular schemes operating or proposed in specific areas that were incorrect.[40] The word 'botched' was used often in debates, as it has been time and again, with no definition of any kind – simply as an emotive anti-comprehensive catchword.

When it came to assessing how reorganization was proceeding, who could really say for sure? Just one example will illustrate. In the month that 10/65 had asked for all plans to be in to the DES – July 1966 – the *Sunday Times* and the *Observer* each assessed the situation on the same Sunday (10 July). Colin Chapman in the *Sunday Times* wrote that only a handful of the 160 or so authorities were *not* going comprehensive, and he named 115 LEAs which had submitted or were just about to submit schemes. Stuart Maclure, on the other hand, in the *Observer*, said only forty authorities would be sending in schemes on time, and half would be incomplete. In the end, again it was left to an independent organization – the Comprehensive Schools Committee – to keep track of the national picture. Their regular surveys showed how incredibly complex the picture was and how urgently needed was more and better information from the department.

Further problems

So far we have dealt with the politics of the reform – and with the policy of the government and the department in promoting it. We have suggested that had this been more positive and coordinated there might have been more success. But we have omitted to discuss three factors that were crucial: the campaign against the comprehensive, the campaign for the preservation of the grammar schools (not the same thing), and the problem of finance.

Before circular 10/65 most of the obstructive campaigning was directed specifically against the idea of the comprehensive school itself. Objections were mainly centred on size and associated difficulties. R. A. Butler dismissed comprehensives as 'soulless, educational factories'.[41] In those early days, this was all that was required in the way of argument, although from the first a consistent argument against the whole comprehensive reform had been carried on by such journals as *The Times Educational Supplement*. The objections set out in its leading articles in the late 1940s were written and rewritten for twenty years. Recently, 'backlash' minority groups, and some of the mass media, have returned to many of these old themes.

But for the majority the view began to change. By the time the Labour government came to power in 1964, and 10/65 was imminent, there were many who were prepared to support comprehensive schools. Even earlier opponents were prepared to support them just so long as they were 'purpose built, and so long as there are no other good schools in the neighbourhood'.[42] It had become evident that the real argument was not going to be about whether comprehensives were good or bad, but how far they could encroach on the intake to the 'good' schools, particularly the grammar schools. The campaign against the comprehensive idea then embraced a much wider set of arguments.

This was necessary, for quite obviously many of the old arguments against reorganization were self-contradictory. For example, comprehensives would 'lower the level of the brighter child',[43] but at the same time comprehensives would concentrate upon the brighter child and ignore the 'ordinary child'.[44] Comprehensive schools were too large; comprehensive schools were too small to have viable sixth forms.[45] Comprehensive schools would be one-class schools; comprehensives would promote social mixing and this was not the proper aim of educational institutions. The argument was against the one-class school but in favour of comprehensives *only* in so-called one-class areas: like council estates. The argument was against the 'soulless factory' but entirely in favour of the exceptionally large purpose-built school rather than adapted smaller schools. What was not contradictory, however, were the arguments that could be mustered for the 'proven worth' of the grammar schools. And it was here that the campaign against comprehensives could far more respectably concentrate.

Although there were sporadic and sincere arguments in favour of the excellence of the secondary modern school, this campaign never got off the ground – too many of the staff and parents of these schools wanted to see them evolve into comprehensive schools. By contrast, many staff and parents of grammar schools wanted to see them remain outside reorganization. Thus around the individual grammar schools sprang up the defence societies, the 'save our schools' committees, the preservation societies, the grammar-school action groups. The fighting funds and the fighting associations of the prestige grammar schools were fully operational whenever local authority planning of reorganization looked like taking place. In towns like Leicester, Flint, Liverpool, Enfield, Ealing, Bexley, Dudley, and dozens more, they organized. A national grammar group was born through the Old Boys' Association of Hampton Grammar School – calling itself the National Education Association – but it was almost superfluous. Local groups could take care of themselves. The grammar schools themselves were the actual centres of campaigns. Headmasters provided facilities for meetings and urged parents to sign or circulate petitions, sometimes sending pupils home with anti-comprehensive leaflets. Old Boys' and Old Girls' Associations campaigned against the reforms. The more prestigious the school, the bigger and better its support – both financially and otherwise.

By contrast those who wished to campaign locally for the comprehensive reform had no centre, and had no ready-made allegiance to a school to draw upon. The Comprehensive Schools Committee did much to redress the balance nationally, but locally the grammar groups practically always had the editorials of the local press to help. Most of these media were editorially pro-grammar or anti-comprehensive, but even those which were editorially neutral always took as the central news-reporting question: should the grammar school go or stay? It was rarely: what kind of comprehensive system shall we adopt?

Reporting was intensely emotive. The *Daily Express* spoke of the comprehensive 'drawing into its maw every child over eleven'.[46] Grammar schools were never to be 'extended' or 'evolved' into comprehensives. They were always to be 'destroyed', 'annihilated', 'assassinated', 'got rid of' and 'wiped off the map'. Even an article in *The Times* spoke of grammar schools being 'liquidated'.[47] Grammar-school staffs not only defended their own selective institutions but projected questionable motives on to those who would end selection at eleven, in one case accusing them of 'unscrupulous barefaced self-interest and trickery'.[48] Respectable local councillors compared comprehensive reorganization to the political system 'of Nazi Germany', comprehensive schools being designed to 'tyrannize the minds of the young' and 'create animal farms where all units receive such teaching as the State Commissars see fit to give'.[49] This prejudice reached its most ludicrous in the reports of the Queen's first visit to a comprehensive school, when one national newspaper next day assured its readers that naturally 'the word "comprehensive" was not mentioned in Her Majesty's presence'.[50] All this popular press propaganda reinforced the idea that comprehensive schools were rather dangerous or unacceptable institutions.

But more insidious was the impression given by the press that the grammar-school lobby represented 'the people', while those who supported comprehensive schools represented only the doctrinaire bureaucrats. The claims of the 80 per cent of parents and children who never had got near a grammar school were rarely put in the popular press. And it was only some journals, like *The Times*, that spoke disarmingly of the alliance between the grammar schools and the middle classes. *The Times* frankly admitted that schools should transmit 'manners, codes, attitudes, ideas and learning' from one generation to the next, and that it was now up to the middle classes to 'insist' upon a fight for their own schools.[51]

Whether it was a battle on behalf of the middle classes, as some saw it, or on behalf of all the 'little people', as others described it, the skirmishing of the gallant grammars were daily serial in many papers. The *Bristol Evening Post* proudly claimed to have devoted more column inches to the grammar/comprehensive controversy in that city in 1965 than to any other issue in any year in all its history.[52] Nationally too, most influential newspapers were committed to grammar schools (although their papers' educational correspondents were often far fairer to comprehensive schools than their editorials), as were a host of influential national figures, ranging from those with powerful university interests across to a battery of peers who regularly spoke up for selection, the grammar schools and the public schools – all three causes now united under one banner.

The grammar schools were also able to count on large sums of money and the services of able legal advisers. These two advantages enabled them to pursue their obstruction of reorganization into the High Court. In the Enfield decision they were rewarded with judgement against the local authority. The case turned on the necessity for an authority to 'post notices' of change in school-age range, but probably not one person in ten thousand knew this was the issue, nor knew that many authorities had previously failed to 'post notices' in similar reorganization schemes.[53] Such was the press campaign and propaganda about the 'people' and their fight against 'authority' that the judgement – in these David and Goliath terms – was read as a victory for the grammar school and for the principle of selection at eleven. In contrast, those who favoured the Enfield reorganization scheme did not fit into the press-manufactured projection of David and Goliath; as a result, their case got very little attention.

Far more important legally to reorganization was the now relatively overlooked Ealing Case two years earlier. The local grammar lobby wished to test whether comprehensive reorganization denied parents their right to have their children educated according to their 'wishes', as guaranteed by section 76 of the 1944 Act. In this case judgement was given for the authority, whom the High Court said had the duty to organize its schooling as it thought best. Parents' 'wishes' could not be taken as a right to control LEA policy or curriculum or school entry arrangements. The later decision in *Cumings* v. *Birkenhead* – upholding the right of the authority to direct Roman Catholic primary-school pupils to Roman Catholic secondary schools – strengthened local authority control still further.

All this intense controversy – expressed in local authority debates, in national parliamentary debates, and reflected in bitter legal wrangling – was bound to be reflected as well in government and departmental policy. If the department had been 'non-committal' and the government bent on 'kidology' before Enfield, they redoubled their efforts to remain cool afterwards. Ministers kept proclaiming that everything was going well when it was not, and that legislation was not needed when a good case for it could always have been made, which got stronger and stronger as time passed, until of course it became inevitable.

Against this background of anti-comprehensive campaigning, the remarks of those who kept insisting that finance was and is the main reason why the pace is slow seem particularly naïve.* It is extremely doubtful if grammar schools would have enthusiastically agreed to reorganization even if an extra sum had been set aside to assist them.

All the same, finance was crucial to reorganization – even if it is very difficult to know just how much reorganization schemes 'cost'. Local costing of schemes in the various LEA plans was worked out differently from authority to authority. In some cases very little costing was done, but very commendable plans were submitted. In other cases – Wigan and Hillingdon – schemes were commendable but were found by the DES to work out as too expensive and so were returned. But these cases were rare. When one comes to look at areas that went comprehensive in those years and those that declared they were 'unable' to do so, the factor that rarely comes first to mind is the 'cost'. Failure to reorganize was, and is, almost always linked to the question of local political or educational initiative.

We are not talking about areas with plans that they are unable to carry out because they are waiting for building allocations; these are genuinely held up through lack of finance, and this was far more of a problem in every way when the Conservative government elected in 1970 introduced a policy of cutting down new secondary school replacement building. We are talking of areas that have refused to plan, or to go ahead with reorganization, because the 'cost' is too much. Surrey was once such an area. It costed all six of the 10/65 schemes in its original submission and found them all too expensive. No doubt Surrey could not have gone comprehensive overnight, but its failure to work out any plans for so many years must have been linked to local political and educational initiative rather than to the 'cost' of reorganizing. This conclusion is reinforced by the fact that another Surrey authority, Merton, was able to begin reorganization in 1969 – ironically enough using the scheme that Surrey had declared was the most 'costly' by far of all six in 10/65: middle schools, and by the fact that once a 'political' majority was gained in favour

---

* See, for example, speeches by both William Alexander and Edward Boyle reported in *Education*, 25 October 1968.

of reorganization, Surrey itself, began reorganizing some areas using middle schools.

Finance determines the speed at which projects can be executed – that is indisputable. Because of this the original decision not to set aside special funds for reorganization was most regrettable. (From 1969 to 1970 a small sum was allowed each year for this purpose.) It meant that the process must be very slow in some areas. But finance does not determine the original decision to go ahead nor the planning of each step in the process. No one expected reorganization would be immediate. But what could certainly have taken place by 1970 was the *planning* of reorganization in detail for all areas, showing how reorganization would be carried through against the day when funds would be available. It was the need to effect planning and to marry reorganization building with R O S L A building allocations that legislation was so urgently needed to meet during all these years – and indeed, the reason why the Labour government finally introduced it in 1970.

But even though the national economic uncertainties prevented an initial decision to support this major reform with special funds, and even though many authorities have been able to reorganize successfully within the context of their ordinary educational expenditure, there can have been little excuse for the severe cuts in education in 1968, and the postponement of the raising of the school-leaving age. These were particularly hard for reorganization, for many plans were inevitably bound up with funds set aside for the raising of the leaving age, which were the key to reorganization. Many authorities had made their decisions to reorganize early enough to use R O S L A money in preparing and equipping all schools to receive pupils of all attainments, but in equally as many, because no decision was available, and no long-term plans ready, R O S L A funds were used merely to 'up-date' or 'enlarge' secondary modern schools, leaving grammar schools alone (henceforth with the excellent excuse that they were not 'equipped' to deal with all-ability intakes). The failure to insist that R O S L A funds and reorganization be coordinated closely – which would have been one of the objectives of early legislation – probably delayed meaningful reorganization by a decade in many areas.

Undoubtedly a definite commitment of resources for reorganization should certainly have been part of the policy of any government seriously bent on a major reform of this nature, but undoubtedly too – and important though adequate funds are – the real barrier to reorganization has not been finance, it has been policy. Circular 10/65 made reorganization permissive rather than mandatory. Some authorities rushed to reorganize; some went at reorganization steadily; some stalled; a few balked; but many more remain locked in indecision and stale controversy. The cuts in local-authority spending and the postponement of the raising of the leaving age did not stop reorganization, they merely stretched out the stalling and intensified the uncertainty.

We would not wish to give the impression that 10/65 made no impact. On the contrary, it was a great step forward. Local initiative, where it stirred, was given every encouragement. This had not happened before. The effect of this circular was immense and immediate. Paradoxically, it was its success that accounted for its difficulty. The encouragement it gave stimulated dozens and dozens of authorities to produce schemes, revealing a high level of support for reorganization in every area of the country, throughout the teaching profession, and in all political parties. It revealed equally how strong was national feeling against the 11-plus examination and all its consequences. It was precisely because the ending of the 11-plus selection procedure was so massively supported that the delayed decision to give circular 10/65 adequate legislative support, and the continuing failure of the department to back the reform at the centre with continuous information, a coordinated research policy, and long-term planning, seems so faint-hearted.

The comprehensive school as a positive policy seems never to have been fully campaigned for by either the Labour government or the department. Yet from the beginning public opinion polls – both NOP and Gallup and many smaller surveys[54] – showed that comprehensive schools enjoy majority support, while, even more important, anti-comprehensive opinion has stayed fairly steady around the 20 per cent mark, the percentage of the national population taken into the grammar schools. Moreover, public support has been shown to rise steadily as comprehensive schools are actually introduced into specific areas.* As comprehensives go on increasing in numbers they provide a centre, an institution, round which the pro-comprehensive campaign can coalesce. For ordinary citizens it need no longer be a vague idea about widening opportunities and choices; it can become allegiance to a specific school and to a known opportunity and educational policy. This means that when the real crux comes – as it inevitably must in all areas where systematic selection and coexistence remains – the majority versus minority nature of the comprehensive argument becomes clearer. And the growing numbers of comprehensive schools can individually and collectively work together to forward their interests, as they are now doing.

* See the New Society/Research Services National Survey, *New Society*, 26 October 1967. It showed that support for comprehensive schools rose to 73 per cent of the population in areas where comprehensive schools have been introduced and to 85 per cent of the population in areas where those questioned had children in comprehensive schools.

Notes

1. Joan Thompson, *Secondary Education Survey*, Fabian Research Series 148, p. 8, 1952.
2. *The Politics of Education*, Edward Boyle and Anthony Crosland in conversation with Maurice Kogan, 1971, p. 188.
3. Michael Stewart, House of Commons, 12 November 1964.
4. Croydon suggested the idea in 1954 but later withdrew it; see also the memorandum of 1942 by J. Idwal Jones, now MP, formerly a Denbigh-shire headmaster, to headmasters of Denbighshire Central Schools.
5. Roger Cole, *Comprehensive Schools in Action*, 1964, p. 201.
6. See research into Wakefield's guided-choice system by G. H. Whalley, published in DES, *Trends*, 1971, no. 18.
7. Thompson, op. cit., p. 8.
8. Cole, op. cit., p. 200.
9. Teeside National Union of Teachers statement, July 1968.
10. A. Griffiths, *Secondary School Reorganization in England and Wales*, 1971, p.72.
11. ibid, p. 75.
12. Speech by A. Crosland, 7 January 1966.
13. Public Schools Commission, Second Report, vol. I, 1970, p. 113.
14. ibid., p. 54.
15. ibid., p. 55.
16. ibid., p. 135.
17. Henry Clother, *Plebs*, October 1965.
18. A. Crosland, reported *Evening Standard*, 9 May 1966.
19. Crosland, ibid.
20. Christopher Price, *New Statesman*, 25 October 1968.
21. *Education*, 23 August 1968.
22. Marsden, Denis, Fabian Society Tract 411, *Politicians, Comprehensives and Equality*, 1971, p. 17.
23. East Sussex, July 1966, p. 2. The long-term intention, however, was to reorganize.
24. Peter Preston, *Guardian*, 13 January 1966.
25. 'Political concerns behind educational upheaval', *New York Times Series*, reprinted in *Cincinnati Enquirer*, 9 January 1969.
26. DES, *Middle Schools*, Building Bulletin no. 35, p. 1.
27. Written Evidence of the Department of Education and Science, 1967, p. 14, section 63.
28. A. D. C. Peterson, 'Comprehensive reorganization', *Comparative Education*, June 1965, p. 169.
29. Anne Corbett, *New Society*, 10 October 1968.
30. Boris Ford, Ford Report, Bristol, 1965, p. 6.
31. John Eggleston, *New Society*, 22 December 1966.
32. See *Going Comprehensive* by Richard Batley, Oswald O'Brien, Henry Parris, 1970, passim.

33. ibid., p. 40.
34. Kogan, op. cit., p. 191.
35. F. Willey, 1 July 1964, House of Commons.
36. M. Rees, 1 July 1964, House of Commons.
37. T. G. W. Miller, *Values in the Comprehensive School*, p. 14, 1961.
38. Cole, op. cit., p. 63.
39. *Inside the Comprehensive School*, Schoolmaster Publishing Co., 1958, pp. 155–6. See also E. Halsall (ed.), *Becoming Comprehensive*, 1971, p. 56.
40. See, for example, the debate in the House of Commons, 27 November 1964.
41. R. A. Butler, *Yearbook of Education*, 1952, p. 35.
42. Gilbert Longden, House of Commons, 3 November 1964.
43. Anthony Grant, House of Commons, 21 January 1965.
44. *The Times*, 18 January 1965.
45. *The Times Educational Supplement*, 21 July 1967.
46. 22 May 1965.
47. 18 January 1965.
48. B. L. Wilkinson, of Balshaws Grammar School, Leyland, article in *Lancashire Evening Post*, 15 January 1969.
49. Worcester Councillor Halstead, quoted in *Worcester Evening News* report of Council debate, 5 January 1966.
50. *Sun*, 26 November 1965.
51. Editorial, 18 January 1965.
52. Editorial, 12 May 1965.
53. Department of Education and Science Press Release, 3 November 1967.
54. See, for example, Stephen Hatch, 'Parents' attitudes to comprehensive schools', University of Essex, 1965.

Chapter 4
1970: One Step Forward, Two Steps Back

Labour's last year

By the start of the 1970s it was quite clear that unless positive steps were taken to secure the comprehensive reform in law, it could not be completed. The legislation that many argued should have been introduced at the beginning of a Labour government was not in fact introduced until its very end – in February 1970.

The 1970 Education Bill was ill-fated. Unforeseen absences of government MPs during an important committee-stage vote slowed its passage through Parliament, and the general election in June intervened before the measure reached the statute book. Had it done so, it would have been repealed by the newly elected Conservative government, of course; but even if a Labour government had been returned, there were many who were not happy with it. They saw it as window dressing, a 'bull dog with rubber teeth', as one researcher called it.[1] Even a Conservative member of the committee said it gave the impression that it would alter the situation overnight but did not have the power to do so.[2]

To a degree these critics were correct. It certainly required no one – neither minister nor local authorities – to actually get up and do anything. But it would have been a step forward in two respects. It would have permitted a determined Secretary of State to require plans from an authority if he wished to do so, and it provided that planning could be looked at regularly – by either authorities or minister – at five-year intervals.

The drawbacks, however, outweighed the assets. Firstly, it did not actually require local authorities to end 11-plus selection – only that in drawing up any reorganization plans they would have to have 'regard for the need' to have secondary education 'only in schools where the arrangements for admission of pupils are not based . . . on selection'. Secondly, it did not require authorities to prepare (or complete half-finished) plans; it just gave the Secretary of State of the day the right to ask for plans if he felt he should. This would, of course, have made every single request the subject of controversy, a policy likely to ensure maximum argument, minimum result. A Bill designed to secure the comprehensive reform is more likely to achieve results if it requires all authorities to reorganize all their schools, not just those authorities any individual Secretary of State decides at any given moment in time he wants to single out for a confrontation.

The Bill had two more defects. Although the Secretary of State could require an authority to prepare plans, he could not actually require them to put the plans into action. Two Labour members of the Committee accordingly sought to introduce an amendment which would have given an authority five years in which to begin its reorganization. This was not accepted by the government on the grounds of cost and because the voluntary aided grammar schools could not be brought in under the present law. This admission that local authorities were powerless to reorganize schools they were already maintaining – even if they wished to do so – was instructive in itself, and another measure of the inadequacy of the Bill. Voluntary aided grammar schools, like direct grant schools, will only be able to participate fully in a comprehensive system when the law is changed specifically in respect of these categories of schools.

The last defect in the Bill was that it permitted some schools to retain selection, since section I made it clear that the principle of non-selection only applied up to fifteen plus. Sixth-form 'colleges', sixth-form 'departments', and schools with sixth-form 'classes' were expressly exempt from the requirement not to select by ability. This was perhaps the most opposed part, especially by those comprehensive campaigners inside schools who were fighting hard, and with no little success (see p. 280), to get the principle of an 'open' sixth form accepted into educational practice. Even in 1970 it was becoming widely agreed that the 'sixth form' should become the 'sixth year', open to any student who cared to stay on, as previously the fifth year had been open to those who wanted to stay beyond the leaving age. The whole argument that further raising of the school-leaving age to seventeen or eighteen is not necessary because boys and girls who wish to stay in school would always be able to do so, is undermined by giving local authorities the right to keep selection for the sixth year of education. To find selection in any form underwritten in a Bill to bring in a comprehensive reform was somewhat dismaying.

Just how much of this Bill was a departmental draft and just how much the clear thinking of the Labour government, is again hard to say. But it is not without interest that a DES private secretary was later to comment of the Labour Secretary of State in charge at the time: that he was one of the Labour ministers who 'left Whitehall feeling that officials cheated them of their purpose'.[3]

When the first edition of this book appeared, in 1970, a few reviewers felt it was far too kind to the Labour government.[4] One even said it had criticized the Department of Education for the failure to bring in a genuine comprehensive reform 'when . . . (it) . . . should have been blaming the Labour Party',[5] a perfectly fair criticism in theory, since ultimate responsibility for a failure to legislate, to direct, to consolidate, let alone to complete, the reform must be the Labour government's. But in assessing the 1964–70 Labour government's record over the comprehensive reform, it is often extremely difficult in practice to disentangle departmental from governmental policies. But over one point there was no difficulty in agreeing: the Labour government had failed to bring about a comprehensive reform. Critics from the right found that Labour's comprehensive policy was wrong because it had tried to be coercive about comprehensives; critics of the left felt it was wrong because it had not been coercive. Researchers in the middle merely noted that both the policy and its instruments were 'scarcely revolutionary'.[6]

A number of interesting studies have been written which throw light on the matter, including a history of the Labour Party's wrestle with secondary reorganization from 1918 onwards.[7] These traced the indecision and disagreement which has characterized Labour on this issue from the first. They also showed that the majority of the Labour leadership never took much interest in education as a major plank of socialism. It was always left to a small group of educators within the party. The result was not so much any lack of agreement about broad objectives as disagreement about how central education policy was, is, and should be. As a result of the failure to bring education into the centre of the Party's thinking, it was usually left to the professionals. The 1945–51 Labour government clearly left conduct of much day-to-day, month-to-month, sometimes even year-to-year policy with the Ministry; and there is little disagreement about this by any historian. The 1964–70 Labour government is harder to assess in this respect, although critics have not been slow to point out that the Labour government came to office in 1964 without having thought out 'what political definitions of equality meant in terms of the everyday workings' of the educational system;[8] that is, had not thought through any concrete strategy for implementation of a comprehensive-school policy. Fewer, however, might agree with this author that accompanying this unpreparedness was 'evidence of a lack of commitment to the ideal of reducing equality in society', plus a 'failure to appreciate that economic and structural changes left to themselves will not reduce and may increase inequality'.[9]

Whatever the reasons, lack of a full strategy meant that there was no choice but to rely on the DES for a great deal of policy implementation. Naturally, the DES itself had its own continuing policy on comprehensives. Departments, especially older and long established ones, always have their well-developed lines on matters of importance to the work of their department. A clear account of this continuing policy on comprehensives in the DES is given in Maurice Kogan's book *The Politics of Education*. Kogan, himself a former private secretary and administrator in the DES, interviewed ministers from both political sides about education

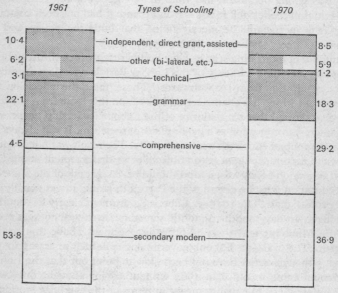

Secondary Education 1961 – 1970

Percentage of total pupil population in secondary education, England and Wales*

Shaded areas: selective, fee paying or independent sector
Clear areas: non-selective sector

1961	Types of Schooling	1970
10·4	independent, direct grant, assisted	8·5
6·2	other (bi-lateral, etc.)	5·9
3·1	technical	1·2
22·1	grammar	18·3
4·5	comprehensive	29·2
53·8	secondary modern	36·9

*1961 figures from p. 124, *Social Trends*, HMSO, 1970; 1970 figures from vol. 1, p. 2, DES *Statistics*, 1970.

Figure 4.1

during the 1960s and provides an introduction on the department's workings. It is possible to read this book straight through without realizing that the comprehensive issue was particularly controversial. The DES policy was clearly to get as much agreement as possible about it by pursuing a concensus line: comprehensive schooling is an irreversible, inevitable trend which will continue, its rate of progress depending upon the policies, tactics and personalities of various ministers of various governments. This is very different from agreeing, as many Labour government, and most comprehensive-reform supporters, had assumed would be agreed, that the comprehensive reform was to be characterized by a *real* change in the basic system of secondary education – abolishing an ability selection – to be carried through in all schools within a definite period of time. Without a clear idea of how they would accomplish this, however, a Labour government naturally had to put itself in the hands of the DES and accept their strategy of an accelerated rate of growth for comprehensives within a bipartite structure rather than any real change. Figure 4.1 (p. 86) illustrates how slow even this 'more rapid' acceleration was during the 1960s. Only 4 per cent of the total grammar-school population had shifted, for example. 'The making of policy', Kogan comments, 'is continuously in the hands of civil servants'[10] but, he adds, only in the matter of 'low-frequency policy waves'. The 'high-frequency waves' are those brought by the ministers. It is clear from his account that the DES's role was to see that political ministers' high-frequency waves married well with the prevailing DES low-frequency ones. For example, when it came to circular 10/65 some of the political ministers wanted comprehensive plans 'required', but the DES (and the Secretary of State) wanted them 'requested' only.[11] That they were requested is itself not so much of importance (the circular itself had no statutory powers) as revealing the way the DES 'line' prevailed.

It is also clear, and this is more important, that the DES was against legislation on the comprehensive issue from the first. The very curious reasoning behind this is given: that had a Labour government '. . . sought a change in the law there might have been a major political row attracting support to the comprehensive issue' from 1965 onwards.[12] This, Kogan reports, was also the minister's 'own view', and no doubt it was every political party's wish to have its policies accepted with as little argument as possible, but on the comprehensive issue, unless one was very inward looking during those years, it is impossible to ignore the fact that even without legislation there was probably going to be – as indeed there was – a 'major political row' over comprehensives from 1965 onwards, which did in fact attract and consolidate support for the comprehensive-school reform. The pity of it all was that the whole long dragged-out argument took place – both nationally and locally – without having the benefit of a secure reform at the end of it which legislation might have made more certain. As one critic of the period has written since:

Whatever else Labour learned from its first post-war spell in office, it should have been manifest that controversial change could not be entrusted to the DES to accomplish. Yet this is substantially what happened.[13]

The Labour government must ultimately bear the responsibility of having failed to transmit its own 'high-frequency waves' adequately on this issue. After 1970's defeat reaction to the government's record was swift and bitter, perhaps too much of both. Thus in the *New Statesman*:

Not more than four or five previous British governments offered such promise for education as this one. . . . Yet none, measured by the practical opportunities on the board, and by the ideals they accepted, was such a spectacular failure.[14]

Again the comprehensive failure was cited as among the most spectacular, again because of the 'indecision' which left matters to the DES officials.

A longer hindsight will probably be fairer to the Labour government, which was not without its educational successes, especially in the comprehensive arena (see p. 80). Certainly it will be less inclined to dump all the blame on the ministers of education themselves, for the problem was wider than this. The comprehensive issue was simply not given anything near the priority of importance it would have had to have had to succeed. Education itself, for example, was hardly ever discussed in cabinet, as, for example, regional policy was discussed and made central to all kinds of decisions. One Labour Secretary of State admits he brought only two educational items before the cabinet in two and a half years;[15] further, that when comprehensive education was debated in Parliament during the late 1960s attendance was poor and interest small[16] (Labour MPs nowadays, he added, are more likely to be interested in higher education[17]); and that although there were 'occasional differences' with Labour back-benchers over the 'comprehensive thing',[18] generally there was agreement within the Parliamentary Labour Party that things were going well. Lastly comes the interesting fact that never once during this minister's two and a half years of office, during a time so crucial to the comprehensive reform itself, did he ever discuss – either formally or informally – any education matter at all – let alone comprehensives – with the man who was ultimately responsible for the conduct of Labour Policy, the Prime Minister.[19]

Although individual Labour spokesmen tried to keep the comprehensive issue to the fore, and although outside Whitehall and Parliamentary circles the comprehensive debate raged as no debate on any educational issue in this country – except perhaps that during the years 1902 to 1910 – there was clearly a need to 'raise consciousness' on this issue inside the Labour government. Towards the end of their period of office the line got noticeably tougher, culminating in the introduction of the Comprehensive Bill and the preparation of a major Act which would have been floated in a green paper in the summer of 1970. But by then it was too late. The Labour government was dismissed in June after a general election which hardly once touched on educational issues.

The Conservative government

A Conservative government was elected in June of 1970 with a Prime Minister who had made it clear six months earlier that he would withdraw both comprehensive circulars 10/65 and 10/66. This pledge in itself was an indication of the hardening of Conservative attitudes on the comprehensive issue, for although Edward Boyle, the Secretary of State in 1964, has been widely given credit for being far more pro-comprehensive than he ever really was, he had at least said that a Conservative government, if returned, would not necessarily withdraw the Labour government's circulars.

But the 1970 Conservative government was less equivocal. It not only withdrew the circulars as its first act of government, but did so without the customary consultations with the educational world usually observed on these occasions. A candid new Secretary of State made it clear why: 'consultation is only meaningful if you enter into it in a state of mind where you intend to be influenced by the representations'.[20]

Whereas Labour's circular 10/65 had been laboriously drafted and had taken 'months and months',[21] the Conservative's circular 10/70 appeared almost overnight, its contents betraying its hurried birth. It was a non-document bringing a non-policy, or, as the editor of *The Times Educational Supplement* called it at the time, '. . . a dishonest . . . substitute for a positive line'.[22] It did not forbid comprehensives, neither did it encourage them. It treated them almost as though they did not exist. The new Secretary of State elsewhere questioned the validity of 10/65, which she called legally meaningless, and the existence of any meaning to the word 'comprehensive' – other than the meaning in the 1944 Act where local authorities are enjoined to provide a 'comprehensive' range of education to meet the needs of children of all ages, aptitudes, and abilities,[23] the only meaning of 'comprehensive' on the statute book. Circular 10/70's guidelines on secondary policy were, therefore, to be 'educational considerations in general, local needs and wishes in particular, and wise use of resources' – all phrases which could mean anything, nothing or a little bit of both. 10/70 also said no existing pattern of schools would be broken up if it seemed to be working well, for it was good schools Conservatives wanted, not schools conforming to any one monolithic pattern. Under 10/65, even though meaningless legally, Conservatives felt authorities had been under a compulsion to organize education in one way. Under 10/70 they were free to organize as they wished.

Reaction to circular 10/70 was generally hostile, for it was widely publicized as an attempt to undermine comprehensives. All kinds of individuals, organizations, leader writers and professional bodies quickly discovered

that they were, and always had been, pro-comprehensive. Many protested in addition: the TUC, the Association for the Advancement for
State Education; the National Association of Head Teachers eventually
voted in favour of comprehensives for the first time. Spokesmen for the
NUT kindly overlooked enough about the Union's own internal disagreements on this issue to come out and declare that it had been pro-
comprehensive and resolutely pursuing such policies from 1943 onwards.[24]
Even the unprovokable Council for Educational Advance was roused to
admit it wished the government had not been so hasty. All over the
national press leader writers who had for years knitted their brows over
this difficulty or that in the comprehensive reform, trotted out righteous
indignation at the threat to halt it so abruptly.

All this support encouraged comprehensive campaigners in local areas.
Believing the comprehensive reform threatened, local campaigning suddenly took on a new lease of life, spreading well out from the centre as it
never had before. Stop The Eleven Plus (STEP) groups formed almost
overnight in the most conservative towns and villages, new comprehensive
groups blossomed in factory darkened towns, and this upsurge of local
activity, combined with the new national assurances that almost everyone
had always been against the 11-plus anyway, led – ironically – to an overall
situation of very little change. Some local authorities withdrew their plans
to go comprehensive, of course; but others produced new ones. As far as
the numbers of schools becoming comprehensive each year went, there
was little change either. For the time being the reform merely pursued its
slow, slow pace. It could even be argued that the appearance of 10/70
stimulated authorities already far ahead with planning to get in 'under the
wire' and go comprehensive at once. Most authorities who had been long
planning to go comprehensive in 1970, 1971 and 1972 – and building
accordingly – went right ahead, and there was thus a slight 'spurt' in
schools going comprehensive in these years immediately before ROSLA.
At the same time the picture of long-term planning – for the middle and
late 1970s – showed a waning impetus.[25]

Long-term planning was no longer required, of course, and the gradual
grinding to a halt of the reform over the next decade was an obvious new
danger. It was also the case that LEAs had no real assurance that plans
prepared for going comprehensive would get accepted. What would be the
policy towards comprehensives themselves by the new government? A
quick acceptance of Leeds's agreed plans to reorganize raised hopes. But
later the earlier predictions about lack of a positive policy seemed more
likely. The editor of *The Times Educational Supplement*, for example,
found the Conservative's early comprehensive policy resting on 'muddled
thoughts on coexistence and parental choice',[26] but as time emerged and

individual decision upon individual decision piled up into a dossier of comprehensive case law, it was obvious that there was a basis for secondary-school policy: the 1944 Act. This was the rock to which the new government was clinging, revealing how clearly antiquated the old granite had become. But granite it remained, since no other major law had supervened.

The 1944 Act gave the new government no power to organize secondary education in any particularly new way, but the government did not wish to 'organize' education in any way at all.[27] The new policy was that local authorities should be free to be comprehensive or selective or both at once. The pro-grammar lobby welcomed the restoration of the basic rights of parents to choose between 'selection and non-selection' in education.[28] From conservative educationalists generally came satisfaction that the government no longer intended to 'impose' a 'uniform pattern' on secondary schooling and that 10/70 was lifting the 'restrictions on the character of secondary building' previously imposed by circular 10/66 (which had said all new building must be compatible with a comprehensive system).

On the face of it, the policy was one which should have made many more converts than it did. The reason why it failed to win new supporters was probably due to the very long argument which had already gone on about comprehensives. Everyone remotely interested in the subject knew the pros and cons by now, however crudely. It might sound sensible to say parents should be able to choose between selection and non-selection but by 1970 almost everyone realized that only those with children passing the selection process were free to 'choose' selection. And although it sounded magnanimous to say building restrictions would be lifted, almost everyone knew enough about the connection between new building and ability to 'go comprehensive' to know this rang hollow in the face of the vigorously pursued policy to give complete priority to replacement of primary-school buildings, thus running down the secondary-replacement programme to a standstill. In reality this was far more restrictive of secondary education than asking new buildings to be compatible with a comprehensive system, and it fooled few in its negative aspects (to stymie reorganization without actually appearing to have any connection to it) as much as it pleased many in its positive side: primary-school replacement.

Lastly, although the banner of knightly variety crushing the dragon of enforced comprehensive uniformity might once upon a time have caught the public imagination – by 1970 everyone was sophisticated enough to know it was a myth. Firstly, as *Education* remarked, 'The Labour Party, the Liberals and most Conservatives who are active in local government . . . long ago concluded the only practical resolution of the 11-plus dilemma

is in comprehensive secondary schools.'[29] But secondly, and this is probably the most crucial point, the real problem left by the policy of circular
10/65 was not uniformity, but the very opposite. By 1970 observers were
saying 'The present situation is near anarchy' and was in fact 'chaotic'.[30]
What was needed was not yet more licence but order at last. Soon after
10/70 was issued the Chief Senior H M I gave his opinion that the rampant
variety in school types which had been allowed to develop was a problem
for secondary education and that some day a government would have to
step in to take some 'hard decisions ... about the limits within which
experimentation with organizational limits can be accepted'.[31] He tactfully put the date in the late 1970s for this, but his worries about unlimited permissiveness had relevance to the situation in 1970 and to the
aftermath of a policy of under-coordinated and under-directed development of secondary education in the years 1965 to 1970. By the beginning
of 1970 schools with no less than twenty-one different age ranges were
operating in Britain, and this was without the half-promised new arrangements for fifteen year olds in FE colleges or many of the cooperative
schemes with colleges of further education from 16 to 19: 5–11, 5–7, 8–11,
11–18, 11–15, 11–16, 5–12, 12–18, 12–16, 8–12, 9–12, 9–13, 10–13, 11–13,
12–14, 11–14, 13–15, 13–16, 13–18, 14–18 and 16–18. As well as the age-
range problem, all shades of selectivity – from the outright rigidity of the
old one-day 11-plus exam, to 'hidden' forms of directing pupils to
'academic' and 'non-academic' comprehensives at various ages from
eleven through fourteen, were operating widely.

The continuation of selection within the system was not likely to stir
the new Conservative government, however. They did not disown selection, they merely said that eleven was 'too early'. This in itself, of course,
was a step forward and enabled progressive local conservatives to press for
reforms in their own local authorities. For, after the introduction of
circular 10/70, it was the Conservative Party's turn to fall to internal
bickering about the comprehensive issue. Rows had broken out earlier
between 1965 and 1970, for example in Middlesbrough and Torbay. In
other areas – like Leeds, Richmond, Sutton or Harrow – 'progressive'
Conservatives had the hard job of 'persuading' their more conservative
colleagues, confident that many ordinary Conservative voters were with
them. This impression was confirmed in those areas – like Barnet or
Buckinghamshire – which took the trouble to consult the public with
referenda on the issue. To everyone's intense surprise, not least, one
suspects, the officers of these traditionally Conservative voting areas, the
votes were overwhelmingly in favour of going comprehensive. Earlier,
in Bedfordshire, there had been a by-election for a traditionally Conservative seat – by chance at a time in 1970 when Bedfordshire Council was

having to make up its mind whether or not to withdraw its laboriously planned comprehensive scheme in response to circular 10/70. There was a lot of council members' pressure to withdraw as well as support to press ahead, and the final decision to go ahead was undoubtedly influenced by the by-election result when the Conservative seat was lost to the pro-comprehensive-reform Liberals in a contest almost exclusively about the comprehensive-education issue.

After these early pro-comprehensive victories, few Conservatives ever said in public, as the Bedfordshire candidate is said to have done, that he was against comprehensives on principle and in favour of public and grammar schools, which he put in 'opposition' to comprehensives. Any outright opposition to comprehensives as such was more likely to be behind the scenes, or in the endemic far right fringe groups of education which continued to press for selection. For the next few years, questions of pressure and counter pressure were to be those of a 'private' nature directly on the ministers: a 'right-wing minority' from the Barnet Council who had the minister's 'ear' or a formidable lady stalwart in Surrey who had got to the minister at a tennis-club party one afternoon.[32]

The pettiness of these exchanges drew attention away from serious decisions which were being made by the government on comprehensive plans, on a basis very different from that of the previous six years. Under a Labour government, 'schemes' for whole authorities and whole areas – involving many schools – had been requested, and were examined and passed as a whole. But under the Conservative government – even where a 'scheme' was sent in – schools were looked at individually, school by school. This was a crucial distinction in policy which was to tell greatly on comprehensive planning.

Of course schools individually had had to be approved by Labour Secretaries of State under section 13 of the 1944 Act – certainly after the Enfield decision in 1967 – but this was a formality once schemes as a whole had been cleared. Under the Conservatives, however, section 13 clearance for each school individually became the heart of the procedure. Thus the process of school-by-school analysis meant that no area's plan was examined as a whole, and therefore no coherent policy for a local authority was either expected or encouraged. Practice of school-by-school approval – where some could be rejected, some accepted – tended to nullify coherent planning. Barnet is a good example, an authority which had passed and sent to the DES a coherent scheme for reorganization of almost all its secondary schools in 1970. It was not examined as a total plan, however. Instead, some of the proposed new comprehensives were accepted, others were rejected and had to continue as grammar or secondary modern schools, making nonsense of the authority's 'plan', and making it impossible to end 11-plus ability selection, since the schools 'not passed' continued to require it. Inner London at the same time sent in a list of about a dozen new comprehensive schools, mostly mergers of existing schools. Again, some were accepted, some rejected. As time wore on, it became obvious that very few authorities' full plans were likely to be accepted as they stood; there were usually some schools turned down.

What was even more worrying than the new part-acceptance policy, however, was that little educational reasoning could be discerned behind these decisions. True, some of those schools rejected were to be on separated sites, had aroused local objections, were costly, or were of an age range not the orthodox one of 11–18; and these were the reasons given for turning them down. But it was equally true that some of those the Conservative government accepted were costly, were on separated sites, were of the very same 'unorthodox' age ranges and had also had objections (since almost every comprehensive scheme has both its supporters and its objectors). Why some schools accepted to go comprehensive, and not others? It was quite impossible to tell. This left an air, if not of arbitrariness, certainly of uncertainty. And it made it even harder for a local authority to plan ahead, with a reasonable assurance that its school plans would pass.

It was true that overall not many schools have been actually rejected under section 13 – only about fifty in the first two years of the Conservative government – but all a scheme needs is to have one or two grammar schools 'left out' to be converted from a scheme abolishing the 11-plus to one which must retain it. In 1972 the rejection of the request for Kidderminster's three grammar schools to be allowed to go comprehensive was an example. But there were many others. Thus the school-by-school vetting process of the 1944 Act, perfectly serviceable in the days when the 11-plus was acceptable by everyone, was an actual barrier to planning a comprehensive reform by 1970, when hardly anyone any longer accepted the 11-plus. Comprehensive reorganization with all its attendant needs – e.g. the need for institutions to cooperate for the 16–19 age group or for incorporation of all schools in any given scheme, grammar as well as secondary modern – requires a legal directive that enforces a look at a whole area's needs and the way existing educational institutions could meet them. The new local-government reorganization will require this over-view planning even more urgently. The 1944 Act's provisions cannot meet this need.

But uncertainty did not lie merely with difficulties in coherent planning or the mystery over which criteria were really used for passing or rejecting individual schools as 'comprehensive'. Far more important, schemes sent by LEAs for approval where the grammar schools had been left out –

Walsall's 1970 scheme for example – found acceptance without question. The Conservatives' coexistence policy soon became a standing educational joke, as the following item from *This England* column makes clear: 'The new scheme, which has taken months to prepare, will mean a completely comprehensive system, except for grammar schools.'[33] As time went on, it slowly dawned on observers that in general what won approval for reorganization was enlargement of secondary modern schools as comprehensive, while what was often disallowed were local authority requests for changes to grammar schools. So much for the promise that local authorities would be free to organize their own pattern of education as they wished. So much too for many authorities' pledges to end the eleven plus, since without government approval to evolve grammar schools in the same way as secondary modern schools, they were forced to keep selection against their will. *Education*, commenting on this problem of coexistence, found the Conservative government had a 'sorry record' which 'pointed to a quite negative attitude to the elementary necessities of efficient local administration and to a reckless application of indigestible doctrines'.[34]

This then was the third way – the first two having been finance and uncertainty over planning criteria – by which the comprehensive tide could be turned to nought: simply encourage the reorganization of the secondary modern sector only, leaving the grammars largely alone. This was the negative side of the new government's positive policy of 'coexistence': that is, of comprehensive schools along with, and in the middle of, the old system – which in the end is, and always has been, the greatest threat to the comprehensive reform. As comprehensives were the controversial topic of the 1960s, so coexistence becomes that of the 1970s.

A coexistence policy not only encouraged the retention of grammar schools, but it lead to such controversial actions as the government's directive to Surrey to retain the 11-plus in an area going comprehensive (because grammar schools existed still in neighbouring areas). It also encouraged the government to give extra funds to the most selective of all the grammar schools: the direct grant schools. Unfortunately, the two million pounds for the direct grant schools came just about the same time – Autumn 1971 – as the government had turned down building projects which included the new Thomas Calton Comprehensive in Inner London, a prototype community school which had been planned for long and hard. The two acts were compared and seen by many as a policy which supported the grammar schools at the expense of the comprehensives. At the same time too it was becoming clear that the clampdown on secondary-schools replacement was holding up even the meagre future comprehensive planning that was still in the pipeline. In early 1972 it was estimated that half the comprehensive schools then definitely planned were unable to give firm dates for starting because of uncertainty over building money.[35]

Important though funds for building are, however, it was once again not building money which was the main cause of the difficulties facing the comprehensive reform: it was the policy of the government, particularly their underwriting of the policy of selective schools existing alongside comprehensive schools. A Conservative government could easily decide to go ahead with a few Thomas Caltons or to give some funds for special aspects of reorganization. Many hoped that as the government wore on, it would adopt a more positive approach to the comprehensive school. But if at bottom a policy of coexistence prevails – then all the extra smiles and pennies will not be enough, because selection at 11-plus or 12-plus or 13-plus will have to continue between schools. Legislation to end selection and to require all schools to reorganize to meet the needs of pupils of all abilities – with funds and positive help in meeting problems – still remains the corner-stone of a successful comprehensive-reform policy.

Many are of the opinion that the reform must await the return of a Labour government for completion. Much will depend therefore upon whether the Labour Party's educationalists and teachers, parents and ordinary workers can convince its leadership to make education a central, rather than a peripheral, issue from now onwards; and upon whether the overworked party secretariat, and its working party on education, can evolve a successful strategy in time. The spectacle of a few local Labour Parties being returned to county halls in the early 1970s after long periods out of office, no further forward with ideas for going comprehensive than when they left office in the mid-1960s – was hardly a heartening precursor of national Labour activity. On the other hand, those newly elected Labour authorities which had taken a firm policy decision to go comprehensive and were ready to argue their well-prepared schemes through, despite a growing scepticism about the government's assurances that they could organize as they wished, gave encouragement to all around.

But the comprehensive reform is far bigger than a single political party, and always has been. In any case major reforms scarcely can be secured by a single political party, nor would the majority who support the comprehensive reform expect it any more than they had a right to expect the DES to alter its own comprehensive policy in 1964 just because an incoming Labour government had forgotten to do its homework. Those who claim it is the Labour Party's 'historic role' not merely to 'articulate and guide, but actually to arouse and lead a popular demand for equality in education',[35] tend to forget that as a whole the Labour Party has rarely aroused or lead anyone anywhere on education. But it has always managed to listen well, and it has usually followed the lead of educational advance fairly persistently. To ordinary teachers, students, and the many thousands of others who care about a proper comprehensive reform, the lesson is plain: work it out for themselves, and press all the political parties and other centres of influence both nationally and locally – as hard as they can, as often as they must.

Reorganization has been able to take place as much as it has to date because local pressure has been successful just as much as because central governments have given any lead or help. It has also been able to take place inside the present artificial local-authority boundaries, with very little cooperation across those boundaries being necessary – because reorganization is a neighbourhood matter in most cases. It involves a 'natural' area, limited by how far the pupil population can travel, or by the existing educational institutions and their traditions of serving the local community. Enlarging local authorities will mean a new look at how certain of these institutions – the technical colleges, for example – will serve a wider population, but it will not alter the need to plan fully comprehensive schooling for each neighbourhood individually.

The net effect of both the Labour government's circular 10/65 and the Conservative's 10/70 has been to force the demand for comprehensives, and the campaigning, down to the local level. The local community is the essential building block of the educational system, where participation in education is most possible for ordinary citizens. But there is a limit to what the local authorities or the local pressure groups can do alone. The time is long overdue when central government aid, central government coordination and direction, central government advice, central government legislation, and central government long-term planning – with fair criteria and coherent standards laid down for comprehensive schools of all kinds, together with the extension of these criteria to all secondary schools – must be made. It is a comprehensive system which is required, not merely a few more comprehensive schools; and only a national decision will make this possible. Without this necessary national action, the reform will always remain half way there.

Notes

1. A. Griffiths, *Secondary School Reorganization in England and Wales*, 1971, p. 104.
2. W. Van Straubenzee, quoted in *Education*, March 1970, p. 281.
3. Maurice Kogan, *The Politics of Education*, 1971, p. 44.
4. See, for example, reviews by Margaret Miles, Edward Blishen and Anne Corbett.
5. Anne Corbett, *New Society*, 17 September 1970.
6. A. Griffiths, op. cit., pp. 72–4.

7. M. Parkinson, *The Labour Party and the Organization of Secondary Education 1918–1965*, 1970.
8. Denis Marsden, *Politicians, Comprehensives and Equality*, Fabian Society Tract 411, 1971, p. 2.
9. ibid., p. 15.
10. Kogan, ibid., p. 42.
11. ibid., p. 189.
12. ibid., p. 51.
13. Marsden, op. cit., p. 15.
14. Brian Jackson, 'Where Labour went wrong', 4 June 1971.
15. Kogan, op. cit., p. 160.
16. ibid., p. 166.
17. ibid., p. 165.
18. ibid., p. 165.
19. ibid., p. 35.
20. Margaret Thatcher, House of Commons, 8 July 1970.
21. Kogan, op. cit., p. 189.
22. Stuart Maclure, *The Times Educational Supplement*, 3 July 1970.
23. Interview with *Sunday Times*, 15 November 1970.
24. Edward Britton, *Teacher*, 17 July 1970.
25. See C. Benn, *Comprehensive Schools in 1972; Plans to 1975;* p. vii.
26. Stuart Maclure, 3 July 1970.
27. See Secretary of State's speech to North of England Conference, reported 15 January 1971.
28. NEA, 'Hiccoughs in education', 9 October 1970.
29. *Education*, 17 July 1970.
30. A Griffiths, op. cit., pp. 99 and 104.
31. William Elliott, 'School or college from 16–19?' Address to the Education Section, The British Association, 8 September 1970.
32. Debate in House of Commons, 5 November 1971, col. 501 and passim.
33. From the *New Statesman*, and quoted also in the House of Commons Debate, 5 November 1971, col. 591, Hansard. The newspaper in which it appeared was the *Coventry Evening Telegraph*.
34. 3 March 1972.
35. C. Benn, 1972 *Survey of Comprehensive Plans*, op. cit., p. 8.
36. Marsden, op. cit.

Part Two
Schemes and Schools

Chapter 5
The Transition

State of play

At the start of the decade 1970 there were well over 1300 comprehensive schools in Britain. Almost a third of secondary-age pupils were in comprehensive schools. By 1975 the number of schools is likely to be in the region of two and a half thousand, with half the secondary-age population.

Of course, many of these schools are in 'interim' comprehensive schemes, where selection is retained. Many more are competing with grammar schools: sometimes with 20 per cent of the 'top ability' population selected out of the comprehensive sector. There is a growing belief that comprehensive schools in these situations should not be called 'comprehensive'.* If a *very* pure definition of comprehensive school were used, therefore, applying only to fully developed comprehensive schools in situations where all selection at eleven and throughout the secondary stage had been completely abolished, the percentage of the secondary population receiving comprehensive education in 1970 was very much smaller: not more than 10 per cent. By the mid-1970s it is likely to be no more than 20 per cent.

Nevertheless the number of comprehensive schools continues to rise each year. The increase in comprehensive schools since 1950 is shown in Table 5.1. What is not shown, however, is what is likely to happen in the middle of the decade, where on present planning figures from local authorities, the reform could begin to slow down. The following figures were taken from local authorities' forward planning in 1971, and show the position of uncertainty at that time.[1]

1972 238 comprehensives planned to open
1973 141 comprehensives planned to open
1974   55 comprehensives planned to open
1975   20 comprehensives planned to open
Planned, but with no dates for opening: 600

What was crucial here were the 600 additional comprehensive schools agreed and planned in 1971 which could not at that time give firm dates

* See chapter 19.

Table 5.1 Growth of comprehensive schools in England and Wales, 1950–73

Year	1950	1955	1960	1965	1966	1967	1968	1969	1970	1971*	1972*	1973*
Number of schools	10	16	130	262	387	507	748	960	1145	1370*	1585*	1825*
Percentage of secondary-school population in comprehensive schools	0·3	0·6	4·7	8·5	11·1	14·4	20·9	26	31	35*	41*	46*

* Figures and percentages for these years approximate only. For 1960 to 1968 percentages given by Minister of State for Education and Science, House of Commons, 15 May 1969. Percentages for 1950 and 1955, and numbers of schools from 1950 to 1970, derived from, or given in, DES, *Statistics*, vol. I, p. viii, 1968 and vol. I, 1970.

for opening, mainly because of uncertainty over new building, but also because local political decisions to go ahead were still awaited.[2] If these 600 schools materialize by the end of the 1970s, about 75 per cent of the nation's pupils will be in comprehensive secondary schools.* Radical changes in government policy, or a new government, of course, would alter the position considerably. Many hope that such changes will occur, for a system that is still 25 per cent non-comprehensive would present almost insurmountable problems in many areas. Had a genuine comprehensive reform been undertaken in 1965, with the legislation and funds to support it, the end of the 1970s would be seeing the final stages of its completion, rather than yet another crisis of confidence over the retention of a selective sector, shrinking so very much more slowly than the comprehensive sector is growing. Figure 4.1 shows this particularly clearly, especially the extremely slow state of decline of the total grammar-school population. All the same, it is now certain that comprehensive schooling will be the majority schooling by 1980 and it is for this reason that the development of the comprehensive school is of such importance to the country.

How schools and authorities make the change

As we saw earlier, decisions about when and how to actually reorganize have always been left to individual local authorities. These are two obvious ways for an authority to 'go comprehensive' – and between these two poles there are many gradations. The first is all at once: all schools change over in a single September. The second is to change over one school at a time.

The school-by-school method is not as simple as it sounds – for this approach can be adopted by authorities with every intention of reorganizing fully but anxious to take the process step by step, as well as by authorities which have no intention of adopting a fully comprehensive system but which are not averse to one or two comprehensive 'experiments' here and there. Gloucester and Buckinghamshire were examples of the last type of authority in 1972. For authorities planning on full reorganization, but unable to do it all at once, Leicestershire is a good example. Reorganization began in Leicestershire in 1957. It slowly involved more and more schools and in 1969 Leicestershire completed its changeover. The merit of the slow changeover is obvious. No upheaval occurs; the operation of a single school can be observed before proceeding. Organization, architecture or teaching can be corrected or changed on the basis of experience.

In theory it means a tranquil transition. But in practice it sometimes

* These figures, and others in this section, relate to England and Wales only. For Scotland, see page 393.

turns out to be too tranquil. For example, when a scheme is the victim of local political change or of political decisions to delay. Many of the pioneer comprehensives in the big cities have been left in the position of stranded experiments by such piecemeal policies of transition. As said earlier, a school-by-school changeover can be indistinguishable from almost no reorganization at all, although there are 'legitimate' reasons why some authorities must go slowly. One is because of the necessity to await building allocation money. What counts, therefore, in school-by-school reorganization, and what distinguishes it from non-reorganization, is the clear decision to proceed along comprehensive lines in respect of *all* existing schools on firmly fixed dates with a clear order of priority.

It was partly observation of the pitfalls that could await one-by-one changeovers, but partly too a desire to effect a meaningful and definite reorganization that led many authorities – reorganizing after 10/65 – to decide on the first form of changeover: where all schools in an area change together. Quite obviously this is a process that is easier done in boroughs than in counties. With the best will in the world schools in counties are often so scattered that reorganization must take place area by area. In very big counties it is usually new-town or new-growth areas first. Essex is a good example here. Harlow came first – as a new town. Basildon and the overspill areas followed. The rural divisions are coming along much more unevenly and the tranquil towns – like Colchester – very slowly indeed, if at all.

In many of these large counties – Lancashire, Kent and Cheshire, for example – the extreme unevenness of the reorganization process is the most formidable argument for legislation requiring an end to the 11-plus as a means of requiring areas to make firm plans for all schools. While fierce arguments rage in one part of a county about whether to have a comprehensive school or not, a few miles away in another part of the same county all schools may have been comprehensive for a decade. In still further authorities – with no comprehensive schools at all as yet – the charade of plans forwarded, plans returned, plans voted in, plans voted down has reached Gilbertian heights. Legislation is essential here as a means of effecting definite decisions. It is also necessary to save money, for decisions which are taken, reversed and retaken are costly, and become vastly more so when they occur after building has already begun. In London a decision to form a new comprehensive out of a merger of an existing old-building comprehensive and a grammar school (next door to each other) was taken under one political party, but reversed later under another, and the new building necessary started – in the form of a new upper school for the comprehensive, the grammar remaining alongside it. Later came another change of local government and another change of plan, but this time after the roof was already on the new building. The new project was comprehensive and the main building had to be reconverted to change it from an upper school into a lower school. The extra cost was considerable, and with a firm policy of reorganization from the start the problem need never have arisen.

By contrast, those authorities that make the change resolutely and uniformly – although they may have a short local 'storm' at the time – sometimes find that in the end this is the easiest solution. Very large towns that did this were Manchester in 1967, Sheffield in 1969. Even so neither's reorganization was complete, for the Roman Catholic, Church of England and Jewish secondary schools were not included in Manchester and direct grant schools also remained in both. An authority where *all* schools change over, and where no selective schools of any kind are left in the area of the authority, is rare.

Of course even in the once-for-all method it is possible to change without actually reorganizing. This can happen where an authority decides to adopt a different age of transfer – say, from eleven to twelve – but still retains selective schools at the *new* point of transfer. Legislation to end the 11-plus will also have to be able to deal with this kind of evasion to be fully effective.

The argument against once-for-all change is that it is too precipitate: there is no room for adjustment as experience of reorganization proceeds. It is true that once all schools have ceased to be selective, it is hard to reintroduce the 11-plus. But it is not true that adjustments cannot be made. Even a wholesale changeover is only in respect of the first year's intake. It takes a full seven years for most reorganization schemes to go through completely – whether begun by taking in a first year only to a newly built school or by arranging for all-ability intakes into previously existing schools. It would be a rare authority that did not use the seven years of the actual reorganizing process to observe, to monitor, to adjust. The way to gain 'experience' of reorganization is not by having isolated comprehensive schools in among selective schools for a decade; this experience can be gained best within the schools *as* they reorganize – adjustments being made constantly, as they have been in hundreds of schools in dozens of authorities.

Reorganization is not a mechanical process, it is living and evolutionary. As one local authority document says, 'No two secondary schools will develop exactly alike – they must be adaptable and responsible to the environment they are in.'[3] Moreover, nothing should be regarded as truly final in comprehensive reorganization – except, perhaps, the decision to abolish selection. Within the framework of genuine comprehensive provision for all local pupils, each area and each school should be free to develop

the form of reorganization that best meets its own special needs and traditions. It is in this way that individuality and local initiative – hallmarks of
British educational practice – will both shape, and respond to, this
historically inevitable expansion of educational opportunity.

Foundation problems

Just as there are two ways for local authorities to make the transition to
comprehensive schools, so we found from our smaller sample of schools that
there were two definite points of view about the best way to go comprehensive from a previously existing school situation – whether the change is
an enlargement of a single school, an amalgamation of two schools, or
moving into an entirely new school. The first, and the one favoured by the
majority of our smaller sample (as well as by those writing on the subject
in comprehensive school literature), was that it is best done slowly. 'Any
development would have to work itself out at the top'; or again, a head
with nineteen years' experience of three comprehensive schools: 'transition must be gradual, avoid shocking the traditionalists' and 'keep up
standards in all sorts of ways'. Successful amalgamations must be carefully planned: as one London head has written, 'a new school must be
created, it doesn't just happen'.[4] Many mentioned the need for adequate
time. One school felt the new head should have six months in the new
school situation before he was called upon to run it and that the 'former
head should be kept out of the new school completely'. Another school
also felt 'the need for time, to plan, to integrate, to adjust, and most
important of all, to allow those staff who wish to do so to find fresh
appointments, so that you can find the "right people" to replace them'.

But there was another view on the changeover that ran counter to this:
it should be immediate. One can compare the two patterns in the case of
the two sixth-form colleges in our survey. In the case of Rotherham, for
example, the existing pupils in the grammar school remain and 'work out
at the top of the school', the lower years dropping out one year at a time,
with the new intake coming in at sixth-form level instead of at eleven. At
Luton, however, the change was made overnight, between ending one
school year and beginning the next. The pupils in the designated college,
except for the sixth form, were rehoused in another school. The 'college'
then accepted all the town's sixth-formers immediately in a single September. No one can say that as an institution Luton's college did not get
off to an excellent start. One of the heads in our smaller sample of schools,
this time of an 11–18 school in Liverpool, also felt this method was right.
It is 'ridiculous to allow previous entries to work out', he said. 'Transition must be immediate: the old school must be killed stone dead.'

What were opinions about the kind of previous school it was 'best' to have emerged from? In *Comprehensive Education in England and Wales*, 1968 (referred to hereafter as the First NFER Report), T. G. Monks showed that in 1965 35 per cent of comprehensive schools derived partly or wholly from grammar schools.[5] Of our smaller sample of schools, thirteen were previously partly or wholly grammar schools, much the same percentage.* In the past it was always argued that a comprehensive school should have its 'grammar core'. Much of the argument about the early comprehensive schools was whether or not they were to be allowed to have a zoned area around them to ensure an intake of both selective and non-selective pupils. In the literature about comprehensive schools, it is also assumed that a grammar core helps to ensure a good start.[6] Specialist staff are easier to recruit and parents are more ready to support the school. This was confirmed by many of the heads and staff of our fifteen comprehensive schools that grew out of grammar schools. These schools said they had standing in the community and often that they had a higher proportion of graduate staff than would be the case otherwise. The Second NFER Report *Comprehensive Education in Action*, edited by T. G. Monks, 1970 (hereafter referred to as the Second NFER Report), revealed too that grammar-type allowance structures tended to persist in comprehensive schools derived from a selective base,[7] and also that pupils in these schools spent an average of an hour a week more in academic lessons than did pupils in comprehensives 'grown' from a new or non-selective base.[8] It is probably for this reason – the more 'academic' tradition associated with grammar schools – that some secondary moderns, when they 'go comprehensive', take such trouble to secure graduates to head their departments, while a grammar school going comprehensive may not be so worried about this. Several studies comparing the experience of schools going comprehensive from a grammar, as against secondary modern, base bring out several distinctions of this kind.[9]

The disadvantages that came with starting from a grammar school were confined to one point in the main: getting an 'academic' oriented staff to take an interest in the 80 per cent of pupils who were not 'academic'. Case studies of schools going comprehensive show that grammar staff were also more likely to be hostile to the idea of reorganization at first than staff from other types of schools.[10] They were occasionally likely to be rather

* Comprehensive schools in our smaller sample used for this analysis had been formed as follows: eight were previously secondary modern schools; six were previously grammar schools. Seven were purpose-built. Four gave no information in answer to this question. Eighteen were founded from an amalgamation of two or more schools. Of these amalgamations: six were grammar-modern, four were central-secondary modern, four were two secondary moderns, one was three secondary moderns, one was two grammars and one secondary modern, and one was a secondary modern and selective intermediate merger.

rigid too. One head of a grammar school that changed to comprehensive in 1969, put it this way:

all too many grammar schools which become comprehensive take in their new quotas of the less able in a rather condescending way, and try to turn them into failed grammarites. I am determined that we shall integrate them in a new school.

This head had been planning his school's enlargement to comprehensive status for many years, seeing to it that all his staff had regular planning sessions, that they visited existing comprehensive schools, and were visited by those who had already made the change. Once again, the key to success is put in the province of staff attitude and cooperation. But not all schools, unfortunately, planned for reorganization in the careful and positive manner of this particular head. Had they done so, some transitions might have been more easily accomplished.

Those whose schools were developed where there was no grammar school spoke of the advantages that came with a raised 'status' for the school in going comprehensive. Staff were much easier to attract. Of course, this was not always the case if a secondary modern became comprehensive in a 'coexistence' scheme. Said one: 'The worst possible start is to enlarge a secondary modern school . . . where the existing grammar school is retained . . . the position becomes impossible.' Close second to bad starts from another head: 'The worst way to go comprehensive is to build on an existing grammar school with a hostile staff.'

Among other disadvantages mentioned in developing from a secondary modern was that sometimes the actual buildings were old, and it was hard to convince parents that academic standing was as high as the grammar school. A few heads, too, said that at first it had been hard to attract highly qualified staff. But more usually, the complaint was not that staff were not qualified but that they tended to think small, to be approaching the comprehensive situation with bipartite glasses. Getting staff to think about the possibilities of teaching the full range of ability was frequently mentioned, and not always in connection with former grammar staff. A 'major' problem, said one head of a comprehensive school in a large northern city, was to get former secondary modern staff to think wide. 'There is no doubt about their ability to teach children of all abilities once they break out of the "modern" pattern and become adventurous and more demanding in the standards they set.'

Where schools had been an amalgamation of both grammar and modern, there seemed to be fewer complaints about difficulties of starting than where they had grown from one or the other. One of the points that stood out to us was how very carefully two amalgamating schools had often planned their joint 'new' school, especially where the school was on two sites, and what a contrast this made to the relative lack of planning in some areas with 'tiered' individual schools, which were sometimes physically just as close and, of course, together taking the same age ranges as the amalgamated individual schools.

Although schools reported various initial disadvantages and advantages to a foundation that was grammar or secondary modern or both, schools that had been established for some years – say a full school generation of seven years – said the initial start was by then of no consequence. The previous status seems to help or hinder only temporarily. After a school generation you are on your own. Schools that were formerly grammar schools find that this prestige beginning does not, after a while, give them the edge over their co-comprehensives in recruiting staff. Schools that were formerly modern schools find that lack of a grammar core does not hold them back in the long run and that other factors are far more important: community support or LEA helpfulness in staffing or in securing an all-ability intake. Many of the country's most successful comprehensives – with very large sixth forms – started without any grammar base of any kind: Allerton Grange in Leeds began as a secondary modern with a sixth form of only three in 1958; today it has over 300. Holland Park school in London began in 1958 as a merger of secondary modern and central schools. Today it has 200 in the sixth.

Whether heads or staff were actually writing from purpose-built schools – or only wishing they were – most agreed this would be the 'best' way to begin. The ideal way to begin even then is one year intake at a time, starting with the first year. But purpose-built schools are not necessarily counted successful by those who work in them because of their physical amenities or facilities, as we shall see shortly, nor even because they are 'new'. It was obvious to us that purpose-built comprehensive schools are successful because of recruitment of staff. The new or purpose-built school is able to attract teachers who positively wish to teach in a comprehensive. As one head put it, it is not because the school is purpose-built, but because the staff is 'purpose-recruited'.

In Scotland there appear to be far fewer foundation difficulties of the kind we have been discussing. Getting under one roof there is a much easier problem, since so many schools in Scotland have always had selective and non-selective pupils in the same school. There, as one head said, the 'major problem' is the introduction of the common first year, a problem likely to be less trouble in England and Wales. On the other hand, social mixing problems would be less likely to trouble Scottish schools – at least outside the big cities. In English schools this can occasionally be a problem – especially in the cities and especially in the early years of an amalgamation of two schools. 'The modern school people treat the grammar school pupils as cissy book-worms and the latter treat the former as layabouts,'[11] was one pupil's comment.

Observing this hostility in an amalgamated school, a staff member wrote: 'some schools in this situation will never become "one school" in the true sense of the word until all the children that now attend it have left'.[12] These difficulties are also sometimes noticeable where comprehensives still coexist with grammar schools or where strict streaming is the rule.* 'We in 4I have very little in common with pupils below 4V. Our ambitions and hobbies and interests are completely different so that we have nothing much to talk to each other about,'[13] was another comment from an amalgamating school.

Most schools amalgamating or enlarging to comprehensive status say they do not experience very serious social difficulties, but in schools where they can be shown to exist, there seems to be no shortage of observers ready to hold them up as proofs of the 'failure' of the comprehensive school. This may come from those who favour segregated schooling anyway or from those who have somehow imagined that the mere act of reorganization in a single school immediately will – or should – solve all social tensions.

A comprehensive school is not a social experiment; it is an educational reform. In a society with class and race differences, a school that reflects all sections of a local community – and reflects them in the proportions in which they are represented in the local community rather than in the artificial proportions in which they were usually represented in public, grammar or modern schools – will often reflect these differences in the school. Indeed, it may be that pupils meet other points of view from which in some cases previously they were protected and that although 'new ills are being caused by comprehensive reorganization, perhaps', as one teacher has written, 'long-standing ones will be gradually eradicated'.[14] The comprehensive school does not offer pupils a chance to hide from society, but the opportunity to learn in the conditions of social reality that prevail in the wider community. Where there are tensions, the opportunity to come to terms with them or to effect improvements through them, are just as likely to be realistic and, in the end, lasting, when approached in years to come by men and women who have had a comprehensive, rather than a segregated, education.

Everything points to the fact that the time of transition to fully comprehensive status is the most precarious time for a comprehensive school – though not necessarily the most difficult. It is also a period of intense

* This is borne out in part by Julienne Ford's research into social mixing in one streamed ILEA school, reported in her book, *Social Class and the Comprehensive School*, 1969.

Table 5.2 **Year of foundation (first comprehensive intake) of schools in the 1968 survey***

	Number of schools ounded	% of total	Number of schools in Scotland	% of total Scotland	Average % of top 20% of ability 1968	Average % staying on after leaving age 1968
1945	3	0·4	0	0	19	50
1946	6	0·8	1	1·5	11	57
1947	1	0·1	0	0	3	50
1948	2	0·3	0	0	10	45
1949	3	0·4	0	0	21	71
1950	4	0·5	0	0	11	44
1951	1	0·1	0	0	5	75
1952	4	0·5	0	0	10	44
1953	7	1·0	1	1·5	11	55
1954	8	1·1	2	3·0	10	47
1955	17	2·3	0	0	14	62
1956	14	1·9	1	1·5	13	54
1957	22	3·0	1	1·5	12	53
1958	24	3·3	5	7·0	15	57
1959	21	2·9	0	0	11	51
1960	10	1·4	1	1·5	11	50
1961	14	1·9	2	3·0	16	55
1962	18	2·5	3	4·5	12	60
1963	19	2·6	1	1·5	16	64
1964	62	8·5	2	3·0	15	59
1965	82	11·2	0	0	15	46
1966	92	12·6	3	4·5	16	46
1967	201	27·6	22	33·0	16	51
Other and unknown†	93	12·9	22	33·0		
Totals	728	100	67	100		

* For explanation of categories used in this and later tables, see questionnaire, p. 547 ff.

† Scotland 'other' were almost all pre-1945; England and Wales 'other' were those not answering this question or founded in 1968–9.

hard work. As one head in Derbyshire has written, 'Going comprehensive is like having a baby in the house: you wonder what you did before.'[15] Certainly it seems that schools intensify their traditional aspects during the transitional phase, the more so in areas where the problem of 'selling' the comprehensive is most urgent. In matters of uniform, speech days and the stress of GCE academic attainment to the exclusion of other forms of excellence, it is almost as if comprehensive schools are saying: 'We can easily beat selective schools at their own game.' How much of this is conscious it is hard to say, but it seems to be a necessary phase in the dynamic of reorganization. After schools are well established and accepted in the 'traditional' sense they often undergo a radical re-examination of methods and practices. We can see the results of this re-examination in many of the comprehensive schools that have been established for two and three school generations; and some of these new departures we discuss in this book.

But most comprehensive schools are still in their first generation, as can be seen from Table 5.2 showing the years of foundation of the 728 schools in our survey. Even though this table shows that many more comprehensive schools *now* say they have been 'comprehensive' for a far longer time than is officially agreed to in departmental statistics,* it is still true that 40 per cent of all the survey schools in 1968 took in their first comprehensive intakes in the two years 1966 and 1967. Further, half the comprehensives in existence in 1972 were established after 1968. It is these facts more than any other which illustrate the interim nature of the picture of comprehensive education in Britain that we are presenting: a reform very much in midstream.

Future planning

Before looking in detail at the comprehensive schools we surveyed in 1968, it is interesting for a moment to look ahead to the future. Even though many authorities' plans are extremely indefinite, enough are now submitted to show us that it is no longer possible or practicable to talk about reorganization in terms of circular 10/65's six types of schemes. As long ago as 1966 the Comprehensive Schools Committee named twenty-one variations in local authorities' plans for the future; and the First NFER Report in 1968 located twelve different types of scheme and seven different systems already in existence in 1965.[16]

Nor are these variations final. New schemes are likely to emerge yet, especially in the field of school and further-education cooperation. Schemes already operating will change, of course. For example, a school that is today taking an age range of 11–13 may well be taking 11–14 or 9–13 in five years' time. Many schools now 11–16 will become 11–18 all-through schools. And some of those that are 11–18 will shrink to become 13–18.

---

* Compare figures from this Table 5.2 with those for the years 1950 and 1955 in Table 5.1. In 1955 official statistics counted sixteen comprehensive schools in England and Wales, but thirty-five schools from England and Wales answering our survey claim to have had comprehensive intakes by 1955.

Circular 10/65 may not have been entirely effective in securing a comprehensive system, but it has certainly permitted and encouraged authorities to organize and adjust to meet local need, and to take account of experience, in a way that has rarely been possible in the recent past.

One outcome is a final laying to rest of those many early fears that comprehensive education would mean an imposition of a single monolithic pattern of schooling upon the British secondary system. If anything, the fear is now the opposite. The variety of schemes is so great that it may well have an adverse effect on pupil transfer arrangements, and on teacher promotion and career structure. For, from a state of affairs with only a single age of transfer – eleven – it will shortly be possible to transfer from lower to higher secondary or intermediate schools at the age of eight, nine, ten, eleven, twelve, thirteen, fourteen and sixteen. If new arrangements for working with further education colleges are put through, the age of fifteen may well be added. But it is not only that individual authorities have different schemes. It is also that in about half of the local authorities more than one scheme will operate in different areas in the same authority. In a few more authorities, even the same area will have different schemes: as, for example, where Roman Catholic schools operate one type of scheme, and maintained schools another, right in the same neighbourhood.

These developments, which are already very well advanced, mean that the question of importance now is not which 'type' of secondary school are you sending your child to, but in what age range does your child come? As one educationist, Alec Ross, has put it, the 'fundamental point' in education is now this: 'what kind of schooling' is right for each age range?[17] What, for example, may a teacher of a child of twelve expect in the way of facilities and pupil numbers in the classrooms and in the school? What may a parent of a child of twelve expect in the way of curriculum or play space? Should these expectations differ if the twelve year olds are in the 'last' year of a 9–13 school, the 'first' year of a 12–18 school, or the second year of a 10–14 school? Obviously, they should not differ. And an instructive speech by the Secretary of State in 1971 suggesting that they do differ should be noted carefully.[18] This is why continuing and central guidance on parity of provision between *types* of comprehensive school, including, perhaps, legislation requiring such parity, is so urgently needed.

Since 1968 there has come considerable evidence about the problem of parity between types of comprehensives arising out of the present Burnham structure, which gives advantages to comprehensives with sixth forms over those without (and incidentally to selective schools over comprehensives). The Second NFER Report shows up this disadvantage for the non-sixth comprehensive, the problem compounded when the schools are in poor areas, and/or are rather small.[19] That one form of reorganization should find itself penalized by the present structure, and another not, is yet another reason why the whole system needs re-examination to ensure parity.

There is also the equally serious problem of lack of parity between individual local authority support for comprehensives. Authorities can differ widely in the degree of support they actually give their comprehensives, and it is often this degree that makes or breaks a scheme. The Second NFER Report provides some really dramatic evidence to illustrate this difference between 'weak' and 'strong' local authority support for comprehensive schools. They give one example of two schools of the same size, in the same type of area, with the same size of sixth form, and with the same spread of ability in the intakes but where Authority A awarded £13,000 in additional allowances and there were twelve Grade E (top grade) posts each worth £700, while Authority B awarded only £8000 and allowed only two Grade E posts.[20] The NFER suggests there may be a case for the allowance structure to be 'reviewed', which is putting it mildly. There is now an overwhelming need to review the whole school system, including allowance structures for all types of schools within a policy of comprehensive reform for all schools, and as part of that same policy.

Possible patterns

Although the future development of reorganization may be various, it must not be imagined there is no pattern emerging from the plethora of schemes. It has long been possible to reduce this variety to three basic schemes. The first is the orthodox all-through school taking all pupils from age eleven (or twelve) straight through to eighteen or nineteen. The second is the tiered scheme, where there are upper and lower schools and a 'break' in between tiers between the age of eleven and the leaving age. The third is the separate sixth-form scheme, where there is a 'break' in some or all schools at the age of sixteen. Table 5.3, which is based on the plans for the future that were available from all local authorities in 1968, gives an approximate indication of the likely future popularity of these three basic types. Of course, it must be remembered that some authorities had not submitted their plans by 1968; and that some of those that had will change them – either slightly or drastically – as they reorganize. But from the present vantage point, as we get to the mid-1970s, it seems likely that in terms of schools, the three schemes may well divide up fairly evenly. Table 6.1 (p. 118) shows the way the new comprehensive schools opening in the year 1971/2 broke down in terms of type. As can be seen, it is remarkably similar in some respects to the long-range forecasts calculated in 1968. Of course, the all-through schools, having more pupils, will

Table 5.3 Future reorganization pattern – England and Wales
Based on local authority long-term plans operating, approved and submitted by 1968*

Type of scheme		Number of existing schools involved in planned schemes, 1968		Percentage of total planned schools
All-through	11/12–18	1524		38% All-through
Tiered	9–13/13–18	792	20%	25% Tiered
	11–14/14–18	197	5%	
	11/12–16+Sixth form college			
Separate Sixth	11/12–16 coexisting with	374	9%	32% Separate Sixth
	11/12–18	901	23%	
Selective Interim	11/12–15/16 coexisting 13/14–18	207		5% Selective Interim
Total		3995		100%

* For further information, see The Comprehensive Schools Committee's *Comprehensive Reorganization Survey, 1968/9*, p. 6, from which this table is derived.

command a greater share of the pupil population than other schemes. But even so, this table makes it clear that we can no longer talk about comprehensive education exclusively in terms of the all-through school. However the final pattern divides in terms of numbers of schools, it is obvious that all three basic schemes need to be equally seriously studied. Let us therefore take them each in turn.

Notes

1. C. Benn, *Comprehensive Schools in 1972*, p. 8.
2. ibid.
3. Reorganization in Gosport, 1966, p. 1.
4. Rhodes Boyson, 'Creating a new comprehensive', *Comprehensive Education*, Autumn 1967.
5. First NFER Report, 1968, p. 90.
6. *Inside the Comprehensive School*, p. 125: and *The Comprehensive School: An Appraisal from Within*, p. 24.
7. Second NFER Report, 1970, p. 32.
8. ibid.
9. See, for example, 'Changing to comprehensive status', *Comprehensive Education*, Autumn, 1971.
10. See, for example, case studies in *Becoming Comprehensive*, edited by Elizabeth Halsall, 1971, pp. 7 and 116.
11. Michael Cullop, 'From grammar to comprehensive', *Comprehensive Education*, Summer 1967.
12. ibid.
13. ibid.
14. ibid.
15. Halsall, op. cit., p. 102.
16. *Comprehensive Reorganization Survey* (CSC), pp. 3–4, 1966–7; First NFER Report, Appendix 5.
17. Alec Ross, 'Symposium on middle schools', *Comprehensive Education*, Summer 1968, p. 7.
18. 16 April 1971. A large part of it was devoted to middle schools.
19. Second NFER Report, pp. 27, 34 and 35.
20. ibid., p. 35.

Chapter 6
Basic Scheme 1:
All-Through Schools

Foundation of schools

The words 'comprehensive school' make most people think of a large, new 11–18 age-range school with thousands of pupils. In fact, as our survey figures confirm, most comprehensive schools today are not excessively large, not particularly new, and may not eventually cover the age range 11–18.

The 11–18 school, however, the 'orthodox' comprehensive, has until now held pride of place. Until 1957 it was the only type and therefore it is the type of comprehensive by far the best documented in literature and research. The NFER's major research project is almost exclusively about these schools. Robin Pedley's landmark, *The Comprehensive School*, was mostly about schools of this kind. So, too, were the National Association of Schoolmasters' and National Union of Teachers' publications of the 1950s and 1960s.[1] So, too, were the local authority publications that particularly stand out: Firth's on Coventry's schools, and the ILEA's on London's;[2] and lastly, the books on individual schools: Harriet Chetwynd on Woodberry Down and Margaret Miles on Mayfield in London, or Harold Simmons on Bedminster Down in Bristol. Many of the schools described in these pioneer publications were large, a good proportion were single sex, most had house organizations, many were purpose-built, and almost all were 11–18.

It is hard to realize that this type of comprehensive school might not remain in the majority. Table 5.3, showing LEAs' long-term plans as of 1968, indicates that only 38 per cent of all schools were being planned as orthodox self-contained 11–18 schools in England and Wales. In our own survey of schools in 1968 we found that this trend is indeed already taking place. Table 6.1, which shows the percentages of different types of comprehensive schools founded year by year from 1963 to 1967, shows what a remarkable drop there has been in the percentage of comprehensive schools that are all-through. For example, 68 per cent of the schools founded in 1963 were all-through; but in 1967–8, the year of our survey, this was down to only 43 per cent. 1972 saw the trend maintained (see Table 6.1).

Table 6.2 sets out the various types of comprehensive school in our

Table 6.1 **Percentages of each type of comprehensive school founded 1963 to 1967 and 1971/2**
Types of comprehensive school by age range

Year of foundation	11/12–18 Type I	11/12–18 Type II*	11/12–16	11–13	11–14/15	13–18	14–18	Sixth-form college	Total number of schools founded in each year
1963	68	0	5	0	21	0	5		19
1964	47	3	3	19	13	8	6		62
1965†	35	6	23	2	26	1	5		82
1966	41	2	36	3	8	5	3	1	92
1967	43	6	34	4	5	5	2	0·5	201
1971/2	48**		35	6	6	5	5	1	223***

* With regular transfer of pupils from other schools at sixteen for sixth-form or higher certificate work.

† One school omitted from analysis because type unknown.

** 1971's analysis did not distinguish between Types I and II, and this figure is for both types 11/12–18 schools in that year.

*** The number of schools opening as comprehensives in 1971 and giving information on their age range in the survey of reorganization:

C. Benn, *Comprehensive Schools in 1972*, published by the Comprehensive Schools Committee, 1972.

Table 6.2 **Types of British comprehensive schools of various age ranges, 1968**

Age range of school	Number of schools	Percentage of total schools	Number of pupils	Percentage of total number of pupils	Average size of school	Percentage of average intake in top 20% of ability range	Percentage of pupils staying on beyond statutory leaving age	Average number of O-level (or O-grade) subject-groups offered	Average number of A-level (or H-grade) subject-groups offered
11 (or 12)–18 (type I)	389	53·4	369,578	65·0	950	14	55	14	7
11 (or 12)–18 (type II*)	31	4·3	33,539	5·9	1081	25	62	15	9
11 (or 12)–16	154	21·2	90,383	15·9	586	13	37	7	
11–13	29	4·0	9762	1·7	336	12			
11–14/15	70	9·6	34,798	6·1	497	15			
13–18	34	4·7	18,295	3·2	538	25	63	14	8
14–18	16	2·2	9397	1·7	587	17	76	15	9
16–18 or sixth-form college	2	0·3	1164	0·2	582				10
Unknown	3	0·4	1810	0·3					
Totals	728	100	568,726	100					

* With regular transfer of pupils from other schools for sixth-form or higher certificate work.

survey of 1968. We see here that of the 728 schools replying, 53 per cent are all-through schools. This is rather a drop from the percentage of all-through schools replying to the NFER survey of 331 schools two years earlier: 74 per cent.* In the NFER survey the all-through schools contained 84 per cent of the total number of pupils covered by the survey.† In our 1968 survey this percentage had fallen to 65 per cent. In England and Wales just over half the schools were all-through, as Table 6.3 shows. Moreover, the picture continued to be remarkably stable for these types of school between 1968 and 1972. As can be seen, there is no difference in the proportion of the total of schools which are all-through, nor in the short-course comprehensives of 11/12 to 16. The percentage of sixth-form colleges is about the same too. The only changes are those taking place in the tiered systems. Lower schools have declined from 14·3 per cent of the total to 10·2 per cent, and upper schools have risen from 7·5 per cent to 11·6 per cent. Thus tiered schemes are as popular as they were before but they are being organized differently. Most of the 13–18 schools introduced in the last four years have 9–13 middle schools feeding them rather than 11–13 ones. Many of the 14–18 schools being introduced are being paired with a single lower school of 11–14 rather than being fed by two or three such schools. In the next few years the proportion of the total of schools of the 13–18 range will gradually rise, since so many are being planned. The proportion of short-course comprehensives might also show a rise, and since whether a school has or does not have a sixth form is of some importance, it is hoped that the DES *Statistics of Education* will give this information in future. Up to 1970 they did not, and lumped both 11–18 and 11–16 schools together under the one category of 'all-through'.[3]

Survey schools

In our survey we divided 11/12–18 schools into two types: those that were self-contained all-through (type I) and those that regularly took in additional pupils for sixth-form or higher certificate work (type II). The latter type of 11–18 or 12–18 school – sometimes called a mushroom-top – is therefore, strictly speaking, part of the separate sixth-form scheme outlined as one variant of circular 10/65's scheme. But even adding these second type to the orthodox all-through Type I comprehensive schools (Table 6.2), we see that the full total of schools of this age range still only represents together 57 per cent of all the schools in our survey. And from Table 6.1 we see also that even together, both types do not total more than

* 246 out of 331, NFER Report, p. 13. Excluding schools that were not comprehensive schools, the figure was 79 per cent (p. 229).

† Six per cent were in 13–18 schools and 10 per cent in schools of other age ranges (NFER Report, Table 90, p. 95).

50 per cent of all schools founded in any one of the last four years up to 1968.

Table 6.2 sets out further basic facts about all-through schools. We see that for type I the intake of the top 20 per cent of the ability range is only 14 per cent. The average for the survey schools as a whole was 15 per cent. On the other hand, we see that the percentage of pupils staying on beyond leaving age is 55 per cent (56 per cent for England and Wales, see p. 522). This compares most favourably with the national average for England and Wales as a whole, which was 50·4 per cent in the same year.[4] There is no doubt that these figures prove the success of the all-through school in holding pupils in full-time education.

The second type of 11/12–18 comprehensive school – the mushroom – as we see from Table 6.2, is 'more than comprehensive' in its intake of the top 20 per cent of ability: taking in 25 per cent. No doubt this is because these schools are in so many cases ex-grammar schools providing the 'sixth form' for neighbouring secondary schools and because some too may be still part-selective at the age of eleven. Their percentage staying on beyond the leaving age is 62 per cent, much higher than the survey average and nearly 12 per cent higher than the national average.

Size

Another point of difference between these two types of 11–18 schools and between these and other types of comprehensive, of course, is their size. They are very much the biggest schools. The all-through school (type I) had an average size of 950 (970 in England and Wales: see Table A.1, p. 522), and the sixth-form centre 11–18 school (type II) had an average size of 1081.

This problem of size in a comprehensive school is crucial; and is also involved closely in problems of future planning. We discuss the size of types of comprehensive school other than all-through schools, and of sixth forms, in separate sections of this book, since, of course, they present separate size problems. We also deal with size when dealing with the location or siting of schools. Indeed, anyone going through the tables in this book – or through the large number of further tables we have collected but, for space reasons, are unable to print – will see at once how very much the 'size' factor of a comprehensive school varies according to the circumstances, sex, denomination, geographical location or age range of a comprehensive school. In this section we shall deal with the size problem in general, but particularly in relation to the all-through or orthodox comprehensive school in England and Wales, for it is this school over which there has been most controversy.

Generally speaking, for the first twenty years comprehensive schools were opposed because they were too big – and felt to be inhuman – but for the last ten years because they might be too small – and unable to support a 'viable' sixth form.

Taking the first fear first: there has always been a tremendous amount of controversy over the idea of 'big' schools because the traditional British secondary school has always been small. Even in the 1950s the average size of the grammar school was only about 400, the modern school about 300. In other countries large size is not quite so unusual. The French lycée and the American high school not infrequently reach sizes of 3000 to 4000.

At first the comprehensive school too was thought of as, of necessity, very large. London's 1944 decision to go ahead with comprehensive schools of 2000 set the seal for a long time ahead. Although the Ministry of Education came out officially for a slightly smaller size of 1600 in its 1947 circular,[5] a chief officer now retired has told us that in 1946, when his own authority was attempting to introduce comprehensives, the Ministry insisted on 2000. The reasons given by the Ministry for having a comprehensive of such a large size were that to provide effectively for 'all the senior children' in an area a comprehensive must be the same size as 'the multilateral school', and 'the normal minimum size for a multilateral school should be ten- to eleven-form entry (1500 to 1700 places)'.[6] The key is in the words 'senior children', for in fact the large size was calculated on the basis of pupils likely to remain to the sixth form and on the number likely to make a viable sixth-form size. All during the 1950s political ministers – especially David Eccles – stuck to the 2000 size.[7] Even as late as 1965 Quintin Hogg was still insisting on this figure of 2000,[8] and so were many of those writing about comprehensive schools.* In some publications and in recent 'backlash' comment it is obvious this very large figure was only quoted as a way of discrediting the whole idea of comprehensive education.[9] As H. C. Dent has observed about the 1944 London decision on size, it did 'more than any other cause to sway opinion against the comprehensive'.[10]

In the beginning there were few who questioned the necessity for large size, although some areas suggested much smaller schools. Middlesex,[11] for example, suggested just over 900 in 1946 (about the average size of today's 11–18 comprehensive) with a sixth form 'shared' between schools – a plan also used in some areas now. In 1947 the Scottish Advisory Council suggested 800 as a good size for comprehensive schools. But these suggestions – at least in England and Wales – did not have much imme-

* In 1967 one speaker at a conference suggested 2500 was necessary to maintain an adequate sixth form (*The Times Educational Supplement*, 21 July 1967).

diate effect upon planning; and Middlesex's suggestions were turned down by the Ministry.

Two developments, however, changed the outlook. One was the success in the 1950s and 1960s of many very small comprehensive schools, far below the official minimum size. These were schools in areas with limited population: Scotland, Wales, Dorset, Isle of Man and Cumberland. We see from Table A.2 (p. 523) that even today the average size of the comprehensive school in the towns and villages and in the countryside is much smaller than in the cities and towns. For example, 11–18 schools in our survey in England and Wales have an average size of 1028 in the big city, but only 667 in the village.*

But the smaller comprehensive school has also become possible because the percentage of each year group staying on after leaving age and going on into the sixth form has increased far more rapidly than had been anticipated by any of the planners – including the Ministry; and later, by the Department of Education and Science, which had to revise its official forecasts of pupil numbers upwards in 1967–8. This was the second development. In many areas now because of this it is hard to pronounce categorically that a school is 'too small'; and the literature about comprehensive schools describes many small comprehensive schools that are run successfully.[12] Our survey also turned up comprehensive schools – in remote areas, like that on the Scilly Isles – that are as yet less than 100 in size, and flourishing. Several other schools we visited in rural areas – with less than 500 – were able to provide a good range of subjects right up through A-level. We are led to believe here that where selection has been completely abolished and the LEA generously supports the school, particularly in allowing extra staff – perhaps a bonus of four or five over the quota – and where the timetable is well prepared, with after-hour periods used, and staff prepared to specialize in more than one discipline, the 'too-small' comprehensive can succeed perfectly well.

The success of so many of these small schools has necessarily raised the problem of 'what is too small' for a comprehensive school? In early comprehensive school literature there was as wide a disagreement as there is now. One writer defined 'small' as a two/four-form entry school (500): while another defined it as six/seven-form entry school (1000).[13] Circular 10/65 itself came out for 'six or seven' form entry as the minimum size for an all-through school and, in most circumstances, this is assumed to apply to 11–16 schools also. No official minimums were ever given for middle schools or upper schools and some of these, as we discovered, are very small.† But even though an official minimum was supposedly laid down in

* See Appendix 1, Note 3.
† See Table A.2, p. 523 for example.

circular 10/65, it was not always agreed to. Local authority planning abounds with categorical statements that only eight-, or nine-, or ten-form entry schools are 'acceptable' as absolute minimum sizes. In some areas these decisions of minimum size appear to have been taken on the advice of the local inspectorate.* In others, they were taken on advice from education officials. In any case the DES rarely turned down reorganization plans between 1965 and 1970 during the years they were 'requested' because schools were too large. On the other hand, there are numerous examples of DES refusal of whole plans and of individual schools because they were too small. Many authorities submitting plans including just under the minimum of six-form entry 11–18s in 1966, 1967 and 1968 were told they would have to bring these schools up to six or seven-form entry before they could be accepted for reorganization. Yet in the middle of all this, in 1967, the DES suddenly accepted Hertfordshire's reorganization plan, where *all* the 11–18 schools were to be allowed to be five-form entry. This naturally confused everyone.

Nor was Hertfordshire the only area where the department appears to have contradicted itself. In 1967 Ealing's first plan for 11–16 schools and three sixth-form colleges was turned down because both the size of the 11–16s (at four-form entry) and the size of the colleges (300 each, working up to 600 each) were too small to offer a wide enough range of courses and facilities. The refusal of the sixth-form colleges was particularly interesting, because the department had accepted Tynemouth's 1966 plan for a sixth-form college when Tynemouth had only 250 pupils of sixth-form age at the time and would be working up to only 350/400.[14] Later, in 1970 – after reorganization ceased to be national policy – we are let into DES thinking on this subject. Thus from the Chief Senior HMI for Schools, William Elliott, we hear that

A group of us in the Department of Education and Science decided that ... a college for traditional sixth formers ... would need at least 400 students.[15]

To include 'new' sixth formers, he adds, it would have to be much larger, probably 600. But these sizes, as William Elliott makes clear, are calculated on a staffing ratio of 1:12.

Of course, circumstances differ in different areas, and what may work in one place may not work in another. No one argues with this. But no explanations of guiding principles were ever given from 1965 to 1970, nor was the reasoning behind the differing DES decisions for the differing

---

* See Berkshire reorganization document, June 1966, p. C75, where the inspectorate advised eight-form entry minimum. In Cheshire's document, 1 November 1965, nine-form entry is regarded as a minimum; in Birkenhead's, July 1966, p. 13, it is twelve-form entry.

Table 6.3 Types of comprehensive schools, 1968 to 1972, England and Wales as percentages

	1968	*1972*
11 (12)–18	56·2	56·2
11 (12)–16	21·0	21·1
11–13	3·9	2·2
11–14/15	10·4	8·0
13–18	5·1	7·6
14–18	2·4	4·0
Sixth form college	0·5	0·7
Totals	100·0 (661*)	100·0 (1532**)

* This column compiled from Table A.1, p. 522. It includes three schools classed as unknown age range.

** This is the number of schools giving information about age range in 1972 in C. Benn, *Comprehensive Schools in 1972*.

areas ever made clear to schools and committees and authorities who were still in the middle of planning reorganization. To this day many of them do not know what 'size' is generally workable for each age range of school, let alone what circumstances the sizes proposed would or would not have been accepted by the DES.

The size position in respect of all-through schools is complicated further because there are two very opposing camps on this matter among those working for reorganization locally. The first group – and these are mainly schools in the countryside or in low population areas – are anxious to get approval for comprehensive schools below the 'official' minimum. They see this as the only chance to get reorganization off the ground in their localities in view of their small population or their own relatively recently built smaller-size secondary schools. They are therefore anxious for every scrap of proof about the 'success' of the small school in maintaining an adequate GCE course, for it is the necessity to provide for GCE pupils that usually conditions decisions on 'too small' or 'too large'. Investigations – like those of Dr Halsall[12] – suggesting that three-form-entry comprehensives can succeed well in this respect are naturally very eagerly studied.

The second camp are struggling against the imposition of a small size upon them – usually of five-form entry or below – by their local authorities. These are usually schools in populated areas and in areas where local authorities run grammar schools close by. The 1969 controversy in Hertfordshire over the proposal to split the twenty-year-old ten-form entry Mountgrace comprehensive school into two separate five-form entry comprehensive schools, and the 1969 ILEA decisions to reduce some comprehensive schools to four- or five-form entry, are examples here. Comprehensive schools in these circumstances urgently require a large enough entry to staff and equip their schools to compete with the co-existing grammar schools – and in a few cases with the very large comprehensive schools in the area.

The various circumstances of individual comprehensive schools make it imperative that decisions about individual schools' size be taken by those who have a good knowledge of the local conditions and problems faced by the schools, and especially of the future reorganization planning in the area. All too often the DES has given the impression that its decisions were taken on paper or before plans for all local schools were in – or, as in the case of Hertfordshire, with regard to local political, just as much as to educational, circumstances.[16] Local politics became much more of a problem after the introduction of circular 10/70 in 1970 which lead to more decisions about schools being taken individually, rather than decisions being taken about plans as a whole, when considering a change of status to comprehensive at national level. It was also complicated by the not-always-rational press agitation about 'giant comprehensives' – and the Secretary of State's suddenly expressed desire in 1972 to go for 'small' comprehensives where possible, without defining exactly how small was small.

But perhaps the two most instructive findings on size of our survey – whatever may be the 'ruling' about official minimum size or desired maximum, and whatever may once have been the necessity for having very large comprehensive schools – were that many of the comprehensive schools that are actually established and working in this country are well below supposedly official minimums and few schools are of the gigantic size thought necessary up until so very recently. The giant school in particular is clearly out. Only four schools of the 728 in our survey are over 2000. Of 11–18 (type I) all-through comprehensives, the great majority fall between 600 and 1200 in size (58 per cent). Only about a quarter (23 per cent) are over 1200. On the other hand, about a fifth (19 per cent) are under 600.*

Table 6.4 sets out the size position in terms of form entry in England and Wales. We see that 101 of the 11–18 schools (of type I, the vast majority) – 30 per cent of the total – were in fact *below* the circular 10/65 minimum of six-form entry in 1968.† No doubt many of these were

---

* See Appendix I, Note 3.

† By contrast, only 11 per cent of 11–18 (type II) schools were under six-form entry for England and Wales (see Appendix I, Note 3).

Table 6.4 **Size by form entry of comprehensive schools in England and Wales, 1968**

	11–16 schools		*11–18 (type I) schools*	
Form entry	*Number of schools*	*Percentage*	*Number of schools*	*Percentage*
1	2	1·5	3	1·0
2	5	3·5	9	2·5
3	11	8·0	21	6·0
4	32	23·0	27	8·0
5	34	24·5	41	12·0
6	23	16·5	53	15·5
7	10	7·0	38	11·0
8	11	8·0	68	19·5
9	4	3·0	22	6·5
10	4	3·0	24	7·0
11	0	0·0	10	3·0
12	1	0·5	17	5·0
13	0	0·0	4	1·0
14	2	1·5	6	1·5
15	0	0·0	2	0·5
16	0	0·0	0	0·0
Total	139	100	345	100

schools with first- or second-year intakes only; no doubt many more were schools that will grow as local population grows and as the percentage of those staying on increases. But not all of them are like this. Rather a significant proportion of all-through schools are probably going to be below six-form entry for good.

Schools without sixth forms

Even more instructive – and in many ways far more crucial – is the comparable proportion of 11–16 schools that were below six-form entry; eighty-four schools, or 60 per cent of all short-course schools. Fifty schools of this age range (36 per cent) were in fact four-form entry and below – the size that the Secretary of State said could not be allowed in the case of Ealing's returned plans. What is crucial about these 11–16 schools' smaller size is not so much that they are actually much smaller than would have been forecast or desired at the time of circular 10/65, but that they differ so radically in this matter of size from 11–18 schools. For many feel that both 11–16 and 11–18 schools should have the *same* form entry. As we show later in the section on separate sixth-form schemes, one of the problems in reorganization that needs immediate attention is the disparity between the 11–18 and the 11–16 comprehensive school. Although it is not just a disparity in size, obviously size influences or conditions many of the other differences between these two types. It is one thing to say that the giant comprehensive is quite obviously no longer necessary and unlikely to prevail, but it is another to say that the size factor can be completely ignored in a 'hope for the best' manner by those responsible for reorganization locally and nationally.

The average size of the comprehensive school in 1965 in England and Wales in the NFER Report was 865.[17] In our survey of 1968 this had dropped to 789 (it was 703 in Scotland) (see Table 6.5). In part this was

Average size of all comprehensives 1955–70*

1955	1960	1965	1966	1967	1968	1969	1970
993	991	915	806	803	810	803	818

* DES, *Statistics*, vol. I, 1970, p. viii.

probably due to the fact that non-responding schools in our survey were on the whole the larger ones (see p. 516), and to the establishment of so many comprehensive schools in the years since 1965 that were not 11–18 schools but of much shorter age range. If we look at Table 5.6, which

Table 6.5 **Comprehensive schools, 1968: averages**

Average size of all schools in survey	781
Average size of all schools, England and Wales	789
Average size of all schools, Scotland	703
Average size of all 11 (12)–18 schools, England and Wales	983
Average staying on beyond leaving age	51%
Average staying on beyond leaving age, England and Wales	52%
Average staying on beyond leaving age, Scotland	43%
Average staying on in all comprehensive schools with sixth forms, England and Wales	59%
Average percentage of top 20% of ability range in all schools in survey	15%
Average number of O-level or O-grade subject-groups offered per school	12
Average number of A-level or H-grade subject-groups offered per school	7

compares school sizes in our 1968 survey with the 1965 NFER school sizes, we see that the size ranges which show the most increase in terms of numbers of schools are those in the 200–400 and the 600–800 size range. At the same time the overall picture, as reflected below in DES *Statistics* over the years, shows that the average size of comprehensive school, though fluctuating, has been going down and down over the years. The number of middle schools is also increasing.

Table 6.6 **Size of British comprehensive schools, 1965* and 1968**
Percentages of schools within each size grouping

Size of school	1965 NFER Report England and Wales		1968 Survey All schools		1968 Survey England and Wales	
	Number* of schools	Percentage of total	Number of schools	Percentage of total	Number of schools	Percentage of total
1–200	0		19	2·5	14	2
201–400	16	5	90	12	80	12
401–600	92	28	174	24	160	24
601–800	56	17	155	21	141	21
801–1000	72	22	106	15	97	15
1001–1200	37	11	84	12	75	11
1201–1400	21	6	43	6	38	6
1401–1600	12	4	22	3	21	3
1601–1800	13	4	23	3	23	3
1801–2000	10	3	8	1	8	1·5
2000 and over	2	0·5	4	0·5	4	1
Totals	331	100	728	100	661	100

* First NFER Report, p. 88.

But although the average size of the comprehensive school generally has fluctuated up and down, the average size of the all-through comprehensive school has risen. The average size of all 11–18 schools in the NFER Report of 1965 was 958.[18] In our survey (Table A.1) type I 11–18 was 970 for England and Wales; type II was 1137. Combined: the average size of all 11–18 schools in England and Wales was 983 (see Table 6.5). This increase in average size in just two years of twenty-five pupils – or nearly one form entry – is marked and undoubtedly shows that the rate at which all-through schools are tending to grow means that the fears for their 'small size', and thus unviable sixth forms, may well be overplayed. We would not wish to give the impression that size of a school is not important. The rationale behind reorganization is that the single school of 1000 can provide three or four times the opportunities as two schools of 500. We are also well aware of the acute problems faced by small-size comprehensive schools in areas where the local authority is running grammar schools alongside, and to the problems of very large schools with inadequate administrative help. In fact, nowhere has the size problem been more overplayed than in respect of large size, where recent press and grammar-lobby agitation has tended to suggest that giant size is a hallmark of the comprehensive school and that large schools are always problem schools. Table 6.6 shows quite clearly – and the 1972 position is little different – that *very* large comprehensive schools are in a tiny minority: less than 6 per cent of comprehensives are even over 1600; and over 85 per cent of comprehensives are 999 or under. Over-agitation about 'size', therefore, can sometimes be an oblique attempt to criticize the comprehensive principle itself by linking comprehensive schools to giant size and then linking large size to other difficulties. That large comprehensives run as efficiently and effectively as small ones was a firm finding of the Third NFER Report in 1972.

The success of the comprehensive school – in so many size ranges – is proof of the fact that the factor of size cannot be allowed to be overriding when so many other factors are obviously just as crucial in determining a comprehensive school's success.

First external examinations in comprehensive schools – achievements and trends

If size has been a controversial feature of comprehensive schools, 'academic results' have been even more so. Those who seek to discredit the comprehensive idea rely especially heavily on stirring fears that comprehensives might 'lower standards', and there have been many and varied attempts to show this is so, as well as attempts to discredit the statistics put forward which show how well comprehensives are doing in this respect. Some of these attempts are less naïve than others, but all arise out of a concern that academic excellence be maintained in our school system. In a way this anxiety is understandable, for hard facts about examination entries and passes are one of the ways in which many people measure success in schools. Some obviously place far more reliance on these measures as guides to 'excellence' in education than others. In the comprehensive-school movement it is probably true to say that while examinations are important, they are not the be-all and end-all that they are in many selective schools. They are taken in stride – as important, but not so all-important that other forms of excellence and other measures of attainment are neglected or downgraded.

Comparing comprehensive schools to grammar schools in examination entries and pass rates on a one-to-one basis is obviously not possible, since a grammar school's intake is made up exclusively of that range of ability which is 'capable of examinations', that is, of the top 20 per cent or so of the ability range, while comprehensive schools take in the full-ability range: those who are in the top 20 per cent as well as the other 80 per cent who are *not* supposed to be of GCE or 'grammar ability'. Thus grammar schools should in theory have a 100 per cent success in GCE examinations – at least to O-level, while comprehensives, if they are all genuinely comprehensive, should have one of 20 per cent. But it is well known that the comprehensive sector lacks its fair share of high-ability pupils. All research reports from the National Foundation for Educational Research (1968, 1970 and 1972) showed this to be so, and in the Second Report the NFER was able to add the results of attainment tests administered to the comprehensive schools' intakes in 1968.[19] This showed that on average the comprehensive schools in the study had only 12 per cent of the expected top 20 per cent of the ability range, that is – only 12 per cent of the intake was of 'grammar' and 'GCE' ability.[20] With these facts in mind, let us look at the latest figures.

Percentages of leavers with GCE passes, 1970

	Grammar schools 100% *of intake of GCE/grammar ability*	*Comprehensive schools Approximately* 12% *of intake of GCE/grammar ability*
Attempted O-level	93·7	36·8
Obtained 3 or more O-level passes	79·0	21·4
Obtained 5 or more O-level passes	63·9	14·5
Obtained 1 or more A-level pass	48·4	11·1
Obtained 2 or more A-level passes	39·3	8·2

DES, *Statistics*, 1970, vol. 2, p. 2.

Since the GCE examination is supposed to be only for pupils in the top 20 per cent of the ability range, it could well be argued that any percentage over 12·0 in the comprehensive column was a measure of the way the comprehensive pupils had exceeded their expected pass rate of 12 per cent based on their approximate percentage of 'grammar/GCE' ability pupils, while anything under 100 in the grammar column was a measure of the way grammar-school pupils had failed to show the pass rate expected of pupils chosen specifically for their 'ability' to take GCE examinations. But of course, it has long been known that not all pupils classed as of 'grammar ability' at 11-plus actually go on to get five or more GCE O-levels – as the percentages in the grammar column make clear. Only about two thirds do so. This is confirmed conversely by looking at the DES *Statistics* for secondary modern schools, where GCE success to a more than modest level is recorded – from these schools which only twenty years ago we presumed were incapable of any GCE courses at all.[21]

All the same, the grammar schools in 1970 were on the whole probably more selective in their intakes than in previous years – since the general trend in reorganization has been to incorporate the 'lesser' grammars (in terms of academic selectivity and prestige) leaving the most selective still outside reorganization. Certainly the most highly selective grammar schools of all – the direct grant grammar schools – where very often only the top 5 per cent of the ability range is admitted, also reveal that 100 per cent success is not assured even here to five or more GCE O-levels, for in 1970 only three quarters of their leavers were able to obtain this qualification.

The comprehensive sector – as Figure 4.1 (p. 86) showed earlier – is largely made up of pupils from the ex-secondary modern sector. Furthermore, as mentioned above, the comprehensive sector probably lacks its share of higher ability pupils by about 8 per cent of the top 20 per cent of the ability range. If we accept that only pupils of 'above average ability' pass GCE, we would therefore expect 12 per cent to pass at the five or more O-level stage, but in actual fact we find that 14·5 per cent did so. Thus the comprehensive-school pass rate could be said to exceed that 'expected' by 2·5 per cent, while the grammar school is less than the 'expected' pass rate by 36·1 per cent. At A-levels too it could be said that three quarters of the 'grammar-ability' group in the comprehensive schools obtained two or more A-levels (8·2 per cent), while in grammar schools only two fifths was able to do so (39·3 per cent). But, of course, these comparisons are built on expectations which arise out of the 11-plus mentality: that at the age of eleven a system can sort out those who are of grammar ability and those who are not, and can decide in advance who is 'capable' of examination success and who is not. This philosophy is rejected by most of those who support the comprehensive reform; but for those who still think in these terms, it is instructive that the comprehensive sector compares so well.

If these excellent pass rates in comprehensive schools are anything to go by, the difference which a genuine comprehensive system could make to raising academic attainment in this country could well be very great – with the real problem, far from being one of comprehensives depressing attainment, one of more and more pupils passing external examinations each year to a point where the real problem becomes the pressure upon entrance to further and higher education, as indeed is now already taking place. A genuine comprehensive system could well increase this pressure very greatly by permitting and encouraging a far higher percentage of pupils to achieve examination success.

One indication of this very real possibility is seen in attainment levels in genuine comprehensive schools in the research Robin Pedley carried out in 1963 and again in 1968. To get a 'fair' comparison with the maintained system, he included only comprehensive schools which had been in existence for at least seven years. He also tried to include schools where, as far as possible, there was no creaming by nearby grammar schools of high-ability pupils, although it should be added that even so in some cases in 1963 there was 5 per cent creaming, and in 1968 10 per cent.[22] As can be seen below, the comprehensive schools compare extremely favourably with the all-maintained system for both years.

Percentage of leavers gaining GCE passes at O-level GCE

		1 or more passes	5 or more passes
1963	comprehensive schools	32	16
	all-maintained schools	26	13
1968	comprehensive schools	39·4	20·1
	all-maintained schools	32·1	17·6

Concentration upon pass 'rates', however, tends to obscure the enormous increase in the actual numbers of pupils passing GCE examinations from comprehensive schools over recent years. For example:

Numbers of leavers (thousands) obtaining one or more GCE and percentage increases over previous year

	1968	1969	% inc	1970	% inc
Comprehensive	39·02	43·69	11·97	55·78	27·67
All-maintained	179·81	187·67	4·37	193·50	3·11

DES, *Statistics*, vol. 2, p. 21 (1968), p. 22 (1969), p. 18 (1970).

As has been observed more than once, the improvement rate in the comprehensive sector exceeds that of schools as a whole. For example, from the *Teacher* in 1970, commenting on examination results just published:

The figures show an increase in academic standards in all types of school, but the improvement in comprehensive schools was markedly better on all counts than the improvement in the country as a whole.[23]

In numbers sitting examinations too the comprehensive sector has continued to increase its share, as the table below confirms

Numbers entering GCE Ordinary-Level Examinations only[24]

	1968	1969	1970
Comprehensive	31,480	38,987	49,362
All maintained	191,222	189,391	188,182

As we see, between 1968 and 1970, there are 17,882 *more* pupils who sat GCE only in the comprehensive sector, but 3040 fewer sitting it in the maintained sector.

Quite clearly the comprehensive sector aims to give as many pupils as possible a chance to sit external examinations, a policy which can sometimes lead to a lower pass rate than in a policy of stricter entry (only those a school is sure will pass are permitted to enter) but may in the end produce more actual passes. Quite clearly too any 'loss' to the all-maintained sector of GCE takers because schools are being reorganized as comprehensive is more than made up by the 'gain' in the comprehensive sector.

CSE

But there is a further important aspect of examination trends, perhaps the most important, which we have not yet considered: the CSE, the Certificate of Secondary Education. The rise of this examination and its growing popularity in all parts of the school system has been remarkable. Even the grammar school sector now sits nearly one third of its leavers in CSE examinations.[25] And in 1970 for the first time the DES *Statistics* included pass rates in CSE examinations in the same table with those for GCE.[26]

Obtained grade 5 or better in three or more CSE subjects, 1970
Percentage of leavers

Comprehensive schools	All-maintained schools
29·5	26·0

It would thus appear that despite the handicap of not having their 'fair share' of high-ability pupils, when it comes to CSE, the comprehensive sector more than holds its own.

But yet more interesting still is the table below showing the way trends have taken place in the three categories of first external examination: (1) CSE only, (2) GCE and CSE combined and (3) GCE only:

Table 6.7 **Candidates for CSE and GCE examinations as percentage of leavers**

		Comprehensive schools	All-maintained schools
(1) *CSE only*	1968	18·0	14·3
	1969	20·9	16·3
	1970	20·6	18·0
(2) *CSE and GCE*	1968	28·7	21·5
	1969	29·5	22·9
	1970	30·9	25·1
(3) *GCE only*	1968	27·4	34·0
	1969	26·8	33·1
	1970	27·6	32·9

DES, *Statistics*, vol. 2, pp. 79, 73, 67, in 1968, 1969 and 1970 respectively.

Two trends stand out here. Firstly, a greater percentage of comprehensive school leavers than those from the maintained system as a whole sat both for (1) CSE examinations only and for (2) the combination CSE and GCE in *all* the years, while in the GCE only category (3) the reverse was true. This is another way of registering the 'preference' of the comprehensive sector for the CSE examination.

Secondly, the percentages of leavers in the country as a whole taking (3) GCE only is *falling* each year in the all-maintained sector (and is roughly steady in the comprehensive) while in the other two categories (1) and (2) it is *rising* each year. This is another way of registering the growing preference of the school system overall for CSE. Certainly these figures record a slow but steady trend away from the GCE examination towards the CSE, thus underlining in practice what many have argued for in theory: an end to the double examination system and its replacement with an examination based on the present CSE.

Table 6.8 **GCE O-level and SCE O-grade examinations, Summer 1968**

Percentages of schools with pupils in 13/14–15/16 age range entering one or more pupils for each subject. Excluding O-levels taken in the sixth form.

	*All schools	All schools presenting any pupils at O-level	Schools with sixth-forms*	11(12)–18 type I*	11(12)–18 type II*	11(12)–16*	13–18
Art	84	93	95	94	93	61	94
Technical drawing	68	75	76	75	80	53	58
Typing/Commerce	35	39	41	42	50	21	27
Latin	43	47	59	54	77	2	73
Physics	78	87	93	90	90	47	97
Geography	84	93	96	94	93	63	97
Woodwork/ Metalwork	69	76	79	78	77	48	64
Cooking/Domestic science	68	75	79	78	93	44	64
Needlework	57	63	68	68	80	32	48
English literature	80	89	93	91	87	54	97
French	77	85	91	88	83	47	97
Chemistry	74	82	91	87	87	37	97
Mathematics	86	96	97	95	90	68	97
Religious knowledge	55	60	65	61	67	29	66
History	84	93	96	94	90	61	97
Biology	79	87	92	90	90	51	91
Music	51	57	65	61	70	18	85
Language (other than French, English, or Latin)	56	62	74	70	83	13	82
Total number of schools	621	561	436	373	30	150	33

* Including all or some of the sixty schools as yet not fully developed enough to sit any pupils for GCE O-level or SCE O-grade in 1968, usually because entries have not yet reached the fifth year.

14–18*	Roman Catholic*	Church of England*	Scotland 12–18 type I*	England and Wales 11(12)–18 type I*	Mixed schools 11–18¹*	Girls' schools 11–18¹*	Boys' schools 11–18*
87	67	67	100	94	94	91	95
87	52	50	100	73	80	3	90
27	31	25	84	36	40	27	20
87	38	8	91	49	51	48	36
93	62	42	98	91	93	64	95
93	72	67	95	95	94	97	95
87	48	42	86	78	86	0	93
87	44	50	91	77	87	85	3
73	34	50	70	68	75	88	3
87	70	42	100	91	91	91	90
93	66	50	98	89	88	94	88
93	57	33	98	87	84	64	93
93	74	67	93	96	96	97	98
87	38	50	16	70	71	88	48
93	70	58	95	95	95	97	98
93	61	42	84	92	92	94	90
87	30	42	70	60	61	64	48
80	46	33	93	68	68	76	60
15	61	12	44	330	257	33	40

Comparing comprehensive schools' examination offerings

While we are convinced that, given a fully comprehensive intake and a fully staffed and equipped comprehensive school, academic achievement will – as Robin Pedley's figures, official statistics and others,[27] show – continue to underline the comprehensive claim to raise educational standards, we were, however, anxious to discover in addition the extent and range of the various external examinations taken in comprehensive schools in 1968 in a wide variety of subjects. In our survey we therefore asked all schools for information about subjects in which they were able to enter at least one pupil at GCE O-level and A-level in England and Wales and at O-grade and H-grade in Scotland. In this chapter we shall deal with O-level and O-grade examinations only, A-level and H-grade being dealt with in later chapters.

Table 6.8, which sets out the information about O-level and O-grade examinations that we collected, indicates only the percentage of schools with either the courses or the ability intake or the age group to enable entry of at least a single pupil in the subject-group for GCE O-level or Scottish O-grade in a single year, 1968. These figures do not measure performance, nor do they include a full range of possible subjects. For example, we omitted GCE English language, since almost all schools will sit pupils in this subject. We also grouped subjects together, so that some of our single categories are in fact representative of a number of individual GCE subjects.

In presenting our O-level and O-grade figures here for 11–18 or 12–18 schools, and for all other types, we are well aware that, as a number of schools told us, pupils were presented in 1967 for a specific subject, or would be presented in 1969, but were not presented in 1968. In addition, these O-levels are those taken in the fifth year only; they do not include any O-levels that were taken in the sixth form in the same year. Lastly, many other schools – and this is perhaps the most important factor – were not yet developed enough in age range to present any pupils for examinations (since no pupils of examination age were yet in the school).* All these factors must be remembered when judging schools' GCE offering in our survey. These figures cannot be used to compare schools in this survey to other types of schools. Their main use is for comparison of comprehensive school types within our survey.

Our findings can also be used to compare schools in our national survey to those in the NFER's 1965 survey in respect of four of the subjects that the NFER chose to ask their schools about and about which we also

---

* Table 6.8 (p. 136), in fact includes schools as yet unable to present any pupils at all in GCE O-level or O-grade. There were sixty such schools.

inquired at GCE O-level: art, physics, French and biology. The NFER's figures were in respect of fully developed comprehensive schools only, of course.[28] We have no comparable category of 'fully developed', but for this comparison we have used the category 'All comprehensive schools with sixth forms in England and Wales'.* The comparative figures for O-level presentation between the two years are given below in Table 6.9.

Table 6.9 **Percentage of schools in England and Wales presenting a pupil in subjects at O-level**

	NFER 1965 *(191 schools)*	Our survey 1968 *(391 schools)*
Art	99	94
Physics	91	92
French	94	90
Biology	92	93

These figures show that the comprehensive school is very definitely holding its own in the matter of presentation for GCE O-level. In physics and biology the percentages have even increased slightly.

When we look more closely at all-through schools, we can see from Table 6.2 (p. 119) that these schools in general have a higher than average offering of O-level GCE subject-groups than the average of twelve for all schools in the survey: fourteen for type I 11–18s and fifteen for type II. Since an average of twelve subject-groups per school could well mean sixteen individual O-level subjects (not counting English language, which we did not include), this will be seen to be quite satisfactory.

Table 6.10 examines the total numbers of subject groups in which schools were able to enter pupils at O-level and O-grade. We see from this that 3 per cent of 11–18 (type I) are as yet unable to present any pupils for GCE O-level or O-grade. This will usually be because entries have not yet reached the fifth year. On the other hand, all type II 11–18 schools are able to sit for exams. Moreover, 76·5 per cent of type I 11–18 and 91 per cent of type II 11–18 schools are able to present an above average number of O-level subjects-groups – thirteen or more. Again, very satisfactory.

When we look at Table 6.8 (p. 136) to see the percentage of schools able to present pupils in the individual subject-groups, we see at once that over 85 per cent of both types of 11/12–18 schools were able to present pupils in all the major academic subjects and over 90 per cent for a number of these (with the exception of Latin, discussed later). We see too that the

* See Appendix 1, Note 3.

vocational skill subjects – technical drawing, woodwork/metalwork and domestic science – were all presented by 75 per cent or over. An even higher percentage of Scotland's all-through schools presented pupils in all subjects (except for religious knowledge).

There are a few differences between the two types of 11–18 school that might be noted, however. The 11–18 (type I) orthodox comprehensive has slightly higher presentations in mathematics, English literature, French and history, but lower ones in Latin and other languages, than the 11–18 sixth-form centre comprehensive (type II). Again, the second type of 11–18 presented a significantly higher percentage of pupils in cooking/ domestic science, needlework, and music than the 11–18 type I, probably partly because this category contains only mixed and girls' schools – and no boys' schools at all (see Table 18.3, p. 411).

Here we might comment for a moment on the relatively lower percentages of the orthodox 11–18 (type I) schools presenting pupils in the vocational than in the academic subjects, and the relatively lower percentages presenting them in music (61 per cent) than in art (94 per cent). These two contrasts are noticeable over the whole range of types of comprehensive schools, as can be seen in Table 6.8, and are not just a feature of all-through schools. Altogether in the 621 schools with pupils within the age group 13/14 to 15/16, only 254 presented pupils for *all* the vocational subject-groups at O-level or O-grade: technical drawing, needlework, cooking/domestic science and woodwork/metalwork. Naturally those schools that were single-sex would be unlikely to provide all these subjects together, but the number may seem to some disappointingly small compared to academic subjects. So too might the number of schools in this category that were able to present pupils in *both* art and music together: only 310 (but see paragraph below on CSE music).

Although it may be assumed that more schools will present pupils in *all* these subjects in the future, it should also be remembered that presentation or not in the O-level or O-grade examination in any of these subjects gives little indication of the prevalence of, or study of, or interest in these subjects inside the individual schools. It must be remembered further, as far as many vocational subjects are concerned – commerce, typing, domestic science, technical drawing – that the GCE O-level and SCE O-grade provision is often influenced by, and related to, the availability of courses in these subjects in other local educational centres, particularly in the further education colleges. These GCE figures must also be put beside the growing use of the CSE examination in comprehensive schools – both alongside, and in preference to, the GCE. For example, as we show in the section on the 14–16 age range in comprehensive schools in chapter 10, many schools sit pupils for CSE in preference to GCE. The

Table 6.10 **GCE O-level and SCE O-grade examinations, Summer 1968**

Percentages of schools with the 13/14–15/16 age group entering one or more pupils in the eighteen subject-groups.

	England and Wales	Scotland	All Schools Age range of comprehensive schools				
			11(12)–18 type I	11(12)–18 type II	11(12)–16	13–18	14–18
Entering in 18	7	5	9	17	0	0	20
17	14	26	19	37	1	12	33
16	11	21	15	20	2	21	13
15	14	15	17	10	4	24	13
14	8	8	8	7	6·5	15	13
13	9	5	8·5	0	8·5	21	0
12	7	6	6	0	11	3	6
11	4	3	4	0	7	0	0
10	3	3	1·5	3	7	0	0
9	3	3	3·5	0	5·5	0	0
8	2·5	0	2·5	0	5·5	0	0
7	1	0	0·3	0	4	0	0
6	2	0	0·5	0	4	0	0
5	0·2	3	0·5	0	0·5	0	0
4	0·7	0	0	3	2	0	0
3	1	0	0·5	0	3	0	0
2	0·7	0	0·3	3	1	0	0
1	0·9	0	0·5	0	2	0	0
0	11	2	3	0	25	3	7
	100	100	100	100	100	100	100
Total number of schools	559	62	375	30	150	33	15

single subject for which CSE is used most often in preference to GCE in schools in our survey is music (A3, Table 3, p. 567). All the same, it is perhaps fair to conclude that some comprehensive schools in 1968 were apparently better equipped to offer traditional academic subjects more frequently than some of the traditional vocational subjects.

Another subject that calls for comment is Latin. It will be seen that it is the 'academic' subject least often presented in the 11–18 type I comprehensive – the type of comprehensive in the great majority. Even in the fully developed comprehensive in the survey – that with a sixth form –

Latin O-level at GCE or SCE O-grade was offered in 1968 by only 59 per cent of schools, as compared to 95 per cent offering art or 96 per cent offering history or 97 per cent mathematics. Table 6.8 shows that in all schools in the survey – with and without sixth forms – Latin was offered by only 43 per cent. It is not hard to conclude that in contrast to all other academic subjects Latin is obviously not thought of as a major academic subject in many comprehensive schools. Colleges and universities that hope to increase their intake of pupils from comprehensive schools will no doubt note this, for in view of these figures, any widespread insistence on this particular subject as a qualification for many university courses will certainly discriminate against comprehensive-school pupils.

For those traditional academics who find this discouraging (although it is a trend that is at least 200 years old), there is the encouraging fact that in almost all categories of comprehensive school – and certainly in all-through 11–18 comprehensives – the subject most often presented at O-level is mathematics. Ninety-seven per cent of fully developed comprehensives presented it, and 95 per cent of (type I) 11–18s.* The other sciences – physics, chemistry and biology – are high in percentages as well. In view of the widespread alarm raised about the availability of mathematics and science staff for Britain's developing comprehensive schools, these O-grade and O-level figures for mathematics and the sciences are exceptionally encouraging.

Extra-curricular activities

When discussing examinations, there is always the danger of leaving the impression that academic success is the be-all and end-all of education. In the comprehensive school exams are important but at the same time kept firmly in their place. Furthermore, no account of the life in existing comprehensives would be complete without some sketch, however short, of the incredible diversity of activity inside these schools today. We talk later about the high quality of art work throughout the comprehensive schools in the country; most visitors to comprehensive schools are aware of this the minute they walk around a school. Music too flourishes. In our visits we also met the usual clubs – for drama, chess, swimming or choir – but in one school we also found a group making its own machine tool to make its own tools, in another a group building a boat, a third learning silversmithing, a fourth designing (and making and modelling) its own high fashion clothes, a fifth organizing lunchtime pop concerts with the

---

* Since 5 per cent of this category as yet present no pupils for GCE O-level or Scottish O-grade (Table 6.10), it is safe to say that in all-through schools with the age range developed up to O-level, virtually 100 per cent of schools were able to present pupils in mathematics.

school's own pop groups, and a sixth making and showing its own 8-millimetre films.

Much of the activity in comprehensive schools involves the wider community. Bicester School's production of *Boris Godunov*, for example, drew in many local residents to help in the staging and the performing of the opera. For many years Ruffwood School ran an annual steam-engine rally for local enthusiasts. In other schools there are imaginative links between school and community as an extension of classwork. Henleaze School's leavers spent a term carrying out a survey of parking accommodation on their council estate (which Bristol Council was later able to use). At Counthill School in Oldham fifth-year pupils spend three weeks at the end of the summer term teaching in local primary schools (both to see if they like teaching as a career and to help the schools).[29] In another comprehensive the domestic science department runs a playgroup in the school itself for toddlers – for the benefit of both pupils and local mothers.[30] In Hull, comprehensive-school pupils provided an 'escort service' for infants from the local primary schools to and from the medical clinic – ready to meet the telephoned requests of the primary-school heads.[31] In April 1969, Wood Green School hired a hovercraft to take a whole year's pupils out to the Goodwin Sands for the day for a lesson of on-the-spot geography. The examples are endless – all of them imaginative and, in the widest sense, educative.

There is obviously small danger that comprehensive schools have developed as stereotyped and uniform institutions in the way critics predicted with such prejudice. Equally obviously comprehensive schools specialize. Not in the old sense where some schools 'specialized' in academic work while others 'specialized' in slow learners who didn't want to bother about examinations – this is just another name for bipartite segregation. As indeed are schemes where one school 'specializes' in foreign languages and academic sciences while nearby another one specializes in craft and technical subjects. Where all comprehensive schools provide a wide range of the basic subjects, academic, technical and craft – and where there are equal opportunities within the different schools for pursuing a wide variety of activities – then uniqueness and diversification arise naturally out of the particular enthusiasms of the staff and pupils or the special tradition of the school and its community. Wandsworth School's special choir work is one example here, but there are dozens more.

Nor have we yet touched on physical education. Many comprehensive schools have encouraged sports of all kinds in a new way because their amalgamation into larger schools or their purpose building has enabled them to enlarge the range of their facilities, equipment and instruction.

Particularly well developed seems to be interest in 'individual' sports: swimming, running, canoeing, climbing, sailing, gymnastics, skating, golf, tennis, judo and fencing. Team sports continue, of course, and in some schools they are strong – Holloway School in London had Mike England of Tottenham as a part-time coach, for example – but they seem to have less dominance than in many selective schools. Comprehensive schools too are developing mixed-sex classes in physical education and many sports, a long overdue development, many think.

Because comprehensive schools are large and therefore usually organized in smaller units within the school, because the staff and pupil body is so various and the subject range so wide, there can be little attempt in most schools to mould pupils to a common pattern. It is ironic that in the old days anti-comprehensive cartoons showed comprehensive school pupils as identical robots. In many ways the comprehensive-school pupil is the hardest pupil to spot, while the public-school-boy or the grammar-school-girl or the secondary-modern-bunch have often become the stereotypes. Because the emphasis in the best comprehensive schools is upon the individual pupil and his or her own uniqueness – whatever the attainment and whatever the home background – comprehensive schools may well be able to produce a generation of pupils far more individual than the schools of the past.

Combined schools and single-site schools

Probably the biggest prejudice against the developing comprehensive school is the belief that a school situated in two buildings, or on two sites, is a 'botched' school and not properly a comprehensive school. Since the majority of schools which are 'split' in this way are the larger all-through schools, this question is naturally of concern in this section.

The reasoning behind amalgamations is that two nearby schools that formerly tried to cope independently with the 11–16 or 11–18 age group but could not provide a wide range of subjects because of their limited overall size and staffing, could, if joined as a single school, with the lower years on one site and the upper years on another, offer far wider subject options and opportunities to the combined school population.

Critics usually say that these schools should 'wait' until they can have completely new purpose-built premises. When one amalgamated comprehensive head in north London was asked if this would not have been better, his answer was, 'No' ... said with deep conviction ...

It would have meant that a whole generation of children would have been deprived of the benefits that two smallish schools could not have afforded: three sciences instead of 'general science', a choice of Italian, modern Greek and Turkish as well as French, not to mention courses in engineering and commerce.

In the secondary modern days most children left at fifteen, now 78 per cent stay on ... in the combined school there are enough staff for some to concentrate on helping the individual child with social and personal education.[32]

Those who condemn 'combined schools' will often admit to never having visited such a school to watch it at work. Nor do some of these critics have any idea how many comprehensive schools – of long-standing and national reputation – have operated successfully as 'combined' comprehensives. The first NFER Report said 22 per cent of all comprehensives in 1965 were split, half of them more than one mile apart.[33] Our 1968 survey (Table 6.11) showed a slight increase of schools on split sites over 1965: 24 per cent. In Scotland the average was higher: 31 per cent; and in the ILEA too: 32 per cent. In some sectors, i.e. Roman Catholic schools, it was lower: 18 per cent.

Are these schools on two sites so very much disadvantaged? Looking purely statistically at Table 6.11, which compares schools on one site with schools on two or more sites, we see that if anything split-site schools are more advantaged in certain ways: their O-level and O-grade total average is higher than one-site schools, for example. So is their A-level and H-grade. Their sixth forms are bigger. Otherwise, their intake of the top 20 per cent of ability is the same as single-site schools – so too is their staying-on rate. There is nothing to suggest in this table that split-site schools are disadvantaged.

Which schools were split? As can be expected, mostly 11–18 schools. There were only one 11–14, three 13–18s, and five 11–14/15s that were on two or more sites in our survey.* Only 10 per cent of 11–16 schools were on more than one site. But 27 per cent of the first type of 11–18s were split and 41 per cent of the second type.* It is worth noting that the second type of 11–18 is so often on two sites, for this kind of school has, as we see in Tables 6.2 (p. 119) and 9.2 (p. 197), a particularly large sixth form, a very high percentage staying on, a high ability intake, and a higher than average A-level and O-level subject-group offering. For those who think these things are very important, it is interesting that being a combined school or 'botched', as some call it, would seem to be no hindrance of any kind but rather the reverse.

As one might expect, schools on two sites make rather less use of the house system of organization (only 7 per cent had a straight house system) and more use of upper and lower school division (45 per cent had this) than those on single sites. Twenty-two per cent combined house systems with upper/lower divisions; while 38 per cent used a year system.† But

---

* See Appendix 1, Note 3.
† See Table 14.1, p. 329, for description of these methods of internal organization.

Table 6.11 The siting of British comprehensive schools, 1968

	% of all schools (numbers in brackets)	% of schools England and Wales	% of Scottish schools	% of all Roman Catholic schools	% of all ILEA schools	Average % intake of top 20% of ability	Average % staying beyond leaving age	Average size of sixth form	Average no. of O-level or O-grade subject-groups	Average no. of A-level or H-grade subject-groups
Schools on two or more sites	24 (176)	23	31	18	32	15	51	88	13	8
Schools on one site	73 (531)	74	67	82	66	15	51	80	12	7
Unknown	3 (21)	3	2	2	2					
Total number of schools	728	661	67	65	56					

even with sensible divisions, organization was sometimes a headache, as those heads and staff answering questions on split sites in our smaller sample agreed. At least half could think of no advantages to being split rather than on one site. But some heads spoke of units being more manageable when smaller, and pupils finding it easier to settle into second-dary education initially in the small 'lower' unit. The big disadvantages were felt to be wasted time (moving between sites), as might be expected, and difficult communications between sites.

But sometimes, when visiting combined schools, we found that the actual situations were often subjectively assessed. One head had written of his tremendous difficulties in a split-site arrangement; another wrote that although split – actually into three sites – he felt the whole school was much more successful than when the three schools were separate. When we visited the latter school we found that not only was it split into three sites, but each school was over a mile from the other. In addition all were former secondary modern schools; the age range of the new school was only 11–16, which in some eyes might add to disadvantages, and lastly, it was in the heart of a northern industrial town with a 30 per cent immigrant intake. The 'school' was carefully arranged, with 'equal' immigrant intakes, facilities and staff at each site. The head visited each site every day, although each site had its own head in charge. The overall head and the site heads met regularly each week and were in constant inter-site telephone communication daily – each having noted points that needed discussion. Everyone we talked to was anxious to tell us about the increased opportunities, the new courses, the better exam results and higher academic standards, that had come with amalgamated reorganization. Hardly a word was spoken of disadvantages, for all thought was on minimizing these and maximizing advantages.

Shortly after this, we visited the other school – another obviously successful school, but where the head had written at length about the difficulties of being so widely separated from his other half. This school was in a small mining village. There we found not only that the two former schools – one had been a grammar, the other a secondary modern – were almost next door to one another, but that the boundaries were less than fifty yards apart. They had been in addition the only two secondary schools in a fairly traffic-free small town, and had been amalgamated as 'one' school for eighteen years with the upper school having had recent extensive additions. Compared to the first school, the split site here would not be regarded as administratively crucial. But to the head it was; while to the first head it was not. And who is to say that either was wrong or right? Probably most would agree with yet another head that: 'Being split is difficult, but it is, however, more tolerable than selection at 11-plus'.

But even heads who found the split situation troublesome – and they were not all, by any means – were more anxious to explain how they operated than to complain. Several said the chief aid in organization was the telephone and the regular meeting of those in charge of both sites; in other words, constant liaison and good communications. One head said: 'disadvantages of split sites are grossly exaggerated'. Another: 'It is just as easy to keep in touch with a school three miles away as a hundred yards away.' Of Thirsk comprehensive school, split from 1957 to 1961, its headmaster has written:

The situation . . . which involved the use of two buildings, about a quarter of a mile apart, was awkward in some respects but did not present insuperable difficulties. A brisk walk once or twice during the day harms no one, teacher or pupil.[34]

Split-site schools in our smaller sample were organized according to the actual sizes of the two schools in most cases – and by facilities in the rest. The commonest form of organization was lower years – usually the first two – in the smaller of the two schools. Sometimes this was the former grammar school, but usually it was the ex-modern. One 11–16 school, however, organized by facilities, with all pupils on one site, and the second site used for specialist work: labs, art, craft and sports.

Another variation was to split down the middle: half of the first years on one site, half on the other, and continue on up the school – usually until the third or fourth year – and then divide according to subjects or examination courses. For example, one northern all-through school had technical courses and leavers' courses in one site, arts courses and commerce on another. In another, in the South-West, CSE courses were on one site, GCE on another. Yet another variation – used when there were three schools – involved the first two years split between two adjoining sites, and the upper years 14–18 in a single upper school. A London split-site comprehensive adopted a system of 'interweaving years': first, third and fifth years in one building, second, fourth and sixth form in another. This was so successful that even when the school was able to get a second site nearer its first, it still retained this pattern of dividing pupils.[35]

Most schools are limited in the arrangements they are able to make because of the disposition of labs, assembly rooms, offices, gymnasia and specialist rooms in a way that cannot be altered. But the real danger of the split-site school from the point of view of the comprehensive is where the 'split' forces separation into bipartite divisions or where it divides the technical from the academic students. In this sense the split-site school then becomes something like the multilateral or campus school – as in Billingham, Durham – where all the pupils belong to the same organiza-

tion but are separated into various 'sides'. In some amalgamated comprehensives it is temporarily unavoidable, and the lesser of two evils. In a
few it is our impression that the split between academic and non-academic
might perhaps have been avoided.

As for movement between sites, the most common approach was to try
to keep pupils where they were and to have staff do the moving. At one end
of the scale, one northern school reported 90 per cent of staff moved – the
head liked all staff to teach in all parts of school. At the other end, neither
staff nor pupils moved, staff being permanently assigned to one site and
pupils likewise. The DES in its *Comprehensive Schools from Existing
Buildings*[36] listed this latter arrangement as a practical alternative method
of split-site organization; but among the schools we questioned in our
smaller sample, only this one school practised total non-movement. A few
others felt that reducing the percentage of teachers who had to move was
desirable and this they tried to do, but the average percentage of staff who
moved in our smaller sample of split-site schools was still between 20 per
cent and 30 per cent.

Most schools restricted pupil movement as much as they possibly could,
and pupil movement was always lower than staff movement. Only one of
our answering schools gave a figure higher than one-third of pupils who
actually had to move between sites at any time. Schools that had been
established longest were less bothered by pupil movement, however. One
head in a big-city comprehensive in the North said that in the beginning
no pupils had moved, but he 'worried less and less about this now' and let
pupils move for 'double periods' of art. In this connection *Comprehensive
Schools from Existing Buildings* speaks of a new division of subjects in
combined schools: 'long-stay' and 'short-stay' subjects; and this we
found generally true: schools organized movement around the nature of
the subject disciplines. Those pupils and staff who were most likely to
move were those going to take, or to teach, 'long-stay' subjects: laboratory science, technical work, craft, domestic science and sports – subjects
where in most cases half a day could be spent.

Generally pupil and staff movements were arranged at the beginning of
the day for the whole day at one site, or at lunch break for a half-day. If
schools were near enough, everyone walked; if not, staff travelled by car
with car allowances. At one school in Devon a double-decker bus service
goes between the two sites four times a day. Buses also move between sites
at midday in one Inner London split-site comprehensive.[37] All the same,
and despite ingenious and well devised plans, staff were sometimes late for
taking lessons. One school reported a 'supervisor' system to keep the class
at work until the 'late' teacher arrived. And a number of schools reported
cutting the total number of periods a day (seven instead of eight, for

example), because of travel time problems. Many schools now consider it is the local authority's job to provide regular transport between sites for any of its schools operating on more than one site. It is also considered essential that local authorities provide these schools with extensive and adequate *internal* phone lines of their own, so that they do not have to be frustrated by ordinary holdups and breakdowns. This provision of a separate internal phone system is also considered essential by many of those who work in very large comprehensive schools on one site.[38]

Paradoxically, the problems often seem to be greatest for split-site schools the nearer their buildings are to each other rather than the other way around. As one split-site head has written, '. . . the greater the distance between buildings the less the movement problem . . . schools two miles distance can on occasion be easier to administer than those separated by a quarter of a mile'.[39] It is also very evident that due to the fear that split-site schools might present organizational problems, greater care is probably taken in their organization of pastoral care, timetabling, staff communications and pupil organization than in the one-site school, where many of these matters are observed to be approached in a 'casual' way, and not in the 'strenuous' manner that must be adopted by the split-site school 'merely to survive'.[40]

From the point of view of pupil welfare and opportunities, it is obvious that the combined school can be just as successful as the one-site school. From the point of view of administrative organization, it is impossible to judge overall how successful the organization of split schools was generally. It is obvious to us, however, that some schools seem able to cope particularly well with the split-site problem, and these were by no means always those in the 'easiest' situations. As one head said: 'Difficulties make us all do much better.'

Purpose-built and adapted schools

Many heads, staff, pupils and parents without a purpose-built school dream about the purpose-built comprehensive as the ideal situation. They imagine all their problems would be solved. As we wrote earlier, the advantage of purpose building as a method of foundation seemed to be largely because it could attract purpose-recruited staff. Nevertheless, it is also important to find out what actual physical conditions make for comprehensive success.

The First NFER Report was not able to give an exact figure for purpose-built comprehensive schools in 1965,[41] but it was able to say that 23 per cent of comprehensive schools were 'new'.[42] Of the 728 schools in our survey we found that 28 per cent were completely purpose-built (see Table 6.12). In some areas it was more: of the ILEA schools responding,

46 per cent were purpose-built; in Scotland, 43 per cent claim to have been.

Once again looking only at the crude statistics of staying on, at the intake of top ability, and at the size of sixth form, we see that purpose-built schools either score the same as, or only slightly better than, the non-purpose-builts. Although in overall average O-level and A-level subject-groups sat, purpose-builts 'score' higher, their sixth forms were much smaller. Once again the statistics – such as they are – do not, as many might have expected, help much in proving one way or the other the truth of the commonly held assumption: that purpose-built schools are infinitely more advantaged.

But what about purpose-builts in the field where we would expect them to be better: architectural suitability? For just as with two-site schools, an extraordinary number of assumptions have grown up about the purpose-built school. Number one is the belief that it is, in fact, well designed for its purpose. Conversely, schools that are not in buildings designed for comprehensive intakes are supposed to be very badly suited to comprehensiveness.

It is true that the heads of non-purpose-built schools in our smaller sample had complaints about the adequacy of the accommodation.* The main complaint was not so much 'lack of' specific items – although there were plenty of these: labs, gymnasia, assembly rooms, house accommodation, craft rooms – but rather the smallness of what was provided, and above all, the unimaginativeness: no rooms for large groups, or for varied numbered groups; and no circulation space. As one London head said: 'just twenty-six standard-size boxes each to house forty children due to leave at fourteen years of age'. All these complaints were perhaps summed up by another London head who said: 'The non-purpose-built school may be summed up in terms of flexibility: (a) lack of, (b) need for.'

By contrast we would expect those in purpose-built schools to be satisfied with facilities, flexibility and size. But if anything, they were more dissatisfied. Perhaps this is because they felt they had a right to complain when things were not perfect, although when we look back in comprehensive literature we see that complaints from purpose-built-schools have long been common: no curtains, no storage space, no rooms for heads of houses, no sixth-form facilities, no TV rooms and no marking rooms. Designers and architects in the early days were sometimes criticized for 'lack of knowledge about the requirements of a school'.[43] Architects themselves, on the other hand, sometimes criticize comprehensive schools because they feel the regulations governing their building are too outdated

* Forty-two schools from this sample were used for this analysis. The earliest school was built in 1883, the latest in 1966: twenty-three were built between 1956 and 1966.

Table 6.12 Architectural foundation of British comprehensive schools, 1968

	% of all schools in the survey (numbers in brackets)	% of English and Welsh schools	% of Scottish schools	% of Roman Catholic schools	% of ILEA schools	Average % intake of top 20% of ability	Average % staying on after leaving age	Average size of sixth form	Average no. of O-level or O-grade subject-groups	Average no. of A-level or H-grade subject-groups
Completely purpose-built	28 (205)	27	43.5	25	46	15	52	70	13	8
Not purpose-built	70 (512)	72	55.5	75	54	15	51	88	12	7
Unknown	2 (11)	1	1	0	0					
Total schools	(728)	(661)	(67)	(65)	(56)					
Total percentage	100	100	100	100	100					

or because they are themselves given incomplete information about what goes on inside the school.[44] That purpose-built schools were too often 'drawn up by theorists and approved by administrators',[45] or by advice from inspectors,[46] rather than after consultations with working teachers and pupils, has also been a frequent complaint. Sometimes the real complaint is of failure to think big enough: the doors that fell off because 2000 pupils pushed them every day rather than 200; or thinking too big: the plate-glass windows that cost so much to replace.[47]

What is obvious, however, is that purpose-built comprehensive schools can vary in suitability and excellence in just the same way as adapted comprehensive schools. Moreover, the ideal about what is 'best' in purpose-building has changed significantly over the years. In the earliest comprehensives it was often thought essential to have the school under one roof; even one of the heads in our smaller sample still felt strongly about this (he was in a school on two sites). So great was this early belief about one roof that one pioneer comprehensive was actually built as a nine-storey tower block. The lifts ceased to operate regularly soon after opening,[48] and though this experiment in building was impressive in some ways, it was never repeated. Another early experiment criticized as awkward was the large cruciform.[49]

These were criticisms about the efficiency of the purpose-building. Other critics sometimes had doubts about the early comprehensive monolithic-block schools because of the effect on the individual inside the structure.[50] One chief officer said to us that in his opinion the monolithic block 'produces a herd mentality, and can, if mistakes are made, lead to appalling congestion at key points in the building'.[51] This echoes Coventry's Director of Education who very early on said that the two main problems in comprehensive school planning were 'traffic control and loyalties'.[52]

Since the main dilemma for those who build comprehensive schools has been to reduce apparent size,[53] and yet retain community feeling, gradually the purpose-built schools began 'breaking up'. Instead of being in one building, they began to be built in related or connected buildings. In Coventry they had already – early on – been unit-built for purposes of accommodating 'house bases'. Elsewhere, too, there were deliberate attempts to create separate areas of the school as secluded and apart for separate functions or age groups: dining-rooms, libraries or sixth forms. Sometimes these parts of the school were in completely separate buildings. The courtyard motif – several groups of buildings around an open space, as at Malory School in London or Wyndham in Egremont – was one popular variant. This 'breaking up' of the monolith steadily advanced until today many schools are designed in several separate buildings from the very beginning. Kaskenmoor School, Oldham, completed in 1969, has five separate buildings – a craft block, gymnasia, administration/staff, teaching and social/dining. In other schools it is the sixth form that is planned from the first as a separate building, or, perhaps, the first two years. Even where the school is under 'one' roof – the new Pimlico school, in London, for example – the internal arrangement of an arcade is very different from early schools.

One of the heads in our smaller sample who has just moved from a head-ship of an old single-building purpose-built school to a split-site school that is not purpose-built, wrote that if he could build from scratch, he would 'try to embody some organization into smaller units'. What some would call a 'botched' school, a school in two separate parts, has turned out easier to run in some ways. This is a very instructive lesson; and it is backed by another interesting discovery we made. Twenty of the completely purpose-built schools in our survey (10 per cent of the total of these schools) said they were in fact on two sites.*

We would not wish to leave the impression that some of the split schools – particularly those in old premises and particularly those very widely separated in time (i.e. with heavy traffic between sites) equally as much as by distance – are not exceptionally difficult to run effectively as a single school. But equally so, we would not be honest if we did not report that schools in ideal purpose-buildings sometimes found matters far from ideal. One purpose-built comprehensive, winner of a design award, opened in 1964, was described by its head in 1971 as 'consisting essentially of a series of boxes . . . already completely out of date'.[54] And yet another teacher in a purpose-built comprehensive in the North describes how 'ill-thought-out' its plan was; mistakes in the design meant long between-lesson walks for pupils, and buildings not always suitable for their purpose.[55]

The purpose-built schools from our smaller sample had many complaints similar to those in comprehensive school literature, plus a new one that has come along in recent years: severe underestimation of parking space needed. The most common and serious complaint, however, was a lack of facilities for the expanding sixth forms, indicating yet again how underprepared authorities were for the numbers wishing to stay on in comprehensive schools. There were also complaints about inadequate amenities: staff rooms, lecture theatres, specialist rooms, administrative suites and technical equipment. Perhaps the central criticism underlying all this was again one of thinking 'small-school' rather than 'big-school' – and, again, this question of flexibility: a failure to build a new kind of school for a new type of education. Just adding more of the same is not

* See Appendix 1, note 3.

necessarily to build for a comprehensive 'purpose'. A comprehensive school is a multipurpose school: rooms have to be used for purposes never needed in unifunctional schools – for example, as 'bases' or centres of loyalty for year-groups or 'houses'. Just doubling the number of existing amenities for double the numbers is not building for a comprehensive purpose.

The comprehensive school is not the old writ large. It embodies a new approach to the education of the pupils in a given area, and it is an approach that has evolved an equivalently new architectural philosophy. This evolution in purpose-built schools towards breaking up the one-roof school is perhaps one reason why so many non-purpose-built comprehensives, split by circumstances in two or three buildings or schools, have proved to be so successful despite the fact that they were not originally 'one' school. It is not necessary any longer to be in one building to be 'one school'. As the department's architects have so clearly put it, this new architectural philosophy in comprehensive schools – both purpose-built and non-purpose-built –

calls for a clear insight into the real meaning of a unified community, and into the ways in which this can be achieved through the association, within it, of a number of smaller, interdependent communities – all of them aware of the social and educational objectives for which the school, as a whole, stands.[56]

A purpose-built school, meaning a single structure put up to last a lifetime and serving a single purpose, is not really meaningful any longer. Building techniques change, new architectural solutions emerge to old problems, and the purpose of a comprehensive school is constantly being redefined. One comprehensive began in 1935 as a small secondary school for only 110 students. It has had eight additions over the years and now houses 1440.[57] Moreover, it is now more suited to its purpose than many of the genuine purpose-built comprehensives from earlier years.

This whole question of additions is crucial; for every school – whether purpose-built or not – will have additions as time goes by. All but one of our non-purpose builts and all but one of the purpose-built schools in our smaller sample had had additions since opening as comprehensives. And sometimes this can pose a real problem. Where it is a question of replacing a caved-in assembly hall or an urgent addition of extra classrooms, there is no difficulty in deciding what is needed. But more often than not a school has a choice – especially when amalgamating as a new comprehensive, or planning for the raising of the school-leaving age.* Should a great deal of

* In 1969 Hartcliffe School, Bristol, conducted a poll among parents and the local community to find out their views on the use to which money for 'additions' should be put.

money be sunk in specialist facilities that only a few of the students will use: like engineering rooms? Or on something everyone might use: like a swimming pool? Should the basic unit in a new plan be the social one, the academic one or the administrative one, i.e. the house, the subject department, or the offices and staff rooms?[58] What accommodation is needed if the school should want team teaching? Or integrated rather than departmental studies? What balance should be held between specialist rooms and all-purpose rooms? This is a problem for all schools: for sixth form colleges and middle schools no less than for 11–18 schools.

Obviously schools with older buildings must accept many of their existing features – including many units that are similar-size 'boxes'. Only newly planned schools can think entirely in terms of library area, reading area, study area or open-resource areas.[59] But even the latest and newest comprehensive soon gets outdated. For this reason current architectural design plans for change.[60] In the new schools and in additions to schools, we see that nothing remains fixed except the outer walls. Shelving, furniture and inside walls are all movable. Teaching units can be made for groups of one, ten or one hundred; for individual study, seminars or lectures. Nor is the new approach meant merely to meet new needs as they arise. Users are encouraged to 'rearrange' their environment as they wish and to use surroundings to reinforce or to help create policies of teaching or social organization specific to the changing needs of each school and its 'comprehensive' purpose.

Nor need they always be impermanent and over-flexible. The inclusion in new comprehensives of lecture theatres on the old 'Faraday' model seem to be particularly popular at the moment.[61] It is not that schools simply want blank and barren spaces which they can shift about to make what they need, but that what there is permanently installed should be capable of *adaptation* to a wide variety of types of teaching, and a variety of numbers of pupils. Sometimes an 'old' idea takes on new use in a new setting.

Planning to anticipate change is not a feature exclusive to sixth-form centres or comprehensive schools, but applies to higher education as well.[62] It is also in line with emerging beliefs about community planning generally: that only the basic design or siting of facilities and amenities should be laid down in advance by planners. Individual communities – and here we would include school communities – should be left to arrange the details and the smaller units of organization as they themselves wish.

Back in 1960 the Ministry booklet, *New Secondary Schools*, warned against too many architectural decisions taken too early. *Comprehensive Schools from Existing Buildings* in 1968 suggested leaving over some money to see what turns out to be needed, as goals and policies change.[63] This new concept of planning for change is particularly important to the comprehensive school as a reform that is only just beginning on a large scale. How reorganization will develop in detail is not yet known – even to those who work in the schools. Many of us may well change our ideas in five years' time about what is the 'best' way to build or run a comprehensive. Said one of the heads of a small-community comprehensive we questioned:

The only part of a school which should be permanent are administrative and practical facilities. Let us have 'less-bricks-and-mortar complex' and more planning of changeable structures. Why can't we add and subtract as necessary? What we are building at present (made to last for eighty years) no doubt suits the 1970s teacher, but will we be thanked by those who follow us in 1980? I rather doubt it.

Undoubtedly the newly built and the conveniently organized comprehensive school will always enjoy certain advantages over other types of comprehensive school, but these are not automatically over-riding. The all-through school particularly has proved this, having evolved over twenty-five years in an enormous variety of circumstances, locations and situations. It is impossible to pronounce categorically, as some do, that only one-site schools or only 100 per cent newly built schools should be allowed to function as 'comprehensive' schools. The difference between a 1950s secondary modern school that had a sixth-form addition in 1965 and a 1960 purpose-built comprehensive school that has not yet had a much-needed sixth-form addition is not at all great. The difference between a school on one sprawling site that is made up of half a dozen buildings – as some of the newest purpose-built schools are – is not all that far divorced from a 'combined' school on two adjacent sites. Anyone who knows comprehensive schools well, and has visited them at work, knows that categorical pronouncements about 'new' and 'old' and 'one building' and 'two building' – in terms of what is permissible or workable and what is not – are quite impossible to make.

There is no such thing as a typical all-through school any longer. Nor is there any longer any agreed 'best' way to build or to organize or run those that exist – or those that are still to come. The final evolution of the all-through comprehensive school in size and in shape and in architecture, and even in 'purpose', has still to be finally decided.

Notes

1. *The Comprehensive School*, 1964; and *Inside the Comprehensive School*, 1958.
2. G. C. Firth, *Comprehensive Schools in Coventry and Elsewhere*, Coventry Education Committee, 1963; and ILEA *London Comprehensive Schools 1966*, 1967.

3. DES, *Statistics*, vol. 1, 1970, p. viii.

4. ibid. p. 27, 1968.

5. Circular 144, June 1947: 'The organization of secondary education' Ministry of Education.

6. ibid.

7. Speech made on 20 May 1955, quoted G. C. Firth, op. cit. p. 65.

8. House of Commons, 21 January 1965.

9. 'Your child's education', leaflet published by Conservative Association, 19 St James Street, Liverpool 12, undated.

10. H. C. Dent, *Growth in English Education*, p. 78, 1951.

11. Reported in *Education*, 23 August 1946.

12. For example, Elizabeth Halsall, 'Curriculum for a small comprehensive school', *Comprehensive Education*, Spring 1968; 'Small comprehensives', DES, *Trends*, April 1971; and 'Becoming comprehensive: case studies', 1970. See also Michael Armstrong, 'The small comprehensive', *Where*.

13. *Inside the Comprehensive School*, chapter 10 and p. 115.

14. Tynemouth's *Reorganization of Secondary Education*, p. 3, July 1966; and June 1969, p. 8.

15. Address to the Education Section of the British Association, op. cit., p. 8. The Secretary of State gave this figure in the House of Commons in June 1967.

16. See P. Nurse, 'One way to botch a scheme', *Comprehensive Education*, no. 7, 1967.

17. NFER Report, p. 88.

18. ibid.

19. In our survey in 1968 we asked head teachers to estimate the percentage they had in their intakes in the top 20 per cent of the ability range. The average over all for 728 schools was 15 per cent. In the NFER's First Report they asked head teachers to do the same. In the Second Report (p. 187) they give the ability intakes in forty-six schools as estimated by the head teachers in 1966, and next to this they show the *actual* ability intakes obtained from attainment tests administered in 1968 to these same schools. When the heads did the estimating, the average ability intake per school was much the same as for our survey: about 15 per cent. This was 3 per cent more than the *actual* ability of pupils as measured by the attainment tests, and the second NFER Report comments that it is undoubtedly the case that heads tend to overestimate the ability of pupils in their intakes (p. 106).

20. Second NFER Report, p. 117.

21. The figure of 20 per cent as the percentage of the ability range 'capable of GCE examinations' is obviously an under-estimate in 1970 (whatever it may have been when GCE first began) for in that year 33·9 per cent of all-maintained school leavers obtained at least one GCE O-level (Table 5, DES, *Statistics*, vol. 2, 1970). It is therefore at the five or more GCE O-level stage that the 20 per cent figure would seem to be more appropriately applied, since in that year 17·8 per cent of all-maintained leavers and

21·4 per cent of all leavers obtained that qualification. This is yet another indication of the rise in academic standards in recent years, as more and more pupils qualify in GCE every year at all levels of that examination.

22. The figures given in the table are from *The Comprehensive School*. Those for the year 1963 are from the first edition (p. 106), where twenty-three schools were included with 3610 leavers; those from 1968 are in the revised edition of 1969 (p. 109), and include sixty-seven schools with 12,493 leavers. Criticisms of the choice of these schools and refutation of this criticism is dealt with in footnote 1, page 208. The figures for 1968 for all maintained schools are derived from the DES, *Statistics*, vol 2, pp. 1, 21. Those for 1963 are given in the revised edition.

23. *Teacher*, no. 12, 25 September 1970.

24. DES, *Statistics* vol. 2, 1969 (p. 73), 1968 (p. 79) and 1970 (p. 67).

25. It is 31 per cent, compared to 29 per cent in 1969 and 27 per cent in 1968. DES, *Statistics*, vol. 2, pages 79, 73, 67 for 1968, 1969, 1970 respectively.

26. Table B, p. 2., vol 2.

27. See 'Academic results in comprehensive schools', *Comprehensive Education*, Summer 1966 and 'Examination results in fifteen comprehensive schools in 1970', Autumn 1970. For interesting information on favourable comparisons between comprehensive and other schools in Scotland, see *Scottish Education Journal*, 25 November 1966, p. 1124.

28. First NFER Report, p. 125.

29. See report in *Education*, 19 January 1968.

30. *Contact*, Pre-School Playgroup magazine, p. 27. April 1969,

31. Albert Rowe, *The School as a Guidance Community*, 1971, p. 75.

32. Kathleen Gibberd, quoting the headmaster of Clissold Park School, London, in *New Statesman*, 5 May 1967.

33. First NFER Report, p. 91.

34. Stephen King, *Ten Years All In*, p. 11, 1969.

35. The school is St Richard of Chichester in Inner London, described by P. J. O'Connell, in *Becoming Comprehensive*, ed. Halsall, 1970.

36. Building Bulletin 40, HMSO, p. 11.

37. Halsall, ed., p. 61.

38. Halsall, ed., p. 105.

39. Halsall, ed., pp. 60–61.

40. Halsall, ed., p. 70.

41. First NFER Report, p. 22.

42. ibid., p. 90.

43. *The Comprehensive School: An Appraisal from Within*, p. 38, 1964.

44. Speech of Professor T. Markus to RIBA Conference, June 1968.

45. *Teaching in Comprehensive Schools*, IAAM, p. 30, 1967.

46. *The Comprehensive School: An Appraisal from Within*, pp. 96–7.

47. ibid., p. 91.

48. ibid., p. 95.

49. ibid.

50. T. W. G. Miller, *Values in the Comprehensive School*, p. 29.
51. G. R. Pritchett, Chief Education Officer, Oldham, personal communication, 27 March 1969.
52. Quoted in Firth, op. cit., p. 33.
53. Miller, op. cit., p. 29.
54. Albert Rowe, *The School as a Guidance Community*, p. 33, 1971.
55. Halsall, op. cit., p. 77. See also pp. 81–2.
56. *Comprehensive Schools from Existing Buildings*, DES, p. 52.
57. ibid., p. 58.
58. ibid., p. 19, outlines this conflict in detail.
59. See C. R. P. Luckhurst, 'Southampton's middle schools', *Comprehensive Education*, Summer 1968; and DES, *Middle Schools Bulletin* 35, 1966.
60. See DES, Building Bulletin 41, Sixth Form Centre, p. 20, with its stress on building for 'constantly changing needs'.
61. Comprehensive schools in both Derbyshire and Leicestershire mention the usefulness of these theatres in Elizabeth Halsall's case studies; in London the same type of theatre in Highbury Grove School was singled out as especially useful during a visit one of the authors made to the school in 1970.
62. See John Vaizey's plea for flexible building, RIBA Conference, June 1968; also his *Education in the Modern World*, 1967, chapter 8.
63. *Comprehensive Schools from Existing Buildings*, p. 10.

Chapter 7
Basic Scheme 2: Tiered Schools

Foundation of schools

As we saw, all-through comprehensive schools, both purpose-built and combined, are often organized in two buildings. Such a school, divided on an 11–14 and 14–18 basis, is in many respects similar to a tiered scheme where two individual schools, taking the same age ranges (11–14 and 14–18), are organized next door to each other but administered separately under two heads.

This merging of one of the three basic schemes into another is characteristic of reorganization. In fact, the variations on each of the basic three schemes are so many that it is possible rather to talk of a continuum of schemes from single-building self-contained 11–18 schools serving all local pupils, all the way across to units of individual schools: 9–14, 11–14, 14–18 and 11–16 plus a further education college – all in the same area and all serving the same general secondary population in what would then be a comprehensive complex made up of units of all three of the basic schemes.

Table 5.3 (p. 115) shows that in LEAs' long-term plans 25 per cent of all future secondary schools may well be involved in tiered schemes of one kind or another, and these do not include 'interim' selective schemes (10/65 3 or 4) which could well develop as tiered eventually. Our own larger survey of 728 comprehensives in 1968 confirms a rise in schemes involving tiered schools – that is, schools of the 11–13, 11–14/15, 13–18 or 14–18 age ranges. As can be seen in Table 6.2 (page 119), schools in these categories amount to 20·5 per cent of all the schools in our survey. This is about double the figures for 1965.* Table 6.3 (p. 125) shows further that tiered schemes continued to be introduced between 1968 and 1972 at much the same rate as between 1965 and 1968 – with the crucial difference being that the relationship between lower and upper tiers is changing. Recent trends have been away from many lower schools feeding a single upper towards fewer lower schools, and sometimes only one, feeding a single upper. Because tiered schools are generally smaller

* See First NFER Report figures for types of schools, p. 229. Their tiered schools add up to 10·6 per cent.

in size than all-through schools, however, the total school population in them is likely to be far less than in 11–18 schools. In our survey in 1968 only 12·7 per cent of the total comprehensive-school population was in tiered schools.

To make things easier, we will distinguish two types of tiered schemes differentiated by the Department of Education and Science[1] as total-transfer schemes and parental-choice schemes. Total-transfer schemes speak for themselves: *all* pupils in a lower school go up automatically to an upper school. In parental-choice schemes there is selection for those who are to go up to the upper school, only *some* 'choosing' or being 'selected', the rest remaining in the lower school which then runs parallel to the upper school, usually until sixteen. As circular 10/65 made clear, this second type of scheme is not fully comprehensive.

Total-transfer schemes

Let us look at total-transfer types first, where age ranges of 'lower' schools can be 9–13, 11–13, 10–13 or 11–14, with upper schools of 13–18 or 14–18. Sometimes these lower schools are called 'middle schools'. This is a term that has also been used for schools taking the age range 8–12. In this latter case the 'middle' schools are almost always the former junior or primary schools that have had one extra year added. Southampton's scheme is an example here. We have not defined schools of this 8–12 age range as 'middle' in our survey; nor have we included upper schools that are 12–18 as schools in tiered schemes, since this is the age range for the standard all-through school in Scotland and the difference between the 12–18 and the 11–18 age-range school in England did not seem so great as to justify their being assessed as other than all-through schools.

The DES classifies 8–12 schools as primary schools, and 10–13 schools as secondary. When it comes to 9–13 schools – by far the largest category of middle schools – the DES says they can be classed as either primary or secondary; it is up to the local authority itself to decide.[2] In 1970 there were 136 middle schools in England and Wales: 105 were classed as secondary, 31 as primary.[3] Quite obviously it makes a difference to the staffing and facilities of a school whether it is 'classed' as one rather than the other.

We are further reinforced in this view by the fact that the 8–12 'middle' schools in schemes with a twelve-plus break are mostly being organized in existing junior schools, while most 9–13 middle schools and most of those of 10–13 and 11–14 are being planned, or already exist, in the old secondary modern schools. This naturally makes a big difference to the foundation of the 'middle' school – both in terms of staffing and size. Existing secondary schools are generally bigger than junior schools, with more specialist facilities and equipment; and securing secondary staff for the 11–13 age range in these schools may be easier than in a school previously a junior or primary school.

It is worth noting at this point that there seems to be a conflict of opinion here between what authorities are planning – which is often 9–13 middle schools in old secondary school premises – and what the DES in its building bulletin *Middle Schools*[4] assumed would be planned: all 9–13 (and 8–12) schools housed in converted junior schools. No examples are given there of any middle schools converted from secondary schools. Conversion of junior schools is cheaper, of course, and is one reason why the DES perhaps preferred them originally. But junior schools are also smaller. *Middle Schools* gave plans for no schools larger than 480 and some as small as 280. This raised another controversial issue, for there are those who claim that a middle school must be at least 500 in size to provide an adequate academic offering for the 11–13 age range[5] (although in many cases this includes provision for classics, a specialist subject few middle schools will probably want to include in their curriculum). As we can see, the difference between a 'break' at twelve rather than thirteen is crucial, for upon this generally hangs a decision about whether middle schools will be developed out of the existing junior schools or out of existing secondary schools. Frequently it is the available buildings that themselves condition a decision about the age to break.

In this connection, schemes with transfer at twelve have occasionally been criticized as merely meeting the problem of raising the school-leaving age on the cheap – by fitting in the 'extra' year at primary level where it is less costly, rather than at secondary level. It is also unfortunate that certain areas plan a transfer age of twelve but do not plan the abolition of selection. For these reasons twelve-transfer schemes have also sometimes come under suspicion as less than genuinely comprehensive. There is no reason to regard them all as such, however, for in some areas they will be genuinely comprehensive.

In 1970 the DES listed 136 middle schools with 46,241 pupils. The average size overall was 340 – of middle schools deemed secondary the size was 348, and of those deemed primary, 313.[6] At the time of our survey in 1968 there were no schools of the 9–13 age range, but a glance at our table showing future LEA planning (Table 5.3, p. 115) shows that schemes with schools of 9–13 followed by 13–18 schools may well be adopted by a large number of areas: one-fifth of present planned secondary schools may well be involved in schemes with this age range alone. The thirteen-plus break is to date more popular with authorities planning tiered schemes than the fourteen-plus break.

The first authority to begin the total change to middle schools of 9/10–

13 and upper schools of 13–18 was Wallasey in 1968–9. The West Riding
has also started a number of middle schools, the development of one area
being traced in the DES document *Launching Middle Schools*, and Bradford had the first purpose-built middle school for the age range 9–13,
which opened in January 1969. But middle-school units covering the
years 9–13 have existed before inside larger comprehensive units. One is
in the Bartholomew School in Oxfordshire. And, of course, middle
schools of 11–14/15 have existed from the beginning of Leicestershire's
reorganization in 1957.

In our survey of 728 schools in 1968, the only 'middle' schools were of
11–13 and 11–14/15 age range and they were 14 per cent of the total
number. This is a large increase over the 1965 position as reported by the
NFER.[7] These schools were involved in both total-transfer and parental-
choice tiered schemes. Some of these parental-selective schemes have
now evolved into total-transfer schemes, of course. Leicestershire and
Swindon are examples. In other areas, like Hull or Bedfordshire, the
change to tiered schemes has taken place from the traditional break-at-
eleven arrangements, as it also has in areas like Waltham Forest where the
tiers are 11–14 and 14–18, or Swansea, where some are 11–13 and 13–18.
In Scotland the term 'middle school' is used to cover schools with the
age range 11–14. In contrast to England there are few such schools
planned, but one was planned in the late 1960s in Grangemouth.

Choice schemes: free and guided

These are the second type of tiered scheme, the first being the total-transfer type to which we have already referred. Although 10/65 lumped all
parental-choice schemes under numbers 3 and 4 of its six types, it is
obvious, as we have seen, that in one sort the 'choice' is relatively
genuine; in the other it is not.

Let us look at the genuine-choice schemes first. These are usually where
11–14/15 schools ran parallel with 14–18 schools, pupils being given a
choice of transfer at fourteen* to the upper school, or remaining an extra
year in the lower. The special features of this scheme are that parents'
choice is usually honoured, and secondly, that lower schools usually
have no external examinations. Some upper schools may at first have
exerted subtle pressure to prevent large numbers of the 'less academic'
from opting to transfer upwards, but the rate at which this percentage of
transfers rises each year in schemes of this kind shows that the choice in
many cases is obviously free. Long before some of Leicestershire's upper
schools were scheduled to change to a total-transfer scheme, they were

---

* In theory schemes with a thirteen-plus break could also operate in this way, but
most do not.

already receiving 100 per cent transfer of the age group. Stonehill School was one such example.

The merit of the free-choice schemes is that they have allowed the grammar school to expand into its comprehensive role slowly. The head of one of these schools in our smaller sample said that he had no doubt this scheme will 'evolve easily into a fully comprehensive system'. The snag is that those remaining in the lower school sometimes feel left out. One head told us that with 75 per cent transferring upwards, he had 'very little of any value' to give those remaining, who required vocational training. In 1968 there were quite a number of free-choice transfer systems slowly but surely evolving into fully comprehensive tiered systems: Leicestershire, Keighley, Swindon are examples. The raising of the school-leaving age to sixteen has meant the end of most truly-free-choice schemes where upper schools get bigger and bigger every year since they were mostly of the fourteen-plus transfer type and those 'left behind' only stayed one year. Now, with a two-year course required, most areas with these schemes transfer the whole age group. Choice schemes of the guided type, most of which have a thirteen-plus transfer of a minority, however, continue to exist, and new ones to be introduced.

Guided-Choice schemes

These true-choice 10/65 type-3 schemes are very different from the 10/65 type-3 'guided'-choice schemes. And it is around the latter that most of the controversy has arisen. In these guided schemes the upper schools are the old grammar schools, often very little changed, and certainly in most cases not planning to take in more pupils than they can presently accommodate, i.e. not planning to 'grow' to accommodate 100 per cent. Planning documents about these schemes make it clear the grammar school tradition will be preserved and enhanced.[8] Brochures explaining the schemes – from Cumberland and from Kent, for example – make it clear they are still selective, as must be the case since such a small percentage of the school population enter them, usually at thirteen-plus. A Middlesbrough upper school told us it accepted about 15 per cent of the thirteen-plus population. In Cardiff, in the first year of the scheme, only 27 per cent transferred to the upper schools:[9] just a little above the 'old' grammar-school percentage. This is a far cry from the 70 per cent regularly transferring in free-choice schemes – almost all of which have now evolved to total-transfer schemes. In some guided-choice schemes the upper schools actually remain grammar schools in status. In some cases they are maintained (Burnley), in others they are direct grant (Blackburn, Wakefield, Sheffield (R C sector)) Where the upper school is particularly prestigious, obviously the whole problem of 'choice' for entry is somewhat euphemistic. In one area in

1971 only 7 per cent of the boys and 19 per cent of the girls actually 'chose' to transfer at thirteen-plus to the upper schools (direct grant) from the lower comprehensive schools.[10] Research into Wakefield's scheme has shown that parents are often 'guided' so well they do not even realize they have a choice of moving to a direct grant school.[11] Particularly interesting in the Wakefield research was the breakdown of reasons why parents of children judged 'suitable for grammar education' but not choosing the direct grant school had not in fact done so: 30 per cent did not realize they had a choice; 46 per cent had been told by their teachers their child did not really have the 'ability', and 20 per cent felt the direct grant school's status 'too high' for their child.

In almost every scheme with 'guided' choice the upper school remains more or less its former size and retains its former purpose: to prepare pupils for external exams. Some have added CSE, but all concentrate first on GCE. Most of the pupils are expected to proceed to A-level work and in some cases promises are required beforehand that they will in fact do so. Only those pupils are encouraged to opt for the upper school who are willing to study the traditional GCE syllabus. For example, one LEA brochure says:

The grammar school will *not* arrange special courses for children who are unable to cope with an academic course. Arrangements will be made for them to transfer back to their secondary schools if it becomes clear that they are wrongly placed.[12]

The actual choice process is very much guided, as most of the brochures make clear. Teachers do the advising. Most parents do not insist against the advice of the lower-school head teacher in schemes of this kind. If they do, they are sometimes asked to see the upper-school head teacher who explains the different nature of the two 'types' of school in the scheme. But parents do not often protest. In the first year of Cardiff's scheme only forty-four did so.[13] The rest had been willing to be guided between the 'choice' of leaving at fifteen or sixteen (in which case the 'lower' school is advised) or going on to A-level work (in which case the upper school can be considered). In guided-choice methods of transfer there is always appeal against the decision. But the whole appeal structure is likely to be intimidating and probably only confident and usually middle-class parents will want to face it. This is the case also in Scotland, where a parent may appeal against the transfer-board decisions when pupils are allocated between certificate (exam) and non-certificate courses at twelve. Recent research tends to confirm that there, too, those who undertake an appeal 'tend to belong to the higher social classes than those who simply accepted the transfer decision'.[14]

The main arguments against guided-choice tiered schemes – and these apply to guided-choice generally – are firstly, that they are still selective. Secondly, they do not always draw the pupils they want in the way they want. As one northern school head put it to us:

Pupils transfer for irrational reasons or as an act of protest against their lower school, and then apply for premature release. Others do not transfer who would do well. The system depends upon parental interest. In effect, children decide. Only end-on transfer is really fair.

Thirdly, these schemes leave the lower school demoralized, as Alec Clegg outlined in explaining why the West Riding had rejected them: lower schools would consist 'mainly of pupils denied the vital spur of parental aspiration', and would be hard 'to run effectively'.[15] Fourthly, pupils who might 'benefit' by the upper school might also have benefited in the lower school, and settled so well that they did not wish to leave the lower school.[16] Fifth, the 11–16 schools often do not provide the range and extent of courses, subjects and exam opportunities that the upper schools do.* Sixth, where they do, there is a wasteful duplication of courses from fourteen to sixteen. Seventh, these schemes may operate in favour of the middle-class child and against the working-class child.

This last complaint has come up repeatedly. Circular 10/65, of course, warned about parents who might not understand what was involved in 'choice'. Several parent groups have themselves criticized schemes of this type for this very reason.[17] The Advisory Centre for Education, investigating 'guided' schemes of this kind, has said: 'it has now been established that this process can work against the interest of the working-class child even more than selection by an 11-plus exam'.[18] The professional teaching bodies have more than once expressed reluctance about a method of selection that puts so great an onus of choice upon the teacher as does this 'guidance' method. Commenting upon it in respect of tiered schemes in particular, one said: 'The element of parental choice at thirteen-plus seems certain to result in some measure of High School opportunities being decided on social rather than educational grounds.'[19] In Middlesbrough, part of Teesside, where this scheme has operated for some years, there were unofficial reports in the press, never denied, that the percentages of pupils being guided from the middle-class districts of the town are as high as 50 per cent, while from some schools in working-class districts they are as low as 6 per cent.[20]

The introduction of 'comprehensive' schemes of guided parental choice involving 11–16 lower schools and 13–18 upper schools is not only continuing, it is rising. In 1971 there were about 125 comprehensive schools involved in this type of scheme – about 8 per cent of all existing

* See chapter 8, p. 175.

comprehensives in that year in England and Wales. Plans to introduce more such schemes – in Kent, for example – are well in hand. It is therefore interesting to have the comments of a lower school already in such a scheme, where 25 per cent of 'selected' pupils leave the school at thirteen plus for a nearby grammar school, now called an 'upper comprehensive'. The head of the 11–16 school writes: [21]

The stress on obtaining clear academic results by thirteen-plus places undesirable pressures on our curriculum for the first two years. The effects of this emphasis become increasingly negative among those staying with us. At thirteen plus those not transferring lose a sense of purpose at this critical age, and the severe lack of able and talented pupils depresses the expectations of both teachers and pupils.

The age of thirteen plus is no better age at which to make overall forecasts of potential than is eleven plus, and the problems of doing so for boys particularly leads to many dubious decisions. In fact, our system of 'guided parental choice' is markedly socially divisive, and it brings undesirable moral and non-educational pressures to bear on teachers trying to make assessments.

He goes on to say that lower-school morale suffers, staffing is more difficult than it should be, and the school itself loses esteem. Not only that, it has fewer resources devoted to it, and since it tries to prepare its pupils for examinations at sixteen, it is necessarily in competition with the 'upper comprehensive' in doing so, leading to uneconomic use of resources which already exist.

The whole problem of 'guidance' is central to Scotland's secondary system too. The 1962 Act laid down that no parent may choose a course at secondary stage from which, in the opinion of the education authority, the pupil shows no reasonable promise of profiting. In those many areas where 12–16 schools with incomplete certificate courses coexist with 12–18 schools in 'comprehensive' schemes, some pupils transferring at fourteen and some remaining behind, the problem remains. The disadvantages of those remaining behind in respect of later taking H-grade (should they do well at O-grade), the problem of a two-year spell for those who will be transferring at fourteen, and the 'low level of expectation' of those who do not transfer, have all been the subject of comment in Scotland. [22] In Scotland, the short-course schools will remain in existence for a long time, even under a comprehensive system. This makes the problem of a common course inside these schools and the abolition of 'parallelism' in O-grade and H-grade work from the years twelve to sixteen, crucial factors in Scotland's reorganization.

If we make a great deal of this matter of guided parental choice, it is because, as we said, it is not confined to 10/65's scheme 3 or 4. It is being used as a method of selection in other schemes as well – and in particular, to replace the old 11-plus. Many authorities claim to be going comprehensive simply because they have replaced selection-by-examination with 'guided' selection between different types of secondary school. This substitution of a new 11-plus for the old one is discussed in greater detail in chapter 20, but for the moment it is only necessary to point out that 'guided' choice is no substitute for reorganization. As one non-reorganizing authority has rightly claimed: 'it is not necessary to go comprehensive to abolish the 11-plus'. [23] One type of 11-plus can merely replace another.

On the other hand, it should be remembered that as far as 10/65's schemes 3 and 4 are concerned, both provide an extra two or three years' more comprehensive schooling for all pupils than was available before reorganization. This is a real gain and should not be minimized. For those who wish to see the grammar school retain its essential nature and purpose, these schemes 3 and 4 are also appealing. They require grammar schools to make the least changes. But in a number of areas where these schemes have been tried, the difficulties we have set out appear to weigh rather heavily. Cardiff and Blackburn are examples of areas where the schemes have got into trouble or been abandoned prematurely. And the probable general conclusion is that schemes of this kind are too much of a compromise to win in the long run; or, put another way, if reorganization is going to be undertaken, it is best done genuinely.

Lower and upper schools: size and siting

Tiered schemes of both total-transfer and parental-choice type were evolved out of the necessity to use existing school buildings, which were relatively new and could not be replaced for decades, but which were too small for the 11–18 or 12–18 age ranges. A number of areas adopting tiered schemes, however, found positive advantages in separating schools with breaks at thirteen or fourteen. Chief virtue was that the younger age group was so very different from the older teenager of seventeen or eighteen that it was to the definite advantage of both groups to have their 'own' school. This advantage, as we have already mentioned, is one that many schools with 11–18 age range also recognize and one reason why they purpose-plan separate sites or accommodation for different age groups even within new purpose-built 11–18 schools. Several of the heads we questioned mentioned that discipline problems were far easier to handle when the two ages were separated physically. And it is interesting to notice that there has long been a definite trend in the United States to split up the six-year high school into junior and senior schools – in order to contain pupil population in more manageable groups. This has particular relevance in areas where violence and racial unrest is high.

The average size of the 11–13 school in our survey was 336 and of the

11–14/15, 497. The size of these schools, of course, varies with the area
in which they are situated, as do many comprehensives. In both city and
village categories the average size of the 11–14/15 school is 355, but in
suburbs it is 616, almost twice as large. With 11–13 schools, on the other
hand, the size is significantly larger only in the town category (see Table
A2, p. 523).

But size is only one factor in the success of a school, as we shall see time
and again. Equally important is staffing ratio, attitude of staff and head
to the potentialities of the school – whatever its age range – and community and authority support. The 11–13 school is an excellent example
of a school that can either be a total failure – its 'transit camp' disadvantages completely dominating the outlook of those teaching in it – or
can be run with the same kind of enthusiasm that most middle schools of
9–13 are being run. Many of these two-year schools will eventually grow a
top or a bottom and become 9–13 or 11–14 schools, but meanwhile the
two-year schools can be successful – especially where liaison between both
primary school and upper tier school is close. Some Bradford two-year
schools had long records of success. We also talked to parents of pupils
in a two-year school in Flintshire. They were extremely enthusiastic
about their 'new' comprehensive school and when we asked if the two-
year span was perhaps a difficulty, it was obvious this was a factor that
none of them had considered. They even asked what we meant by
'difficulties' involved. A few of the two-year comprehensives have been
outstanding successes, and those who teach in them speak warmly of
the advantages which come in a school with 'a narrow age band' and
'small numbers', for they can concentrate upon a personal, intimate,
family-type atmosphere.[24]

Liaison between schools is a key factor, of course. Many of the tiered
schools we questioned gave as their chief complaint the lack of communications between upper and lower tier. One head in a long-established
break-at-fourteen scheme said he would prefer 'the two schools run as
one, under one head, with both staffs interchanging freely between
schools'. It is interesting that what he preferred, of course, is what many
call a 'botched' scheme, a single school on two sites.

Our experience, therefore, leads us to conclude that the key to success
or failure is not primarily the actual physical arrangements – unless they
are so appalling that no organization could succeed – but the quality of the
provision and administration within the unit and the quality of liaison
between the units in any type of scheme.

The same applies to the arguments about whether it is best to 'break'
for upper schools at thirteen or at fourteen. There are strong arguments
for both ages. A break at fourteen gives pupils three years in the lower

school where the transfer is age eleven. The incentive to stay beyond the leaving age is high when the 'new' school is entered so close to the age when leaving is possible. It is perhaps given more of a chance to 'hold' its pupils. Certainly our own survey figures support this, for the 14–18 schools had the highest average percentage for any type of comprehensive school for pupils remaining beyond the leaving age (Table 6.2, p. 119) – 76 per cent. This is particularly encouraging, for most of these 14–18 schools are involved in genuine-choice transfer schemes rather than in guided-choice schemes. The 'guided' choice upper schools tend to be of the 13–18 age range. In these the percentage remaining beyond leaving was only 63 per cent.

Although most of the 'guided'-choice schemes involving selective upper schools have a thirteen-plus break, it should not be assumed that all 13–18 comprehensive schools are semi-selective, nor, on the other hand, that 14–18 schools cannot be – as a few are – involved in guided, rather than free, choice schemes. The distinguishing feature here is not the actual age range of the schools, it is whether the lower school runs parallel to the upper school at any point, with only some pupils transferring, as against whether the lower school meets the upper school end-on – with *all* pupils transferring upwards.

The number of 13–18 comprehensive schools is growing in the country (see Table 6.3, p. 125), and will probably continue to rise throughout the 1970s. Hopefully, the percentage of the total which are semi-selective will be much less at the end of the 1970s than it was at the beginning.

There are other interesting comparisons to be made between the 13–18 and the 14–18 upper school in 1968. The first striking one is the difference in the proportion of each that are mixed schools. The percentage of all schools in the survey that are mixed was 81 per cent (See Table 18.3, p. 411). In no type of school did this fall below 80·5 per cent – *except* in the case of 13–18 schools. In this category only a minority were mixed: 38 per cent. This supports the assumption that in 1968 many were former single-sex grammar schools that chose to remain single-sex. By contrast, however, 94 per cent of the 14–18 upper schools were mixed (and no boys' 14–18 schools were represented in our survey at all). Considering that many of these 14–18 upper schools were also former single-sex grammar schools, it would seem that reorganization associated with a 'genuine' choice pattern of transfer seems to be far more likely to involve reorganization to mixed status along with expansion of the school to take in all abilities.

There is a further interesting difference between the two sets of upper schools: their size. Since the 13–18 schools have an extra year over the 14–

18s, we would expect their average size to be larger. But in fact it is smaller: 538 compared to 587 (Table 6.2, p. 119). This suggests not only that the 13–18 schools represented in our survey were still highly selective and did not need to be of great size to support adequate GCE and CSE courses, but also that the 14–18 has indeed 'expanded' to meet the greater ability intake that asks to come. Lastly, there was the interesting finding made in our follow-up survey of schools in 1972 when we found that of 13–18 upper schools in the sample two out of the five required qualifications for entry into the sixth form (usually at least one GCE pass) but that all of the 14–18 upper schools replying had 100 per cent open sixth forms, all permitting pupils to enter the sixth form regardless of previous qualifications obtained (see p. 516).

So far we have talked about 13–18 schools as if they were always selective. But this is not the case – even though, for reasons given earlier, it was largely the case up to 1970. As the future pattern of schemes indicates, however (Table 5.3, p. 115), total-transfer schemes – involving fully comprehensive 13–18 schools – will be numerous. And indeed in our survey, a few of the 13–18 upper-tier schools were already of the fully comprehensive total transfer variety. In this connection it is interesting to note that in our survey we found that where 13–18 schools were mixed rather than single-sex, their average size rose quite dramatically: from 538 to 634.* The difference between the average size of single-sex and mixed schools of the same type was not generally as great as this in schools in our survey. The future 13–18 schools, therefore, will probably be rather different from those in existence in 1968. Certainly they will be mostly mixed, as are most comprehensive schools, and they will probably eventually be only slightly smaller in size than the all-through schools.[25]

GCE O-level

In comparing the two types of upper school in the matter of presenting pupils for the total range of eighteen subject-groups at GCE O-level (Table 6.10, p. 141), we see that higher percentages of 14–18 upper schools are able to present pupils in a great number of subjects than 13–18 schools – undoubtedly because they are so often mixed schools and thus able to offer the full range of options inside the school. Both types of upper school, however, compare well in this respect with the all-through schools of 11–18 – both with a higher percentage able to present a full range of thirteen or over than is possible in the 11–18 school. Since many of these upper schools in 1968 were already well-developed grammar schools when they became 'comprehensive', this is not surprising. This is much less the case in the 1970s.

* See Appendix 1, Note 3.

When comparing the two types of upper school in presentation of pupils for the individual subject-groups (Table 6.8, p. 136), we see that both presented pupils for the academic subjects in roughly the same percentages (and these were high in all subjects), but that a far higher percentage of 14–18 schools than 13–18 were able to present pupils in the vocational subjects like woodwork, metalwork, needlework, domestic science and technical drawing – again, perhaps, confirming that 'genuine' choice schools provide more fully for all abilities. 14–18 schools also scored better in this respect than all-through schools, though the difference was not so marked. The upper schools together generally had slightly higher scores than the all-through schools in most of the academic subjects, but these were not significant except in the case of Latin and music.

These comparisons between the two upper schools are instructive. They show that the 14–18 schools – by chance, to date, schools associated with 'genuine' choice more often than with 'guided' choice, and schools where there were great fears for 'academic' success because the entry of pupils at fourteen was so near to O-level – competed most favourably with the (by chance in 1968) more selective 13–18 schools, with their extra year to prepare for exams. It is also worth noting that the 14–18 schools only took in 17 per cent of the top 20 per cent of the ability range, while the 13–18 schools in our survey (Table 6.2, p. 119) took in 25 per cent, the highest, along with the second type of 11–18, for any type of comprehensive school. That the 14–18 school is less than comprehensive, while the 13–18 is more so, does not seem to have impeded the 14–18 school in its academic offering.

It is worth pointing this out again, for many local-authority documents make it clear that schemes of this kind were not chosen because education committees felt 'academic' success would be limited by a mere two-year run-up to O-level. As a result of these fears the existing 14–18 schools have had to concentrate rather heavily on exams. And while no doubt this concentration has helped to ensure a good academic offering, many working in these schools told us they felt that there was far too much exam pressure in them. Undoubtedly a reform of the present double examination structure, particularly abolition of GCE O-level in favour of the CSE, would do a lot to ease the problems of break-at-fourteen schemes, which in so many ways have much to recommend them.

In summing up, it is certainly possible to say that tiered schemes with breaks at thirteen or fourteen – of the *total-transfer* type – can be, and are, fully comprehensive forms of reorganization. Their greatest virtue is, perhaps, their potential 'holding' power upon pupils in the older teenage years – in comparison with schemes where there is a break at the leaving age or at sixteen. But undoubtedly their biggest disadvantage is the difficulty in forming and maintaining proper liaison between the lower and upper tiers. Liaison is a feature of many tiered schemes which has been very much neglected and which needs radical rethinking and improvement before tiered schemes are counted a complete success.

Notes

1. Press release, 22 November 1967.
2. DES, *Statistics*, vol. 1, 1970 p. x.
3. ibid., p. 2.
4. Building Bulletin 35, HMSO, 1966.
5. See submission from Bedfordshire Grammar Schools Representative Committee, Appendix to Bedfordshire's Reorganization Scheme, 1967.
6. DES, *Statistics*, vol. 1, 1970, p. 2.
7. First NFER Report, p. 229.
8. R. E. Presswood, writing about Cardiff's scheme, *Comprehensive Planning*, ed. Stuart Maclure, Councils and Education Press, 1965.
9. David Evans, *Comprehensive Education*, Summer 1967, p. 21.
10. These are the percentages in the RC sector in Blackburn, 1971, given in *Comprehensive Schools in 1972*, C. Benn, p. 4.
11. See G. E. Whalley, University of Leeds, writing up his Research in DES *Trends*, 1970, Issue 18.
12. 'Secondary education in Whitehaven' (Cumberland), a brochure for parents of pupils about to choose whether to transfer up or to stay behind in the lower school, 1968.
13. David Evans, op. cit.
14. A. Valentine, 'Attainment of pupils admitted to certificate courses after parental appeal', University of Glasgow, unpublished M.A. thesis, 1968.
15. Alec Clegg, letter to Comprehensive Schools Committee, March 1967, explaining why the West Riding had decided against these schemes.
16. *Education*, 7 July 1967, p. 11: A. Griffiths, Lecturer in Education, describing the results of research into 11–16 schools that coexist with 13–18 upper schools, makes this point.
17. See Newsletter 13, 1967, of the AASE in Sevenoaks, Kent.
18. *Where*, January 1967 editorial.
19. Teesside NUT Document, July 1968.
20. *North Eastern Gazette*, 28 May 1968.
21. This account appears in *Nine Points of View* (on 11–16 schools), *Comprehensive Education*, Summer 1971, no. 9.
22. *Scottish Education Journal*, vol. 49, no. 9, p. 223.
23. Bournemouth authority publication, 1965, p. 21.
24. Kenneth Rudge, 'The two-year comprehensive school', *Comprehensive Education*, Autumn 1970.
25. C. Benn, 'Middle schools', *Forum*, Spring 1967, gives information on the size of planned schools of this age range.

Chapter 8
Basic Scheme 3:
Separate Sixth Forms

The varieties

Separate sixth schemes are of many kinds: schemes with 11–16 schools and sixth form (or junior) colleges, and schemes where 11–18 schools act as the sixth form for neighbouring 11–16 schools. They also include schemes where post-sixteen work is centred in the local further education or technical college, either in part or entirely.

Separate sixth schemes are likely to be very popular: as we see in Table 5.3 (p. 115), one-third of all schools in planned future comprehensive schemes may well be involved in such schemes. Table 6.2 (p. 119) shows that in our survey of 728 comprehensive schools in 1968, just over 25 per cent of existing schools were already in separate sixth schemes. In 1972 the percentage was just as high (Table 6.3). These schools contained just over 22 per cent of all the pupils in our 1968 survey – almost all of them in schools of the 11–16 and 11–18 (type II) age range. In 1968 as yet only a tiny fraction of pupils – less than a half per cent – were in sixth-form colleges; but this figure will rise dramatically during the 1970s and 1980s. In 1972 there were a dozen sixth-form colleges, and plans to introduce a further sixty schemes of this kind were firmly fixed in about thirty more areas.[1] In the 1968 survey there were only two full sixth-form colleges, although there were a number of embryo colleges – like Preston Grammar School which in 1968 had stopped admitting pupils at eleven but had started admitting into its sixth form instead. Its sixth form in 1968 was only 179; by the mid-1970s it planned to be 500.

What is even more dramatic, as an indication of the trend towards more separate sixth schemes generally, is the fact that of all comprehensive schools in our survey receiving their first comprehensive intakes in 1967, 40 per cent are schools of an age range consistent with separate sixth-form schemes (see Table 6.1, p. 118). The measure of this change is the rise of the 11–16 or short-course comprehensive. In the NFER Survey of 1965 only about 9 per cent of the schools were in the 11–15/16 age range.[2] In 1968 it was 21 per cent – 31 per cent if we include the 11–15 schools that we have put in a different category. In some areas in Britain in our survey – like the South of England – half of all comprehensive schools in

1968 were 11–16.* If we look at the figures for comprehensive schools opening in the years from 1963 onwards, in Table 6.1, we see that as 11–18 schools drop in percentage of the total, so 11–16 schools rise. In 1963, for example, only 5 per cent of all schools opening in that year were 11–16. In 1967, 34 per cent were.

The same trend is evident in the schools opening in 1971 in England and Wales where 35 per cent of new comprehensives were 11–16 (Table 6.1, p. 118). No attempt was made to distinguish between the two types of 11–18 school (one self-contained, the other acting as a sixth-form centre for neighbouring 11–16 schools and thus counted as properly part of a separate sixth-form scheme). If these 'mushroom' 11–18 schools were counted in as well, the percentage of schools in this type of scheme was probably higher in 1972 than in 1968, where the two types are so distinguished (Table 6.1, p. 118).

Among many inadequacies in the DES statistics on comprehensives is the lumping together under one heading of both 11–18 and 11–16 schools. The *Statistics* give the number of schools with a 'middle' age range, and the numbers which can be classed as 'lower' or 'upper' schools, but they do not give exact age ranges, and they 'hide' the percentage of comprehensive schools which are short-course – without sixth forms. Since this long-term trend to comprehensives without sixth forms is a result of policies of concentrating the sixth form, it is essential for a proper evaluation of this policy, and of the way the reform is developing, that these simple statistics, which are certainly available, should be given. The trend towards concentration of sixth forms by introducing more comprehensives without sixth forms is a very controversial one, of course. In areas where local parents and teachers are quite sure they have the numbers and the form entries to justify a sixth form – Saddleworth in Yorkshire is one – the policy of concentration of the sixth form – pursued in many local authorities – which tells them they must wait, meets with a good deal of resistance. As a policy, it has both pros and cons, but either way the more information the better, since the controversy about to-have-or-not-to-have a 'separate' sixth will dominate a good deal of local comprehensive planning in the next decade.

The 11–16 school is one of the most controversial of all types of comprehensive, ranging as it does from a large, fully comprehensive school providing a vast range of GCE, CSE and many other opportunities all the way across to a school which 'loses' one-third of pupils at thirteen plus and offers no GCE at all.[3] There is no other type of comprehensive which it is so important to monitor as it develops, since the directions it can take are so wildly various. The differences between 11–18 schools with

* See Table 17.1, p. 390, for information about regions.

ordinary self-contained sixth forms and mushroom sixth forms is also crucial, yet no information is given us about the development of each type, not even simple facts like how many there are of each. That the DES does not even think it important enough to give information of this kind each year is yet another indication of the way in which the reform is handicapped. A national fuss about 'immigration' has led to a startling growth of information in the yearly *Statistics* about pupils supposedly in the immigrant category, but information on the progress of comprehensives – the various types, their age ranges and their sizes – all of which is certainly available, is not thought important enough to print in any detail in the *Statistics*. The NFER's Research project on comprehensives, while valuable, does not chart the *growth* of the reform or the way it is developing since it is limited to schools and school types which were in existence in 1965. A great deal has happened in the comprehensive reform since 1965. The most valuable support for any reform is full and continuous information; this the comprehensive reform has never had.

Cooperation with further education

Before we examine the 11–16 school, however, let us look at the possibility of cooperation between schools and local colleges of further education and technical colleges. Circular 10/65 gave only a bare hint that this was a possibility, and even less far-sighted, it talked about such cooperation only in terms of sixth-form colleges. As we know, such 'cooperation' is just as important for other types of comprehensive's sixth forms.

What we are more in the dark about, however, is just how much of it actually goes on. Oxfordshire has three 'centres' for advanced studies, Melton Mowbray has a 'centre', the South Berkshire Technical College is developing 'links' with schools, and Wiltshire has 'area committees' of heads of schools and principals of further education colleges. Chapter 12 gives examples of some of these individual schemes in operation, but overall these do not yet represent practice in a large number of schools, although ROSLA schemes operating in the mid-1970s will no doubt increase the flow of school pupils who will spend one or two days a week at a local further education or technical college. But the flow is usually one way – few technical college or FE students flow into the schools. And the flow is also very much confined to pupils in the 'less-academic' sector of the comprehensive – at least it was in the early 1970s. It is the girls who are sent out of comprehensive schools to the local technical college for secretarial work in Gloucestershire or the boys sent for 'workshop practice' from a Leicestershire comprehensive,[4] or boys sent for building trades, or girls for office arts.

Thus while the closer cooperation of schools and colleges can lead to many advantages – and may be cheaper – it also carries dangers. One DES publication assumes that where comprehensive schools and colleges cooperate, the schools will keep the academic pupils and the colleges will have the technical pupils.[5] Several individual local authority schemes have also said that cooperation at sixteen between comprehensive schools and colleges will be on a basis of colleges having the 'less able',[6] the 'mature late developer', those who require 'vocational education',[7] or who are 'less academic',[8] while all imply that the academic will stay in the schools. The concentration of all post-sixteen work in a further education college, as is now being developed in Barnstaple (Devon) and Exeter, is not the radical proposal it must seem to many whose only knowledge of post-sixteen education has been the enclosed and traditional sixth form in a selective school. Similarly, the extension of the grammar school itself to fill the role of a sixth-form college, is proving a much more natural evaluation of the school's role than many had forecast. Some sixth-form colleges (e.g. St Austell) hope to 'cooperate' fully with the further education colleges; others make it quite clear that they will retain a 'school' ethos, and that colleges are for 'vocational' work; and some even say those at the college doing A-levels are quite 'a different type of student' from the school sixth former doing A-levels.[9]

Apart from the fact that it is very doubtful that the majority of technical and further education colleges will enthusiastically support this role for themselves as maxi-modern schools, there is also the danger of splitting academic work from vocational, and arts from technical studies, just at the moment in history when many realize that some of the difficulties in industry and society arise from previous arbitrary divisions of this kind: between, for example, research and its application. New divisions between 'academic' and 'technical', or between arts and sciences, or between specialist and general – at the sixteen-year-old level – would be unhappy at this point in time. The problem will be more acute if legal changes allow pupils to take part or all of their education in colleges from age 14/15 onwards. For reasons of this kind separate sixth-form schemes are sometimes viewed with suspicion, and only time will tell if these suspicions are justified.

Whatever one's opinion about these separate sixth developments, the reshaping of post-sixteen education represented by these schemes is once again an example of local initiative making its pressure felt. Nor is this present pressure coming from the authorities alone. It is the teenage students in many cases who have been 'voting with their feet' and choosing to take post-sixteen schooling in colleges even when their own schools could provide the teaching or the courses. Local further education and technical colleges have been aware of this trend for a long time. Loughton

College of Further Education in Essex, for example, found that 40 per cent of its students for A-level came from schools with their own sixth forms.[10] Our own investigations in several other colleges tell us they expect this trend to continue. Our impression is that students who leave school in this way are often very independent. In many cases the reasons for leaving had more to do with the authoritarian nature of the secondary school than the magnetic pull of the college.

Advantages and disadvantages

The trend to separate sixth-form schemes – whether because students themselves want a change or because authorities concentrate all post-sixteen work in a few institutions – is deplored by many. It is particularly deplored by existing 11–18 comprehensive schools, many of these the early and most comprehensive of the comprehensive schools. Many local authority documents also dislike 'break-at-sixteen' schemes, especially those who have chosen to go for all-through schools. The objections are these: 11–16 schools, inevitable in any 'break-at-sixteen' scheme, cannot be true comprehensive schools. They are too small to provide the courses and their lack of sixth-form work will not attract the better-qualified staff. As one authority puts it, 'they will be regarded as inferior in status to the full comprehensive 11–18 school'.[11] Second, the break at sixteen will discourage pupils from continuing education after sixteen.[12] One head of an 11–18 school that was threatened with 'decapitation' wrote:

Our young people of promise will not be inclined for the most part to continue their education beyond the age of 16 unless they continue to enjoy the unbroken personal contact with teachers . . . who have known them for 5 years in the main school course.[13]

Third, sixteen-plus selection will rapidly develop. (This is already happening in many areas – and is a growing problem, as we show shortly). Lastly, in all kinds of situations and areas, existing comprehensive schools have built up a new and successful pattern of truly comprehensive sixth-form education. The advent of the break-at-sixteen movement seems to many to be threatening it.

To counter these arguments, there is the view that at sixteen many students are too mature for the 'school' atmosphere, that they welcome a break in institutions, and that they enjoy and respond to the more adult atmosphere of a sixth-form college, junior college or further education college (although the degree of 'adult' status given varies enormously between the colleges). Secondly, these new separate sixth institutions are able to provide a much wider range of courses than is possible in many small-school sixth forms, which, if the sixth forms were removed from them, could concentrate more effectively on meeting the needs of the 11/12–16 age range. Thirdly, concentration of post-sixteen work in one school is more economical and 'conserves' scarce resources, both of staff and of facilities.

Undoubtedly there will be different answers in different areas to the problem of to-break-or-not at sixteen. In some areas, especially de-populating country areas, where a nearby town has a flourishing sixth-form college, there is often little point in trying to keep a sixth form in the face of great staffing shortage and falling pupil numbers. Concentrating on the 11–16 age range and providing this with a truly comprehensive curriculum and courses may eventually seem more sensible. Nor is the loss of the sixth always traumatic. We visited a school that had 'lost' its post-sixteen pupils in a scheme that was developing a centralized college. It had, frankly, feared the effect on the school and on the staffing position. But no staff had left. And contrary to fears for the restricted nature of the age range, we were told that the fifteen/sixteen year olds in the new situa-tion had suddenly become much 'older' and more responsible now that they were the top of the school.

But the problem is very different in an area – say a town or in a countryside development where numbers are rising – where demands for post-sixteen education will continue to be high. The argument that asks for concentration of resources here is less logical and very often a dis-guised argument for retention of grammar schools – as schools 'specializing' in sixth-form work. Even if the initial intention is not one of evading comprehensive reorganization, there is a danger that if sixth forms are too concentrated in too few institutions they lead to an inevit-able sixteen-plus situation. This is already happening in some areas. At Luton, for example, where the separate sixth scheme was established in 1966, the sixth form from the first was concentrated in one highly selec-tive college, asking for four O-levels for entry. What was to become of the pupils with three O-levels: or two: or one: or five non-grade-1 CSE? It is likely that the post-sixteen overflow must 'back-up' into the 11–16 school. One of Luton's 11–16 schools told us that barely two years after the scheme began, they already had a 'sixth form' of thirty-nine pupils – most sitting for either CSE or GCE examinations. Those sixth-form colleges being planned along the Luton lines – qualifications asked for entry, and more or less general concentration upon traditional academic work – will probably have to become more and more selective as time goes on, and overspill sixth forms will have to develop alongside. Or, as we showed earlier, the local technical and further education colleges have to step in and catch those who fall through the selective net. In areas where this kind of a situation is developing it is probably true that the sixth-form college is *more* selective than ever was the old grammar school.

But some colleges are being planned as 'open', as indeed are many of the sixth forms in all-through and upper comprehensive schools. It is in the all-through sector that the tradition of the 'sixth form' meaning the 'sixth year' has taken hold firmest. All pupils are accepted: both examination and general-course pupils; O-level retake and first-take O-level courses are also provided in addition to a wide range of A-levels. How long areas planning these 'open' policies can persist in them remains to be seen. It depends upon available finance for buildings, how accurately they predict demand, and how efficiently they expand to meet it. Stoke's chief officer was quoted as saying as long ago as 1966 – of the sixth form that eventually became the centre for the separate sixth scheme in that city and which was then 'open': 'it might be necessary to impose some qualification later if the number of students wishing to take up sixth-form studies exceeds the accommodation the College will provide'.[14] And indeed that is just what has had to be done in Stoke on Trent.

But it is not only sixth-form colleges which impose restrictions; it can happen in the ordinary sixth form of a comprehensive as well. Overall in our 1968 survey 74 per cent of the schools in England with sixth forms operated an 'open policy' – that is, no qualifications called for entry to the sixth year of education. In Wales, however, only 27 per cent were open, and in Scotland it was even lower: 13·5 per cent. Thus confirming that both Welsh and Scottish comprehensives were more internally selective at sixth-year level in 1968 than comprehensives developing in England.[15]

In 1972 when we re-examined the entry policies for sixth forms we found an increase in the percentage which were 'open' (see p. 184), but within the overall picture schools in separate sixth-form schemes were more selective at sixth-form level than those with sixth forms attached (see p. 185). Since 1968 too the pattern of sixth-form colleges has emerged more clearly. On the one hand, there are the colleges of Luton and Stoke, which are highly selective – 'A-level Academies' they have been called – requiring four GCE O-levels for entry. Others are open, with no entry qualifications, usually offering O-level work, CSE and special non-examination work as well. Most sixth forms (and colleges) are probably between these two ends of the spectrum, and many are trying to avoid the problems by cooperating with each other and with the further education sector.

In those areas where some schools find their sixth forms have difficulty in building up numbers there have been attempts to 'pool' resources and for schools to cooperate together – to make use of scarce specialist staff, or to form larger teaching groups in individual schools. But they have rarely met with success. Sometimes it is the old monastic notion that a school should be a self-contained institution, but more often than not it is the timetables which clash. If 'consortia' policies could be developed in time, it could well be one of the ways to avoid depriving some comprehensives of their sixth-form work, and to avoid the selectiveness of some of the separate sixth-form schemes now developing.

It is because of the desire to avoid a fifteen-plus that many also welcome the solution of centring all post-sixteen education in a further education (FE) college or of formal cooperation between school and technical college. But these are not automatically solutions to fifteen-plus situations. The FE college has an accommodation limit like any other institution. Unless correct assessment of future demand is made for *all* post-sixteen courses – full- and part-time, in schools or in colleges – and expansion planned, any separate sixth scheme could well have to become selective.

What percentage in school from 16 to 18?

How far ahead and how realistically are most authorities planning to meet the demands of those wanting sixth-form education in the 1970s and 1980s? Local authority reorganization documents rarely touch this subject; when they do they differ a great deal. One sixth-form college in Essex tentatively planned to take only 12½ per cent of the age group – even in 1981.[16] One Lancashire area planned on the basis of 15 per cent wanting sixth-form education in the 1970s,[17] Herefordshire predicted 30 per cent,[18] and Ipswich 35 per cent.[19] In many of the comprehensive schools we questioned and visited, these higher percentages already apply. In 1968 Fishguard school in Wales, for example, 40 per cent were already staying on into the sixth.[20] In Myers Grove in Sheffield almost 30 per cent. In many southern comprehensives it is now well over 50 per cent.[21] Since forecasters have always fallen short of actual targets when predicting demand for education – and this includes the Robbins Report on Higher Education and the DES itself, whose late 1960s forecasts of numbers in schools in the 1970s had to be revised upwards – it is obvious many local education authorities originally also underestimated the demand for sixth-form education. One example is the city of Manchester. The Chairman of their Education Committee wrote in 1971:

The city's reorganization plan provided sixth-form accommodation in each school for 20 per cent of its annual intake and it is assumed that this figure will probably be too low. We are now thinking in terms of 40 per cent.[22]

Some estimates of percentages made in the early years of reorganization were very small, as we show above. Those introduced after the start of the

1970s, however, such as the Harrow or Ipswich plan – start by assuming 50 per cent of the age group would want entry by the time the colleges there were in full operation.

Yet official opinion continues to be sceptical about the demand for sixth- and seventh-year education. An HMI writing in 1970 was of the opinion – even at this late date – that institutions providing a two A-level course or equivalent 'will be needed for no more than a quarter of the age group, perhaps for less'.[23] He also adds that 'ours is a society that sets a strong guard on entry to a third stage of education for reasons that have nothing to do with education itself but derive from economic necessity and social tradition'. Whether this 'low-percentage outlook' will prove to have been justified in a decade's time, who can say. Many feel it will not, and that even the number staying for a two-year course must be drastically upgraded. For example, in 1971 one local authority was already planning for 40 per cent of the age group to remain for a *two-*year period (and many more for only one year).[24] And many comprehensive schools already have half an age group entering the sixth form as it is.

But there are two further important facts. The first is the raising of the school-leaving age which may well result in a larger percentage of pupils wishing to remain in school after sixteen. The second is that comprehensive reorganization itself will encourage pupils to stay beyond leaving age in far greater numbers. Our survey of 1968 found evidence to suggest this is so. The average percentage of pupils staying on beyond statutory leaving age in the 621 survey schools with the 13–16 age group was 51 per cent – 52 per cent for comprehensive schools in England and Wales, 1·6 per cent higher than the same year's figure (50·4 per cent) for maintained secondary schools in England and Wales. In the all-through schools in England and Wales in our survey it was 56 per cent (type I) and 60 per cent (type II). For all comprehensive schools in England and Wales with sixth forms it was 59 per cent – more than 8 per cent higher than the national average figure. That the percentage of those staying on beyond statutory leaving age in comprehensive schools is directly related to the size of the sixth form – and that the bigger the sixth form, the greater the staying on – can be clearly seen in Table A.3 (p. 524). That the more 'open' the sixth-form entry practice and the less streamed the school, also mean that more will stay on is equally likely. In 1968 comprehensive schools with sixth forms operating a policy of open entry to their sixth forms (no qualifications asked for entry) had a 6 per cent higher staying on rate than those operating a selective policy (at least one GCE O-level required).[25] Staying on rates were also higher (by 4 per cent) if schools with sixth forms permitted pupils to study O-level work only in the sixth (did not require all sixth formers to be on A-level work).

Many of the 'new' sixth-formers, of course, are taking a much wider course than the traditional two- or three-A-level sixth-form course – a fact that must also be taken into account when planning future accommodation. In fact, one of the most startling trends evident in education in the last four years is the rise in what the DES calls the 'new sixth former' – in 1969 already 13 per cent of the total of sixth formers.[26] The numbers in the higher years of schooling in the 1970 DES *Statistics* were presented in a new form in that year, but it is possible to see that over a quarter of the sixteen year olds in schools were following courses other than A-levels.[27]

All these facts added together should warn us that we may well not be planning enough places for post-sixteen students in 1980. Restriction of opportunity because of a conscious policy of selectivity in separate sixth-form schemes or because of failure to expand limited college accommodation, is almost inevitable unless, from the beginning, separate sixth schemes are deliberately planned as open-ended institutions that can expand to meet demand as it rises. One good example of such expansion is the way most Leicestershire upper schools expanded to meet post-leaving age demand throughout the 1960s.

But open sixth-form planning is necessary in all types of comprehensive schemes. Although the selection-at-sixteen problem is nothing like as urgent in all-through or upper schools as in separate sixth schemes, in comprehensive school literature there are many examples of complaints from all-through schools of failures on the part of authorities to anticipate the 'present trend towards larger sixth forms'.[28] Heads of 11–18 schools we ourselves questioned in our smaller sample of schools about current accommodation difficulties listed overcrowded sixth forms as their most urgent problem more often than anything else. The Second NFER Report comments on the fact that in many schools sixth forms '. . . were considered hopelessly inadequate by their teachers, there being no place where the sixth could meet together as a form or socially, and in some cases the sole base of a sixth-former was a locker in a corridor'.[29]

Whether it was because of overcrowding or not, in the schools in our 1968 survey we found that 31·5 per cent of all schools in England and Wales with sixth forms required at least one O-level pass for entry to the sixth – and thus were not genuinely comprehensive sixth forms (see Table 12.1, p. 280). In the eighty-five comprehensive schools with sixth forms re-surveyed in 1972 this percentage had gone down to 2 per cent – 73 per cent were now 'open' – indicating a continuing trend towards greater openness.[30] What was most interesting too about this follow-up survey was that it asked the question about open *v.* closed entry in terms of the type of scheme, and when this was examined it was found that it was 'open' in 72 per cent of the schools that had sixth forms attached, but only in one-third of the schools where pupils had to proceed elsewhere for sixth-form work, e.g. leave 11–16 schools to transfer to sixth forms in 11–18s or to sixth-form colleges. The schemes with 'separate sixth forms', therefore, are in danger of being more selective, and this is a disadvantage which will have to be watched very closely.

This need to expand post-sixteen facilities finds itself in direct conflict with arguments from those who fear the multiplication of sixth forms – for traditional academic reasons associated with A-level GCE – and who wish to see the sixth forms concentrated further rather than expanded. Most notorious of those who put forward these arguments were the twenty-five university vice-chancellors who wrote to *The Times* * to state fears that academic standards would decline because sixth forms in grammar schools were being 'broken up' during the process of reorganization. They gave no example of where this had occurred † – indeed, it is rare for a reorganization scheme to remove sixth forms from schools – but their academic standing and the gravity of their accusations were such that they consolidated the arguments of those – like *The Times Educational Supplement* of the 1960s – who had long since opposed reorganization wherever it meant any alteration in the role of the grammar school. The shortage of 'good' maths and science graduates to teach in sixth forms was another point made at this time that also carried weight.[31]

These campaigns led to a general loss of nerve in reorganizing authorities about all-through schools, many of whose sixth forms must necessarily be small in the first five years of existence (until the comprehensive entry works its way up to sixth-form level) ‡ – with the result that many authorities back-tracked to say they would not after all have all-through schools, but would 'concentrate' sixth-form work in existing sixth forms instead,¶ leaving some comprehensive schools to develop to 11–16 only. About the same time, too, the government was facing economic difficulties which eventually led to the temporary cut-back in building allocations to authorities. And, of course, some authorities

---

* *The Times*, 3 June 1967. See also reply by distinguished academics on 10 July 1967.

† See also *Comprehensive Education*, Autumn 1967, which reports having written to each of these vice-chancellors to ask for examples, and receiving from the only six who answered only one example.

‡ See Table A.21 (p. 545), which shows how the percentage of schools with very small sixth forms declines sharply after schools have been established as comprehensives for five to six years. See also chapter 9 for evidence about the growth of comprehensive sixth forms between 1968 and 1972.

¶ Berkshire is an example here. See the resolution passed in June 1967.

planning fully comprehensive schemes changed hands politically and used these kinds of arguments to keep two 'kinds' of comprehensives – with and without sixth forms – as a way of avoiding real reorganization. All these events conspired to bring forward in large numbers a second version of the sixth-form college scheme 5: where 11–18 schools coexist with 11–16, the sixth forms concentrated in the 11–18. After 1970 the newly elected Conservative government cut down completely on the replacement of secondary schools (except where new population needs could be demonstrated), a policy which obviously further encouraged a policy of 'concentration' rather than one of 'expansion'.

The 11–18 grammar school as a sixth-form centre was not new, of course. Mexborough in Yorkshire had been running such a scheme for some years; so too had Roseberry Grammar School in Surrey. In the late 1960s both were highly imaginative breakthrough arrangements and in many ways pioneered a new type of sixth form. But neither was part of a comprehensive scheme. They, and schemes like them, either ask for a good number of O-levels for entry or they operate in areas where the 11-plus still exists. Sometimes both disadvantages apply. In reality they were merely extensions of the old transfer principle, where pupils from secondary modern schools – usually those who had achieved a certain number of O-levels – could transfer to the local grammar-school sixth form. They also resemble many of the 'interim' comprehensive arrangements already existing in many authorities, such as that at Kingswood, Gloucestershire, where the old grammar school coexists with four or five ex-secondary modern schools. Schools in these plans are no longer labelled grammar and modern, but as the Kingswood brochure states, there is a 'wide overlap in the range of ability for which all schools will provide'.[32] Behind the 'overlap' in many schemes of this kind it is well known in the area that the ex-grammar school takes the very brightest and provides a far wider choice of subjects to examination level at sixteen than do the ex-secondary moderns, which are still known to be retained for the non-academic. Indeed, the Kingswood brochure explicitly states that these ex-secondary modern schools specialize in the 'slow learner'.[33] Schemes of this kind are often designated as 'short-course' and 'long-course' schools. Pupils are distributed between each by 'guidance'. The dangers are obvious: some areas will adopt these schemes merely as a cloak for remaining bipartite; others will adopt them as a 'stage' on the way to reorganization but in fact settle for them permanently. This can lead to local cynicism about what comprehensive reorganization really amounts to,[34] especially where parents are told: grammar schools will remain and 'secondary modern schools have in effect become comprehensive schools'.[35]

On the other hand, there is no reason why this version of a separate sixth scheme could not be genuinely comprehensive. If each long-course and short-course school had non-selective entries at eleven or twelve, and if the form entry was much the same for all schools, and if the provision of subjects and staffing was the same for the years 11–16 in all schools, and if the entry to the 'concentrated' sixth was genuinely open to all pupils – the scheme could be comprehensive in design. But the difficulty is that all these combinations of factors are hard to secure all at once – and the temptation to concentrate 'academic' work in the 11–18 and 'slower-learners' in the 11–16 indefinitely is great. This temptation is one of the major threats of reorganization today and raises in acute form the real problem here, making the 11–16 or 12–16 age range one that is exciting and attractive. It is interesting that so much educational excitement has been generated by the 9–13 'middle' school and that these schools show such confidence in being able to attract qualified staff, while such an impoverished attitude exists in circular 10/65 and most LEA documents towards the 11–16 school.

There is no reason why the enthusiasm for the middle years cannot extend to sixteen. Undoubtedly a single examination – suitable for the majority of pupils – rather than the present two, would help the situation in the 11–16 schools as in other comprehensive schools. Since the 11–16 school is likely to be smaller anyway than the years eleven to sixteen in the 11–18 (Table 6.2, p. 119, shows the extreme average size difference in 1968), the difficulties in the way of provision of a full range of courses in 11–16 schools, in both CSE *and* GCE, are obvious. The disadvantage for the pupils in the 11–16 school, when it comes to gaining the 'necessary' GCE qualifications for transfer to sixth forms of 11–18 schools, is also obvious. But undoubtedly the biggest single problem is the fact that these 11–16 schools in almost every case are old secondary modern schools – with no sixth-form tradition – and correspondingly disadvantaged locally (especially in staff recruitment) compared with the former grammar schools which become the 11–18 schools.

Coexistence of short-course and long-course comprehensive schools: the dangers

The figures we have collected about the 11–16 comprehensive would seem to bear out its disadvantaged position in 1968 in some important ways. We see from Table 6.2 (p. 119) that its intake of the top 20 per cent of ability is lower than the survey average of 15 per cent – it is only 13 per cent. We see too that the percentage of pupils in 11–16 schools staying on beyond leaving age overall is also low: only 37 per cent compared to 51 per cent for all schools in the survey in 1968 and 55 per cent for type I 11–18s. That it is not the age range 11–16 itself that conditions low staying on is proved by looking at Table A.2 (p. 523), where we see that this staying-on percentage differs enormously in 11–16 schools according to the population situation of the school. That is, when the 11–16 school is in a big city it is down to 27 per cent staying on, but when the 11–16 school is in the 'town and surrounding countryside' category, for example, staying on rises to 52 per cent. This suggests that 11–16 schools need not be disadvantaged schools, and that what makes them so is not their intrinsic age range but their situation relative to other types of secondary schools in their areas. It is well known that in many big cities the 11-plus continues and grammar schools remain.

The 11–16 school is also disadvantaged on the question of size. This stands out particularly in relation to the all-through schools. We have already seen its position relative to these schools in the matter of form entry (Table 6.4, p. 127): 70·5 per cent of all-through schools were at or over the minimum six-form entry size, while only 39·5 per cent of 11–16 schools were. Table 6·2 (p. 119) shows the difference between the average size of 11–16 schools on the one hand and all-through 11–18 schools on the other: 586 for 11–16 but 950 average for all-through 11–18s (type I).

But the type of 11–18 with which the 11–16 will be most often competing is not the 11–18 all-through, it is the 11–18 type II, the school that acts as the sixth-form 'centre' for neighbouring 11–16 schools. It is when we compare the average size, ability intake, staying-on and examination percentages between the 11–16 and 11–18 schools of this second type that we see the greatest gulf: 586 for 11–16 and 1081 for 11–18; 13 per cent of the top 20 per cent compared to 25 per cent; 37 per cent staying on compared to 62 per cent; an average of only seven O-level (or O-grade) subject-groups for 11–16s compared to an average of fifteen for 11–18s. In Table 6.10 (p. 141) we see that exactly a quarter of 11–16 schools aren't yet able to present a single pupil for any of the eighteen O-level or O-grade subject-groups, while all type II 11–18s can; and, at the other end, only 7 per cent of 11–16 schools are able to present pupils in fifteen or more subject-groups compared to 84 per cent of the 11–18s. Although we have only compared 11/12–16 schools to 11/12–18 schools here in the matter of GCE O-level and SCE O-grade offering, percentages staying on after leaving age, and intake of top 20 per cent of ability, the same type of comparison can also be made between 11–16 schools and upper-tier schools. Since 11–16 schools frequently must 'coexist' with upper-tier schools, particularly 13–18 schools, in interim reorganization schemes, it is important to note that comparisons between 11–16 and upper-tier schools on all these points show an *even greater difference*.

In the matter of putting forward pupils for the individual subjects,

we see from Table 6.8 (p. 136) that only a minority of 11/12–16 schools
were able to offer pupils for GCE O-level or SCE O-grade in some of
the major academic subjects (and in all the vocational subjects except
technical drawing) and that percentages for all academic subjects were
significantly lower for 11/12–16 schools than for all other types of comprehensive school. Percentages were particularly low in languages (Latin
2 per cent, French 47 per cent and other languages 13 per cent). It is some
consolation, however, that the percentage able to present pupils in mathematics was the highest of any of the eighteen subjects: 68 per cent.

We would wish to emphasize again that we are not talking about
academic performance but only about academic offering in 1968; and that
undoubtedly, as we have said before, many 11–16 comprehensive schools
were just building up their numbers. The significance attached to these
figures will also vary with the amount of emphasis readers place on
examinations in comprehensive schools, particularly GCE. For 11–16
schools undoubtedly find the CSE examination far more congenial, and
all but six of them sat pupils for CSE examinations in 1968.* But the
disadvantages listed here are probably severe enough to make many worry
about the disadvantaged position of the 11–16 school as it now operates
in certain schemes. Many of the disadvantages still existed for some of
these short-course schools in 1971, as a study of the courses and local
authority support of nine such schools showed.[36] Since all separate sixth-
form schemes depend in one way or another upon the 11/12–16 schools
that form the majority of schools in *all* schemes of this kind, separate
sixth schemes as a whole are never going to win public confidence while
such comparative disadvantages exist in short-course schools. This
problem is particularly acute when these short-course schools must
coexist with 11–18 or 12–18 or 13–18 long-course schools. Merely saying
to parents and staff that there is 'equal opportunity' to take 'GCE
courses' in 11–16 schools is a very far cry from an opportunity to take
them in the range of subjects that is met with in the 11–18 or in the
upper-tier school.

We point out these difficulties not to bring down opinion against the
11–16 comprehensive – for many are very successful and some are fully
comprehensive with a full range of subjects – but to underline the inherent difficulties in the hope that parents and staff and education committee members with 11–16 comprehensive schools in coexistence
schemes will press authorities to attend to their needs. It is very obvious
that the type of support a local authority chooses to give its short-course
school is probably the single most important factor in its success.[37] The

* 133 out of 139 England and Wales 11–16s sat for CSE, 331 out of 345 11–18s as did
25 out of 27 11–18s sixth-form centres, and 47 out of 50 upper-tier schools.

four areas most requiring attention are staffing, facilities, curriculum development, and genuinely comprehensive intake. 11–16 schools also need their buildings brought up to scratch. Only 12 per cent (19) of all the 11–16 or 12–16 schools in our survey were purpose-built as comprehensives, compared to 42 per cent (162) of all-through comprehensive schools.* The exciting new departures implicit in all separate sixth schemes, including the flexible arrangements permitting cooperation of schools with further education colleges, and, of course, the success of all sixth-form or junior 'colleges', all depend upon 11–16 schools. Many will fail unless the 11–16 school and its problems are radically and immediately attended to.

Summary

To sum up, the separate sixth-form schemes are facing three dangers. The first is selectivity at sixteen with denial of opportunity and waste of talent, especially to pupils who achieve just under the 'requirements' for centres or colleges, who need longer to achieve these requirements than is usual, or who wish to pursue a general or untraditional sixth-form course rather than the traditional academic one. These difficulties could be obviated by devising colleges or centres that are genuinely open – where O-level work, general work, part-time, full-time work and vocational work are all provided in addition to traditional academic or A-level work. But even then great care will be needed to see that the 'break' at the crucial sixteen-year mark does not discourage pupils of talent and ability from carrying on to the 'next stage' of schooling. The second danger is the divorce between academic and vocational work or between 'pure' studies and technical courses – in both concentrated sixth forms and in schemes where schools cooperate with further education colleges. The third is that reorganization will, in fact, never really take place – with grammar/modern segregation merely replaced by coexistence of 11–16 on the one hand and 11–18, 12–18 or 13–18 comprehensive schools on the other, with guidance between the two 'types' taking place at eleven or twelve or thirteen.

The principle at stake in separate sixth schemes is really no different from that involved in any other comprehensive scheme: how far are provision, staffing, size and facilities equal in *all* schools in the scheme? How far is the intake to all schools in a scheme genuinely non-selective? How far are pupils in all schools in any scheme encouraged to continue their education to the next stage of schooling regardless of paper qualifications? How far do all schools provide a wide variety of courses and options for all pupils, using community resources to the full? How far does coopera-

* See Appendix 1, Note 3.

tion and liaison take place between all schools in any scheme, and between primary and further education and comprehensive schools in all areas? Where separate-sixth-form schemes can answer all these questions satisfactorily, they can be as comprehensive as other schemes. But there is no doubt that for all the reasons we have given, it is going to be more difficult for them to do this – especially at sixth- and seventh-year level – than for the other two basic schemes.

Notes

1. C. Benn, *Comprehensive Schools in 1972*, Appendix, lists all the areas planning sixth-form college schemes in 1972.
2. First NFER Report, p. 229.
3. For a description of these many types, see 'The short-course comprehensive school', Nine Case Studies, *Comprehensive Education*, Summer 1971.
4. Halsall, ed., op. cit., p. 15 and p. 119. See also the Series on Raising the School Leaving Age, *Comprehensive Education*, Spring 1971.
5. DES, Building Bulletin no. 40, p. 35, 1967.
6. Wigan, reorganization document, 1968.
7. Chester document, p. 4, 1969.
8. Wolverhampton document, para 12, January 1968.
9. Halsall, op. cit., pp. 224–5.
10. Loughton College of Further Education, 'Survey of full-time students', p. 2, September 1967–8.
11. Caernarvonshire reorganization document, p. 3, 1967.
12. See John Eggleston, 'Some environmental correlates of extended secondary education in England', *Comparative Education*, March 1967, which tends to prove the validity of this question.
13. Willenhall School memorandum on the 11–18 school's need to retain its sixth form, 18 January 1968.
14. Quoted in 'Comprehensive reorganization', p. 11, 1967–8.
15. See C. Benn, 'School style and staying on', *New Society*, 24 June 1971.
16. Essex reorganization document, Thurrock, p. 7, March 1966.
17. Lancashire Division No. 7, Memorandum of Working Party, 1967.
18. Reorganization document, p. 10, 1967.
19. Report of Education Committee, October, 1966.
20. Fishguard School brochure, 1968.
21. Many Inner London comprehensive schools already report this.
22. Norman Morris, SEA Bulletin, Spring/Summer 1971, in an article on school progress in Manchester.
23. David Hopkinson, 'The 16–18 question', DES *Trends*, no. 20, 1970.
24. Reorganization Document for Redbridge, 6 July 1971, Appendix B.
25. C. Benn, 'School style and staying on', op. cit.; this article reproduces material from the authors' 1968 survey which was not in fact used in the first edition for reasons of space.

26. DES press notice, 'Biggest sixth form population ever', 7 December 1970.
27. DES, *Statistics*, 1970, vol. 1, p. 42.
28. *The Comprehensive School: An Appraisal from Within*, p. 104.
29. NFER, Second Report, 1970, p. 93–94.
30. For details of the Re-Survey, see Appendix I, p. 516. The number of 11/12–16 schools was twenty-three.
31. D. N. Roaf, *Comprehensive Education*, Spring 1968.
32. Kingswood brochure, Gloucestershire, 1967.
33. ibid.
34. Letter to *New Observer* (Gloucestershire), 9 May 1968.
35. Gloucestershire Education Committee, 'To Parents', 1965.
36. 'Short-course comprehensive schools', *Comprehensive Education*, Summer 1971.
37. ibid.

Chapter 9
The Sixth Form

In this chapter we will look at the sixth forms in all three types of comprehensive scheme from two points of view only: size and GCE A-level and SCE H-grade subject offering. We discuss the work of the sixth form in chapter 12 and in chapter 8 we examined in detail different ways of concentrating sixth-form work.

In chapter 8 we also discussed the whole question of national planning for the 16–18 age group, showing how differently different local authorities are going about it – especially in terms of estimating the percentage of the age group each expects to want full time education in the 1980s. We saw too how the policy of concentrating sixth-form work in certain schools as against developing them in all schools will certainly bring dangers of selection at the sixteen-year level – when the country is gradually adapting to the idea of turning the old 'sixth form' of schooling – selective and higher-education directed – into the new 'sixth year': a true comprehensive collection of pupils working on many different kinds of courses, and open to all who wish to stay on in full-time education regardless of qualifications.

Size

Before the Second World War the average size of a grammar-school sixth form was about twenty. In the late 1940s the Ministry of Education was concerned to provide comprehensive schools with an 'equivalent' sixth form to a three-form entry grammar school. This was then about forty. From resulting calculations it was determined comprehensive schools must number at least 1600 to produce this figure. This approach was questioned from the beginning. But areas proposing smaller comprehensives – Middlesex was one – found that most of their proposals were turned down by the Ministry. In the 1950s very small comprehensive schools – Windermere with 220 and Castle Rushen with 450, many of the small bilateral schools in Wales, and many of the 'omnibus' schools of Scotland* – showed they could provide adequately for all pupils, including those staying on to enter university. Nevertheless, the Ministry

* This point was made by Lady Simon in *Three Schools or One*, 1948.

continued to rule out small comprehensive schools and it was not until the first phase of the Leicestershire experiment was launched in 1957 that an effective way was found of circumventing this insistence on very large comprehensives. Here older pupils were concentrated in an upper school for the 14–18 age group.*

Since circular 10/65, of course, both these trends outlined above – smaller all-through comprehensive schools and tiered arrangements – have continued. In many ways the question had shifted now to the actual size of the sixth form itself and away from the overall size of the school. There is no official policy on sixth-form size, but several recent documents from local authorities indicate that a comprehensive-school sixth form should number at least forty to be what is called 'viable' – that is, to provide economical teaching groups for A-level or H-grade I subjects.†entify This in itself is a rather static and short-sighted view of viability – for a comprehensive can have twenty pupils in its sixth form in one year and 100 pupils four years later. Moreover, the standard two- or three-A-level GCE is a very narrow measure of sixth-form work. Some pupils will be studying O-levels only in many comprehensives. Therefore some authorities – like Inner London– suggest forty in each year as the minimum 'viable' number. But concepts of the sixth form are changing so quickly and comprehensive sixth forms themselves are growing so quickly, as we show below, that the whole idea of a magic 'viability' may be over-played. As the Chief Senior HMI, William Elliott, remarked of comprehensive schools 'emerging and founding sixth forms', they will 'gain confidence and strength; meanwhile that unnecessary word "viable" has become the Homeric epithet of the sixth form'.[1]

The First NFER Report (1965) (p. 96, Table 10a) found the mean size of sixth forms in their category of 'fully developed' comprehensive schools (187) to be 70.‡ When a further eleven schools were dropped because of 'incomplete' information, the mean rose to seventy-five. Our inquiry of 1968 did not separate fully developed comprehensive schools from others. Nevertheless, we found that in the 391 schools in our survey with sixth forms in England and Wales the average size of the

---

* The Chief Education Officer of Leicestershire said his plan was to have the advantage of comprehensive education while avoiding large schools (S. C. Mason, *The Leicestershire Experiment and Plan*, 1964, p. 9). By 1970, however, the average size of the thirteen upper schools was 782, and two of them, in rapidly growing dormitory areas, were over 1000; a few upper schools are now being planned for 1500.

† See, for example, Wolverhampton's 1968 reorganization document. Other documents – for example, those from Inner London – suggest forty in each year of the sixth is necessary.

‡ For information on the NFER definition of 'fully developed' in this context, see p. 14 of the report.

sixth form was eighty-three. This is an increase of an average of thirteen pupils in two years. In our first edition we said that were this increase to be maintained, the comprehensive-school sixth form in 1972 in those 391 schools would have an average size of 109 (see below how accurate this forecast turned out to be). The raising of the school-leaving age to sixteen is bound to increase the demand for post-sixteen education in the future.

There was also an increase in the size of the sixth form specifically in the all-through school between 1965 and 1968. Our 1968 survey found that both types of 11–18 school in England and Wales had an average of seventy-seven pupils in the sixth form (as compared to the NFER's figure of seventy) – again a significant increase. It is even more significant when we remember that our figure includes *all* the all-through schools – including several that have only a single pupil as yet in their sixth form – and not just the 'fully developed' schools as was the case in the First NFER Report. (An analysis of schools with sixth forms of less than twenty shows that the bulk of these were established very recently (Table A.21, p. 545). The really comparable increase is therefore likely to be even higher and it is an important finding to underline. It means that authorities in doubt about whether to go ahead and establish comprehensive schools with sixth forms can know that there is a good chance that they will grow in size fairly quickly.

Growth of comprehensive sixth forms, 1968–72

For the school year 1971–2 we made a follow-up study of fifty-six comprehensive schools from our 1968 survey in six local authorities: Bristol, Oxfordshire, Swindon, Flint, Haringey, West Riding and Bradford (see Appendix I, p. 516). The results are printed here:

Table 9.1 **Sixth-form growth 1968–72**
Fifty-six Comprehensive Schools with sixth forms – England and Wales

1968	1972
Average size	*Average size*
84	107
Percentage increase in pupil numbers: 27.2	

At this rate of growth the average size of the comprehensive sixth in 1980 would be about 153 – fifteen more than the size of the average direct grant school sixth form in the Public Schools Commission Report, 1970.[2]
The increase was greatest in Oxfordshire at 69·4 per cent and lowest

in Swindon at 8·6 per cent – but Swindon's average size sixth form in 1968 was already very large at 184. There was also a below average gain (19 per cent) in the West Riding because once again the average size of their sixth forms in our 1968 survey was high at 118. Bradford had a sixth-form size below average in 1968 but between that year and 1972 twelve schools replying to both our surveys had increased their total sixth form numbers by 48 per cent, again a striking gain.

Eight schools with a total of 928 pupils in their sixth forms also gave information about the numbers in the first-year sixth who were not engaged on the traditional two A-level course for two years, but doing other work, e.g. taking or re-taking O-level, or on another type of course altogether. The percentage of the total which were 'new' sixth formers of this kind was 22, a very large proportion. It is this part of the comprehensive sixth form which is going to grow so rapidly, especially in those schools which encourage these 'new' sixth-form pupils to stay on. Since the conception of a sixth form which does include the 'new' sixth former is itself so new, it makes it doubly difficult to make categorical pronouncements about what size is viable, or what will be viable three or ten years from now.

The raising of the school-leaving age may well increase this new sixth-form population very significantly in the mid and late 1970s. If the comprehensive school is to be as good as its name, it must be ready both to encourage, and provide for, this increase.

Six schools answering in 1972 said their sixth forms had decreased in size. The reasons given were various: two because of population decline, and two because they had previously been able to draw from all over the city but now, because of reorganization elsewhere in their area, they were restricted to a catchment area. They found smaller numbers wanted to stay on. But other schools, similarly placed, had a different experience. As one wrote:

In 1968 our sixth form was (partly) the product of . . . a grammar school intake, drawn from a wide area . . . our present sixth form is completely 'unselected' and drawn entirely from the local council estates. My fear with reorganization was that our 'grammar' pupils would be reduced by half. This has not happened. . . . The present size of our sixth form is 196.

Most of the schools speak optimistically of the growth they expected in the years to come – particularly towards the end of the 1970s.

Meanwhile, we realize what a wide variety of comprehensive sixth forms already exist. Table 9.2 gives information about comprehensive-school sixth forms in a wide variety of types of school and situation in 1968; from this it is easy to see how variable the numbers are, depending upon the type of school and scheme. For example, 11–18 schools of the

Table 9.2 **Average sizes of sixth forms (and Higher Certificate Classes) in British comprehensive schools, 1968**

All schools	82
England and Wales	83
England and Wales 1972 sample	107
Wales	75
Scotland	71
All 11 (or 12)– 18 schools (both types)	76
11–18 Type I	70
11–18 Type I. England and Wales	71
11–18 Type II	150
11–18 Type II. England and Wales	157
11 (12)–18 (both types – England and Wales)	77
13–18	110
14–18	125
Sixth-form colleges	459*
Non-denominational schools	84
Church of England schools	46
Roman Catholic schools	58
Schools competing with grammar schools	75
Schools competing – England and Wales	75
Not competing with grammar	88
Not competing with grammar – England and Wales	92
Schools on two or more sites	88
Schools on two or more sites – England and Wales	91
Schools on one site	80
Schools on one site – England and Wales	80
Purpose-built schools	70
Non-purpose-built	88

* One sixth-form college is not yet up to full size, hence the discrepancy between this figure and the overall average size for both colleges of 582 given on p. 131.

second type (acting as sixth-form 'centres') have very much larger sixth forms than all-through 11–18 schools (type I): an overall average of seventy for the latter and 150 for the former. Upper-tier comprehensives generally have much larger sixth forms too: their combined average is 115.

Effects of coexistence on sixth-form size

But perhaps the most significant figures in the table are those which show the differences in sixth-form average sizes in areas with and without 'competing' grammar schools; in England and Wales an average of seventy-five where grammar schools coexist, but ninety-two without. This is a difference of nearly 20 pupils, which obviously is crucial to many schools in reaching that magic 'viable' number of forty. Our figures therefore suggest that coexistence with grammar schools is a vital factor in depressing sixth-form size in comprehensive schools.

There is the problem also of direct grant grammar schools in certain of our big cities. Their existence is coming to be seen as every bit as much a discouragement to the development of the comprehensive system as maintained grammar schools, as the second report of the Public Schools Commission has pointed out. Only 3 per cent of secondary schools and only 10 per cent of sixth formers may be in direct grant schools, but that is overall. Everyone knows that these schools tend to be concentrated very heavily in certain cities. And it is in some of these that we see the way they can affect a comprehensive scheme.

In Newcastle upon Tyne, for example, the maintained system was reorganized comprehensively in 1967. In 1968 the size of sixth forms would not represent their full potential, of course, since 'comprehensive entries' had not had any chance to work their way up to sixth-form level as yet. But the existing sixth forms gave a general idea of the total sixth-form population at the time in the maintained sector: which was about 450 pupils.[3] In the same year the Public Schools Commission figures show the direct grant school sixth-form total to be 892.[4] Thus at the age of eleven, about 18 per cent of the secondary age group in Newcastle goes into direct grant schools,[5] but by sixth-form level 66 per cent of the pupils still in school were in the direct-grant sector.

Looked at another way we found that the average size of sixth form in Newcastle comprehensives in 1968 was forty-four pupils; in the direct grant schools 148. If the combined totals of pupils in both sectors are added together and divided by the total number of schools (ten comprehensive, six direct grant) Newcastle would have an average of eighty-three in each sixth form – exactly the survey average for 1968 in comprehensive schools. Of course, it would not turn out that each school had exactly the average number – it would depend upon its area and its circumstances – but there is no doubt that without the direct-grant 'concentrations' the available sixth-form population would be more equitably spread between schools than it then was, and that the individual sixth forms would have a greater chance to be viable and continue development on genuine comprehensive lines.

The same kind of calculation can be made for such cities as Manchester, Bristol, Bradford and (counting voluntary aided grammar schools) Inner London, although none show quite the imbalance that Newcastle does – simply because their proportion of voluntary aided and direct grant schools to maintained comprehensive schools is less. But in most of these other cities the argument about the highly selective schools undermining the work of the comprehensives is being made more and more loudly.

The same can be said of Scotland's cities. Figures for Edinburgh were given in the House of Commons to illustrate that at transfer age to secondary school 23 per cent in Edinburgh go to state fee-paying schools. By the fourth year it is 40 per cent in this sector and by the sixth year it is 75 per cent.[6] The coexistence of state aided selective schools – of any kind – quite obviously affects the comprehensive system severely and must always be kept in mind in any consideration of any area's sixth-form opportunities. What is obvious now is that the most crucial effect of coexistence comes at the sixth-form level, an effect made much worse in those areas where the direct grant schools seek to 'help' the comprehensives by taking in even *more* sixth form pupils at fifteen plus. However helpful on a short-term basis in a few cases, this kind of cooperation is against the interest of a long-term comprehensive system and is increasingly being seen as such.

Sixth forms and school types

Sixth-form size was also related to type of school. Table 9.3 gives the number and percentage of schools in England and Wales that have sixth forms of various sizes. A rather coarse grading of sixth form size by units of sixty is given since this brings out clearly the main differences.

Table 9.3 **Size of sixth form by type of school (two sixth-form colleges excluded), England and Wales, 1968**

Size of sixth	Type of school 11–18 Type I		11–18 Type II		13–18		14–18	
	No.	Percentage	No.	Percentage	No.	Percentage	No.	Percentage
1–60	166	52·5	3	12·5	6	20·0	2	13·3
61–120	113	35·8	6	25·0	15	50·0	5	33·3
121–180	23	7·3	6	25·0	8	26·7	5	33·3
181–240	10	3·2	3	12·5	0	0	3	20·0
241–300	2	0·6	4	16·7	1	3·3	0	0
301–360	2	0·6	1	4·2	0	0	0	0
361–420	0	0	1	4·2	0	0	0	0
Total	316		24		30		15	

This table brings out what one would expect: that 13–18, 14–18 and 11–18 (type II) schools tend to have larger sixth forms than 11–18 (type I)

Table 9.4 **Size of sixth forms in both types of 11–18 all-through comprehensives related to the total size of the schools, in Britain, 1968**

	Size of sixth form										
Size of schools	*1–20*	*21–40*	*41–60*	*61–80*	*81–100*	*101–120*	*121–140*	*141–160*	*161–180*	*181–200*	*201–220*
1–200	2										
201–400	2	1									
401–600	4	10	3	1							
601–800	8	15	16	6	2	2		1			
801–1000	13	20	19	10	4	4			1		
1001–1200	9	8	17	16	12	3	4	1			1
1201–1400	5	10	16	9	12	15	4		2	1	1
1401–1600	2	3	5	6	7	6	1	2	1	2	2
1601–1800	1		3	1	3	3		3		2	
1801–2000	1	2		4	1	3	3	3	1	1	1
2001–2200	1				2		1		2	1	
2201–2400						1	1		1		
Total	48	69	79	53	43	37	14	9	8	8	5
Percentage of total schools	12·4	17·9	20·5	13·7	11·1	9·6	3·6	2·3	2·1	2·1	1·3

221–240	241–260	261–280	281–300	301–320	321–340	341–360	361–380	Total number of schools	Average size of sixth form	Percentage of total schools
								2		0·5
								3	18	1
								18	33	4·5
							1	51	51	13
								71	48	18·5
	1					1		73	72	19
							1	76	82	19·5
		1						38	100	10
1		1	1					19	130	5
1	1				1			23	132	6
	1							8	138	2
				1				4	184	1
2	2	3	1	1	1	1	2	386		100
0·5	0·5	0·8	0·3	0·3	0·3	0·3	0·5	100		

schools. It should be remembered that on the whole these are schools which have developed from grammar schools, so these will be subject to a distortion towards larger numbers than may be the case when they all become 'fully developed'; similarly 11–18 schools will be subject to the opposite distortion, since several of these, as we shall see, are only beginning to develop their sixth forms.

This table does not give information about sixth forms between one and

Table 9.5 **Sixth-form proportions in comprehensive schools in Britain, 1968**

Sixth-form proportions	England, Wales and Scotland	England and Wales	Scotland
	No. of schools	No. of schools	No. of schools
1 : 10	145	127	18
1 : 20	171	153	18
1 : 30	55	52	3
1 : 40	17	15	2
1 : 50	11	10	1
1 : 60	11	11	
1 : 70	6	5	1
1 : 80	4	3	1
1 : 90	1	1	
1 : 100	2	2	
1 : 110	3	3	
Between 1 : 200 and 1 : 450	4	4	0
Between 1 : 650 and 1 : 1830	6	5	1
Total	436	391	45

sixty pupils, however. How many schools had more than, and how many less than, the forty thought to be necessary for an 'adequate' sixth? Among the 436 schools with sixth forms in Britain, 28 per cent had fewer than forty, while only 12 per cent had fewer than twenty.* Table 9.4

* See Appendix I, Note 3. It is worth noting that, in 1939, 'a sixth form of ten to twenty was normal' in *grammar* schools. A. D. Edwards, *The Changing Sixth Form in the Twentieth Century*, p. 50, 1970.

shows the position more precisely in respect of 11–18 schools only. This table gives the position for England, Wales and Scotland in terms of size of school (measured in units of 200) and of sixth forms (in units of twenty). Although the table indicates a positive relationship between size of school and of sixth form, it will also be noted that schools of similar overall size have sixth forms of very different numbers. Similarly, the forty-eight schools with very small sixth forms (one to twenty pupils) vary in size across almost the entire range (from the category of under 200 pupils to that of over 2000). This is to be explained by the fact that many of the schools concerned are former secondary modern schools now being built up as comprehensive.

Another index which may prove a useful tool for a more refined analysis is the proportion the sixth form bears to the total number of pupils in the school as a whole. This will tend (probably) to be lower for 13–18 and 14–18 schools than for 11–18 schools. A school with a 'sixth-form proportion factor' of 1:20, with 2000 on the roll, will have a sixth form of 100; if the proportion is 1:10, it will have a sixth form of 200. In general, schools with sixth-form proportions of up to one in twenty may be said to have a healthy situation. Thus 316 of the 436 schools with sixth forms – or three-quarters – in our survey had a healthy sixth form. This is a very encouraging picture (Table 9.5).

There were 35,746 pupils in the sixth forms of the schools in our survey in 1968.* The biggest sixth forms were obviously those in the sixth-form colleges. One had 520 and the other had 389 students in the sixth form, but both will eventually grow well above the minimum size thought necessary for a sixth-form college: 400 (see p. 124). Most colleges are being planned at around 500 in size, but some well above this. It is not unlikely some will reach 1000 eventually.

After the sixth-form college, the biggest sixth form was in an 11–18 type II school: 370. The largest sixth in a 11–18 type I school was 325, the largest in a 13–18 school was 260, and in a 14–18, 205.

GCE A-level and SCE H-grade

The all-through schools were clearly the most important schools with sixth-form provision. Type I accounted for 82 per cent of all the sixth forms in our survey of 1968, type II for 6 per cent, and upper-tier schools for 10 per cent. We can see from comparing Table 9.7 with Table 6.8 (p. 136), that at A-level there is not the very great discrepancy between types of comprehensive school in percentages presenting for most individual subject-groups in contrast to O-level, where, as we saw, the inclusion of the 11–16 school with so relatively 'low' a presentation in

* 36,013 when 'unknown' categories added.

individual subject-groups, tended to pull down any of the categories in which it was included. It is perhaps interesting to note, however, that at A-level and H-grade the Scottish schools, the upper-tier schools, and 11–18 (type II) schools consistently presented a higher percentage of pupils for most of the academic subject-groups than the 11–18 all-through school. In some subject-groups the difference is not significant, but in

Table 9.6 **GCE A-level and SCE H-grade examinations British comprehensive schools, Summer 1968**
Percentages of schools with sixth forms presenting one or more pupils for examinations in eleven subject-groups

	All schools	England and Wales
Presenting in		
11 subject-groups	21	17
in 10	15	14
in 9	21	22
in 8	15	17
in 7	7	7
in 6	3	3
in 5	3	4
in 4	3	3
in 3	2	3
in 2	2	2
in 1	3	3
in 0	5	5
Total number of schools	100 (436)	100 (391)

four groups – chemistry, physics, zoology/botany/biology, and languages (other than English) – it is.

A greater percentage of schools of 11–18 (type II) and 13/14–18 upper schools were also able to present pupils in nine or more of the eleven subject-groups than were all-through schools (Table 9.8).

In looking at A-level and H-grade, however, it must be remembered that many of the all-through schools – in contrast to the upper-tier and sixth-form centre schools – are as yet not fully developed. The fact that roughly a quarter (28 per cent) of the comprehensive schools with sixth forms in 1968 in our survey were as yet not developed enough to be

Table 9.7 GCE A-level and SCE H-grade examinations, British comprehensive schools, Summer 1968

Percentages of schools with sixth forms presenting one or more pupils in each subject or subject-group*

	All schools	11 (or 12)–18 type I schools	11 (or 12)–18 type II schools	13–18 + 14–18 schools	Scottish schools	Roman Catholic schools
Physics	81	78	96	93	85	59
English literature	89	88	93	100	92	76
Chemistry	78	75	93	91	90	53
Art	85	84	96	86	85	68
Mathematics (single or double subject)	85	83	96	95	94	71
Zoology Biology or Botany	78	75	93	91	79	59
History or Geography	89	88	93	100	92	82
Language (other than English)	77	74	93	93	88	62
Technical or geometrical or engineering	52	51	71	46	90	44
Metalwork or woodwork	41	39	68	38	60	24
Needlework Cooking or Domestic science	45	42	71	57	75	24
Total number of schools	436	356	28	45	48	34

* Including twenty-one schools as yet not developed enough to sit any pupils for GCE A-level or SCE H-grade.

'viable' – i.e. were under forty – would even suggest that this same percentage of schools would be unable to sustain an adequate GCE A-level or H-grade course to examination level. But we find this was far from true. Table 9.6 shows that just about 80 per cent of schools with sixth forms were able to present pupils in seven or more subject-groups in 1968. Seven subject-groups was the average for all schools in the survey and, since we have grouped so many subjects together under individual head-

Table 9.8 **Percentages and (in brackets) numbers of comprehensive schools with sixth forms in England and Wales, presenting pupils in nine or more GCE A-level subject-groups, Summer 1968**

11–18 type I	*11–18 type II*	*13–18*	*14–18*
48 (151)	83 (20)	70 (21)	80 (12)

ings at A-level, these seven could well represent some fifteen individual A-level subjects. Since about 80 per cent of all A-level subjects taken in sixth forms are generally known to be drawn from eight standard subjects (and these were all represented in the survey), it seems likely that a high percentage of comprehensive schools are able to make a very adequate A-level and H-grade offering.

When we examine the individual subject-groups (Table 9.7), we see that well over 80 per cent of all schools with sixth forms were able to sit pupils in such subjects as physics, English literature, art, mathematics and history (or geography) – and very nearly 80 per cent in chemistry, zoology-botany-and-biology, and a language other than English. It is obvious from these figures that some of the very small sixth forms (under forty) must have been able to provide a good range of academic subjects to A-level or H-grade. The vocational subjects, however: technical, geometrical, or engineering drawing, metalwork, woodwork, needlework, cooking or domestic-science – were presented by only about half of comprehensive schools sixth forms. This did not apply to the second type of 11–18 or to the Scottish comprehensive schools, both of which were able to present pupils in the vocational subjects in a majority of schools. But in general we saw at A-level and H-grade what we also saw at O-level and O-grade: schools in general better equipped to present pupils in the academic than in the vocational subjects.

When considering the fact that all these A-level and H-grade figures (particularly for the academic subjects) were taken when reorganization was in midstream – and that just over half the schools in our survey (375) were comprehensive schools *less* than four years old – this is a remarkable showing.

Recent DES statistics for England and Wales bring out another point – the rapidity with which comprehensive-school sixths are growing. In 1967 there were 23,260 students in comprehensive-school sixth forms; a years later, in 1968, there were 37,137 – an increase of 13,877, or 60 per cent. At the same time grammar school sixths fell by 4210.* In the next

* DES, *Statistics* 1968, vol. 1, *Schools*, pp. 58–9.

two years the comprehensive school figure doubled – to over 74,500, while the grammar schools remained stable.* Some of the increase of comprehensive school sixths is due to reorganization, but, since there is such a big difference between the two sets of figures (an overall increase of over 50,000 between 1967 and 1970 cannot be accounted for by reorganization alone), it seems clear that most of it must be due to the extra holding power of these schools with their 'open' sixth forms (see chapter 12). The number of students entering for GCE A-level examinations has also risen greatly – from 2560 in 1964 to 7235 in 1967 and then to over 18,000 in 1969 (the latest available figure) – that is, by over seven times in five years only; the percentage increase for grammar schools over these years was 17 per cent (from 48,040 to 56,300). The comprehensive-school expansion represents a really dramatic rise.†

What of A-level results themselves? The rate of increase of students gaining two or more GCE A-levels is higher in comprehensive schools than in maintained grammar schools. In 1964, 1370 students were successful according to this criterion in comprehensive schools; in 1969, 10,600 were – nearly eight times as many. Over the same period the grammar-school increase was 4860, from a base of 35,560; an increase of one-seventh.‡

Estimates of comparative success have been made by Robin Pedley on two occasions, as we have already seen as regards O-levels, page 132. He showed that in a sample of twenty-four comprehensive schools (mostly in rural areas) in 1962–3, 7·5 per cent of the leavers obtained two or more A-level passes as compared to an average of 5·3 per cent for all-maintained schools in England and Wales. A larger sample of sixty-five schools which had been established as comprehensives for at least seven years, and which did not lose more than 10 per cent of their pupils to local grammar or independent schools, was identified in 1968. Thirty of these were in 'educationally disadvantaged' areas where O- and A-level results are below the national average. Pedley found that the percentage of leavers obtaining two or more A-level passes in these schools was 9·7 per cent. Since his book was published, the national average for all maintained schools in 1968 has become available. This gives a figure of 9·6 per

* DES, *Statistics* 1970, vol. 1, *Schools*, p. 42. The DES *Statistics* no longer gives a breakdown under 'Sixth forms'; instead it presents statistics for all fifteen-plus pupils under the heading 'Older pupils'. The figures given in the text are calculated from the DES tables, but *excluding* all pupils aged fifteen except those following GCE A-level courses. This figure probably approximates to the 1968 criterion of 'sixth-form' pupils, though it may exaggerate it slightly in the case of both grammar and comprehensive schools (since some pupils aged sixteen might have been in fifth rather than sixth forms).

† DES, *Statistics*, 1967, vol. 2, p. 3; 1964, pt 3, p. 29; 1969, vol. 2, p. 1.

‡ Calculated from DES, *Statistics* 1964, pt 3, p. 29; 1969, vol. 2, p. 1.

cent gaining two or more A-level passes in all maintained schools. In so far as these figures cast any light on the situation, then, it seems that these comprehensive schools, *in spite of losing up to 10 per cent of their higher ability intake to other schools*, are holding their own satisfactorily in terms of this criterion.*

In sum, it seems that, in spite of the inevitable teething troubles reorganization must bring about, in spite of the extent of coexistence schemes and other difficulties, comprehensive-school sixth forms are increasing rapidly in size, offering a varying but wide range of subjects at A-level, and holding their own in academic achievement by the criterion of A-level passes. We have taken care to give full details of comprehensive schools' academic successes both in this section, and in chapter 6, because it is important that those just beginning reorganization should know that standards have been maintained during this difficult period of transition. But at the same time there is a danger in over concentration on examination success – measured by GCE. First, because it implies that examination success is the main object, or main measure of success, of the comprehensive reform, when it can only be one of them. Second, because it takes as a measure of examination success – the GCE examination itself. The GCE examination is one that is now widely criticized and rapidly becoming obsolete. It was designed to meet grammar-school requirements twenty years ago, and both grammar schools themselves, and many universities, are now busily engaged in scrutinizing this very examination to see how its manifest shortcomings, at least in its present form, can be overcome. If comprehensive schools accept this examination at A-level in too uncritical a spirit, they will not be able to make the contribution to its reform that so many of them, so well placed in their experience of the 'new' sixth form that is emerging in Britain, could make.

The 'facts' about schools and schemes which we have been discussing in this entire Part are in many ways purely external. The size and age range of a comprehensive are important, of course, and the range of academic offering as well. But when assessing a comprehensive scheme,

* For full details, see Robin Pedley, *The Comprehensive School* (revised edition, 1969), pp. 106 ff. The figure of 9·6 per cent for all maintained schools is calculated from the information given in DES *Statistics of Education*, 1968, vol. 2, p. 1, Table B. The figure there given for comprehensive schools is not comparable to the grammar/modern results for a number of reasons, one of which is that the DES list of comprehensive schools, from which it is calculated, naturally includes a large proportion of schools coexisting with, and 'creamed' by, maintained grammar schools. This completely invalidates any such direct comparison. Attempts have been made to discredit Robin Pedley's sampling technique, and so the validity of his conclusions. These have been answered conclusively by Michael Armstrong in the *Spectator*, 8 and 22 November 1969.

or planning a new comprehensive school, it is not enough to be satisfied with the external 'pattern', or complacent because the age range 'fits' the numbers, or the pupils in the sixth are more than 'viable'. External factors will always have only a limited importance. The intake policy, teaching policy, facilities, staffing, total curriculum, the attitude of staff, the support of the authority and the community for the school, the invisible quality of life there reflected in individual pupils, and the kind of encouragement each one is given to make the most of the education that the school has to offer – all this is equally, if not more, important in any school. And it is to these matters that we now turn.

Notes

1. William Elliott, 'School or college after sixteen?', op. cit.
2. Public Schools Commission, 1970, vol. 2, p. 65.
3. There were ten comprehensive schools with sixth forms in Newcastle in 1968. Nine replied to our survey. The total sixth-form population they contained was 354. Since the tenth school might have had well above the average size of sixth, we have allowed it a sixth of ninety-six, if anything possibly over-populating the maintained sixth. There was also a technical school in existence at the time, which is not included in the figures.
4. Public Schools Commission, Second Report, vol. 2, Appendix 2.
5. This is calculated from the 1970–71 Yearbook of the Education Committees from the total maintained secondary population and the total direct grant school population. These figures do not include any of the independent schools in the area. If they did, the 'selective sector' would, of course, represent a higher percentage than 18 per cent.
6. Figures given in House of Commons, 5 November 1971, col. 588.

Part Three
Internal Organization: Teaching and Learning

The transition to a comprehensive form of secondary education, now taking place in many countries, will be seen by future historians as a response to the technological and scientific revolution of the mid-twentieth century, and to the rising standard of living and parental aspirations associated with it. They may also point to a recognition, at both national and international levels, that the advancement of a few at the expense of the majority could no longer be defended as viable policy. Even from a narrowly economic or political standpoint a general raising of educational standards is the prerequisite to controlling an increasingly complex environment for human ends.

It is not only the technological revolution, or 'social needs', that must be taken into account, but also the explosion of new knowledge, up to and including a new understanding of the psychology of learning and of how to use new methods and resources which can facilitate, even alter, the former course of learning by the child. All these point to the need for new forms of educational organization. Whereas it has been customary to think of school as a place where children are taught specified subjects in classrooms, easily to be defined and allocated in timetables, those subjects are now undergoing basic revision while at the same time new ones are claiming entry. We must keep in mind what will be the pattern of life after the year 2000 when the child, starting school in the 1970s, reaches adulthood. To do so is to turn from traditional classroom questions to the much more complex problems of equipping children with the techniques of learning, so that their education corresponds to the new demands likely to be made upon them in adult life.

Comprehensive schools, representing a new form of organization and faced with the task of educating the whole child population of an area at the secondary stage, have been more sensitive than others in preparing to meet these new demands. They recognize that education has to do with a child's whole experience in school and must provide adequately for his all-round development (not only intellectually in class and physically on the playing field). They have necessarily looked for new methods. But to do so involves also making a way out of the thicket of much antiquated educational thinking and practice, which reflects the confusions of a whole era of resistance to reform on the necessary scale.

The cornerstone of this resistance has been a determination to preserve intact the traditional academic school. This has meant that 'academic excellence' continues to be equated with current grammar-school practice. Thus the ethos of this type of school, the methods of teaching in use, have been taken for granted, and children have been expected to fit into the given pattern; should any fail, this was to be ascribed to lack of the requisite ability. Not only has this approach resulted in waste of intellectual talent but it has insulated the grammar school as an educational institution, for grammar schools have been responsive mainly to influences from the university level. This, then, was one strand in the inheritance of the comprehensive school – a conception of secondary education for a selected few on traditional academic lines; with, as ultimate proof of excellence, examination successes, notably the securing of the maximum number of places for sixth-form pupils at universities, preferably Oxford and Cambridge.

The other strand in their inheritance derives from attempts to throw off the straitjacket of 'elementary instruction' imposed on the majority of the population since the establishment of compulsory education. This has been inspired by a variety of theories, whose particular emphases tend to be reduced to the single (if complex and often far from clear) concept of 'child-centred' education. The child must be free to develop, to follow his own interests, to realize his own powers. The positive aspect of this approach can be seen in the practice of good junior schools, which have released children from desks without abdicating educational direction and planned teaching. The negative aspect, or even perversion of the basic intentions, is to be discerned in the official ideology of the 'modern school' (and parts of the Newsom Report), which emphasizes the limited powers and interests of the average child; or in current arguments that, since the majority of children lack intellects capable of development, education should be mainly directed to their emotions, the shaping of social behaviour, preparation for simple vocational tasks, or the right 'use of leisure'.

This represents a facile acceptance of the facts of social deprivation, or inequalities, as if they were the outcome of social laws to which education itself must also conform; as, indeed, it has done in the past. It is one of the chief purposes of the comprehensive school to break out of this vicious circle, to substitute for what has been abdication of the educational function a new tradition of secondary education for all.

The basic intention of those establishing comprehensive schools has been to provide a common educational experience. This such schools do to some extent by their very existence and methods of recruitment, and can do in a more active sense by means of many activities. But how should this principle be applied when it comes to grouping pupils for the purpose of teaching? This has turned out to be a crucial question for comprehensive schools in Britain, as it has also in other countries.

Most early comprehensive schools, established in the midst of the selective system, recruited pupils who had sat the 11-plus examination. The doctrine of 'intelligence' still had full force at this time; one of the main tasks was to prove that the comprehensive school could educate those who would have passed the selection examination as well as the grammar school, besides giving due attention to all its other pupils. Consequently, it was usual for the intake to be streamed (on the basis of 11-plus results, or junior-school reports and an internal examination), and streaming was sometimes prismatic in larger schools, with graded forms ranging from 'A' to 'L'. The LCC Education Committee and teachers in the London schools were influential in securing development on a new course, primarily by advocating the need for a 'common core' to the curriculum in the early years. These teachers worked out a common curriculum for certain basic subjects to be taught to *all* pupils, sometimes at different levels (streaming or setting), but occasionally in unstreamed classes. This opened the way for new thinking about the inner structure of schools, which in turn was greatly stimulated by the collapse of the doctrine of 'intelligence' in the late 1950s.

By now the children entering comprehensive schools quite often came from junior schools which had greatly modified, or even abandoned, the practice of streaming. The question soon arose, therefore, of doing so in the entry classes of the comprehensive school, as one aspect of attempts to coordinate more closely the work of junior and secondary schools; and this extended also to modifying the content of the first years of the secondary course. It is, of course, from similar developments that there has gradually evolved the idea of a 'middle school' from nine to thirteen.

Parallel with these changes went a variety of new approaches in the middle and upper sections of the comprehensive school. Just as, in tackling the problems of young entrants, the comprehensive schools began to evolve their own methods (drawing on, but not merely imitating, the positive experience of junior and modern schools), so at the other extreme they developed a distinctive approach to the organization and work of sixth forms. It is these developments, as brought to light by our survey, that will be examined in this section, in relation to different age ranges: first, ages 11–14, or the lower school; second, ages 14–16, the middle school; finally, ages 16–18, the upper school. The section concludes with a chapter on the relations between comprehensive schools and higher education.

Note

1. *The Organization of Comprehensive Secondary Schools* (Suggestions), pp. 9, 19, 1953; *Survey of Sixteen Schools*, p. 34, 1961.

Chapter 10
11 to 14 Years in the Comprehensive School

The common course

It was a significant new development when teachers in the London 'interim' comprehensive schools began to work out a common syllabus in the main subjects at the first stage of secondary education. This was designed to cover the main fields of knowledge and skills in such a way as to cater adequately for a comprehensive intake – of children who would formerly have been classified under the headings 'grammar' or 'modern'. The survey published by the Inner London Education Authority in 1967 defined the three-year general course now in operation in many of its schools as including all the normal subjects at this stage of the secondary course: 'English, mathematics, science, history, geography, art, music, drama, handicraft (for boys), housecraft (for girls), religious instruction and physical education.'[1] During the intervening years many other schools had been working on similar lines.

Our questionnaire asked whether all pupils pursue 'the same basic subjects, even if at a different pace or depth', without asking for its content to be defined. Of 606 schools in England and Wales answering this question, 488 (or 80·5 per cent) had a common course for all pupils in the first year.* Of these, 235 (48 per cent) maintained the common course for three years, from 11 to 14; 145 (30 per cent) for two years, eighty-seven (18 per cent) for one year.† In Scotland, where pupils are recruited at twelve, fifty-three schools (79 per cent) stated that they provided a common course, twenty-two for two years (41·5 per cent) and thirty for the first year only (56·5 per cent).‡

A specific problem which arises in this connection is that of a second language; the ILEA itself draws attention to the difference in approach here, saying that 'in many schools all the pupils start a second language in their first year, while in others only a proportion do so', adding that

* For detailed figures, with a breakdown by type of school, see Table A.4 (p. 525).
† An additional nine schools stated that the common course was maintained for four years, five for five years. See Table A.5 (p. 526).
‡ One school answered incorrectly. See Tables A.4 and A.5 (pp. 525–6).

'apart from this subject distinction, the curriculum is a common one for all forms'. [2]

Our survey shows that 97 per cent of 11- and 12-plus comprehensive schools in Britain offer a foreign language in the first year (650 out of 673).* But a considerable proportion of schools stating that they provided a common course for all pupils in fact do not provide a second language for all pupils. This is indicated in Table 10.1.†

Table 10.1 **Schools claiming to provide a common course for all pupils, England, Wales and Scotland, 1968**

Proportion of pupils studying a foreign language in the year a foreign language is first begun	Number	Percentage
0–25 %	13	2·5
25–50 %	50	9
50–75 %	88	16·5
75–90 %	154	28·5
100 %	227	42
Unknown	9	1·5
Total	541	100

It may be argued that the exclusion of a second language for a proportion of children does not basically distort the concept of a common course for all pupils. Nevertheless, there are clearly many comprehensive schools that regard the teaching of a second language for all pupils as a question of principle, and it is, therefore, worth drawing attention to this difference of approach at this stage. At the same time, too hasty conclusions should not be drawn from this evidence; one headmaster of a medium-sized comprehensive school in a rural area, who firmly believes in the concept of a common course for all pupils, is unable to provide it since he has insufficient French teachers on his staff. [3] It may be worth stressing at this point that where a second language is *not* available to some of the pupils, the differentiation is often resented by those who are

* See Table A.6 (p. 527).

† For the breakdown of type of school, see Table A.7 (p. 528). It is noteworthy that a smaller proportion of 11–13, 11–14/15, and 11–16 schools provide a second language for 100 per cent of their pupils than 11–18 schools.

excluded. This is one of the main reasons why many comprehensive schools deliberately include the subject for all children, including (often) the most backward, utilizing audio-visual aids and other modern techniques of teaching where these are available.

Another related subject leading to early differentiation is Latin – a subject that presents particular problems. It appears that Latin is taught in the early years most generally only in those comprehensive schools which have developed from grammar schools – and in this case the pupils are normally streamed from the start as it is seldom, if ever, taught across the entire ability range. The survey conducted by the Association of Assistant Masters in 1967 found that three of the thirty schools surveyed introduced Latin in the first year, four in the second. 'Where the school does not stream or set its pupils', runs the report, 'Latin is unlikely to be taught.'[4] It is evident that the teaching of Latin to a minority of pupils and the provision of a common curriculum are incompatible, and that, as in the case of many grammar schools, the teaching of Latin is likely to be postponed until the fifth or sixth forms. The IAAM survey found that early differentiation was particularly related to language teaching; the common course in the schools they surveyed was normally of two years' duration, and some differentiation of subject matter related normally to languages occurred already in the second year; the ILEA, however, found in 1966 only 'minor curriculum changes' in the third year – again normally related to language teaching;[5] already in 1961 the LCC found that the practice of delaying specialization until the fourth year had become very widespread in the London schools.[6]

Grouping of pupils: streaming, setting, banding and mixed ability

Methods of grouping pupils – the inner academic structure of the comprehensive school – are clearly related to the question of the common course. If a differentiated curriculum is provided from the start, then the form of grouping must give effect to this decision, in which case differentiation of pupils must be built into the academic structure in the first year. If, on the other hand, the aim is to provide a common curriculum, then the grouping structure remains an open question; it can be provided at various 'levels' through streaming, or it can be adapted to the character of mixed-ability classes. But before examining the methods actually found in use in each case separately, the overall situation may be presented.

Question 19 of the survey asked: 'How is your first year grouped for teaching purposes?' It provided seven possible responses, one category being reserved to cover all 'other' methods. In fact 93 per cent were able to answer within the named categories, as shown in Table 10.2.* A sample survey to check the dynamics of development was conducted in December 1971 for the second edition, and this information is included in the Table.† The significance of the changes there indicated will be discussed shortly. In the meantime a few words should be said about the information in this Table, and about each of the categories used.

The first category, utilized by 19·5 per cent of the schools (but only 4·5 per cent of the 1971 sample): streaming by ability, involves the division of pupils into a series of forms (A, B, C, etc.) graded according to an assessment of the pupils' intellectual ability – the classic method of streaming as it developed in Britain from the mid-1920s. This method reflects the concept that a child's intellectual capacity is largely inherited, fixed and unchanging; it seeks to provide 'homogeneous' classes, of roughly the same level of ability, and to keep these classes stable for all the teaching (or learning) activities of the school, whatever the subject or activity the class is involved in. It was this method – the traditional method of class organization in most junior, secondary modern and grammar schools – that was taken over by many comprehensive schools from the past.

In some of the larger grammar schools, however, and in some modern schools, streaming has been combined with setting to allow a less rigid – or more flexible – structure, and this form of organization is used in various ways in comprehensive schools (category 4). The system of 'setting' is one whereby pupils are rearranged in ability groupings in each of the main subjects in the curriculum, particularly those normally considered more 'difficult': for instance, mathematics, a foreign language, science, and sometimes such subjects as English, history, geography. It is theoretically possible, of course (given sufficient teachers), to regroup pupils according to some assessment of their 'ability' in each of the subjects of the curriculum, which means that each pupil may be in a different class for each subject. In fact, in 1968, 5·5 per cent of the schools stated that children were 'setted' for most individual subjects (category 3), but many more (14·5 per cent) stated that pupils were organized 'in a combination of streams and sets' (category 4). This system is, then, an attempt to ensure that, in all the main subjects taught, a higher degree of homogeneity of ability is achieved than is possible where streaming only is used. In other words, the system of setting is a refinement of streaming, having the same objective, but attempting a more precise classification of pupils across the subjects, and based on the same principles or theoretical

* The position for schools in England and Wales and for Scotland is given separately in Table A.8 (p. 529).

† For details of sampling, see p. 516.

Table 10.2 **First-year grouping by type of school in Britain, 1968, and 1971 sample survey (schools with 11- and 12-plus intake only)**

Method of grouping	Percentage of schools (numbers in brackets)					Total number of schools	Percentage 1968	1971 Sample survey Percentage of schools
	11/12-18(I)	11/12-18(II)	11/12-16	11/12-13	11/12-14/15			
1 In streams	17·5	13	20·5	34	23	130	19·5	4·5
2 In broad ability bands	34·5	32	27	21	26	210	31	45
3 In sets	4		8	7	10	36	5·5	3·5
4 Combination of streams and sets	12	16	18	14	17	96	14·5	5·5
5 Mixed ability (1) (no more than two subjects settled)	5	10	8	14	1	42	6	10
6 Mixed ability (2) (remedial pupils separated)	14	13	9·5	10	7	80	12	18
7 Mixed ability (3) (for all subjects and pupils)	5	6	2		6	29	4	6·5
8 Other method	7	10	6		6	43	6·5	7
Unknown	1		1		4	7	1	
Total number of schools	100 (389)	100 (31)	100 (154)	100 (29)	100 (70)	673	100·0	100·0 (111)

outlook. Paradoxically, however, setting may be used as a stage in the transition towards non-streaming, as in category 5. Indeed the 1971 sample survey suggests that this is happening.

The second category, involving 'broad ability bands', contained in 1968 the largest proportion of schools in any single category: 31 per cent, of which a high proportion were all-through 11–18 schools (of both types); the 1971 sample survey indicates that the proportion of schools using this system is now even higher (45 per cent). This system was first pioneered by comprehensive schools in the early 1950s. These rejected the practice (or concept) of precise or 'prismatic' streaming, holding that it was not consistent with the comprehensive principle; on the other hand, they did not wish to move over to the other extreme of complete non-streaming, or mixed-ability grouping. That 'banding' is a widely used, popular method of organization is evident from the figures given; the system has certain organizational advantages for the large comprehensive school in particular.

In essence this system can be regarded as a coarse, or modified, form of streaming – or alternatively, as a stage in the transition towards non-streaming. Instead of dividing, let us say, a twelve-form entry intake (360 pupils) into twelve streamed classes, graded from A to L, the intake is divided into two, or more usually three (or sometimes four) broad bands of pupils, but again based on 'ability' assessed according to some criterion; in the case of a three-band school of twelve-form entry, there might be three groups of four classes (120 pupils), or any variant: for instance, an 'A' band of three classes, a 'B' band of five classes, and a 'C' band of four classes; or a 5:5:2 distribution (with two remedial classes).

Within these bands, various structures are possible; in particular the group of pupils in any particular band can either be graded in streams or arranged in 'parallel' forms. It seems likely that the latter is the more usual arrangement, and it is for this reason that the system of banding may be regarded as a transitional stage towards non-streaming. In this case the pupils in each band are arranged in classes each of which reflects the spread of ability in the band as a whole – in other words, the pupils are unstreamed, but only *within the band*. A three-band school, therefore, may be seen as a three-stream school, but within each of these broad 'streams' there may be two, three, four or five classes of similar make-up.

According to the 1966 ILEA survey, the number of schools using this system has increased as compared to those using precise streaming.[7] This survey also makes the point (not covered by our questionnaire) that setting across the ability block (or band) is also extensively used. When the school is large, the division of the school into two or, better, three ability bands facilitates setting, since the timetable can be 'blocked' for different years within the bands without introducing too great a rigidity into the timetable as a whole. If only some three, four or five classes have to be blocked together to allow setting, the provision of sufficient teachers to teach the different sets at the same time does not present the same problem as would be the case if setting were organized across a year group as a whole.

Categories 3 (setting) and 4 (combined streaming and setting) have already been referred to. The next three categories, however, may be taken as a group, since all relate to various forms of non-streaming, or mixed-ability grouping, a comparatively recent development. In these cases the basic form unit for teaching and for activities generally is a class whose composition reflects (normally) the distribution of ability in the school as a whole; each class, in other words, theoretically contains an equal proportion of pupils of high, medium and low intellectual ability as assessed according to a given criterion – hence the somewhat unsatisfactory phrase 'mixed ability'. Mixed-ability grouping is normally equated with non-streaming, but the latter phrase has, strictly speaking, a broader connotation, since it allows for the grouping of children by other criteria than that of 'ability'; for instance, by forming friendship groups (using sociometric tests), by grouping on the basis of neighbourhoods, or alternatively by mixing neighbourhoods, etc. Alphabetical grouping is a common form of non-streaming, random sampling may be used. Examples of these forms exist, but for our purposes, all may conveniently be grouped under the heading of 'mixed ability'.

The first of the three categories (category 5), containing 6 per cent of the total in 1968 (but 10 per cent of the 1971 sample), is the method of grouping found in schools which have rejected the concept of streaming (and banding) as the main principle of organization, but in which the staff teaching the more 'difficult' academic subjects wish to form homogeneous groups in their own subjects. In this case, to organize the pupils in non-streamed (or mixed-ability) classes for the majority of their work, but to regroup and 'set' them for certain subjects – normally mathematics and a foreign language – provides a comparatively simple solution; the school retains its basically non-streamed character, even if the pupils experience a form of streaming for part of their work.*

Category 6, containing, as we put it in our first edition, the surprisingly large number of eighty schools (12 per cent of the total), fifty-seven of them being 11–18 schools, represents another solution. Here also the 1971 sample indicates a swing to this method – to 18 per cent. In this case the school has moved over to non-streaming in all subjects for nearly

---

* A number of schools use non-streaming, but set for *three* subjects rather than two; this was the most usual reason for indicating category 8 ('Other method').

all the pupils, but a group of the slowest or those with special learning problems are segregated and taught separately for all (or most of) their work. This, it is argued, facilitates non-streaming since very slow-learning children, who present particular difficulties, are not involved; these may be taught together at an appropriate pace and with appropriate materials by teachers either specifically trained to teach these children, or particularly interested in their problems. The whole question of teaching very slow children in the comprehensive school is a complex one, and will be discussed more fully later.

Finally, category 7, containing twenty-nine schools in 1968 (4 per cent of the total), twenty-two of which are 11–18 schools, includes those which involve *all* pupils, including the most backward, in a system of non-streamed classes. Here also the 1971 sample survey shows an increase, if a small one. These schools also have to make special arrangements for the slow learner, as will be described later; at present it is sufficient to note that for the bulk of their activities they are organized in non-streamed classes along with all the rest of the children. This represents, therefore, a complete system of non-streaming. The first comprehensive school to be organized on this system was Vauxhall Manor School in London, which established it in 1957 under its then headmistress, Miss Ingram. Another school to begin early unstreaming was the David Lister school in Hull which opened under its headmaster, Albert Rowe, in September 1964. Since then, as the figures show, the number has increased.

Looking first at the 1968 figures, we see that at that stage the systems of streaming and banding were the most widely used (340 schools). If to these are added schools using the systems of setting and of combined streaming and setting (132 schools), the preponderance is considerable (472 schools or 70 per cent of the respondents). Nevertheless we pointed out in our first edition that the most striking feature of Table 10.2 was the comparatively large number of schools utilizing one of the three forms of mixed-ability grouping. There is no doubt whatever that the most striking feature of the 1971 sample survey is the indication it gives of a relatively massive swing away from streaming (in its various forms) towards non-streaming or mixed-ability grouping. Category 1, the strict classical form of streaming, has dropped enormously, as also has category 4 (combination of streams and sets); on the other hand both broad banding and each of the three forms of mixed-ability grouping show increases. While the results of sample surveys must be interpreted with caution (the sample was chosen as representative of all types of comprehensive schools in all regions of the country) the swing indicated in the Table, over the short period of three school years, seems remarkable.

A few years ago very few schools used this form of organization which was considered radical and impracticable, except for the 'non-academic' subjects such as art and religious instruction. In his survey *Comprehensive Schools Today* (1954), Robin Pedley found that the schools then existing took special pains to test, to classify, and then to arrange their pupils in 'homogeneous groups'.[8] A *Survey of Sixteen Schools* published by the London County Council in 1961 stated baldly that 'None of the schools bases its organization on the impracticable assumption that teaching groups covering the whole range of ability are suitable or desirable.'[9] Two years later G. C. Firth found that all the Coventry comprehensive schools used either the system of streaming or that of banding, although some of the schools – in particular Caludon Castle – used mixed-ability grouping quite extensively for non-academic subjects.[10] Yet already by 1968, the period of our main survey, the position was transformed; a significant number of schools definitely moving over to non-streaming. It seems clear that this movement is still gaining pace.

The National Foundation for Educational Research (first report) also analysed grouping procedures, using a somewhat different category system. Their data was gathered in 1965; in fact two school years earlier than our 1967–8 survey. They found roughly the same proportion of schools using complete non-streaming – just over 4 per cent (though, obviously, fewer schools). But the *trend* towards non-streaming was more clearly brought out in the response to our 1968 survey. The figures both in category 5 and category 6 represented decisive moves towards mixed-ability grouping, while a high proportion of those using 'other methods' (category 8) also used non-streaming, but with three subjects setted. Adding categories 5, 6 and 7 together, the proportion of schools using predominantly mixed-ability forms of organization in 1968 rose to 22 per cent – a total of 151 schools, 103 of them being 11–18 schools. The 1971 sample survey, as already indicated, shows a further move; 34 per cent, or one third of all schools in the survey, now using predominantly mixed-ability methods of grouping in the first year.

The type of school showing the highest proportion using one of the three forms of mixed-ability grouping in the 1968 survey was the 11–18 (type 2) school (29 per cent), whereas the 11–14/15 schools showed the lowest proportion (14 per cent); it may also be noted that in Scotland as many as 42 per cent of schools used some form of mixed-ability grouping (see Table A.8, p. 529). If that proportion of category 8 schools using mixed-ability grouping but setting in three subjects (thirty schools) is added, the overall percentage using non-streamed forms of grouping during the first year in Britain as a whole in 1968 rises to 27 per cent of the total, over one school in four. If the same calculation is made for the

1971 sample survey, the figure rises to 36 per cent, or well over one third. Whatever the exact proportion moving over to mixed-ability grouping, there seems certainly a remarkably rapid shift in this direction.

The 1968 survey revealed further interesting data relating to grouping presented in Table 10.3.

Table 10.3 **Percentage of top-ability intake and average percentage staying on analysed by method of first-year grouping, England, Wales and Scotland, 1968***

Method of grouping	*Percentage in top 20% of ability range*	*Average percentage staying on beyond school-leaving age in 1968 in schools with 13–16 age range*	*Total number of schools*
1 In streams	13	43	130
2 In broad ability bands	16	52	210
3 In sets	14	52	36
4 Combination of streams and sets	14	50	96
5 Mixed ability (1) (two subjects setted)	16	55	42
6 Mixed ability (2) (remedial pupils separated)	14	55	80
7 Mixed ability (3) (for all subjects and pupils)	27	63	29
8 Other method	14	51	43

* The seven schools in the 'unknown' category (see Table 10.2) are omitted.

This table shows, first, that schools using categories 2 to 6 had between 14 and 16 per cent of top-ability pupils, but two categories stand out: schools using streaming had the lowest percentage (13 per cent), while schools using complete non-streaming had by far the highest proportion of any category (27 per cent). Second, the table relates the percentage staying on beyond the school-leaving age (15) to first-year grouping. Again, schools using categories 2 to 6 varied between 50 per cent and 55 per cent (the national average was 50 per cent), but schools using streaming had the lowest percentage, 43 per cent, while schools using complete non-streaming had the highest, 63 per cent. The average staying-on rate for schools using the three mixed-ability methods was 57 per cent, well above the national average, and above the rate for schools using any of the differentiating forms of grouping.

A more refined analysis of grouping procedures may be made by differentiating schools which provide a common course in the first year from those which do not. (The subsequent analysis in this section refers to 1968 survey figures only.) Of 11-plus comprehensive schools in England and Wales, 108 (18 per cent) differentiate the subject matter from the start; of these, forty-one (38 per cent) stream pupils in the first year, thirty-three (30·5 per cent) use ability bands, four (4 per cent) use setting and fourteen (13 per cent) a combination of streams and sets (a total of ninety-two schools). Only seven (6·5 per cent) use some form of mixed-ability grouping; none are entirely unstreamed.*

The proportion of schools using differentiating systems in this case (85 per cent indicated categories 1–4; 6·5 per cent indicated mixed-ability categories) is, of course, higher than for the schools as a whole. Conversely, the proportion of schools using mixed-ability systems is higher for schools which provide a common course (69 per cent indicated categories 1 to 4; 24 per cent indicated one of the three mixed-ability categories).† In Scotland the percentage using mixed-ability categories now rises to 49 per cent.‡ These figures underline the point already made, that acceptance of the concept of the common course inevitably raises the question of grouping in a new way. Many teachers have felt that to provide a common course logically involves the transition to non-streaming, since a common course at differentiated 'levels' may be regarded as a contradiction in terms.

As we saw earlier, some schools carry the common course through the first year only (87), some through two years (145), and half through three (235). (See Tables A.4 and A.5, pp. 525, 526.) Though widely accepted (especially in 11–18 schools), this latter practice is not yet universal. But of particular interest is the number (or proportion) of schools that both provide a common course for three years, and adopt some form of mixed-ability grouping throughout this period. Such schools may be said to be attempting to realize the full advantages of comprehensive organization in terms of equal opportunity and an undifferentiated educational experience for all their pupils. The survey showed that a total of forty-two responding schools in England and

* One school answered the question incorrectly, eight indicated 'other method'. See Table A.9 (p. 531).
† See Table A.9.
‡ See Table A.10 (p. 532).

Wales fell into this category; thirty-four of these were 11–18 schools, six 11–16 schools, and two 11–14/15 schools. A further forty-two schools utilizing mixed-ability grouping provided a common course for two years (and twenty-four for one year only). (See Table A.11, p. 533, which gives the breakdown also for Scotland and Wales separately; only one out of the fourteen Welsh schools using mixed-ability grouping maintains the common course for three years.)

New developments in teaching

New developments in teaching in the early years of the comprehensive school are closely linked with the movement towards non-streaming, which has prepared the way for related changes in the content and methods of education. The designing of a common course, in the eyes of many teachers, itself provided an impetus for structural reorganization, since a common course implies no basic differentiation between groups of pupils. Instead, it was held, the objective should be to provide broadly similar and relevant educational experiences for all the pupils, while allowing scope for each individual child to make his own contribution. Just as those primary schools which moved over to non-streaming in the 1950s began to evolve new flexible classroom structures, usually embodying a combination of class, group and individual work, so comprehensive schools, taking the same direction with their eleven year olds, began to evolve new techniques both of classroom organization and of grouping.

But the process has been a gradual one; schools have tended to move over to mixed-ability grouping as a result of their own experience and of the educational objectives of the head and staff. In some cases this transition, and the reasons for it, have been documented. At the Woodlands school, Coventry, with an intake of between 250 and 300 boys a year, a gradual transition was carried through over a period of four years, each stage involving a closer approximation to complete non-streaming. The performance of the pupils in mixed-ability classes was compared with the position (or stream) they would have achieved had they been streamed on Verbal Reasoning Quotients (the only statistic resulting from an objective type test used in the 11-plus examination), and in each year a wide measure of discrepancy was found 'between performance in the 11-plus type of test and work done subsequently in the secondary school'. Some did much better than could have been predicted, some did less well – and in general there was a low positive relationship between the VRQ rank order at entrance, and examination positions in six basic subjects one term later ($r = 0.53$). These results, which covered pupils over almost the entire ability range, suggested that the assumptions on which rigid streaming is based are fallacious, and confirmed the advantages of mixed-ability grouping in providing a flexible situation allowing for differences in the intellectual development of children. Similar results were observed and described by Harold Simmons of Bedminster Down School, Bristol, who also documented his school's unstreaming experience. The transition to non-streaming in both these schools was, then, based on a form of operational research, and the process could have been halted or reversed at any point, had the results suggested it. These researches, carried through by the heads of the schools, were published in 1965 and in 1969, and were one of the factors leading to an acceleration of this movement.[11]

If this was the course taken by some heads, others proceeded from their own convictions usually supported by a good proportion of their staff. Thus Miss Hoyles, who took over Vauxhall Manor School in London – an unstreamed comprehensive school – in 1964, was already a 'firm believer in non-streaming' which she had introduced in her previous school, a secondary modern school.[12] She saw her task as to take the school 'a stage further on the path it has begun', and, with the aid of her staff, this is what she has done. An example where the pressure has come from the staff is that of a second London school, established in 1961, which, the ILEA reported in 1967, had been unstreamed since 1962, using setting for French and mathematics, 'but', the survey continues, 'on the strong recommendation of the departmental heads this was dropped after one year', while the staff is reported as welcoming the fully non-streamed form of organization.[13] In 1966 and 1967 the movement towards non-streaming gathered way with considerable rapidity, being supported by a number of well-attended teachers' conferences where the whole issue was thoroughly ventilated.* The publication, again in 1966, of the booklet *The Flexible School*, by Michael Young and Michael Armstrong, which strongly advocated non-streaming, undoubtedly assisted this movement. In September 1967 an educational journal (*Where*) listed fifty-eight comprehensive schools experimenting with non-streaming, while the response to an inquiry in 1968 by the Comprehensive Schools Committee on the research necessary in the comprehensive situation made it abundantly clear that, in the eyes of many heads, this

---

* For instance, *Forum*/CSC conference on 'Non-streaming in comprehensive schools', June 1966 (transcript available from CSC and report in *Forum*, vol. 9, no. 1), and similar conferences on the same topic organized by the Nottingham, York, Exeter, Reading Institutes of Education (or universities) and by some local authorities and colleges of education, all held in 1966 or 1967. It was noticeable that, in its 1966 Survey, the ILEA dropped the remark in their earlier report (LCC, 1961) that non-streaming in academic subjects was 'impracticable, etc.' (see p. 223).

was the most important immediate issue requiring research data.* How rapidly the general outlook on this question is changing is indicated in a recent article by the head of a Roman Catholic school in the city of Durham which went comprehensive in September 1971. Feeling that the first year of existence was not the time to introduce widespread innovations, the head planned to use a rough streaming system in the first year.

However, discussions among heads of departments soon revealed a unanimous opinion that this was a situation quite at variance with our duty, contradicted the school's name, and, therefore, was not to be tolerated any longer than strictly necessary. An immediate beginning was made to prepare for an unstreamed situation in the first years. I do not feel that we jumped on any mixed-ability 'bandwaggon'. Put as simply as possible, I would have been ashamed to say to the pupils on the first day of term that they were in streams F G H.[14]

The effects of the transition to non-streaming at the Woodlands School, Coventry – on staying on rates, candidature for examinations, success in examinations, and other indicators – is now being intensively analysed retrospectively by the headmaster, Mr Thompson. Preliminary studies indicate that the transition to non-streaming has been accompanied by a large increase in the proportion of non-selective pupils staying on to complete a fifth year at school, together with a significant tendency for non-selective pupils to do better in O-level GCE examinations than they did while streaming persisted. In fact, *both* selective *and* non-selective pupils have improved their performance at this examination, the success rate of the latter, however, tripled (rising from 8 per cent to 24 per cent of the non-selective intake gaining one or more O-level passes). 'It would appear,' writes Thompson, 'that the abandonment of streaming was not only accompanied by an increase in the percentages of selective and non-selective pupils who were entered for and passed O-level but that a higher proportion of the increased entry was successful than in the previous period', adding 'a comparison between the number of subject passes gained by selective and non-selective pupils indicates a highly significant tendency for the transition to non-streaming to be accompanied by a large increase in the number of passes gained by non-selective pupils.' This statement applies both to GCE and CSE. In 1961, before the transition to non-streaming started, 23·4 per cent of the intake gained one or more GCE O-level passes, while 32·4 per cent gained one or more CSE passes. In 1965, after the transition to non-streaming had worked its way through, 47·2 per cent of the intake gained one or more GCE O-level passes, and

* An analysis of the replies to this inquiry was made by Douglas Holly, Secretary, Comprehensive Schools Committee's Research Advisory Panel; see *Comprehensive Education*, no. 11, Spring 1969.

56·9 per cent gained one or more CSE passes.* It seems clear that the transition to non-streaming at this large 11–18 comprehensive school has led to a significant improvement of standards throughout the school – as measured in the traditional terms of success in external examinations.

Most schools, taking the initial steps towards non-streaming and starting logically with the first year, have tended to retain the traditional subject divisions and to seek new teaching methods which would allow for a more flexible approach to the teaching (or learning) of individual subjects. Over the last few years a number of articles have been published, as part of the general discussion on this issue; in many, but not all, cases, these are concerned with group and individual methods within the class-room as well as with class teaching. While it is the general experience that subjects such as English, history and geography can be well adapted to teaching in the non-streamed situation (more particularly if timetables are blocked, worksheets provided, and films, tapes, film-strips, slides, etc., made available), more difficulties have been found with subjects having a linear development: for instance, some sciences, mathematics, foreign languages. However, here also teachers have pioneered non-streamed teaching, sometimes using programmed learning techniques (which allow group and individual work on a sequential pattern) as an auxiliary. A wealth of experience has now been gained on the whole problem of teaching unstreamed classes at the early secondary stage, and many articles, study groups and conferences have been devoted to this question.[15] The 'resources' approach to learning has added stimulus to the whole move-ment. Though it is generally accepted that there are many problems still to be overcome, it is unusual to find schools which, after attempting un-streaming, have reverted to previous methods. The general consensus appears to be that the gains made, particularly in pupil–teacher relations and social development generally, as well as in the encouragement of independent learning, far outweigh the difficulties, and that these latter can be overcome, given further study and experience and, above all, the provision of suitable resources to meet the needs of the schools. Perhaps the best example of a carefully planned and systematic transition to non-streaming as an essential concomitant to comprehensive reorganization on a whole county basis is given by Fife, where a team of teachers, supported by the authority, has worked out relevant approaches to the teaching of a common curriculum in mixed-ability groups for all first-year pupils in secondary schools; these, it should be remembered, are aged twelve to thirteen in Scotland – the equivalent of second-year pupils in England.[16]

Some comprehensive schools have taken the further step of accompanying

* Personal communication from D. Thompson, headmaster, the Woodlands School, Coventry.

non-streaming with the development of an integrated first-year course involving a team of teachers, each of whom spends a considerable proportion of his time with one class. This method has a twofold aim, (1) to provide a stable social unit for first-year pupils whose entry into what is often a large secondary school can be bewildering, and at the same time to preserve some continuity of teaching methods by using the more informal (flexible) junior-school approach in the early stages, and (2) by breaking down subject barriers to evolve a more relevant education for eleven and twelve year olds. An example of this approach, covering about a quarter of the teaching time, is the first-year project developed at Hartcliffe School, Bristol, a school of 2000 pupils, carried on under the aegis of a member of the staff designated as head of the 'Discovery Department'. The aim here is to move over to a new general 'open-plan' learning situation and the introduction of team teaching.[17]

Swinton comprehensive school in Yorkshire provides an example where an integrated approach, using a team of eight teachers, has led to the establishment of a 'Foundation Year' for 250 first-year pupils. Building on the experience of team teaching both with the fourth year and the sixth form, a team of teachers drawn from history, geography and science have developed an experimental course comprising large themes such as man's place in the universe, the nature of our planet and the evolution of life; the search in human societies for law and order, both in natural phenomena and in community life; and the agricultural, industrial and scientific revolutions. The aim is to develop a sense of perspective as a basis for later more specialist studies. The technique of the key lesson, given to all 250 pupils by one member of the staff, is used, together with the provision of carefully thought-out materials for follow-up work in the different classes. Teamwork of this character, involving cooperation, mutual understanding, and a readiness to learn from each other, is a new feature in teaching (normally an isolated activity); it is introducing a new dimension into the inner life and activity of comprehensive schools.[18]

Experience shows that new developments in teaching and learning, of the kind outlined above, are dependent on modifying the more rigid structures of the past – in particular the system of subject teaching to 'homogeneous' classes supported, usually, by hierarchical forms of government and control. While the data presented in this chapter, including the sample survey, indicate that the swing to non-streaming is retaining its momentum, the majority of schools still use one or other form of ability differentiation in grouping pupils. It may be some years before non-streaming spreads generally up the school to include later age-groups. That this is already the trend of development is, however, clear. It opens up new prospects of great significance for the future of education.[19]

Middle schools

The developments so far described concern largely the early years of the 11–18 comprehensive schools. But many authorities are planning various forms of middle school, spanning the traditional break at eleven (see pp. 162–4). These include the Plowden type covering the years 8–12, the 9–13 school first proposed by the West Riding, as well as schools commencing at ten. The Leicestershire 'high' school comes into this category, taking pupils from eleven to fourteen (some to fifteen), and these have been established in Derbyshire and other areas.

The bulk of the Leicestershire schools cover only the secondary age range, so that problems of the fusion of primary and secondary approaches have not been posed in so acute a form as in the new middle schools. However it is now the county's policy to lower the age of intake to ten, and three schools have already had two years' experience of this situation. The general trend described in this chapter is particularly noteworthy in the case of the Leicestershire schools, some of which have been in existence for fifteen years. Here also the tendency has been towards the modification of the more rigid forms of streaming to complete non-streaming of the first, and in some cases the second, year. In a report on the first year at Hinckley, where the Leicestershire Plan was first introduced in 1957, the high school head then noted that the intake was divided into five forms, of which two took French, one Latin, while one did special remedial work – these divisions were made on the basis of the 11-plus results, still taken at that time.[20] By 1964 Stewart Mason, Director of Education for Leicestershire, could stress that rigid streaming was avoided, the main aim of each high school being 'to keep its organization as flexible as possible' while in the coming year at least two high schools would be experimenting with non-streaming.[21] Several of these schools are now unstreamed in the first year; among these are Kibworth, Bushloe, Ferneley, Oadby Manor, Roundhill and Belvoir high schools, each of which is striking out on its own path and developing new approaches involving integrated studies, team teaching, inquiry and discovery projects in a basically non-streamed situation.[22] The fact that schools of this type are entirely free from external examinations certainly leaves more scope for initiative on the part of head, staff and pupils than is the case with 11–18 schools. Our evidence indicates that developments similar to those under way in Leicestershire are taking place in equivalent (11 to 14) schools elsewhere.

The transition to recruitment at ten in Leicestershire high schools raises some interesting questions. In the first place it is worth noting that this move is linked with the unification of the primary school taking children from five to ten (as the move to 9–13 schools involves a single 'first school' for the five to nine year olds). At Belvoir high school, Bottesford, where ten year olds entered for the first time in 1970, primary methods, although including team teaching and some specialist teaching, are used with the new age group, who are supervised by a permanent team of three teachers working closely together. There is no streaming. Half the time is spent in the first-year base pursuing integrated studies, utilizing different resource areas in a flexible structure; specialist studies (French, music, drama, woodwork, etc.) are taken by specialist teachers in different areas of the school. The year's work has been carefully thought out to provide a bridge between primary- and secondary-school approaches. However this may be, there is no doubt that the introduction of this age-group has had a stimulating effect on the work of the school as a whole, and present experience indicates that the transition to the 10–14 high school will further reinforce positive educational change throughout the high school system.[23]

9–13 schools are, of course, an entirely new venture. The first of these opened in September 1968, in the Hemsworth area of the West Riding (thirteen schools, which operated in their first year only as 8–12 schools), in Wallasey (ten schools) and at Bradford, where a single 'model' purpose-built middle school was opened in January 1969. Since then many other authorities have opened 9–13 schools (for instance, Northumberland opened twenty-three in 1969 and 1970), and, from the forward planning data available, it seems clear that approximately one-fifth of all schools involved in reorganization plans will be of the 9–13, 13–18 variety (see Table 5.3, p. 115). These schools will, therefore, form an important element in the reorganized educational structure coming into being. Since they cut right across the break at eleven with its built-in division between two distinct stages of education, 9–13 schools pose quite new educational problems.

This was recognized in the initial discussions preceding this development. At this stage, two points of view were in evidence: some saw these schools as providing an opportunity for extending the integrated, form-teaching approach of advanced primary schools into the secondary age range; others saw the opposite opportunity – that of extending specialist teaching, structured and perhaps subject-centred in character, down into the primary age range. Both these views are closely linked with certain practical considerations. Where the schools are developed from secondary modern schools, with the main nucleus of the staff initially coming from the school now adapted, the latter view is likely to prevail – and plans indicate that in fact most 9–13 middle schools will be brought into being in this way. Where, on the other hand, the schools are adapted from existing primary buildings, the main nucleus of the staff being experienced in primary education, the former view is likely to be favoured. Only where the middle school is purpose built, and a new staff recruited, do the conditions exist to implement fully the new conceptions of education now considered appropriate to this age range.

The Delf Hill School, Bradford, was one of the first to be purpose-built, and its planning indicates the pattern of organization. The school contains four centres – one for each year; centres 1 and 2 being grouped together (for 9–11), as also 3 and 4 (11–13). Each pair of centres provides accommodation for groups of various sizes, spaces for shared teaching, bays for group projects and experiments, as well as enclosed rooms, again of various size and differently furnished. Centres 3 and 4, for the older pupils, include additional equipment: for instance individual work places for audio-visual language teaching, provision for science and mathematics, and so on. There is in addition a large studio/workshop area linking all the centres, and other facilities.[24]

This planning allows the work of each year group, consisting in this case of three classes, to be planned as a unit, the class teachers forming a team together with the year group leader who normally carries a graded post. A report on the West Riding schools (*Launching Middle Schools*; DES Survey 8, 1970) which also encourages this approach, specifically notes the effective team work developing in year groups of this kind, stressing that teachers are encouraged to think in terms of the year as a whole rather than a class. The conditions exist therefore for the development of integrated studies, but drawing on the expertise of all the teachers in the year group, together with other specialist teachers. A new pattern of delegation is developing in these schools. Timetabling for the school as a whole is often confined to the use of specialist facilities (the hall for physical education, the music room, etc.), the year-group leader then working out with the rest of his year staff (and specialist teachers) what the pattern of work will be for the year group as a whole. This is resulting in a much greater delegation of responsibility than exists in most junior schools, and allows the flexibility of organization essential for the implementation of discovery and child-centred approaches to education. The head, however, once he has set up this organization, is free to move around the school and take an active part in the work of the year groups; since few middle schools contain more than 500 to 600 pupils, the schools are still small enough for the head to play this role.

Another purpose-built middle school – that at Grimethorpe in the West Riding, is also designed to facilitate the year-group organization, though the school is designed to focus more specifically around the practical activity areas than at Delf Hill. These tendencies are reinforced in one of the latest purpose-built middle schools to open, Pollards Hill middle school in the London borough of Merton. Here, while plans originally involved a division of the 9–11 and 11–13 age groups, each with different facilities (as at Delf Hill), this concept was abandoned during the planning stage and the school designed architecturally as a unified school allowing the maximization of communication and easy access by all age groups to specialist facilities, now placed at the centre of the building, together with resources areas, stores and study bays. This school is specifically designed to allow maximum flexibility, both immediately and in the future. Apart from the specialist facilities, the teaching area consists of 'two large uninterrupted spaces' of sixty metres by ten metres, carpeted and equipped with a specially designed system of moveable screens allowing for class teaching, enclosed bays for group and seminar work, or large open-planned areas for up to 150 children. This makes possible day to day reorganization to meet immediate varying needs, the fundamental restructuring of the whole teaching area in response to major evolutions of teaching policy, and even the expansion of the building to enlarge single departments or the school as a whole. This school opened in January 1972.[25]

A good deal of creative thinking has clearly gone into the planning and design of the new middle schools. Equally impressive has been the careful planning by which the transition has been made to the new system in most (if not all) areas. In the West Riding, for instance, a carefully worked out programme of in-service training, much of it under the control of the teachers themselves, preceded the transition, the proposal to set up teachers' study groups to tackle specific problems gaining an 'overwhelming response'[26] – these study groups played a very important part in working out the new educational approaches now being implemented. The same careful preparations have been made in Dorset and other areas, and the apparent success of many of these schools is clearly partly due to the high level of teacher involvement in this preparation. Reports from many areas, for instance, Northumberland, West Riding and elsewhere indicate that 9–13 schools are very popular with the teachers, generating very positive attitudes among the staff – a sense of excitement arising from the feeling of participating in an important educational innovation.[27]

It is too early yet to define any single organization or plan emerging as general in middle schools – each school is working out its own solutions in relation to the specific conditions and problems it faces. The DES West Riding survey goes further when it states that it soon became apparent that 'no set pattern' would emerge: 'all schools have used the first year as an exploratory period and none, as one would expect, has evolved an organization which it would regard as settled'.[28] There are almost as many patterns as there are schools, writes the CEO of Northumberland about the twenty-three schools in his area.[29] Nevertheless the year-group 'team', or better, perhaps, 'cooperative-teaching' approach seems fairly general, and represents a new feature in English education which may well have implications for schools with older pupils. Another point deserving attention is the clear swing towards unstreaming which has been very marked in the planning of schemes. 'There is one point of near unanimity in the proposals for middle schools', states the DES pamphlet *Towards the Middle School* (1970), and that is the 'strong preference' of most middle-school working parties for classes of mixed ability.[30] This is clearly a crucial matter for the inner organization and structure of these schools. It is specifically the move to non-streaming that makes possible the planning of year-group activities in a flexible manner, varying the groupings appropriately in relation to given activities. 'The school is entirely unstreamed', writes the head of Delf Hill school, Bradford. 'Indeed the open plan of the school would permit no other solution.'[31] It seems that all, or nearly all, middle schools are planning to make use of this new flexibility, whether they are purpose-built or not.

The width and variety of activities which may be organized in schools of this age range will clearly be limited by the size of the school, the availability of staff, staff–pupil ratios, the actual facilities in the buildings and similar factors. It seems that the tendency may be to maintain the primary school form-teacher system for the first two years, though stiffening it with a certain amount of specialist teaching, or at least the advice of a specialist to a team of teachers responsible for a year group. In the upper part of the school a gradual introduction of subject-teaching may take place. Schools planned with four single-year units allow for a group of teachers to be responsible for each year, and so also for a progression of appropriate techniques for each age level throughout the school. The brief experience of these schools to date indicates that the 9–13 middle schools are likely to adopt this form of organization, and that the content of education and methods of teaching, as things settle down and these schools develop their own particular ethos, may well reflect that of advanced primary schools on the one hand, and the movement towards non-streaming and interdisciplinary teaching at the upper levels.[32]

This is not to say that these schools do not have their problems. There has been considerable difficulty in converting primary schools into middle schools, in view of the new levels of equipment and facilities now necessary; further, teachers have protested about the inadequacy of capitation grants, the shortage of library and reference books, the lack of equipment for science. In the West Riding these protests led to the doubling of capitation grants for two years, to be followed by a revised scheme allowing more generous allocations. It is clearly essential that this new venture should not be frustrated by lack of the elementary requirements which the more flexible approaches appropriate to these schools render absolutely necessary.

9–13 schools originated in proposals put forward by Alec Clegg; accepted by the then Secretary of State (Edward Boyle), the way was cleared by the Education Act of 1964 which abolished the statutory requirement for a transition to secondary education at eleven. Both the Leicestershire 10–14 schools and the 8–12 middle schools proposed in the Plowden report of 1967 were made legally possible, as it were, by this Act. The Plowden proposal was, of course, linked with their plan for 'First schools' covering the age range 5–8, and was intended to operate throughout the country. As things have worked out, however, many authorities are finding other solutions, and, at the time of writing, only some twelve authorities are planning 8–12 schools covering the whole of their area. Sheffield established eighteen schools of this type in 1969 (as part of their overall reorganization policy), while four authorities opened schools of this type for the first time in September 1970 (Birkenhead, Southampton, Stoke-on-Trent and the Castleford area of West Riding).[33]

The clear intention of the Plowden committee was to retain the primary–secondary sequence in terms of school organization, but to enlarge the primary sector by the access of an extra age group. This proposal marks a less radical change than the establishment of 9–13 schools. Plowden type middle schools are normally based on primary schools. They lose their first year's intake but retain the eleven to twelve year olds; the main problem, therefore, becomes that of effective provision for the extra year group within the primary context. Nevertheless here also much preliminary planning has, and is, taking place in those areas making the transition. At Southampton, for instance, where twenty-three 8–12 schools were established in September 1970 (as well as seventeen middle departments in combined first/middle schools), this transition was preceded by four years' detailed planning, involving 500 teachers in inservice courses, as well as many teachers' study groups examining and making recommendations across every aspect of the new schools' activities. In addition the design of four new buildings was worked out by a team of architects, teachers and advisers supported by study groups meeting at the Curriculum Development Centre; these examined in detail the aims and objectives of these schools as well as problems of organization, staffing, building and resources.[34] Adaptations and extensions have been made to existing schools, a major consideration for both old and new buildings being again to ensure maximum flexibility in the use of the entire school area.

The transition to 8–12 schools at Southampton has resulted in new developments in environmental studies, in the teaching of French, mathematics and science (for which considerable additional aid has been made available), as well as in other areas. Some twenty secondary school teachers have moved into the primary sector and are learning new approaches appropriate to the new situation. While a report on the first year's working indicates once again that no set pattern has yet developed – since the year has been largely one of exploration, and in any case schools differ as to their buildings, staff and children – one feature that is stressed is the success of new patterns of 'cooperative teaching' now emerging here as well as in the 9–13 school. An experienced head writes that

this past year has been enormously successful without the brilliance of any individual teacher. This has proved that cooperative teaching is far more successful than flashes of genius based on one type of activity. In my forty-two years' experience I would consider that a greater advance has been made in the last twelve months than at any time during those years.

Essential to the success of this approach has been 'the opportunity for frequent discussion and planning sessions by members of the team'. Teaching methods have been transformed through the use of resources areas adjacent to the classrooms so that 'the teachers begin to think in terms of a year unit rather than a class'. In the fourth year the lower teacher–pupil ratio that was made possible clearly improved the type and quality of the work, 'allowing more scope for individual discovery, first-hand experience and creativity'. This is not to deny that new problems also emerged – particularly those arising from the teaching of the new fourth year in one-stream schools, where the demands on the teacher have proved excessive.[35]

With the Plowden type 8–12 school we enter the area traditionally thought of as primary – and this, as we have seen, was the objective of this particular proposal. The 9–13 and 10–14 schools gradually shift the emphasis towards secondary education; but at the same time, methods and organization traditionally seen as secondary are breaking down in all types of school towards more flexible approaches over this entire age range. A good deal of attention has been devoted in this edition to these new types of school coming into being as part of secondary reorganization. The establishment of middle schools has undoubtedly released a fund of energy, enthusiasm and innovation which is a clear gain. As we point out later, however, this whole development not only leads to a great variety of ages of transfer in the system as a whole; it also raises sharply the question of determining the appropriate provision for each particular age group, under whatever system. The DES now categorizes middle schools into two groups, those 'deemed primary', and those 'deemed secondary'. However this categorization may be made, it is clearly important that equal educational provision is made (or at least aimed at) for each age group throughout the country, whatever the particular system in specific areas. One very positive result of this entire development is that the middle schools are breaking down the dichotomy between primary and secondary education and the educational process is now at last beginning to be seen as a unity. This could have far-reaching results in the schools.[36]

Remedial groups

An important issue, so far little discussed in the literature on comprehensive education, concerns arrangements for pupils with learning difficulties. Some would estimate that about 10 per cent of children are in need of special educational treatment; allowing, of course, for regional and local differences. Some comprehensive schools will have a larger proportion, and some a smaller. Most established comprehensive schools have remedial departments responsible for their teaching and organization.

Surveys[37] show a remarkable variety of practice in the definition and staffing of remedial forms and departments. In one school of 1000 pupils, for instance, thirteen pupils only were classed as 'remedial', while in another of the same size, 160 were so defined. In another school all the early leavers were the responsibility of the remedial department – a practice which seems to indicate some confusion of thought to say the least. Departments in some large 11–18 schools contain up to 230 pupils, though the usual size in ILEA schools varies from thirty to ninety. Staffing varies likewise – from one or two teachers up to six or eight. There are wide differences also in the facilities available and the proportion of the capitation grant allocated to the remedial department.

Differences of opinion, and practice, exist also as to the degree of segregation of remedial pupils considered necessary or desirable, as also about the necessity for express streams – segregation of the 'very able'. At some schools, slow learning children are taught together for all subjects by the remedial department staff; this policy was advocated by the late Cyril Burt over the last forty years.* This system may also lead to the social segregation of the backward, although most schools rely

* 'The first and most important step is segregation, the formation of separate classes or of separate schools expressly for the backward child. Segregation sounds like a drastic measure; yet it is needed in the interests alike of the other children, of the teachers, and of the backward themselves', Burt, *The Backward Child*, 1964 edn, p. 574.

on clubs, house activities, games and assemblies to provide opportunities for social integration. More usually remedial pupils are segregated only for the academic subjects – for instance, English, history, geography, mathematics, French – but are grouped with other pupils for classes in art, woodwork, metalwork and so on.

Schools which have moved over to non-streaming have already been discussed; here a major question for decision is whether to continue to segregate the slowest learners and treat them as a differentiated unit, complete in itself with, where possible, its own teachers, or whether to integrate them fully with the mixed-ability classes. As we have seen, both techniques are used. In the former case the remedial department continues to operate as a unit in the traditional way. In the latter case children are withdrawn as individuals or small groups for specific remedial work, the department's teachers functioning in a new way. The most comprehensive survey so far undertaken on this question, by Olive Sampson and P. D. Pumphrey (Manchester University), brings out very clearly the extent to which remedial teachers in comprehensive schools wish to integrate both themselves and their pupils into the mainstream of the schools' activities – 'integration not segregation', writes Olive Sampson, 'is implicit in the comprehensive school'. In answering questionnaires, many remedial teachers 'gave uninhibited expression to strongly held views' on this question; 'again and again they applauded and sought integration for their pupils and particularly abhorred the segregative results of rigid hierarchical organizations'. Two typical answers are given: 'No pupil should feel he is in the lowest stream'; 'I think it is better in the long run to keep as many as possible with a large assortment of their contemporaries.'[38]

The most workable method of avoiding segregation is the system of withdrawal, referred to above. Albert Rowe, until recently head of the David Lister School (Hull) explains this method as follows:

At present we withdraw pupils who need extra help for up to twenty out of forty weekly periods for individual work with remedial teachers. The amount of time they are withdrawn will depend upon their own needs, e.g. some will only be withdrawn for English and mathematics. The groups will always be small, giving opportunity for individual and specialized attention, but will differ in size and composition according to whether pupils are withdrawn from English, mathematics, geography, history or French. The appropriate syllabuses are followed, for the object is to feed them back if possible into their mixed-ability forms after they've been 'remedied'. For the remainder of their weekly timetable they are with their own forms, taught by individual and small-group methods appropriate to mixed-ability forms, including graded homework.

This method avoids the no doubt unintentional but inevitable hiving-off that comes from putting them into separate remedial classes and shows them how much they have in common with their fellows, not how different they are, a view borne out by their personal assurance and social competence.[39]

This system of withdrawal is used at other non-streamed comprehensive schools, and is clearly in line with the general outlook of such schools which seek, through their organization, to avoid a fundamental segregation of any group of pupils. This is an issue on which there is a considerable division of opinion among the supporters of non-streaming, although Olive Sampson's survey indicates that it has wide support among remedial teachers themselves in comprehensive schools, even though she found (and this is in line with previous surveys) that 52 per cent of the schools she surveyed (205 comprehensive and 65 modern schools) in fact segregate 'remedial' children full-time. These children are not (or should not be) actually certifiable as E S N (educationally subnormal). Their learning difficulties may not be qualitatively different from those of more advanced children. But if they are to be taught together with others in mixed-ability classes, the teachers require a knowledge of the special skills and techniques that are needed, or remedial teachers need to participate in the normal activities of the classes. Some schools are adopting this approach and are now reducing even withdrawal to a minimum; the remedial staff working with other teachers responsible for a year group – or a particular subject area – as members of the whole team responsible for an area of work. This is a feasible system and can be put into practice in schools like Countesthorpe (Leicestershire) where much of the work is carried on in individual or small-group settings under the aegis of a group of teachers; limited withdrawal for special tuition can, of course, be combined with this method which has the advantage of reducing to a minimum overtly differential treatment of remedial children.[40]

This is an issue on which research data is urgently required, so that different approaches can be compared and the most effective determined. In addition, improved training opportunities for teachers specially interested in this work, plus fairer allocations of resources to remedial departments are both necessary. The present heterogeneity of organization 'suggests a lack of certainty as to what remedial departments are for', writes Olive Sampson, and the extraordinary variety of practice described at the start of this section bears out this conclusion – there is an urgent need to clarify objectives and evaluate different procedures.* There is no

---

* This point is also stressed in the HMI's survey, *Slow Learners in Secondary Schools*, 1971, which, however, was more concerned with secondary modern than comprehensive schools: 'The uncertainties are obvious', they write. 'Uncertainties about the nature of (the children's) potential, about the nature and extent of their disabilities, about the most appropriate organization, about suitable educational methods and techniques, about the nature of a suitable curriculum' (p. 21). This survey

doubt that the burning issue among remedial teachers in comprehensive schools is precisely this question of integration and segregation; such at least is the conclusion Olive Sampson draws from a study of the views of a cross-section of 'the most alert members of the remedial profession'. It is clear that the whole question of the organization of remedial classes and departments offers a particular challenge to the comprehensive school.

In connection with the idea of 'withdrawal' lessons, it is interesting to note that this approach has been advocated on behalf of the very advanced pupils as well. In a sense it is already practised in some ways for pupils learning musical instruments – they are 'withdrawn' for individual tuition at stated periods of the week. Professor Herman Bondi has advocated withdrawal lessons within the comprehensive schools for pupils especially gifted in a particular subject: mathematics, for example. He is of the opinion that the brilliant mathematical child would be better served by individual lessons within a comprehensive school than by being placed in a thirty-pupil 'stream' in a grammar school.[41]

Liaison with primary schools

The new systems coming into operation involve transfer between schools at a variety of ages between nine and sixteen. The key transition point in England and Wales, however, remains that at eleven, in Scotland, twelve.

It has long been recognized that transfer from primary to secondary school marks an important change for the pupil. It involves a transition from the form-teacher system to specialist teaching, so that pupil–teacher relationships differ, as also do the curriculum and teaching methods; moreover, the secondary school is usually considerably larger than the primary school and children may be overawed. It is generally recognized that the process of transfer should be eased by special measures to familiarize children with their new school. How far this is actually done in grammar and modern schools it is difficult to say: few studies of any value have been made.[42] In the case of comprehensive schools, the problem of transfer is posed in quite a new way.

There are two reasons for this. First, comprehensive schools, even if creamed, are usually neighbourhood schools, taking in all, or most, of the children from particular primary schools. This is a new feature. Second, the 11–18 schools tend to be large so that specific steps have been taken to ease the transition. There are two aspects to this question. First, what

also stresses 'the almost infinite variety of organization' (p. 7) and the fact that the term 'slow learners' (derived from the Plowden report) 'was capable of a wide variety of interpretations' (p. 2).

arrangements are made *before* the pupil is transferred, and second, what is done to ease the transition *after* transfer – in terms of the structuring of the new intake and its activity.

Our smaller sample of schools was specifically asked for information about arrangements for liaison and for familiarizing pupils with their new school before transfer. From the replies it is clear that considerable attention is given to this; but one point stands out very clearly. Where the secondary school serves a neighbourhood, recruiting its pupils from specific local schools, such liaison is greatly facilitated as compared with the position where elaborate guided-choice selection or ability banding directs pupils to a wide variety of secondary schools.

Thus, one headmaster of a London (ILEA) school states that the situation is 'bedevilled by the fact that under the ILEA arrangements only a small minority of feeder schools can feel an established relationship (i.e. only those "very near")'; another head from the same authority states that he has forty feeding primary schools, and that, although he visits several of these to meet parents, he has to 'avoid too much contact for fear of offending other secondary heads' who 'rather disapprove of visits which could seem to be canvassing for pupils'. A system of specific feeder schools, however, presents quite a different situation, one head of a long-established comprehensive writing that liaison arrangements are 'magnificent': 'two primary schools supply 80 per cent of the intake'; transfer of information is, therefore, 'easy, automatic and as full as could be desired', while the pupils have 'many opportunities to learn of school before they come'. The head of a large comprehensive school in Wales makes the same point:

Since complete reorganization it has become possible to establish a close relationship with our contributory primary schools. The head of the lower school visits the junior schools to talk with staff and pupils. The pupils spend half a day here (each week) enjoying themselves in the swimming pool. The parents are invited to meet the staff here.

There is also interchange of visits by heads of departments and staff. All this 'was not possible when individual primary schools sent pupils to as many as four secondary schools under the bipartite system'. The value of proximity, and of having specific feeder schools, i.e. of acting as a neighbourhood school, is brought out time and again in the replies.

It is clear that a good deal of effort goes into developing workable and effective systems of liaison. Many heads of comprehensive schools visit their feeder primary schools for discussions with the head and staff, and also to meet the pupils in their last year, who will form their intake. This task is sometimes the responsibility of the head of the 'lower school' or the 'First-Year Tutor' in the comprehensive school. The head of an 11–18 school (serving a county rural area) writes that 'The Director of Junior Studies visits each of our twenty-one contributory schools to meet prospective pupils, then for the last fortnight of the summer term groups come in daily to spend a day in school.' The majority of our smaller sample referred to such visits. In some cases the heads of houses at the secondary school visit the junior school to discuss the coming intake, and allocate children to houses on this basis; several others said this also.

It appears to be a common practice for junior-school pupils to visit the secondary school during their last year before transfer; fourteen schools reported this procedure. 'Parties from contributory schools visit the school in the summer term before entry as a "shock-absorber" for a one-day programme', writes one head. A Leicestershire high school writes of 'frequent two-way visits by staff and pupils for half-days or whole days', of 'very close consultation and exchange of information'.

Parents' meetings have already been mentioned. It is clear that a good deal is done by the schools in our smaller sample to help parents to get to know the new school. A typical answer is that parents are invited to an evening meeting 'to have the organization and aims of the school explained, to meet staff and especially house staff'. One school asks parents to fill in a confidential questionnaire 'to familiarize us with details concerning health and physical defects, parents' place of work and telephone number, etc.'. Others organize parents' evenings, tours of the school or individual interviews. Parental involvement of this kind may seem an obvious step, but it was often evaded under the bipartite system.

The main purpose of visits by the head and other members of the staff to the junior schools before entry is both to meet the staff and pupils and to gain information about the new intake – many junior schools keep record cards of children's progress, and these are handed on. Some heads obtain information about friendship groupings in the school and use this in forming class groups in the secondary school.

But in addition a primary function of all such activity is to provide for the mutual discussion of joint problems. In several areas arrangements are made for regular meetings between heads or staff of both junior and secondary schools; in one case primary-school heads attend a monthly meeting to discuss educational topics; in another the progress of the first-year intake at the secondary school is discussed with the junior heads, and in still another regular meetings with primary-school heads are attended by heads of departments at the secondary school, and consultations take place on various issues, such as the form of the record card to be used.

Another joint concern lies in the content and methods of education – particularly the former. Heads were specifically asked what arrangements are made 'for coordinating teaching method or curriculum'. It is, perhaps, symptomatic of the gulf between primary and secondary education that only one in four of our smaller sample replied to this question. Those who did so referred to joint meetings and discussions (sometimes to study groups) on the teaching of mathematics, languages and science. But only two schools reported special arrangements involving, in one case, freeing heads of departments for one afternoon a week to visit feeder primary schools 'principally to discuss and ensure continuity of method in English, mathematics and French'. On the other hand, there was a general recognition that current practice falls short of what is needed. 'Full information is passed on about pupils', writes the head of a large urban comprehensive, 'but coordination of teaching methods, or even subjects, is impossible'; the illustrative example given is that some junior schools do not teach French, some do, but without necessarily covering the same ground.

As the age of transfer now varies widely, it is of growing importance to establish appropriate educational experiences for each year group, whatever the type of school – whether for ages 9 to 13, 10 to 14, or 11 on. This applies with particular force to the 11–13 age groups, since these may be housed in a variety of types of school. The more informal, flexible structure now being developed in the first years of the Leicestershire high schools and the 9–13 middle schools represents a deliberate attempt to extend into the 'secondary' years the best of the new practices in primary education. It would be wrong, however, to underestimate the difficult educational problems of 'marrying' the systematic, specialist (or 'sequential') approach of the traditional secondary school with the more informal primary-school practice. Particular interest attaches, therefore, to the steps taken by established 11–18 comprehensives to smooth the transition from primary to secondary teaching techniques. These include the formation of relatively small first-year groupings, approximating to those with which children have been familiar; and modification of the school organization to enable younger children to be kept together as a group (now a fairly common procedure). So far as academic organization is concerned, the form-teacher system of the primary school may be continued with first-year entrants (if in a modified form); first-year entrants may be grouped in classes on the basis of friendships formed in primary school; all the first-year forms may be treated together as a unit. This last pattern, as we have seen, is followed in many schools.

In sum, with the establishment of the comprehensive school there can be a much closer liaison between what have been separate stages of schooling than has been possible in the past. This has already been recognized and useful steps have been taken, but it is important that they should be fully recorded and studied for there are complex problems involved. There should not be undue differences between the education of the same year group within different forms of school organization. Given the variety of ages of transfer between schools, the task is now to determine the guide lines for each age group, within which individual schools can work.

Notes

1. ILEA Survey, p. 59, 1967.
2. ibid.
3. 'Non-streaming in the comprehensive school', report of CSC/*Forum* Conference (transcript), p. 19, 1966.
4. *Teaching in Comprehensive Schools: A Second Report*, p. 65, 1967, hereafter referred to as IAAM Report.
5. ILEA Survey, p. 59, 1967.
6. LCC Survey, p. 34, 1961.
7. ILEA Survey, p. 58, 1967.
8. R. Pedley, *Comprehensive Schools Today*, pp. 2, 24, 1954.
9. LCC Survey, p. 32, 1961.
10. G. C. Firth, *Comprehensive Schools in Coventry and Elsewhere*, pp. 78ff. 1963.
11. D. Thompson, 'Towards an unstreamed comprehensive school', *Forum*, vol. 7, no. 3, Summer 1965, and 'An experiment in unstreaming', vol. 11, no. 2, Spring 1969. H. W. Simmons and R. Morgan, *Inside a Comprehensive School*, pp. 99–101, 1969.
12. 'Non-streaming in the comprehensive school', p. 9, 1966.
13. ILEA Survey, p. 62, 1967.
14. William D. Cavanagh, 'St Leonards', *Comprehensive Education*, no. 19, Autumn 1971.
15. See, for instance, 'Teaching in unstreamed secondary schools', report of conference at the Exeter University Institute of Education, January 1967; 'Non-streaming in comprehensive schools', report of CSC and *Forum* conference, 1966 (and see *Forum*, vol. 9, no. 1); 'Unstreaming in the comprehensive school', *Where* Supplement 12 (1968). For articles on subject teaching in non-streamed comprehensive schools in *Forum* see: vol. 9, no. 2 (Mathematics, by Brian Clayton; History, by R. D. Lobban; English, by George Robertson); vol. 9, no. 3 (Mathematics, by P. Herbert; Science, by D. P. Bosworth; Languages, by P. I. Pole and G. B. Handley); vol. 10, no. 3 (Science, by D. F. Hamilton); vol. 12, no. 3 ('Two and a half years on', by Joan Leighton); vol. 13, no. 1 (Mathematics, by Anthony Bailey; Modern languages, by Elizabeth Halsall; Science, by John Darke; Biology, by Donald Reid); vol. 13, no. 2 (French, by Tony Warnes; English, by Brian Hankin); vol. 14, no. 2, ('Curricular developments in Fife', by William Breslin). See also Maureen Hardy (ed.), *At Classroom Level* (1971), a collection of articles bearing on this question in both primary and secondary schools, and Michael Tucker, 'Organizational change: the process of unstreaming', in M. G. Hughes (ed.), *Secondary School Administration*, chapter 9. For a review of available literature on

non-streaming, see Clyde Chitty, 'Non-streaming in comprehensives: a review', *Comprehensive Education*, no. 12, Summer 1969.

16. William Breslin, 'Curricular developments in Fife secondary schools' *Forum*, vol. 14, no. 2, Spring 1972.

17. W. A. D. Williams, 'Unstreaming and subject integration in a comprehensive school', *Forum*, vol. 10, no. 3; see also John Sealey 'Interdisciplinary studies', *Forum*, vol. 13, no. 2, for a description of a similar approach at Dunsmore School, Rugby.

18. J. H. Parry, 'What to teach', *Forum*, vol. 11, no. 1; and see also J. H. Parry, 'Framework for the first form', *Trends in Education*, no. 11.

19. Basil Bernstein, 'Open schools, open society', *New Society*, 14 September 1967; and 'On the classification and framing of educational knowledge', in Earl Hopper (ed.), *Readings in the Theory of Educational Systems* 1971, pp. 184–211.

20. G. Baxter, 'The Leicestershire experiment: first year at Hinckley', *Forum*, vol. 1, no. 1.

21. Stewart C. Mason, *The Leicestershire Experiment and Plan*, p. 32, 3rd edn, revised, 1964.

22. See C. J. Hetherington, 'A Leicestershire high school: a view from within', *Forum*, vol. 5, no. 1, and 'Unstreamed methods in the "middle school"', ibid., vol. 8, no. 3, both articles on Kibworth High School; Constance Redfearn, 'Programmes and projects in history' (on Bushloe High School), ibid., vol. 11, no. 1; Donald Atkinson, 'An active experiment', ibid., vol. 11, no. 1. See also Dennis Smith, 'Design for a flexible high school', ibid., vol. 9, no. 2, which relates to the new principles of design incorporated into Manor High School, Oadby, which opened in September 1968; and Walter Higgins, 'Blueprint for progress', ibid., vol. 12, no. 2, January 1970, which describes the first year's working of this school.

23. Personal communication from A. W. Reed (headmaster, Belvoir High School, Leicestershire); report by A. J. Simpson (coordinator of studies, first-year base), November 1971.

24. See J. S. Nicholson's article in Elizabeth Halsall (ed.), *Becoming Comprehensive* (1970) for a full description of this building and its potentialities.

25. *Education*, 24 September 1971.

26. DES Surveys, *Launching Middle Schools* 1970.

27. ibid., pp. 6–7.

28. ibid., p. 12.

29. Personal communication from Michael H. Trollope, C.E.O., 30 November 1971.

30. *Towards the Middle School*, DES Pamphlet no. 57 (1970), p. 25.

31. Personal communication, 18 January 1969; on this question the head has since outlined some of the 'fundamental principles' determining the planning of the school's activities. 'First, the school will be entirely unstreamed. . . . If we are to unify the school the divisive effect of streaming would seem to be an odd way to set about it. If we believe in parity of esteem by accepting our children for what they are, then we must give them that parity by not putting them into inferior positions with the

self-fulfilling labels of B, C, D etc.' Elizabeth Halsall (ed.), *Becoming Comprehensive*, 1970, p. 157.

32. Problems of the organization and structure of middle schools are discussed in School Council Working Paper no. 22 entitled *The Middle Years of Schooling* (1968); also in Building Bulletin no. 35: *Middle Schools* (DES, 1966). See also *The Middle School: a Symposium* (NUT, 1967); *Middle Schools* (West Riding Education Committee, 1969); *Middle Schools* (University of Exeter Institute of Education, 1968, report of a conference); Caroline Benn, 'The middle school: which way', *Forum*, vol. 9, no. 3; *Comprehensive Education*, no. 9, Summer 1968 (special number on middle schools); *Forum*, vol. 11, no. 1 (special number on 9–13 years), Autumn 1968; J. Johnson, 'The organization of middle schools', Hertfordshire County Council, 1968; *Launching Middle Schools*, DES Survey 8, 1970; *Towards the Middle School*, DES pamphlet no. 57, 1970.

33. *Towards the Middle School*, p. 61.

34. C. R. P. Luckhurst, 'Southampton's planning for the middle school', *Comprehensive Education*, no. 9, Summer 1968.

35. N. M. Griffiths, 'The first year of middle schools in Southampton', report dated 27 August 1971. Our thanks are due to D. P. J. Browning, CEO Southampton, for allowing us to see this memorandum by the Senior Adviser for Primary Education.

36. Our thanks are due to Michael H. Trollope (CEO Northumberland), to Eric Davies (Leicester University School of Education) and to Jack Johnson (Educational Research and Development Officer, Hertfordshire) – in addition to those already cited – for documents and assistance bearing on middle schools.

37. We are grateful to W. R. Davies and to C. F. O. Howitt for allowing us to see their dissertations on remedial education in comprehensive schools. These are entitled respectively, 'The role of special education in the comprehensive school' (Caerleon College of Education, 1967–8), and 'The ESN child in the comprehensive school – patterns of organization' (Maria Grey College of Education, 1966–7). See also reports of the survey undertaken by O. C. Sampson and P. D. Pumphrey referred to below, and the recent survey by a group of HMIs, *Slow Learners in Secondary Schools*, Education Survey 15, 1971.

38. Results of this survey are reported in O. C. Sampson and P. D. Pumphrey, 'A study of remedial education in the secondary stage of schooling', *Remedial Education*, vol. 5, no. 3/4, October 1970, and in Olive Sampson, 'Children in a world apart', *Special Education*, vol. 60, no. 2, June 1971, from which the quotations in the text are taken.

39. Personal communication from Albert Rowe. See Peter Blacklaws, 'Slow learners in comprehensive schools – inclusion *versus* the special group', *Forum*, vol. 12, no. 1, Spring 1969.

40. This approach is being developed in Fife; William Breslin, 'Curricular development in Fife secondary schools', *Forum*, vol. 14, no. 2, Spring 1972.

41. Professor Herman Bondi, *Education*, 11 February 1966; see also 'Mathematics, the universities and social change', *Universities Quarterly*, September 1966.

42. But see the study by Colin Lacey, 'Some sociological concomitants of academic streaming in a grammar school', *British Journal of Sociology*, vol. 17, no. 3, September 1966, pp. 245–62; this is now reprinted in Colin Lacey, *Hightown Grammar*, 1970.

Chapter 11
14 to 16 Years in the Comprehensive School

Since the first edition of this book was published (in 1970) the government has taken the necessary steps to raise the school-leaving age to sixteen. Provision was made for this in the 1944 Education Act, and the Labour government proposed to implement it in 1970, but then postponed the measure for two years. The direct effect will be felt in the schools first at the beginning of the Summer term, 1973; since those who would previously have left at the end of the Easter term that year will spend an extra year in the schools. The same is true, of course, of the summer leavers that year, so that the full effect of raising the school-leaving age will be felt in the Autumn term, 1973. At this point it is worth making clear that the old system of two leaving dates is unfortunately to be retained.*

Since the latest figures (for 1970) show that approximately 55 per cent of fifteen year olds stay on voluntarily at school, the raising of the leaving age means that the number of fifteen year olds in school will be roughly doubled from the autumn of 1973; an addition of about 300,000 pupils. While this works out at an *average* of sixty pupils per school, the impact of this measure will, of course, be felt differentially; comprehensive schools tend in any case to have a higher voluntary staying on rate than secondary modern schools, and this is particularly the case with 11–18 schools (see Table A.1, p. 522). In many cases the proportion staying is between 60 and 80 per cent, so that the effect of raising the leaving age may quite easily be absorbed by the school (the same is true of 13–18 and 14–18 schools).

The significance of this reform, particularly for comprehensive schools, is, however, immense. It makes possible a full five year course for most (but not all) pupils between the ages of eleven and sixteen, and therefore fundamentally alters a situation which presents comprehensive schools with particular difficulties. These arise from the fact that a comprehensive school, in so far as it is genuinely comprehensive, contains children who were previously either in secondary modern or in grammar schools; and

* Those whose sixteenth birthday falls between 1 September and 31 January (inclusive) may leave at the end of the Easter term; the rest at the end of the Summer term (circular 8/71).

must cater for a much wider range of abilities and aspirations than either type of school under the divided system. In secondary modern schools the great majority of the pupils (75 per cent in 1970) leave at the age of fifteen; in grammar schools, on the other hand, the majority stay till seventeen or eighteen. Since the comprehensive school includes, or should include, all secondary pupils in a given locality, its inner structure must inevitably be more complex than either of its antecedents; especially with the early leaving age of fifteen and an examination structure that reflects the tripartite system. Nevertheless the objectives of comprehensive schools are also different, and this has led to new forms of organization.

It may be as well first to point to the new perspectives that the raising of the school-leaving age opens out for comprehensive schools, in spite of all the difficulties with which we are familiar. To gain full value from this measure, and to make possible the development of a unified secondary course for all from eleven to sixteen, two further steps may be envisaged. First, the fixing of a single leaving date (the end of the summer term), so allowing a full five-year course for all, and not a truncated course for about half the students; and second, the provision of a single system of examinations – or set of objectives – catering for *all* at the age of sixteen, in place of the present three-level system of GCE, CSE and non-examination pupils. This latter is a matter of extreme importance, and one that we return to later in this chapter – it is enough to stress here that these are necessary conditions for overcoming the divisions now forced on the schools by a system of examinations created for quite a different situation than now exists, and so of unifying the comprehensive school in its internal structure.

The need for thinking in terms of the five-year course, or at least in terms of a fundamental 'reconstruction of the curriculum for all pupils between the years from thirteen to sixteen', is stressed by the Schools Council in a recent paper concerned with raising the school-leaving age.[1] This correctly emphasizes that the problem facing schools is not merely that of what to do with the 'extra year'; in the long run, this approach is sterile. If schools reject this standpoint, as many are doing, and if the reforms outlined above can be brought about, the whole existing middle-school pattern in the comprehensive school may be fundamentally altered, especially in relation to the process of pupil differentiation which normally takes place in the third year (at thirteen to fourteen), a process now forced on the schools by the character of existing examinations.

This is a difficult moment to be writing on the fourteen to sixteen years in the comprehensive school, since it is clearly a period of transition. The school-leaving age is about to be raised, but the concomitant reforms are only now the subject for discussion among educationists. Schools are preparing for the change, but they have not yet made it. Because of present constraints, many schools are clearly still thinking in terms of the 'extra year' – of the extension of existing 'leavers' courses', and so on. Indeed, given the present examination system it is difficult to break out of this situation and develop a genuine secondary education for all in the unified school, although, as we shall see, some schools are ingeniously attempting to, and in so doing showing the way forward. An analysis will, therefore, be made of the existing situation – the background from which these changes are being made or planned. From this it is hoped that the way forward in the future will emerge.

In the typical comprehensive school at the moment (1972) just under half the pupils leave shortly after they reach the age of fifteen, just over half stay on. Of the latter group, some will stay for one year (to sixteen), some for a sixth year, and some for a seventh and possibly an eighth. While many schools try to keep all options open, some of the pupils can best be served by the provision of two-year courses leading to GCE O-level or CSE examinations, leaving at sixteen. It is for this reason that the third, or sometimes the fourth-year tends to be the point at which differentiation of pupils, already under way in some schools through such techniques as streaming and setting, becomes actual and recognized in terms of differences in courses and direction. It is this situation that will surely be modified as a result of raising the school-leaving age, though at the start it seems likely that this general pattern may still be maintained.

Early differentiation of this kind is due fundamentally to factors external to the school: specifically to the occupational structure of society at the present stage of technological and socio-economic development – a structure which, in a complex manner, directly affects pupils' aspirations through a web of parental attitudes, local employment opportunities, wage and salary differentials, and higher education requirements. At present the examination system provides the means through which these external requirements are mediated to the schools.

With a leaving age of fifteen it has been the practice in most comprehensive schools to make special provision for 'school leavers'; those who have already decided, in the fourth year, to leave at fifteen. These courses have usually been differentiated from the arrangements made for the rest of the pupils. For this reason these 'leavers' courses' will be dealt with first, since many of them will be continued (though extended) into the new phase. It should be remembered, however, that the raising of the school-leaving age will inevitably transform the situation described. Some of the arrangements made are suitable for extension for another year; others less so. Indeed it could be argued that the whole idea of separate leavers' groups is already obsolete, and certainly it will become so in its present form after 1973.

School leavers

Our inquiry indicates that arrangements for school leavers (at fifteen) fall into three main groups. First, schools in which a specific department is in charge of the courses; second, schools where no special department exists, but where specific courses, taught by the different subject departments, are arranged, sometimes with one member of staff responsible for co-ordination; and third, schools which deliberately do not provide special courses for leavers, but set out to integrate them with the rest of the school. Each of these groups was represented in roughly equal numbers in our smaller sample.

The first group includes some schools which give the responsibility for the school leavers to the 'remedial' department; a matter of convenience, presumably, since, although many 'remedial' (or 'backward') pupils leave at fifteen, all those who do so cannot possibly be classed in this way. Thus, one head writes that for the last three years there has been a separate 'Leavers' Department', but that the post has now been extended to include 'responsibility for remedial work throughout the school'. In one case this responsibility lies with the 'Basic Studies Department' which looks after 'remedial' needs in the first three years, and the 'Newsom area' in the fourth and fifth year. The head of another school writes that the school leavers' department must be 'labelled' by directive of the local authority, and is called the 'modern and remedial' department. All this seems to indicate considerable confusion of thought and practice.

Schools with special departments (whether remedial or not) organize many specific courses for school leavers, often of the Newsom variety – that is, involving some work experience or activities out of school. Most courses are structured to include continued general education as well as a vocational element. A typical example is a course involving forty periods a week of which fifteen are devoted to social studies, two each to mathematics, science and 'careers', four to physical education and games, three to 'leisure' activities (e.g. drama); the remaining twelve periods, based on vocational choice, being spent either on engineering, agriculture, clerical work or home economics. Both the engineering and agriculture courses involve one day a week at the local technical college. 'The course', writes the head, 'is inspired by some of the recommendations of the Newsom report, and is regarded as a bridge between three years of secondary schooling and x years at work.' At another 11–18 school with a 'Newsom Department', the pupils are grouped into mixed-ability forms for the basic school subjects, taught by masters 'specially chosen for this task'; half the timetable is made up from a series of options, 'usually of a practical nature', including technical studies, motor engineering, catering and gardening.

Integrated social studies courses, sometimes with a 'community orientated curriculum' involving team teaching, genuine option choices, outside experience and visits, feature in several of the replies from schools. The deputy head of a Sheffield comprehensive writes of the 'short courses' offered to leavers:

These are largely practical in character, and contain some of the most interesting and forward-looking developments in the school, including the team-teaching of 'General Studies' which includes English, religious education, and social, geographical and historical subjects.[2]

In another large 11–18 school with a Department of General Studies which is in charge of courses for leavers, the head writes that:

The timetable comprises twenty general-studies periods plus twenty option periods – the latter, where possible, of a vocational nature (e.g. typing, building). The general course, meant to fit pupils for life in the wider community, is team-taught and usually based on a theme which changes every third week. There is great emphasis on community service and the school has a community service volunteer attached. He, in conjunction with the General Studies Department, organizes the rota to enable all these pupils to spend some time on community service – e.g. helping old-age pensioners with gardens, shopping, decorating, etc.

In view of the discussion of the comprehensive school as a 'community school', this direction of work is interesting.

In Scotland also, 'Brunton'-type courses are provided for school leavers and others in comprehensive schools. The late head of Glenwood School, Glasgow, for instance, stresses their wide development and success; 'pupils are pleased with a scheme whereby they are placed in a situation in works or shops where they can see the relationship between what happens in school and in the world outside'.[3] R. F. Mackenzie, now head of a comprehensive school in Aberdeen, has, however, expressed sharp criticism of a 'paper-mill' course the local authority suggested he conduct, as being altogether too limited in scope and outlook.[4]

The second main grouping consists of schools with no special department, but where the teaching of the school leavers is done by the staff as a whole. This method, which is sometimes controlled by a coordinator responsible for planning, may still result in specific courses for leavers. In one case, for instance, blocked periods are devoted to such activities as 'community service', 'school service' or 'project work'. Another school, without a special department, is designing a course including elements of community service and work experience for young leavers. At another school, leavers take a local leaving examination, each department making its own arrangements for teaching the pupils, though three members of staff have the responsibility of designing suitable courses. 'There is collaboration by several departments in a course along "Newsom" lines for fourth-year pupils – not all of whom leave at fifteen', writes another head . . . . 'This can be followed in the fifth year by a Mode III CSE in social studies.'

The third main grouping consists of schools which deliberately make no differentiation between 'school leavers' and other pupils. The rationale behind this system has been expressed recently by Kenneth Macrae, lately head of a Glasgow comprehensive school, who pointed out that one of the *main concerns* in devising school curricula must be to reduce the number of young school leavers; it is, therefore, 'dangerous to differentiate between courses for those staying on at school and those intending to leave at the earliest possible date'. Instead, curricula should be devised for the whole school, catering as far as possible for the interests and characteristics of each pupil 'without committing him to leave at a particular stage'.[5]

It is clear from the answers we received from our smaller sample that many heads agree with this point of view and feel that the segregation of pupils implied by the organization of specific 'terminal' courses is not justified within the comprehensive school. At a London girls' school, for instance, where a basic core of subjects is taken by *all* fourth-year pupils together with a number of options chosen by the pupils, the head replies that they have no special leavers' courses. The system at this school mixes together pupils from every group (or 'level'), whether they wish to stay on or not, and provides each with a viable course which aims to meet the particular interests of each girl. One result, it is reported, is that more pupils stay on to the end of the fourth year than would otherwise be the case, while some pupils, who originally intended to leave at the end of the year, are encouraged to stay on to the fifth year.[6] The head of another 11–18 school writes that there is no specific leavers' course in his school: 'Every timetable in the fourth year is an individual one.'

An inquiry made in the autumn of 1971 among a sample of twelve schools from our original smaller sample indicates that several are thinking along these lines, in preparation for the raising of the leaving age. The head of a Bristol comprehensive (11–18), for instance, stresses that there are no separate courses for leavers; only a basic course for all with a variety of options. School leavers are integrated into the main stream of academic organization of the school (the school is unstreamed for the first three years). Another head writes that 'leavers' courses as such have been abandoned' so that the structure planned for the leaving age of sixteen is already there; 'all pupils are integrated into the main stream' of studies – there are no 'courses' as such, but a free choice of subjects within the children's capabilities. At another school in a market town, where some 80 per cent of fifteen year olds already stay on, all courses are already planned to last two years (14–16); the school has been preparing for this change for some years, and pilot schemes tried out and modified. The objectives are to provide similar opportunities to all pupils – all courses contain a common element and a choice element. An 11–16 school head writes that the fourth year is already treated as a single entity and no distinction made between leavers and those wishing to complete the fifth year. Other examples could be cited; but these indicate the trend towards unification.

With the raising of the school-leaving age many of the truncated 'terminal' courses will no longer be viable or relevant, and there is bound to be a move towards integration along the lines cited above. Such a move should reduce the very difficult behaviour problems some comprehensive schools face at present which are certainly reinforced by the segregation of pupils into specific courses, as research has shown. It is the general experience in both primary and secondary schools that the reduction of streaming (and leavers' courses are a form of streaming) enables pupils who would have been placed in low streams to identify more closely with the school's objectives.[7]

The fifth year

The academic structure of the fourth and fifth years in comprehensive schools is often extremely complex, both in 11–18 schools and in 11–16, 13–18 and 14–18 schools. With a leaving age of sixteen it should be possible to simplify it, although it may be some years before the full potential is realized. We can assume that the large majority of pupils will, at first, leave at sixteen; some without any qualifications whatever in the form of examination results or a certificate of some kind, some having taken GCE O-level in a number of subjects, some with CSE, and many with a mixture of both. A proportion will continue into the sixth year (16–17) with the aim of extending their general education, preparing for A-level GCE examinations, and/or taking or retaking GCE O-level or CSE examinations. Some of these will leave after one year in the sixth, some after two, and a few after three years. Some of these pupils will go on to higher education, others straight out to work. The academic organization of the school must cater for the varying needs of these different groups of pupils in a dynamic situation in which the aims, aspirations, and indeed the abilities of pupils change and develop.

Our inquiry indicates that comprehensive schools today are in a state of transition in the provision they make for these age groups. There is now a clear tendency to move from a system of precisely defined courses, often having partially vocational objectives and usually graded according to the 'ability' of the pupils, towards a more flexible structure allowing (within certain limits) a high degree of individualization of programmes through the use of electives or options. This reduces sharp differentiation according to predetermined decisions, and aims specifically at keeping further educational possibilities open as long as possible. This development is in line with the 'comprehensive' nature of these schools.

At fourteen (or sometimes thirteen), the common course gives way to a new structure which invovles the guidance of pupils towards choice of a particular course or grouping of subjects. Whatever the system used, the choice made determines the character of the pupil's education in the coming period. It is therefore largely decisive in terms of career prospects, so that this point of differentiation is of key significance. This is widely recognized in comprehensive schools which have to cater for a cross-section of the entire age group, and have, therefore, responsibility for guiding pupils across the whole range of employment possibilities – a situation that no previous type of school has had to face. Educational guidance assumes a new importance in the comprehensive school.

How are pupils assisted in making their choice of courses? The replies to this question, specifically asked from our smaller sample, together with the documents prepared for pupils and their parents to explain the system which were sent us by many heads, made it clear that this function is normally taken extremely seriously.

The general approach can be described quite briefly. Most 11–18 schools adopt some variant of a system which includes explanation of the choices available both to pupils and parents, discussion between pupils, parents, and the responsible staff members involving youth employment officers where appropriate. The process of choice-making often takes four or five months during the third year, choices being finalized by the end of the year in most cases.

We may take two examples from 11–18 comprehensive schools – the first in Bristol. Here the 'middle-school' options are explained to pupils in February of the third year. At this first stage the pupils state their preferences. In March, writes the head, these options are analysed. 'Do they fit the usual pattern?' If not, can this be changed to meet pupils' preferences? (This may be prevented by staffing and accommodation difficulties.) At this point the senior master invites comments from heads of departments as to the suitability of the choices made. In April, the third stage, consultation takes place with the parents; this is arranged at a meeting of parents of third-year pupils, but permits many individual interviews. In June the final decisions are made and communicated to the pupils.

The head of the second school (in Oxfordshire) describes a six-stage process lasting from February to May in the third year. In February the year tutor explains to the pupils what choices will be open to them. This is followed by talks from careers masters, youth employment officers, career advisory officers, relating choices to career prospects. A letter is then sent to parents outlining the choices, and a parents' evening held to discuss the child's development: his reports, progress and the choices to be made. This is followed by individual interviews held by the heads of schools, careers master and year tutor with parents and children who require further assistance. The choice sheets are then returned and any outstanding problems resolved.

Many similar examples could be given, varying only in details. Some stress that the material on the options is available in written form (in duplicated documents or booklets) both to pupils and parents. Others, that all pupils and parents have an interview with the teacher responsible (for instance, the third-year teacher and/or deputy head) to determine options. One school stresses that the pupil's direction is decided as a result of two years' diagnostic work, as well as discussions with pupils and parents. In schools with a house system this guidance is sometimes a function of the house staff; where the school is organized on a year system it may be the function of the year teacher and attached staff. In some schools the process of guidance is linked with careers advice and lessons throughout the period of choice (February to July). In others, particular teachers act as careers advisers and play a special part in the process; a more recent development is the employment of school counsellors who include careers advice and guidance as one of their functions. In general, heads made it clear that the pupil's choice is the main item to be considered, although choices may be modified by guidance – some heads said that the final decision is the school's (one writing that 'the school has the last word but never needs to say it!').[8]

In Leicestershire-type upper schools (14–18) transfer takes place at fourteen (the end of the third year), so that the choices have to be made when the pupil is still at the high school (11–14). A Leicestershire upper school we visited described the process, which involves talks to parents in the feeder high schools in the third year to explain the structure of the upper school's organization, the distribution of duplicated material to all pupils describing what the school can offer and asking for choices, together with guidance material. The teachers in the high schools play an important role in aiding the pupils' choices, and three weeks are allotted to the process in the Easter term. The upper school attempts to be as flexible as possible in meeting pupil requirements and, since it has been growing by some eighty pupils a year over the last few years, the additional staff recruited each year have increased the variety of offerings. Staff recruitment is therefore functionally linked with pupils' study preferences.

Whatever the variation in method, by the end of the fourth year at the latest pupils have chosen the various courses or options that the school offers. We may now examine the curriculum arrangements in more detail.

Curriculum arrangements: courses, options and required subjects

The response to question 24 in our survey indicates the variety of methods used in arranging the curriculum in comprehensive schools. Only the total figures for all schools in the survey are given in Table 11.1, the breakdown by type of school, and for England and Wales, and Scotland, separately, may be found in Appendix 2 (Tables A.12, A.13, and A.14, pp. 535–7).*

Table 11.1 **Curriculum arrangements in comprehensive schools with 13/14 to 15/16 age group, England, Wales and Scotland, 1968***

Curriculum arrangements	Total	Percentage
1 Required subjects plus options	420	68·5
2 Complete course choices	84	13·5
3 Free choice from option groups	53	8·5
4 Other systems (or combinations of above)	48	8
5 Unknown	8	1·5
Total	613	100

* Five 11–13 schools which answered this question (perhaps because they were still 'fading out' their older pupils) and three schools which could not be identified by type are omitted.

In this table, 'complete course choices' indicates a structure comprising clearly differentiated courses (e.g. commercial, general, academic/GCE/ CSE, pre-nursing, etc.), while the first and third categories indicate systems based more on the principle of individualization of programmes.

* These tables may be compared with a similar analysis made by the NFER: see *Comprehensive Education in England and Wales*, pp. 123–4.

An example of the first category (given in the survey as a guide) would be a system where mathematics and English are required of all pupils, but another five subject options are chosen from five groups of subjects. The third category carries the principle of individualization furthest, since it requires no specific subjects to be studied.

The striking feature of this table is certainly the very high proportion of schools falling into the first category, as well as the sizeable group based on completely free choice of subjects in a number of different option groups. This is certainly a recent phenomenon; it was, however, already becoming noticeable during the last few years. The ILEA 1966 Survey specifically stressed the need for a sophisticated form of organization involving diversity and flexibility in order both to meet the varying needs of pupils and to enable schools to react quickly to new situations and demands. Examples were given of schools which had evolved from a form or 'course' system towards greater flexibility and pupil choice of options.[9] The IAAM Report of 1967 reflects the same trend.

An important factor promoting flexibility of structure has certainly been the establishment of the Certificate of Secondary Education. The new possibilities this examination has opened up have greatly altered the situation in comprehensive schools; indeed, its full impact on internal academic structuring has certainly not yet been felt. Although originally designed for pupils of 'moderate' intellectual ability, it is now clear that the examining techniques it permits are equally appropriate for advanced pupils; recognition of a grade 1 pass in CSE as equivalent to a GCE pass has made it possible for schools to substitute this examination for the more rigid GCE examinations. CSE examinations can be specially designed to reinforce the objectives of particular courses; project work and other forms of course work can be taken into account in assessment, and, under Mode III, the examination can be adapted to the work done in a particular school or group of local schools. This built-in flexibility, under the control of the teachers themselves, means that course subject matter need not get ossified, as has certainly happened in the case of GCE both in science and other subjects, preventing innovation and putting a premium on memory and rote learning. There is no doubt that the CSE type of examination offers new opportunities to the schools, and that the techniques which may be used (provided the teachers take the initiative)* are well adapted to pupils of all levels of achievement, including the most advanced.

A specific question in our survey (question 26) revealed that the vast majority of comprehensive schools in England and Wales which include

* Recent statistics show that Mode III entries to CSE constitute as yet only about 14 per cent of the total. DES *Statistics of Education*, 1969, vol. 2, p. 77.

pupils between the ages of thirteen and sixteen sit pupils for CSE: 543 out of 551.* By providing an attainable examination objective to many more pupils than before, the CSE has made it possible to overcome the distinction in the fifth year, in comprehensive schools, between examination forms and forms taking no examination. The IAAM Report, in pointing this out, adds that its introduction has pushed away overclouding expressions like 'failure' and brought success 'within the reach of almost all'. The experience is that some pupils discover their ability only in the process of working for the examination itself. Not only has this examination reduced the number of early leavers but 'there will be more boys and girls, delightedly surprised to find how capable or competent they are, who ask to stay on for a sixth-form course'.[10] In one of the schools we visited – Brislington, Bristol – *all* pupils staying on for the fifth year work towards some examination, even if only in one CSE subject.

The continued existence of two parallel school examinations, however, creates its own difficulties, especially in comprehensive schools.† How are decisions to be made as to whether a particular pupil sits for one or the other? It is partly to meet this difficulty, and to provide a variety of alternatives, that a flexible structure in the middle school is now encouraged. Indications of the move away from rigid forms of differentiation were given in answers from schools in our smaller sample as to whether different sets of options were available to the higher- and lower-ability groups in comprehensive schools.

A number of heads confirmed that this was the case, pointing out that some pupils take public examinations, others do not; others pointed out that ability differences are reflected in course differences – some pupils take GCE, others CSE, some take Latin and other languages, others not. In some cases 'high-ability' pupils have a wider choice of academic subjects. Another group of schools, taking up a middle position, said that in general there are no differences in options between higher- and lower-ability groups, but that there are exceptions – again especially for languages and to some extent for science and mathematics.

A third group, however, claimed that there were no differences in the options available – all the options are available to all. Thus in one case the head pointed out that, although options are available at different levels, the choice of an academic option in one field 'does not entail acceptance of academic options in other fields', while the converse also

---

* With a further eight 'unknowns'.

† Examination candidates are fairly evenly split between the two examinations in comprehensive schools; in the 1969 summer examination, 38,987 candidates sat for GCE O-level, 42,949 sat for both CSE and O-level, and 29,570 sat CSE alone. DES *Statistics of Education*, 1969, vol. 2, p. 73.

holds true. Another head writes that no differences are made 'but individual children may be advised against choices too demanding or not demanding enough for their abilities'; another school without differences in the option system writes that 'all children receive guidance according to their aptitudes', adding that 'it is usual for clusters to form; but no individual is denied a programme because it is for the more able or for the less able'. In one case the head writes that there are no differences in the options provided; to arrange things in this way would be 'contrary to the principle of the school'.

The ILEA 1966 Survey lists four main types of five-year courses provided in London comprehensive schools; these are defined as (i) academic studies, (ii) commercial studies, (iii) technical studies and (iv) 'Newsom courses'. The large 11–18 comprehensive school is, of course, equipped and staffed to offer a wide range of courses and, in some cases, the internal structure of the middle school still reflects the older concept of multilateralism. Within each of these broad areas, however, a considerable variety of provision can be made – the technical area, for instance, sometimes covering a variety of directions, e.g. engineering, building, retail distribution, catering, horticulture, dressmaking, millinery and pre-nursing courses for girls. Some London comprehensives now also have an 'academic and technical' course, designed for pupils who have higher education, particularly engineering, in mind.

The Newsom courses are often related to occupational interests but also contain elements of the other three areas. The authors of the ILEA Survey recognize that the description presented can give the impression of a multilateral set-up, 'with pupils hived off into one course or another and following separated programmes', but claim that most schools avoid this, partly by using techniques described below.*[11]

Our survey indicates that the system of offering choices of complete courses is followed by only 14 per cent of the schools covering this age range (eighty-four schools), another 3 per cent (twenty schools) combining complete course offerings with an element of options.† An example of a school organized on a complete course system is provided in our smaller sample by an 11–16 school working in three buildings; one of these is designated for 'academic' studies, one for technical (mainly boys), and the third for 'commercial and business' studies (mainly girls). Pupils are placed on entry in what is considered the appropriate building, and although transfer at fourteen is possible, it is not encouraged. Another example is given by a large 11–18 comprehensive school in Wales which

---

* We found pupils in London comprehensives, however, very much aware of their separation into distinct courses at fourteen.

† See Table A.12, p. 535. The percentage is lower in Scotland (Table A.14, p. 537).

makes eight divisions in terms of courses; these include a four-year O-level course for thirty pupils (6 per cent of the age group), five-year O-level courses for 120 pupils (27 per cent of the age group) – these overlap with CSE courses and include technical subjects, domestic science, etc.; five-year CSE courses for 120 pupils (which in turn overlap with GCE); two special technical courses involving O-level, CSE and RSA for fifty pupils, or 12 per cent of the age group; general technical courses for fifty pupils (12 per cent); commercial courses involving different ability groups for sixty pupils (14 per cent); and finally special courses 'for pupils of low ability' for forty pupils (8 per cent). The head points out that the structure is complex and that a study of the complete timetable would be necessary to produce a fair picture of the position, but it is clear that course structure determines the nature of middle-school organization.

Some schools combine a system of complete course choices with options, as the school already described does to some extent. A Gloucestershire 11–18 school working on two sites until recently grouped all O-level work together in one of these because of the specialist facilities available. In September 1969, however, the school reorganized into a junior and senior group each in its own building, so that fourth-year options are now open to all 'and a cross-section of all courses can be taken instead of opting for a course'; there are five courses available. Other schools combining courses with options organize specific leavers' or 'Newsom' courses and arrange the rest of the school in terms of O-level 'courses' (with four- and five-year courses) and a separate CSE course, within which a number of options are offered.

In general, from the material received from schools, it seems that a course structure with broad divisions persists in some schools, although a variety of methods are being used to soften the divisions between courses and arrange a more flexible structure.

The survey shows clearly that the great majority of comprehensive schools of all types have moved over to a system of middle-school organization involving a very free choice of options by the pupils together with a core of required subjects – a total of 420 of the 613 schools categorized in Table 11.1 indicating this method. A breakdown makes it clear that this is the preferred system in all relevant types of school, whether 11–18, 11–16, 13–18 or 14–18 (see Table A.12, p. 535). In some cases, as we have seen, the options available to the more advanced pupils differ from those available to the lower groups, but in others they do not.

We may give one example out of many to make the system clear, in this case of a school in a large northern industrial city which makes no basic differentiation between the pupils at this stage, although where subjects are offered at both GCE and CSE level the pupils are placed in the relevant groups by the staff 'on the basis of previous work'. In this case each pupil takes English, mathematics, religious education, 'careers' and physical education – these are the required basic core for all. Subjects are then arranged in five 'pools', being offered in some cases only at O-level GCE, in others only at CSE-level, and in many cases at both levels. The pools from which choices are made are listed in Table 11.2.

Examination of the composition of the pools will indicate that subjects 'lost' in one pool because of a preferential choice may be picked up in another pool. Clearly the number of possible permutations is enormous, allowing, so far as staff and accommodation conditions permit, a very high degree of individualization.

There are a number of variations on this system. The core subjects, which are compulsory, may either be basic subjects such as English and mathematics (as in the case given), or they may be subjects which, grouped together, form the essential ingredients of a given course; to that extent the option system merges into the course system already described. At a London school, for instance, six courses with different biases are arranged (literary, science, engineering, commercial, art and general), each of which contains relevant required subjects around which the pupils add their own choice from optional subjects – these provide both for pupils preparing for GCE and for CSE.

Another variant broadens the extent of required subjects – that is, provision is made to ensure a balanced choice of options so that a viable educational course emerges. One head, for instance, writes that all those who stay on beyond the fourth year must take English, mathematics, religious instruction and physical education, while the majority also do French. 'The choices look wide', he adds, 'but in fact everyone must choose one (in some cases two) "practical" subject, must choose history and/or geography (or social studies), must choose at least one science.' The rest of the subjects may be freely chosen and taken at O-level GCE or CSE level, or 'need not be studied with an examination objective at all'. In other words, 'a large number of permutations is possible'. Mayfield School, London, has recently moved to a pattern giving fifteen periods to the basic core, twenty to electives (the standard practice now in Swedish comprehensive schools). A variation of this is the system in a Liverpool comprehensive where the week of forty periods is divided half to required subjects (six mathematics, six English, two physical education, one music, one religious education, two games and three complementary subjects – a system of balancing unbalanced choices) and half to options, five of which are chosen, each of which is allotted four periods. Pupils can make any choice they wish. At a Staffordshire school the provision of

Table 11.2 Subject pools for options in the fifth year in a large 11–18 comprehensive school*

1		2		3		4		5	
18 French	o/c	23 History	o/c	23 Geography	o/c	30 Chemistry	o/c	20 Physics	o/c
8 Spanish	c	4 Typing	c	9 Chemistry	o/c	15 Physics	o/c	35 Biology	o/c
37 History	o/c	8 Technical drawing	o/c	11 Biology	c	11 General science	c	14 General science	c
37 Geography	o/c	8 Metal work	c	8 Typing	c	4 Economics	c	14 Art	o/c
		8 Engineering	c	6 Scripture	c	15 Social studies	c	9 Typing	c
		24 Domestic science	o/c	14 Art	o/c	9 Music	c	8 Accounts	c
		10 Needlework	o/c	14 Technical drawing	o/c	9 Typing	c		
		7 Catering	c	7 Domestic science	c	7 Accounts	c		
		8 Woodwork	o/c	8 Engineering	o				

The figures give a rough indication of the percentage of pupils choosing the subject in each column in a typical year.

o = GCE groups. c = CSE groups.

* These optional subject pools do not, of course, include the required subjects which all pupils must study (English, mathematics, religious education, 'careers', physical education).

six option groups in the fourth year is structured to provide some twenty courses, combining both general and vocational subjects – within these options some pupils prepare for GCE, some for CSE.

When it comes to the part required/part optional pattern that most comprehensive schools have been building up in the 14–16 years, the subjects 'required' are naturally of great importance. They differ markedly between schools. Although English and mathematics are the base of most schools' requirements, the additional subjects often differ greatly. In some schools French (or another language) is required as well; in others it is a science subject. The difference between a language or a science as the standard discipline required for all pupils in this age range is important and of obvious significance for the pupil's future. This is a subject that needs careful study and one that is of wider, national interest.

Only a few schools – fifty-three in all (9 per cent of the total) – claimed that their curriculum structure for the fourth and fifth year involved a complete free-choice system based on option groups, though the proportion indicating this system was higher in Scotland than in England and Wales. The school which comes nearest to this in our smaller sample is a Cornwall upper school (developed from a grammar school) which, in 1968, began its transition to an 11–18 comprehensive school. Even here, however, English and mathematics are required subjects for all pupils; it seems probable that a number of schools which placed themselves in this category do in fact make some compulsory requirement, even if the overall system is a free-choice system.

Some aspects of the method used in this school may be described, since it represents a variant on that already given. Each pupil is assigned to one of six mixed-ability forms in the fourth year. These are not teaching groups, but 'convenient units for registration and pastoral care', i.e. they have primarily a social function; each form is a unit in one of the three houses which make up the school. Each pupil builds up an individual timetable consisting of five periods each of mathematics and English and five options (a maximum of thirty-five periods). Each pupil has five periods in which he works on his own. The option groupings in 1968–9 are given in Appendix 3 (p. 568) together with the (estimated) number of pupils attending each.

The headmaster, who supports the concept of non-streaming, points out that this system allows heads of departments to set their pupils (if there are enough) or to teach them in mixed-ability groups if they so choose. In 1967–8 setting was used in the science subjects and French, each of which was offered at both GCE and CSE level. Some subjects – for instance, Latin and German, which are not started until the fourth year – do not have sufficient pupils to allow for differentiation, and are reserved at this school for GCE candidates. In history, geography and metalwork, however, the forms were arranged on a mixed-ability basis, preparing for both examinations – this is in line with the tendency to find means of putting off the moment of decision as to which examination will be sat as long as possible; the GCE is still regarded by many as the most rewarding examination in terms of career prospects, and it is a growing experience that pupils may develop unexpectedly during this year.

This structure, which stands in sharp contrast to the more rigid course systems of the past, aims to enhance motivation and the pupil's sense of 'involvement', allowing for unusual combinations not previously regarded as practical. 'Since we became comprehensive', writes the head, 'and introduced a completely flexible series of options ... I think no two pupils of the 144 in Form IV have exactly the same timetable.'[12]

Examinations

Heads of schools in our smaller sample were asked to make some assessment of their examination achievements in the middle school. The relevant question asked for information about GCE O-level examination policy and performance, and for comments on this subject.

Most schools replied to this but in varying ways – the actual figures given cannot have any general significance. For one thing, the percentage of passes in either GCE or CSE examinations will be affected by the school's policy as to entry, as was pointed out in some replies: 'I refuse to produce percentages even for the governors', wrote the head of a large school,

In this way I safeguard the staff who on my request may have put too many candidates, for what we think good reasons, in for, say, the O-level examination. If the school is to be judged on percentages then it is quite easy to make this 100 per cent passes, by restricting entry. Many borderline pupils would suffer and the whole policy of the school would change.

A similar point was made by other heads.

Another complication arises from the fact that comprehensive schools enter the same pupils for some subjects in GCE and for others in CSE – as a deliberate policy to achieve courses adapted to individual pupils' needs. As a result overall comparisons are difficult to make.*

Some heads, however, gave useful information or comments in reply to

* One 11–18 school gives the following information which makes the complexity of the situation clear: 'This year, of 168 examinees, only six were entered *only* in GCE; sixty-five only in CSE; ninety-seven had mixed entries. The maximum number of GCE entries for one pupil was eight. Only thirty-four were entered in five or more GCE subjects, but 102 were entered in five or more CSE subjects. The average GCE entry was for 3·73 subjects (103 pupils); the average CSE entry was for 4·84 (162 pupils). The average *total* entry was for 6·95 subjects (168 pupils).'

this question.* Developing schools whose 'comprehensive' intake had not yet reached the fifth year reported success with 11-plus failures; in one case 10 per cent of these obtained four or more O-level passes at one sitting, while in another 'approximately 10 per cent of the secondary modern intake' achieved five or more passes in GCE. Schools whose comprehensive intake had reached the fifth year tended to report encouragingly on their results: 'There is no doubt that the school's academic record has improved enormously over the last five years', writes the head of an 11–18 school after saying that 20 to 25 per cent of those entered for GCE gain five or more passes (thirty to forty out of 150 pupils), 'particularly gratifying is the number taking CSE and achieving good grades.' The head of a grammar school which has become a comprehensive upper school reports that 'the figures are no worse than when we were a grammar school', adding that 'many of the ex-secondary modern pupils do better than the selected 11-plus children'. An interesting point is brought out by the head of another upper school which developed from a grammar school. Reporting that 22 per cent of his first 'comprehensive' fifth year gained five or more O-level passes (or grade 1 CSE), he adds: 'the evidence for this one year shows that the children who originally passed the 11-plus (and who were later joined by those who failed) did better than their predecessors in the grammar school'.

Differences in the quality of the intake, or in the socio-economic characteristics of the catchment area of the school, naturally affect pass rates in external examinations – another reason why small-scale comparisons are invidious. Thus, a large comprehensive school in a working-class housing estate in Wales reports that, of an original year's intake of 340 pupils, eighty-two sat GCE (24 per cent); of these forty passed in five or more subjects (11 per cent). A long-established 11–18 comprehensive school near London, however, with a 25 per cent selective entry, has achieved an average of 40 per cent gaining five or more O-levels over the last twelve years, 'Proof positive (were it needed)' writes the head, 'of the efficacy of the comprehensive school ethos as far as "examination success" is concerned.' A Scottish school writes in a similar vein: this was a junior secondary school now developing as comprehensive, which reports that the O-grade results have been 'first-class' – 20 per cent of school leavers gaining O-grades in five or more subjects. 'Remember', writes the head, that as a junior secondary school, 'we presented pupils who were previously denied the opportunity of staying on at school.' Another Scottish comprehensive reported 30 per cent gaining five or more O-grades, and another 76 per cent. The variations in percentage are probably due partly to differences in policy as to entry.

* It must be remembered that all the figures in this section refer to 1968.

One school (11–16) replied to this question by saying that no pupils gained five or more O-level passes because 'CSE is the school examination at present for *all* fifth-year pupils, most of whom take from six to eight subjects', O-level entries being restricted to pupils 'whose parents wish them to enter where certain qualifications are needed for their prospective careers'. This raises sharply a problem already referred to: the existence of two parallel and indeed overlapping examinations for pupils of the same age group.

We saw earlier that almost every comprehensive school in our survey entered pupils for CSE. A further question (26A) asked whether there were 'any subjects in which *all* pupils hoping to sit for an external examination in these subjects now (or will from the next school year onwards) sit for the CSE examination rather than the GCE?' Of the 521 schools replying to this, 38 per cent – a total of 199 schools – replied in the affirmative, a very considerable number. The proportion of these schools which have moved over entirely to CSE in 1968 in different subjects is given in Appendix 3 (p. 567). The table shows that subjects for which fifty or more schools in our survey now enter pupils only for CSE include basic subjects like English, geography, mathematics, as well as practical or vocational subjects like domestic science, woodwork, technical drawing, metalwork, typing and commercial subjects, and needlework. In addition, music, which has the highest percentage of these schools (42 per cent) and art (33 per cent) figure among those where the swing to CSE is greatest.

We probed the opinions of heads in our smaller sample about external examinations generally, as also on the question of the two examinations. Heads were asked whether they had 'any views about external examinations and their place in the comprehensive school? (e.g. whether CSE should replace GCE in some subjects?)'. One rightly pointed out that this was a leading question; but it certainly revealed a strength of feeling beyond that released by any other question, together with many interesting comments and proposals for the future.

The strongest views were expressed by seventeen heads who stressed the need to replace the two examinations by one; in most cases CSE was favoured, very often 'Mode III' which allows schools to develop their own syllabuses and carry through their own assessment, though the procedures used are subject to external moderation. A sample of these is given:

'The CSE/GCE position is gradually becoming intolerable.' 'I look forward to the day when CSE (preferably Mode III) will replace GCE O-level.' 'The two O-type examinations is one too many – either GCE O-level should go or CSE should. I would prefer to retain CSE.' 'GCE O-level and CSE should merge.' 'CSE for all.' 'CSE should completely replace GCE at O standard.' 'CSE should replace O-level in all subjects in the comprehensive school.' 'Scrap O-level!' 'They are a menace. The existence of two examinations designed for pupils of different ability is a major stumbling block. O-level and CSE should both be replaced by a new internally assessed, externally moderated exam (based on Mode III CSE methods)' – a point made by other heads as well.

This strong demand certainly represents the majority view of respondents. But some heads saw some point in retaining GCE, at least for the time being. One reason given was the need to establish the 'image' of the comprehensive school: 'It is vitally necessary to secure results in external exams, comparable with those the pupils would have gained in grammar schools'; a few other heads seemed satisfied with the present position: 'I cannot really see that CSE need necessarily keep out GCE or vice versa. Use both, and use them correctly for their true purpose.' 'I prefer to retain both GCE and CSE', writes another head. But several, while wishing to retain GCE for the time being, prefer the CSE examination: 'Syllabuses are more interesting.' There is 'greater flexibility in devising integrated syllabuses'; the examination is 'very valuable with children of average academic ability'; but the GCE should continue for the academically able until entrance requirements to higher education and the professions 'become more flexible in their admission arrangements'. Others, while wishing to retain GCE, stress that this examination should use the new techniques being developed by CSE (use of course work, new forms of assessment, etc.); yet others propose that GCE be abolished and that CSE develop a 'superstructure', that is, an optional element 'such that candidates who wished to demonstrate higher ability could do so'. Proposals are also made for the development of an A-level CSE examination, an idea which is now gaining wide support, particularly among the CSE Regional Examination Boards.

As to the place of examinations as a whole in the comprehensive school, most heads suggest that these are needed while wishing to move over to the CSE type of examination as being better adapted to new approaches in education and to the requirements of individual schools and even (with Mode III) of individual pupils. One head typically writes that he thinks much less about examinations

than the whole ethos of the school. If examinations are necessary to qualify for certain basic training, then take them. *But* the school must adopt the attitude that all children are individuals and therefore different, so the development of personality is just as important as that of skill. If a school is large enough to run CSE and O-level courses (he adds), this must be done. In general, for many children, the CSE approach is better than the GCE O-level.

Some heads who wish to retain GCE hope that it may change: 'It seems to me that the spirit of the CSE is already permeating GCE to the latter's great advantage', writes one head. While recognizing the necessity for some form of assessment of pupils, many heads clearly wish to reduce the dominance particularly of external examinations of the old type. 'I feel that CSE should replace O-level in all subjects in the comprehensive school', writes one head. 'I feel, too, that pupils should take the minimum number of examinations possible.'

New developments

We have already indicated that some schools, in an attempt to provide an objective suitable for the majority of their pupils and avoid the necessity for differentiation in the middle years, have moved over entirely to the CSE examination in a number of subjects. There is little doubt that this movement is gaining momentum. An interesting example is the Desford upper school, Leicestershire, where the forward planning has been recorded by the staff in *School for the Community* (1971). The staff committee concerned with planning for the fourth and fifth years (and teaching in the grammar school that was to be transformed into a comprehensive upper school) 'quite early in its deliberations . . . unanimously rejected streaming' – several departments wanted a situation where teaching could be in mixed-ability groups, whether the objective for individual pupils was GCE or CSE; in any case the aim was to avoid a situation that would lead to 'a disguised 14-plus' in the school. The conclusion was that there should be a common core of studies for all pupils, together with a flexible system of options; departments were to be left free to use setting or non-streaming as they wished. Several decided on the latter – for instance, the English department decided at the outset that 'we didn't want any form of streaming and we wanted to reduce examinations to a minimum'. In particular they wished to avoid the GCE O-level in English literature which 'seems almost to be designed to stifle the enthusiasm of teacher and pupil alike'; 'accordingly we banished it; . . . having made that decision, we had removed a major obstacle to the proper working of the mixed-ability group'. As a result an entirely new syllabus was worked out as a Mode III CSE, to be continuously assessed by the teachers themselves. While this may be more easily achieved in certain subjects, other departments in the school are following the same course, and all are concerned to find the means of reducing differentiation to a minimum.[13]

Other schools are seeking similar solutions, given the present examinations set-up; for instance Countesthorpe College, another Leicestershire upper school, is seeking the means by which all pupils can be retained together in the same learning situation throughout these years. Ingenious methods are being tried out to overcome present divisive forces. An example in this case is the design of a new social studies GCE course, in line with the school's overall objectives, which has been worked out by the school and accommodated to the social-studies examination offered by one of the GCE examination boards. At the same time a Mode III CSE syllabus has been developed which focuses on similar topics, and which will be internally assessed (with external moderation). Non-examination students can be comprised within this structure, since the topics themselves are those which these students in any case should study. Given this situation, together with the use of the resources approach to learning for which this school is well known,[14] involving small group and individual work in addition to some full class or year activities (films, dramatic presentations, and so on), it is possible to keep all students and groups together, even if the examination objectives differ. This is more particularly the case where teachers (including remedial teachers) work as a team all of whom cooperate together in the different teaching/learning areas at the appropriate times. This kind of structure embodies an approach that should become easier to establish in the near future, given the raising of the school-leaving age and the examination changes referred to below. Similar approaches for instance for the integrated humanities course at Rossington school, Doncaster, which leads to three CSE Mode III examinations across a wide area of studies – allow for great flexibility of study by individuals and groups while retaining a common objective for all students.

Hedley Wood School, Brentwood, an 11–18 comprehensive, moved over to non-streaming in 1965 in preparation for just such a unification of the internal structure of the school. Experimenting first with interdisciplinary studies in the humanities in the years 11–14, the school decided to extend this approach (including self-motivated inquiry and group cooperation methods) into the fourth and fifth years, negotiating with both GCE and CSE examining boards to achieve a common syllabus covering four subjects (English, history, geography and religious knowledge). Similar developments are taking place in other areas of the common curriculum – for instance in mathematics and science – while plans are being formulated to cover a number of optional subjects. 'The importance of this new breakthrough', write the head and director of studies, 'cannot be minimized.' It means that

all fourth/fifth-year pupils (and not just the so-called Newsom rejects) could take a humanities course . . . really relevant to their needs. . . . Most important of all, it means that the social groupings to which the children had become accustomed as they moved upwards through the school could remain undisturbed so that there would be no division between sheep and goats, between leavers and academic streams (so-called), between accepted and rejected.

Examination results, with a wholly non-selective intake taught in complete mixed-ability classes for five years, have been remarkable. 'There is no separation of any kind', writes the head, 'each teaching group contains pupils of abilities ranging from low CSE grades to high GCE O-level grades.'[15]

It is in the light of these developments that the Schools Council's proposal for a single examination at sixteen plus needs to be assessed. The Working Party's report, *A Common System of Examining at 16 plus* (1971) certainly goes some way to meeting the long felt need of comprehensive schools for a single examination in place of the present dichotomy. If the proposals are accepted by the Council, the scheme is to be submitted to the Secretary of State for approval in the summer of 1973; the first examinations on the new syllabuses will become optionally available in the summer of 1975, and in 1977 the first examinations will take place completely under the new system. This at least holds out some perspective, even if the timetable is somewhat long drawn out.[16]

However, the main contentious issue raised in the report is the proposal to limit the design of the new examination to those at present (in theory) covered by GCE and CSE – that is, to the top 60 per cent of the age group – leaving 40 per cent unprovided for. The argument against providing an objective for *all* pupils (except perhaps some 5 per cent) is that sufficient experience of examining across the whole age range has not yet been gained, so that 'some largely novel methods of assessment might well need to be devised'. It is argued, in addition, that the lower limit is not 'a rigid cut-off level of general ability', since the percentile range applies separately to each subject examined; thus 'pupils below the 40th percentile in general ability may, nevertheless, achieve grades in a small number of subjects', while new syllabuses may extend the range even further 'to less able pupils'. Finally the working party add that their proposal is only for 'the initial adoption' of the percentile range 40 to 100, and this 'would by no means preclude the possibility of a downward extension at some later date if it was generally agreed to be desirable'.[17]

But this proposal, while providing the means for overcoming *one* of the divisive factors in comprehensive schools, must clearly lead to an even sharper division than now exists between those pupils – now the majority – whose work will have a clear objective defined by the new examination, and the non-examination rump of the school. It is for this reason that many comprehensive teachers have already protested vigorously against the scheme. 'I am convinced that the proposed restriction to the percentile range 40 to 100 would be a calamity', writes Pat Daunt, the very experienced head of the Thomas Bennett school, a large and long-established comprehensive at Crawley. 'No doubt many schools would do their best to ignore the constraint, as they have already done with CSE; but equally, many would not, and the total effect would be one of a gratuitously missed opportunity.' It is already known, Daunt adds, that we can devise, 'and successfully test, purposeful courses for the "under Forties" over the whole curriculum including the major so-called academic subjects'.[18] What Pat Daunt, and those who think like him (several letters in support were published in *The Times Educational Supplement*) fear is the imposition of a sharp division in the schools, whereby some 40 per cent of pupils are, as it were, written off from the start, and provided with educational experiences unworthy of their potential.

As we have already made clear, there is a trend in this direction built in to the present situation, whereby many schools are planning to extend so-called 'leavers' courses' for a single year, retaining the present differentiating structure in the third year. Thus we can expect a proliferation of non-examination or 'non-academic' courses lacking intellectual content. The aim is often the laudable one of building a course around the immediate experience and interests of pupils, sometimes linked with vocational objectives; and it is easy to see why, with the present tripartite examination structure, schools feel this to be necessary. But it may well be that the conditions already exist for schools to break out of this modern school/Newsom syndrome and recognize the advantages, both for the school itself and for individual pupils, of raising their sights higher in terms of all their pupils.

The danger is that non-examination courses, developed out of the best motives to meet the present situation, may become institutionalized and so difficult to transcend at a later date. A case in point is the establishment of a 'Record of Personal Achievement' now being developed for 'school leavers' at Swindon. The aim is to provide 'a worthwhile and realistic incentive for pupils aged fourteen to sixteen who cannot reasonably be made to work for examinations'. Designed specifically for 'less academic youngsters' (the bottom 40 per cent of the age group), the RPA, as it is called, aims to provide the opportunity for encouraging the development of personal qualities, since 'what employers do want to know is something about personality'; it also enables teachers to put the emphasis on activities in which these students can achieve success. The record, it is claimed, will provide employers with a more realistic assessment of personal qualities than any normal examination, and will be 'a reliable guide to the interests, the aptitudes, the talents, the values, of each individual who takes it'.[19]

The relevance of such proposals to the proposed new examination structure is already made clear:

The outcome of the present debate about combining and extending the GCE and the CSE will do little to provide for the needs of pupils at present languishing in the non-academic streams of secondary modern and comprehensive schools, and currently leaving at the earliest possible date.[20]

The RPA is designed to meet precisely this situation.

Such proposals accept the concept of streaming; of the division of pupils into 'academic' and 'non-academic'. But history tells us how dangerous it is to accept current diagnoses as regards the distribution of 'ability' as holding good for all time. 'Many of those who now hold CSE Certificates, for example, can read with amusement the passage in *Early Leaving* (1955) about the "absurdity" of their ability group taking an external examination', and this was only fifteen years ago.[21] To take one's stand, and determine school organization for the future, on the basis of the criticality of the 40th percentile is just as questionable as all similar attempts in the past have proved to be. In every case these arbitrary divisions, institutionalized in the school system, have acted as brakes on advance, very difficult to overcome. The IQ cut-off point of 115 for a grammar-school education is a case in point.

Many comprehensive schools have realized this and are planning to move in the opposite direction – towards integration, on the lines already indicated. 'Leavers' courses' are being jettisoned as unnecessary in the new situation. This does not mean that comprehensive schools will not continue to offer a variety of directions to their pupils; they clearly will, but the general pattern will be on the lines of a common core of studies (or, better, educational experiences) for all pupils at least up to the age of sixteen, combined with a variety of optional studies, some of which may be combined to provide a specific direction, but all of which will make up a balanced course both of general and specific education; one which also keeps the doors open to further education for all pupils.[22]

Because many comprehensive schools have already developed a flexible structure which makes this possible, many are looking forward to the statutory leaving age of sixteen as providing the conditions for a genuine move forward. The main concern of these schools is not with the problem how to differentiate earlier and more accurately, but how to develop the school as a single, unified entity in the new situation. Thus a typical response to our query as to the significance of ROSLA (to a sample of our smaller sample) runs:

I think it will be of benefit to the children. They will all have a chance of reaching maturity and experiencing some of the freedom and responsibilities of fifth-form life before they leave school. We shall not be really affected either in terms of academic studies or social organization since most of the children stay at school now to complete the five full years.

From this point on, writes another, all fourth-year students should be in a position 'to regard themselves as equal'. While the age remained at fifteen 'some early leavers tended to feel that they were inferior notwithstanding our efforts to remove this feeling'. The main impact, however, 'will inevitably be felt in the sixth form where numbers are bound to increase'. Many similar quotations could be given. It seems clear that comprehensive schools generally arc looking forward to the new possibilities optimistically, conscious of the opportunities they present for bringing about a decisive change in the middle years of secondary schooling.

A note on mathematics

Particular interest attaches today to the teaching of mathematics and this was probed in the survey, question 18 asking whether mathematics is taught to all pupils in each year in the school and, if not, at what stage pupils are excused (see Table A.15, p. 538). Replies indicated that in 63 per cent of schools (a total of 463 respondents), all pupils are taught mathematics in each year. The proportions in the 11–13, the 11–14/15, and the 11–16 schools were (fairly naturally) higher than in schools taking pupils to 18, but even here the proportion answering affirmatively was reasonably high (49 pcr cent of 11–18 type I schools); though it is noteworthy that 13–18 schools showed a considerably higher percentage than 14–18 schools (59 per cent as compared with 37·5 per cent). One unexpected result was the picture coming from Scotland which is roughly the reverse of that for England and Wales; only 33 per cent of Scottish schools answered affirmatively by comparison with 67 per cent. This difference may result from the fact that the Scottish sample contains a higher proportion of 12–18 all-through schools than does the sample for England and Wales; but the supplementary question made clear that this was not the whole story.

This asked at what stage pupils were excused from mathematics, if the subject was not taught throughout the school. Over half the respondents (59 per cent) kept mathematics as a compulsory subject up to and including the fifth year. But here again there is a sharp national difference. In England and Wales over two-thirds adopt this policy; but two-thirds of the respondents from Scottish schools reported that pupils are allowed to drop mathematics in the third year (equivalent to the fourth year in England) (see Tables A.16, A.17, and A.18, pp. 540–42).

It may be of interest to note that 155 responding schools (21 per cent of the total) claimed to be teaching both maths to all pupils in each year, and a foreign language to all pupils in the year when this subject is first introduced. Over half of these (86) were 11–18 schools: only eight were Scottish schools (see Table A.19, p. 543). The average staying-on rate in 1968 for schools both requiring mathematics and teaching languages to all pupils was high – 55 per cent as compared with the average of 50 per cent for England and Wales and our survey average of 51 per cent (or 52 per cent for England and Wales).* This double requirement in some schools represents a trend towards retaining a common core of subjects through the school. This is of particular interest since it shows that, in spite of the differentiation now forced on pupils in the fourteen to sixteen age group by two sets of examinations (and the traditional sifting of pupils in preparation for their occupational roles in later life) there is now a clear movement towards providing a common course for all pupils – at least in part. The groundwork is now spontaneously being laid for such a course for all pupils to sixteen, as the basis for the higher educational levels which will certainly be required in the future.

Notes

1. *The Schools Council and the Young School Leaver.*
2. Anthony Bullivant, *The Why and How of Comprehensive Reorganisation,* official handbook of the Ashton-under-Lyne Association for the Advancement of State Education, p. 21, 1968.
3. James M. Gardner, *New Era,* vol. 47, no. 3, March 1968.
4. *Scottish Educational Journal,* 24 June 1966.
5. *The Times Educational Supplement,* 30 August 1968. The IAAM Report stresses the danger of simply accepting a pupil's declared intention as regards leaving, and the need to keep further options open through curriculum design. IAAM Report, p. 80.
6. ILEA Survey, pp. 74–5, 1967.
7. David Hargreaves, *Social Relations in a Secondary School,* 1967.
8. Guidance systems in comprehensive schools have been analysed in B. M. Moore, *Guidance in Comprehensive Schools: a study of five systems,* NFER, 1970.
9. ILEA Survey, pp. 69–70, 72, 118ff.
10. IAAM Report, pp. 88–9.
11. ILEA Survey, pp. 70–71.
12. Ralph G. Crow, 'Old ideas die slowly', *Forum,* vol. 10, no. 1, Autumn 1967.
13. Timothy Rogers (ed.), *School for the Community,* 1971, pp. 57, 111.
14. Tim McMullen, 'Countesthorpe College, Leicestershire', *Forum,* vol. 14, no. 2, Spring 1972.
15. Arthur Gregson and Bill Quin, 'Quiet revolution', *Dialogue,* no. 10, Spring 1972. The article gives full details of GCE/CSE examination results in 1971.
16. *A Common System of Examining at 16 Plus,* Schools Council Examinations Bulletin 23, 1971.

* See Appendix 1, note 3.

17. ibid., pp. 10–11.
18. *The Times Educational Supplement*, 12 November 1971.
19. Donald Stansbury, 'The record of personal achievement', *Secondary Education*, vol. 1, no. 3, Summer 1971, pp. 18–19.
20. ibid., p. 19.
21. C. Benn, ibid., p. 11.
22. It remains to be seen how effectively the many Schools Council/Nuffield projects can be used in this context. See Schools Council Working Paper 33, *Choosing a Curriculum for the Young School Leaver*, 1971.

Chapter 12
16 to 18 Years in the Comprehensive School

Provision for post-sixteen study in comprehensive schools has developed rapidly over the last few years. In many comprehensive schools the traditional sixth form has been radically expanded, both in number and in content of curriculum.

In Part Two we discussed schemes for separate sixth forms and the nature and variety of GCE offering in various types of sixth forms in 1968. In this section we are concerned with the general educational approach between the years of sixteen and nineteen in the upper years of all types of comprehensive school. In the light of answers to our questionnaires we shall consider, firstly, the conditions of access to sixth forms in existing comprehensive schools: are they 'open' or do they require qualifications? Secondly, we deal with the related question of recruiting pupils for the upper school and the assistance given them in choosing courses. This leads on to an analysis of the structures of upper-school studies, to the relation of sixth forms with further education, to the new types of sixth-form colleges, and to the special characteristics of the 'new sixth' developing in comprehensive schools.

Access and recruitment to the sixth form

The main new feature of the sixth form of comprehensive schools, as compared to the traditional grammar-school sixth, is the deliberate opening up of the sixth to pupils who would not normally have qualified – or have wished to stay on – in the past. The ILEA Survey (1966) describes this evolution. As their comprehensive schools matured, they naturally began to develop traditional sixth forms; pupils, on completing their GCE O-levels, moved into the sixth forms to study for A-levels, many of them preparing for entry to higher education. But 'the larger range of courses for which these schools are staffed and equipped', together with the varying standards of academic achievement, led to a significant change in recruitment to the sixth form. Some pupils described as 'average and below average' now stayed on; some remained to tackle their O-levels one year later than normally (in the sixth year). As a result, pupils in their sixth year now include not only those who have completed their O-levels and are now studying for two-, three- or four-A-level examinations, but also many pupils with only a few O-levels who wish to add more, and even pupils with no O-levels at all.[1] This is a relatively new phenomenon in English (and Welsh) education, though some girls' grammar school sixth forms have included non-examination pupils in the past.

The development of sixth forms in the pioneer comprehensive schools, made up in different ways (often, in London, from amalgamating secondary modern and central schools), often working in cramped and difficult conditions and sometimes inadequately staffed, forms a story in itself which we cannot embark on here. Nearly all comprehensive schools in urban areas, as we have seen, are in any case heavily creamed, and it is worth recalling that many of these schools built up their original sixth forms almost entirely from pupils who had failed the 11-plus examination and therefore been rejected for a selective education. Eleven of the London schools surveyed in 1964-5, with sixth forms varying from thirty-three to 102 and a total enrolment in the sixth of 547 pupils, contained not a single pupil in the 'advanced academic' group (at eleven) from which the grammar schools are normally recruited.[2] Or, if we go to the opposite extreme, and examine the development of the sixth form at Wandsworth School, London, a grammar school which first took in a 'comprehensive' intake in 1956, we find that, although only sixty-two of the original 410 entrants had the IQ of 115 or over that distinguishes the 'grammar category', 130 entered the sixth form five years later, including boys originally placed in every one of the fourteen first-year streams. In these conditions, a much higher proportion of pupils was staying on to the sixth form than before.[3]

In January 1966, the ILEA Survey found that there was a total of 5594 pupils in London comprehensive-school sixth forms. The authors stress the point made above as characteristic of the comprehensive-school approach – that all pupils in their sixth year are regarded as sixth-formers, whether they are staying for A-levels, O-levels, or following a general or vocational course. This definition of the sixth form, which marks a definite break with tradition, is now widely agreed and has been accepted by the Schools Council in relation to their proposals and planning of sixth-form studies.[4]

The same point is stressed by the IAAM in their second report on comprehensive schools. The lower sixth, it is stressed, is first and foremost the sixth year of the school. In other words, the traditional sharp break at sixteen in grammar schools is deliberately being overcome. It may include – as well as those taking A-levels – students intending to stay for one year only (re-sitting O-levels, taking a commercial course, taking O-

Table 12.1 Percentage of schools allowing entry to sixth form without any O-level passes, 1968 (total number of schools in brackets)

	11/12–18 Type I	11/12–18 Type II	13–18	14–18	16–18	Total number of schools	Percentage of total number of schools
England and Wales							
Schools allowing entry	69	58	53	80	50	261	67·5
Schools not allowing entry	30	42	47	20	50	122	31·5
Unknown	1					4	1
Total	100 (316)	100 (24)	100 (30)	100 (15)	100 (2)	387	100
Scotland							
Schools allowing entry	12·5	25				6	13·5
Schools not allowing entry	87·5	75				38	86·5
Total	100 (40)	100 (4)				44	100
Wales							
Schools allowing entry	23		50			15	27
Schools not allowing entry	77		50			41	73
Total	100 (47)		100 (8)	100 (1)		56	100

level GCE after passing CSE, taking O-levels for the first time after six years in the school, perhaps taking one A-level – usually art – at the end of one year).[5] Because the comprehensive-school sixth form contains such a variety of students, including a combination of those who in non-reorganized areas would be in grammar *and* modern schools, comparison of results between grammar and comprehensive schools is extremely difficult.

A key aspect of the comprehensive-school sixth form, then, is the new freedom of access which obtains in most schools, though our survey shows that a considerable minority of schools still definitely require a number of O-level passes before pupils are permitted to transfer (question 29). The position is set out in Table 12.1.

This indicates that nearly two-thirds of the schools in England and Wales allow entry to the sixth without O-level passes; the proportion is greatest in the case of 14–18 schools and least in 13–18 schools, with the two 11–18 types lying between. The sharp reversal of the proportion for Scotland, as also for Wales when considered alone, is remarkable, English schools clearly adopting a more flexible policy as regards entry to the sixth than either Scottish or Welsh schools.*

A similar picture is given in relation to sixth-form pupils working for O-level examinations only (question 30), as Table 12.2 shows.

Table 12.2 **Percentage of comprehensive schools with sixth forms that include pupils working for O-levels only, 1968 (total number of schools in brackets)**

	England, Wales and Scotland	England and Wales	Scotland	Wales
Schools with sixth-form pupils working for O-levels only	71	76·5	20	34·5
Schools without sixth-form pupils working for O-levels only	29	23	80	65·5
Unknown	0	0·5	0	0
Total	100 (436)	100 (391)	100 (45)	100 (58)

Whereas 76 per cent – just over three-quarters – of schools in England and Wales recruit pupils to the sixth form for this purpose, only one-fifth

* The analysis for England alone showed that 74 per cent of English comprehensive schools with sixth forms in our survey allow entry to the sixth without any O-level passes. See Appendix 1, Note 3.

of Scottish schools do so. Here again Wales lies between the two figures, with just over one-third of the schools permitting this practice. This reinforces our overall impression that, at the time of our survey, the internal organization of comprehensive schools in England tended towards a greater flexibility than those in either Wales or Scotland, although of course individual schools in Wales, Scotland and England provide open structures in different degrees.

The difference in practice between open and restricted access is well brought out in the answers from our smaller sample and in some of the literature sent by responding schools. Restricted access is indicated in some replies as to qualifications required for entry to the sixth – two schools ask for four O-level or CSE grade 1 passes for academic courses. The majority of replies however, indicated open access, as the following examples show:

'all who have completed a fifth year and are prepared to work' are accepted; 'all comers are welcome unless they grossly distract other pupils'; 'any who wish to join the sixth form may do so'; 'No conditions. All are welcome if there is a course they can profitably take'; 'It is an "open" sixth. We admit anybody who wants to learn, even if they have no O-levels'; 'No qualification is required other than evidence of interest to work to the best of ability. We regard the sixth year as the sixth year of secondary education and a natural continuation of years one to five'; 'At the moment we admit anyone who wants to stay. No one in the sixth has passed the 11-plus.'

It is clear enough that the development of an open sixth form is deliberate policy on the part of the majority of comprehensive schools, and this impression is reinforced when attention is given to the care taken by very many comprehensive schools to encourage their pupils to stay on. Many schools produce printed or duplicated booklets or hold open evenings directed at both pupils and parents, describing the specific opportunities offered in the sixth, the nature of sixth-form study, career prospects, and often giving much other relevant information. The abundance of this literature is extraordinary. Special steps also are taken to advise the potential sixth-former about his programme of work, and to assist him (and his parents) to make the right choices from among what is often a wide variety of options.

We may take one example only from the literature available, the booklet *Why go into the Sixth?* produced by Hartcliffe School, Bristol. This is addressed to fifth-year pupils 'to assist them in their thinking about the Sixth Form'. It consists of eight sections, beginning with a clear statement on what pupils should find out about the sixth, which teachers to see to discuss what issues, and so on. The different opportunities offered are then outlined; A-level courses, new O-level subjects, one-year courses to convert a CSE pass into a GCE pass at O-level, and finally, a general course which is not examination-oriented but can be tailored to fit individual choice. The different life and work of the sixth-former is outlined, the opportunity for specialist study, for independent work, for student–teacher partnership, and the exercise of leadership in the school. There is a description of the way the individual student's curriculum is built up, and various combinations of subjects at A- and O-level are related to careers. Advice is provided about grants and other financial assistance for higher education, and another section gives in diagrammatic form the study pattern for particular careers: teaching, engineering, agriculture, business studies, medicine. This attractive and well-presented booklet concludes with a form which each pupil is asked to fill in, according to the decisions he has come to.

Many schools produce similar material. Ounsdale School, Staffordshire, for instance, produces *Opportunity Ounsdale* specifically for parents, an illustrated, printed booklet. This explains the nature of the sixth form, its beginning in 1960 with eight pupils and subsequent expansion; the corresponding development of the range of courses. 'Of particular importance', it is stated,

has been the establishment of courses for pupils who normally would not be considered for sixth-form education. A comprehensive school has a special responsibility to develop such courses as, if it is to be true to its name, its sixth form must be as comprehensive as the other part of the school.

This booklet also outlines the form organization and courses available, links suggested examination combinations with possible careers, discusses O-level and 'minority-time' courses, the sixth-form council and its functions, and the whole field of higher and further education, dealing with student grants available. It includes a bibliography 'which may be of interest and of value to a sixth-former and his parents'. Here, again, is a conscious effort to bring knowledge and understanding of sixth-form work to pupils and also to parents who, in most cases, will not have experienced it themselves. It is evident that a new and quite unprecedented effort is being made by comprehensive schools to recruit a wide variety of pupils into their sixth forms.

Assistance in choosing courses

One of the features of comprehensive-school sixth forms is the *variety* of courses available, particularly where the sixth form is reasonably large, but also sometimes in quite small schools. This has already been noted in the previous section; essentially it comprises opportunities to study both for A-level and O-level GCE in a number of subjects, as well as, in many cases, for taking courses with a particular vocational orientation – for instance, secretarial or technical. In some schools CSE courses are offered and in others a general course which is only partially examination-orientated. In most cases each individual student will build up his own personal timetable from the variety of options offered, and this will be determined both by his own interests and abilities, and by career prospects. Just as guidance and assistance is needed to help third-year pupils determine their options and courses for the fourth (and fifth) years, so expert assistance is now required to ensure that fifth-year pupils wishing to stay on to the sixth make correct choices.

The booklets and duplicated material made available to pupils and parents normally set out the various options available, but many schools also arrange a series of interviews and discussions as part of the process of guidance. These normally begin in the fifth form to ensure that all pupils have enough time, information, and advice to make an intelligent choice of sixth-form courses. Some schools also attempt an assessment of their pupils' abilities – building up (as at Hartcliffe) a system of record cards. Some arrange for their pupils to go out of school for one day a week in their fifth year on a job closely related to their sixth-form work.

The actual process of guidance varies from school to school; the following quotations from replies to a question on this topic to our smaller sample are probably the best way of conveying a general impression as to procedure:

'Interviews are held with the Careers Advisory Officer in the fifth year – pamphlets are consulted in the careers room – advice is asked from sixth-form tutors – parents and pupils visit the school to discuss careers one evening during the fifth year'; 'a week of discussion and interviews' involving the 'head of house, parent and sixth-form tutor'; 'A printed booklet is distributed in the fifth year. The head of the upper school sees all potential sixth-formers and their parents and holds a general evening meeting'; 'By interview with careers master and the year teacher'; 'This procedure is a long one in the fifth year. It is covered by a parents' and staff evening meeting, talks from the staff, the careers staff, etc.'; 'Each (potential) sixth-former is a member of a tutor group (fifteen pupils per group). The tutor has the responsibility for advising pupils about their sixth-form subjects – naturally, the pupils also discuss their sixth-form subjects with the respective specialist teachers. In the case of particular difficulty, the matter is referred to the headmaster'; 'Lectures by careers advisory officers; discussion with tutor, careers master, head (if they wish) before returning after the fifth year; in September full individual discussion with head, who sends them to heads of departments and the senior master for special advice.'

These excerpts are given at some length as they indicate not only the care generally taken on this question, but also the variety of people involved in this vitally important process of decision-making. Pupils, usually parents and the headmaster are normally involved, but in addition careers masters (where they exist), housemasters (or year masters), tutors, the head of the upper school or sixth-form tutor. This variety reflects differences in the social organization of comprehensive schools, analysed in chapter 14.[6]

The structure of sixth-form studies

It is certainly impossible to give a single, simple description of the structure of sixth-form studies in comprehensive schools, and this for two reasons: first, many 'comprehensive' schools, especially those which have emerged from non-selective schools, are only just beginning to establish sixth forms, so that several 11–18 schools have not as yet developed these, and second, because, as we have noted, new groups of pupils are now staying on into the sixth form so that the structure developing even in well-established comprehensive schools is in a state of transition. We may start, however, with the survey undertaken in London in 1966.

This showed that 41 per cent of sixth-formers in the thirty-two schools studied were preparing for A-level examinations; some of these were also studying for some O-level papers. A second large group – rather less than half of the total – were following O-level courses alone; some of these were re-sitting papers in which they had not been successful in the fifth form, others preparing to take these examinations for the first time. A third group were preparing for CSE or its then equivalent, RSA (Royal Society of Arts) examinations, following pre-nursing courses and a variety of secretarial, commercial, and some technical courses (for City and Guilds examinations), or following homemaking courses. The survey found that thirteen schools offered twenty or more subjects at O-level in the sixth form (three offered thirty or more), and that some offered less than thirteen.[7]

The majority of those staying for a sixth year to tackle O-level, CSE or similar courses left at the end of one year in the sixth, so that 84 per cent of seventh-year pupils (in thirty-five non-grammar schools surveyed) were following A-level courses, there remaining 'a small minority' following O-level courses only. Some pupils, of course, stayed a further (eighth) year, either to re-sit A-level examinations, or prepare for S-level examinations and open scholarships.[8]

The IAAM Report (1967) also reflects the developing situation in its description of sixth-form structures. Programmes combining both A- and O-level courses are 'very much a normal and expected thing in a comprehensive school'; such planning is easier in a comprehensive than a grammar school. Referring to the course choice process already described, the IAAM reports that 'everything is done to ensure that no one starts

in the sixth form with a feeling that he is a misfit'. There is no suggestion
of a single standard course, in which all have to move at the same pace.
The sixth form in the comprehensive school contains many so-called
'non-academic' pupils – in spite of low IQs on entry, many gain A-level
passes. 'It is something of an achievement', they write, 'that in a comprehensive school a division into "academic" and "non-academic" can
be avoided.' The comprehensive school, it is claimed, is better equipped
than the grammar school to combine study for A-levels with the O-levels
required for entrance to higher education. O-levels can be taken at the
end of the first year, if needed – or at the end of the second year. 'Much
use is made of the opportunity to start new subjects in the sixth form,
taken at O-level at the end of two years' – for instance, in metalwork,
technical drawing, a second language (e.g. Russian). Coherent one-year
courses – for instance, secretarial – are being experimented with. 'As a
demand for something new or something different arises in order to
provide an appropriate individual timetable, there is in comprehensive
schools a determination to satisfy the demand.' In describing the grouping
of subjects for choice, the authors write: 'We are reminded by those in the
schools concerned, "these lists are altered each year to accommodate the
wishes of intending sixth formers".' This flexibility is a new feature in
sixth-form organization and is possible primarily due to the variety of
expertise available in a large staff.[9]

Our own investigation underlines these points. First, the present,
transitional phase of comprehensive-school sixth-form development is
clearly brought out in an analysis of the number of A-level subjects
offered in each type of school. This matter has already been discussed in
chapter 9 (pp. 203–4), but a summary table may be given here. The
relevant figures for England and Wales are given in Table 12.3.

This table reveals, for instance, that seventeen 11–18 comprehensive
schools with sixth forms offered no A-levels at all in the summer of 1968 –
these are all schools which are developing as all-through schools, but
which have not yet had pupils sitting A-level examinations (i.e. completing two years in the sixth). Those offering one, two or three A-levels are
schools at a slightly later stage of development, but which have not yet
got a fully developed sixth form. Taking an offering of six A-levels in
Table 12.3 – which could cover, for instance, physics, chemistry, mathematics (as a single or double subject), history, geography, French,
German, Latin (or any other language), English literature: a total of ten
subjects in practice – as the cut-off point for an adequate A-level offering,
then a total of 315 (of the 387 schools represented) were, in 1968, beyond
this threshold, seventy-two below. But it is clear that, within these
general categories, facilities differed quite widely.

Table 12.3 **Number of A-level subject-groups offered by comprehensive schools with sixth forms in England and Wales, 1968***

Number of A-levels	Type of school					Total number of schools
	11/12–18	*11/12–16/18*	*13–18*	*14–18*	*16–18*	
0	17	0	1	1	0	19
1	9	1	0	0	0	10
2	8	0	0	0	0	8
3	10	0	0	0	0	10
4	10	1	0	0	0	11
5	14	0	0	0	0	14
6	12	0	1	0	0	13
7	25	0	4	0	0	29
8	60	2	3	2	0	67
9	61	6	12	4	1	84
10	42	2	8	3	0	55
11	48	12	1	5	1	67
Total number of schools	316	24	30	15	2	387

* This table does *not* give a fully accurate picture of the number of A-levels taken, since the survey (question 32, Appendix 3, p. 554) grouped subjects together for purposes of analysis. For instance, zoology, biology and botany are grouped as *one* subject, also history and geography. But it certainly gives a fair estimate of the differences in the *extent* of offerings in different schools. (Three 11–16 schools and one unknown which answered this question are omitted from this table.)

The different structures of sixth forms can perhaps best be illustrated by extracts from answers (from our smaller sample) to the question 'Could you describe how your sixth form is organized, and say approximately how many pupils are involved in each division, if you have divisions (e.g. how many pupils in O-level sixth, how many in A-level work, vocational courses, etc.)?' We may start with comprehensive schools which have developed from (or include) a grammar school and which therefore include a high proportion of students following traditional A-level courses:

1. 100 doing A-level work.
30 doing a general course, i.e. O-levels with the possiblity of one A-level and general studies. 20 following a secretarial course.

2. 100 in the sixth (50 in each year). Of these no more than half a dozen in the lower sixth have been taking only O-level courses. Next September (1968) we anticipate the lower sixth will be nearer 70, and a higher proportion will be following non-A-level courses.

3. Five or six parallel forms of mixed subjects and ability in the sixth year (say 150). Two or three parallel forms of mixed subjects and ability in the seventh year (say 70).

4. 6R – O-level course with one A-level – 27 pupils. Lower sixth art – mainly arts A-level – 31 pupils. Lower sixth science – mainly science A-level – 22 pupils. Upper sixth arts – mainly arts A-level – 42 pupils. Upper sixth science – mainly science A-level plus third-year sixth – 45 pupils.

These examples reflect different stages of development. Schools 1, 2 and 4 have developed as comprehensive schools only during the last three or four years; school 4, a 14–18 school, bears all the marks of the traditional grammar-school organization, with the 'new sixth' form (6R) developing alongside the traditional structure. School 2 also shows the 'comprehensive' sixth only in embryo – though expected to develop. School 1, however, shows a fuller development in this direction with the addition of general and secretarial courses alongside A-level work. School 3 is also a long-established comprehensive school, this time in London.

Turning to comprehensive schools which have not developed from grammar schools, we find a different, but still various, picture. We may divide these into three groups, first, schools whose sixth forms are about average in size or slightly below (60–75), but which contain a high proportion of students studying for GCE O-level or CSE:

1. 75 boys in sixth. 55 studying for O-levels or CSE; 20 studying for two or more A-levels.

2. 62 girls in sixth. 20 studying for O-levels and additional CSE; 36 studying for A-levels; 6 studying vocational subjects principally.

3. 70 in sixth. 30 studying for O-levels and occasionally one A-level. 20 studying for two or three A-levels (lower sixth); 20 studying for two or three A-levels (upper sixth).

4. 60 in sixth. 15 studying for O-levels, some following a commercial course. 20 in lower sixth, all studying for A-levels and some doing O-levels as well; 25 in upper sixth, also studying for A-levels and some for O-levels as well.

Schools of this kind represent the new sixth-form structure now developing; their sixth forms are being built up, often on the basis of 11-

plus failures, through extended opportunities for O-level and CSE studies in the sixth year; alongside these the number of students preparing for A-levels is increasing. Schools at this stage are developing towards the situation found in the second group, with relatively large sixth forms of 100 or more:

1. 108 in sixth. The lower sixth contains two groups, one studying for O-levels only (30 students), and one for A-levels and some Os (35 students); the upper sixth contains 43 students studying for A-levels and some Os.

2. 100 in sixth. 80 following A-level courses; 20 other courses.

3. 180 in sixth. In the first-year sixth are 41 studying for O-levels, 33 in the commercial sixth, 5 following the first year sixth technical course (boys), 4 following first year sixth technical course (girls), 31 studying for A-levels in arts subjects, and 20 for A-levels in science.

In the second-year sixth are 22 studying for A-levels in arts, and 20 in science (some of these are in their third year of sixth-form studies); also 4 studying for the second-year sixth technical course.

4. About 150 in the lower sixth and 150 in upper sixth (total, 300). Of these, about two-thirds are studying for O-levels, with or without A-levels. The rest are studying only for A-levels.

In these cases A-level studies have built up further, but the sixth also caters for considerable numbers pursuing other objectives. School 1, a long-established comprehensive school, covers a wide rural area in Yorkshire. School 2 is a Roman Catholic school on a housing estate outside a large northern city. School 3 was established several years ago on a large housing estate in Wales – it is not creamed by a local grammar school – here the sixth form is highly developed with a complex structure involving commercial, technical and O-level ('General') courses alongside the traditional A-level structure. School 4, a well-established comprehensive in a suburban area of a large provincial city with a sixth form of 300, has a very high proportion of 'new' sixth-form members.

Finally, a third group may be isolated: schools which had not developed, or were only just developing, sixth forms at the time of our survey (1968). A girls' school in Liverpool which became 'comprehensive' in 1964 has eight pupils in the Lower Sixth studying a total of five subjects only; 'one cannot describe it yet as a sixth', writes the headmistress. Another slightly further developed school in the same city expected a total of thirty in the sixth in 1968–9: ten following a vocational course (pre-nursing or commercial), ten O-level courses, and ten A-level work – a typical comprehensive-school structure in embryo. Another head in a provincial city writes that his sixth form is 'very new ... and too early to comment', and another in a Midlands market town, 'Not representative at this stage.' It must be remembered that the first pupils of many 'comprehensive' school sixth forms – as, for instance, the two Liverpool schools cited – will be 11-plus failures, since these schools are evolving out of secondary modern schools and 11-plus selection continues in the city. In many cases it will be some years before the first 'comprehensive' intake of such schools reach the sixth form. Even then their intake will have been subject to creaming in many cases by local grammar and direct grant schools, where the schemes of 'reorganization' allow these to 'coexist'.[10]

One aspect of the new comprehensive-school approach is the inclusion of vocationally oriented courses in the new sixth forms. In a sense, all courses might be so described, including A-level courses which qualify students for university, college of education or technical college. But, just as earlier vocationally oriented courses were developed in comprehensive schools to give purpose and direction in the 14–16 age range, so similar courses on a higher level are now being established in sixth forms, a practice likely to develop when the leaving age is raised. Several of these are referred to in the examples just quoted. A further question to our smaller sample, however, elicited more specific information. Several schools have developed commercial courses, often combining shorthand, typing and commerce with a general education. Pre-nursing courses for girls are sometimes provided, as well as courses in dressmaking and catering. But most schools do not run specific courses as such (commerce is an exception here); rather they offer a variety of options and then recommend particular combinations appropriate to specific vocations – engineering apprenticeships, secretarial work, preparation for art and domestic science colleges, and the like. This method extends into the sixth form the general flexibility which we found to be typical of the middle-school years (14–16).

School/college cooperation

Discussion of vocationally orientated courses in school sixth forms inevitably raises the question of the relation between comprehensive schools and local technical colleges and colleges of further education, since both sectors provide in parallel for the same age-group – the 15 (or 16)–19s (see chapter 8). Relations between these two sectors are likely to grow closer in the near future with the development of 'linked' and 'work experience' courses for the fifteen to sixteen year olds; circular 8/71 (ROSLA), while stressing that full-time education for this age group can no longer be legally provided in colleges of further education, specifically encourages the development of linked courses whereby pupils spend one or two days a week in local colleges, following activities normally with a vocational element.

The whole question of the relation between these two sets of institutions is likely to become of crucial importance as a higher proportion of sixteen year olds seeks extended education. In 1969 Edward Short, then Secretary of State for Education, stressed that the time had come 'when we really must advance from the concept of 10/65 in which the sixth-form college type of organization alone had to take account of what was being done in the further education college'; provision in both institutions must be 'dovetailed to form a coherent pattern'.[11] In the autumn of 1969 the Secretary of State accepted both the Exeter and the Devon plans to centre all post-sixteen studies, both full- and part-time, in colleges of further education; the early experience of both these institutions is discussed below – since then many similar proposals (for instance at Preston, Street, etc.) have been accepted by the DES. But first, we may examine shortly schemes where schools and colleges cooperate together, but where both retain their independent existence.

An ambitious scheme of this kind, based on very careful forward planning, already operating and introducing some quite new features, is that at Banbury in Oxfordshire. Here a school of some 2000 pupils, formed by amalgamating three secondary modern schools and a grammar school, was established in 1967 and took in its first comprehensive intake in September 1968. From an early stage, planning involved both members of the staff of the amalgamated schools and of the North Oxfordshire technical college, both of which required new buildings. A new feature is the structure of the school itself, which consists of three four-form entry 'halls' (the original amalgamated school buildings, three of which are on the same site) for pupils aged eleven to fifteen, and a fourth hall for pupils aged fifteen to eighteen (the upper school) which opened in a new, purpose-built building in September 1969. Each of these halls has a head (one of whom acts also as head of lower school), a deputy head, a senior master or mistress, and a tutor-group system, while the whole is presided over by a Principal, assisted (on the academic side) by a Director of Studies. Each of the lower halls contains just under 500 pupils while the upper school at present has 350 students, but this is expected to rise to 600 when the school-leaving age is raised.[12] The inclusion of the fifth form in the upper school is an important feature of this scheme, providing an effective base for a very wide variety of options and activities.

But the most interesting feature for our purpose is the degree of joint planning, joint working and activity between the school and the technical college, situated one mile away. This college itself has some 400 full-time students, and, of course, a very wide range of equipment, facilities and staff. In its planning, the education committee has adopted a policy of partnership between school and college, and this finds expression in many ways. For instance, both institutions provide a very wide range of fourth-year optional courses, many of these taking place, on a block release pattern, on the college premises; both school and college staff are, therefore, involved in joint counselling of third-year pupils, assisting them in choosing fourth-year courses at both college and school. A similar exercise is carried through with all fourth-year pupils wishing to remain in full-time education beyond the school-leaving age; some of these transfer to the college at the end of the fourth year to follow vocational (and some general) courses, and some remain at the school. Joint counselling of fifth-year students in the upper school also takes place on the choice of courses available for the sixteen to eighteen year olds; the school acting as the 'focus' for O- and A-level work in most of the 'academic' subjects (though subjects like economic history, economics, law, as well as art are provided at the college), while the college offers a very wide variety of vocational courses, many directed at OND (Ordinary National Diploma), together with more broadly based commercial, technical and agricultural courses. A-level art courses are jointly staffed and the school of art facilities at the college (which provides an extensive range of specialist art courses) are made available to students from the school studying the subject together with academic subjects; courses in art are now (for an experimental period of two years) the definite responsibility of the college. Minority-time courses (for example, in engineering projects or contemporary studies) are open to students from both college and upper school. A substantial element of many fifth-year school courses are provided by the college.[13]

At Banbury, school and college work 'in partnership'; from September 1971 much of the daily working timetable of the upper school has been integrated with that of the college, so that, as an explanatory brochure puts it, students belonging to either establishment 'have a free . . . choice of subjects and courses offered in the other establishment as well'; this means, it is claimed, that sixteen-plus students at Banbury 'will have a wider choice of subjects than could possibly be offered in any comparable sixth form or technical college'; it also means, it is added, that 'the waste of publicly providing the same thing twice for two groups of students a mile apart will be avoided'.

Formal machinery of cooperation is provided in this case by a small management committee of senior college and school staff, to which a number of specialist advisory panels report (for instance, on subjects of common interest, like catering and engineering).

The close-linked cooperation developed here may well provide a model for the future, particularly if steps can be taken to avoid the danger of perpetuating a sharp division at sixteen-plus between vocational and academic courses.

If the Banbury pattern of 'partnership' is perhaps the most highly developed scheme of this sort, there are other examples, though mainly concerned with relations between sixth-form colleges and further education colleges. At Scunthorpe, for instance, the sixth-form college and technical college are on two sites 500 yards apart; working parties have been set up to consider joint A-level and OND courses, though so far these have proved impracticable under the different regulations that apply to schools and colleges. The sixth-form college has, however, decided not to develop secretarial or narrowly vocational courses, while the technical college has dropped the small-scale A-level courses they ran before the sixth-form college started. The notion of cooperation – or rather, the division of responsibilities – is there, but little has been achieved as yet. The two colleges are aiming, however, to develop joint work, and have asked for a joint refectory, some shared classrooms and servicing facilities; and are considering asking for a joint library. They are planning an A-level engineering science course, to be taught jointly.[14]

At Darlington, where the sixth-form college (Queen Elizabeth College) is situated close to the college of technology, both planning and practice is further ahead. The courses available at both colleges are presented together to prospective students in a single booklet; students can take courses at both colleges simultaneously while some staff work across both sites (particularly those involved in home economics, wood and metal crafts, and drama). Students working at both institutions are mainly those pursuing GCE A- and O-level courses; for instance, college of technology students may take a number of subjects (e.g. classics, music, some science courses, statistics) at the sixth-form college, while those from the sixth-form college may take technical drawing, metal and woodcrafts, surveying and drama at the college of technology. Similar opportunities exist for 'minority-time' subjects. Although there was little response in the first year that this possibility existed (1971–2) it is expected that the following year will see significant numbers of students following combined academic/vocational courses at the two colleges.

This development clearly has many potential advantages, though existing conditions make it difficult to gain full value from this cooperation at present. Facilities available at the college of technology for certain key activities (wood and metal work, craft technology, etc.) are strictly limited, while these are not available at the sixth-form college. At the same time the limited facilities which do exist at the college of technology are under very heavy pressure from the 11–16 schools to provide linked courses, and this may increase in the future. Finally, while the two institutions cooperate, both still provide parallel GCE O- and A-level courses, resulting in small classes at both institutions. No definite directive as to the division of responsibilities in this area has been issued by the LEA. A merger of the two colleges was, however, approved by the borough council early in 1972, to take effect from September 1973 (subject to the approval of the DES). The total facilities are, therefore, now being considered and planned as a single unit; together with the new facilities required to meet present deficiencies.[15]

Sixth-form colleges

We have seen that cooperation between schools and colleges is relatively little advanced, except where joint planning has been evident from the start of reorganization plans, as at Banbury and at Darlington. The original concept of the sixth-form college certainly did not envisage cooperation except in the negative terms of a strict division of the territory between the two institutions, the sixth-form college focusing on full-time academic studies, leaving the further education colleges to deal with full-time and part-time studies of a strictly vocational nature. Before considering examples of the full merger between sixth-form colleges and colleges of technology, we will turn to consider the sixth-form college itself.

Sixth-form colleges of this kind, which received added momentum at a critical time from the notorious Vice Chancellors' *Times* letter of June 1967,* have been brought into being in a number of areas, and others are planned. Two of the best known are those at Stoke-on-Trent and Luton. The Stoke college, originally planned in the mid-1950s, was seen as the keystone of comprehensive reorganization in Stoke. It was strongly argued by the Chairman of the Education Committee that a concentrated academic college was a necessary concomitant of comprehensive organization ('especially in the older industrial areas') in order that local students could be prepared to compete successfully for places in higher education.[16] Somewhat similar arguments were used at Luton.

The Stoke sixth-form college opened in specially designed buildings in September 1970, although experience had been gained of a large sixth form at Longton High School over seven years, since this school first offered sixth-form facilities to students from local high schools in 1963. Both the junior high schools and grammar schools in the city have now been reorganized as neighbourhood comprehensives for pupils aged twelve to sixteen, and the entire sixteen plus output from these schools

* *The Times*, 3 June 1967; but see also the reply by a number of university teachers and administrators, *The Times*, 10 July 1967.

who qualify for sixth-form studies on the criterion established (see below) and who wish to enter proceed to the college. At Luton the school structure is precisely similar. At both places, therefore, the colleges of further education operate quite independently of the sixth-form colleges, concentrating on part-time studies for those going out to work.[17]

Although the Stoke college was designed for 750 students (in spite of consistent protests by the authority as to the inadequacy of this number) already in 1971 it had a student roll of just under 900; makeshift arrangements have had to be made, but extensions have already been approved to raise the total to 1000 probably by September 1974. The total number of students at Luton (1971–2) is 592. Stoke has a staff of ninety, Luton of fifty-four (plus four part-time).

Both institutions offer a very wide variety of courses, carried through in a 'college' atmosphere. At Stoke, every student must take three A-levels, together with general studies, and English, while one afternoon each week is set aside for games. The requirement of three A-levels is now recognized as imposing a heavy load on some students, and modifications are planned for September 1972. O-level courses are also offered to run alongside these. At Luton students may study for one, two or more A-levels, or may follow an O-level course only (for one year).

The college at Stoke is divided into six major departments (English, languages, social studies, mathematics, science, general studies), in each of which several subjects are involved. The department of English studies, for instance, is subdivided into a department of English literature, of general English, and of drama and spoken English; that of languages, into departments of French, German, Spanish, Italian, Russian, Classics (Latin and Greek); that of social studies into departments of history, geography, geology, economics, British constitution. Scientific studies include departments of biology, chemistry, physics, engineering science. A total of twenty-eight subjects are offered at A-level, not including general studies (often taken at A). Although Luton is considerably smaller, it also offers a wide variety – of twenty-four A-level courses. Both colleges use the system of blocking option groups, the student making a free choice (with guidance) from four blocks of subject groups (Luton also has a system of minor subjects grouped in five option blocks, mostly for O-level).

The Stoke purpose-built college ('designed specifically for young adults preparing for university or college') includes a large lecture theatre for 300–400 students, four small theatres for sixty–seventy, classrooms for about thirty students, others for about fifteen; tutorial bases for meetings of three or four staff or students, and private-study carrels. Science provision is on an open plan; specialist rooms are provided for geography, history and geology, as well as a language laboratory. The Luton college cannot boast a new building, being located in a pre-war boys grammar school (although extensions are now in hand), but as already indicated, the new building at Stoke is itself already proving inadequate. The use of lectures, small-group tutorials and individual work, characteristic of higher education, is encouraged at both colleges. Both have also developed tutorial systems of pastoral care and student welfare; at Luton tutors have responsibility for the welfare and guidance of about twelve students each – at Stoke the tutor groups are larger, up to twenty, and here the pastoral side is tied in with the departmental structure, the tutor meeting his group twice daily before the morning and afternoon sessions.

The Stoke college was specifically designed to act as a specially high-powered grammar-school sixth form – this was the concept from the start. Although it does not insist on four O-level (or grade 1 CSE) passes as a condition for entry, it does attempt to ensure that all entrants can benefit from study for three A-levels, and therefore only accepts applicants with fewer than four O-levels if they are supported by the feeder high school; in this way, writes the head, 'we have admitted many excellent students who would have been excluded by a rigid entry requirement'. High-school students, as a result of 'expert advice and guidance' (well developed at Stoke) opt either for employment on leaving school, for further education college, or for the sixth-form college. Those applying to the college with four or more GCE passes are exempted from a *second* interview; those without need both the support of their school and of the sixth-form college at the interview. The head writes that the four GCE O-level figure is simply chosen to reduce numbers (for interviews) to manageable proportions. Nevertheless it is clear that there is not open entry at Stoke, nor is the college designed to meet the needs of those who are not aiming at university or college entry. At Luton, although four O-levels was originally insisted on, this has now been modified; according to the head, the college is 'still admittedly academically biased, with the emphasis lying on the A- and O-level pattern of studies'; since September 1971, however, the college has admitted its first non-A-level group; until then the head's brief to contributing schools making recommendations for entry stressed (i) degree of motivation, (ii) public examination performance where relevant, and (iii) those who would 'benefit from an A-level course'.

Both colleges, as might be expected, send a high proportion of their students to full-time courses in higher and further education; at Luton the overall figures have been between 120 and 140 each year over the last four years (in 1971, output to universities alone was seventy-one); at

Stoke about 60 per cent go on to higher education – the principal expects this to rise shortly to 85 or 90 per cent.

Stoke and Luton are examples of academically directed sixth-form colleges, aiming specifically at higher education, and at present selective in character and outlook. Colleges of this kind represent one specific solution to the problem of the sixteen to nineteens, whereby all 'non-academic' educational activities are relegated to different institutions – to the colleges of further education, with which there is little or no liaison, although there is no reason in principle why such liaison should not develop in some areas of study as at Darlington and as is the intention at Scunthorpe. Where liaison does take place, however, the division is likely to be on academic/vocational lines; but this, of course, has definite implications in terms of the social status and standing of the two institutions, given the high prestige of academic studies today. Such schemes, in other words, run the danger of institutionalizing a deep division at sixteen plus.

The open sixth-form college

A contrast to the Stoke/Luton model is provided by those sixth-form colleges which allow *all* who wish to to enter (or, at least, with very few exceptions). A well-developed scheme of this kind operates at Southampton.[18] Here three grammar schools were legally established as 'open access secondary colleges' (as they are called) in 1967, taking in at sixteen almost everyone who wished to continue their studies. Between September 1966 and 1970, the numbers in the sixth forms in these colleges increased from under 800 to over 1300 – an increase of 62 per cent. Those transferring to the secondary colleges from the high schools, all of them 11-plus failures, have increased from a total of 121 in 1966 to 434 in 1971 – well over three times.

The Southampton school system is similar to that at Stoke and Luton (as we have already seen in chapter 10), with neighbourhood comprehensives taking all pupils from twelve to sixteen. Since comprehensive reorganization started five years ago the secondary colleges, based on grammar schools, now for the first time (1972) have no pupils aged eleven to sixteen (they have all passed into the college). The three colleges, housed in what are now ex-grammar school buildings, have a total of 144 teachers plus forty-eight part-timers and six foreign language assistants; their average size in 1972 is 452.

The steady growth of these colleges over the last five years is expected to continue, especially after the raising of the leaving age. Southampton has, in any case, a good record for staying on – in 1971 this stood at nearly two-thirds of all fourteen–fifteen year olds. During the last five years there has been a consistent improvement in qualifications on entry to the colleges – the number with five O-levels (or grade 1 CSEs), for instance, has more than doubled (from 61 to 129); it must be remembered that all these students were 11-plus *failures*.

The chief interest in the Southampton scheme lies in the working of open entry. A memorandum by the Chief Education Officer (July 1971), accepted by the Education Committee, deals fully with this point, and argues very strongly indeed against the imposition of any formal entry requirements. The position is that pupils can transfer from neighbourhood comprehensives 'without any formal requirements', the only condition being that the student himself wishes to pursue full-time education beyond sixteen and is prepared to apply himself; what matters, says the CEO, is the *degree of motivation* on the part of the students; this is of 'the greatest importance for future success, and more so than any measure of intelligence or academic attainment at any previous stage of a child's development, whether eleven-plus or sixteen-plus'. Unanimous support for the principle of open access came from all organizations consulted, including the Joint Four (the grammar-school organization), the local NUT, and the head and staff of all three colleges. The principle, it was held, was 'educationally sound and vital to the continued development of comprehensive education in Southampton, in the interests of pupils of all abilities at all stages of the educational system'.

It is worth remembering that the system of comprehensive secondary education and open access colleges only became fully developed in Southampton in September 1972, when the first comprehensive intake of 1967 reached sixteen-plus and provided all the entries to the sixth forms of secondary colleges. In preparing for this situation, the heads of the three secondary colleges expressed themselves as 'strongly opposed to restriction of open access by specifying minimum qualifications for entry at sixteen'. All the evidence, it is claimed, supports this contention; experience has shown 'that many other factors operate in relation to degrees of success achieved by sixth-form students'. These benefits 'are by no means only to be assessed in terms of examination results, although the latter may be far better than their previous academic records might have suggested'.

This is supported by data from individual colleges. Referring to the Southampton College for Girls, the memorandum shows, for instance, that 153 girls who transferred between 1964 and 1968 (11-plus failures) with three or fewer O-levels (or CSE grade 1 passes) added another 380 passes, making an average for each of these girls (the weakest group on entry) of 4·2 O-levels; while in addition forty-one obtained one A-level, eight two A-levels and one three. But for the 'open access', states the report, 'none of these girls would have been able to enter the sixth form. ... On leaving, they entered a much wider and better range of careers than would have been open to them at sixteen. No less than forty-two went on to colleges of education to train as teachers ... one proceeded to university, twenty-eight entered the nursing profession.' At the Richard Taunton College, where fears were initially expressed as to the effect of open access on standards, the report states that the head is 'now able to declare that open access has not involved the college in serious difficulties nor has it led to any decline in standards'. An issue of the college journal is quoted in support; this summarizes an analysis of the results of the first group of transfers (11-plus failures) in 1967.

Of sixty-eight entrants, forty-one completed a course containing at least one A-level pass, although on entry attainments at least fifteen of them would not have been admitted to sixth-form work in a selective school. Thirty-three attained at least the minimum qualification for university entrance, and in fact twenty-one are proceeding to degree courses, six to HND (Higher National Diploma) and three to colleges of education: up to twelve of these thirty would not have received sixth-form education under the old scheme.

Reference is then made to the small number who were unsuccessful; and to two remarkable cases, first, of a student who transferred with one O-level and two CSE grade 1 passes who gained three A-levels and two O-levels at the college and went on to university, and, 'still more remarkably, two students who were not even entered for GCE at their secondary schools and came to us with two CSE passes each', these both gained the identical qualification of two A-levels and five O-levels at the college and won university places. 'It is almost incredible but true to add that one of these two ... despite finding time for a Ford Trust travel scholarship and taking a prominent part in college drama, was awarded distinction marks in both his A-level subjects.'

All three college heads can quote many cases, it is reported, of students with four or more O-level passes who were less successful in their sixth-form course than those entering with three or fewer passes

One reason for retaining open access, in the view of the CEO, is very relevant. If access were limited in terms of examination qualifications, he argues, 'there would undoubtedly be strong pressures on secondary schools to ensure that pupils achieved the prescribed number of examination passes, with dangers of "cramming" and restrictive influences on the curriculum and non-examination activities of the secondary schools, i.e. creating a "sixteen-plus" situation in these schools comparable to the "eleven-plus" limitations on the primary schools'.

The Southampton experience has been given at some length, in view of the importance of this question as a result of the decision of so many authorities to develop the sixth-form college pattern. Open access has, of course, operated elsewhere than at Southampton; at Mexborough, for instance, a West Riding grammar school that takes in students at sixteen from the surrounding area. 'It is a cardinal principle', writes the head, 'that a place will be available for all who want to come whatever their ability' – and this principle is being adhered to.[19] At Scunthorpe, the borough education officer writes that all who wish to continue at sixteen-plus 'will be admitted, as of right, to the college. There is no eleven-plus and there will be no 16-plus.'[20] Decisions as to whether access should be open to all, or whether a system of selection at sixteen-plus should be operated, are clearly of vital importance for the school system as a whole. In developing genuinely open access, Southampton and other authorities are in line with the parallel development of the 'open sixth' in comprehensive schools generally.

The junior college

The most radical solution to the problem of the parallel provision for sixteen to nineteen year olds is certainly that being considered at Darlington and elsewhere, and first put into practice at Exeter and Barnstaple – the single, unitary college (or 'junior college' as it has come to be called) for *all* students, both full-time and part-time.*

The case for the junior college has been powerfully argued since the mid-1960s on educational, as well as 'cost-effective' terms. That it permits rationalization of the use of resources, both in terms of teachers and buildings, is evident and, as we have seen, several authorities are encouraging cooperation between separate institutions with this in mind. But the single junior college, it is argued, has further advantages. As D. E. Mumford, for many years its most energetic protagonist has put it, 'if the educational system is to be reorganized, then the undesirable social and educational aspects of selection at eleven-plus must not be allowed to reappear at a later stage'.[21] Sixth-form colleges which focus on full-time academic studies, whether selective or open access, in fact imply 'separateness' – the division of sixteen-plus students into two streams. The junior college provides the means by which this can be overcome.†

The argument, however, is taken further. The division between secondary and further education arose when the distinction was one

---

* Both Preston and Street (Somerset) plan to open such colleges in 1973.

† The name 'junior college' carries different meanings. If it is confined to colleges catering for sixteen to nineteens, both full- and part-time (some are planned), it should not be used to describe the Exeter/Barnstaple schemes, which include full- and part-time students of *all* ages. The 'open college' might be a better description.

between full-time and part-time education. But recently, 'with the rapid growth of full-time courses in further education this distinction is no longer valid'. Fusion into 'a single institution with a wide choice of courses of recognized value, meeting the needs of the whole age group, and with the flexibility needed to allow for differing rates of individual development' is now a more rational solution, one which 'maintains the full comprehensive principle'.[22]

Similar points are made by Joslyn Owen, the deputy CEO for Devon, a county authority which has brought a college of this kind into being at Barnstaple. Owen gives five main sources for this development: (i) that the concept – and overall purposes – of the sixth form is changing, (ii) that the traditional distinction between academic and vocational studies 'is increasingly an unreal one', (iii) that many students may be lost to higher education because after sixteen they want 'a course of studies which is not fully orientated towards higher education nor wholly vocational in character' – there is room for the opportunity 'to offer a better mix of studies', (iv) comprehensive reorganization is designed to diminish social divisions at eleven: it seems right, therefore, 'to prevent the reappearance of that division at the age of sixteen', and (v) this particular solution may have local administrative advantages, in relation to overall provision.[23]

Although the Exeter scheme only comes fully into operation in 1973, the college of further education took in its first group of sixteen-plus students (who would previously have moved into a school sixth form) in 1970; at Barnstaple the first sixteen-plus intake entered a year later – in 1971. Since Exeter has the longer experience, we may concentrate first on that.[24]

Already before amalgamation, the college at Exeter catered for a large number of both full-time and part-time students; indeed the increase in full-time students at the college over the last three years has been striking. These students are offered both 'typically vocationally orientated courses' and 'the more academically directed courses typical of sixth forms', for instance O- and A-level courses were provided and attended by students leaving secondary modern and grammar schools at sixteen plus, the latter consisting often of students who preferred the freer atmosphere of the technical college.[25] In addition young people 'wishing to continue in education without any of these objectives' were catered for; for instance, those wishing to repeat or to take additional O-level subjects. Planning for 1971 indicated that the 850 full-time students already studying at the technical college would be augmented (when the scheme becomes fully operational) by a further 360 students from the schools in the city, and thirty from neighbouring county areas.

It is impossible here to go into detail about the planning by the college for its new role. The implications of acting as the single centre for all post-sixteen studies have been given careful consideration, particularly as regards providing for the fusion of the best elements of the 'sixth-form ethos' in the college: the development of new areas of the curriculum (notably music, drama, art, physical education, and including also religious instruction and classics); the enrichment of some already established curriculum areas to support the ideals of scholarship (particularly in terms of library provision and the development of facilities for private study and discussion); the provision of an adequate resources centre, accommodation for tutorial consultations, seminar discussions and individual work. All these matters are under discussion. At the same time the whole structure of tutorial and advisory services are being overhauled, with the aim of ensuring effective careers and guidance services as well as a tutorial structure. The college is certainly able to offer an immensely wide variety of courses ranging across the whole spectrum from specifically academic to specifically vocational – an interesting feature is the proposal, in the light of this variety, to establish a structure of common courses to give coherence and balance in a system which makes possible so wide a choice of options.

It is plainly too early yet to draw any conclusions from the Exeter experience, particularly because, quite apart from the sixteen-plus transfer scheme, the college is experiencing a very rapid expansion in the demand for full-time education, and this 'has created an unprecedented demand for certain types of course'; particularly a really insistent demand for GCE A-level arts courses. Due partly to this situation, the average size of A-level classes is rather large (fourteen) – though not necessarily larger than in sixth-form colleges proper. The college is aware of the dangers of oversize groups, which 'often imply little individual attention, over-crowded classrooms, overworked teachers and an insufficient supply of equipment, books and materials'. This concern is fully understandable in view of the predictions of the likely growth in numbers, particularly in relation to open access from the neighbourhood 12–16 comprehensive schools. It is now estimated that an additional 300 full-time students may join the college in 1972, and a further 200 in 1973 (when the transfer scheme becomes fully operative) – a total of 500 extra full-time students from this source alone in two years. It is fully realized that this will mean additional demands on guidance, tutorial, counselling, welfare, library and other staff, and make necessary not only a very considerable increase in staff (it is estimated that an extra fifty are required), but also a great deal more teaching space.

The college at Exeter is a pioneer venture, and it is clear that, while some hard thinking has been done in preparation for the change, new problems, particularly in terms of the explosion of demand, are also arising. (These may, of course, be the penalty of success.)

It is too early yet to make any estimate of the Barnstaple initiative; but it seems unlikely that this area of the county (north Devon) will experience quite such a high level of demand (in terms of growth).* The total number of sixth-form students in Barnstaple (before reorganization) was 240; at the technical college there were a further 100 students following A-level courses in a total of 500 full-time students, as well as 2300 part-time students. The Barnstaple initiative, which seems to 'fit' the requirements of north Devon very appropriately, has also been very carefully prepared as the key feature of the overall secondary reorganization in the area.[26] Discussions, consultations and a whole programme of in-service training preceded and is accompanying the transition, which has been worked out by the authority in close relation with the teachers in the area and of the college itself. Here also the concept of the united institution has been thought out in detail, in advance, both in terms of planning and administration, and in terms of the content of courses, their relations to each other, and the methods of teaching to be used. The actual material provision required has also been thought out in advance, and much of it provided in the new purpose-built college, which stands high on a rise above the river overlooking the town.

The 'new sixth': its characteristics

We have looked at the wide variety of solutions being found to the education of sixteen-plus students under 'comprehensive' reorganization; here we have to assess their educational significance.

The principle of comprehensive education implies the elimination of selectivity in the school system as a whole. This is the significance of the move to end streaming and other divisive practices between the years eleven to fourteen (chapter 10), and, equally important, the extension of this approach into the middle years of schooling, ages fourteen to sixteen (chapter 11). The parallel development at sixth-form level is that of the 'new sixth' within the comprehensive school; but this concept is now being taken further both through cooperation with the colleges of further education and, more particularly, by the setting up of junior colleges catering for all students who wish to continue their education, whether full-time or part-time.

This latter solution is, however, a very recent development, and so far confined to areas where the advantages of concentration are evident.

* Though the two colleges are in Devonshire, they are, at present, the responsibility of different authorities – the Devon county council (Barnstaple), and the Exeter borough council (Exeter).

Consideration of this solution should not blind us to the very positive developments that are taking place within comprehensive schools, both of the all-through and the tiered variety, which mark a radical break with the past, and which so far educate at sixth-form level very many more students than are catered for either in sixth-form or in junior colleges.

The benefits of the new comprehensive-school sixth forms are, as the IAAM pointed out as much as five years ago, 'open to a wider range of pupils than in any grammar school'. The consensus view of the group from whose experience this report was compiled – former teachers in grammar schools – was that

all the traditional methods used to develop personal qualities, encourage judgement, etc., could be applied more successfully to many more pupils than previously. It was felt (the report continues, looking to the future) that the comprehensive school would probably do this better than the average grammar school because of its size and the consequent wide variety of opportunities.

In comparison with the grammar school, the comprehensive-school sixth 'is an open society. If you're old enough you're good enough. Being in a sixth form is more of a natural completion of continuous education.'[27]

The fact that a fully open policy for entry to the sixth is now being consciously pursued by some comprehensive schools was brought out in our survey. Table 12.4 analyses the answers to the question: 'Are there any pupils in your sixth form taking a general course only (i.e. not studying for any external examinations)?'

Of the 436 schools with sixth forms, 15 per cent answered 'yes'. While this is still a small minority, it indicates a new trend in sixth-form studies,

Table 12.4 **Comprehensive schools with, and without, pupils taking a general course only in sixth form, 1968**

	England, Wales and Scotland	England and Wales	Scotland	Wales
Percentage of schools with such pupils	15	16	11	19
Percentage of schools without such pupils	83	82	87	79
Unknown	2	2	2	2
Total	100 (436)	100 (391)	100 (45)	100 (58)

and underlines the general direction of development stressed by the IAAM.[28]

That comprehensive-school sixth forms in England and Wales contain a much higher proportion of pupils who have stayed on for purposes other than A-level studies as compared with grammar schools, is clearly brought out in the DES statistics for 1970:[29]

Table 12.5 **Pupils in grammar and comprehensive-school sixth forms following and not following GCE A-level courses England and Wales, 1970**

	Pupils following GCE A-level courses	Pupils not following GCE A-level courses	Percentage not in GCE A-level courses
Grammar schools	121,398	10,406	8·5
Comprehensive schools	56,980	17,686	31·0

Heads of schools in our smaller sample underlined the new approach to the composition of the sixth form in comprehensive schools. Asked, 'Do you feel that the comprehensive-school sixth form is in any way different from a selective-school sixth-form?' the response was almost unanimous. Typical answers were:

'It is different in that it contains a broader spectrum of society, and the aims of its members are much more diverse'; 'Yes, it is broader in ability range and pupil background'; 'Yes – greatest range of courses in breadth and depth to meet the needs of the more extensive ability range of students'; 'Yes. The false aura about the term "sixth form" should be dissipated. A comprehensive-school sixth form is as good as the rest of the school since it is merely a continuation of the work of the fourth and fifth years'; 'Yes. There is obviously a greater opportunity for sixth-formers in view of the greater variety of provision – especially on the practical side.' 'Of course. The comprehensive sixth form has the same social advantages as the comprehensive school has over the selective school.' 'Yes, it is very different. It must offer an increasing number of subjects and options. It must aim at broadening the pupil's outlook.' 'Undoubtedly. At the moment the proportion studying academic as opposed to non-academic courses is 2 to 1. I expect this proportion to be reversed in the next few years (hoping that more will be doing non-academic courses as well).' 'The sixth form must be open to all, irrespective of previous academic attainment. The only criterion for admission is that there is a course from which the pupil can profit'; 'In my case, yes. We shall go on "open" sixth lines with provision for plenty of O-level work in addition to A-level.' (And, finally), 'Yes. Our sixth form, by definition, is every pupil who has been at school five or more years.'

These quotations have been given at some length, since they convey an atmosphere – and a clear sense of direction. The broader base of the sixth form, its variety and new multidirectional purpose is bringing into question the traditional examination requirements which still determine its structure. Some heads are already looking forward to the separation of A-level examinations from university entrance, so that it can 'either be replaced or developed to meet the needs of *all* sixth-formers'; another suggests the development of CSE-type A-level work including project work, conjoint technical college courses, and so on. Such developments, which are operating, for instance, at Banbury, will clearly be extended in the future (it would be quite irrational not to do so), though a delaying influence may well be the in-built tendency for institutions such as schools to retain a certain isolation and separation – a tendency that is reinforced by the different regulations under which schools and further educational institutions operate – so that there is likely to be strong resistance to cooperation, even where the situation clearly demands it. But developments of this kind would allow sixth-form work to be further broadened, and begin to overcome the division of vocational (technical) and academic studies with all that this implies educationally in terms of that one-sidedness which is perhaps the chief bane and weakness of English educational practice and theory, as well as the separation of students who wish to continue their studies into two main streams divided at 16-plus – those pursuing full-time studies at school and those pursuing part-time studies at colleges of further education. In this connection both the open sixth form, and genuinely open access to sixth-form colleges, diminish the danger of the imposition of competitive differentiation (or selection) at sixteen-plus, which is not only undesirable in itself, but is also bound to push selective pressures down into the high schools catering for the eleven or twelve to sixteens, as pointed out by the Southampton CEO (p. 299).

On the face of it, the junior-college solution seems the most 'comprehensive' of all in that it brings all students together into the same institution, though such students are bound to be internally divided in the courses they follow within that institution (given a leaving age of sixteen). But it is too early as yet to come to any firm conclusion as to the effectiveness of this solution in terms of specifically educational criteria. Much will depend on the ability of large colleges of this kind to provide an effective social setting for the students' development – perhaps particularly in terms of guidance, pastoral care, and the general 'life' and ethos of the institution. If these colleges can succeed in fusing the most positive aspects of both school and college they may well prove successful. But the general conditions of life and study facilities at these institutions may need careful watching – particularly if the primary motive for this development is simply that of cost-effectiveness derived from the concentration of resources; and there are indications that this may be a real danger. Somewhat similar considerations apply to sixth-form colleges proper, although the main argument here at present is the need for concentration specifically on *academic* studies. It is worth noting, however, that there is now a growing feeling among many educationists that smaller units have multiplied educational advantages; and some large schools (e.g. Countesthorpe) are testing out, or preparing to test out, the formation of relatively small sub-units within the school as the central learning and social unit for individual pupils; a standpoint which has recently been argued by Michael Armstrong and Elizabeth Halsall (the latter citing a good deal of research evidence in support).[30] It could, however, be argued that large colleges are as well able to break their students down into smaller learning/teaching pastoral units as are schools.

The general conclusion must await further experience of the different types of sixth-form provision only now coming into being. Whether the solution is found in separate or fused institutions, however, the move is inevitably towards some form of integration for this age group, whether by means of cooperation between institutions specializing on different objectives, joint working, and possibly joint control, or through the development of single institutions for all. It is as well to remember that the solutions found can only be provisional; the long-term historical trend to stay longer at school will certainly continue in spite of the 'deschoolers', so that the problem itself, and the institutions concerned, will inevitably change in character. Once again, then, the final conclusion must be that whatever the provisional solution, flexibility of structure is the key.

We have already given a good deal of data on the size of comprehensive-school sixth forms (chapter 9). The latest DES estimates indicate that the number of sixth formers who will have at least two A-levels in 1980 is likely to be 40 per cent higher than was previously projected – a total of 170,000 rather than 120,000 (in 1967 the total was 70,140). This reinforces the conclusion reached above – that the structure evolved must be capable of absorbing the massive growth expected through the 1970s – and beyond. It is the dynamics of the situation that need to be considered, rather than achieving 'cost efficiency' at the present level. It is precisely this that the developing sixth forms in comprehensive schools make possible, and it is from this standpoint that they should be assessed.

Notes

1. ILEA Survey, 1967, p. 77.
2. ibid.
3. H. Raymond King, 'Comprehensive school: a pattern of achievement', *Forum*, vol. 5, no. 1, Autumn 1962.
4. ILEA Survey, p. 77.
5. IAAM Report, p. 99.
6. The NFER (Second Report) also found a wide variety of provision in a sample of nineteen schools studied, claiming that 'there were about as many systems (of careers guidance) as there were schools', and linking this to differences in local career prospects; T. G. Monks, *Comprehensive Schools in Action*, 1970, p. 83. One of the most clearly worked out systems is that at West Bridgeford Comprehensive school, Notts, where, in addition to the departmental system and year-tutor teams, there is a 'guidance team' of seven staff; two covering higher education, two the 15/16 year old leavers, one the middle school (years three to five), and one the lower school (who also acts as primary-school liaison and as a general counsellor). The team is the responsibility of the 'director of guidance'; it has its own office together with interview rooms and space for a careers library and permanent displays (information from P. M. S. Cornall).
7. ILEA Survey, p. 78.
8. ibid., p. 79.
9. IAAM Report, pp. 100–103.
10. A rather similar analysis of comprehensive-school sixth forms has been made in the NFER Second Report; this is based on a sample of eighteen schools. T. G. Monks (ed.), *Comprehensive Schools in Action*, 1970, pp. 85ff.
11. Speech to the annual conference of the ATTI, 24 May 1969.
12. H. G. Judge (Principal) and S. Moore (Director of Studies), 'Banbury school development plan', revised 1967. See also Anne Corbett, 'The future of the sixth', *New Society*, 10 July 1969.
13. H. G. Judge, 'Banbury: the upper school and the North Oxfordshire technical college', July 1969. Material in this and the next paragraph is also derived from the 'Guide to opportunities for students in Banbury, 1971–2' and other documents kindly made available by the Principal.
14. Information from E. Charlesworth, Principal, John Leggott College, Scunthorpe; see also J. V. Edmonds, 'Unstreaming at Scunthorpe', *Education*, 1 October 1971.
15. Information from L. G. Reedman, CEO Darlington; see also, 'Educational opportunities at the Queen Elizabeth College and Darlington College of Technology', March 1971.
16. R. B. Cant, *Forum*, vol. 7, no. 3, Summer 1965; see also Joan Simon, 'The swing to comprehensive education: Staffordshire', ibid.
17. Material in this and succeeding paragraphs on the sixth-form colleges at Stoke-on-Trent and Luton is based on personal communications and very full documentation provided by the two Principals, H. Beynon (Stoke)

and B. D. Dance (Luton), to whom our thanks are due. See also F. D. Bailey, director of education, Luton, 'Broadening the scope at Luton', and A. H. Little, 'Good groundwork at Stoke-on-Trent', in *Education*, 1 October 1971.

18. Material on Southampton is based on documents kindly made available by the CEO, D. P. J. Browning, to whom our thanks are due. The documents, from which quotations are made, are two memoranda, 'The development of open-access secondary colleges in Southampton', 2 July 1971, and 'Secondary school and secondary college numbers and staffing September 1971', 1 November 1971, both by the CEO.

19. S. W. Shield, 'Mexborough Grammar School, Yorkshire', in Elizabeth Halsall (ed.), *Becoming Comprehensive*, 1971, p. 170.

20. J. V. Edmonds, 'Unstreaming at Scunthorpe', *Education*, 1 October 1971.

21. D. E. Mumford, 'The junior college', *Forum*, vol. 7, no. 2, Spring 1965.

22. ibid.

23. Joslyn Owen, 'A 16 to 19 Solution', *Education*, 27 March 1970.

24. Our thanks are due to P. H. Merfield, Principal of the college at Exeter for material on which the following paragraphs are based, including a memorandum, 'Plan for reorganization', by J. L. Howard (Director of Education) and related documents, and a memorandum by R. A. Lord dated 18 November 1971.

25. See Jean Floud's evidence to the Robbins Committee, 1963.

26. Our thanks are due to D. Cook, CEO, Devonshire, for material on the Barnstaple college.

27. IAAM Report, p. 98.

28. ibid.

29. DES *Statistics*, 1970, *Schools*, p. 42. The same conditions apply to the statistics given in this table as are indicated in the note on page 208.

30. Elizabeth Halsall, 'The small comprehensive school', *Trends in Education*, no. 22, April 1971, pp. 12–17; and 'The small comprehensive flexible and open-ended?', *Comprehensive Education*, no. 8, Spring 1968.

Chapter 13
Higher Education and the Training of Teachers

Comprehensive schools and higher education

There is little information on the relation of comprehensive schools to higher education, even as regards such comparatively simple but important matters as the number and proportion of students going on to universities, colleges of education or technical colleges. This is certainly an area where further research is needed, particularly as the 'new' sixth in the comprehensive school builds up, as it is bound to do with increasing rapidity. What are the implications of this development for higher education, and what effect, for instance, do present university entrance requirements have on comprehensive schools' sixth forms? How successful are comprehensive-school pupils when they reach university or college, and how do differences in the academic structure of these schools affect this? These are some of the questions which must arise and which require an answer, particularly as comprehensive schools become more widespread. We obtained data on some of these matters from our smaller sample.

The only source of information about the output from comprehensive schools to higher education is contained in volume 2 of the annual DES *Statistics of Education*. These give the destination of school leavers in England and Wales, separating comprehensive from grammar and modern schools. This information must, however, be treated with care. First, it is gained from a 10 per cent sample of all leavers in all types of school, and second, it represents their *intended occupation as known to the head teacher* at the beginning of the autumn term after they have left school. The sample figures are grossed-up by multiplying the data for each pupil by a carefully calculated factor.

This procedure means that the total figures given are subject to sampling errors. Further, there can be no guarantee that those intending to proceed to higher education actually get there, though all have been offered and have accepted a place at specific universities. In fact, in 1968, 97·5 per cent of those offered places in universities took these up.* The

* Information from the Universities Central Council for Admissions (UCCA).

figures given, then, are not completely accurate for this reason also, but are probably a near approximation. Certainly it may reasonably be assumed that most heads would be able to make an accurate statement of the intentions of their pupils as regards higher education.

With these warnings, we may examine the information given for England and Wales covering the four years 1967 to 1970 (the latest information available).* This is presented in Table 13.1, together with some

Table 13.1 **Output to full-time higher and further education from comprehensive and other schools (England and Wales), 1967 – 1970**

	1967	1968	1969	1970
Number leaving comprehensive schools	76,750	114,980	145,340	178,240
To universities	2260	4240	5000	6770
To colleges of education	2140	3440	4450	5320
To other full-time further education*	4130	6950	9450	12,490†
Total to full-time further and higher education	8540	14,620	18,910	14,390
Rest of leavers from comprehensive schools	68,060	100,360	125,980	153,650
Number leaving grammar schools for full-time further and higher education	51,730	49,850	50,190	47,370
Ditto for modern schools	24,630	24,660	25,360	24,460
Total grammar-school leavers	111,210	105,160	103,900	99,370
Total modern-school leavers	312,420	290,910	274,150	249,130

* This includes *all* full-time further education courses, ranging from degree courses to GCE O-level and OND/ONC courses.

† This includes 2320 going to polytechnics (data available for the first time in 1970).

comparative data covering maintained grammar and modern schools. The figures bring sharply to notice the relatively small proportion of school leavers from all types of school who go on to full-time higher and

* Details of the sampling and other techniques used in compiling this information are given in DES *Statistics*, 1967, vol. 2, pp. xi–xii and later volumes. Source: DES, *Statistics*, 1967, vol. 2, Table II; 1968, 1969, 1970, vol. 2, Table I (in each case).

further education (a total of approximately 96,000 out of 526,000 in 1970 – or less than one-fifth).

As far as comprehensive schools are concerned the Table shows that the proportion of leavers going on to all forms of full-time higher education has increased from approximately one in nine in 1967 to one in seven in 1970; a similar increase is recorded in the proportion going on to universities and colleges of education combined – from approximately one in seventeen students in 1967 to one in fourteen in 1970. In the case of university entrants alone, output from comprehensive schools has tripled over the three years (1967–70); that is, has grown at a greater rate than the total number of leavers over the same period; and this at a time when the total number of leavers from all types of school going on to universities has increased only slightly (during 1968 and 1969 this remained static).* Output to colleges of education increased at a slightly slower rate, but this may reflect the actual decline in entrants which took place in 1969. Output to all other forms of full-time further education, however, increased more rapidly than the total number of leavers.

This is objective evidence, if of a general kind, that comprehensive schools are fulfilling their function in terms of the output of highly qualified students to the various forms of further and higher full-time education. It seems likely, for a number of reasons, that in future polytechnics may prove more attractive to comprehensive-school students than other colleges and universities, but it is too early as yet to make any comparative analysis.† While the figures for comprehensive school leavers going on to further and higher education shows a consistent increase in all sectors, those for other types of school have remained static, or show a decline. This is, of course, only to be expected in a period of reorganization, but it indicates the extent to which comprehensive schools are supplanting the bipartite system in a crucial sector of public education. In this connection, while the relative proportions of leavers going on from comprehensive and grammar schools may seem disparate, the highly selective entry to grammar schools must be borne in mind; also that the bulk of modern school leavers aim at further education at various levels – in 1970 only 100 (out of a total of 249,000) gained places in universities.

If we examine those intending to proceed to universities in greater detail (at least we know that these will have been offered places at the university of their choice) we find that, in 1970, 420 were aiming at Oxford and Cambridge (380 males and only forty females), 620 for London university, 5300 for other universities in England and Wales,

---

* At 36,800. DES, *Statistics*, 1969, vol. 2, p. viii.

† Evidence pointing to this conclusion is given in *2001 Sixth Formers* (1971), Brunel Further Education Monographs 2.

and 300 for Scottish and Irish universities (100 were untraceable, while forty aimed at universities outside the United Kingdom).* In addition, 960 were intending to follow degree courses at non-university institutions, and a further ninety to take up a place at a university in the following year. Others were intending to follow Higher National Diploma and Certificate courses at technical and commercial colleges.

It is likely that, in 1972, all the figures for entry to higher and full-time further education will be greatly expanded as sixth forms develop in comprehensive schools, sixth-form and junior colleges come into being, and as more areas move over to the comprehensive system. The state of transition in comprehensive-school sixth forms is well reflected in answers to a question which asked our smaller sample for information as to the number of pupils proceeding to universities, colleges of education, or to professional courses in technical colleges. An ex-secondary modern school reports three students to colleges of education; two others report none yet sent on to higher education; on the other hand, an established comprehensive school reports 'practically all from the upper sixth'; another (for October 1968) reports fourteen acceptances at universities or colleges of education, of whom twelve had failed the 11-plus examination; another, seven to universities, thirteen to colleges; another long-established school sends twenty-five a year to degree courses, and another fifty a year to colleges of education, as well as ten to twenty a year to Dip.A.D. and professional diploma courses. A fairly typical entry from a well-established medium-sized comprehensive gives an average of nine a year to university, seven to colleges of education and five to colleges of technology. Output from the new sixth-form colleges is also building up; Luton sends on roughly 120 a year to full-time higher education (in universities, polytechnics and colleges of technology, and to colleges of education); the 60 per cent of the Stoke college leavers now going on to full-time higher education is expected to increase (p. 297), while the Southampton colleges clearly expect an increased output as their comprehensive system becomes fully established. It is from the sum of such disparate situations, reflecting specific stages of development and socio-economic catchment areas, as well as different types of institutions, that the overall totals are made up.

Such surveys as have been made of the social origin of university students from comprehensive schools indicate that a significantly higher proportion are of working-class origin than is the case for university students as a whole. This appears to be true also of sixth-form students.

* DES, *Statistics*, 1970, vol. 2, Table 1, pp. 8–9. The slight discrepancy between the total figure intending to go to universities and the sum of its elements is due to the DES method of rounding in tens in this table.

Table 13.2 **Proportion of sixth-form pupils from manual workers' homes, by type of school, England and Wales**

Type of school	Percentage of pupils from manual workers' homes
Independent boarding schools	4
Independent non-boarding and direct grant schools	21
Grammar schools	34
Comprehensive schools	51
Technical and 'other' maintained schools	51

The intensive study carried through by the Schools Council Sixth-Form Survey (based on a sample of 4377 pupils from 154 schools) specifically draws attention to the 'very marked differences between the proportion

Table 13.3 **Social-class origin of sixth-form students, by type of school, England and Wales**

| Social class of parent | Type of school | | | All schools |
	Grammar	Comprehensive	Independent boarding	
Professional	9	6	42	14
Managerial and Senior technical	38	26	47	38
Clerical and sales	15	11	4	13
Skilled manual workers and foremen	26	35	3	24
Partly and unskilled	8	16	1	8
Unclassified	3	7	3	4
Total percentage	100	100	100	100

of pupils from homes of manual workers in different types of school'. This is indicated in Table 13.2.*

* *Sixth-Form Pupils and Teachers* (1970), vol. 1, p. 67. The survey was carried through in 1965–6. Secondary modern schools were excluded, as well as schools with sixth forms of less than twenty. No sex differences in social-class distribution were found.

The social-class distribution of sixth-form students is broken down in more detail in Table 13.3, taken from the same source.*

The higher proportion of working-class students in sixth forms appears also to be reflected in university entrants from comprehensive schools. Two recent investigations bear on this question; the first, concerning those students following a general-studies course in the first-year intake at the university of Surrey (a total of 514 students) found that 'more than half the students coming to the university from comprehensive and secondary modern schools had fathers with marginal "white collar"

Table 13.4 **Social-class origin of university students by type of school, England and Wales* (percentages)**

Social class No.	Total	Grammar	Sec. Mod.	Public	Independent	Comprehensive	Other†
1, 2, 3	62	64	54	86	66	49	53
4, 5	22	24	24	5	18	43	31
6, 7	9	7	17	1	7	6	15
8	1	2	1	1		3	
Number of students %100	514 100	265 100	70 100	75 100	27 100	37 100	40 100

Class 1, 2 Professional, managerial executive
      3 Lower professional, managerial, proprietors
      4 Supervisory grades, self-employed
      5 Highly skilled and skilled manual workers
      6 Relatively skilled (unapprenticed)
      7 Semi-skilled
      8 Unskilled manual workers

For further details of this classification, see *Comparability in Social Research*, ch. 4 (Social Science Research Council/British Sociological Association), 1969.

* A small proportion of replies were unclassifiable; for this reason the percentages in all columns do not add up to 100.

† Mainly overseas students who failed to recognize the nomenclature of school type.

or manual occupations, whereas two-thirds of the grammar school and independent school fathers had professional or managerial level occupations'.[1] The breakdown, which is based on an eight category system, is given in Table 13.4.

As the author points out, it would be improper to generalize from the

* *Sixth-Form Pupils and Teachers* (1970), vol. 1, p. 68. The original table includes similar data concerning independent non-boarding and direct grant schools, and technical and 'other' maintained schools.

results of so small a sample as that represented in Table 13.4. They are, however, borne out by the results of a second survey of nearly 1000 students from comprehensive schools in England and Wales who entered universities in October 1968, carried through by Guy Neave as part of a much wider study of the relations between comprehensive-school sixth forms and universities.* Table 13.5 compares the social-class composition of these students with that of all entrants to universities in 1968. It indicates that a considerably higher proportion of comprehensive-school students come from manual working-class homes than is the case generally.†

Table 13.5 **Social-class origin of university students from comprehensive schools, England and Wales**

Social-class origin	Percentage of comprehensive-school entrants, 1968	Percentage of all student entrants, 1968
1. Professional	17	24
2. Managerial and senior technical	31	20
3. Clerical and sales	15	26
4. Manual	38	28

We were interested to know whether the heads of comprehensive schools felt that their pupils had an equal chance of acceptance by institutions of higher and further education as equally qualified pupils from other types of school. The consensus of replies was positive, implying no discrimination – one head writes that he finds that 'in fact most universities are anxious to extend their contact with comprehensive schools', another that he gets the 'vague impression' that in the case of some universities and colleges 'it is an advantage to have come from a comprehensive school', but, he adds, 'I have no real evidence to substantiate this'. There is a division of opinion, however, about Oxford and Cambridge, one writing that she was at a meeting with chancellors and vice-chancellors of these universities who said 'they were anxious to have

* We are grateful to Guy Neave for permission to publish these results from his survey.

† The figures for 'all student entrants' are calculated from UCCA, *Statistical Supplement*, 1968–9. The social-class categories are collapsed differently from Table 13.4. Referring to the list of classes on that table, horizontal column 1 on Table 13.5 corresponds to social class 1; column 2 to social classes 2 and 3; column 3 to social class 4; and column 4 to social classes 5 to 8 inclusive (i.e. *all* manual workers).

entries from comprehensive schools, especially girls'; another reports that in his experience universities 'and especially Oxford' are very fair.* The head of a long-established school, however, does not agree. He finds no discrimination against his students 'except for Oxbridge', adding, 'It clearly needs the Old Pals Act to gain admittance to Oxbridge. I'm *not* kidding.' Several comprehensive-school pupils and junior staff we talked to definitely reported discrimination at many universities against comprehensive-school pupils. One girl told us that the opening remark made to her at her interview for a northern university, by the professor, was: 'So you come from a comprehensive school? We do not think much of comprehensive schools at this university.'

No follow-up studies have been carried through to assess how effectively comprehensive-school students succeed in higher education, though records have been kept in some schools.† Heads expressed themselves well satisfied with students' progress. 'By and large, they appear to do quite well', writes one head; 'none so far has either been given up or sent down'. 'Usually they do pretty well', writes another; 'very few fail at training colleges – only one in fifteen years. This year two former students gained upper second and two lower second honours.' Others comment more generally: 'We seem to have had an encouraging degree of success' writes one, and another: 'From return visits, in every case satisfactory.' One head writes that progress and development 'have in most cases been greater than we anticipated, e.g. first-class honours degrees obtained by students for whom we would have forecast upper seconds at most. Particular satisfaction has come to us from pupils "non-selected" at 11-plus making a great success of courses in higher education.' In several of the schools we visited – as distinct from those answering the questionnaires – we noticed that bulletin boards carried local newspaper cuttings of the schools' students who had taken first-class honours degrees at various universities. Several successful pupils, it may be added, were non-white.

It is becoming increasingly apparent that new developments in the schools, particularly at sixth-form level, call for an adaptation of university entrance requirements; and, also, indicate the need for a unification of higher education to enable adequate planning to accommodate the grow-

* The Franks Report (Oxford University) devoted attention to this question, and showed a definite concern to establish entry conditions suitable for comprehensive schools. *Oxford University: report of commission of inquiry*, vol. 1, pp. 79–85, 1966. The figures given on page 312, however, seem to indicate that this may not be working out.

† This and related matters are now being researched, for the 1968 university entry, by Guy Neave. Interviews and comments by students are reported in *Comprehensive Education*, no. 19, Autumn 1971.

ing numbers of qualified entrants which the open policy in comprehensive schools is bound to bring forward.[2]

Who teaches the sixth?

It was not our intention to make an analysis of the staffing of comprehensive schools, a matter covered by the NFER report on the position in 1965. But a point of particular interest is the extent to which non-graduates are now teaching in sixth forms and taking A-level work. It was once generally held that teachers in secondary modern schools (for the most part non-graduates) were incapable of teaching O-level GCE – in practice they proved the contrary. Now it is held that, except in one or two subjects, only graduates can effectively teach at A-level, and this argument is being used in support of restricting the development of sixth forms. But this supposition is already crumbling.

We may look, first, at the overall position in 1969 – the latest year for which the DES has produced comparative statistics (Table 13.6).[3]

Table 13.6 **Graduate and non-graduate teachers in maintained schools, 1969, England and Wales**

	No. of teachers	*Graduate*	%	*Non-graduate*	%
Modern schools	63,274	10,167	16·1	53,107	83·9
Grammar schools	34,967	26,157	74·8	8810	25·2
Comprehensive schools	37,222	14,630	39·3	22,592	60·7
Total	135,463	50,954	37·6	84,509	62·4

The different proportion of graduates and non-graduates in each case is striking. Only the comprehensive school has a roughly equal balance between the two. It is evident that, as comprehensive schools multiply, the proportion of graduates teaching in them may diminish slightly. An earlier report from the DES – from a sample of schools in 1965–6 – makes possible a detailed analysis of the distribution of teaching power for external examinations between the two groups of teachers.[4] If we start with O-level GCE (taken in the fourth and fifth years) we find that in secondary modern schools 23·5 per cent of the total tuition time was given by graduates (or graduate equivalents), as compared to 76·5 per cent given by non-graduates. In grammar schools the proportions were reversed, 83 per cent of the total tuition time being given by graduates, and only 17 per cent by non-graduates. In the sample of comprehensive schools 59·3 per cent was given by graduates, 40·7 per cent by non-graduates. (The overall figures were 62·1 per cent graduate, 37·9 per cent non-graduate.) These figures make it clear that the comprehensive school was already six years ago making good use of non-graduates in teaching O-level both in the fourth and fifth forms – and, incidentally, in the sixth form, where just over 40 per cent of O-level teaching was done by non-graduates in the sample of comprehensive schools.

Moving now to A-level, in which we are particularly interested, the DES sample survey revealed a trend which is likely to grow in the future: A-level teaching by non-graduates. But first it is worth pointing out that this already had a base in those relatively few secondary modern schools which had developed A-level work, the survey revealing that just over 55 per cent of all such teaching in the sample modern schools was done by non-graduates. In grammar schools the comparable figure was only 8·1 per cent (probably mostly woodwork, metalwork and technical drawing). In comprehensive schools, however, the figure rose to 18·6 per cent – almost one-fifth of all A-level work.[5]

Heads in our smaller sample were asked a specific question on this issue: 'Are any A-level courses taught by non-graduates? If so, which ones?' The answers gave some indication of more recent developments. As in the case of grammar schools, metalwork, woodwork and technical drawing are normally taught by non-graduates, as well as art (in some cases). It is likely that such subjects are more highly developed as sixth-form subjects in comprehensive schools, so this may account partly for the higher proportion of A-level work taught by non-graduates in comprehensive as compared to grammar schools in the DES survey. 'If you count fully qualified art, metalwork, woodwork and technical-drawing teachers as non-graduates (an invidious distinction) then there are four', writes one head; another points to 'divinity, needlework and commercial subjects', another to 'woodwork and housecraft', another to 'housecraft, needlework and art', another to 'music, art, engineering', another to 'metalwork and housecraft'. But there is evidence also in the replies of a growing acceptance of non-graduates as teachers of general subjects also. In one school, biology is so taught; another head replies that English, French and biology are taught by non-graduates, the first two 'very well', the third 'well'. In another school with a very large and successful sixth form, English, history, mathematics, art, engineering and religious instruction are taught to A-level by non-graduates; in another school mathematics is so taught, the head noting 'this is not for lack of graduates'. Another school uses non-graduates for science and mathematics 'to a limited extent'. Although a few schools in our sample (six) use no non-graduates for teaching at A-level, it is evident that this situation is changing, and, as already noted, is likely to change further in the future. The head of a Leicestershire upper school visited in the course of this survey was, for instance, very definite on this point. With a staff of about 55 per cent graduates, he stressed that non-graduates on his staff were quite capable of taking sixth-form A-levels and many do so. The converse, he pointed out, also applies – citing a science graduate who concentrates on first-year science teaching (14–15) and the general-science courses.

In this connection it is worth pointing out that a growing proportion of college of education students have now gained between one and four A-levels (65 per cent of entrants in 1970); that all now (since 1963) follow a three-year course in which at least one 'main' subject is studied throughout. Such teachers, if prepared for secondary schools, should be quite capable of teaching to A-level standard, quite apart from the new graduate (B.Ed.) output from the colleges (nearly 3000 in 1971 alone).*

In addition, some university schools of education are now providing in-service training for non-graduates whose schools are going comprehensive, and who will, therefore, have the opportunity to teach at sixth-form level for the first time. The Bristol School, for instance, recently provided a two-year part-time course for teachers of technical and engineering drawing, and another, shorter, course for teachers of English (both graduates and non-graduates). Those who succeed at such courses, writes the tutor concerned, 'are well able to teach to A-level', adding that this procedure could well be applied to other subjects. 'Such people', he concludes, 'are going to play a very full and very useful part in the development of the comprehensive schools of the future.'[6]

Training of teachers for the comprehensive school

As a school of a new type, the comprehensive school makes new demands on teachers. In so far as schools are genuinely comprehensive, each will usually include children from different social and home backgrounds, with a different linguistic development and at widely different levels in terms of knowledge and skills. This represents a situation radically different from that in the divided system of the past.

It is evident that teachers who have taught in grammar or modern schools, accepting the assumptions upholding this differentiation, may find the transition to teaching in a comprehensive school difficult – especially, perhaps, in relation to the new possibilities that arise. 'The first thing for people used to teaching in grammar or modern schools', writes one head, 'is to discard preconceived ideas about the "type of child" who normally used to go to one or the other', to clarify their ideas about the educability of the normal child, and be prepared 'to adopt versatile approaches with children of a wide range of ability'. Another writes:

* The number of college of education students gaining the B.Ed. since its inception in 1968 is as follows: 1968, 219; 1969, 1388; 1970, 2260; 1971, 2872. Total, 1968–71, 6739.

Staff who have been teaching in grammar schools for a long period find very great difficulty in adapting themselves to the spirit and method of comprehensive education. What is required is acceptance of the idea that it is worthwhile to teach one's subject to classes of varying ability, and to recognize that this requires greater professional skill and a more profound social consciousness.

This problem of adjustment is clearly widespread and now affects teachers everywhere and in a variety of ways. Non-graduates wish to increase their qualifications – inquiry by the NFER has revealed that as many as 80,000 non-graduate teachers wish to take a degree; graduates want to learn more of the problems of the more backward – or more deprived – pupils. A national conversion process such as is run in Sweden, to assist teachers to equip themselves to meet the new situation, is not only necessary, but entirely practical. The Open University, in cooperation with universities and colleges, is in the best position to carry through an operation on the scale required; one that should be planned in the closest connection with the schools, and aimed at meeting their current requirements at each stage of development.

The transition to comprehensive education also has direct implications for the training of teachers; especially if current trends continue (as is likely) and the schools move towards the modification of streaming and new approaches in the content and methods of education. 'The idea of the closed classroom door and of the teacher as an expositor and conveyor of knowledge has to give way to the concept of the teacher as mediator of learning resources', as one head writes, and this involves a new expertise, as well as a new adaptability and flexibility. The young teachers who are needed now in comprehensive schools, writes another, must be able to contribute a specialist knowledge to as high a level as they are capable but also be able and willing to work as part of a team in a group project or interdisciplinary study. Above all the teacher must not only be prepared to teach across the ability range – part of his professional preparation must involve concentrated study and understanding of recent research findings as to the nature of intellectual ability and the conditions fostering its growth. This involves familiarity with recent advances in the psychology of human learning, as well as relevant research in sociology. 'For goodness sake', writes a head, 'let us rid ourselves of the old language and stop thinking in easy categories. *Forbidden terms:* "failure, stream, top-stream, Newsom child, a remedial, bottom of the class", etc. Let us stop making easy assumptions about individuals and groups.' Teachers in comprehensive schools, according to another head, must be 'very energetic and prepared to teach pupils of widely varying ability – and to adapt their approach continually from lesson to lesson in a more flexible way than under the tripartite system'. They should 'become more familiar with the techniques of mixed-ability teaching and less conventional in their approach to subjects', writes the former head of a grammar school; 'the problem is finding graduate teachers capable of taking A-level courses who have sufficient interest in the welfare of children of average ability'.

Answering a question on teacher training in this way, heads of comprehensive schools underlined the new demands from these schools – for new techniques, approaches, attitudes, sympathies, for an open mind as well as an informed one, for readiness to innovate. Stress was also laid on the need for training to take account of the social aspects of the comprehensive school: the role of the house or form tutor, guidance and counselling. Certainly the time has come for conscious acceptance by university departments and colleges that their task is to prepare students for *comprehensive* secondary education, with all that this entails. Another thing seems clear. Such training must be carried on in much closer cooperation with the schools than has formerly been the case. It is in the schools that the new developments are taking place, and it is the teachers in these schools who are responsible. Training institutions need to establish the closest contact if they are effectively to induct students in the new ethos of the comprehensive school. That there is a firm desire on the part of the staff of schools to play a much more positive part in the preparation of new entrants to the profession comes out time and again in our questionnaire replies, particularly in relation to the supervision of teaching practice. Could not experienced teachers act as teacher-tutors (on the pattern introduced by the University of Leicester school of education), asks one head, so that 'the school itself becomes directly responsible for the student-teacher while on school practice', the students being allocated only to good departments whose head in turn receives an honorarium? Could there not be closer integration through secondment of 'our best teachers' ('and we all know who they are') for three-year periods? Would not a three-year sandwich course of training be better than the present concurrent course at colleges, the second year being spent in school? All these suggestions both express the desire to play a more responsible part in training recruits to the profession and indicate how a constructive relationship could be established.

In addition, teachers – both those in service and those in training – need to be given the opportunity to learn more about new developments in educational technology, especially in connection with specific problems involved in reorganization.

Teaching the full-ability range at secondary stage requires new techniques of teaching – for example, greater emphasis on group and individual work. To assist this, teachers naturally look for help to the new technology

– for example, to the multi-media approach involved in the use of tape recorders, films, slides and television. These aids can be used individually or combined in a 'package' programme of learning. Teachers also need to master the new processes of learning made possible by such developments as teaching machines, language laboratories and computer-assisted learning. The effectiveness of many of these has not yet been fully assessed, but clearly each has inherent possibilities provided it is properly integrated in a total learning programme in a school which has clear educational objectives.

It is for the colleges and universities, in turn, to assess the new requirements and work out new approaches, as some are already doing.* In the meantime we may note a radical shift of interest, on the part of university graduates, in teaching in comprehensive schools. The Donnison commission found that whereas in 1966 the government social survey showed that the grammar school was 'the most popular' type of school in which to teach, an investigation at the University of Leicester School of Education three years later (1969) showed an overwhelming preference for teaching in comprehensive schools (of 157 students, ninety-seven stated that the comprehensive school was the type of school in which they would *like* to begin their teaching careers); independent investigations by the Commission at the Manchester and Oxford departments of education in 1970 confirmed this shift, if not quite to the same extent: 46 per cent at Manchester saying they would prefer a comprehensive school 'for the major part of their teaching career', and 41 per cent at Oxford (compared to 36 per cent and 25 per cent opting for grammar schools – the type next most preferred – respectively). It seems clear, therefore, that the comprehensive schools of the future will not be short of their share of graduate teachers.[7]

In this connection, it is increasingly recognized today that teaching is a highly skilled job, and that this is the case whatever the age-level. It could well be argued that the greatest expertise is required today in the primary schools, since so much of the most advanced research into the psychology of learning finds its direct application in these schools which,

---

* Some areas are more fortunate than others in this respect, but an inquiry in 1965 (by the NUS) revealed that 71 per cent of those leaving college that year had not even visited a comprehensive school, let alone learning about teaching in one. 'Report on the three-year course in the colleges of education', NUS, March 1966. A later survey (1969) indicated that 48 per cent of a sample of college of education students training for secondary schools found the course on teaching in comprehensive schools inadequate (or the topic altogether ignored), though teaching about the comprehensive-school system itself was rated more highly. *The Future of Teacher Education*, National Union of Teachers, 1969. Unfortunately the James Report on teacher education (1972) produced nothing whatever on this question.

therefore, call for special knowledge and skills. Now that secondary schools partly as a result of comprehensive reorganization, are also beginning to operate on the basis of *educational* criteria, the essential unity of the process of education as a whole is beginning to be realized. Any attempt, therefore, to hive off the colleges of education to produce primary teachers on the cheap, and to break their connections with other sectors of higher education and especially the universities, as was in fact proposed by the James Committee early in 1972, can only set the clock right back by perpetuating divisions in teacher education just beginning to be overcome. Progress must rather be made in precisely the opposite direction.

Another point is equally clear – the unification of secondary education makes nonsense of the division of training into graduate and non-graduate – a leftover from pre-war days before the Education Act of 1944. Both are doing precisely the same job in secondary schools, and, if we are serious about the need to maintain standards (the quality of education), then this dichotomy should be overcome as rapidly as possible. All teachers in secondary schools (and we would add, in primary as well) should follow a course of degree standard, though not necessarily with the present content. The unification of secondary education points inevitably to such a unification at the level of higher education, and in particular, to a fusion of the colleges with universities as was proposed in the Robbins Report. This would provide the ground base from which teacher education could be lifted to a new level. It would also bring the universities into direct relation with the school system as a whole, including the primary sector where there are some of the most complex problems. It remains to work out ways of attaining this objective.

Notes

1. Margaret Westwood, 'University course: how comprehensive students compare', *Comprehensive Education*, no. 17, Spring 1971. Table 13.4 is taken from this article.
2. R. Layard, J. King and C. Moser, *The Impact of Robbins*, 1969, especially chapter 3, 'The upsurge at A-level'.
3. DES, *Statistics*, 1969, vol. 4, p. 18, Table 15.
4. DES, *Statistics*, Special Series 1965–6, pt 1. *Teachers*, pp. 100–101, Table 18.
5. ibid., p. 100, Table 18, provides the material for these two paragraphs.
6. Harold Knowlson, 'Forward to the sixth', *Forum*, vol. 10, no. 3, Summer 1968.
7. Public Schools Commission, *Second Report*, vol. II, 1970, pp. 78–85; the University of Leicester investigation is reported in M. T. Whiteside, G. Bernbaum and G. Noble, 'Aspirations, reality shock and entry into teaching', *Sociological Review*, vol. 17, 1969.

Part Four
The Comprehensive School as a Community

Chapter 14
The Internal Social Organization

Although the very large comprehensive school of 2000 is now no longer necessary or likely, the average comprehensive of 800-plus is still – for Britain – larger than is traditional. It still poses a problem of how to adapt the school organization to make the individual pupil count.

The realization that comprehensive schools would have to adopt new forms of social organization came more slowly than the realization that they would have to adopt new academic organization. From a head:

In the first comprehensive I knew . . . nobody so far as I knew raised the issue of a special social organization during the first few years of its existence. . . . It was assumed traditional methods would meet the needs of most pupils. Things, I fancy, would be different today.[1]

Indeed, they are. Most comprehensive schools realize that the traditional social organization – the form with its form teacher – is inadequate for a comprehensive school. It is inadequate partly because of the larger size of the comprehensive, partly because of the wider variety of guidance that the wider variety of pupils will require at different ages.

If the traditional form-and-form-teacher structure of the grammar or secondary modern school is not adequate, and if the head teacher cannot, as he sometimes could in a small school, be familiar with all the pupils and their problems – what form of organization will best permit the large school to be broken down into manageable, homely units, where pastoral care may be exercised and pupils known as individuals? There is no real agreement here. Firstly because schools differ in age range and in size. What is required for a 1500 all-through school is not always that which will suit a 500 upper school. The layout, shape and size of the school's buildings will also have an influence on the framework adopted, as will the school's educational policy generally. But the case for social units is not just for the sake of administrative convenience or pastoral care. As one head has written: 'There is a realization that the social institutions of the school can serve a positive educational role, when education is taken, as it generally is in this country, to imply the education of the whole person rather than merely academic instruction.'[2]

Speaking very generally, the two main ways of breaking down schools into small units are horizontally – into upper, middle and lower divisions (or, more finely, into individual years) – and vertically – into units that contain a cross-section of pupils from youngest to oldest. Table 14.1 sets out our findings about the main forms of internal social organization used in comprehensive schools in 1968.

House systems

The most widely discussed and described vertical grouping in the comprehensive school in Britain has been the house system. This is partly because it is familiar, the idea of the 'house' having come from the public schools, and partly because it is associated with some of Britain's pioneer comprehensives. The First NFER Report found that 299 of its 331 responding comprehensive schools in 1965 had house-system organizations.[3] This was 90 per cent of all comprehensive schools in 1965. No wonder so many educationists and sociologists assumed – even as late as 1968 – that house systems were standard practice in comprehensive schools.

The surprising feature of Table 14.1, showing the 1968 position, is that the pure house system – with no other forms of social organization – was used in only 17 per cent of British comprehensive schools. Even when combined with other forms (upper and lower school division and year organization) the house system was used as the main form of organization in only 37 per cent of comprehensive schools. In Scotland only seven schools used the house system as their sole form of internal organization, and only twenty (30 per cent) had any form of house system. The Second NFER Report of 1970 modified their 1965 findings a good deal, for reasons we deal with later. Their Second Report on 59 schools showed only one in five with strong house systems, and only 36 per cent with any form of house system – findings roughly comparable with our own.[4]

Before examining the reasons for this dramatic change – for there has been one – in recent years, let us first look at the development of the house system.

The establishment of the house system as a physical entity was Coventry's major contribution to the evolution of the comprehensive school – and a model for others to follow. Each of the eight comprehensive schools which Coventry built between 1953 and 1959 was organized on a house basis, designed at the outset to be the day school's equivalent of the residential houses in public schools. It was intended that all these schools would ultimately contain ten houses, each supervised by a housemaster or housemistress assisted by several other members of the school staff. Much thought and care went into the planning of Coventry's compre-

Table 14.1 **Internal social organization of British comprehensive schools, 1968**

Method used	All Schools		Scotland		Percentages of each type of school with each method							
	No.	%	No.	%	11/12–18 Type I	11/12–18 Type II	11/12–16	11–13	11–14/15	13–18	14–18	16–18 or sixth-form college
Houses	122	17	7	10·5	20	3	19	14	10	6	19	0
Lower + upper school (or lower/middle/upper)	86	12	0		17	16	9	0	1·5	0	0	0
Years	291	40	44	65·5	28	26	47	79	64	65	56	0
Houses and lower/middle/upper schools	111	15	7	10·5	18	35·5	14	0	4	11	19	0
* Years and lower/middle/upper	34	5	2	3	7	10	0·5	0	1·5	3	0	0
* Houses and years	34	5	6	9	4	3	3	3·5	11·5	6	6	0
Others and unknown	50	7	1	1·5	6	6·5	7	3·5	7	9	0	100
		100		100	100	100	100	100	100	100	100	100
Totals	728	100	67	100	389	31	154	29	70	34	16	2

* These two categories added for computer coding on basis of additional written information supplied by schools in answer to this question.

hensive schools.[5] The house provision consisted of an assembly room (which was also to be used as the house dining room), a study room, a small staff room, a housemaster's or housemistress's room, as well as cloakrooms and lavatories for staff and pupils. The houses were built in pairs, with accommodation for one house in each wing, the aim being for each school to have five pairs – ten houses of 150 pupils each. Some houses were regarded solely as social centres and were built without accommodation for teaching. From the experience of others, however, it was found that certain advantages derived from the association of at least four teaching spaces with each house. In the first place, registration was simplified. Secondly, teaching in mixed-ability groups could be more easily arranged; and facilities existed for quiet recreational activities and house-society meetings during the lunch hour and when school was finished. In comprehensive schools outside Coventry house systems have sometimes been introduced primarily for teaching, rather than for social, purposes. This is particularly true in Wales, where house systems are less the rule. The David Hughes School in Anglesey, for example, introduced a house system primarily as a means of organizing mixed-ability teaching groups. Whether used for teaching purposes or not, in most schools in the country where house systems are used, houses are of mixed ability.

House tutors are expected to show a real concern for the pupils in their care and are encouraged to refer problems of discipline and work to the house heads, who have authority to deal with them without further reference elsewhere. An inquiry into Coventry's house system showed that the houses in the Coventry schools also provided many opportunities for pupils of all abilities to shoulder responsibility.[6] A good house system does much to help children with special difficulties overcome their problems. E. F. McCarthy, late headmaster of Malory, the first London comprehensive to be built on Coventry-like house basis, wrote: 'it is for its effect and influence upon the social rebels that the house organization is most justified'.[7] Giving older pupils responsibility for younger ones within the vertical house grouping has been commented upon frequently by schools as one of the benefits of this system. One of the Coventry heads reported that:

Backward readers are coached by me with the help of sixth-formers who are interested in welfare, and I often find an older pupil patiently explaining some knotty problems to a younger member of the House.[8]

In the earliest comprehensive schools – especially those that grew up as large schools and in urban areas with mixed populations – there is no doubt that the house system played an important part in creating a true community within the larger school. They seem also to have happily avoided the rigid hierarchical structure of their counterparts in the public schools. Coventry's example was followed, together with provision of actual house blocks, in West Bromwich, Walsall, Nottingham, and in some of the later LCC schools. One headmaster, writing in 1958, described the house and tutor-group system as 'the best feature of the English public-school system', which, when transferred to the comprehensive school, solves, among other things, 'the vexed problem of continuity'.[9] This idealism about the house system, and faith in its ability to overcome the problems posed by size, carried through into the 1960s. In his book *Comprehensive Schools in Action*, published in 1964, Roger Cole wrote that 'parents whose children attend a comprehensive school which has a house system should realize that the houses are a *sine qua non* of the life of the school'. 'A house organization', he continued, 'is in practice effective, as a means of giving each child a place within a unit smaller than the school as a whole'.[10]

But as time went on, it became obvious that the house system was not the answer to all problems. For one thing, in a few schools where it was adopted, it was wrongly assumed that it would take care of all social and educational guidance. It was left to the house tutor or house staff to deal with all problems that arose – academic, social, vocational and medical – and this most were not equipped or prepared to do. Perhaps the most important factor was that there was not enough time. Generally those who are in charge of houses or tutor groups are supposed to be given a lighter teaching load than other staff. But some schools do not do this. In our own smaller sample of schools, we found that out of the thirty-six schools answering the question as to whether a lighter teaching load was given to staff with pastoral duties,* eleven schools did not allow the staff in charge of social unit groups *any* lighter teaching load at all.

Practice in the twenty-five schools allowing time off varied according to the scope of the duties. When the schools interpreted this question to refer to the large social unit (house head, for example), we found practice varied from complete freedom from any teaching duties (especially for heads of whole organizational units like lower schools) in a small number of cases across to the majority pattern: only a half to one-third time off the usual teaching load. When schools answered this in respect of the smaller unit, the 'tutor-group' or 'year-group' leaders,* of the fifteen schools giving some time free for these tutors: five gave five fewer periods a week, two gave four, five gave three, and three gave two. A number of schools among those not giving any free time to social unit staff said they wished they could give it, but staffing shortage would not permit it. Even

* This question was asked of all schools – both those with house systems and those with one of the other forms of organization.

many of those giving time off said they found it was quite inadequate. The Second NFER Report also reported that teachers in charge of houses were heavily timetabled for ordinary teaching, a finding that indicated 'a need for senior staff to have sufficient time free from classroom teaching to undertake other duties'.[11] It also found that the demands of subject teaching left the allowances far too thinly spread over those with social-unit responsibilities.[12] There is no doubt that the pastoral staff – whether in house or year systems or horizontal sectioning – need a substantial portion of their time free from teaching, and adequate allowance recognition of their many heavy extra duties, to do their jobs effectively. In most comprehensive schools they are probably not getting this. For a house system in particular, this is undermining and may well be one of the factors contributing to the decline of this system.

Schools vary a great deal, not only in the amount of 'free' time they give staff to deal with social units to which they are assigned, but also in the practice of paying extra allowances for this work and in the assignment of staff themselves. Some schools allot every staff member to a social unit, others do not. Some schools assume the social unit will merely deal with routine matters of registration or 'teams' for games, others hope that it will encompass all the pastoral and educational guidance needed during the whole school life. This policy towards the social unit obviously affects actual social organization deeply. An American researcher, Ralph Pounds, in his study of the house system in Britain,[13] characterized three types of house system: strong, weak and medium – on the basis of the percentage of activities and tasks of guidance that were organized in the house as against those organized outside it. A strong house system almost always had physical units around which it could build, but this need not always be so. Highbury School in London is an example of a strong house system without specially built house blocks. It is strong because of the policy of organization:

the house is a very real home to each boy; he wears its flash, he plays sport for it, and he receives his academic reports, his medical cards, and all educational and pastoral guidance through it. The house room is open before school; at morning break for talk and a canteen; at lunch for meals, for games and talk; after school for over an hour for games, talk or a place to do homework; one or two evenings a week each house has a Club Evening until 9.30. . . . There is no School Parents' Association, only House Associations.[14]

A weak house system, on the other hand, organizes only for games or for Eisteddfod competition. A medium system will come between, sometimes organizing discipline and guidance within a house, sometimes not. Pounds found that those schools indicating decreasing use of house organization in the school – or abandonment of it altogether – were always those with medium and weak organization.[15]

As our survey results indicate, the house system is used by only a minority of schools. As we found out in visits, and as is obvious in recent comprehensive school literature, the house system has not turned out to be the panacea early pioneers expected it would be. Where house staff were over-worked or where organization of courses, subject guidance, or welfare was dealt with systematically outside the 'social unit' of the house, it was obvious that the house unit declined in importance. In some schools it declined precisely because its medium or weak organization left it unable to cope with the wide variety of social and educational needs that came crowding in. The NFER's Second Report gives another reason for a fall in house systems, for it comes to the conclusion that it has 'not usually been possible to organize a strong house system in schools adapted from existing buildings'. They will only really succeed where there are purpose-designed and built house units.[16] Even for purpose-built comprehensives, today's stringent financial situation rarely permits the 'lavish' construction of separate house units on the early patterns – each with their own kitchens and assembly hall.

But there is another important reason why house systems have not been able to stand alone. As we have seen, developing comprehensive schools have tended to separate their schools into sections. The most important section to be divided off has been the sixth form, which has expanded rapidly in all types of comprehensive schools. This need for the sixth-former to have separate quarters and a separate social 'life' was recognized very early.[17] Over the last five years more and more schools – due to the large increase in pupils staying on – have either separated their sixth-formers or devised special areas of the school for them. In some schools, like Duffryn in Wales, the sixth form has its own separate building. In others, like Brislington in Bristol, a new floor has been added to the top of the school for the sixth form. At Elliott School in Putney and Monks Park in Bristol – and in many others – it is a new block that has been built with ROSLA funds especially for the sixth and seventh years of the school. Among the early Coventry schools some have now provided sixth-formers with their own common rooms and libraries and study rooms – even though they are retained in 'houses'.

At the other end of the age range the same thing has happened. Many schools have deliberately adopted a policy of separating out the first year or the first two years of the school – partly to ease the transition from primary to secondary school curriculum, partly to get pupils used to a 'big' school, and partly to make the individual ages easier to manage. Several of the schools replying to us spoke of the success of these arrangements, one head saying he would now defend them against any who 'want to mix ages in artificial groupings'. The method of separation differs in different schools. Wyndham School at Egremont has a reception block for newcomers where they remain for one year (although the head feels this is too short a time). At Fishguard School in Pembrokeshire the first year's intake of 150, coming from fourteen different primary schools, is housed in the old grammar-school building under a separate master in charge. Netherhall School, Cumberland, has a Foundation House for the first two years. So does Wandsworth in London, although the boys are also at the same time members of one of the six houses of the school.

Many of these upper/lower systems that we have been describing occur when the school is in two buildings. Sometimes schools are purpose-built in two buildings, sometimes the two-building arrangement is the result of amalgamation of two existing schools. But quite obviously the house system pure and simple is harder to operate in a school that is divided among more than one building. It is natural to organize the younger (or older) groups separately in the 'other site', and the rise in the percentage of combined comprehensives since 1965 no doubt partly accounts for the fall in popularity of the pure house system in recent years.

Horizontal sectioning: lower, middle and upper schools

In describing the changes that have taken place in the house systems over the years, it is evident that they involve schools moving imperceptibly to a form of organization in broad horizontal bands: of lower-and-upper or lower-middle-upper school. As we can see in Table 14.1, this broad-band horizontal form of social organization is used by 12 per cent of schools in our survey as the only form of organization. When combined with some of the other forms, it is used by 32 per cent.

Perhaps the best-known example of a pure horizontal system in action is that used in Birmingham's Sheldon Heath comprehensive, which began life in 1955. This is divided into lower, middle and upper schools, each possessing its own assembly hall, library, staff room and class-rooms in three- and four-storey blocks, the upper school being centrally placed, with through communication to the other schools. The lower school at Sheldon Heath is for all children between the ages of eleven and thirteen. At the end of their second year, the boys and girls move on to the middle school which will be the final section for those who leave the school at the end of their fifth year. The upper school is for those pupils who elect to remain at school beyond the present statutory leaving age. These senior pupils, while having their own building, are expected to set an example of maturity and serious study to the whole school. Each school has its own 'teacher-in-charge'. It is obvious that recent separate building developments – in both purpose-built and amalgamated schools – as well as the recent rise in 'tiered' schemes generally where separate schools are linked in steps, mean that the division of schools into horizontal age units will be developed much further in years to come.

Year systems

The big rival to the house system and the broad-band horizontal system is the year system. More schools use the year system than any other form of social organization, as we discovered. Forty per cent use it as the only form of organization, and this rises to 50 per cent when used in combination with houses or horizontal sectioning.

This is an interesting and curious development, and it is difficult to relate it to past practice. This is because three years before our survey – in the National Foundation Survey of 1965 – no question was asked about the year system.[18] It may be that many schools would have answered with 'year system' had the NFER included questions on it in their 1965 survey. It may be that some schools answering the NFER survey called their year groups 'houses'. It may be, too, that a house system is something that takes time to build up and that the nearly double number of comprehensive schools between 1965 and 1967–8 had not yet developed house systems to the point where they could name them as operating. But it is unlikely that any of these is the full explanation for these changes. We must also look for a subtle shift away from the house form of organization in some schools that had adopted it – and have now abandoned it – and, also, an inclination in newly-formed schools not to adopt it at all. This is especially true in schools where the age range is other than 11–18, so many of which have been established in recent years. In its Second Report the NFER included year systems in its investigations, but it also had a category called 'school systems' – a horizontal unit based on age, within which year systems could also operate.[19] It was not always clear, however, exactly what was being described by the terms used – perhaps because schools differ so in their use of terms and in their individual practices. It is also true that schools are continually evolving in this respect, and can alter their own practices from year to year, as well, perhaps as their system's names.

Table 14.2 shows quite clearly how strongly 'year-system' organization increases as schools get smaller in size (while other forms, like a combination of houses and upper/lower division, increase in frequency as schools get larger in size). We can also see from Table 14.1 that year systems are far more popular in the shorter age-range schools – 11–13, 11–14/15 or 13–18 – and less popular in the all-through schools.

Table 14.2 **Internal social organization of British comprehensive schools by size, 1968**
Percentage of schools using each method

Method of organization	Size of school				
	Small 1–600	Medium 601–1200	Large 1201–1800	Very large 1801+	Total no. schools
Houses	14	19	19	17	122
Upper/lower or upper/middle/lower	5	15	21	8	86
Years	60	30	19	8	291
Houses and upper/middle lower	9	18	22	42	111
Years and upper/middle/lower	2	5	11		34
Houses and years	4	5	5	8	34
Other and Unknown	6	8	3	17	50
	100	100	100	100	
Total number of schools	283	345	88	12	728

It must also be remembered that the house system works better in schools with actual physical houses than in schools where it is super-imposed upon an ordinary physical organization – although quite a number of schools, particularly in London, will say they operate successful house systems even without 'physical' house dining rooms, assemblies, common rooms.[20] Other London schools, however, have had doubts. A house system, wrote the head of Woodberry Down, 'in a day school ... has tended to be a weak, artificial imitation of the real purposeful organization of the public school'.[21] The head of Mayfield argued: 'Without such physical bases, the development of a house system feeling is very difficult; makeshift meeting places instead of house rooms or house blocks emphasize the unrealistic side of the house system.'[22]

Others have found that although from the school's point of view there could be successful house systems without actual houses, they were not always supported as meaningful social units by pupils in these same schools.[23]

Analysis of recent changes

It is not surprising, then, that a number of publications, and a number of schools in our own inquiry, report the abandonment of what many reluctantly have come to regard as 'artificial' social units.[24] Some of the schools we questioned made the move deliberately:

Before the two schools were amalgamated, both had their own house systems, but these were not of any real significance. For one year as an experiment we strengthened the house system in the grammar school and implemented a year system in the modern school, to compare the two. The house system had much to commend it, but because of the advice we were given at other comprehensive schools, and the design of our buildings, we settled for the year system which we now have.

This was an 11–18 school in a country town. Southgate County School in Hertfordshire also changed over from a house system to a year system in September 1968. The headmaster found it impossible to operate an effective house organization with the school divided into a lower school (for the first three years) and an upper school situated in different buildings one mile away. It proved very difficult to maintain close contact between housemasters/mistresses and the pupils in their house. In moments of individual crisis, it was never easy to bring house tutors who were in the other part of the school to interviews between headmaster and parents. Under the new system now in operation, year staff are largely restricted to one part of the school and are available on the spot to help children with day-to-day problems. The headmaster and his staff know exactly which teacher is responsible for each year, and can more easily exchange information and discuss problems. In this connection it is interesting that the NFER's Second Report said that individual advice to pupils was more likely in schools that were sub-divided,[25] rather than in schools left to operate on the old form-and-form-teacher basis. It did not matter whether it was in horizontal or vertical units; what mattered was that there be strong sub-units.

Most schools that abandon house systems go over to year systems. As we have seen, many more schools – half of all comprehensives in our survey, in fact – adopt year systems as their main form of social organization.

Mayfield School in London, which developed out of a three-form-entry grammar school in 1955, will serve as a useful example of a strongly developed year system.[26] Each year contains twelve forms of thirty – 360 girls. The form tutors in each year are directly responsible to the head of year, or year mistress, who carries a special responsibility allowance similar to that of housemistress in other schools. Her status in the school is high, for she is responsible for the academic and social well-being of each girl in her particular year and will be consulted by the head and the deputy on all matters concerning their general discipline and pastoral care. She may call assemblies of the girls in her year whenever she wants to, and will hold regular meetings of her form tutors at break or during the lunch hour. Year mistresses and form tutors remain, year by year, with the same group of pupils as they make their way through the school. This establishes continuity and avoids a situation where information has always to be passed on from one set of teachers to another.

The year is also the unit at Mayfield for the organization of social service and extra-curricular activities, the third-year drama festival and the second-year music festival being good examples of popular events organized on a year basis. A disadvantage of the year system, conceded by Margaret Miles herself, is that it is not always desirable to have pupils of a narrow age range experiencing things together. On the other hand, it avoids a competitive spirit, with the idea that 'our house' must be the 'best house', which, in the opinion of Miss Miles, is 'immature and unfruitful of real educational and social development'.[27] It is obvious that girls' schools are particularly less partial to the house system – perhaps because of this element of male 'competitiveness' – for, as we see in chapter 18, many fewer girls' schools operate a house system than do boys' or mixed schools and more girls' schools have abandoned house systems than boys' schools.[28]

But a further reason for the rise of the year system is the general movement towards student participation in the running of schools. This has led to a desire of schools to enable pupils to participate within their own group. Participation for all pupils is harder in a 'house' system which automatically gives leadership to the older pupils or prefects only. As one headmaster has observed, the year system by contrast fosters 'leadership from *among* and not from *above*'.[29] This head hopes his own school will develop a year system that will 'be centred on the development of a grass-roots democracy in each of our year groups'. It is significant, too, that this particular headmaster is one who has visited the United States. The American high school is year-based – each group entering a high school, in fact, being given the name of the year when it will reach the 12th grade (or upper sixth), i.e. a year group entering a six-year school in 1970 would be called throughout 'the class of 1976'. It is assumed that everyone will stay until eighteen – that it is abnormal for anyone to leave before 1976. In the United States the year system has assisted in focusing pupils upon the 'goal' of their school life and has – along with the existence of a single qualifying diploma available for the vast majority of secondary age pupils at the end of the twelfth grade at eighteen – helped to achieve almost 80 per cent staying on until eighteen.

The year system in this form, however, is unlikely to be suitable to Britain, for in this country the traditional sixth form is now far too well entrenched as the natural 'top' of any school. But it is certainly possible that the sixth form will be the goal that the majority of pupils in Britain will one day stay on to achieve. Any social organization in the comprehensive school must therefore build on this expectation.

In summing up, it is perhaps true that some comprehensive schools have been more determined in their efforts to organize the academic side of the comprehensive school than the social side. But this is changing rapidly. Most schools we visited or questioned are now fully aware that a system of social guidance needs every bit as firm and systematic an approach as academic work. The system adopted by schools varies enormously, and in a growing number of schools a mixture of all three basic forms of organization is the solution adopted. In Appendix 3 (p. 569) we give two versions of 'mixture' systems in two all-through schools, showing in detail how elements of the house, the year, and the horizontal system may be combined.

No single method of organization can be said to be the best one any longer, but it can be said that no system adopted will succeed unless *time* is given to its needs – time in terms of working out a social policy for the school as a whole and time in terms of staff given freedom from teaching duties to undertake their pastoral duties adequately. Nor will any method really succeed unless it is systematically organized and carefully administered. The NFER's Second Report on fifty-nine Comprehensives, as we have shown, provides disturbing evidence that comprehensives do not receive the support they should – in terms of adequate staffing and allowances – to permit staff the time and financial rewards needed to run their social subdivisions with maximum effectiveness. Comprehensive schools are sometimes big places and sometimes seem impersonal. This is why it is important to work out carefully the internal organization to give to each boy and girl a feeling that somebody cares, that there is somebody to whom he or she may turn for help and advice, and that there is some constant and congenial unit through which he or she may participate and to which he or she can really belong. Some schools still have a long way to go. But to give adequate pastoral care – especially in urban areas – they will have to have extra help.

Notes

1. P. M. P. Cornall (Headmaster, West Bridgford Comprehensive School, Nottingham), 'Social organization in the comprehensive school' (document) 1968.
2. ibid.
3. First NFER Report, p. 41.
4. Second NFER Report, p. 37.
5. See Geoffrey C. Firth, *Comprehensive Schools in Coventry and Elsewhere*, 1963.
6. These opinions were collected by means of a questionnaire to all heads of houses in all comprehensive schools. For a full discussion of the results of this inquiry, see Firth, op. cit., pp. 111–30.
7. Writing in *Malory School Magazine*, 1967.
8. Firth, op. cit., pp. 128–9.
9. *Inside the Comprehensive School*, 1958, p. 29.
10. Roger Cole, *Comprehensive Schools in Action*, 1964, pp. 89, 91.
11. Second NFER Report, p. 46.
12. ibid. p. 39.
13. Ralph Pounds, 'The house system in comprehensive schools in England and Wales', US Office of Education, 1968.
14. Rhodes Boyson, 'Breaking down barriers', *Education*, 9 May 1969.
15. Pounds, op. cit., p. 56.
16. Second NFER Report. p. 40.
17. Robin Pedley, *The Comprehensive School*, p. 125, 1963.
18. Question 25, p. 196, could be interpreted as year organization, but it is not specific.
19. Second NFER Report, pp. 37–8.
20. Cole, op. cit., p. 133, comments on Eltham Green School.
21. H. R. Chetwynd, *Woodberry Down*, p. 90.
22. Margaret Miles, *Comprehensive Schooling*, p. 27, 1968.
23. Pounds, op. cit.
24. ILEA, *London Comprehensive Schools*, 1966, contains several examples, with reasons.
25. Second NFER Report, p. 47.
26. Miles, op. cit., pp. 27–31, gives a detailed account of the year system as it operates at Mayfield.
27. ibid., p. 31.
28. See, for example, ILEA Survey, 1967, p. 50. See also NFER Report, pp. 40, 41.
29. Cornall, loc. cit., p. 8.

Chapter 15
Administration in a Comprehensive School

Guidance and counselling

In the last chapter we discussed the comprehensive school's social organization. But there are a great many other matters that a school must organize on behalf of its pupils besides day-to-day social welfare. The extent to which any or all of these matters will be dealt with inside the social unit – the house, section or year – varies with the school. For example, record keeping and matters of discipline are sometimes the province of the social unit, sometimes of the subject department or central office. The social unit in many schools can cope with a great deal, but in most schools some guidance has to be organized alongside, or in conjunction with, pastoral care.

An example of an important set of problems that arise is the choice of subject or course that needs to be made at specific points in school life. Should the exam be CSE or GCE? Should the choice be another language or engineering drawing? Another example is when outsiders must be called in: a psychologist to perform tests or to help in a behaviour problem, a youth employment officer to assist in job placement, or a welfare officer to deal with trouble in the home. Then there are all the uncategorized problems of school life: truanting, bad eyesight, bad company, lost property, or change of mind about a career. There is the boy or girl who wants to leave school whose parents won't let them; the ones who want to stay but whose parents want them to start work.

In schools where the social unit is limited only to daily social life – registration, games or meals – specialist staff and outsiders must be organized alongside to give the necessary guidance or help. The problem with this method is that too fragmented responsibility and widespread distribution of expertise can be inefficient and confusing to all concerned. On the other hand, if too much is centred on the social 'pastor' – the house or year staff – they may well be overburdened with work, and unable to discharge every duty as they would wish. In any case, some guidance tasks are so specialized that pastoral staff cannot take them on even if they wanted to try.

The fact that neither method of organizing pastoral care and pupil guidance (and incidentally a centre of information for parents in respect of each child) is perfect, has led many schools to experiment with new methods, or to try organizing existing staff in a new combination of existing methods. A reorganizing school in Nottinghamshire set up a 'team of staff members under a leadership of a Director of Guidance' to organize specialist help in advising on (a) higher education, (b) careers, (c) courses in the school, and (d) special problems in the lower school.[1] An additional solution – and one certain comprehensive schools have already adopted, e.g. Longslade in Leicestershire – is to add specially recruited and trained guidance counsellors to the staff. This kind of appointment is widely used in other comprehensive systems – particularly in the United States, where the whole field of 'pupil personnel services' is highly developed inside comprehensive schools.[2] There a guidance counsellor is attached to a pupil when he enters the school and stays with this pupil for the whole of his school life. In the counsellor are centred all the aspects of guidance and pastoral care; most do no teaching at all. In Britain, however, the training for counsellors (furthest ahead at the universities of Keele and Reading)[3] aims to equip practising teachers with the skills and knowledge required, reintroducing them in the schools after what amounts to professional in-service training.

Sometimes this training is carried out locally. Netherhall comprehensive school, Cumberland, together with neighbouring comprehensive schools, and in collaboration with Workington college of further education, runs its own in-service courses on counselling for the school's own house staff. The head has written that

Since all of the staff are involved in the exercise of pastoral care, much of the social worker's approach is permeating the structure of the school and an increasing number of teachers are looking at education from a child-centred point of view.[4]

Fourteen of the staff at Netherhall have attended courses, and, says the head, 'we have already noticed a significant reduction in the incidence of juvenile delinquency'. A London comprehensive head also commented on the success of what she called her 'extremely permissive' method of dealing with social problems. She had no discipline problems, she said, because 'we aim at strengthening the desire to conform to an accepted pattern of courtesy and cooperation'. On the other hand, many schools would find the 'social-worker' approach too unstructured, although a few recognize that if properly carried through it might work. As another London head, commenting on the extreme hostility to education generally in much of his pupil population, said: 'Extreme insolence to staff presents acute problems and makes staff unwilling to try new methods. Yet it is the use of inappropriate methods that leads to the hostility.'

Many schools admit to not having found the best way of dealing with behaviour problems. But many authorities – especially urban ones – are now facing the task presented by children with special difficulties. Inner London's special report on this subject, published in early 1972, estimated some 17 per cent of pupils could be in need of special help with behaviour or handicap problems, and it gave notice of a number of projects to be started in schools in an attempt to find the combination of aids and services most helpful to teachers in dealing with children 'in difficulty'.

In some schools the problem is lack of communications; the difficulty goes undetected or is delayed in getting reported to staff and to the home. Nor have some schools been able to deal with the problem of getting out vital and necessary information to all parents and pupils. Although great care is taken, as we saw, in writing leaflets and explaining options – especially at thirteen or fourteen – there is no doubt that in some schools this information just does not reach the parents. Several parents and pupils in schools we visited, told us that they had had no systematic guidance at thirteen/fourteen years of age. Lack of guidance for sixth-formers is mentioned less frequently, but others have found evidence that this too could stand improvement.[5] So too could advice to comprehensive pupils intending to go on to higher education.[6]

On the matter of employment for those leaving schools, while the youth employment officers were praised highly in some areas, we found parents in other areas with very severe criticism about the quality of the help schools and officers had been able to give – especially in finding employment for boys of sixteen.[7] Sometimes the help or the information may have been there, but pupils and parents did not know where to find it. Part of the difficulty, of course, is that many schools just do not realize how complicated their inner workings seem to parents and pupils. Very few arrange for any systematic follow-up study of the effectiveness of their own procedures.

In this connection we collected some interesting insights into procedures from our smaller sample of schools. We asked them about two situations: one academic, the parent who had a child who was having trouble with mathematics; the other social, a child the parents suspected of truanting. We wanted to know about practice in schools for parents making an approach to the school. For parents are often very diffident about coming to school, especially about asking for, or seeing, the head.

We also wanted to see – and this was very important – if the parent had to see a different person for each query; that is, if one person was seen for a school-work query and another for a social-problem query. If practice was to see different persons for different items, this could be confusing.

The answers to the questions were interesting. Here are a few. For truanting one school said the parent should see the 'head, senior master or form master or mistress – any or all'. Another school said, 'At the moment head of upper school.' Yet another said, 'Doesn't really apply to me, but the parent could come to see me.'

The majority of schools gave more than one person to whom the parents might go. Moreover, two-thirds of the schools answering had a different procedure of inquiry for social problems (truancy) than for educational ones (maths). The answers showed that schools cared and that they were anxious and willing to help in problems of this kind; and that parents were always welcome. But for the parent who was diffident, unsure or apathetic, the lack of system in some schools, the complexity of the process, the *ad hoc* nature of the method, and the uncertainty about whether in the multifarious alternatives there would be any one person 'up at the school' who really would take a *continuing* interest – these left question marks. A pupil does not need merely a permanent physical base in relations with the school, he needs a human base as well.

There are many ways to solve this problem, but what is certain is that it cannot be left to chance – or to the parent. And many of the schools we visited feel that help in organizing some kind of formal arrangement for counselling is now required, for this is once again an area where a school may be tempted to carry over past practice into the comprehensive situation and where it may be inadequate. It was traditional in the English school, either grammar or modern, for administration, instruction and all specialized services to come under the list of duties with which the head-master was supposed to cope.[8] Sometimes this informal and *ad hoc* method worked well: choices were understood and made without undue difficulty; behavioural problems were quickly sorted out. The traditional hierarchy of head, deputy, senior staff and 'visiting' help was all that was needed in many cases.

The difficulties of administering comprehensive schools due to lack of adequate support in staffing for pastoral and clerical work and the failure of some schools to delegate effectively or to devise workable means to ends – can be just as confusing for staff as parents. The Second NFER Report illustrates the case of an assistant geography teacher who was a form master in the lower part of a school and taught in the upper. He was required to send matters concerning academic progress of GCE fifth formers to the head of the geography department, those concerning misbehaviour in his registration form to the head of the lower school, but misbehaviour in his geography lessons to a house master, and communications on choice of subjects for a third former making future fourth year choices to the deputy head. When this criss-cross of responsibilities concerns a staff member, he at least is part of the organization – hopefully with a voice in it. But when it involves a pupil or a parent, the effect can be totally bewildering. Not only that, the systems evolved, as this criss-cross indicates, are fairly complex. What can often happen therefore is that advice for commonly arising queries or common problems gets regularized and has a system for dealing with it – but those with an odd problem fall through the net. And every pupil will have at least one odd problem during his school life.

A comprehensive school, therefore, requires something more than the old unifunctional school. Not only because of its large size and the variety of interests and ambitions its pupils will have, but also because this is one of those key points where the school meets the wider world, both in the person of the parents and in its relationship to other schools, to the services and personnel of local organizations and industries, and to further and higher educational institutions. Since the world outside is changing continually, and both the job situation and higher education are getting more and more specialized and complex, a school's organization of advice and information in these fields must keep pace. In addition, writes one specialist on the subject, there is a continuing need for all pupils at a school to have the 'benefit of a personal and confidential relationship with a congenial adult' who will help them 'to attain a realistic understanding of themselves'.[9] These tasks cannot be left to operate on the old informal basis.

Developmental, social or other problems of adjustment, e.g. at the beginning of the secondary school period, can seriously divert a pupil's energies and attentions from academic pursuits. Such problems arise not just for the odd pupil but for all children to some degree . . . it soon becomes obvious that nothing short of systematic organization can hope to cope successfully with the formidable array of tasks involved.[10]

The key words here are 'systematic organization'. We do not know yet which arrangement of social unit works best. We are not yet fully knowledgeable about the outcome of the use of guidance counsellors in British comprehensive schools to know how successful they will prove. But what is already certain is that the tasks that both counselling and social organization are devised to carry out – throughout the whole field of pupil-life – are tasks of the greatest importance that must be systematically organized within each school. A search for the most efficient and effective method within each school situation is now the urgent task of those running comprehensive schools.

Quite obviously one of the big problems is whether we have been right to insist that in general counsellors should also teach, for in the 'under-staffed' situation at all comprehensive schools the counsellor soon finds he or she is spending most of the time in the classroom, unable to practise counselling. As Anne Jones, who has been a full-time counsellor in London, writes of one who has had counsellor training but is not actually counselling: 'it is frustrating and galling not ... to exercise ... new skills', and in many cases to get less allowances than he had formerly.[11] If the problem is solved by employing the counsellor as a full-time counsellor, this post usually has to come off the teaching quota itself – and few schools want to reduce the number of class teachers. What is more, to be truly effective, a counsellor will need, as one who has been a success-ful full-time counsellor knows, 'a room of his own, a telephone, secretarial assistance, his own filing cabinet, ... a flexible timetable so that he actually has time to see his students, staff or parents'.[12] There is lastly the problem of supervision by the local authority, and what Anne Jones has called 'lack of directive or policy at a national departmental level'.[13] To a certain extent too, there is also confusion about whether a counsellor should be primarily orientated towards social work, psychological servicing or careers guidance? Probably some of each, more or less accord-ing to the school. Probably too – more integrated with the school staff than in the USA. But even these major uncertainties should not disguise the fact that someone somewhere in comprehensive schools has got to respond to the 'counselling' needs arising. That the needs are greatest in the large schools and in the schools in the big cities and in those areas where comprehensives coexist with a well defined grammar sector still – is brought out very well in the Second NFER Report which shows that comprehensive school teachers in precisely the latter situations averaged each week *four* hours less teaching and *three* hours more on welfare matters than teachers in, say, Welsh or rural comprehensives.[14] The educational implications here are important and clearly point to the need for counsellors in specific school situations as a matter of some urgency – with a national departmental policy a further essential.

But in the drive for more efficient and well-organized pastoral and educa-tional guidance, the basic social unit of each school will take care not to become a mere mechanism. Nor will it be too inward looking. Since the comprehensive as a school is one that is more outward looking in every way than were the institutions of the past, many feel that social units in particular function most effectively when they have a purpose outside the school as well as inside it. One house in a school we visited in Lancashire organized a snow-shovelling brigade, ready to turn out and clear paths to old people's cottages whenever snow began to fall. In another school it is an adventure playground that one school 'year' undertakes to supervise. In others it is an international relief agency, a school for spastics, or help with traffic warden work in the area. This 'attachment of the social group to a matter of general humane concern' – as one observer puts it[15] – is something that is an essential part of any school's sub-social-unit. This can draw a social group together in a way that traditional internal 'rivalries' often fail to do today, and can give a social unit a purpose and an ideal that will attract many pupils anxious to contribute to society in some immediate and fundamentally useful way and who find the usual goals of a school 'house' or 'year' rather narrow. This is but another example of the way in which comprehensive schools, as they develop, forge further links with their own communities.

Staff organization

The larger and more complex school presents problems of organization for staff as well as pupils. A school of 1600 will have a staff of eighty or ninety – more if some are part-time. This requires sub-groupings and deliberate measures designed both to involve staff directly in the wider responsibilities that arise from comprehensive education and to develop a structure of staff organization which enables rank-and-file staff members to participate in the functioning and decision-making of the school.

The development of such a structure is, of course, given greater emphasis by some heads than by others. But whatever the case, the resultant system is still the decision of the past or the present head. There is no statutory requirement in this country that any form of staff council or committee structure must be set up, with definite powers over the curriculum and functioning of the school, as there is, for instance, in Sweden, the USSR and elsewhere. Hence a considerable variety of structure exists. It is possible, however, to discern certain overall patterns, particularly in the 11–18 schools, and these we will describe in detail later. But in the smaller units of the two-tier system, it appears from such evidence as we have gained that very often the traditional informal systems are retained: the head exercising his historical functions and utilizing the traditional staff meeting, called at his own initiative, to discuss those aspects of school affairs that he determines; this system is, however, being modified in those middle schools where considerable responsibility is devolved on year group teams and their leaders (chapter 10).

Practice also varies in 11–18 schools in this matter of full staff meetings. We asked our smaller sample of schools how often the whole staff met together. Thirty-one schools answered this question: one school had a staff meeting weekly; six had it monthly; eight half-termly; seven termly;

and seven on an *ad hoc* basis. The bigger the school, the less frequent the meetings.

But it is obvious that in the larger comprehensive the department has become the meaningful unit and departmental staff meetings are as important as full staff meetings. Staff are involved in a given department team which forms one 'leg' of the staff structure. At the same time, as we have seen, they are also involved in the social unit – in charge of a year group, or of a tutor group attached to a house. These social units, too, hold staff meetings and form another 'leg' of staff structure.

The departmental side of big comprehensive schools is generally very well developed. In some schools these form schools within schools. Department heads are in charge of the content of the education (syllabuses), teaching methods and general coordination of the work of the department. In some comprehensive schools a decision about whether to stream or set in a particular subject or not is left to the department head. Thus a school may have highly streamed (or setted) maths work, but totally unstreamed English, or vice versa. This is a measure of the importance of the department within the larger comprehensive.

The average number of departments per school, in the schools of our smaller sample, was fourteen. The staffing ratio average was 1:19·31. What subjects 'rate' department head status in the comprehensive? Forty schools answered the section on department heads. All had department heads for English and for mathematics. The other subjects (with head of department status) in diminishing order of frequency were history, geography (both thirty-seven), art (thirty-six), physical education (thirty-one), domestic science and music (both thirty-one), science (thirty), religious education (twenty-nine), technical (twenty-eight), remedial, biology (both twenty-seven), foreign language (twenty-six), physics (twenty-five), commerce (twenty-four), chemistry (twenty-three), French (twenty), classics (ten), engineering (nine), Newsom (seven), German, building/boys' crafts (both six), needlework (five), Welsh, economics (four). Below four: careers, rural studies, general studies, office arts, woodwork, environmental studies. It ought to be mentioned that some subjects in some schools 'shared' a head, i.e. geology with geography. What is of interest, perhaps, is the higher numbers of department heads in the arts (music and art) and in sciences (maths, science, physics) than in languages (classics, French, other foreign).

How often did department staffs meet together? Thirty-nine schools answered this. Sixteen said they met *ad hoc*, seven met every three or four weeks, six met weekly, four met termly, three met 'regularly' but did not specify intervals, two met twice termly, and one never met. Practice in this respect seemed remarkably various, and in some cases casual, considering the importance and size of individual subject departments in most comprehensive schools.

This lack of any 'standard' practice is the case in much else as well. For example, in distribution of capitation grant money. Some heads had an informal policy: 'traditions and special pleading' was a typical answer. Others had a precise formula: 'number of subject periods by number of pupils by allowance . . . with 50 per cent increase for practical subjects'. One head allocated money according to the proportion of 'time' given to each subject in the timetable; another gave more for 'lower-ability groups'. One said it was given according to staff size of the department. Those without special policy here – and this was the largest group – said that it was just a matter of re-discussing 'last year's allocation' each succeeding year. But quite a few admitted to special demands from various quarters receiving special attention.

Comprehensive schools vary a great deal also in the matter of staff organization between the social unit (house or year) and the teaching or departmental unit. Two reports on comprehensive schools – the ILEA and the IAAM[16] – give some idea of this variety. Even though schools vary in the amount of importance and autonomy given to subject departments as against social-group units within a school, and a single staff member is usually a member of both, he often has a double set of obligations. He has to attend meetings of both departmental and 'house' or 'year' staff. The ILEA report stresses the lack of time available for staff meetings of any kind. But it gives examples of how schools cope. At one school (Forest Hill) coordination of tutors' work within houses takes place at a monthly meeting of only fifteen minutes. At Wandsworth there are weekly meetings of house masters, but only monthly meetings of house tutors and departmental staff. In Wandsworth, too, the senior masters – of both social and departmental units – meet twice a term in a sort of 'inner cabinet'.[17] This inner-cabinet principle is common in many large comprehensive schools – and, as we found, is sometimes resented by junior staff who feel all the 'big' decisions are taken without their being able to participate.

Many schools, however, have made systematic attempts to organize their staff structures in such a way that all staff are involved. The IAAM report gives many examples. Some of the schools had formed a staff council. In one school this was in addition to the permanent committees of heads of departments and senior house masters. The staff council includes the head, the deputy head, the chairman and secretary of each of the two committees, and ten elected members. Each house block elects one member (representing two houses). Five more are elected by the staff as a whole. 'This council meets monthly and any members of staff may submit items for discussion and decision, and attend in person to present their case.' The council in this school is, in fact, the main policy-making body 'and can overrule the head'.[18]

Our second questionnaire devoted a section to staff organization, one question specifically inquiring whether the school had staff committees, and, if so, what the membership and function was in each case. None of the 11–13, 11–14 or 11–16 schools claimed any particular form of staff committees – answers were either a straight negative, or, for instance, 'No – the staff room is very informal and I would wish it to remain so.' These schools are, of course, in general relatively small.

On the other hand, 11–18 schools – there were thirty in the sample – showed a considerable variety of practice, from schools which had little or no formal organization to schools with a complex committee structure. Only a handful had no structure, such as a large Welsh comprehensive, whose head answered that problems involving only some staff members are dealt with by means of *ad hoc* meetings. The most typical system is that already described: a committee of heads of departments, another of heads of houses or years, and sometimes a higher committee or 'inner cabinet' containing the senior masters and mistresses and some represent-atives from each of the two committees. A few schools go further than this, having deliberately established a system providing opportunities for innovation among the staff. A fairly typical organization, presenting most of these features, is the following, reported by one head. In this case each committee has a defined area for discussion and action.

1. A monthly meeting consisting of the head, deputy heads of schools (lower, middle, upper) as well as year masters (or tutors), the senior mistress and counsellor. Purpose: discussion of general questions of policy.

2. Heads of departments, with the headmaster and heads of schools, meeting monthly to discuss policy questions relating to the curriculum and other academic matters.

3. A weekly meeting of year tutors with the heads of the upper, middle and lower schools respectively, to discuss matters of day-to-day organiza-tion.

4. A so-called 'diary meeting' of the head, deputy, the three heads of schools and the bursar, to discuss week-by-week organization of the school.

5. A number of *ad hoc* committees consisting of selected members of the staff (selected by the head) to discuss educational issues such as 'non-streaming in the first year', 'team teaching' or 'CCTV', and to make

recommendations to the headmaster. This is a large home counties school organized on the horizontal system.

Other schools in our example had a similar pattern, if not quite so well defined. One reports a tripartite arrangement:

1. 'Pastoral and discipline' committee, consisting of house masters, senior master, deputy and head, which meets weekly in school time.
2. A 'curricular' committee consisting of heads of departments (together with the librarian and teachers responsible for drama and engineering), the senior master, deputy and head, meeting monthly after school.
3. 'Staff affairs' committees set up by the staff to discuss specific educational issues.

In another school the two main committees are called the 'tutorial board', concerned with pastoral care, and the 'academic board', to advise on all matters of curriculum organization.

Meetings of departmental staff clearly play an important role in the functioning of the comprehensive school. As one head writes, these meetings are called 'to discuss general matters of department policy, or specific questions of organization. To discuss methods and progress. To summarize discussion for heads of department meetings, and to gather ideas to be put forward at these meetings.' Further issues for discussion at other schools' departmental meetings include 'subject cooperation', the grouping of pupils and their allocation to different streams or sets, the allocation of staff to teaching sets, the ordering of equipment, and choice of textbooks, as well as considering 'the latest educational developments with regard to their subject', examination arrangements and marking schemes, the difficulties of individual pupils' homework, textbooks, apparatus and aids, and general policy.

A school which provides for weekly departmental meetings sees it as an opportunity for all the staff to discuss, through their departmental organization, problems of school policy generally as it affects their subject. The head of department takes the chair at these meetings, one advantage of which is 'that even the youngest or newest recruit to staff can speak his mind on these occasions'. Discussion of syllabus and methods may lead to innovations; thus in one case the departmental meetings take the form of 'workshop meetings to prepare schemes and material' and the discussion of curriculum developments. It seems clear that departmental meetings, when systematically organized, can provide a structure which can serve as a type of in-service training for the staff group as a whole, rather similar to the study group, or 'teacher-centre' type of approach; though for this to be effective, adequate time is necessary.[19]

Enough has been said to show that the large comprehensive school normally functions through a committee structure. In some ways the structure is not unlike that of a university with its oligarchic senate of senior heads of departments, or like the colleges of education, also recently much enlarged. The latter are now for the first time required by law to set up academic boards consisting of representatives of the staff and, sometimes, of students, so that here also the function of the principal is changing in character.[20] In the 11–18 comprehensive school structures described above, junior staff do have the opportunity of participation to some extent through their membership of a department (at departmental meetings), since nearly all staff members, however junior, will be a member of a department.*

Many schools told us that side by side with new patterns of organization they retained the traditional staff committees – mainly to deal with the social side of staff life, staff welfare, dining, common-room organization – and also *ad hoc* committees. But there was an increasing need for a parallel structure to coordinate staff and school. One head of an Outer London comprehensive admits that he has taken his effective governing committee structure straight from the model he knew in a training college where he taught for many years. Both consciously and unconsciously, it would seem as though there is an imperceptible development of secondary-school organization towards the more sophisticated and complex pattern prevailing in higher education.

Since the latter is now under attack by students and junior staff, it is as well that a number of comprehensive heads are alive to the problem of devising staff structures which will allow full staff participation, either by meeting junior staff directly, as one head does, or by organizing a regular network of smaller subject, social or project meetings for participation – leaving the 'big' staff meetings, as another head put it, 'for dissemination of information rather than as a forum for discussion'.

Several heads emphasize the value of the full staff meeting as a means of disseminating information. The problem of communication in the large school is a difficult one, and here the staff meeting can play an important role, quite apart from its further extension as a forum for discussion, questioning and policy-making. But clearly even this traditional assembly is not enough in many schools, and in some it is being replaced by a regular staff publication and internal 'news-sheet'.

A new development of interest – already referred to briefly – involves setting up specific *ad hoc* staff committees (outside the formal structure,

* Though university teachers know from experience that where the calling of a department meeting is the prerogative solely of the head of the department, these are often seldom called.

if one exists) to plan ahead, to discuss innovations and new departures.[21] One such committee has already been referred to. Some of the schools in our smaller sample have developed this technique; one in the South-west referring to various committees of this kind 'studying problems of transition and innovation'. Among these is a sixth-form curriculum sub-committee, consisting of sixth-form tutors, teachers of the sixth form, and sixth-formers themselves, working on how to develop an integrated sixth form in spite of the differing aims and courses. At another school the head reports that staff committees arise from suggestions made by the staff-room committee; among these are a sixth-form study group which proposed radical reforms later accepted both by the full staff and the sixth-formers themselves. The staff of this school also formed a 1970 Committee which worked out a curriculum (already being imple-mented) for those likely to be affected by the raising of the school-leaving age. This led to the formation of a 1980 Committee to examine the treatment of the more able children over time.

In a recent article, three members of the staff of an 11–18 school discuss the problem of decision-making in such schools, and describe the method used to build into what is often a somewhat autocratic or oligarchic structure the means of ensuring a continuous process of rethinking current procedures and proposing and developing desired innovations. The method used was to set up a curriculum advisory committee with three members – two retiring each year – to receive problems, information and suggestions from any member of staff, to determine priorities, arrange for report and discussion (sometimes in the form of a teach-in). 'As a result of these reports, which are advisory and informative', write the members of this committee, 'decisions are made.' Junior members of staff are able to express radical opinions (not easy in a full staff meeting) through the committee, and these can be incorporated in the report. By such means as these, some schools are seeking to prevent the ossification that formal structures may reinforce, while at the same time opening up basic educational issues for discussion by the staff as a whole.[22]

An example of an advanced stage of curriculum change and design is afforded by the Thomas Bennett School at Crawley, a comprehensive with 2200 pupils. Here the headmaster, Pat Daunt, has set out consciously to encourage a continuous review of the curriculum and indeed of the whole approach of the school as regards organization, content and methods. He holds that it is not enough 'to encourage innovation in separate subjects on an *ad hoc* basis' – it is also necessary to look at the relation of subjects to each other and to the social aims and organization of the school. Such a commitment has to be communicated, in Daunt's view, to teachers, pupils, parents and the community. It requires organization – a 'cabinet' able to take an overall view and bring together the threads which represent both the social and the academic life of the school (the departments). With this must be constructed a system of consultation bringing in all the staff and the pupils – and also external agencies, the LEA, university, schools council and inspectorate.

To carry this through, the teaching departments have been grouped into seven divisions ('faculties') responsible for innovation with particular emphasis on integrated programmes and the building up of resources. All staff meet regularly in discussion groups to consider major matters of policy and make recommendations to the senior committee of teachers; agendas for this may be created in open common-room discussions. A student–teacher school council, on which students have a large majority, draws up the school code of conduct and has financial powers; student members from this council are included in a working party with parents, teachers and a governor to recommend ways of improving links between school and community. Mode III is now established for the great majority of CSE work, and, in two important areas (Humanities and Design) for GCE as well. At the same time the school has now moved steadily towards a 'consolidated curriculum in the first five years', reducing the previously elaborate system of options 'which encouraged premature specialization'. 'House-teaching', which offers the opportunity for totally mixed-ability groups and already operates for half the curriculum in the first three years, will be extended to the whole curriculum for the first-year children in 1972; further extension is expected in 1973, when integrated work, already well developed within the faculties, is contemplated between faculties for younger children. In this context such reforms as the abolition of selected prefects and of uniform have not been fortuitous acts but part of a planned endeavour to maintain a harmony of attitudes within and beyond the classroom. Such an operation, on a massively ambitious scale, requires in the new situation, teamwork and understanding together with a certain unity of perspective among the staff as a whole.[23]

The most radical innovation in staff participation in running a school, however, is that now being implemented at Countesthorpe in Leicestershire. This is a new school, which opened in specially designed buildings in August 1970. To grasp the significance of its attempt to change fundamentally the learning situation for students aged fourteen to eighteen, it is necessary to see it as the conjunction of a number of significant trends in education, as its first Warden, Tim McMullen, has pointed out.[24]

Some of these trends came together in the thinking of the group involved in the Nuffield Resources for Learning unit, of which McMullen was the first director, and from which both the deputy head and the head of one of the main departments were recruited. The 'resources' approach lead the team to place major emphasis on the development of what is best called 'independent learning' by students; and this involves the promotion of small-group and individual work as the leading technique in place of class teaching.[25] The emphasis, therefore, is inevitably placed on the ability of the school or college to maintain and enhance the student's self-motivation for learning; it demands considerable flexibility of organization, and relies on the initiative of the teachers to find for themselves the most effective pedagogic approaches in the varying situations that are developed.

Another trend arises from the deliberate rejection of what have been called 'meritocratic' objectives in the comprehensive school (leading to streaming, etc.) and the belief 'that all individuals should be equally valued, that the quality of life is all-important, and that an undivided society is desirable'. These values and methods lead, as McMullen has put it, 'to an all-through non-streaming approach, to non-authoritarian relationships, towards curriculum relevant to life, and to participatory types of democracy'.[26] The opportunity to put these ideas into practice came from the conjunction of these ideas with the consistently developing thinking of the Leicestershire education authority under its director, Stewart Mason (now retired), who had called in the Nuffield unit to discuss plans for the physical lay-out of the school (which incorporates many new features), and which appointed the head nearly two years before the school opened, to allow time for the thinking and planning necessary to a new initiative of this type.

Chief interest here attaches to the democratic staff structure; the opportunity that is given for total involvement by the staff in the organization and control of the school – in determining its objectives, both short and long term, and in evolving the means by which these objectives can be realized in practice. The head as warden (the college also acts as a community college on the Leicestershire pattern) has deliberately devolved his authority on to the staff as a whole, acting as the chief executive carrying out the decisions made by the staff, in which, of course, he has a say as all others. This system is carried through every level of decision making: 'The aims of the school led to wholly participatory democracy,' writes McMullen, 'with all *policy* decisions taken by staff either as a whole or in sections; executive actions being left to individual members of the staff according to their functions.'[27] Thus departmental heads carry out decisions made at departmental meetings; year heads, decisions made at year-tutor meetings, and so on. The whole staff meets together regularly for discussion of matters affecting the school as a whole (at what is called the 'moot'), while in addition a full committee structure has developed covering both academic and pastoral sides, as well as other matters affecting the running of the school. New staff appointments and promotions are in the hands of staff committees 'heavily biased with those who will work with the newcomers' – a procedure which has apparently proved successful.[28]

Although Countesthorpe was planned to start as an upper school, it opened largely as a high school with the full range of eleven to fourteens, since the high school planned for the area was delayed as a result of postponement of the raising of the leaving age in 1968. It has now (1972) full fourth and fifth years, but none in the sixth. The new high school is now under way, so that by 1974 Countesthorpe will be fulfilling its originally planned function as an upper school of some 1400 students. Student participation in the running of the school is being developed (students already have the right to attend meetings of the moot and senior students the right to vote), but a full assessment of the significance and success of these innovations will not be possible for a few years. In the meantime it can certainly be said that the system is leading to a very high degree of involvement in the planning and functioning of the school by the great majority of the staff members, whatever their age and experience.

Developments at Countesthorpe are being closely watched as a prototype of the school of the future; it should be remembered, however, that radical innovations of this type are clearly easier to carry through in an entirely new school, where staff can be appointed in sympathy with these aims. To transform existing institutions is a more difficult, or at least a different, kind of task. Nevertheless Countesthorpe clearly represents a breakthrough on a new level; a convergence of trends in the areas of pupil–teacher relations, new methods of promoting learning, and in participatory democracy, all of which are now exerting an influence throughout the school system. In this sense the school has great value as a prototype or possible model for others.

A similar initiative was to have been taken by the ILEA in the careful planning and design of the projected new Thomas Calton school – also seen from the start as embodying advanced thinking, in this case from both sides of the Atlantic.[29] The new building, planned for 1976, was, however, disallowed by the Secretary of State, in spite of the strongest representations by the ILEA and the teachers themselves, with mass support from the locality. This is a pity. As a method of encouraging innovation, the establishment, say every five years, of an entirely new school which sets out to embody the most advanced thinking in education generally, acting as a kind of laboratory test of new ideas in a planned and systematic way, might well prove exceptionally effective. Certainly no one who visits Countesthorpe, or for that matter the Thomas Bennett school at Crawley, can come away other than profoundly impressed by the newness and unexpectedness of the social and educational situation created; perhaps particularly by the nature of the relations between staff and students, but also by the whole ethos and 'feel' of the school.

Special attention has been given here to Thomas Bennett and Countesthorpe as representing the most advanced of new initiatives within the maintained system of comprehensive schools. But other schools not mentioned here are also developing along these lines.[30] The very wide range of methods used to integrate staff and involve them in policy and forward planning in individual schools is a feature of developing comprehensive systems. As with social organization, individual schools will evolve individual patterns. The general tendency, however, is to find the most effective machinery through which all staff and pupils may play a part.

Administrative problems in comprehensive schools

In discussing staff committee structures, the social organization of pupils or the introduction of participation, it is obvious that we are talking all the time about the problem of administration. Administration is central to all these matters. When it comes to running comprehensive schools, more thought has often been put into the teaching policy and the curriculum structure than into the administrative procedures. But neglect of administrative problems can only be temporary. Administration is too crucial to be left for long, as schools have discovered. For one thing, the successful carrying through of social and academic policy depends upon efficient administration. As has been observed often by Robin Pedley, a radically progressive policy can easily run aground because of inefficient administration.[31]

Another reason administration cannot be left out is because a comprehensive school is far more complex than either of the old types of school, the secondary modern or the grammar. It is more complex socially – drawing from all ranges of society and in the proportions that they exist in the local community rather than disproportionately, as was the case in most schools in the selective system. It also has a far more elaborate curriculum, course, and examination structure than either of the 'old' types of school, with obligations to its pupils that are consequently far more various. The sixteen-year-old leaver must be helped to get into meaningful employment at the same time as the A-level student must be guided through the maze of applications for university.

Thirdly, as we saw, comprehensive schools build up a special relationship to their own community – interacting with its agencies, services, industries and organizations in a far more intricate fashion than did either of the old unifunctional schools. All this interaction puts a strain upon a school's administrative procedures. Lastly, the comprehensive is a larger school. This size factor compounds the complexity of the functions already mentioned and it raises in a critical form the problem implicit in all of them: how to provide individual attention and guidance for each pupil in each school.

In well over half the cases of specific complaints about comprehensive schools that we encountered from staff, parents or pupils, the real complaint was not about the architecture, or the siting, or the size of a school, but in fact about its administration. Time after time a school would say, 'We have terrible timetable problems due entirely to our being old, or on two sites.' But schools on one site, and purpose-built into the bargain, also have terrible timetable problems. Sometimes the complaint is about the difficulty of communications between staff: 'One meets the very person one urgently needs to talk to when travelling hot-foot in the opposite direction.'[32] This head was writing of a split-site school and he put the problem down solely to the fact that the two halves of the school were in two different buildings. But staff in single-building, purpose-built comprehensives also have this kind of complaint: witness the teacher who moaned about staff having to 'walk several miles a day' and never being properly organized in one of the early showpiece schools.[33] Practically all the complaints we heard from parents – of pupils in every stage and in schools of every type – could be traced to administrative failure of some sort.

When examining the organizational practices of comprehensive schools, one comes across procedures where the aim is right but the method is hardly practical. In a recently published account of a comprehensive school an example is given of the procedure that is followed when a pupil does good work (the italics are our own):

The teaching master will *fill in* a pink card when a boy has done good work for that boy's ability. Then he *sends it* to the Head of Department who *passes it* to the Headmaster, who *passes it* on to the Deputy Headmaster, who *sends it* to the Housemaster, who *gives it* to the boy to take home. . . . A white card for poor work *goes through the same process*.[34]

A quick calculation tells us that if each pupil in the average size comprehensive school (seven-form entry) did one piece of good (or poor) work a week, this would involve schools in at least 5000 separate passing, noting or filing operations each week. We have already cited the case of the assistant teacher in a comprehensive caught in the cobwebs of multiple administration (p. 344). The NFER's Second Report of 1970 has a good deal of evidence – drily stated but inflammatory in some of its implications – about the *ad hoc* nature of administration in comprehensives, with 'no clear delegation of responsibility for various activities' or so much 'shared' responsibility that problems fall straight through the net.[35] They found heads of sections over-timetabled and staff in the schools with the biggest problems having to meet the biggest demands on their time and expertise. And it must be remembered the NFER did not even bother to look at one crucial part of the administrative network – what they called 'routine office administration, building maintenance, etc.'[36] This may well be an oversight, for the office is as central a contributor to efficiency in a comprehensive as in any other organization. And some comprehensives are as undersupported in this aspect of their work as they are in staffing for teaching or counselling.

It is curious that the administrative problems of the comprehensive school have received very little attention. Few local authorities take a deep interest in management problems, although more are beginning to do so now. So are others. One of the most imaginative was a television series run by Harlech Television for local West of England schools in conjunction with the University of Bristol's School of Education.[37] Another was a lecture course run by the University of Wales at Cardiff. The DES has been slow to encourage research into organizational problems in the comprehensive school. It is true that there has been a growing interest in the department and elsewhere in training courses for heads and other senior staff of schools, but in view of the magnitude of the problem, much of the work seems very inadequate and late in the day. It reflects the general lack of interest in management science and problems of administration generally in Britain – and lack of interest specifically among educationists, when compared to interest in problems of curriculum, teaching or examination policy.

Some authorities, however, have been alive to the problem of secondary-school administration. A recent study by the Organization and Methods Service of the Corporation of Edinburgh reviewed the situation in local secondary schools and found many tasks being done by staff in secondary schools that should, and could, probably be done by auxiliary help. They divided these tasks into three sections: clerical, secretarial and administrative. (A list of duties under the three headings is given in Appendix 3, p. 571.)

In looking more closely at these three categories in turn, we see that many schools badly need more auxiliary clerical help – if only, as the Edinburgh report said, because it 'releases teachers from work which they commonly regard as irritating and irrelevant' and enables them 'to concentrate more efficiently on their teaching function'.[38] The problem of the secretary's duties, on the other hand – which are sometimes clerical, sometimes administrative – is far more complex. The secretary's duties in comprehensive schools have grown out of all proportion to those a school secretary normally should be expected to carry. Very early on it was seen that these responsibilities inside the comprehensive school had grown.[39] But as often as not the pay had not. The job has just become too big and too complex for one person in some schools, as the Edinburgh Report made clear: 'The secretary assumes a responsibility which her grading and status do not recognize.'[40] In addition, a 'secretary's job' can vary widely from school to school and from LEA to LEA, as writers on this subject have found.[41]

The administrative tasks proper are those performed as a matter of routine by the head or his deputy or senior staff. The Edinburgh report felt many such tasks were too difficult, too numerous and time-consuming, and most of the heads and senior staff we questioned were agreed. Many heads in our smaller sample, for example, wanted more time free to think about total school policy or the goal of the school, and to be less bothered about the routine tasks, as we show shortly. Moreover, many tasks were strictly non-educational. In Edinburgh, these tasks 'formed the basis of the justification for the employment of an administrative assistant'. The administrative assistant in this case was a new post, injected in the school at the level of senior staff or deputy head, but with no other tasks but administrative ones. It is too early to say if this pioneering effort – many of Edinburgh's schools now have administrative officers – will become widespread. But there is no doubt that many comprehensive schools would welcome the appointment of such an officer in the school and would not even fuss overmuch if the officer had not had – as is usually asked for anyone at the top of the school hierarchy – much classroom experience. Although the post was set up in Edinburgh as suitable for men, all but one of the appointees have been women. This might help correct an imbalance in running comprehensive schools often complained about: relatively few top posts – except at girls' comprehensives – go to women.

The new thinking in the Edinburgh document, plus similar exercises elsewhere in Scotland, is summarized in a publication of the Scottish Education Department of 1971 advocating a radical rearrangement of the career structure in secondary schools. *The Structure of Promoted Posts* analyses the needs in two directions: those specially required when schools are large, and those required to meet the changing pattern of secondary education. In particular, it recommends that promotion through work in counselling and curriculum direction be recognized as on a par with subject-department work. Its suggestions for new structures for various sizes of schools therefore include senior posts for curriculum directors, directors of studies, counsellors, and welfare directors along with the traditional posts for deputy and senior assistant posts. The net result, of course, is to increase the number of senior positions in the school immediately below the level of head teacher but above that of subject-department heads. But this is precisely where many secondary schools know an increase is needed. They also know, and the Scottish document recognizes this, that large schools need a different kind of help—not just an addition of a few more staff to each subject department. Thus the new structure of posts suggested (p. 19) lays down *five* times as many assistant head teachers for a 1500 size school as for one of 600. In most schools in this country now there would usually only be twice as many for the large school as against the small.

The basic problem is that managing large units is 'sophisticated' work, as William Taylor has called it – inimical to many school teachers whose view of their own work may be professional-minded in the extreme, but whose understanding of the way management systems run can be obstinately amateurish. And this includes heads equally, upon whose say-so the reshaping of the school's management always depends. Perhaps big-school management relies too heavily on ordinary teachers. Some ask why heads and staff should have this burden – completely unprepared or untrained as they are for so many of the duties they now perform in a comprehensive school situation, so different in kind as well as size from the old situation. One head writes quite clearly that his staff just have not 'the time in the day nor the expertise' to deal with the deprived, recalcitrant or abnormal. This work – and so much else – must be 'done properly by a professional, instead of with expensive inefficiency by amateurs like us'.[42]

Another teacher looking at his large, purpose-built comprehensive asked the same question and his answer was unequivocal: 'If comprehensive reorganization relies on finding men able to operate successfully in counter-purpose buildings, or on insisting that the work load of teachers can be increased still further, then it will fail.'[43]

The problem was bad enough before 1970 when at least it was national policy to go comprehensive and some start was being made to identify the different needs such a system might develop. After 1970 it became increasingly difficult with a national policy which saw the comprehensive as just one among many types, taking its chances individually in a hectic melée of LEA practice, in a decade where ROSLA will add to its problems, and with no certainty of reform by a government hardly sympathetic to a comprehensive system, however willing to tolerate a slow rise in the number of such schools as part of a policy of 'variety' and 'parental choice'.

Comprehensive reorganization also requires a new view of non-teaching staff. Many staff – and parents – and education officials are apt to take the non-teaching staff for granted, just as in the same way they take far less interest in administration than, say, teaching policy. We asked our smaller sample of schools about their non-teaching staff: how many they had and what they did. Almost all had secretaries, most had librarians, laboratory technicians and careers masters (though the latter doubled as staff in most cases). Less than half had clerks, adult education officers, welfare or guidance officers, or groundsmen. Very few had carpenters, accountants, bursars or nurse/matrons attached to the school. When we asked what kind of extra non-teaching help they would like if they could have one extra appointment of some kind, of the thirty-eight answering this question, twenty-two named some form of administrative aid: bursar, another secretary or clerical assistant. The second largest category, seven, was for social help – a guidance counsellor or a welfare officer. The remaining requests divided between nurse, handyman, librarian and lab technicians. There is no way of telling how adequate a picture this represents of the needs of comprehensive schools generally, but our guess is that it is not far out in the big percentage that badly needs extra administrative assistance. The NFER's Second Report, in finding that comprehensive schools they studied only averaged twenty-nine non-teaching staff per school, shows up an equally inadequate situation.[44] As one head has put it, 'I cannot think of any comparable institution, in the field of education or outside, which is expected to function with an administrative staff of one and a half.'[45]

The general comments on administration by the schools we questioned in our smaller sample bear this need out even more forcefully. One head-master, commenting on the fact he did the accounts, said flatly: 'It ought not to be my job.' Another commented on how badly school administration fared when put next to that of commerce or industry. He said large schools deserve an entirely new scale of operation: 'too bad factory is a dirty word'. Another said: 'In my opinion most large schools are still run in a fashion that deserves derision from, say, any O and M team.' Yet another:

The complexity of organization in a comprehensive school hardly begins to resemble that in other secondary schools. This complexity involves a basic change in attitude and organization. Unfortunately, too many people tend to think of the new as the old writ large and there is perpetual wrangling to try to change conditions. In this the support of the Department of Education is singularly lacking. There should be some sort of central guidance on the question of administrative staff.

Several heads agreed with the one who put his administrative problem starkly: 'A top quality administrative officer is needed.'

It was not just the big schools that complained either. Plenty of the smaller schools were obviously bogged down in administrative detail. Many said they would welcome particular forms of help – a filing system, an intercom telephone, a photo-copying machine, a bursar – so that, as they frequently said, they could be free to concentrate on policy, and the staff on teaching. Heads frequently said their main job was to delegate. But if the delegation simply left them bogged down with bigger administrative tasks, having jettisoned smaller ones, or overburdened the senior staff to whom tasks were delegated, schools were sometimes no better off.

Certain problems were especially difficult; that of the timetable, for example, was enormous. This has been a constant matter of comment in comprehensive school literature.[46] Schools we visited and the answers to the question about timetable preparation in the second questionnaire indicated that this problem has become even more pressing lately. In about half the schools in our smaller sample the deputy head did the timetable. When he did not have charge of it, it was done variously by the headmaster, heads of 'upper' or 'lower' sections of the school, in one case by a senior mistress, and in two, by the head of the mathematics department. One school said it took three months in each year to prepare. Many said it took a full four weeks. One school said the deputy head was sent away for a week to do this work. Recently a school wrote it must give a senior teacher a whole term off for the work, which takes 400 hours.[47] The loss to any school's efficiency through a senior staff member's yearly enforced absence of a whole term is obvious, and should not be a situation to be tolerated as a matter of course. Yet it is.

Timetable preparation was one of the tasks the Edinburgh Study suggested an administrative officer should take over, and there can be few schools who would oppose this. But it is not just a case of finding another person to whom this task may be delegated. There is a very strong case for relegating the whole process to a computer. No secondary school of the future should be without access to a computer in any case, and although timetable preparation is not yet practicable,* the greater the demands for help of this kind, the sooner will satisfactory programs be worked out. This is a problem that would have to be solved on a local authority basis, rather than by schools individually, since the practical assistance schools would need in processing data and making use of programs (and, eventually also in using computers for teaching purposes) might be too great to leave to schools alone.

---

* A Norwegian program for preparation of timetabling by computer is in the process of being tested by the Local Government Operational Research Unit of Reading. Initial trials have been successful and there is hope of a useable program some time during the 1970s.

There is no doubt that authorities will in future have to give schools far more systematic assistance in all sorts of ways than they have in the past; and that schools themselves will have to work together to solve common problems far more closely. Certainly to date most comprehensive schools have no idea how similar, or even neighbouring, schools are being run. Many comprehensive schools that have operated for years in the same neighbourhoods have rarely paid more than courtesy calls on each other – especially in areas where coexistence of many 'types' of school is the rule. One example of this innocence about each other's practices came in answers to some of our questions. For instance, when asking for the 'special duties' of the deputy head, one school answered 'normal duties'. This was ironic for with the exception of timetabling duties mentioned previously, there was not, for deputy heads, any settled practice that could be called 'normal'. Seven of the deputy heads in our smaller sample had the duty of maintaining discipline and some of these seven also dealt with welfare. Just slightly fewer had as their special province the day-to-day running of the school. Otherwise, there was no pattern. Two said their province was equipment; two more acted as registrars; two more, curiously enough, said their job was to 'deputize for the head'. But other duties also included: agendas of meetings, courses for certificate pupils, stationery, 'voice' of the common room, liaison with male staff, and charge of school policy. In other cases it was fairly clear that head and deputy head were interchangeable in function.

Senior master and senior mistress duties too were even more varied – with one exception: senior mistresses or deputy headmistresses in mixed schools were often in charge of girls' welfare. Three, though, had examinations as their main job. An additional three were in charge of either 'lower' or 'upper' school in a horizontally divided school. Other duties named included responsibility for public occasions, sixth-form applications, careers, staff absences, senior students, timetable, probationer students, parents and staff liaison. It could well be that from among the vast experience now available in comprehensive-school administration, research, or even merely the pooling of practices by authorities or consortia of schools, could well come up with very definite answers to what is the 'best' way to deploy existing staff. Research in this field is badly needed.

We have examined the administrative problems of the forty-odd schools in our smaller sample in some detail because we are convinced they are an all-important key to reorganization. We came across schools whose policy and teaching approach was new – sometimes their buildings also – but whose heads indicated their administrative structure was from the dark ages. Primarily, but not always, this was because it was the same administrative structure that had been used in the small schools that senior staff had served in before.

We would not wish to suggest that most of the schools we visited or questioned were badly run. Considering the administrative problems of reorganization with which they were coping, their administration was spectacular. But heads, staff, parents and pupils in enough of the schools were worried enough about the sheer problems of running the school to cause administration to come to our attention. Several schools told us that they had asked their authority or governors for help. Several mentioned they were having organization and methods studies made of their schools to try to improve matters, and a few said that they had asked their authorities to send them on administrative courses. Several bodies run 'courses' for the heads of large schools: for example, the Department of Education and Science, the College of Preceptors and the University of Wales in Cardiff. Six of the forty-two heads in our sample said they had already attended such courses. Four found then valuable, particularly discussion with other heads. Two did not; one commenting, 'infantile, but fun'. A staff member in one school said his head had gone, but 'no value has been apparent yet' in the running of the school. Four heads who had not been on courses felt they would be valuable for them, and there is no doubt that the majority do find the courses useful. Most courses are derived from ordinary management training, where heads are introduced to imaginary schools and given a full in-basket of 'problems' connected with the school: to solve and to deal with. This 'simulated situation' approach was particularly highly praised by two of the heads in our survey.

But it is unlikely that most heads will have the benefit of courses or, even if they do, that anyone else in the school will have them. Departmental heads in a big comprehensive are sometimes in charge of a unit the size of a small secondary school. Michael Marland's study of the department inside a comprehensive school shows how clearly this unit needs help and support as a school-within-a-school.[48] A department head can have a staff of twenty working under him, including part-timers, is responsible for hundreds of teaching hours a week, an enormous stock of materials, and – if he or she is any good – for planning the work of the department carefully, not just day to day, but in terms of policy for the future, as well, of course, as carrying a near-full teaching load.[47] If the heads and deputies of schools are undersupported and underserviced by unrealistic staffing ratios and inadequate allowance structures, the heads of departments can frequently be more so. But they are even less likely to get any training for, or advice on, this aspect of their work than heads, deputies and 'section' heads, who get little enough. So far, administrative courses for these key posts are rare. In all the schools in our smaller sample only one school had sent a staff member other than the head for a course in administration.

But in any case, training for head teachers and department heads is only a small part of the problem, since in many cases it is the whole administrative structure of the school that needs redesigning. If we return to this theme, it is because it loomed so large in our visits and in the answers of schools in our smaller sample. Several schools said their local authorities and their governors simply did not understand what was happening or had no real idea of the magnitude of the problems involved – partly, perhaps, as one London head said, 'because they have no idea of comprehensive schools' ethos, aims or organization' in the first place. Management training for heads was a start, but it only scratched the surface, said a northern head, 'so long as local education authorities think that a 1700-pupil school merely needs ten of everything more than a 170-pupil school'. This particular head wanted administrative help – and he also wanted help in coping with the welfare of pupils – 'without these *two*', he added, 'we muddle through and frequently run very close to criminal neglect of our pupils'.

The comprehensive school is not just a bigger school; it is not just a school made by joining together the two previous types of secondary school. It is a school that attempts to educate and deal with the whole range of ability and the whole education of pupils from a given area during that period of their lives when they make their most important educational discoveries and decisions. As we have shown, it involves schools in complex and intricate relationships with pupils, parents and with services, agencies, employers and educational institutions outside the school. It takes pupils up to the time when they will go to work or go on to higher education. Not just some pupils. Not just clever pupils. Not just vocationally oriented pupils. But *all* pupils. To imagine that a school can do these tasks adequately with the administrative organization, ancillary support and staffing of the 'old' unifunctional or small school, is to handicap the comprehensive movement from the start. If this book will have done anything, we hope it will have called to the attention of those with the power to assist schools, the urgent needs that exist. They are getting more urgent with every passing day.

Notes

1. P. M. P. Cornall, 'Social organization in the comprehensive school', p. 3.
2. For much of this information we are indebted to P. M. Hughes, lecturer at Reading University, author of 'Guidance and counselling in British

schools', *European Teacher*, July 1968. See also Hugh Lytton and
Maurice Craft, *Guidance and Counselling in British Schools*, 1969, and
Anne Jones, 'What do school counsellors need?', *Comprehensive
Education*, Autumn 1971.

3. Courses are also run at the Universities of Manchester, Exeter and Wales,
and at London's Tavistock Institute.

4. Personal communication from head teacher, T. Davies Hibbard, 28 June
1968.

5. H. D. Dickinson and John McLaren, Report on The Comprehensive
Schools in Bristol, Fabian Society, Bristol, p. 9, 1968.

6. See for example the critical comments of Comprehensive school pupils at
various universities about the guidance schools failed to give,
'Comprehensive pupils in University Look Back', *Comprehensive
Education*, Autumn 1971.

7. See also ibid., where the same observations are recorded from some
schools.

8. Hughes, op. cit.

9. ibid., p. 12.

10. ibid.

11. Anne Jones, 'What do school counsellors need?' *op. cit.*

12. ibid.

13. ibid.

14. Second NFER Report, p. 52.

15. D. S. Stansbury, Curriculum and Study Development Centre, Swindon,
'The social structure of a senior high school', 1968/9. His comments were
about the Park School, Swindon.

16. ILEA, *London Comprehensive Schools*, 1967; IAAM, *Teaching in
Comprehensive Schools*, 1967.

17. ILEA Survey, pp. 35–40, 1967.

18. IAAM Report, pp. 134–5, 1967.

19. A useful book, covering departmental organization in the large school, is
Michael Marland, *Head of Department*, 1971; this is based on the
author's experience as head of an English department in a comprehensive
school.

20. William Taylor, *Society and the Education of Teachers*, pp. 235ff, 1969,
discusses the effect of these changes on the role of the Principal.

21. A good example is the committee structure set up at Market Bosworth
grammar school, Leicestershire, to plan the school's transition to a
Leicestershire comprehensive upper school, as set out in detail in
Timothy Rogers (ed.), *School for the Community*, 1971.

22. R. E. Copland *et al.*, 'Curriculum planning in the large school', *Forum*,
vol. 10, no. 1, Autumn 1967.

23. Report in *Education*, 17 January 1969. See also Pat Daunt, 'Innovation in
the comprehensive school', *Forum*, vol. 12, no. 1, Autumn 1969; Pat
Daunt, 'Opinion and decision in a large school', *Comprehensive
Education*, no. 12, Summer 1969; personal communication, January 1972.

24. Tim McMullen, 'Countesthorpe College, Leicestershire', *Forum*, vol. 14, no. 2, Spring 1972; see also Tim McMullen, 'Flexibility for a comprehensive school', *Forum*, vol. 10, no. 2, Spring 1968; Anne Corbett, 'The school bosses', *New Society*, 15 April 1971.
25. L. C. Taylor, *Resources for Learning*, 1971.
26. Tim McMullen, op. cit., 1972
27. ibid.
28. ibid.; see also D. C. Middleton, 'Staff participation in comprehensive schools; Leicestershire', *Comprehensive Education*, no. 17, Spring 1971.
29. Ron Pepper, 'Planned innovation, Thomas Calton School, London', *Forum*, vol. 14, no. 2.
30. David Howe, 'Staff participation in comprehensive schools: Kingston-upon-Hull', *Comprehensive Education*, no. 17, Spring 1971 (on the Leo Schultz school).
31. R. Pedley, *The Comprehensive School*, 1963 and 1969.
32. 'Split site schools', *Comprehensive Education*, Spring 1967.
33. *The Comprehensive School, Appraisal from Within*, p. 79, 1964.
34. IAAM Report, p. 50, 1967.
35. ibid. p. 47.
36. ibid. p. 25.
37. In connection with this course William Taylor compiled a most useful background workbook for use by schools watching the series: 'Heading for Change'.
38. *O. and M. Review*, Edinburgh, p. 12.
39. *The Comprehensive School, Appraisal from Within*, p. 112.
40. *O. and M. Review*, Edinburgh, p. 7.
41. See Joan Galwey, 'Administration in three comprehensive schools', *Comprehensive Education*, Summer 1969.
42. J. Climo, in *Becoming Comprehensive*, ed. Halsall, 1970, p. 103–4.
43. P. H. Withington, ibid., p. 94.
44. Second NFER Report, p. 173.
45. S. King, *Ten Years All In*, p. 51.
46. *Inside the Comprehensive*, p. 111, for example. See also C. Benn, 'The timetable problem', *Comprehensive Education*, Summer 1969.
47. Halsall, ed., op. cit., p. 91.
48. Michael Marland, *Head of Department*, op. cit. See also NFER Report, ch. 2.

Chapter 16
School and Home

Head teachers

Good administration depends in present circumstances upon a school's headmaster. Governing bodies can sometimes be of assistance and in one or two schools, as we saw, they have been exceptionally helpful. But in other areas there is little doubt that many governors – though they are conscientious in their duties – are far too remote from either the life of the school or the immediate district to discharge their function fully effectively. In some schools they seemed totally unaware of the school's urgent administrative problems. In other areas the LEA itself, as we saw, was unaware. It should be added that there is very little a sympathetic local authority can do and some schools said local officers were exceptionally helpful – if the head of a school does not want help or insists upon running his school as though it were still the same smaller school he perhaps once knew so well. Readers may say no head of a comprehensive, particularly a large one, would even attempt this. But some do, not because they are stubborn or unimaginative but because by and large they are too conscientious. As the Second NFER Report on comprehensives commented, many were still trying to do all the tasks they used to do.[1] All too many of these heads are carrying far too big a burden of their school's success on their own shoulders – because of their desire to live up to traditional ideals of being a 'good headmaster'.

Although there may be a vague appreciation that a comprehensive school, by virtue of its size or its multifunctional nature, might need a different kind of administration, there has been relatively little appreciation until recently of the fact that it may also eventually need a different kind of headmaster than is traditionally associated with a secondary school. No doubt this is mostly because the selective-school tradition of headship is so firmly entrenched and so powerfully maintained as a centre of authority in secondary education: 'Arnold still casts a shadow over ideas of what a head should be.'[2] There is no doubt that the autonomy of the head, 'one of the chief beneficial contributions made by the great public schools to the English tradition',[3] is an ideal that has become part of headmastership generally. Whether this public-school tradition is always 'beneficial' to comprehensive schools is open to question.

From it flows the tradition of the headmaster as captain of his ship, head of his 'order', and from it arises much of the folklore of headmastership. Writings on the subject of headmastership make it clear what are the important qualities required. For example, one article laying down guidelines for headmasters, said the headmaster must be independent, 'vigilant to preserve his position', in charge of the prestige and 'standing' of his school, seeing to it that there is 'seemly behaviour in the streets and public places', maintaining and establishing a 'firm regime of discipline'.[4] A Ministry handbook also notes: 'It is the head's personality that in the vast majority of schools creates the climate of feeling; and that establishes standards of work or conduct.'[5] The headmaster is almost 'magic'. Even in comprehensive-school literature there is mention of the need for the head to 'appear' once a day in each half of a school on two sites to 'show the flag'. His mere presence is seen as sufficient, although anyone knows that unless there is efficient management at each site in a combined school, and machinery for intercommunications, a fleeting physical appearance is going to be no more than a gesture.[6] But the cult of headmastership somehow makes matters like machinery or management seem unimportant. In a comprehensive this could be dangerous.

On behalf of public, grammar or secondary modern schools it might be possible to argue, as has been argued by one educationist, Kathleen Ollerenshaw, that 'more important than variety of courses is quality, and quality of a school derives first and foremost from its head'.[7] But in a comprehensive school variety of courses is essential, more important than a head's personality. The cult of the importance of the headmaster can even be used as an argument to make reorganization itself seem irrelevant. Thus from a debate in Parliament: 'It doesn't matter whether a school is a grammar or a secondary modern or a comprehensive . . . what matters is the head's personality.'[8] This argument that a good head makes selection immaterial, or variety of courses not all-important, expresses an ideal that is incompatible with comprehensive education. It belongs to an outlook that sees schools as unifunctional – whether selective or non-selective. It arose from an era when schools, like public schools, served one section of society with one type of education and one type of training.

It was also an ideal that applied to small schools. For example, one of the special requirements of the ideal head is that he should know all his pupils. Opinion varies a good deal about what number of pupils a head can 'know'. One local authority document says it is doubtful if 'in any circumstances' a head could have personal knowledge of pupils when 'numbers exceed 200–300'.[9] Comprehensive-school teachers suggest that the maximum number for social units is 200–250.[10] Kathleen Ollerenshaw suggests that after 800, a school becomes merely an 'organization'.[11] The word 'organization' here is used pejoratively. Deeply imbedded in the monastic-authoritarian concept of the head is the idea of a school as a single corporate entity with the *esprit de corps* of the closed institution, unique because of a 'living tradition' handed down intact from generation to generation – what a recent publication from public schools has called a tradition of 'godliness and good learning'.[12]

A comprehensive school is not necessarily unique because of its mystic 'comprehensive' *esprit de corps* or its social or academic mix. Its uniqueness is more apt to lie in its special relation to the community it serves – to the particular pupils whose various educational needs it meets locally in the context of the greater national needs of any given moment. To function well it must be efficient within the context of its own community and local organizations and not merely efficient (as was the public school or the grammar school) as an isolated institution. This change of role is very hard to accept. Many heads try to live up to the old all-purpose ideal at the same time as trying to meet the requirements of the new type of education. They try to fulfil all the roles – old and new: fount of authority, policy-maker, discipline maintainer, managing director, teacher, public relations man, tone-setter, chairman of the board and executive chief with his door always 'open'. In a small school (500) or in a very remote area or in a school-in-transition a head may be able to combine all these tasks. But it is unlikely he will succeed in all roles at once – and in a well-established or large comprehensive he could not even attempt them all. In most comprehensive schools a head will have to choose one of these as his dominant role – and delegate the others.

About half the heads in our smaller sample said that what must be learned mostly is the art of delegation, although realizing it was necessary and actually doing it effectively were two different things. In addition, far too many heads felt guilty about actually doing the delegation – because to do so meant that one of the 'essentials' of the impossible ideal of headship was forfeited. Nevertheless, said one of the heads in our smaller sample, the lesson is clear: 'the established head must accept that he cannot do everything and decide on the kind of head he wants to be'.

Many of the heads we spoke to or questioned had done this, even though it was often unconsciously. Here are several individual answers to the question: 'What do you see as the head's role in a comprehensive school?' 'My job is to know the pupils' (Wales). 'I must be a public relations officer' (London area). I am 'controller of policy, decision-maker' (Midlands). A fourth head said he must firstly know and guide his staff (South-west), and a fifth: the head's job is to 'know everyone and listen to everyone' (East).

From the wealth of answers it was plain that there were three main types of head's role: first, that which put coordination of tasks first, i.e. administration; second, that which put public relations first; and third, that which took personnel relations, or the mediator's role, as central. As one said, a head 'needs tact, patience, geniality (at all times) and he *must* have kissed the blarney stone'.

But whatever role is dominant, all comprehensive heads have enormous administrative tasks. We also, therefore, asked the heads in our smaller sample how they divided their day between desk work, teaching and seeing people (whether staff, pupils, parents or visitors). Forty-two answered this question. The highest percentage for any head's desk work was 70 per cent of his time; the lowest 10 per cent. For teaching, the highest was 50 per cent, lowest none at all. For seeing people, highest was 85 per cent of the time, lowest 10 per cent. The average head spent 40 per cent of his time at his desk, 14 per cent teaching and 46 per cent seeing people. This percentage of time teaching was slightly higher than that recorded by the DES sample of comprehensive head teachers in 1966.*[13]

It was our impression that most heads worked far too hard – some dangerously too hard. The 'ideals' of headmastership must change with the comprehensive school, not only for the sake of the health of head-masters, but because the ideals of the public-school or grammar-school head, depending upon dedication to a single, well-defined and narrow goal of education for one section of the pupil population only, are inadequate in the long run for a comprehensive school. The goals of the comprehensive school being widely varied and very much tied to community need, the headmaster's role, both locally and nationally, may well need enlarging or changing. We are not suggesting the traditional head cannot be successful as a head of a comprehensive. He can be and is – especially in the early years of the transition. We are saying that where the new approach is made – necessarily abandoning the strict authoritarian interpretation of the role of head and incorporating more of the managerial and organizational skills required in running complex educational and social units – or where the approach is less that of a head of a restricted 'order' or segregated institution and more a team leader or member of a larger community than a school (in partnership with other heads, with other organizations: racial, educational or industrial), that these new

---

* This asked heads to divide time between teaching duties and others. The comprehensive-school sample was of twenty-eight heads, who spent 11·9 per cent of their time teaching. The average time spent teaching for all secondary-school heads was 16·8 per cent.

approaches should also be recognized as valuable and proper, and perhaps inevitable.

A century or so ago in Scotland the headmaster of a school did not exercise great 'authority over his colleagues'.[14] Schools were organized departmentally in those days, rather like comprehensives today. The head presided over a council of department heads and 'managed internal affairs of the school in a republican fashion'. It may well be that the movement to some form of 'republican' rather than oligarchical control is indicated in today's large comprehensive schools or units. Certainly authority will break up and lodge itself in five men or women where formerly it lodged in one, just as architecturally the monolithic structure of the 'one' school is dissolving into four or five separate buildings or units in many new purpose-built schools.

But this is a slow process. What is observable in schools is a distinct difference between the head's role in schools in transition and schools that are well established. It is almost as if the head-in-transition intensifies his attempt to be the ideal traditional head – just as we noticed comprehensive schools themselves go through a temporary super-traditional phase when making the transition to full comprehensive status – as proof that the comprehensive system can preserve sacred values while at the same time forging new educational paths. But this intensification, so valuable in a school making the transition, may be inappropriate or antagonistic to the thoroughly reorganized school. One head in our sample characterized this as an 'irresolvable conflict between the Ulysses complex and the Telemachus complex'. A 'reformer' or one charged with the transition finds it difficult to run a 'school quietly'. For most comprehensive schools, once over the hump of controversy, run quietly. The fuss of reorganization does not last long.

When a school is running 'quietly' – and when most schools have been reorganized (and the argument about reorganization is over) – then the head's role may change imperceptibly. One head observed this during his own time. He said that at the start his own person was central. The school depended upon his own reputation, and upon his 'own background as an academic'. But now the roles have reversed. 'My own reputation depends upon the school.' The school has become the 'focus of attention . . . without the name of the "head" '.

The head may not wither away, perhaps, but his role may well be transformed by the dynamic of the comprehensive school. The new heads will be less authoritarian, but in many ways far more influential, for their role will spread beyond their school and out into their immediate communities in a way the old heads' never did.

Pupils

The changes in the role of the head within the comprehensive school will be – and in some cases are already being – paralleled by changes in the whole exercise of authority within the school situation itself. We asked our smaller sample of schools who was in charge of school discipline. In most public, grammar or modern schools the answer would naturally be the headmaster. Thirty-six schools answered this question, but only two said the head was in charge of school discipline – although seventeen said he was the ultimate source of it, or shared it with the deputy or the senior staff. Two schools said the deputy alone was in charge; two, the senior master; five, the heads of the school unit (upper or lower school); four, the form teachers; one, the year tutors; one, the house heads; three, a combination of senior staff (minus the headmaster). But nine said the discipline was 'shared' by all the staff in the school. The 'sharing' of discipline throughout all the staff may not sound revolutionary, but in many ways it is. For it is a development quite far removed from the idea that discipline is a matter one must always refer to someone above.

But we should add that in many schools the word 'discipline' was narrowly interpreted. At least half the schools assumed the first meaning of discipline was the enforcing of school uniforms. The smaller the school, the more small-community the school, and the newer the school, the more uniform seemed important. By contrast, many large urban and well-established comprehensives had dropped uniform for the sixth form and some throughout the school. Where uniform was hardest to maintain, schools told us, was among the poorest pupils and those about to leave school for good. It was ironic that so many schools also said they keep uniforms in order that the poorer pupils and leavers should not be made to feel inferior.

It was hard to be sure about corporal punishment in comprehensives. Some comprehensive schools told us they have dropped it altogether, and others say they use it far less. Our impression is that it hangs on strongest in the single-sex boys' schools.

Nothing illustrates the diversity of comprehensive schools more completely – nor their intimate involvement with the traditions and pace of their own areas – than the subject of discipline, or more properly, conduct. Both the headmasters of Fishguard School in Pembrokeshire and Thirsk School in the North Riding, for example, circulate to all parents definite rules of pupil behaviour both for inside and outside the school.[15] The small town comprehensive, as the only school, can perhaps be the arbiter of community conduct in this way. But few big city comprehensive-school heads could lay down guidelines for the hours of

TV to be watched or the amount of pocket money to be allowed each week; far too many conflicting codes of conduct operate in urban areas. For this reason discipline problems were often greatest in the big urban schools. Thirty-five schools from our smaller sample answered the questions on problems of discipline. Thirteen said they had no discipline problems and eight said they had none that were serious. The remaining schools cited various problems, but stressed they were confined to tiny minorities in the school: truanting, pupils before the courts for misdemeanours outside school hours, theft inside the school and vandalism in the school. Two schools, however, reported serious violence or gang warfare and one said protection rackets operated. They were both in the heart of big cities. They were both boys' schools.

In the great majority of comprehensives, discipline seems easily and naturally maintained, but there are a few schools in very special circumstances where some new form of control is obviously going to have to be worked out. In the United States, where extreme violence has broken out in some schools, particularly over racial issues, there are now regular arrangements with the local police and in some cases, parents, for quick and systematic assistance, including permanent patrolling of corridors and classrooms. Situations similar to this have developed in this country. To prevent some of the same consequences, intensive attempts to tackle the underlying problems reflected in indiscipline in such schools are urgently necessary, drawing in all those involved in working out lasting solutions. Inner London's experiments in this direction, helping certain schools in especially difficult areas in a wide variety of ways, are one example of new attempts to meet these late twentieth-century problems in Britain.

As we saw in chapter 11, some schools have tried (with modest success) a permissive approach to discipline problems. But this is unlikely to suit many schools and in others the approach is more organizational: the school is divided up into age groups and each group is handled quite differently. One school described it in this way: the first two years (11–13) have easy discipline based on the parental approach. The middle years (13–16) have firmer discipline; and the upper years (16-plus) are encouraged to discipline themselves and to run their own affairs. In this matter, as in so much else, schools find they must work out their own methods and must modify approaches continually. In the comprehensive sector – perhaps because it is associated with new developments generally in education – there is always the possibility of conflict, as Tyrrell Burgess has written, between the 'old school virtues of loyalty, respect and sportsmanship' held up by teachers, and those 'other virtues' which children of today prize, who 'may be quite heartless in their neglect of the old ones'.[16] There is also the new problem provided by the overlap with further education, for 16–19s under FE regulations are often far freer than 16–19s in a sixth form at school. But even between sixth forms, rules of conduct and behaviour differ widely. In some schools pupils not actually with a class are free to study at home; in others – Rotherham's sixth-form college is one – all sixth formers have to be in school all the time, whether they have a class or not. In some sixth forms, pupils may smoke or wear what they want, or play cards; in others they cannot. Some schools find that as fast as they have relaxed their rules, others have relaxed them faster. Often it is parents who want the tighter rein,[17] not pupils or even necessarily staff.

As we said, severe discipline problems involve only a tiny minority of comprehensive schools. What is likely to involve a far larger number, however, is the extension downwards from higher education of the students' rights movement. Secondary-school students have already begun to organize – in January 1969 they held their first national meeting in London – to protest about uniform, corporal punishment, the prefect system and all the other manifestations of what their spokesmen see as the 'old' authoritarian school system. They also campaigned for the introduction of comprehensive schools and it is not without interest that some of the leaders of this movement are pupils from the selective schools – public and grammar. In these schools the authoritarian regime still holds the fastest. It holds fast in some comprehensives too, of course, but in others it has already relaxed – and relaxed to such an extent that many of the 'reforms' that the secondary-school pupils are hoping to pioneer have already taken place – quietly and without fuss – in comprehensive schools. Co-education is one. From time to time, a boys' public school will announce – with fanfare – that they plan to introduce a few girls into their sixth form as an 'experiment'. These bold breakthroughs are held up as yet another example of the valuable spirit of experimentation afforded by independent schools. Meanwhile, of course, thousands of young men and women in hundreds of mixed comprehensive schools regard this bold experiment as the normal state of affairs. And the same goes for many other experiments as well – all of which are taking place in the context of reorganization and most of which never find their way to the pages of the national press as do so many public-school 'changes'. Longslade School in Leicestershire, for example, has abolished prefects and corporal punishment and is on the way to abolishing prize day. Several comprehensives no longer have formal prize days, but have open days, demonstration lessons or community events instead. Settle School in Yorkshire is one school pioneering this approach;[18] so, too, is David Lister School in Hull.

Many of these activities are encouraged in order to see that all pupils are drawn into active school life, not just the so-called natural leaders. The NFER's Second Report showed a tendency in comprehensives 'for participation in activities to decrease as the social-class scale is descended, but to much less a degree than a tendency for participation to increase as the ability scale is ascended'.[19] A teacher in a large boys' school also found that when he asked his third-year boys about their participation in the voluntary activities of the school, that there was higher joining in the sports and clubs by pupils in the top-ability bands than lower ones, and none at all by those in the remedial forms. There was also very low joining in by immigrant boys who formed a large proportion of the school's intake.[20] This school set about putting this right; but many comprehensive schools probably are not even aware that certain groups are not playing as full a part as they could in school life. Once again active measures to see that objectives in this field are set and reached are required. Involving pupils is not something that can be left to work out by itself.

But what of other forms of pupil participation – where students take a hand in running their own affairs? This too has come far in some comprehensive schools, as was clear in the thirty-nine schools that replied to this question among our smaller sample. Only eight had no form of pupil participation and were not considering any (we did not count prefect systems as pupil participation). Six had none but were considering it, and twenty-four – well over half – already had it. Half the comprehensive schools in the NFER's Second Report had school councils,[21] and many, it was reported, had rejected the old 'elitest' approach to pupil responsibility, although, as the NFER added, 'it was not yet clear what will emerge in its place'.[22] There were many variants being tried. The characteristic of most was student election – rather than staff appointment – of pupils to various bodies: councils, year-group committees, or upper-school or lower-school boards. Among pupil activities undertaken were redesigning of the school uniform, decisions about disposal of general funds, and decisions on all aspects of the running of the school. Some student councils had staff assigned to them; some ran totally without staff. Although it is far too early to pronounce upon the effectiveness of these various forms, it would seem that in many schools the large and formal and staff-attended councils were the least successful – unless, of course, they were underpinned by smaller bodies that operated at shop-floor level. Or, put another way, the big council is best worked up to from the smaller groups. One school gave this account:

One or two year groups, notably fifth and sixth, have tried experimental year committees, either of a general nature, or *ad hoc* (for a dance). Because of their success we are establishing Year Councils throughout the school from this

September. At a later day, if the need arises (and I personally think it will) we shall add to these an Upper-School Council and a Lower-School Council. They will be encouraged to involve themselves in the running of the school.

How much say students – especially older age students – should have in schools' policy-making is a much more controversial point. In most comprehensives they have none directly,[23] but indirectly student influence varies a great deal. In some areas, of course – Sheffield is one – comprehensive schools have a student representative on the Board of Governors. In the 16–19 age group, therefore, it is probable that the students' 'say' will get greater and greater as time goes on.

To those who fear that giving responsibility to pupils will lead to anarchy, we can only report that far from the problem being students pressing for participation, some heads told us that the school was having to push the pupils into forming their own representative organizations. As yet in only a few comprehensive schools are student 'militants' far ahead of the school authorities in their demands. But where they are, the problem for many militant comprehensive-school students, who are often middle-class and in GCE courses, is somewhat akin to those of militant university students in society at large: how to work together with other social groups – particularly with the other 'rebellious' groups in the school situation, for example, the early leavers. The comprehensive militant student inside his school, therefore, has an undeniable advantage (or insoluble difficulty, depending on how one looks at it) of having to work with pupils representing the *whole* spectrum of society – unlike the university student whose fellow students are by definition a select group. Student participation in comprehensive schools is not likely to be successful, therefore, unless it is representative of all sectors in the school, and unless it is given, and genuinely accepts, responsibility for management of many of its own affairs.

Parents

The participation of parents in the comprehensive school – as partners in the enterprise of education – is also unlikely to be wholly successful unless a way is found of involving all parents – not just middle-class parents. But though there may be a danger of domination by middle-class parents in some areas, there is no doubt that the rise of support from such parents has been a crucial factor in the success of comprehensive schools and that it will be of continuing value when it comes to pressing locally for improvements in individual schools and schemes. One of the difficulties of the early years in the comprehensive movement was that the middle-class parent was conspicuous by his or her absence. As one observer wrote of an early comprehensive, there were few children of 'high-level executives, skilled technologists or scientists or senior administrators'.[24] The middle class were much too dedicated to 'their' schools: the grammar schools and the public schools. But gradually middle-class parents (especially in the countryside, and the smaller towns and villages, where comprehensives were the only schools, entirely neighbourhood-based, and where the academic and social achievements of the school were easily made widely known) began to entrust their children to the comprehensive school. The vastly improved parental support of comprehensive schools has been noticed in several recent publications.[25] In some areas now it is absolutely established practice for all pupils to attend the local comprehensive. Several heads we saw told us the comprehensive was now so well accepted that local private schools were having to close down. This acceptance has not yet taken place in most large cities, however, for co-existence of comprehensives with selective schools – maintained and private – persists.

The comprehensive issue generally has brought parents very much to the fore, if only by stirring them up to take an interest in what was often being decided by local or national governments and education officials. Circular 10/65 said parents' views were to be taken into account, but in most local authorities there was no machinery for doing so and parents were rarely involved in reorganization in any systematic way. Their main activity was in organizing protest parties, usually over grammar schools that were involved in plans, or, on the other hand, through bodies like the Association for the Advancement of State Education, organizing support for, or discussion about, comprehensive schools. In this connection it is interesting to report that not a few of the parents we met – enthusiastic about the education their children were getting at a comprehensive – told us that in the beginning they had opposed reorganization but had changed their minds. Very few areas – and only one school in our whole survey of 728 schools – maintained reorganization was 'not working' and was still bitterly opposed locally, and no area with a comprehensive school long established reported that reorganization was still opposed. This build-up of local loyalty to the school as a community school is a factor that will become more and more important as reorganization progresses.

The NFER Report of 1965 reported that 50 per cent of comprehensive schools had some form of parents' association.[26] The Second NFER Report of 1970 showed this had gone up to 62 per cent.[27] Thirty-nine of our smaller sample of schools answered the section on parents. Only nine had no form of parents' association. Of the thirty who had them, twenty-four were parent–teacher associations and five of them were for parents only. If those samples are anywhere near representative of comprehensive schools, this means the percentage of parents' associations in comprehensive schools has risen dramatically since 1965.

Certainly in the schools we questioned and visited, parents played a big part. PTAs were in the main exceptionally successful and their contribution to the school was enormous – especially materially. Libraries, buses, film equipment, a £4000 swimming pool and much plain cash – these are just a few of the items heads reported parents' groups had raised. Several of the schools in our smaller sample said that there was not a single material need not met by the LEA that the parents had not then met themselves by their own fund-raising. Nor were most of these schools in so-called affluent areas – as can be seen by looking at the list in Appendix 1 (p. 517); council-estate comprehensives managed to raise quite prodigious sums. It is quite obvious that the financial support so many endowed and public schools have enjoyed for years – the kind of support that makes a crucial difference to a particular sport or cultural event or course in the school – is very definitely available within the circle of parents and friends of all but the most disheartened or disadvantaged comprehensive school.

PTAs also organized educational functions, but as yet schools claimed these were not as well attended as social ones. At the same time several schools reported that their parents had organized to protest against the continuance of a grammar sector in the area; and in one town, Oldham, the combined PTAs of all the comprehensive schools were able to organize effectively enough to get the education committee to abandon plans for selection for direct grant schools. The most successful PTAs were able to combine business with pleasure, but there is little doubt that for most schools and parents the mainspring of parental involvement to date has been fund-raising activities: fairs, rallies, films, dances and sports events. And although it is fashionable in some intellectual circles to decry fund-raising, there is no doubt that the cooperative spirit fostered as a result of these events and the chance for parents to make contact with staff and with each other are gains not to be minimized. The comprehensive school, as a neighbourhood school and as a big school, has the opportunity to become a leader in the field of parental involvement and support. One school in a new town said the PTA already acted as the town's major social centre, enabling new residents to meet and to get to know each other.

But parents also need to know and understand what the school is trying to do. All the heads agreed that parents could help their children by taking an interest in their work at school. From a West-country head: 'Parents are the most important single agency in a child's education.' Apathy was several times mentioned as being by far the worst parental failing. A few heads took a very traditional, but not unhelpful, view of the parental role. From Scotland: 'To send the child to school regularly, dressed suitably, clean and with the correct attitude – that education is important.' And from a large industrial town: 'Not too much money or TV – not too little sleep, a bit of old-fashioned discipline and a whole heap of . . . conversation.' The conversation most hoped for was the conversation of encouragement. Several mentioned that nagging was most unhelpful. Many heads hoped parents would take an active interest in homework and school work, but most knew this was not always done, and that, as one said, lack of parental interest is a 'major social problem'.

Yet how to encourage it? Parent or parent–teacher organizations can help but often only in a limited way, for sometimes only parents who are already interested take an active interest in the PTA. Several heads we questioned commented that their schools' PTAs were dominated by middle-class parents – by 'CASE types', as one London head put it. Another said, 'It is all too easy for parent associations to become representative of the minority of parents and dominated by middle-class attitudes to committee structures.' But so long as the school is aware of this danger and the school actively plans to make contact with *all* parents, it need not be a reason to mark down PTAs. In some cases, of course, parental disinterest may be linked to school policy: 'I have one grammar stream (A), one best secondary modern (B); and one second best secondary modern (C); and one remedial stream (D). Parents from A and B support the PTA – but C and D parents are quite uninterested'. One might ask: Are C and D parents uninterested because they are C and D or are they C and D because they are uninterested?

The problem of parent power has been raised by many, especially in connection with the domination of parent groups by middle-class parents, whose leadership, so valuable on the one hand, has, on the other, 'motives' that some have seen to be 'selfish'.[28] One comprehensive teacher wrote very bitterly of his school where the parents of 'grammar-ability' children called all the tunes.[29] This experience is not typical, but all the same it points up a danger. In the comprehensive school it is particularly important not to let any one set of parents dominate participation. Any alliance between staff, who are often middle-class, and middle-class parents – with the interests and aspirations of the working-class majority of pupils pushed to the background – would not be in the best interests of the comprehensive school. On the other hand, the ethos or outlook of a particular section of the working-class – sometimes very strong in a particular area – should not be allowed to dominate either. This is especially important in areas where black immigrants or white minority groups may have settled, or where some pupils are exceptionally affluent and from homes where skilled work provides many material benefits, while other pupils may come from homes where circumstances have combined to produce severe cultural or material deprivation. A comprehensive school that takes an interest in each pupil as an individual, seeing to it that systematic provision for personal supervision, regular reporting, and continual guidance is available for each and every one – with no group or section carrying special 'weight' in these respects – will be the one most likely to avoid difficulties of this kind.

Staff and heads who fear the onslaught of opinionated parents, trying to lay down the law on education, is one problem sometimes raised, for no school could tolerate active interference by parents in the job of education. But in only one school we visited or questioned was this problem raised. Complaints were always of the opposite order: parents who never came near the school. But parental interest in a comprehensive school is different – and must be judged differently – from parental interest in a grammar school, where most pupils will have the same aims and objectives. Comprehensive parents have as wide a variety of interests or problems as do their children. One Derbyshire head has wisely commented that it may be a mistake for comprehensive schools to 'still expect *all* parents to support *all* functions'.[30] Nevertheless, since parental choice in a comprehensive system is a choice that will be exercised within each school situation, it is vital that parents know and understand the alternative choices open to their children at *all* stages of school life. In this connection it is interesting to note that in one city, in comprehensive schools where responsibility for choosing subjects at thirteen was left to parents, parental response to schools' invitations to visit the schools for discussion was far higher than in schools where pupils were directed to courses by the schools themselves.* It is also instructive – but somewhat disheartening – to read in the NFER's Second Report on comprehensives that 'seeing parents' was still largely a function heads or senior staff abrogated to themselves (or that, perhaps, parents insist on), and that 'individual contacts between teachers and parents were extremely rare';[31] also, that half the teachers did not even have formal 'parents' evening' contacts.[32]

Again, a PTA can help but, as the educationist, William Taylor, has put it: 'We should be very cautious in assuming that freeing the channels of communication will of necessity make it easier for parents and teachers to work together.'[33] Nor does having a PTA ensure adequate contact with all parents. Michael Tucker of Settle, a head who has made an all-out

---

* H. D. Dickinson and John McLaren reported this (pages 2 and 3) in their 1969 publication, published by the Bristol Fabian Society, 'The Comprehensive Schools in Bristol'.

effort to involve parents in his school, knows that for certain parents 'more active measures are needed'.[34] Many other schools also know that the school itself has to take the lead – and actively organize to go out to parents, or get them to the school. A number of comprehensive schools have now stopped issuing reports on school work: a parent *must* visit the school to hear about his child's progress in all his subjects. In Highbury Grove comprehensive, London, there is no PTA, but rather 'open-ended committees of parents to help in organization and finance'.[35] Here it is the job of the house heads to keep in touch with all parents – even if it means repeated visits to the home of a pupil before the contact can be made. In Croxteth School, in Liverpool, the head said, 'I am convinced the reduction of apathy and complete school acceptance can only be achieved by personal contact.' Last year his school made 850 visits to parents.[36] Another head said his aim was to get the parents themselves involved in the educational process as 'receivers'. For a growing number of schools now realize that the old, formal – even if well-meant – approach, of 'An appointment has been made with you to see X at the school', is inadequate. But many schools still use it. Comprehensive schools still have 'a long way to go' in this matter of working with parents, the head of a recently reorganized grammar school told us.

Everything the staff and the heads said and everything we have learned has convinced us that just having a PTA or parents association or just having an open-door policy or just providing open nights or exciting events at the school – excellent though these are – is not enough. If parental encouragement is as vital as all believe, and if in too many cases it is lacking, then the school must take the initiative. Every single parent at a school should be seen by someone at the school regularly – and if it means going to the parent, then this is something the school must accept.

But in considering this problem we come up against a difference of opinion within the schools themselves. Who should do this contacting? The staff themselves as an extension of their ordinary pastoral work in schools? Some schools strongly believe in this, even suggesting that extra allowance should be given for staff prepared to do home visiting. The schools where this is the policy, as we saw, are certainly pursuing their policies energetically and successfully. But in a few schools there are doubts. One head said: 'I am suspicious of this modern trend to make teachers parish priests and welfare workers.' This is possibly a minority view, but where it exists a school has two alternatives. The first is to make extensive use of local welfare agencies, for no comprehensive will want to be without some means of linking home and school. In some authorities we visited, the welfare officers or educational social workers were very highly praised. In one northern town comprehensive-school staff told us that the authority's welfare workers could be around to a child's home almost before the school itself knew there was any trouble. But the danger in relying on external services of this kind is that they are mobilized only in times of emergency. What most schools felt was required was some form of regular year-by-year contact between home and school – organized on a systematic basis. One educationist, Michael Young, has suggested a second alternative,[37] a new type of social worker – an education visitor.* In this connection the appointment to the staff of some comprehensive schools – South Wigston in Leicestershire is one – of 'community counsellors' is an interesting development.

The comprehensive school has the opportunity to become the centre of education in its widest sense in most communities – not just by virtue of being the only school attended by all local boys and girls, but by actively engaging the community, parents included, in the total educational process and in the life of the school. The great majority of comprehensive schools know that to do this effectively and successfully schools must have a sound administration and be actively interested in their neighbourhoods and accessible to them. An open-door policy is no good if the door is so many miles away that it is hard for parents to get to the school and for staff to understand the many local problems parents face. In this as in all else, the comprehensive must be a community school if it is to gain the support and help of all parents.

Notes

1. Second NFER Report, 1970, p. 251.
2. Paul Ferris, *Observer*, 15 September 1968.
3. Incorporated Association of Headmasters, *The Position of the Headmaster*, p. 1, July 1960.
4. ibid., pp. 5, 6, 7. Notice the list of headmaster's duties in order of importance; attention to governors and important visitors is at the top.
5. *Handbook of Headmasters*, Ministry of Education, p. 97, 1959.
6. See *The Comprehensive School; Appraisal from Within*, pp. 99/101, for discussion of site management problems.
7. Kathleen Ollerenshaw, *Education for Girls*, p. 57, 1961.
8. Lord Newton, House of Lords, 10 February 1965, col. 142. See also Scotland, Memorandum on Primary Education, p. 26, 1965.
9. Southend Plan, Joan Thompson, *Secondary Education Survey* (Fabian pamphlet), p. 19, 1952.
10. IAAM Report, p. 24, 1967.
11. Ollerenshaw, op. cit., p. 58.
12. Governing Bodies Association and HMC Working Party Document No. 135, p. 3, 1969.

* Some Glasgow comprehensives have an appointment of this kind.

13. *Statistics of Education*, Special Series, 1965–6, part 1, *Teachers*, p. 37, Table 10.
14. H. M. Knox, *250 Years of Scottish Education*, pp. 39/40, 1963.
15. S. King, *Ten Years All In*, chapter 10. See also pupils' handbook published by Fishguard School, 1968.
16. Turrell Burgess, HMSO, *Inside Comprehensive Schools*, 1970, p. 140.
17. Halsall, ed. op. cit., p. 213.
18. See Michael Tucker, *Comprehensive Education*, no. 4, 1966.
19. Second NFER Report, p. 159.
20. Robert Moon, 'Interests inside and outside schools', *Comprehensive Education*, Autumn 1970.
21. Second NFER Report, p. 53.
22. ibid., p. 54.
23. ibid.
24. R. Cole, *Comprehensive Schools in Action*, p. 173.
25. IAAM, *Teaching in Comprehensive Schools*, p. 10.
26. First NFER Report, p. 133.
27. Second NFER Report, p. 170.
28. Brian Macarthur, writing in *The Times* on 'Parent power', 12 October 1968.
29. R. G. Gregory 'Change in name only', *Comprehensive Education*, Autumn 1971.
30. J. Climo, in *Becoming Comprehensive*, Halsall (ed.), p. 108.
31. Second NFER Report, p. 43.
32. ibid., p. 57.
33. William Taylor, quoted in John Parham, 'Beyond the school gates', *Comprehensive Education*, Spring 1967.
34. *Comprehensive Education*, no. 4, 1966.
35. Rhodes Boyson, 'Creating a new comprehensive', *Comprehensive Education*, Autumn 1967.
36. Croxteth School document, 1968, p. 1.
37. Michael Young, *New Society*, 4 July 1968.

Part Five
Comprehensive Schools in the Community

Chapter 17
Where the Comprehensives Are

As comprehensive schools grow in size and numbers, new questions arise. We have already talked about the likely differences in the types of schools and schemes and in the methods of transition to comprehensive status generally. But there are many more question marks. How do comprehensive schools differ between town and country or between Scotland and England? In what way is comprehensive reorganization altering the balance between mixed and single-sex schools? How are comprehensive schools to be related to the dwindling selective sector and to their own neighbourhoods? All these questions are fundamental and all of them are questions in one way or another of choice. We discuss the whole question of choice in a comprehensive system in detail in chapter 20, but we also argue in many places in this book that the most important choices in a comprehensive system are those that pupils and parents will make inside the individual schools. It is for this reason that we have urged that all local authorities ensure parity of provision of facilities, courses and subject-options for the same age ranges in all their comprehensive schools or units.

Regional variations in reorganization

But it is not just between different comprehensive schools in the same area that parity of provision is crucial. There are many other differences that might affect a child's chances in education and it is to some of these that we now turn.

Many parents live where there are as yet no comprehensive schools, so that the question of choice inside a comprehensive system does not yet apply. It is not likely that many of us have a choice of the region of the country in which we live, but for those who do, Table 17.1 analyses some of the differences between eight regions of Britain in respect of the 728 comprehensive schools in our survey in 1968. More comprehensive schools in our survey were in the North of England than in any other region: 29 per cent. The region with the least was the East with 5 per cent. Scotland and the Eastern area of England had the most nearly 'comprehensive' intakes – 18 per cent of the top 20 per cent of the ability range – while Greater London had the least comprehensive with only 11 per cent.

Table 17.1 Regional differences in comprehensive schools in Britain, 1968*

	Scotland	Northern	Midlands	Eastern	Greater London area	South	South-west	Wales
Percentage of all 728 survey schools in each area	9	29	17	5	14	7	8	13
(number of schools in brackets)	(67)	(208)	(109)	(38)	(101)	(53)	(60)	(92)
Percentage of top 20% of ability range	18	15	15	18	11	15	16	15
Percentage staying on beyond leaving age	43	46	50	56	61	54	61	47
Average size of the sixth form	71	88	75	90	78	83	93	75
Average O-level (grade) subject-groups	14	11	11	11	12	12	13	12
Average A-level (H-grade) subject-groups	9	7	7	7	7	7	8	9
Percentage of all schools with 13–16 age group able to offer at least 13 O-level or O-grade subject groups	79	58	60	55	68	56	75	71
Percentage of all schools with sixth forms able to offer at least 8 A-level or H-grade subject-groups	87	67	77	59	58	67	83	88
Average size of 11 (or 12)–18 (type I) comprehensive school	787	987	835	675	1,210	759	947	807
Numbers (in brackets) and percentages of 11 (or 12)–18 schools (both types) of total number of schools in each region	(48) 72	(105) 50	(50) 46	(19) 50	(86) 85	(23) 43	(35) 58	(54) 59
Numbers (in brackets) and percentages of 11 (or 12)–16 schools of total number of schools in each region	(15) 22	(52) 25	(18) 17	(15) 39	(1) 1	(27) 51	(9) 12	(19) 21

* For lists of authorities in each region, see Appendix 3, p.570

Inner London's pupils had the lowest attainment in the NFER's Second Report too.[1] The percentage of pupils staying on beyond the leaving age was highest in the South-west and the Greater London area (61 per cent) and lowest in Scotland (43 per cent). It was also rather low in Wales (47 per cent). In the Greater London area 85 per cent of the comprehensives were 11–18 (of both types), while in the South only 43 per cent were all-through. The largest average size of schools of all types of comprehensive was in the Greater London area. Breaking this down further, we found that the largest average schools in neighbourhood categories were council-estate schools in London, the smallest were schools drawing from sub-standard housing areas in Wales.*

As for academic offering, it is interesting to see from Table 17.1 that both Scotland and Wales, despite smaller than average sixth forms and generally smaller schools, nevertheless had higher than average GCE and SCE subject-offerings. In addition, 51 per cent of Scotland's 12–18 and 12–16 schools were able to sit pupils in sixteen or more of the eighteen subject-groups at O-grade compared to only 33 per cent for all schools in the survey in these categories.† The NFER Report of 1965 made similar observations about Welsh comprehensive schools' generally smaller sixth forms.[2]

Considering next the percentage of schools in each region able to present pupils in at least thirteen or more O-level or O-grade subject groups or eight or more A-level or H-grade ones – that is, those whose academic offering in 1968 was above average in these respects for all schools in our survey – we see in Table 17.1 that once again Scotland and Wales do very well at both examination levels. Again, their smaller than average sixth forms do not seem to have been any disadvantage at A-level and H-grade – Scotland with 87 per cent and Wales with 88 per cent of schools with an above average offering. The South-west does well at both O- and A-levels too – with 75 per cent and 83 per cent respectively. The lowest regions at O-level were the Northern (58 per cent), the Eastern (55 per cent) and the Southern (56 per cent). At A-level the Eastern was again low (59 per cent) but Greater London was even lower (58 per cent).

That London should have the lowest percentage of schools able to offer an above average number of grouped A-levels in 1968 is interesting in view of the anxiety in the Inner London Education Authority (where most of our survey's Greater London sixth forms were) about the adequacy of A-level courses, and sizes of A-level classes, in comprehensive schools.‡

* See Appendix 1, Note 3. See also Table 21.1 (p. 474), for description of neigh-bourhood areas.
† See Appendix 1, Note 3.
‡ See the ILEA Report 951, for example, published in 1968.

This inadequacy has been assumed by some to be an intrinsic failure on the part of the comprehensive school as an educational institution. But others have seen this inadequacy as directly related to the fact that Inner London continues to support a grammar-school sector alongside its comprehensive schools, where, it is worth noting, many of the A-level classes are as uneconomic in size as those in the comprehensive sector.[3] In the year of our survey, 1968, for example, not only were just under 19 per cent of eleven year olds still selected for grammar schools in Inner London, but at sixth-form level, of the 10,592 pupils taking A-level courses, 6500 were in grammar schools but only 4092 were in comprehensive schools.[4] The grammar-school sixth forms were thus able to have more pupils and to have pupils in the higher-ability ranges, while the comprehensive-school sixth forms had fewer A-level pupils and these were mainly pupils who had been unable to obtain grammar places at eleven. Both sets of sixth forms were segregated one from the other, and some would say that comprehensive sixth forms were supported as 'second-class' sixth forms because of this coexistence situation. One hundred per cent of Greater London comprehensive schools in our survey in 1968 had to coexist with grammar schools – compared to only 52 per cent of all comprehensives in Britain in that year. In such a 'duplicating' situation the comprehensive school sector was bound to have difficulty building up big A-level classes in all subjects in every school.

Scotland

Perhaps we should say one special word about Scotland, for it has reorganized on a different timetable from England and Wales. The Secretary of State for Scotland issued circular 600 from the Scottish Office in October 1965, asking education authorities in Scotland to prepare initial intentions about reorganization by March 1966, and fuller statements by December 1966. Most were able to do so, although submissions were often short and informal. Like 10/65 in England and Wales, this circular asked for development on 'comprehensive lines' rather than for comprehensive schools, and it also said it aimed to give 'guidance on how development on these could best proceed'. Unlike England and Wales, no long list of schemes was suggested, for there are really only two kinds of reorganization schemes that Scottish authorities were prepared or equipped to adopt for comprehensive schools. The one most would prefer, and towards which most are working eventually, is the 12–18 all-through school. But too many authorities already have too many small schools to make this kind of change possible for a very long time. Moreover, many areas are too thinly populated to support a 12–18 school.

Therefore, 12–16 schools must 'coexist' with 12–18 in the future, as they have in the past. In a very few areas there are experiments with 'middle' schools: 11–14 and 14–18, and some areas – like Stirling – are developing semi-selective interim schemes. Table 5.2 (p. 111), on foundation of schools in our survey, shows that reorganization in Scotland has tended to accelerate noticeably since 1965, very few comprehensive schools having been established between 1945 and 1965.

Table 17.2 **Types of comprehensive schools in Scotland, 1968**

Age range of school	Number of schools	Percentage of total schools	Number of pupils	Percentage of total pupils	Average size of schools
12–18	44	65·5	34,639	73·6	787
12–18 type II*	4	6	2823	6·0	705
12–16	15	22·5	8668	18·4	577
11–13	3	4·5	875	1·9	292
11–14/15	1	1·5	77	0·2	77
13–18	0	0			
14–18	0	0			
16–18 or sixth-form college	0	0			
Unknown	0	0			
Totals	67	100	47,082	100	

* With regular transfer of pupils from other schools for Higher Certificate work.

It has always been traditional for Scotland's education to be considered separately, but there are fewer and fewer reasons to go on doing this. The transfer age of twelve between primary and secondary schooling was the main difference often urged for keeping away from comparisons with England and Wales, but this no longer applies, since so many English schemes will also now transfer at twelve. In questioning heads, staff and parents in Scotland and in reading the Scottish educational journals, it seems obvious that many of the reorganization problems in Scotland are identical to those in England and Wales: lagging authorities, retention of selection within comprehensive schemes, small size of remote schools, and creaming of pupils by the selective schools. This latter problem is especially evident in Glasgow and Edinburgh, and comments by comprehensive heads and staff in these areas are identical to those in the large

English cities. The opposition to educational change – particularly where it endangers the traditional selective schools in big towns – came out very clearly during the debates surrounding the bill to end corporation fee-paying grammar schools in 1968 and 1969, and of course in the Conservative government's repeal of this bill to permit maintained schools to go on charging fees. Inevitably this keeps a firm divide between the fee-paying sector and the non-fee paying, the selective and the non-selective.[5]

But there have been certain differences in Scotland that matter. We know that pupils of the same measured ability have had a higher chance of being placed in a selective course in Scotland than in England: in one study it was found that 38 per cent in Scotland enter selective courses, compared to only 30 per cent in England and Wales.[6]

As far back as 1947 it had been suggested that comprehensive schools were 'the natural way for a democracy to order the post-primary schooling of a given area' in Scotland.[7] Traditionally too, many Scots schools have taken in all pupils in the neighbourhood for education in the single school. Indeed, in our survey Table 5.2 (p. 111), almost a third of the Scottish comprehensive schools were classed 'unknown' because they were unable to give a date for their establishment between 1945 and 1965. When we looked at the dates actually given we saw this was because most of them pre-dated 1945 – one as early as 1836. In other words, they had always been 'comprehensive'.

But although in some respects – 'social' ones foremost – reorganization is easier in Scotland, in others it is harder. For the internal organization of many Scottish schools has always permitted a very marked segregation of pupils. What has mattered in Scotland equally as much as, if not more than, the type of school to which a pupil went has been the type of 'course' to which a pupil was allocated. There was no 11-plus, but there was a transfer test at twelve and on the basis of this pupils were allocated to separate types of schools or to certificate and non-certificate courses inside schools. These represented far greater divisions than exist between Engish 'streams' or even between the 'sides' in bilateral schools. One writer has called this division between certificate and non-certificate courses that of an 'iron curtain'.[8]

Certificate courses lead on to Certificate of Education at higher grade and, since 1962, in ordinary grade as well.* For those who are in schools

---

* But unlike the two grades of GCE in England and Wales, the H- and O-grades in Scotland are not separated by two years' schooling, only by one. O-grade is taken at sixteen or seventeen, H-grade at seventeen, but for many who take H-grade it is common to skip O altogether. One might say that O-grade was in some respects a CSE experiment (except that it is not as widespread in the school population nor is it an untraditional exam), while H-grade continued to be the exam course to which the university and profession-bound students aspired.

with an age range of only 12–16 (with *no* H-grade courses) the transfer to 12–18 schools to take H-grade courses at age sixteen, as sometimes happens, results in their having to study another two years for H-grade, rather than just the one year required of those who are in the 12–18 school from the first. When the 12–16 school has H-grade courses for only two years, transfer must take place at fourteen.* Scottish 'comprehensive' schools are therefore of many different kinds. In recent publications from the Scottish Education Department (e.g. *The Structure of Promoted Posts in Secondary Schools*, 1971, p.7) junior high schools and senior secondary schools are not classed as comprehensive – only schools with 'all courses including H-grade to SV or SVI'. These, therefore, are the schools many feel should be the only ones claiming the title of comprehensive: in which both higher grade, ordinary grade and non-certificate courses are offered all the way through. But since these schools are themselves often 'selective' for pupils from schools outside the area – most commonly at fourteen – this definition is hard to apply universally. Thus, it is obvious that entry into a certificate course at twelve in a 12–18 school puts a pupil at a much greater advantage than entry into a 12–16 school when transfer takes place at fourteen or sixteen. Many feel these parallel schemes discourage the borderliner, the late developer, and the pupil from a home with little encouragement, and that they also offer scope for Scottish education authorities to 'drag their feet' over true reorganization.[9] In our survey we found one-fifth of all Scottish comprehensive schools were short-course comprehensive (12–16) schools, running parallel with long-course schools (Table 17.2). From the school's point of view, when transfer takes place at fourteen from the 12–16 school – like parallel schools in scheme 3 of circular 10/65 – short-course schools 'lose' their ablest pupils at fourteen. It also means that selection at this age takes place inside a school to decide which pupils will transfer – and which remain behind. As far as reorganization goes, therefore, this need to identify those who will take certificates, and in which grades, to separate them and, in some cases, to send them to different schools, makes 'for rather more inflexible parallelism than in English two-tier systems',[10] as one educationist has commented. He goes on to say that it is a 'twist of history' that a country priding itself on the omnibus school

---

* A second category of comprehensive school has years I and II of the H-grade course, and I through IV (or II) of the O-grade, plus non-certificate courses – but H-grade (and sometimes also O-grade) pupils move out at the end of year II (age fourteen) to a school of the first type. A third category has years I to IV of the O-grade plus non-certificate courses, but no H-grade pupils come at all. There are, of course, some secondary schools with no certificate courses at all, but the percentage is small, and dropping as reorganization proceeds.

for so long should devise in these parallel schemes a 'refined system of selection'.

The solution for Scotland, therefore, lies in a comprehensive internal reorganization of schools, and especially in the introduction of a common course for pupils that does away with the rigid division of all pupils into certificate and non-certificate courses. Circular 600 made it clear that these 'rigid divisions' between courses will have to go. A common course is the real crux of reorganization in Scotland. But as Table A.4, p. 525, shows, one-fifth of Scottish comprehensive schools in our large survey did *not* have a common course in the first year. We also found that at fourteen course allocation took place in practically all Scottish comprehensive schools. It is quite true that at fourteen in English schools there are also subject option choices and differentiation of pupils taking GCE, CSE or other courses. But the divisions at fourteen in Scotland are still the fairly rigid and traditional ones that have prevailed since the 1962 introduction of O-grade and before. Some think that reconsideration of these examination courses in the light of the new departures involved in reorganization and the introduction of the common course in earlier years is now required.[11]

Extended courses for the non-examined students have not been widespread. Despite the jump in staying on after the leaving age of certificate pupils that followed the introduction of the O-grade certificate in 1962,* the staying-on rate in Scottish comprehensive schools in our survey is the lowest for any area in Britain, 43 per cent, and more than 3 per cent lower than the 1968 average for Scotland as a whole.[12]

Much pioneering work in education that is relevant for ordinary boys and girls was done by such men as R. F. Mackenzie, formerly of Braehead School. It is feared by some that reorganization in Scotland will merely mean the domination of the comprehensive-school curriculum by the traditional certificate courses and the comprehensive schools themselves by the certificate teachers with an inevitable concentration upon external examinations. Circular 600 talks of the need to introduce vocation-centred courses, which would seem to be an urgent necessity. All these problems point to the need for an examination that a far greater percentage of the school population could take – and that schools themselves could perhaps set, as in Mode III CSE – and, equally, to the need for some kind of reform that will eliminate examination parallelism and enable short-course schools to retain all pupils until sixteen without their being disadvantaged when it comes to transfer to long-course schools for any final examination.

* It went up 17 per cent between 1964 and 1969 (Osborne, p. 221).

Northern Ireland and other areas

Although comprehensive secondary education in the British Isles outside England, Scotland and Wales is not much advanced (with the exception of the Isle of Man, which has long been totally comprehensive), it is being seriously discussed. The two Channel Island authorities have both had the subject raised, but at the time of writing they have not yet decided to introduce comprehensive schools. There, as in Northern Ireland and as in Scotland, the local authority grammar schools are often fee-paying schools. In Northern Ireland, grammar schools comprise less than a quarter of all secondary schools, but 75 per cent of all these grammar schools are fee-paying schools. Thus, the divisions of the ordinary 11-plus segregation are further reinforced by fee-paying in the state system.

Very little agitation on the subject of 11-plus selection and segregated schools has existed in Northern Ireland until the last few years. But it has been apparent, wrote head teachers recently, that there is 'growing disillusion with selection'.[13] The pattern of progress in Northern Ireland is therefore following that in Britain by about ten years. First, a reaction against 11-plus segregation itself, followed later by agitation for specific reorganization.

Already, however, there are pioneering efforts being made in comprehensive schooling. Some areas plan interim selective reorganization schemes (County Armagh was considering a version of circular 10/65's scheme 4). But in other areas – like Fivemiletown in County Tyrone – local secondary schools have been providing all the secondary education for all pupils in the community and so could rightly claim to be comprehensive schools. In fact, one university researcher identified fourteen such schools in Northern Ireland in 1970. His study of their achievements showed how remarkably successful they were, particularly in external examinations.[14] In Eire, comprehensive schools are also just being introduced.

Geographical variations

Another area where differences are likely to occur is between comprehensive schools in different population areas. We asked all our 728 schools: 'From what kind of population area does your school draw the majority of its pupils?' Table 17.3 sets out the results. We see from this table that the largest block of comprehensive schools are no longer in the large cities with populations over 200,000 – as used to be the case; they are now in the suburban areas, defined as areas 'on the outskirts of town or city'. Thirty per cent of all comprehensives were in suburbs, 34 per cent if additional suburban categories are added.* Very closely next in line are comprehensive schools in towns with populations between 5000 and 200,000 (27 per cent). Large cities (over 200,000) have only 19 per cent of schools, while villages have only 14 per cent – with an additional 6 per cent in the town-and-surrounding-country category.

It is sometimes said that comprehensive reorganization will lead to a situation where schools are split between city schools that are disadvantaged and suburban schools that are specially favoured. Do we see many differences between comprehensives in the different geographical areas?

As the NFER found in 1965, we also found that schools in the middle of large cities had the lowest ability intake: only 12 per cent of the top 20 per cent (Table 17.3). We found in addition that the two categories of village and town/country had the highest: 18 per cent. They are neighbourhood schools, of course, and not usually coexisting with grammar schools that would 'cream' them of high ability. Suburban schools fell between, with 14 per cent of the top 20 per cent – not in this respect advantaged.

There was also some difference between the precentage of pupils staying on beyond leaving age in the various categories: town/country schools had the highest: 57 per cent; villages and big cities the lowest: 50 per cent. Suburban schools again fall in between with 53 per cent.

Table A.2 (p. 523) shows the relative sizes of schools of all types in the geographical areas. We see here that the suburban schools for 11–18 and 11–16 age ranges are quite a lot larger than schools in other areas. This is an advantage or not, depending on one's views about size of comprehensive schools.

In sixth-form sizes we see the highest average – ninety-nine – goes to the town category. Suburban schools are only second in this respect.

In general these limited inquiries do not reveal that suburban schools in Britain are particularly advantaged in the way many feared. But what they do show – and this we found confirmed in visits and in questioning schools in addition – is that the big city schools are apt to be struggling the hardest in a number of important ways: to obtain a genuine comprehensive intake, to retain a sixth of adequate size, and to provide a full range of subjects and options and examination courses for all pupils. What limited these schools was not so much the pupil population they might draw from, nor their size. As we see in the section on neighbourhood (Table 21.1, p. 474), all but a few comprehensive schools draw pupils from reasonably varied housing areas, and Table A.2 (p. 522) shows that big-city schools were very often the largest schools. What disadvantaged them was what gave the schools in the villages, the small towns, and

* See note on Table 17.3.

Table 17.3 Population areas from which British comprehensive schools drew pupils in 1968

Population area from which majority of pupils were drawn	Percentage of all schools (numbers in brackets)	Percentage of schools, England and Wales	Percentage of top schools Scotland	Percentage of Roman Catholic school	Percentage of top 20 per cent ability	Percentage of pupils staying on after leaving age	Percentage of schools that are mixed sex, England and Wales	Average sixth-form size
1. From middle of large city (200,000 plus)	19 (136)	19	19	20	12	50	56	76
2. From town (5,000 to 200,000)	27 (199)	28	21	45	16	50	86	99
3. From suburban area (outskirts of town or city)	30 (217)	31	22	20	14	53	77	88
4. From village (5,000 or under) or countryside	14 (100)	12	27	0	18	50	100	60
5. From town and surrounding countryside*	6 (44)	6	6	8	18	57	88	71
Other† and Unknown	4 (32)	4	5	7				
Totals	(728) 100	100	100	100			(523)	

* This category not included in questionnaire, but so many schools wrote it in under 'Other' that we added it.
† Most of the 'Other' category were variations of suburb, i.e. town and suburb or suburb and surrounding countryside; many could theoretically be added to the suburban category 3.

the countryside such immense advantages so very often: they were still operating in authorities that were systematically supporting a grammar-school sector alongside them, while the other geographical categories had to face this problem far less acutely, or not at all. The NFER's Second Report also brought out the crucial importance of 'competition with grammar schools' when it came to differences in pupils' attainment levels, in the intake of high-ability pupils, both of which were affected by this type of comprehensive scheme. They also found that in certain schools teachers' time was taken up with welfare problems far more than in others. Generally, the divide was not regional – but between urban schools and rural schools – in size, intake, methods of organization, allowance structure, and in the amount of time pupils actually spent at lessons. Pupils in Wales, for example, had an average of ninety minutes a week more on lesson time than pupils in comprehensives elsewhere.[15] But this was because they were in largely rural schools as well, schools not so often in direct competition with grammar schools as are schools in the centres of big cities.

There are many versions of the most 'successful' of the comprehensive schools. Articles and books and newspaper reports over the years have nominated a wide variety of schools in Britain. Some are in the countryside, some are in the small villages, some are in the reorganized towns and some are on council estates. Not all are necessarily purpose-built by any means, and many are amalgamations of two 'former' schools. What distinguishes many, however, and what makes them so successful academically, so well staffed, backed by local parents and the local community, attended by most local pupils, and supported 100 per cent by their authorities, is that in all but a few cases they are the *only* maintained secondary school for their own particular community or neighbourhood. Parents and pupils and staff in these communities do not believe their 'choice' has been limited because there is only one school, or in urban areas, only one type of school. On the contrary, most of them know that in terms of subject options, courses, facilities and opportunities choice is wider and far more real inside a genuine comprehensive school than it could ever be in a system where 'choice' was equated with irrevocable segregation at eleven into two types of school.

Notes

1. Second NFER Report, 1970, p. 110.
2. First NFER Report, p. 37.
3. ILEA, *Sixth form document*, 1970/71.
4. ILEA Report 951, 1968, p. 2.
5. See chapter 9, p. 199.

6. J. W. B. Douglas, *British Journal of Educational Psychology*, vol. 36, part 2, June 1966.
7. Secondary Education, A Report of the Advisory Council on Education in Scotland, 1947.
8. N. Dixon, 'Comprehensive education and the small burgh school', *Education in the North*, Spring 1965, p. 19.
9. ibid., p. 204.
10. G. S. Osborne, *Scottish and English Schools*, p. 203, 1966.
11. See the recommendations of some Scottish teachers' organizations.
12. *Scottish Educational Statistics*, 1968, p. 29.
13. Association of Head Teachers of Secondary Schools in Northern Ireland, 'Why not comprehensive?', p. 1, 1968.
14. 'Northern Ireland's comprehensive schools', Terence Donaghy in *Comprehensive Education*, Summer 1971.
15. NFER Second Report, p. 52.

Chapter 18
Some 'Choice' Questions

Denominational comprehensive schools

Denominational school choice was the one largely meant by education-according-to-parents'-wishes in the 1944 Act, and it is the one that local authorities often feel most obliged to meet.

The denominational schools are reorganizing along with all other schools, and in many areas are taking part in the same scheme as maintained schools. In other areas – Luton is an example – the Roman Catholic scheme is different: all-through schools rather than sixth-form college. In still other areas, however – Manchester is an example at the time of writing – maintained schools are reorganized but many denominational schools are not. There is no doubt that overall the denominational schools are reorganizing more slowly than the rest of the country. At the beginning of the 1970s one in seven secondary maintained schools was a denominational school, but only one in ten comprehensives was denominational.

The problem is difficult in some areas, for often diocesan authorities do not coincide in boundaries with the local authority. Sometimes they span more than one local authority, one of which may be reorganizing, another of which may not be. 'What is the poor puzzled papist to do?' in those circumstances, a Roman Catholic peer once asked in the Lords.[1] But just as often it is the poor puzzled LEA that has the problem; for example when the denominational school is far too small to fit into the local scheme and wants a wider catchment area than an LEA can give it.[2] In Salford a reorganization scheme was returned partly because of difficulty about fitting in the denominational schools. Occasionally there was some bitterness over an authority's decision to allow a C of E comprehensive to be built or developed in an area (mainly because it would have a wider catchment area and would become, some felt, a selective school in disguise). We found no opposition from non-denominational schools to having Roman Catholic schools nearby or in the same area, although a few of the schools we questioned were of the opinion that no denominational schools of any kind should be retained anywhere. Others have suggested that the 'ecumenical comprehensive' – already one such school exists, shared by the Church of England and the Roman Catholics[3] – should be the pattern for the future.

The Roman Catholic sector is having an uneven time reorganizing. In some ways it is far ahead: the only direct grant schools and independent schools to have 'gone comprehensive' are in this sector. But in many areas there has been resistance from members of the Roman Catholic hierarchy and occasionally the teaching orders. It can be resistance to a particular reorganization scheme – as from the staff of St Brendan's, Bristol – or it can be, as near Stockton-on-Tees, on the part of a male teaching order to the idea of mixed schooling in a reorganization scheme.

The essential dilemma for the Roman Catholics is that if they fail to reorganize effectively in an area, many Roman Catholic parents will opt for maintained comprehensive schools rather than for the Roman Catholic secondary schools. Church pronouncements on reorganization make this fear clear,[4] and we came across a few Roman Catholic parents who had disregarded their primary head teacher's 'guidance' to choose a Roman Catholic secondary school. On the other hand, when Roman Catholic grammar schools have come into reorganization, there can be problems too. The head of one well-established grammar school, recently reorganized and thus now open to all pupils, said that many parents living in the vicinity were 'suddenly discovering their religious affiliations, which I imagine are influenced by the proximity of this grammar school to their homes'.

Most of the Roman Catholic and Church of England schools we questioned said that although they did not admit many pupils outside their own faith, they would have no objections to doing so. This would be crucial in areas where denominational population is small, for in some areas both denominations are having to discuss the possibility of relinquishing their hold on some of their secondary schools; or, as one typical LEA document said, in certain instances 'it was reluctantly . . . felt . . . it would be better for the Church to transfer its interests from secondary to primary provision'.[5]

But it is not just a problem of numbers or of finance. It is also a question of educational policy. In the Roman Catholic Church in particular it is clear that comprehensive reorganization has opened up a debate on the whole future of denominational education.[6] Some Roman Catholics opposed reorganization. On the other hand, some hoped that Roman Catholic schools would take the lead in reorganization and build up a flourishing comprehensive tradition.[7] A minority, however, are questioning the need for denominational education at all at a time when

Table 18.1 Denominational comprehensive schools in Britain, 1968

	Number of all schools	Percentage of all schools	Percentage of top 20% of ability	Percentage staying on after leaving age	Average size of sixth form	Percentage of total schools that are mixed sex
Non-denominational schools	631	87	15	53	84	81
Roman Catholic	65	9	17	40	58	74
Church of England	14	2	18	45	46	100
Other*	17	2	20	46	75	88
Unknown	1					
Total	728	100				

* Most of these were Church of Scotland.

'it seems almost certain in the long run that all schools will belong to the State'.[8] The reason given in one document for 'liberal Catholic opinion' favouring an end of church schools is the fact that 'the educational level of many church schools falls short of that in ordinary institutions'.[9] Most Roman Catholics would not be in favour of abandoning denominational schools, of course. But many have suggested alternatives to the present situation.[10]

What do our survey figures reveal about denominational schools to support or refute any of the stands being taken in debates about religious schools generally?

Table 18.1 shows that 13 per cent of all the comprehensive schools in our 1968 survey were denominational schools. The percentage of all comprehensive schools in our survey that were Roman Catholic was 9 per cent, the same percentage of secondary schools that is Roman Catholic nationally.[11] Table 18.2 shows that 34 per cent of Roman Catholic comprehensives in our 1968 survey were 11–16 short-course schools – much higher than the national average for this type of comprehensive. The percentage of Church of England schools overall was small: 2 per cent. The 2 per cent that were neither Roman Catholic nor Church of England were Church of Scotland or Jewish.

Denominational schools are generally much smaller than non-denominational (see Table 18.2). The average size of both types of 11–18 all-through non-denominational school in Britain, for example, was 981, the average size of the Roman Catholic was 812.* Church of England schools were smaller still at 620.* The differences in size can be illustrated in another way: only 18 per cent of all Roman Catholic schools were over 800 in size, compared to 43 per cent of non-denominational schools. Or again, only one Church of England school in the survey was over 1000 and only three Roman Catholic comprehensives were over 1300.*

The average sizes of sixth forms in denominational schools were particularly small too: fifty-eight for Roman Catholic schools, compared to eighty-four for non-denominational. The Church of England average size was even smaller: forty-six (Table 18.1). The percentage of pupils staying on beyond the leaving age was also much lower in denominational comprehensive schools: 45 per cent for Church of England schools and 40 per cent in Roman Catholic, compared to 53 per cent in non-denominational schools (Table 18.1). In the limited field of presenting pupils for GCE examinations, no Roman Catholic or Church of England school in the survey presented pupils for all eighteen O-level subject groups and only one each for at least seventeen. At the same time thirty-eight non-denominational schools were able to present for all eighteen, and

* See Appendix 1, Note 3.

Table 18.2 Types and sizes of denominational comprehensive schools in Britain, 1968

Percentage of schools of each type (average size of schools in brackets)

Denomination	Type of comprehensive school by age range of schools								Total number of schools
	11/12–18 Type I	11/12–18 Type II	11/12–16	11–13	11–14/15	13–18	14–18	16–18 sixth-form college	
Non-denominational schools	54 (972)	4 (1099)	20 (614)	4 (331)	10 (498)	4 (526)	2 (598)	0·5 (582)	631 100%
Roman Catholic	49 (809)	3 (855)	34 (475)	3 (412)	3 (400)	8 (624)	0 (0)	0 (0)	65 100%
Church of England	43 (549)	7 (1046)	43 (426)	0 (0)	7 (653)	0 (0)	0 (0)	0 (0)	14 100%
Other	71 (903)	0 (0)	12 (569)	0 (0)	6 (467)	6 (435)	6 (420)	0 (0)	17 100%
Unknown									1
Total	389	31	154	29	70	34	16	2	728

seventy-six were able to present pupils for at least seventeen.* Although they had a common course in the first year in 80 per cent of the Roman Catholic comprehensive schools in the survey, only 22 per cent of the schools kept this up for three years, compared to 48 per cent of schools generally.*

If one examines the individual subjects at O-level and A-level GCE (Tables 6.8, p. 136 and 9.7, p. 205), comparing the Roman Catholic schools only to all schools' average percentages in various categories, one sees a much lower percentage offering by Roman Catholic schools in almost all subjects, but particularly marked at O-level. Church of England comprehensives were just as low (see Table 6.8, p. 136). As we have often repeated in this book when dealing with these particular 'academic' criteria, they are conclusive of very little other than the general range of academic offering in schools at GCE O- and A-level, or O- and H-grade in a particular year (1968) in selected subject-groups. They say nothing about performance in examinations or about offering in previous or subsequent years. But these figures, taken together with the low numbers staying on and the small numbers in the sixth forms generally, might perhaps give those who fear for the academic viability of religious schools some cause for concern.

On the other hand, it should be noted that as far as the intake of the upper 20 per cent of the ability range is concerned, denominational schools were more 'comprehensive' than non-denominational schools, taking in 17 per cent of the top 20 per cent of ability (RC) and 18 per cent (CE) compared to non-denominational: 15 per cent (Table 18.1). Roman Catholic schools were also less likely to be on split sites than non-denominational schools (only 18 per cent were, while 24 per cent of the latter were, see Table 6.11, p. 146).

The future of denominational comprehensive schools as a universal choice for all is most uncertain. The small number of Church of England comprehensive schools speaks for itself (only twenty-three in 1970).[12] As for Roman Catholic comprehensive schools, it will entirely depend upon the area in which a parent lives. There were 104 RC comprehensives in 1970 in England and Wales.[13] It is obvious from Table 17.3 (p. 399) that only Roman Catholic parents living in big cities or in the large towns are going to find it universally possible to 'choose' a Roman Catholic comprehensive school. Just about half of the RC comprehensives in our survey were in the single category of towns. Only 8 per cent were in the category town-and-country and none at all were in the category of village-and-country.

The denominational comprehensive schools most likely to succeed, of

* See Appendix 1, note 3.

course, are those that take part in the local reorganization scheme or that are able to offer facilities, options and opportunities equal to those in non-denominational comprehensive schools in their areas. Some already do, of course, and in visiting denominational schools we were also much impressed by the quality of their care for the whole education of their pupils. But only time will tell if most denominational comprehensive schools will be able to hold their own in the long run in many other ways.

Mixed and single-sex comprehensive schools

A choice between single-sex or mixed education is another some parents insist upon and a few education committees feel they must ensure, although this is getting more and more difficult every year. There are few single-sex schools at primary stage. Equally, there are going to be almost no single-sex sixth-form colleges. And there are almost no single-sex higher education establishments outside the colleges of education, and even these are gradually becoming mixed.

Single-sex schooling is therefore an issue that is confined to the years eleven to sixteen, the years when sex differences become most apparent. Many argue that single-sex schools are necessary for 'academic' progress (in either sex), or socially, for reasons of disparity between the develop-ment of the sexes. But the basic reason for the tradition of segregating sexes in Britain is probably still the long line of influences starting with sexual taboo, reinforced by the beginnings of formal education in monastic and religious institutions, by the 'public school' tradition, by the 1926 Hadow Report recommendation to develop separate secondary schools for the sexes, and by the 1945 Ministry pamphlet encouraging single-sex schools.[14] The situation is complicated in Britain because so many of the old prestige state schools happen also to be single-sex schools, so that many people have the idea that single sexness itself is necessary for academic excellence or for maintenance of order and decency. Research, however, has shown that academic attainment is not lower for either sex in co-educational schools, and for some girls and boys, possibly higher.[15]

There has been very little research, however, into what communities actually prefer. Some authorities claim to have tested opinion locally. Harrow, for example, said they found some years ago that only one parent in three wanted mixed schools. Gloucester conducted a poll in 1968 and found opinion fairly even. Other authorities, however, say they found very little demand for single-sex schools. Demands for single-sex second-ary schools are rarely heard in country districts, where few exist. They are often heard in cities, where most of the single-sex schools are. Thus views are often conditioned by the existing school situation locally.

In the maintained secondary sector of England and Wales in 1967

58 per cent of schools were mixed; in 1968 it was 60 per cent.[16] By 1970 it was 63·5 per cent.[17] These in themselves are rather higher percentages of mixed schools than were originally planned in the 1945 development plans.[18] Thus the trend to mixed schooling was taking place anyway; reorganization has only accelerated it. In the comprehensive sector the percentage of mixed schools is, of course, higher still. In 1968 DES statistics show that about 77 per cent of comprehensive schools (576 out of 745) were mixed[19] with boys' and girls' schools exactly equal at just over 11 per cent of the total each. In our own survey of 1968, 81 per cent of all comprehensive schools were mixed, while 9 per cent were girls' and 10 per cent boys'. In 1970's DES *Statistics* this was up to 84·6 per cent in the comprehensive sector[17] which means the trend towards mixed schooling in the comprehensive sector is now accelerating – probably because so many of the areas now reorganizing are rural and small town areas, where mixed schools are so much more common, and accepted, than in cities. In Scotland 99 per cent of our survey schools were mixed which, since they are included in the total, would raise our survey percentage. But even so, the true overall figure is probably slightly lower for mixed schools, however, due to the fact that in our survey (Appendix I, Note 2, p. 511), as in the NFER Survey of 1965, girls' schools, and probably boys' too, are slightly underrepresented.[20]

In the early days of reorganization the Ministry were very anxious to get very large schools and therefore pushed hard to get some authorities to plan all mixed comprehensive schools.[21] This was in contrast to its general secondary-school policy which, as we saw, urged single-sex schools. Since reorganization is partly a rationalization of resources, it makes more sense in general to have one mixed school of 1000 than two single-sex schools of 500. Many early authorities therefore went ahead with all schools as mixed (Anglesey, Isle of Man). Most county authorities today also plan a very high percentage of mixed schools. For example, only four out of sixty schools planned in 1966 in Nottinghamshire were single-sex.[22] Many other counties will have only mixed schools and even in boroughs there are a good number of authorities – like Keighley or Sheffield – who have only mixed comprehensive schools. In these authorities the question of whether some single-sex schools should be preserved for 'choice' purposes has not been overriding. Nor has there been any great objection raised.

But in other areas – usually boroughs – authorities plan to retain one or two single-sex schools simply in order to meet this point of 'choice'. Very often, however, these single-sex comprehensive schools are the old prestige grammar schools, and one gets the impression that some single-sex schools have been retained in schemes as an olive branch to their grammar staff. In one or two areas schools are being kept single-sex in order to avoid 'zoning' problems, i.e. instead of having two comprehensives in a single town and having to decide who goes to each, the area will retain both as single-sex schools, the 'allocation' problem being disposed of by nature.

In a few areas there is yet another complication. It is the single-sex grammar school that is being conveniently 'left out' of the comprehensive reorganization plans altogether and for which selection will continue – as in Southampton. In areas where large numbers of selective grammar schools remain outside reorganization – Bristol, Coventry, London – they are almost always single-sex schools. In situations like this local citizens naturally have reinforced the idea that high prestige goes together with single-sex status. And this adds to the difficulties in trying to maintain coexistence of a comprehensive system – so often mixed-sex – side by side with selective schools – so often single-sex.

Since 1945 there has been a subtle shift of opinion within the comprehensive movement about mixed versus single-sex schools. In comprehensive literature in the early days there were quite a few who felt that the type of comprehensive most likely to 'succeed' was the single-sex. This was partly because these had been developed out of grammar schools and were thought more likely to succeed because of academic tradition or a 'clear image'.[23] Since so many mixed comprehensives have now succeeded so well – including academically – this view no longer prevails. In some ways it is the single-sex schools that are now on the defensive.

It is also interesting that the early argument over mixed schools was almost always about whether they were best for girls or not. It was assumed mixed schooling was all right for boys but it was often felt that girls would be swamped and overwhelmed in a mixed situation. Mother Mary Norbert, who has questioned the value of single-sex education in the traditional Roman Catholic single-sex schools,[24] nevertheless worried about girls in a mixed situation where they had to endure an atmosphere of 'heavy handed' discipline on account of the boys.* Early comprehensive staff also often worried about girls because of the male domination of staff in mixed schools. They feared that a mixed comprehensive school would merely be a 'boys' school with girls in it'.[25] This is no doubt why many mixed schools give one of the senior staff special responsibility for 'girls' welfare – as if this had to be specially arranged for and could not be trusted to come under general 'pupil welfare'. This provision of a special 'girls' adviser', however, can confuse counselling and pastoral work in a school – and for this reason is now coming into question. The Scottish Education Department, for example, has recommended its

---

* We found in the RC comprehensive sector that a slightly higher proportion of schools are single-sex than in the non-denominational (see Table 18.1, p. 404).

Table 18.3 Mixed and single-sex comprehensive schools in Britain, 1968 (1)

	Number and percentage of all schools No. %		Number and percentage of Scottish schools No. %		Percentage of Roman Catholic schools %	Percentage of ILEA schools %	Average size of schools	Average size of sixth-forms	Percentage staying on after leaving age	Average number O-level or O-grade subject-groups	Average number A-level or H-grade subject-groups
Mixed schools	589	81	66	99	74	39	783	80	50	12	8
Girls' schools	62	9			11	25	725	79	57	11	7
Boys' Schools	75	10	1	1	15	36	811	91	56	11	7
Unknown	2										
Totals	728	100	67	100	65	56					

Table 18.4 Mixed and single-sex comprehensive schools in Britain, 1968 (2)

Average size of schools and percentage (in brackets) of each type of school in each age range

	11 (or 12)–18 type I		11 (or 12)–18 type II		11 (or 12)–16		11–13		11–14/15		13–18		14–18		Sixth-form college	
	Aver-age size	% of total	Aver-age size	% of total	Aver-age size	% of total	Aver-age size	% of total	Aver-age size	% of total	Aver-age size	% of total	Aver-age size	% of total	Aver-age size	% of total
Mixed schools	939	(80·5)	1071	(94)	600	(81)	344	(83)	510	(96)	634	(38)	589	(94)	582	(100)
Girls' schools	909	(8·5)	1238	(6)	514	(9)	288	(7)	0		449	(27)	550	(6)	0	
Boys' schools	1059	(11)	0		541	(9)	305	(10)	208	(4)	500	(35)	0		0	
Unknown						(1)										
Total number of schools	389	(100)	31	(100)	154	(100)	29	(100)	70	(100)	34	(100)	16	(100)	2	(100)

abolition in Scottish secondary schools (see *The Structure of Promoted Posts*, 1971) and several researchers in England have come to the same conclusion: it is no longer necessary to have a 'welfare post' especially for girls.

In visiting comprehensive schools we found many of the traditional attitudes to girls prevailed, sometimes unconsciously, especially about their supposed limited interest in maths and sciences. This was discouraging. On the other hand, we did not notice that girls themselves seemed submerged as individuals in any comprehensive school. Perhaps the early Cassandras were wrong about this? As well as about what girls actually prefer? For example, those who have written about girls' education, both inside and outside the comprehensive movement, have stressed that girls prefer the house system as a social unit.[26] This is no doubt partly wished on girls as a result of tradition in selective schools and partly because of early fears that they might be lost or intimidated in a big comprehensive. But for several years now it has been evident that where the house system has been scrapped, it has usually been in girls' schools.[27] And in our own survey we found that fewer girls' schools have house systems than boys' or mixed schools (only eight out of sixty-two have them).*

We see from Table 18.4 how far mixed schools predominated among all types of comprehensives. Both the sixth-form colleges are mixed, 96 per cent of 11–14/15 lower schools are mixed, 94 per cent of 14–18 upper schools, 80·5 per cent of 11–18 schools of type I, and 94 per cent of type II. The only type of school to deviate seriously from this pattern is the 13–18 school, of which only 38 per cent are mixed. We discussed why this was so in 1968 in chapter 6 (p. 117).

It is interesting to see that boys' schools are larger than girls' or mixed in the 11–18 category type I: average size 1059 to 939 mixed, and 909 girls'. Boys' schools also have larger sixth forms than girls' or mixed schools: average of ninety-one to girls' seventy-nine and mixed's eighty.†
In all categories other than 11–18 or 12–18 schools, however, the mixed schools' average size is largest. Mixed schools are quite a lot larger in most (Table 18.4), suggesting for those who are most worried about size viability that mixed schools might more successfully ensure larger size. Our size figures generally show a change from 1965 when the NFER Report found both boys' and girls' schools to be slightly larger than mixed schools.[28]

* On the other hand, many more girls' schools have year systems: 54 per cent of girls' schools had year systems (thirty-four out of sixty-two) while in mixed schools only 38 per cent had them (226 out of 589), and in boys' schools only 41 per cent. See Appendix 1, Note 3.
† In type II 11–18 schools, girls' schools are larger than mixed schools (Table 18.4).

As might be guessed, single-sex comprehensive schools figure more prominently in urban areas. The city category of comprehensive schools has 26 per cent boys' schools and 18 per cent girls' schools, much higher than the overall average for single-sex schools.* The area with the highest proportion of single-sex schools in our survey was the ILEA: only 39 per cent of schools answering in the ILEA were mixed (Appendix I, Note 3). In the three categories – town, suburb and village – which contain the majority of comprehensive schools, the reverse is the case: more schools are mixed than single-sex. In towns, for example, only 8 per cent were boys' and 6 per cent were girls' schools (Appendix I, Note 3). And the village and countryside category had no single-sex schools at all (Table 17.3, p. 399).

As we saw in Table 18.1, 100 per cent of the Church of England comprehensive schools in our survey were mixed; and in Table 18.3, 99 per cent of Scottish comprehensive schools. Clearly for parents in particular regions or population areas or in particular circumstances, the 'choice' between mixed and single-sex comprehensive is not going to be possible. But it is fair to add that the diminishing number of single-sex schools in the comprehensive sector is not a subject that often provokes disquiet among parents and education committees. The trend towards mixed schooling is accepted as desirable – probably largely because it is obvious that nowadays so many staff prefer to teach in mixed schools.[29]

All the same, it is interesting to compare the single-sex and mixed schools for the benefit of those who might live where there is a choice. Taking first GCE O-level offering in all-through schools (Type I) in England and Wales (Table 6.8, p. 136), we see that, as one would expect, in the girls' subjects like needlework and domestic science the girls' schools score very much higher than the boys' schools, the reverse being true for the boys' subjects like metalwork and woodwork, which boys' schools obviously sit more in. But it should also be noted that in *all* these subjects the mixed schools score high percentages as well. And in some subjects – like typing and commerce – the mixed schools have a significantly higher percentage of schools offering pupils in the subjects. When considering the traditional academic subjects, we see that in English literature, history, mathematics, biology and geography there is really very little difference between all three types of school. All three score high. Significant differences can be found between girls' schools and mixed schools, however, in physics (taken by only 64 per cent of girls' schools compared to 93 per cent of mixed) and in chemistry (64 per cent girls' compared to 84 per cent mixed). On the other hand, the girls' compre-

---

* See Appendix 1, Note 3. Girls' school percentages are probably higher than shown, however, because of lower response rate among girls' comprehensive schools.

hensive schools were able to sit pupils for languages (other than French, Latin or English) in a higher percentage (76 per cent) than were either the mixed (68 per cent) or the boys' comprehensives (60 per cent). A higher percentage of girls' schools were also able to sit pupils in religious knowledge. Far fewer boys' comprehensives, on the other hand, were able to sit boys for Latin than mixed schools (36 per cent compared to 51 per cent for mixed schools). This also applied for music (48 per cent for boys' compared to 61 per cent for mixed schools). Only in chemistry were boys' schools able to present a significantly higher percentage than mixed schools (93 per cent compared to 84 per cent).

As can be seen from Table 6.8 (p. 136), we have deliberately made our comparisons in all-through schools only. This is likely to give a fairer comparison than when 'upper' schools are added – so many of which are single-sex and so many of which in 1968 were recently changed-over grammar schools. In the all-through schools, therefore, it would appear that mixed schools can guarantee a better all-round provision of subjects for both sexes, and that if girls are to be encouraged to become proficient in science and boys in languages to a greater degree than is now the case, that a mixed comprehensive is – on evidence to date – probably slightly more likely to ensure this range would be possible.

But what about other features of school life? Parents arc sometimes anxious underneath that mixed schools will foster precosity in their children. Although we came across schools where there were 'gangs' and occasionally violence, where there were discussions about the length of the girls' skirts or the boys' haircuts, where vandalism was a real problem and truanting endemic, we can truly say that in all the schools we visited and have personal knowledge of – and with all the comprehensive pupils, staff, heads and parents with whom we have talked – there was one subject conspicuous by its absence: problems of promiscuity. This used to be raised in the early debates as a campaigning point against the introduction of comprehensives.[30] No doubt all comprehensive schools – like schools anywhere – have to cope with the general problem of changing codes of behaviour among young adults. But the fear that comprehensive schools – being mainly mixed – would bring special new sex problems is quite unfounded.

We also asked our smaller sample of schools about the mixed versus single-sex issue. Most of those who were mixed were quite categorical about its being preferable. Three wrote identical answers: 'Thank goodness, not single-sex.' Several said a single-sex school cannot be comprehensive. A comprehensive is a school 'for *all* children in a given area, not half of them', wrote one. Another: 'All comprehensives should be mixed. Families are.' Another said a mixed school is best as a 'natural preparation for life'.

On the other hand, two heads felt there should be a 'choice' of single-sex schools for families who preferred them. One was a Roman Catholic head. Those who had single-sex schools themselves were in two minds. One big city head said:

We are a girls' school but I feel the full advantages of comprehensive schools can only be experienced in mixed schools. It is very difficult to staff girls' schools without permanent professional men teachers.

But another head of a girls' school, also in a city, said that being single-sex meant she had more opportunity to plan to suit girls' needs and greater freedom to experiment. The disadvantages were entirely social. A Roman Catholic boys' school felt that their own 'social disadvantages' were offset by their having a 'sister' school nearby for plays and dances, and that having a mixed school was not always 'an unmixed blessing'. Another head said that a mixed school led to 'uneconomic use of practical spaces and hence staff time'. But being single-sex was not always to be isolated. We found several single-sex schools in our survey had 'paired' off with a nearby school of the opposite sex – e.g. the two John Kelly Schools in the London borough of Brent shared sixth-form facilities and some classes as well. The new sixth-form building between Hammersmith County Girls and Christopher Wren Boys in London, where they share a site, will also be used by both – in fact this 'link' now makes this campus one of the biggest comprehensive 'schools' in Britain.

There is no doubt that mixed schools are more complicated to run and that some of the single-sex schools are freer to tailor their courses and activities to the specific needs of pupils of their sex. But there is equally well no doubt that most of those we talked to and met preferred working and being in mixed comprehensive schools. Pupils in mixed schools were particularly enthusiastic about the school being mixed (where this was recent) and quite happy about it where it had always prevailed. Pupils in single-sex schools were also enthusiastic about not having the 'other sex' around. But this enthusiasm waned noticeably as the pupils approached leaving age. Several single-sex school sixth-formers said they were dissatisfied with the school's single-sex status. Several pupils in mixed comprehensives told us they had transferred to the school solely because it was mixed.

The trend of reorganization planning makes it quite clear that mixed schools will continue to predominate. It is not unlikely that by 1980 only one school in ten in the comprehensive sector will be single sex. Since the education of most pupils will be in a mixed comprehensive situation –

where course options are far wider than in any single-sex situation – this transfers the question of choice from one between types of school into a different arena: choice in the school itself. One of the factors that one would not expect to limit choice within a mixed comprehensive school is that of sex. Unfortunately we have found out that it sometimes does.

We asked all 589 mixed schools in our survey if there were any subjects in the school that could not be chosen because of sex, i.e. 'Are there any subjects or options open only to boys: or open only to girls?' 50 per cent of all mixed schools said there were some subjects limited to boys only, 49 per cent had them only open to girls.* A few wrote that they would be willing to change this practice if there was 'a demand'. Some said there had been a demand, but the staff in question wouldn't consider it. 'The metalwork teacher said he won't have girls in his class', said one. Where changeovers had been allowed, it was generally in response to boys' requests to be allowed to do cooking or tailoring.

On the other hand, several schools wrote to tell us that their options were open regardless of sex and that several girls in each school had opted for technical drawing, woodwork and engineering, and boys for cooking. In Table 6.8, (p. 136), we even see one girls' school had presented girls for technical drawing at O-level, and one boys' school for domestic science. So there must be some 'demand', even if it is entirely masked in many schools.

We asked mixed schools restricting subject by sex to list the subjects in their schools that were so restricted. There were about a dozen subjects altogether not open to boys, among them catering and clothes design.† There were over a dozen subjects in mixed comprehensives that were not open to girls, among them engineering and gardening.‡ It should perhaps be added that a few mixed schools added that pupils of the 'wrong' sex were sometimes admitted on special application. In others they said pupils were admitted 'in theory', but none in practice. We found it rather disquieting that such a long list of subjects should be restricted by the accident of sex in so many mixed schools. The value of a mixed school should be precisely in wider options. If the same sex restrictions are

* In Scotland it was 70 per cent limited only to boys, 68 per cent to girls.

† In order of number of schools naming them (numbers in brackets) there were: needlework (186), domestic science (140), typing (thirty-four), cooking, shorthand (twenty-seven), and (with twenty-five and under) dress design, catering, nursing, girls' crafts, jewellery making, hygiene, dancing and human biology. One school put 'Mother-craft' with large exclamation marks, which was, perhaps, fair.

‡ The subjects and numbers of schools were: woodwork (160), metalwork (159), technical drawing (102), and (under twenty-five): building, gardening, rural science, navigation, engineering, physics with chemistry, pottery, surveying, technology and boys' crafts.

continued as in single-sex schools the special value of mixed schools is much diminished.

As long ago as 1923 British schools were urged to organize their curricula so that girls could try boys' subjects and boys girls', and so that girls could have more attention paid to their proficiency in the 'men's' subjects like maths and physics.[31] But all signs point to our schools having moved very slowly in this direction. What is perhaps most noticeable is the failure to educate girls not so much in maths and chemistry and physics – though this could stand improvement – but more particularly in the many engineering sciences. This failure in engineering was once referred to as Britain's 'national disgrace'.[32] The only way in which it can be righted is by encouraging girls in the study of science subjects more than we do and by permitting them, in addition, to opt for technical subjects or engineering while still at school. The comprehensive reform has a real chance to encourage this development, and the mixed comprehensive school is the most likely school in which all this can best be done. For this reason it was disquieting to find so many mixed comprehensive schools timetabling options to prevent girls' choices of so many subjects. It was also discouraging to find some schools with the traditional outlook upon girls' 'natural' talents. This was not school policy, of course, but it came out in many subtle ways. For example, one thirteen-year-old girl in a mixed school told us that she had recently complained to the physics teacher because he never looked at the girls' section of the room when he taught. 'It was as if he unconsciously assumed we could not possibly be interested.'*

But the choice-of-options problem is wider than just the training of girls in the traditional academic disciplines. It also bears on the whole question of providing a varied and stimulating course – for both boys and girls. This is especially important for girls whose chances of apprenticeships and day release are so few. In the early days in the comprehensive school, one reads of worries about what to do for the 'non-academic girls' for whom nothing, it was said, could be provided but 'domestic science'.[33] This now seems an impoverished and traditional outlook, just as the assumption that girls will find 'their personal satisfaction' in the art and music departments, in 'painting, design, embroidery, pottery, printing, weaving and basket work'[34] seems limited. In another early account of the comprehensive we find someone writing quite rightly of the way comprehensive schools could make up for pupils' lack of skills. But one

---

* In this respect it is interesting to note that, as this girl's report makes clear, it is customary for girls to sit on one side of the room and boys on the other in the early years in most comprehensive schools we have visited. We often asked if this was school policy, but were always told it was spontaneous.

example given, 'in the commercial field for girls and in engineering for boys', begs the question again about the alliance of certain skills with certain sexes. This is rather dangerous with its art-for-girls, sciences-for-boys implication. The limitations are probably more serious for girls, who generally have fewer opportunities inside schools and far fewer day release and employment opportunities outside. If the comprehensive reform is going to be successful it must alter this. There is no reason why girls, if they wish, cannot learn car maintenance, technical drawing, gardening or engineering – subjects many mixed schools restrict to boys only. There is no reason why boys should not learn typing or tailoring or catering, subjects that were closed to them in many schools. It is to be hoped that the timetable difficulties, which we know are severe, will nevertheless not be used as excuses in mixed schools for failing to provide the opportunity for both girls and boys to have a full 'choice' of all subjects and courses. Once again, the real choices that are going to matter in the comprehensive system are those that are available inside the school. But real choice across the sexes does not just happen; it must be actively organized.

Boarding

Boarding in state schools has long been established practice,[35] and from the beginning some comprehensive schools have had provision for boarding. One of the oldest is the boarding house at Crown Woods comprehensive in South London. This is a separate house in the school grounds provided for boarders – many of them weekly – where they have separate sleeping and eating accommodation and common rooms for after school and weekends. During the day, however, the pupils are part of the population of this large school. The boarding, like the school, is mixed. Crown Woods is in a large urban area. But boarding wings also exist in other cities and in many rural comprehensives. The Dukeries School in Nottinghamshire has a boarding wing. Boarding wings in new comprehensive schools are expensive. Sometimes they are asked for but are not possible financially.[36]

Quite a few of the comprehensive schools in our survey had boarding wings, or special houses reserved for boarders. Some were schools previously grammar schools – like Midhurst in Sussex or King Edward VI in Devon. Others were schools previously non-selective. Local authority planning shows further that quite a number of presently non-comprehensive schools – with boarding accommodation – will eventually be brought into the comprehensive system of schools.[37]

Discussion and correspondence we have had with several heads of comprehensive schools with boarding wings or houses gives us to understand that sometimes boarding places are undersubscribed. Yet we hear and read of the need for boarding that is 'unmet' in the country. It was partly because of this 'unmet' need that the Public Schools Commission recommended making public schools places available to certain pupils at state expense. The explanation of what seems to be a contradictory set of facts here may well be that comprehensive-school boarding is not organized in any systematic way and depends upon individual local authority practice (about which little may be known more widely), while public-school boarding is well organized nationally. It may be that, instead of meeting any general boarding need by recourse to using the independent or public schools, it might well be in the comprehensive school interest to investigate and organize a system of boarding within the comprehensive schools themselves.

Unfortunately, Ministry policy for many years has been to encourage LEAs to use independent and public schools for boarding pupils[38] and it is a continuation of this policy that no doubt still encourages those who see a solution to the problem of state pupils' boarding needs by recourse to the independent schools – a solution that has a number of difficulties for all concerned, not least the problem of fitting in many ordinary boys and girls to the 'hothouse' regime of the average public school. Even selective schools themselves have already admitted that what they call the 'newer type of parent' would be happier 'sending his boy to a boarding school with day pupils which was part of the local community which he already knew, and the boy himself similarly would be likely to adapt more easily to these surroundings'.[39] Boarding units attached to ordinary comprehensive schools would seem to offer more normal and more familiar circumstances in which to provide for this need. There is a lot of experience of this kind of boarding to be found up and down the country upon which any new systematic attempt to organize large-scale comprehensive boarding could draw. For example, there are not only the boarding sections attached to ordinary day schools, but also hostels. Some – like that in Dunoon in Scotland – offer a modern solution to the problem of residential accommodation for pupils away from home.* They are mixed sex, small, relaxed, and without the strict rules associated with the usual 'public'-school boarding situation.

A few pupils have to board. In addition, boarding itself in some circumstances and for some children might well be of benefit. There are possibilities to be explored for weekly or termly boarding or even a year's boarding for ordinary comprehensive-school day pupils – partly for reasons of healthy change (to give city children one term in the country), and partly for academic reasons (to give students at a special stage in their

* About 1800 Scots pupils board – often because of remote location of their homes, too far from any school. See article by Lois Mitchison, *Guardian*, 9 January 1969.

work the chance of a concentrated period of teaching and study away from distraction). Oxford has pioneered short-term boarding in some of its schools, and other authorities suggest experiments along this line in connection with reorganization.[40] There is no reason why this practice could not be enlarged, especially in connection with schools in large urban areas, where problems of home accommodation are sometimes great. Many comprehensives know the very great benefit pupils in less-than-advantaged areas of the country can get from having their 'own' boarding house in another district. One teacher writes of the old mansion his school bought in a peaceful Welsh valley and what 'residential education in a beautiful, peaceful valley' meant to children from a 'raw, new industrial town in the north'.[41] It is not boarding itself that so many comprehensive-schools, parents and staff object to, it is its traditional association – in Britain – with the exclusive, expensive, selective, single-sex, upper middle-class schools in which it has up to now been chiefly available.

On the other hand, a few comprehensive schools have already formed 'links' with particular public schools and this kind of experiment is now being pursued further in the case of such schools as Dartington School. Here the 'cooperating' comprehensive is not the local school but one that is many miles removed. In the case of Dauntsey's School, however, the cooperation is local. The difficulty involved in these situations (especially where boarding schools like Dauntsey's will offer places in their sixth form for selected pupils from a neighbouring comprehensive school that will *not* now develop a sixth-form of its own) is that they often meet the needs of, or offer advantages to, only a minority of pupils from the comprehensive school. Sometimes it is just to the 'academic' minority, as in the case of Dauntsey's.

The dilemma in all cases of cooperation between comprehensive and public schools is this: if it is the kind of cooperation that is in the best interest of all the comprehensive-school pupils, or the comprehensive school as a whole, it is liable to undermine the efficiency of the public school. It is also hardly likely that the parents of the pupils in the public school are going to feel it is worth paying large fees for advantages the comprehensive-school pupils receive for nothing, or, alternatively, to wish to 'subsidize' comprehensive schools. It would take a most exceptional public-school headmaster, or governors and parents to weld a public-school and a comprehensive-school community into one – even in a limited area of cooperation. This is not to say it could not be done some day; it is only to warn of the danger that the comprehensive might always remain just the 'poor relation' in any such union, or that the 'benefits' derived for the comprehensive are so minimal, or limited to such a few pupils, or so obviously likely to perpetuate selection or unfairness at a particular point in the comprehensive school itself that the association is hardly worth its name. These dangers are the reason why so many of those involved in the day-to-day running of comprehensive schools feel that if large-scale boarding is required, it might be better organized within the comprehensive system itself – possibly on a regional basis in the new, larger local authorities.

Special education

Special education – usually for pupils with disabilities, e.g. deafness – has traditionally been provided by the state separately from normal education. But there has always been a borderline between pupils who were 'slow' learners and those who were educationally very subnormal. Recent controversy has surrounded this subject again because so many black children are in ESN schools in some areas, raising the question of racial disadvantage; or, as others see it, of one form of discrimination. There is also no doubt that in some areas pupils are in ordinary secondary schools who in other areas would be in 'special' schools.

Until recently most accepted this separation of the special pupil into separate institutions as right. But more and more it is coming to be questioned. A special kind of attention is undoubtedly needed for pupils who have particular disabilities – special apparatus in classrooms for pupils unable to walk, for example – but many feel that there is no particular reason why many 'special' pupils cannot take most, if not all, of their schooling within the context of a normal school. Some could be integrated in the ordinary school-class situation from the first. In other cases, and this no doubt the majority, pupils would have to be withdrawn for special teaching in especially equipped classrooms. But a particular comprehensive school might have attached to it a special unit for, say, the blind pupils of a certain area. Some lessons would be separate, but not most, and other activities – choir or debating – could be pursued in common with the rest of the school. One comprehensive in the South-west already has a section set aside for handicapped pupils in the area. In London, Sedgehill Comprehensive has a unit for the partially hearing fully integrated within the school, as do several other schools. Not only is this kind of an approach better for many 'special' pupils, but it might also help the normal boy or girl to understand the problems of the handicapped in our society and to be more realistic and accepting towards them.

Recently the Jewish Free School comprehensive school in London accommodated a totally blind pupil within the ordinary school timetable for a number of years. His special braille books and tape recorder were supplied by a philanthropic body,[42] but in all other respects he was part of school life. He successfully completed examinations and gained entrance to London University. The school felt this was a worthwhile experiment and that it 'posed the question as to whether or not it was possible to integrate more handicapped pupils in normal schools'.[43] This example is proof once again that the common claim that independent schools are the only schools really free to experiment, is one that is quite out of date. Comprehensive schools are experimenting in every direction, and the field of special education is one in which comprehensive schools might well do so further.

Notes

1. Lord Iddesleigh, House of Lords, 10 February 1965.
2. See, for example, Chester LEA document, p. 3, July 1968.
3. 'Anglican reorganization', Roland Morant, *Comprehensive Education*, Autumn 1971, p. 30.
4. Joseph, Bishop of Clifton, pastoral letter quoted in *Bristol Evening Post*, 3 March 1969.
5. Nottinghamshire's Plan, p. iv, July 1966
6. See 'The schools debate', *Catholic Education Today*, 1967, vol. 1, no. 2.
7. Brian Whicker, *Guardian*, 'Schools for separatists', 14 April 1966. See also deputy head of St Bede's writing in *Bristol Evening Post*, 6 August 1964.
8. *Search*, vol. 6, no. 2, p. 69, June 1967.
9. ibid.
10. See *Catholic Education Today*, vol. 1, nos. 1 and 2: in particular the reported suggestions from Father Rochford, Anthony Slade, A. C. F. Beales and Mother Mary Norbert.
11. *Catholic Education*, Catholic Education Council for England and Wales, p. 211, 1969.
12. DES, *Statistics*, vol. 1, 1970, p. 32.
13. ibid.
14. *The Nation's Schools*, pamphlet no. 1, 1945.
15. R. R. Dale, *Mixed or Single Sex School*, p. 230, 1949. On page 53 Dale gives information on the research projects substantiating these results. Dale's own research is in selective schools, of course, but research including comprehensive schools has not to date shown otherwise. See also J. W. B. Douglas and J. M. Ross, 'Single sex or co-ed?', *Where*, no. 25, 1966.
16. DES, *Statistics*, vol. 1, p. 2, 1967 and 1968.
17. DES, *Statistics*, 1970, vol. 1, p. 2.
18. J. Thompson, *Secondary Education Survey*, 1952, p. 27. Here it was predicted that by 1965 57 per cent of county schools would be mixed, but only 30 per cent of borough ones.
19. DES, *Statistics*, vol. 1, p. 2, 1968.

20. NFER Report, p. 236. The NFER Survey showed 80 per cent mixed and 10 per cent single-sex each.
21. Thompson, op. cit., p. 23.
22. Nottinghamshire reorganization document, 1966.
23. *The Comprehensive School, Appraisal from Within*, 1964, p. 111.
24. 'Coeducation and the catholic girl', *Catholic Education Today*, vol. 1, no. 2, pp. 27–8.
25. *The Comprehensive School, Appraisal from Within*, p. 88.
26. Ollerenshaw, *Education for Girls*, op. cit. p. 60.
27. See also chapter 14, p. 325.
28. NFER Report, p. 20.
29. Dale, op. cit., passim.
30. See House of Commons debate, 27 November 1964.
31. *Differentiation of the Curriculum between the Sexes in Secondary Schools*, Consultative Committee of the Board of Education Report, p. 137, 1923.
32. E. Short, Secretary of State for Education, quoted in *The Times Educational Supplement*, 28 March 1969. Figures given include these: in France one engineer in twenty-eight is a woman, in Norway one in ten, in the USSR one in three. In Britain, however, it is one in five hundred.
33. *The Comprehensive School, Appraisal from Within*, p. 86.
34. ibid., p. 87.
35. See Royston Lambert, *The State and Boarding Education*, 1966.
36. See Henry Swain, address to the RIBA, *Forum*, vol. 12, no. 1, p. 7.
37. See Suffolk, Kent and Northumberland reorganization documents.
38. Circular 83, 1948, and Circular 90, 1952.
39. Governing Bodies Association/Head Masters Conference Joint Working Party, Document 138, 1969, p. 3.
40. Bromley's reorganization document, Appendix, paragraph 606, 1966.
41. Halsall, ed., op. cit., p. 93.
42. Jewish Society for the Blind.
43. S. Conway, 'Experiment in integration', *Education*, 6 September 1968.

Chapter 19
The Coexistence of Grammar and Comprehensive Schools

The most controversial of the questions involved in reorganization is whether grammar schools should remain alongside comprehensive schools. To some, coexistence seems a sensible solution. The traditional grammar-school type of pupil will continue attending a school with special academic education from which he will supposedly benefit, while those not selected for grammar schools will have a chance to enter a comprehensive school (or a secondary modern school), where courses for the so-called less academic are available as well as, where possible, courses for the whole range of ability.

In the early days of reorganization, coexistence was not a hot issue. Most comprehensive heads were concentrating upon the success of individual schools and were not yet concerned about whether grammar schools also continued nearby. Many were satisfied if their authority was willing to grant them a slightly wider catchment area than other non-selective schools and slightly better staffing. A few, however, felt that coexistence was impossible, although their pleas were restrained. One Welsh headmaster wrote in 1958:

I consider it an essential condition for the complete success of the comprehensive school that for its own definite catchment area it should be the only school where education, usually associated with the secondary phase, is provided.[1]

Now that the comprehensive school itself has been accepted and endorsed in principle by every political party and almost every educational body in existence in Britain, the argument is necessarily about how comprehensive these schools really are. Does the continued coexistence of a grammar-school sector alongside comprehensive schools prevent them from developing as genuine comprehensive schools? Later writing was less restrained. Thus a Yorkshire comprehensive head wrote in 1969:

I think it is sheer hypocrisy and double talk to suggest that a 'grammar' school and a 'comprehensive' school can coexist in one locality: if the grammar school takes its traditional 'cream', the comprehensive school is merely a secondary modern school.[2]

Gradually the early attitude of indifference has changed. During the 1950s and early 1960s – especially in big towns, where coexistence was systematic and well enforced – comprehensive schools began to realize that their chances of success were limited. The relative success of comprehensives in areas without coexistence – the thoroughly neighbourhood schools in the small towns and countryside areas of Anglesey, Staffordshire, Dorset and Yorkshire – widened the gap and pointed up all too clearly what a comprehensive system (as against individual comprehensive schools in a bipartite system) can really achieve.

Requests for reform were made behind the scenes, but none were too emphatic because at about the time this problem was just becoming acute it was thought that a Labour government would shortly be elected – a government committed publicly to a comprehensive system, not just to augmenting comprehensive schools. But as chapters 3 and 4 have shown, the comprehensive reform has not altogether succeeded. The trouble is that it has succeeded enough to underline the problem even more emphatically: there are now such a large number of comprehensive schools being systematically undersupported in areas with coexisting selective schools that their position is becoming increasingly difficult. Privately, many education officers and department officials recognize the seriousness of the problem. Publicly it was recognized by the Labour government in its decision to legislate for ending selection. But the grammar, direct grant and public-school lobbies – united on this issue – are powerful, with powerful support in national and local editorial columns, in the Department of Education and Science, in the universities, and among local and national Conservative politicians and conservatives generally. Though many would not oppose comprehensive schools, all would oppose a comprehensive system. The traditional advantaged positions of the grammar and public schools in the educational structure – traditional in the sense that they have always enjoyed better staffing ratios and higher expenditure per pupil than other schools, as well as in the sense that they draw disproportionately from the higher income and higher IQ section of the population for their intakes – these depend upon coexistence of the two types of school being acceptable.

The Labour government – by failing to bring about reform – allowed a system of coexistence to develop, but for the Conservative government, elected in 1970, coexistence became official policy. As the new Secretary of State said, when challenged as to how you could have the two side by side: comprehensive schools 'coexist with grammar schools already, and always have, how can it be impossible?'[3]

The answer points up a genuine conflict about what a comprehensive school really is. Back in 1947 circular 144 defined it as a school 'which is intended to cater for all the secondary education of all the children in a given area, without organization into three sides' (see page 512 for further definitions). By the time of the NFER's comprehensive research project of 1965 the objectives had changed substantially to a school that eliminated selection by 'gathering pupils of the whole ability range . . . representing a cross section of society . . . into one secondary school'. The first definition specifically says *all* the pupils in an area must be in the school, the second does not. It merely says the school must have a full-ability range, which is very different and quite compatible with an isolated comprehensive sector in the middle of a bipartite system. By 1970 the DES had streamlined its earlier definition of comprehensives down to 'schools . . . intended for all secondary pupils in a district'.[4] The operative word is 'intended' – the school does not have to have all the area's pupils, just that it should be able to provide for them, if it did. Bound up in these two definitions too is the conflict of a neighbourhood intake as against the engineered mix, which we discuss at length in chapter 20.

The question of coexistence is now the crucial question for comprehensives, as evidence continues to pile up concerning the difficulties and disadvantages comprehensives face where they must coexist with grammar schools. Some of these we have already discussed in chapter 18, and in the two chapters on sixth forms: 8 and 9.

The NFER Report of 1965 presented interesting statistics to support the hypothesis that competition with grammar schools prevents comprehensive schools from developing fully. Their findings were mostly in respect of lack of higher-ability pupils – those in the top 20 per cent of the ability range[5] – but it was not always possible for them to draw detailed conclusions owing to their subdivision of comprehensive schools into fully and not-fully developed categories for many analyses. Their report established fairly certainly, however, that almost all comprehensive schools had their fair share of, or more than their share of, pupils in the middle (20 per cent to 80 per cent) of the ability range and in the lower 20 per cent. Their report contains many statistical analyses of the distribution of these three sets of pupils – labelled X, Y and Z – within the comprehensive schools covered by the report.

In the NFER's Second Report on fifty-nine comprehensive schools this evidence is stronger still, for not only are those comprehensives which are in 'competition' with grammar schools shown to have lower intakes of high-ability pupils than those without (only fifteen out of the forty-five schools even had 15 per cent of the top 20 per cent of the ability range – and no comprehensive competing with a grammar was among these), but also that attainment of pupils inside comprehensives in the fourth and sixth year of schooling was adversely affected by competition with grammar schools.[6]

Only nine out of the forty-five schools examined had a 'normal distribution of ability'.[7] It wasn't only that 'high-ability' pupils were absent, but that the schools were overcrowded with low-ability pupils. Although the Second NFER Report did not say so in so many words, plainly the situation had got no better since the First Report.

Another example of this unequal distribution is given in connection with the Public Schools Commission Second Report in an interesting table of the distribution of ability by type of school in a large urban education authority. Some schools were grammar schools and some comprehensives – as well as a good number of other secondaries. One example of divisions then operating was revealed by the figures showing that the direct grant school had no pupil with a score of less than 110. The comprehensive schools had all their pupils (with three exceptions) under 110.[8]

The Second NFER Report in 1970 compared the attainment of pupils in the first, fourth and sixth years of comprehensive schools 'competing' with grammar schools as against those 'not competing'. It found that the

differences in mean scores are highly significant when the schools are divided ... and this was so for test results in all three year groups, the 'not competing' group of schools having the greater mean scores (p. 108).

This was proof positive of the way continuation of coexisting grammar schools prevents comprehensive schools from attaining their full potential.

In our survey of 1968 we confined our question about ability intake to the top 20 per cent of the ability range, since this was the range in doubt. We found that the average intake of this top 20 per cent for all 728 schools in the survey was 15 per cent – according to heads' estimates (for *actual* ability intakes in 1968 see note 19, p. 158). When the distribution of this top 20 per cent is analysed further, we see in Table 19.1 that there is no central concentration of schools at the 15 per cent mark. (Only 10 per cent of the comprehensive schools in England and Wales actually had *exactly* 15 per cent of the top 20 per cent of ability.*) Rather, there is a cluster of schools with low intakes at one end, and, at the other, a cluster of schools with rather high intakes: thus, an uneven picture.

We further found that if we match our 1968 figures of this top 20 per cent of ability intake to the same percentage groups used by the NFER in 1965 (Table 19.2), there appears to have been little change in two years. This is interesting in view of the fact that in our survey there were

---

* See Appendix 1, Note 3.

Table 19.1 **Distribution of top 20 per cent of ability range in British comprehensive schools, 1968**

Intake of top 20% (as percentage of total intake)	Number of schools	Percentage of total number of schools
0%	3	0·5
1–5%	179	24·5
6–10%	102	14·0
11–15%	119	16·5
16–20%	196	27·0
Over 20%	129	17·5
	728	100

over twice as many schools and the schools of Scotland were included in addition.

When we asked the schools in our smaller sample, however, if they felt their schools reflected the distribution of ability in their area, we saw that when it comes to reflecting local-ability distribution, a greater percentage of schools say they are comprehensive than would say so if asked if their

Table 19.2 **Distribution of top 20 per cent of ability range in comprehensive schools, 1965 and 1968**

	0–5%	6–15%	16–25%	Over 25%
1968	25%	30%	35%	9%
NFER, 1965	24%	34%	34%	9%

intakes represented general- or national-ability distributions. This was something the NFER Report found as well.[9]* This was further confirmed in their Second Report, where in addition it found that of all first-year pupils tested, only 12 per cent came in the 'able' category, where we would expect 20 per cent.[10] When we asked schools in our smaller 1968 sample that did *not* have a cross-section of local ability why they felt they did not have it: eight said it was because their intake was creamed by

* For example, well over half the NFER heads felt they had intakes between 16 per cent and 25 per cent of the top 20 per cent when asked in respect of local ability, but only one-third thought so when estimating nationally. At the lower end only 4 per cent of NFER head teachers felt they had 5 per cent or less speaking locally, but about a quarter said they did when speaking nationally (First NFER Report, p. 26).

selective schools, two because their own catchment area was itself un-representative of national ability, and nine said their local authority policy was unhelpful: it 'filled' the grammar schools before it started admitting to the comprehensives. Five schools in addition said they were creamed by fee-paying schools as well as grammar schools.* In most cases, there-fore, coexistence was to blame.

Coexistence and creaming are undoubtedly factors in the overall 'shortage' of higher-ability pupils in comprehensives. But to measure the precise effects of this shortage it is necessary to look more closely at how comprehensive schools with and without competing grammar schools compare in certain important ways. The NFER Report could not be quite certain about how many comprehensives coexisted with grammar schools in 1965, but it was able to say that 42 per cent of 11–18 schools (the vast majority of comprehensives in their report) were competing.[11] In our first questionnaire we asked all schools, 'In addition to a compre-hensive school, do some pupils in your school's catchment area also have the choice of attending a local grammar school?' In England and Wales 54 per cent (355 schools) said 'Yes'. In Scotland it was much less: 34 per cent (twenty-three schools). In some authorities, on the other hand – like the ILEA – it was 100 per cent.† Overall, therefore, a greater percentage of comprehensive schools were probably having to compete with grammar schools in 1968 than in 1965.

What difference might this make? Table 19.3 sets out a few compari-sons between coexisting and not-coexisting comprehensive schools. Firstly, we see clearly how coexistence depresses the intake of high-ability pupils. Coexisting comprehensive schools in the survey had only 12 per cent of the top 20 per cent of ability. The average ability intake of comprehensive schools with *no* coexisting grammar schools, however, rises dramatically to 18 per cent in England and Wales, and 20 per cent in Scotland. This difference is extremely significant.

It means that in England and Wales 8 per cent at the top of the ability range is missing in comprehensive schools where grammar schools co-exist, but only 2 per cent is missing where a comprehensive system prevails. This means that coexisting comprehensive schools are being denied what many regard as the real top ability, the pace-setters – or, to put it in other terms, pupils of 121 IQ and above. It is now more or less clear that this particular missing percentage is the one over which the argument will be taking place. How important is it to the success of comprehensive schools? There is wide disagreement on the subject.

* The number adds to more than fifteen because some schools ticked more than one reason.

† See Appendix 1, Note 3.

Table 19.3 British comprehensive schools with and without coexisting grammar schools, 1968

	Number and % of all schools		Number and % of schools in England and Wales		Number and % of Scottish schools		% of top 20% of ability	% of top 20% of ability, Scotland	% staying beyond leaving age	Average size of sixth form	Average size of sixth form, England and Wales	Average number O-level or O-grade or H-grade subject-groups	Average number A-level subject-groups
	No.	%	No.	%	No.	%							
Comprehensive schools coexisting with grammar schools	378	52	355	54	23	34	12	14	51	75	75	12	7
Where comprehensive schools are the only schools	322	44	281	43	41	61	18	20	52	88	92	12	8
Unknown	28	4	25	3	3	5							
Total	728	100	661	100	67	100							

In one or two ways a full range of ability does not appear to make a great deal of difference to a comprehensive school. For example, the percentage of pupils staying on beyond leaving age does not appear to have a direct relationship to ability intake in comprehensive schools as many of our tables make clear,* nor to size.* There is only 1 per cent difference in staying-on percentages as between a comprehensive that has, or has not, a competing grammar school (Table 19.3).

On the other hand, as Table 19.3 shows, comprehensives without competing grammar schools have a better A-level offering than those with. There is also a clear relation between the percentage staying on and the size of the sixth form (see Table A.3, p. 524), and as we saw in chapter 6 and can see again in Table 19.3, the coexistence of a grammar school does make a difference to sixth-form size in a comprehensive school. In England and Wales, for example, coexistence depresses the average size by almost twenty pupils: a critical number in many schools that are just building up their sixth forms and – this is the most vital – trying to attract staff. This is the most important single point about having a full-ability range: it attracts staff. Keen staff come to a school they know has the full-range of ability from its area – in other words to a genuine comprehensive school. And good staff benefit all abilities. Table A.20 (p. 544) shows strikingly how the proportion of comprehensive schools with full-ability intakes rises when there are no competing grammar schools, but drops when grammar schools coexist. There are many who therefore say that no comprehensive can succeed, nor can all-round educational standards be raised, without the full-ability range in the area.

In chapter 8 on the sixth forms we showed how seriously the coexistence of selective schools could effect the members in comprehensive schools, particularly at sixth-form level. Under the coexistence policy now being nationally supported, plans for local authority reorganization are being accepted which build in this imbalance. Thus at the time of writing, in Walsall, where two grammar schools will be retained alongside comprehensives, to 'provide academic courses', comprehensive schools are also going to be encouraged to build up their sixth forms, the implication being that this is perfectly possible alongside grammar schools. It is pointed out that only 6 per cent of the 11-plus entry will be sent to grammar schools, but in small print – which must be calculated from figures given – it appears it is also envisaged that by A-level time 40 per cent of the LEA's sixth formers will be in the grammar schools, which will 'specialize' in sixth-form work.[12] What chance will the thirteen sixth forms in the remaining comprehensive schools have in this situation?

* See Table A. 20 (p. 544).

We have seen by examining those areas – including all those retaining large separate direct grant sectors – which already operate the policy (p. 198) how seriously it affects development of many comprehensive schools. Even the Public Schools Commission had to admit that although in some areas the actual loss in numbers of high-ability pupils may be small, 'nevertheless, the loss of even a small number of this calibre (all of them potential sixth-formers) must have an effect on comprehensive schools in the area'.[13] And the Commission goes on to add that 'in some areas it will be impossible to carry through comprehensive reorganization or to achieve the benefits reorganization can bring if direct grant schools continue in their present role'.[14] If this was true of direct grant schools in 1968, it is even more true of maintained grammar schools in the 1970s, where the percentages creamed off are so much higher.

Arguments against coexistence are in direct conflict with those which say top-ability pupils need a different kind of education in a different kind of setting from all other pupils. Some who advocate this have always felt that 11-plus selection itself was right, but others argue that a selective sector can 'coexist' with comprehensive schools so long as comprehensive schools can be persuaded to be content with less than the full-ability range. They are inclined to offer theoretical percentages of 'high-flier' or 'academic-ability' pupils that require special education apart from their fellow students. For the coexistence argument in the end is merely a matter of percentages, and one of the difficulties seems to be that there is no real agreement on the percentage of pupils that really requires this special education.

There are few left who would categorically state that the old 'grammar school' percentage of 20/25 per cent is the exact percentage of the population that needs to be educated in separate schools apart from everyone else. But there is no shortage of those prepared to name lesser percentages – 10 per cent, 8 per cent, 7 per cent, 5 per cent or 1 per cent – as the proportion of the pupil population whose academic needs require their separation from the general child population at eleven years of age. The task of finally deciding on a percentage is complicated further because some of those who believe in special education for the 'top' pupils have actually lowered their definitions of 'top' in recent years. William Alexander, secretary of the Association of Education Committees, for example, argued for 5 per cent in 1954, but in 1969 he had come down to 2 per cent or 1 per cent.[15]

In other arguments for coexistence special pleading seems to play as much a part as theory. Thus, for example, bodies that represent very selective or fee-paying schools sometimes suggest that eventually 'in the national interest' 5 per cent of pupils should be educated selectively. By chance, this percentage coincides roughly with the percentage of the school population able to be accommodated in the schools represented or championed by such groups.[16]

In many local authorities, too, the percentages are hardly theoretical but obviously directly derived from the percentage of pupils likely to remain in the grammar schools that local politics has decreed shall be 'preserved'. Thus, Christopher Chataway, when Education Committee majority leader in London, always argued for a rather high percentage of pupils to be educated separately (reports of his speeches vary from 7 per cent to 10 per cent) because when he was leader in London it was agreed to retain forty-one grammar schools in coexistence with comprehensive schools, eventually taking about 10 per cent of secondary pupils.[17] On the other hand, Wolverhampton's 1968 plan for reorganization argues that 4 per cent is about right for a special academic sector, since by chance this is the percentage that will remain in the two local prestige grammar schools that plans of that time hoped to retain in permanent coexistence with comprehensive schools. In Walsall grammar schools were to take in 6 per cent under the comprehensive plan. In Liverpool in the early 1970s a figure of 15 per cent was being advocated – to conveniently embrace the percentage in selective schools which was to remain permanently. One of Birmingham's many rejected plans in the 1960s also called for a 15 per cent selective sector. The Gifted Children's Association is widely claimed, however, to believe that only 2 per cent of the population is 'gifted', and it is significant that the minority of the Public Schools Commission which did want some separate selective sector to remain (the majority did not) also went for 2 per cent.[18] However, this percentage is not steady. Edward Boyle, speaking to the Gifted Children's Association in April 1972, put it as 2 or $1\frac{1}{2}$ per cent. It is getting smaller all the time.

Quite obviously there is no 'holy' percentage of pupils that is agreed by all to be one that needs to be specially provided for apart from everyone else. This makes some ask if there is any special reason why any pupils should be educated apart in different schools at all. Clearly this is an argument that will be prolonged far into the future.

But even if a percentage can be agreed upon, how is it to be selected? And how is this selective procedure to be defended as accurate and fair to all social and economic groups when the 11-plus has proved so fallible? And how will comprehensive schools and primary schools feel about it? For the Wolverhampton document also contains an interesting phrase: 'the more selective a selection process becomes the easier it is to select'; the 4 per cent is just 'optional'. There are many who might say that the more selective grammar schools become, the more competitive entry will be and the more primary schools will groom their leavers to pass.

There is certainly very little evidence that as systematic selection slowly declines, comprehensives themselves get less hostile to creaming and co-existence; much to suggest they get more so. Even in the early days of reorganization it was the areas with the least grammar coexistence that had the most objections. Coventry, with only 5 per cent systematic creaming, felt it invidious to be deprived 'of that element that might be expected to set the pace in academic pursuits'.[19] Head teachers felt frustrated and disappointed and the effects on sixth forms were noted. In Oldham in 1968, where all secondary schools were fully reorganized and comprehensive, we might expect that there would have been no fears about 'coexistence'. But the argument in that city over the proposed plan to reintroduce selection for direct grant schools caused a storm that was just as bitter as any argument ever raised over maintained grammar schools. The combined Parent–Teacher Associations of the comprehensive schools organized themselves very effectively to get the proposals withdrawn, an example of what must have been one of the first groups organized by and for the welfare of comprehensive schools. They felt coexistence would harm comprehensive schools by:

1. Money taken away, at least £65,000 a year. 2. The best pupils (pace-setters) taken away. 3. Discouragement for the best teachers who will undoubtedly leave our schools.[20]

Nor is Oldham an isolated phenomenon. Many LEA reorganization documents recognize that in the long run 'coexistence' is impossible. Berkshire, not even half reorganized, nevertheless says coexistence is a

policy which would nullify the comprehensiveness of all schools purporting to be comprehensive. It would create an imbalance in such schools between the number of children in the high-ability range and those in the lower-ability range.[21]

In many other authorities, too, there is evidence that parents, staff and local education committees argue that once you have reorganized, *any* selective schools are incompatible. In many areas it has already been decided that selection for any state schools remaining outside the maintained system (i.e. direct grant) will cease once the comprehensive system is established. Inner London and Manchester have already taken this decision. Bristol took it in 1965, only to find it reversed again when party political control of the Education Committee changed hands a few years later. Coexistence and creaming are now firmly in the centre of the party political battle, as was probably inevitable.

Those who have observed comprehensive education for some time are also inclined to feel that genuine comprehensive schools are hard to organize where coexistence or creaming takes place. In 1959 one observer saw it as a distinction between comprehensives with a small c, where the school was coexisting, and those with a big C, where it was the only school and 'took in all boys and girls from the whole ability range in a given neighbourhood'.[22] *The Times* educational correspondent distinguished between 'pure comprehensives' and 'pseudo comprehensives'.* The pseudo comprehensive was forced to coexist, the pure comprehensive was 'not forced to compete with a grammar school and to concentrate upon academic success to overcome parents' fears while at the same time being deprived of pupils of grammar ability'. He said that comprehensive education worked at a school he had recently visited (Withernsea, Yorkshire), because 'it is enabled to work. The school is the only secondary school in the area serving 100 square miles. All the pupils in the area go to it.'[23]

If genuine comprehensive schools are defined as schools that are the only secondary schools for an area, the most serious coexistence problems are naturally in urban areas where so many grammar schools are retained. Many of the big city comprehensives pioneered comprehensive schooling in many important ways. It is for this reason that those associated with them have for so long said nothing about the serious situation developing in respect of coexistence. No head of a comprehensive school, anyway, wants to say in public: my school is not comprehensive. But from about 1967, a few heads in London and Coventry – to name but two areas – decided to tell the truth.[24] There is no doubt that the campaign for a genuine comprehensive intake to, and 100 per cent education committee support for, comprehensive schools will get more energetic – rather than less – as the percentage of grammar schools slowly declines.

In 1968 we found a great deal of bitterness among staff and among parents in comprehensive schools about policies of 'coexistence'. They felt that education committees expected them to operate as fully comprehensive schools while these same education committees were systematically selecting for, and supporting, grammar schools in the same areas. They were asking comprehensive schools to show excellent examination results right up through A-level and scholarship level, yet at the same time they were saying to them that, as usual, 10 to 20 per cent of all top-ability pupils will be going to grammar schools (or 'long-course' comprehensive schools, as some selectively 'reorganized' areas now call them). There are many people who now feel that the word 'comprehensive' should not be allowed to be used for schools that are not truly comprehensive[25] – i.e. that are coexisting with grammar schools.

---

* This distinction is not to be confused with that between 'pure' and 'not-pure' comprehensives in the NFER Report. There the difference depended on more factors than coexistence.

The loss of morale, the effect on staffing and on the size of the sixth form, were all cited by comprehensive schools as results of coexistence policies. But perhaps the most overriding argument – and one that included all others – was that of efficiency. Coexistence by definition is duplication. If a school is equipped and staffed for *all* abilities, it is wasteful and expensive for an education authority to go on duplicating staff and facilities and classes for the top ability in addition in other schools in the same areas. Many have pointed out that those who argue against comprehensives because of a fear of duplicating sixth-form work never see that duplication can be caused because grammar schools have not been brought into reorganization.[26]

In many areas this policy has inevitably forced certain comprehensive schools into a second-class role. Despite much discouragement, many of these nevertheless do magnificent work, making us realize the standards they could achieve were they really supported systematically by their authorities and education committees and backed by a national comprehensive policy. But others are struggling against the odds. It is hard to maintain a wide range of GCE O-levels or a big sixth form when well-established grammar schools or selective 'comprehensive' schools coexist in neighbouring streets. When creaming makes the ability intake low in traditional academic pupils, staff get discouraged. Many prefer to go to a genuine comprehensive – and who can blame them? And who can blame parents for shying away from a comprehensive school that can no longer offer a normal range of GCE and CSE courses? The fault in these cases is not that of the 'less popular' comprehensives, who so often are made the scapegoats, but of a policy that permits comprehensive schools to continue to try to function as comprehensive in a situation where selective grammar schools are systematically organized and systematically selected for immediately alongside them.

But not all coexistence systems are as bad as those that exist in certain of Britain's large cities; and not all 'cream' the traditional grammar-school 20 per cent away from comprehensives. We asked all the heads in the smaller sample, therefore, their opinion about 'creaming' generally. Was it acceptable? If so, at what percentage? Just under four-fifths (twenty-six out of thirty-five) of those answering this question said no creaming was acceptable if the school was to be a comprehensive school. They were quite definite about this. But three said 5 per cent creaming would be acceptable, and one each said: 1 per cent, 2 per cent, 3 per cent and 10 per cent: 'there are special schools for the bottom 1 per cent, why not for the top 1 per cent?' But even some who favoured creaming seemed doubtful: '1 per cent? 2 per cent? but where would it stop?'

In one case – where a head said he would accept 10 per cent – opinion was related to the present state of the school, which had 25 per cent creamed off. In this connection it was interesting that very often those who were least creamed were those who were most adamant that no creaming should take place at all.

Because so many comprehensive schools are being supported as second-class schools by education committees and authorities, and because the position of a few is now so critical, supporters of comprehensive reform are naturally tempted to say that all coexistence is incompatible with comprehensive education. But the situation may well be different when a comprehensive system is well established and supported as the only maintained system by all authorities, and all state-supported schools have been given a choice of coming 'in' or staying out. It is not coexistence itself that is so damaging (although many in the comprehensive movement would prefer its total abolition), but the systematic support of a selective sector by an authority, or within an authority, at the same time as the community purports to be supporting a comprehensive sector. The key word in all coexistence questions, therefore, is the word 'systematic'. The Oldham parents who objected to direct grant schools coexisting did not object to parents sending children to direct grant schools, while they continued to exist; what they objected to was systematic support by their LEA of the whole selective procedure, including withdrawal of £65,000 for fees which otherwise would have been spent upon the maintained schools, and the reintroduction of 11-plus testing in primary schools.

More and more of the primary schools in these situations are beginning to object as well, for the whole coexistence problem is as much their concern as that of the secondary schools. It is probably primary schools whose pressure will count most in the end, for a systematic coexistence policy means that *some* form of local-authority-organized ability selection must continue within the authority at transfer age. This is so even if there is only *one* grammar school – as in Southampton LEA. There, education committee support for this one school has meant that ironically a large part of the first brochure to parents explaining the new comprehensive system in Southampton was taken up with explaining the *ability-selection procedure* for this one coexisting grammar school. How large a part a selective process for a single school will play, and how damaging to the local comprehensives, remains to be seen. In areas with more than a single school the outcome is less in doubt, for a good number of coexisting selective schools ensures not only that the whole apparatus of selection must be retained, including primary school preparation for 'passing' it, but that a good percentage of the most able pupils and most highly qualified staff will remain in the selective sector and will not be found in comprehensive schools; and that education committees (and taxpayers and ratepayers) will have to support two sets of academic centres for the same age group in the same area.

As we have already shown, the difficulty for comprehensive schools occurs most severely at the sixth-form stage, for only a very few selective schools – taking in relatively few pupils at eleven – can, five years later, monopolize sixth-form work in an area – all the more so if they are 'cooperating' with comprehensive schools by actually taking in 'academic' comprehensive-school pupils at fourteen or sixteen. This simply results in grammar schools being even better staffed than comprehensives than they were already, and, of course, risks comprehensive schools losing the older-age pupils who count so much under the present school grouping structure, thus disadvantaging them further.[27]

In questioning our smaller sample of schools we found that where creaming was casual – rather than systematic – there was less objection. In the North: 'Frankly I don't mind if I've no cream. All I want are good kids with good Mums and Dads'; or from a school in the South-west:

We lose fewer pupils to independent or direct grant schools than we did when we were a grammar school. The ones we lose are not top-ability pupils, but just pupils of top people.

Sometimes there must be some coexistence while authorities are making the transition to comprehensive systems. If that were the only problem it would not be so serious. But many authorities are undertaking reorganization so limited or so piecemeal as not to be worthy of the name, or are planning permanent and systematic retention of a selective school sector for the higher-ability pupils immediately alongside their comprehensive schools. Until legislation is effective in introducing a comprehensive system rather than just augmenting comprehensive schools, the majority of comprehensive schools (which inevitably are in the urban areas where selective schools are most entrenched) will never develop fully.

The coexistence problem for individual comprehensive schools is obvious. But nationally the danger of a permanent coexistence system is equally great. The grammar schools (and 'selective' comprehensive schools in interim schemes) could easily join forces with direct grant schools and with many public schools as well (the link with the latter provided by those public schools always anxious to widen their intakes and reinforce their incomes by providing places for 'selected' local authority pupils at ratepayers' expense). They would form a new super-selective sector, far more formidable than any in the past, and with this kind of an alliance, the comprehensive reform would be meaningless, however many schools there were with the name 'comprehensive'.

What is much more likely to happen, however, is that comprehensive schools go on growing slowly but surely, and grammar schools go on shrinking – but far more slowly. What will probably emerge – if no new policies or legislation intervene – is a system where 75/80 per cent are in comprehensive schools, but 10/15 per cent are in highly selective schools, and 10/5 per cent in old small non-selectives which cannot be fitted in anywhere. The wheel will have come full circle and from a similar starting position of 80 per cent in non-selective and 20 per cent in selective schools in 1945. All that will really have happened in many areas is not comprehensive reform, but an updating and upgrading of the secondary-modern sector. But it is also likely that sometime before or after 1980 a national decision to complete the comprehensive reform will be firmly taken, and selection by ability for schools ended, along with a two-sector state system. The point has been widely taken that a coexistence system in the end means that genuine comprehensives are impossible in many areas. In no other area has opinion hardened more in recent years than over coexistence's crippling effects.[28] They are more pernicious than lack of financial support in the long run. And inadequate finances has only under-lined the acute position. There are many who look forward to seeing all comprehensives allowed to function as genuine comprehensive schools, if only because the education of almost all of this nation's children, and thus its future, will depend entirely upon their effectiveness.

Notes

1. T. Lovett of Holyhead School, in *Inside the Comprehensive School*, p. 48, 1958.
2. S. King, *Ten Years All In*, p. 203, 1969.
3. House of Commons, 8 July 1970.
4. DES, *Statistics*, vol. 1, 1970, p. x.
5. NFER Report, pp. 227–8.
6. NFER Second Report, p. 112, 117.
7. ibid., p. 107.
8. Public Schools Commission, vol. II, Second Report, Appendix 8, Table 7.
9. ibid., p. 25.
10. NFER Second Report, p. 117.
11. NFER First Report, p. 26.
12. Walsall Reorganization Document, p. 10.
13. Public Schools Commission, Second Report, vol. I, p. 118.
14. ibid., p. 119.
15. Speech reported in *Education*, 5 March 1954; but see *Towards a New Education Act*, 1969, p. 25.
16. See, for example, reports prepared jointly by Association of Governing Bodies of Public Schools and the Headmasters' Conference, 1969.
17. *Setback in Education*, Conservative Research Department, p. 46, 1968.
18. Public Schools Commission, vol. I, Second Report, p. 15.
19. G. C. Firth, *Comprehensive Schools in Coventry and Elsewhere*, p. 75.

20. Parent–Teacher Associations of Oldham, letter to Secretary of State for Education, 30 October 1968.
21. Berkshire LEA, reorganization document, June 1967, p. C67.
22. W. G. Jackson, address to Cooperative Association, Easter 1959, p. 95.
23. Brian Macarthur, *The Times*, 1 August 1968.
24. E. F. McCarthy, 'The comprehensive myth', *Forum*, vol. 11, no. 1, Summer 1968, and H. H. Tilley, 'The Fakes' Progress', ibid., vol. 11, no. 3, Summer 1969.
25. See, for example, Michael Walton speaking for the Liberal Party, 'Towards a new education act', CSC Conference, 1969, transcript, p. 26.
26. Howard Glennerster and Tyrrell Burgess, 'Sixth forms and reorganization,' *Comprehensive Education*, Autumn 1967.
27. NFER Second Report, p. 27. Here it shows the disadvantages of comprehensives with a small sixth form or sixth forms.
28. See the *Comprehensive Education*, no. 20, 1972, feature on 'Coexistence and creaming', for the facts and feelings about the depressing effects of coexistence policies on comprehensives.

Chapter 20
Choosing Schools in a Comprehensive System

In general terms everyone is in favour of choice in secondary education. Politicians of all parties, secretaries of state, parents, and education officials will agree it is a fundamental right and must be safeguarded. The difficulty about 'choice' in education is that many of us are talking about entirely different things when we use the word. Those who are strong supporters of the public schools or fee-paying state schools frequently speak of the necessity to guarantee parental 'choice' in education by having schools of this kind. The choice they are talking about – freedom of parents with money to buy places in fee-paying schools – is limited to about 5 per cent of the population. Those who argue for retaining the grammar schools as a separate selective sector often use the argument that this will retain 'choice' within the state system of education. This is yet another kind of choice: one limited to types of school only, and again, to a minority: the 20 per cent or so of parents whose children pass the 11-plus or whose primary head teachers recommend them in 'guided' systems. Others use the word 'choice' when they mean the right of religious parents to opt for a school of their own denomination, again a choice that cannot be universal; or the right to have single-sex schooling; or boarding schooling; or out-of-the-area schooling – choices even less likely to be universal.

Many who talk about choice believe that the 1944 Act guaranteed parents' choice, which is not true. It really said that parents' wishes about the way they wanted their children to be educated was one of the factors local authorities should take into account when allocating pupils to schools. The 'wishes' the 1944 Act had most in mind, of course, were the wishes of parents for denominational schools, i.e. Roman Catholics. For this was the big issue settled by the 1944 Act. But this could be taken more widely, and almost immediately after the 1944 Act the Ministry found it necessary to issue a circular to clarify the position.[1] This circular on 'Choice' made it clear that decisions about allocation to schools rested with local authorities, not the parents. It was the authority which 'determined the type of secondary education most appropriate to the individual child'. But it could take into account the parents' wishes in respect of denomination, single-sex schooling, convenience or distance of school from the home,

expense to the authority, and something called 'educational conditions' –
the type of advanced work available at the school.* The circular recognized that there might be trouble if too many parents insisted on having
their wishes respected when there were no places, or upon a type of
education the authority felt was not 'appropriate' for their children. It
therefore made it clear that in the end 'the remedy lies in the refusal to
admit the child to the school concerned'.

Even though this is prevailing practice, and even though the law is quite
clear on this point of parental choice, and was made clearer in the case of
Cumings v *Birkenhead* in 1970,[2] the last two decades have seen a growing
insistence on parental rights of choice. Those who think we have it,
argue it should be kept. Those who feel we don't have it, argue we should
get it. It has become part of the campaigning associated with the rise of
middle-class use of, and interest in, state education. In this connection it
has often been observed that it is middle-classs parents whose wishes
about 'choice' of type of school are especially respected in practice.[3]

In any case, the growing insistence on rights of 'choice' has meant that
many authorities have had to come out into the open much more clearly
and say that respecting wishes of parents does *not* mean that parents have
a right to have their child admitted to the school of their choice (Wolverhampton's 1968 brochure is an example here). With or without reorganization this clarification would have had to occur, for although slogans about
respecting absolute free choice for all parents everywhere are attractive,
and no authority likes to stress the negative side of things, a brief reflection
will make it clear that no system of education could work if absolute right
of choice of school were ever systematically guaranteed to all parents. If
there are two schools of 750 places in a town and every parent chooses the
first, it could not possibly accommodate 1500. Nor could the second school
and staff be left idle. Some method for deciding must be brought into
play – or, to put it in the words of a ministerial manual:

Authorities would be faced with an impossible task unless they could assume, as
in fact they can and do safely assume, that the great majority of parents will be
content to send their children to the school which has been provided for their
district.[4]

This is the prevailing pattern in primary schools (which are all comprehensive, of course): parents are assumed to wish to use the nearest school
(and most do) unless they opt otherwise. But there are many who resist the
same pattern when it comes to secondary education in Britain. 'As soon as
you get ... all comprehensive schools, there will be no choice', said one

* This last condition, of course, has been made the basis of some selective reorganization schemes where 'academic' and 'non-academic' comprehensive schools coexist.

Conservative Minister of Education,[5] who later argued that grammar schools must be retained because 'freedom of choice' is a 'mark of an advanced society'.[6] Here the simple parents' wishes point is much expanded to include overtones of free-world philosophy. In other 'choice' arguments against the comprehensive system, free-enterprise philosophy is added, and competition of all types of schools urged. A writer in the *Daily Telegraph* objected to a comprehensive system on grounds of impairment of choice, adding, 'choice of schools is important, like many have choice when shopping'.[7] This consumer approach finds its cul-de-sac with those who argue – as did the headmaster of Winchester – that the answer to the problem of the 11-plus selection was to 'build more grammar schools'.[8] But consumers' rights arguments are not only used by those who oppose reorganization. The Advisory Centre for Education in its *Guardian* fortnightly education columns frequently counsels parents to push for adequate 'choice' of schools in comprehensive systems. Rhodes Boyson, headmaster of a London school, has frequently gone on record as urging that parents be given the right to choose whatever school they prefer – popular comprehensive schools flourishing and unpopular schools 'suffering contraction' or being 'taken over by a popular school' as 'would be surely right in a consumer-choice society'.[9]

Certainly all those who favour reorganization want as much choice as possible to remain, but it might be true to say, however, that many think the critical choices – in a fully comprehensive system – are less and less likely to be between individual schools and more and more certain to be those that are available inside a given comprehensive school itself. In a fully comprehensive system, what is most important is that parents and pupils should have real and meaningful choice of courses, subject options and facilities inside each school or unit – and, moreover, that they should be informed adequately enough and in good enough time about the implications of all these choices and their importance in respect of future employment, higher education or careers.

Many factors limit choice: lack of knowledge, lack of interest or lack of provision within a school of the basic courses and subjects and facilities for the major disciplines and skills. It is because we wish to see every parent given an adequate and genuine choice in education that we have urged that provision of courses and subjects and facilities be made as equal as possible for the same age range in all types of comprehensive schools in each authority, for this is the only way *all* parents can be assured of choice.

But there still remains another question: What kind of choice should there be between individual comprehensive schools in a fully comprehensive system? This problem of allocation is fundamental to the comprehensive school and so far has been little investigated – one might almost say it has been avoided. Even as late as 1969 the National Foundation for Educational Research's *Trends in Allocation Procedure* still concentrated exclusively upon the methods used in authorities to determine 'between those who are designated as suitable for grammar education and those who are not'.[10] They found in 1969 that the 'open' 11-plus attainment tests were being replaced by verbal reasoning tests and teachers' assessments. As we have seen, these methods are being used in 'hidden' 11-plus selection in conjunction with 'guidance' for parents in many areas where two types of school remain.

But what about areas that have dropped selection altogether because they have abandoned two 'types 'of school? Although the 1969 NFER *Trends* found there were twenty-six out of 162 authorities using no selective allocation procedures, and a further 104 who indicated they intended to abolish them eventually, no information was given about how allocation between comprehensive schools was made or planned in those authorities. Nor in the earlier NFER Report on Comprehensive Education published in 1968 was there much information on the subject of allocation to comprehensive schools – either in areas where selection had disappeared or in those where it still existed.* The Second NFER Report of 1970 contained even less.

The difficulty in the way of any assessment of allocation procedures in a comprehensive system, as distinct from procedures for 11-plus selection, is that in so many authorities so many comprehensive schools 'coexist' with grammar schools that the two kinds of allocation get hopelessly confused. Or, put another way, a method of allocation used in a system where all schools are comprehensive is naturally different from the same method used in a system where 11-plus selection is taking place between two 'types' of school.

In our 1968 survey of all comprehensive schools we were interested to find out the methods of allocation actually being used for comprehensive schools in Britain. Table 20.1 sets out the results of answers to the five main methods of allocation that we listed and details associated with each:
1. Feeder schools (where all pupils from a primary school usually move up *en bloc* to the secondary or upper school).

* Of comprehensive schools answering the First NFER Report's question on 'choice of schools' in 1965, 54 per cent said pupils had had choice of school, but it was not clear if this was between different comprehensive schools or between selective and non-selective schools (see pp. 24 and 184). Nor was it clear what kind of 'selection' had taken place in the 159 schools indicating they had had 'selective procedures' associated with entry to their schools (p. 23). Was it the traditional 11-plus or one of its replacements? Was it for external or internal purposes?

Table 20.1 Methods of allocation used in British comprehensive schools, 1968

Methods used	Percentage of all schools (numbers in brackets) No. %		Percentage of England and Wales schools	Percentage of Scottish schools	Percentage of ILEA schools	Percentage of RC schools	Percentage of top 20% ability	Percentage staying beyond leaving age	Percentage of schools coexisting with grammar schools using each method	Percentage of schools not coexisting with grammar schools using each method	Average no. GCE O-level and O-grade subject-groups	Average no. GCE A-level and H-grade subject-groups
1. From specific feeder schools	(142)	20	19	27	1·5	38	15	46	17	23	11	8
2. Catchment area (natural geography)	(83)	11	15	13·5	3·5	11	18	51	7	17	13	8
3. Catchment area (zoned by LEA)	(176)	24	23	31	11	18	14	49	20	30	12	8
4. Guided parental choice	(130)	18	20	0	62·5	8	14	60	25	9	12	8
5. Balanced ability or part selective	(78)	11	11	4·5	16	11	15	54	14	7	12	7
Other	(34)	5	5	3	4	6			} 17	14		
Unknown	(85)	12	11	21	1·5	8						
Total number of schools	(728)	100	100 (661)	100 (67)	100 (56)	100 (65)			100 (378)	100 (322)		

2. Catchment areas determined by geography (where there is only one school in the area and all pupils normally attend it).

3. Catchment areas drawn by an authority (in populated areas where more than one school would be possible for many pupils to attend).

4. Guided parental choice (where parents are assisted in choosing a secondary school by primary heads, staff, or the authority).

5. A combination method where feeder or catchment area applies for some but others are admitted from outside the area on a selective basis; either because the LEA operates a balanced ability policy for comprehensive schools or because the areas outside have no GCE courses.

It will be seen that the majority of comprehensive schools (55 per cent) use one of the first three methods: feeder schools or catchment areas. Only 29 per cent use the other two methods: guided choice or part-selective. But it should also be noted that there is rather a large percentage of schools in the 'other' and the 'unknown' categories (17 per cent). When these were analysed separately, it was found that fifty-nine of these schools ticked a double combination of one of the first three methods. This would bring the use of feeder schools and catchment areas up to almost two-thirds of all existing comprehensive schools (63 per cent).

1972 methods of entry

1430 comprehensive schools in 1972 gave information about the method used to enter them.[11] These were classified somewhat differently from the entry methods in our 1968 Survey, but the comparison between the two years is of some interest.

Catchment-area entry was still the most popular form of entry and this has gone up from 34 per cent to 48 per cent. Feeder-school methods have gone down from 19 per cent to 15 per cent, but if feeder and catchment methods are added together they make up 63 per cent – the same percentage calculated as using these two methods overall in 1968.

The 1972 methods are categorized somewhat differently from the Survey of 1968, so a direct comparison of the remaining methods is not possible, but it is interesting to see that in 1972 a total of 125 schools were partly 'selective' in their entry. This usually meant they were comprehensive schools for the immediate area, but grammar schools for a larger area. Sometimes they were overtly selective – e.g. the sixth-form colleges of Stoke and Luton.

To these 'selective' methods must be added the category of guided parental choice, for in the 1972 figures this category refers to those areas where selection into academic upper schools was used or where choice by guidance was used in a system still retaining two types of secondary school: selective and non-selective. 139 schools were operating this method, but far more schools were associated with it, of course. In St Helens, for example, only two schools (the academic upper schools) were

Table 20.2 **Allocation methods**

		1972 1430 schools	1968 661 schools
Catchment area		48%	34%
Catchment only	33%		
Catchment plus organized parental options	15%		
Feeder systems		15%	19%
Feeder only	7%		
Feeder plus organized parental options	8%		
Parental choice		19%	
Guided parental choice		10%	20%
Selective		8%	11%
Catchment plus selection	5%		
Part selective	3%		
			16% (Other)
		100%	100%

entered by guided parental choice, but eleven other schools operated in the scheme: the 11–16 lower schools from which pupils transferred at thirteen plus. Thus it is probably true to say that if guided choice and selective entry were taken together something like one in five comprehensive schools are still associated with eleven-plus or thirteen-plus 'selection' procedures, however informally these may operate.

Choice – free or guided

The 1968 survey did not distinguish between free and guided choice. But the 1972 figures not only distinguished between these two very different forms, but show how 'choice' can also be associated with catchment-area and feeder-school systems as well.

Choice methods are obviously extremely complex, not least because they can be used where selection between two types of school remains as well as where all schools are comprehensive. Sometimes it is hard to distinguish between 'free' and 'guided',* but a closer look soon reveals the rationale behind the use of the different terms. In comparing London and Manchester in 1972, for example, both had roughly the same percentage of their secondary age group in comprehensive schools (about two-thirds) but in Manchester comprehensive schools are entered by 'free' choice, in London it is 'guided'. This is because in London the authority itself still took responsibility in 1972 for doing the selecting for the grammar schools, and children were still 'tested' and 'assessed' for the purpose of letting their teachers know their ratings so that they could 'guide' their choice. In Manchester teachers gave no help, unless asked. There was no grading and sorting, and the grammar schools which remained did their own selecting. It would be interesting to know which method resulted in a 'better' spread of ability in the comprehensive sector, and how long-term parental satisfaction compared. But at the time of writing no research of any kind was being undertaken in this field.

Almost one-fifth of the comprehensive schools in 1972 were entered exclusively by parental choice methods. But even where there were catchment-area methods and feeder systems operating, parental options were often organized in addition or in conjunction, as the table shows. When *all* the parent choice methods are added together, the total comes to 42 per cent of all the comprehensive schools in 1972 entered by some degree of parental choice. Quite clearly these were mainly those in cities or big towns, where pupils were close enough to more than one school to make 'choice' realistic. Most were probably in England or Wales. One of the most interesting findings of the 1968 survey is that none of the schools in Scotland made any use of allocation by choice at all – either free or guided (Table 20.1). This seems to be a predominantly English tradition.

Up to now in this book we have talked about 'guided parental choice' as a method of replacing selection at eleven-plus, or at twelve, thirteen and fourteen, where there are both selective and non-selective schools. The kind of selection we had in mind is illustrated by the following excerpt from an authority leaflet which described how pupils were selected between grammar and other secondary schools before the comprehensive system.[12]

as a result of some three and a half years intimate knowledge of the child's work and development the head teacher will arrange his or her pupils in descending order of suitability for selective education and the placing of children in secondary schools will be determined by this order. There is therefore no question of

---

* The First NFER Report, p. 24, distinguishes three types of 'choice': free, parental and guided. A description of 'guided' is given, but not of the difference between 'free' and 'parental'.

the child's future being decided on the basis of performance in an isolated examination.

Parents in this scheme are then asked to give their choice of school, which will be met (provided, of course, the school chosen is one of a type found appropriate to the capabilities of the child as revealed by the transfer procedure). If parents choose a type that is not suitable, continues the brochure, in some cases 'direction to the other type ... will be necessary'.

Many of the 130 schools ticking 'guided' choice in 1968 were from London. As the 1969 London brochure to parents said,[13] selection is based 'on the careful record which has been built up of your child's attainments and interests, special aptitudes and abilities and promise for the future'. One is struck here by the word 'interests', which, of course, are very different from attainment and often reflect home background. When it comes to the 'choice' upon which the pamphlet assures parents there is 'no restriction', we find that parents must nevertheless

consider most carefully the advice and guidance of the head of the primary school ... who ... will be able to suggest, from a full knowledge of each child, the secondary schools where your child is most likely to be accepted. The head can also help you avoid choosing a school which may not be suitable for your child.

Clearly, parents did not make their choice in London between the grammar schools, the comprehensive schools and the 'other' secondary schools until they were told of the likely prospects of acceptance. The percentage of first choices granted in London are obviously choices made *after* the impossible choices have been tactfully excluded by the head teacher. As the editor of *Education* wrote in 1967, of parents in schemes of this kind, 'if guidance is brought in and they choose as guided, it is hard to see how this differs from the selective system'.[14] In addition in London guided choice was not the only method used at transfer. Method 5, a balanced ability allocation, was used as well. But only one London school named *both* methods as the transfer system in London, and only 16 per cent of the fifty-six schools named balanced ability at all.

If comprehensives in an authority are unable to name the methods used, it is no wonder parents are often confused as well. Inner London changed the operation of its method in 1972 (reducing the ability bands from seven to three and having divisional offices, rather than heads' choice, allocate pupils to maintained schools) and at this time a group of London parents produced a leaflet about the new method and how it differed from the old. Just these explanations took them eight close-typed pages;[15] and even then there may have been some parents who still did not fully understand.

Not that the ILEA was the only authority answering us in 1968 where the situation was complex and confusing – mostly because the systems were still having to have ability selection at some point in secondary education. Schools from Bradford and Cardiff – to name but two – disagreed widely in describing the allocation method actually in use in their own authority's scheme in 1968.

In London only one school could be chosen, but in many other authorities a parent may list three choices. This listing of more than one choice, however, does not necessarily mean that the system is 'free' rather than 'guided'. It may be choices are made (as in London) only after parents have been heavily pre-advised about the 'type' of school to name; or it may mean that all parents start with an equal chance of their 'choice'. Sometimes there are conditions – for example, in Wolverhampton in 1969, one of the three schools parents could list *had* to be a secondary modern school. Thus, in many areas parents are highly likely to receive one of their choices; and this is why figures regularly released by so many authorities about the high percentages of parents getting 'their choice' – including the figures given in the NFER Report of 1968[16] – need to be read with such caution. Choice is not by any means always 'free'. As one of the heads in our smaller sample commented on his own area: 'Yes, there is free choice, which means that parents do as the head teacher advises.'

In this connection we met a great deal of adverse comment – as there has been from the beginning of reorganization[17] – about the hostile attitude of some primary-school head teachers to comprehensive schools. In the 'guided'-choice systems in areas where grammar schools still coexist, a great deal of 11-plus power is theirs. This is a serious problem especially where they specifically 'guide' the higher ability pupils away from comprehensive schools, as comments from head teachers make plain.[18]

When we examined the schools using method 4 (guided parental choice) in 1968, we noticed that their ability intake showed that there was a cluster of schools down at the lower end, with a low percentage of high ability pupils, and another cluster of schools up at the top with a high percentage – over the 20 per cent mark, in fact.* This suggests that schools using the method can be classed into those where 'guidance' was *away* from them (to selective schools in the area) or towards them (where they were themselves selective schools, i.e. 13–18 schools in 10/65's scheme 3). This is further confirmed in the case of 13–18 schools by observing that 50 per cent of them had this method of allocation – the highest percentage (along with 11–13 schools) for any type of school using this method.*

* See Appendix 1, Note 3.

The correlation between this method 4 and selective transfer generally can also be seen from Table 20.1, showing that where guided parental choice is used by comprehensive schools 'coexisting' with grammar schools, it rises in frequency to use by 25 per cent of schools, but that when it is used in a comprehensive system – where there are no grammar schools in the area – it falls to use by only 9 per cent of comprehensive schools in this category.

Free-choice methods can be distinguished from guided ones by the absence of any selective schools in the area – at any age. In areas where all schools are comprehensives (at least in the maintained sector, direct grant school selection is another matter) and where the local authority wishes to use a 'parental choice' method of entry, very often parents are given a list of all the schools in the area and asked to name three choices of school. This is the system in Manchester, in Oldham and in Newcastle upon Tyne. These are the way their choices worked out in these areas in 1969.

First choices obtained:
Manchester 78%; Oldham 89%; Newcastle 87%.

Free-choice systems can 'work' successfully because the majority of parents now, as always, actively wish to choose the school for their area. Obviously choice systems work best in local authorities where all the schools – although individually each different – are thought to be of comparable standing in the community and able to offer a comparable range of opportunities.

In other areas there have been complaints about the use of 'free-choice' methods to mask the great inequalities in comprehensive schools which are developing locally. Although the choice is not 'guided' in the systematic way it is in areas where grammar schools still remain, or where selective comprehensive schools take in only some of the pupils rather than all of them, it is sometimes suspected that choice methods are used to cover the continuing entry of able children to one school, less able (or less interested) to another.[19]

The problem of inequalities between schools is frequently raised when free-choice methods are discussed for comprehensive-school systems. The dangers of too much 'free choice' in a comprehensive system have been pointed out frequently by both teachers and parents. The NUT has written firmly that the 'existence of the comprehensive school can be undermined by unrestricted parental choice'.[20] A group of CASE parents in one reorganized local authority also wrote that 'a system where transfer is based *entirely* on choice is likely to produce its own inequalities'.[21]

Basically, these are where some schools become more and more favoured and, perhaps, overcrowded, while others are so weakly supported that they become 'residue' schools. It has also been felt that this method tends to make schools 'more class and colour segregated',[22] and since not every parent gets first choice, those who will in fact get it will be largely those parents who are most aggressive or knowledgeable or influential. As has been found in other countries with fully comprehensive systems, other methods of allocation are eventually adopted in place of choice. As one Danish educationist has written, 'The maintenance of liberty of choice for some must delay development of the many.'[23] This is not to say that all 'choice' of individual schools need be banned in a comprehensive system. All authorities and all teachers and parents will always want to allow as much individual choice as is possible within the limits of any allocation method. But it must be clearly recognized that an allocation procedure based on the systemization of the 'choice' factor alone has dangers and limitations.

In any case, in any system, including a free choice one, some method of deciding who goes to which school must be worked out when there is over-subscription to a particular school. This is the crux of all allocation procedures, and of free choice ones in particular. Here it is of interest to note that throughout the comprehensive sector in Britain – in schools visited by us and in the reorganization plans of local authorities using every type of allocation method – the procedure most often used to resolve this dilemma is simple geography. Those who live nearest a school have priority.

The fact that free-choice systems do present dilemmas, and that they lead to imbalances and perhaps to hidden advantages for certain groups over others, has sometimes resulted in their introduction becoming a matter of party political argument. In both Newport and Newcastle upon Tyne this has been the case, with the Labour Party favouring a 'controlled' system of entry (zoning in the case of Newport and feeder schools in the case of Newcastle) while the Conservative Party favoured the completely free-choice method. The issue was debated in both these areas, although in other areas – Manchester is one – the Labour Party favours free choice equally with the Conservatives. In general, however, it might be true to say that choice systems are more favoured by the political right, by the middle class (of all political views), by the consumer-oriented bodies like CASE and ACE, while it is opposed (although some choice is retained) by the political left, and by many teachers and most administrators. The conflict seems to be between the rights of the individual to have his freedom and the duty of the community to protect the collective good.

Education administrators are often those who express concern at unlimited free-choice systems. The deputy education officer of Hampshire wrote that any local education authority had 'a responsibility for the education of those children who are not lucky enough to have articulate and discerning parents' as well as for those who were.[24] Like the NUT, which favours a 'public policy' about allocation, which may include choice but is not exclusively based on it, education officers often feel that it is an 'authority's responsibility to avoid' polarized situations of good schools and bad schools by trying wherever possible to give each school a 'reasonably balanced intake', usually by drawing catchment areas in such a way that this is more possible. Others argue for controlling choice on the grounds of the vast expense involved in allowing it to run free. Thus Alex Clegg: 'The only way I know of meeting parental choice that I can think of is to make all the schools twice as big as we need them and at the same time shut half of them down or keep them only partially filled.'[25]

Many local authorities, therefore, after they have gone fully comprehensive, try to work out a 'public policy' on allocation, sometimes zoning schools, sometimes arranging feeder schools for entry, each feeder school drawing from a different area of housing, or the catchment area drawn in order to take in a wide variety of housing. Usually there is a degree of choice in addition, but these methods aim to give each school as 'balanced' an entry as local circumstances permit and to avoid an entry that draws exclusively from one area, or that is monopolized by parents-in-the-know from far away to the exclusion of parents who live nearby.

The issue of parental rights is by no means simple itself, however. A conflict can often arise between the right-to-choose-a-particular-school, often insisted upon by the middle class, and the right-to-attend-the-school-which-is-nearest, often asked for by working-class parents.

When problems of over-subscription to any individual school (the crux of all allocation systems) arise, the school may be 'informally zoned', with those who live nearest given priority. This is 'negative' zoning, used to resolve too many choices at a popular school. But there is also 'positive' zoning, where a definite area is deliberately created for a school to draw from in order to give it a balanced intake. Many comprehensive-school teachers and heads – among them Harold Simmons and Albert Rowe – argue for this method in their writings. Sometimes odd shapes of areas for schools result, which is why their schemes are sometimes referred to as 'piece of pie' or 'octopus' zoning. Bristol is an area using positive zoning, each school with its own area and the whole city covered contiguously. But in addition Bristol also permits parents to opt for a school other than the one in their own area. In 1969 79 per cent of Bristol parents chose their area school, and of the remainder all but 4 per cent got their first choice – thus 96 per cent could be said to have got their choice of school. Bristol's record is thus the best of any city for 1969 and is higher than the percentage of first choices satisfied in the 'free'-choice systems. Thus, paradoxically, a 'controlled' method of entry – zoning plus choice – may well result in more satisfied parents, than a truly 'free-choice' system, and, possibly, more balanced entries as well.

Balanced-ability methods of allocation

If the free-choice method seems to be the most *laissez-faire* of the allocation procedures, the survey's fifth method – part selection/part other method – is the most controlled. One version has a catchment area for local pupils but allows 11-plus passes (or, in some schools in Scotland, those selected for certificate courses) in from outside the comprehensive's normal area. Another version aims to 'balance' the intake to get a cross-section of ability into each comprehensive. Our analysis of schools' answers in the 'other method' category in 1968 shows a further twenty-four schools which could be said to be operating this method 5. Many of these twenty-four schools classed themselves as 'other', however, because they were planning to change from method 5 to a straight catchment-area or feeder system, but had not yet done so.*

Only 11 per cent of schools in our survey used method 5. It was natur ally used by certain types of comprehensives more than others; for example, by the second type of 11–18 school (acting as a sixth-form centre for a wide area).† Like method 4 (guided parental choice), this part-selective method was strongly associated with comprehensive schools that had to compete with grammar schools. When there were no competing grammar schools, Table 20.1 shows that use of this method dropped to only 7 per cent of schools.

As more and more schools become comprehensive, the use of a comprehensive as a selective school for 'out-area' pupils is declining. The balanced ability intake version of method 5, however, has become more talked about. This method lays down fixed percentages of each ability range that may be taken into each comprehensive school with the aim of filling each 'band' so that the school has a cross-section of ability. This may sound simple, but it is not. Is ability to be measured by hypothetical

---

* A few more schools had yet another system that could be classed under this method. All pupils in the area may opt for the comprehensive, but those who opt for a grammar school outside and fail to obtain a place, may not then come back for a comprehensive place. This method helps to establish a comprehensive school locally as a sought-after school, but it is often misunderstood by parents. It is not a growing practice.

† See Appendix 1, Note 3.

national ability scales or by known local ability distribution? We have already seen how these two scales can differ in schools' estimations. How many 'bands' are to be recruited into each school, what percentage of ability is each band to have, and how many pupils are to be assigned to each band of each school? If distribution of social class or race is attempted in addition, how are these factors to be assessed? Come to that, how is ability to be assessed in the primary school so that it too may be distributed evenly in the secondary? What is to be done about those many areas of the country where a national cross-section is out of the question? A school in a Welsh mining town, for example, is going to differ substantially from one in a private housing estate in the Midlands, and no allocation engineering can change this. All these problems mean that some areas in the country could not possibly adopt this method, and that those that could are necessarily involved in a number of important decisions, and, in carrying them out, in a very complicated procedure as well.

Very few areas use balanced-ability methods as an allocation method for the whole of their school system. Quite a number, however, have balanced-ability entries for individual comprehensives which exist, usually alone, in the middle of a still bipartite system. Some authorities, like Hull, with a fully comprehensive system, are measuring abilities of pupils at thirteen to monitor upper schools' intakes to achieve better balance (within a parental-choice system). Haringey is another authority which tried earlier to introduce banding, but which has now virtually abandoned it in favour of parental choice. Inner London is the longest-standing user, although it never tried to use the system for 'racial mixing',[26] as did Haringey, a policy which brought balanced-ability allocation into the arena of extra-educational controversy, as well as raising all the usual queries about 'choice' and the way the system would operate in respect of ability itself. In London the method has been operated hand in hand with the 11-plus itself, and this has meant that although a few comprehensive schools get their fair share of the system's top band of ability, this band is itself not representative of the top ability that is naturally available in the schools' neighbourhoods – since 18 per cent of eleven year olds were still selected for grammar schools in the year of our survey, 1968. Not surprisingly only five of the fifty-six London comprehensive schools taking part in our survey claimed to be comprehensive, i.e. to have the top 20 per cent of ability, and two of these were denominational and two were single-sex. The intake of higher-ability pupils in the Greater London area comprehensives generally was, of course, the lowest for any region in Britain – as we saw earlier (Table 17.1, p. 390). This was further confirmed by the Second NFER Report on comprehensives in 1970, which found Inner London's comprehensives to have the lowest 'high-ability' intake of schools in their project.[27] Whatever else a balanced-ability policy has done for Inner London in terms of keeping a few comprehensives from hogging all the high-ability pupils available to the comprehensives sector – essentially a 'negative' use of banding – it has not been able to secure a balanced-ability intake to comprehensives as a whole, which would be the 'positive' objective of such a method – partly, of course, because grammar schools still remain.

Comments we had from four ILEA head teachers in our smaller sample illustrate the problem even more clearly:

'grammar schools are . . . filled before one comprehensive, i.e. pupils from the best-ability bands are directed to grammar schools'. 'We reject higher-ability pupils only.' 'I find this task of rejecting the most difficult thing I have to do.' 'The ILEA policy is soul-destroying.' .

It is not merely that the 'top' ability must be fixed at an artificially low figure because of the large percentage of pupils still selected for grammar schools that aroused complaint in London, but also that all allocation adjustments made in response to normal pupil population fluctuations are made in the comprehensive schools sector *only* because banding is used only for comprehensives. In London in 1968 and 1969, for example, because of a fall in pupil numbers, all comprehensive schools had their intake of the higher-ability ranges reduced even further and some comprehensive schools had their overall numbers cut as well. There was no corresponding reduction or cut made in grammar schools' intakes, of course: a good example of the double standard that must apply when a coexistence policy is pursued by an authority. While grammar schools and the 11-plus remain in an authority, it is fair to say that a balanced-ability policy in respect of comprehensive schools is simply a contradiction in terms.

There is also another risk. Even in a fully comprehensive system balanced-ability methods might run the risk of over-emphasizing the old ability classifications at eleven which the comprehensive reform is designed in part to eliminate. In Inner London in 1968, for example, we found evidence that the balanced-ability method – which lays such stress on testing and grouping pupils into good-bad-and-indifferent academic layers – seemed to correlate rather strongly with the use of streamed methods of organizing the first years of comprehensive schools. When Inner London's fifty-six schools in 1968 survey were analysed separately, the following emerged:

	Inner London Comprehensives (fifty-six schools)	All 11–18 schools (389 schools‡)
Streamed*	88%	68%
Mixed ability†	13%	24%

Not only were more Inner London schools found to be using streamed methods more generally than comprehensives as a whole, but exactly half its schools were organized into 'broad bands' of ability, compared to only about a one-third who used the method overall in 1968. It seemed to be the case that using a balanced-ability method not only makes schools obsessed with each child's 'band', as anyone who knows London's schools will confirm, but this in turn makes it more likely that more rigid methods of grouping pupils inside the comprehensives will prevail once the actual transfer process is over.

It is not hard to see that existing balanced-ability systems have not been given anything like a fair trial in respect of comprehensive schools. But even an ideal balanced-ability policy has drawbacks. Bolton submitted one in 1967[28] with the aim of making each comprehensive a 'replica of the whole town' rather than representative of the character of its own neighbourhood. Although parents were assured they would have the 'maximum' degree of choice, it was plain from the detailed explanations of the system's workings that the method must involve a good deal of direction – continued year in and year out – to keep the comprehensives as 'mixed' as those in charge would feel desirable. The document recognized that there could well be a 'feeling of unfairness' because 'children from the same street may attend different schools due to vacancies in one ability band as against another'; and it admitted that the method would call for a good deal of 'public explanation'.

It is hard to escape the conclusion that some balanced-ability methods are mere contortionist attempts to obviate neighbourhood schooling rather than attempts to obtain 'ideal' mixes. This could well prove unpopular, since most parents like to feel their neighbourhood school is theirs if they want to use it. But even where ideal 'mixes' are the object, the method's operation will still depend upon community agreement that a comprehensive is not a comprehensive unless all abilities (and perhaps all social or racial groups as well) are represented in each school equally and upon that same community's agreement that the object of comprehensive school allocation policy is actively to engineer these mixes and that the

* Adding together methods 1 through 4, which were basically streamed, see chapter 10.

† Adding together methods 5 through 7, which were mixed ability.

‡ Taken from Table 10.2, p. 264, excluding 8 per cent 'other'.

LEA be empowered to take the necessary steps, including central direction, to keep the engineering machinery operating.

Two definitions of a comprehensive?

Consideration of banding and balanced-ability methods of allocation forces us to recognize that there are two prevailing, and in some senses contradictory, definitions of a comprehensive school in Britain. A first definition – one that has been put forward by the DES itself and by the NFER,[29] and one that underlies all balanced-ability methods – defines a comprehensive as a school in which pupils of all abilities and all social classes are represented; or, as the NFER's working objectives specify, it must 'collect pupils representing a cross-section of society'[30] together in a school in a purposeful way so that a 'mix' is obtained. Considering this is one of the objectives, it is curious that the giant NFER project has made virtually no attempt to examine allocation procedures, or to see which ones actually produces this 'mix' best.

A second definition – used in all earlier Ministry documents[31] – defines a comprehensive school as a school providing secondary education for all the pupils in a given area. Between these two poles are a number of intermediary definitions of a comprehensive like that in the First NFER Report: 'A school making a substantial effort to cater for the whole ability range'; or the definition in the DES *Statistics*: 'A school intended for all the secondary-age pupils of an area.'[32] Both these definitions are qualifications of one or other of the main definitions. That is, a school may not have *all* the pupils in an area (since grammar schools have some) but it is '*intended*' it should. Alternatively, a school may not have the whole ability range yet (or have it but not have a full provision for it), but nevertheless it makes a '*substantial effort*' to cater for it. Both qualifications reflect the realities of a system of coexistence, when grammar schools still remain, of course. But this should not obscure the fact that these are two variations of two very different alternatives: to provide for all the pupils of a given area, whatever their ability, as against a school for all classes and abilities, whatever their area. The distinction between the two definitions is fundamental. Decisions about allocation methods usually involve a decision in favour of one rather than the other.

Very early in reorganization one head wrote:

> It might be interesting to consider whether controlled entry is the best method of building up a school, or whether a disproportionate balance of ability may be ignored for the sake of striving to serve a neighbourhood completely.[33]

This is not to say that many heads and staff of schools we questioned were not in favour of schools that contained a wide ability range – i.e. certainly the full range that existed in the area without selection – but many would question the desirability of artificial attempts to manufacture 'comprehensiveness' in schools. The objective of the comprehensive school is to educate pupils. As even *The Times Educational Supplement*[34] has said: 'Social mixing is unrelated to education. It is an encumbrance to it.' Few would agree with the *Supplement* that the comprehensive school will make 'no difference' to existing social divisions in the long run, but many would agree that a social unity artificially created might sometimes defeat its own ends. Getting a cross-section of ability that is naturally available in an area properly apportioned between two or three schools is one thing, and even this is sometimes difficult – but policies of strict balanced-ability intakes, operating over large areas, though not impossible, may well be one of the hardest ways to achieve comprehensiveness. Certainly to date they are one of the least popular.

Random draw

In recent years a few areas have taken to the old-fashioned draw as a method of solving problems of oversubscription to individual schools. No one as yet has advocated allocating all places by random draw, although it could probably be done – and scientifically too, with as good a chance, if not better, of obtaining as perfect ability-mix as any of the balanced-ability methods with their elaborate eleven-plus testing. Both Rotherham, for a single school, and Manchester for any school oversubscribed, used the method of having an Education Committee member draw numbers out of a hat when too many pupils are chasing too few places. In Bedford, where selection by guidance for two direct grant schools and two public schools will continue even in the new 'comprehensive' scheme, the computer is doing the drawing if there is oversubscription.

Random draws may be fair, but they are also impersonal. The advantage of catchment areas or parental choice, or mixtures of both, is that they can build upon maximum parental support for each school in its own local area.

Catchment areas

If balanced-ability methods depend upon a comprehensive school being defined as a school that has engineered its mix of pupils in hopes of getting all schools a full-ability range, the two catchment-area methods in our survey – methods 2 and 3 – depend upon the second definition: a school for a given area. Almost a third of all comprehensive schools in Britain – and almost half in Scotland – were entered by one or other of these two catchment-area methods in 1968 (see Table 20.1). In 1972 it was up to

46 per cent: (see p. 448). In contrast to both balanced-ability methods and guided-choice methods, use of catchment-area methods drops in frequency when comprehensive schools coexist with grammar schools but rises when they do not (Table 20.1). In other words, these two catchment-area methods are strongly associated with genuine comprehensive systems and in fact were used by at least half of all comprehensive schools in Britain in 1968 where there were no competing grammar schools.

Catchment-area policies are ones we are familiar with already, as they are the method of allocation used in Britain's other comprehensive sector, the primary schools – which may well be why so many comprehensive systems use them. Parents are presumed to want to choose their local school except where they choose otherwise. Sometimes this opting out – or 'choice' of other school – can be allowed, sometimes not. It will depend upon the accommodation in all the area's schools. In some areas, as is well known, well-defined catchment areas for primary schools have to be drawn. This is accepted by practically everyone as necessary – and there has never been strong opposition to this.

But there has often been argument about a catchment area for a comprehensive secondary school. The policy of the Conservative government in the 1950s was against allowing a comprehensive school a special 11-plus-free zone from which to draw. This was because it might upset the intake to other schools, especially to grammar schools. Therefore, when zoning was asked for, it was often turned down on the grounds that a comprehensive school should not be able to 'enjoy a monopoly of the able children within its area'.[35] The 'choice' here was one that was given only to the children who passed the 11-plus. Zoning a comprehensive school is therefore still a difficult – one might say impossible – allocation method when there are selective schools in the same area.

But where all schools are comprehensive, zoning can be used in a positive and creative way without becoming an artificial engineering method. In several areas we were told zoning had been used to enlarge, or restrict, a school's intake when the school was in danger of over-crowding – or of falling numbers – or to prevent a particular school from becoming a 'residue' school and to retain staff. Zoning can also be positive in highly populated areas, where there are always two or three possible choices of a 'natural' zone. By simply extending the area served by a school a little to the north at the expense of the south, for example, a totally different kind of housing area can often be taken into the school's catchment area. In many big cities affluent and non-affluent areas exist very closely together. Some of the problems of advantaged versus disadvantaged schools in some areas can be, and are certainly being, solved by zoning, so that a good variety of housing areas can contribute to each school. Several parent bodies urge zoning for the same reasons.[36] Local education committees, too, accept zoning far more willingly than they used to: 'Comprehensives cannot develop properly unless they have their quota of able pupils. This is fundamental. If zoning is required to produce this, it must be accepted.'[37] Circular 10/65 recognized zoning would be necessary and urged LEAs to draw boundaries so that intakes would be as varied as possible.

Most 'zones' are in a circle around a school. But Harold Simmons, in his book on Bedminster Down Comprehensive,[38] suggests that in some cities zoning could be on the wedge principle: the city cut like a piece of pie, so that the comprehensives, which tend to be on the outskirts, each have an area that extends into the city centre – a way of preventing a knot of schools in the decaying centre, a problem that is so often faced in modern urban areas. This suggestion has also been put forward elsewhere, where it has been variously called the piece-of-cake or orange segment plan.

But while zoning can be creative, there is also a limit to what zoning can do. Too rigorously or artificially drawn zones would end up with weaknesses of the balanced-ability intake methods discussed earlier. And there are other variations to zoning which may also need watching. Usually, catchment areas involve only one school. Some authorities, however, divide a town up into large zones, each with a certain number of comprehensive schools – 'choice' between the schools taking place within the large zone. If all schools in the zone are equally equipped and staffed as comprehensive schools, this can work well. But where some are 'more comprehensive' than others – one school with GCE O-level and another without, one with a sixth form and another without – this 'choice' can rapidly become a process of 'guided selection' between two types of school.

Schools in authorities – like Bristol – with clear and definite zoning policies were the ones in our survey most likely to agree among themselves about the allocation method being used in the authority. Bristol has been observed by those who have studied its comprehensive system, to be a city without many of the problems that exist in other areas: excessive social tensions in schools or hosts of very poor comprehensive schools and a few that are highly favoured.*[39] Although it has been said that there is a 'complete absence of class barriers in the school situation',[40] it is true that some in Bristol will say 'Ah, but the schools are in a definite league table.' What was interesting to us was that the league table named by

* We are talking here of the genuine comprehensive schools, not the schools still involved in interim schemes, coexistence situations or as yet unreorganized.

Bristol university professors was quite a different one from that given us by BAC workers or even local comprehensive staff. A league table problem is only acute when *all* parents and staff have the same order of priorities.

Catchment-area allocation is sometimes feared because authorities are afraid it smacks of Big Brother – a fear that has undoubtedly been fostered by the negative attitude to catchment-area allocation in the Ministry of Education. 'Zoning should be kept to a minimum', said a 1946 circular.[41] Because of this prevailing attitude, here and elsewhere, a few authorities therefore devised all kinds of elaborate ways around zoning. Many are imaginative. One area had to decide whether its two existing schools would become two separate comprehensive schools or a single 'split-tier' school; it chose to be a single school to avoid zoning problems. In yet another – in Leicestershire – allocation is done alphabetically: last names with letters A to M in one school, N to Z in another.

Reorganizing authorities adopting zoning are sometimes unnecessarily over-fearful. They fail to realize that – as has always been true, and has been observed over and over again – most pupils and most parents prefer the school in their own area. When Luton reorganized, very strict zoning was in force with 'choice' for parents within the zones allowed for only very special reasons. But so few parents actually opted to change schools that the authority is now much easier about allowing 'choice' outside the area. In Bristol, too, as we saw, the percentages after nearly ten years of comprehensive schooling suggest that over a period of time catchment-area zoning and parental choice can be reconciled successfully.

Most of the schools in our smaller sample strongly supported zoning. Many of these were schools in urban or suburban areas. A few supported it with regret, for they did not like to have to refuse entry to *any* pupils. They had had to begin using it, they said, because they were now too 'popular', or because the LEA had had to avoid a pecking order situation. But most said they favoured it because they had it and it worked well. A few said they did not have it and wished they had. 'Our experience is that zoning works very well indeed.' And again: 'We allow free choice but most parents choose within their own area.' Another said: 'freedom of choice is an attractive slogan, but zoning works'. Only three heads favoured 'choice' as a method of allocation. One was in a country area and said he favoured choice just so long as parents paid the transportation. The reason he wanted it, he admitted, was that he 'might want more than his fair share of musicians' for his school. About half of those who favoured zoning also favoured regular local boundary reviews by the authority. As one said, and as others have observed before, 'The answer lies with the town planners.'

We also asked heads in our smaller sample what they did if they became oversubscribed. On what basis did they reject and accept pupils? Most had the same method, though they described it differently. One said that those living closest got first choice, or 'geography decides'. A number said free choice was allowed, but each school had a fixed intake and when it was reached, zoning was applied. Another said existing boundaries were re-arranged when there was oversubscription – in other words, re-zoning. Only a handful appeared to have no policy. One said 'first come, first served'. Another: 'I take all pupils in my catchment area irrespective of whether I have room for them or not. If overcrowding becomes severe, I would ask for, and probably get, temporary buildings.' Another said: 'We occasionally have to suggest to Roman Catholics that they go to a school some miles away.'

There is no doubt that catchment-area allocation has so often been approached in a negative manner in the past. The many creative possibilities for using it to build up community support for a school and to ensure a fair and workable allocation policy within a comprehensive system have scarcely begun to be explored by the majority of local education authorities, although each year catchment areas rise in popularity.

The feeder-schools system

The second main form of allocation method within a 'comprehensive system', and one that, unlike zoning, is not common to primary schools, is that of a feeder system (method 1 on our large survey): where certain designated schools (either primary or lower secondary) automatically send all their pupils to certain designated all-through or upper schools. As we see in Table 20.1, about one-fifth of all comprehensive schools used this method in 1968, but only 15 per cent in 1972 (p. 448). Rather more Scottish schools use it than English, and more Roman Catholic schools than any other group (38 per cent). Like zoning, it rises in incidence when there are no grammar schools (Table 20.1). It is most strongly associated with 14–18 schools (38 per cent use it)* and with 11–16 schools (30 per cent).† Its virtues are that it affords excellent liaison possibilities between lower and upper schools and that it is quite flexible as a system of allocation. For example, if a comprehensive school becomes over-crowded or has the opposite problem of falling numbers, the authority could plan to 'add' or 'subtract' a feeder school. Two schools reported that this had already happened to their great advantage. One local authority in England tried out a very controlled system for a while in the late 1960s: classing primary schools as A, B or C according to the type of

* Since so many of these are schools in 'guided parental choice' schemes, it is interesting that feeder system was the method named rather than 'choice'.
† See Appendix 1, Note 3.

intake each had and the areas of housing each served. Each secondary school was then assigned one A, two Bs and a C as its 'feeder' schools so that each would have a balanced intake.[42]

The flexibility of feeder-school schemes is one advantage that has led to its also being tried out in other countries. In the United States for example, where all schools are usually strictly 'districted', the feeder system, called 'cluster schooling', aims to associate together in a particular complex, schools that differ rather dramatically – usually in matters of racial make-up. Thus an all-negro primary or lower school will be switched from its association with an all negro upper school and become one of the lower schools feeding a predominantly white upper school in the same general area. In cases of very severely disadvantaged schools, or where a local community feels its schools have too narrow a range of pupils, a feeder-school method of allocation could have its value in associating together lower and upper schools that draw from different housing areas, so that comprehensive or upper schools would become more varied. But there is obviously a limit to the arrangements that can be made on these lines, for as we have already discussed and will see in the next chapter, pupils mostly prefer neighbourhood schools and sending too many pupils too far out of their own district is not always popular. The Chief Officer of Sheffield writes, in explaining the linked system there, that 'parents have found it difficult to understand why their children should be asked to pass one or two secondary schools to go to one further from their homes'.[43] This is an obvious problem and does sometimes conflict with widely held parental preference for the neighbourhood school. It may well be one reason why feeder systems, with so many obvious educational advantages, have not grown in popularity since the 1960s in the same way as catchment-areas systems have.

It goes without saying that because feeder schools are so easy a system to manage the temptation may be arbitrarily or summarily to attach lower schools to upper schools without consultation or notice. This must obviously be avoided. No allocation system – zoning, choice and balanced ability included – and no boundary reviews or re-zoning should be undertaken by *any* authority without full explanation to parents and to staff of all schools involved, and any changes decided on should be announced, and given time for discussion and appeal a good way in advance.

Community controlled

For there is one last fact about allocation procedures that we discovered that is of extreme importance and marks a contrast between schools in a bipartite system – especially many grammar schools – and many schools in developing comprehensive systems: in about half the schools in our smaller sample, decisions about entry to schools were entirely in the hands of the authority or education committee and not in the hands of the head or staff of the comprehensive school. Since 1968 this move has accelerated, Inner London's significant change in 1972 from head-teacher choice to Divisional Office allocation under close Education Committee supervision, being a major example. This means that decisions about entry to schools are gradually moving away from being school-and-head teacher controlled to being community-controlled. But it also means that the authority and its education committee will have to make allocation procedures genuinely responsive to, and explicable to, local parents and staff in the schools. What has always held up zoning and feeder-school policies of allocation in the past, and made many prefer 'free choice' systems of allocation even when they know these present identical difficulties, has been the unnecessary association of zoning and feeder schools, but particularly zoning, with arbitrary and dictatorial laying down of the law from the centre. Allocation procedures to comprehensive schools in comprehensive systems are procedures upon which consultation within the school community is always required. They are matters upon which the wider community must also be consulted, and perhaps, upon which it ultimately decides itself. They are also a field which urgently needs research – if only to discover whether, in fact, the allocation methods adopted in each area actually do meet the objectives set for them; or, perhaps for an even simpler reason, in order to help us clarify these objectives themselves.

Notes

1. Circular 83, 1946.
2. The High Court ruled against the Birkenhead parents who had disputed the authority's direction that RC primary pupils were to proceed to RC secondary schools as an infringement of parents' right. They upheld the authority's decision to operate its own allocation policy.
3. For interesting proof see R. Saran, 'Decision-making by a local authority', *Journal of Public Administration*, Winter 1967.
4. DES, *Manual of Guidance*, no. 1, 23 August 1950.
5. David Eccles, 20 May 1955, quoted Firth, op. cit., p. 65.
6. David Eccles, House of Lords, 10 February 1965.
7. 14 June 1966.
8. Speech to Bristol Grammar School by Desmond Lee, reported *Bristol Evening Post*, 21 October 1965.
9. Rhodes Boyson, letter to *Sunday Times*, 16 March 1969. Dr Boyson gives a full account of his views in *Education*, 18 July 1969. His arguments were answered and continued in subsequent issues (August 1969).
10. NFER, *Trends in Allocation Procedure*, p. 13, 1969.
11. This was derived from the information given by local authorities in C. Benn, *Comprehensive Schools in 1972*, published by Comprehensive Schools Committee, 1972.

12. Newcastle-upon-Tyne, 'Roman Catholic secondary school entrance', leaflet, p. 7, 1967.
13. ILEA, 'Advice to parents', 1969.
14. *Education*, 17 March 1967.
15. Camden Association for the Advancement of State Education, 'A guide to the selection of children for Inner London Secondary Schools in 1972'.
16. Second NFER Report, p. 24.
17. H. R. Chetwynd, *Woodberry Down*, pp. 162–3.
18. See also *Forum*, vol. 11, no. 3, Summer 1969, article by H. H. Tilley.
19. See a correspondence between a parent and a chief Education Officer about this problem 'The parent and the chief officer', *Comprehensive Education*, Spring 1971.
20. NUT, *Into the Seventies*, p. 10.
21. CASE, 'Middle schools in Merton', 1970.
22. Christopher Price, House of Commons, 3 November 1967.
23. 'A Danish view', SEA *Journal*, p. 10, Autumn 1965.
24. G. R. Potter quoted in 'Allocation methods in a comprehensive system', *Comprehensive Education*, Summer 1970.
25. Quoted in 'Allocated methods in a comprehensive system', *Comprehensive Education*, Summer 1970, reprinting a letter in *Education*.
26. 'Review of comprehensive education', Haringey Education Committee, p. 6, 1969.
27. Second NFER Report, p. 269.
28. Bolton Reorganization Document, 1967. The plan itself was returned by the DES because the school bases to which pupils were allocated were themselves selective.
29. See the DES Definition of a Comprehensive in its evidence to the Royal Commission on Local Government, 1967, p. 5; and the definition of a comprehensive in the objectives set out by a working party guiding the NFER project, p. xi of First NFER Report, 1968.
30. First NFER Report, p. xi.
31. Ministry of Education Circular 144, 1947.
32. DES *Statistics*, 1970, vol. 1, p. viii.
33. *Inside the Comprehensive School*, p. 15, 1958.
34. 19 July 1968.
35. *Secondary Education for All, A New Drive*, White Paper, December 1958.
36. Midlothian AASE, *Scottish Educational Journal*, 13 May 1966, p. 470.
37. Gosport, Reorganization Document, p. 4, 1966.
38. H. Simmons, *Inside a Comprehensive School*, 1969, pp. 53/4.
39. H. D. Dickinson and John Maclaren, *The Comprehensive Schools in Bristol*, p. 8, 1968.
40. ibid.
41. Circular 83, January 1946.
42. 'Linked primary and secondary schools' C. Benn *Comprehensive Education*, Spring 1971, p. 28.
43. ibid.

Chapter 21
The Neighbourhood School

In the last chapter we saw that since most parents and pupils usually prefer a school near their home, catchment-area and feeder-school policies of allocation – including the same kind of 'choice' already available in the primary sector – have generally been successful in secondary comprehensive schemes and are the allocation systems used by the majority of existing comprehensive schools. These particular allocation methods underline the natural neighbourhood character of comprehensive schools.

This raises a difficulty for some people who oppose reorganization because they oppose neighbourhood schools. They argue as though non-neighbourhood schools have been the tradition and as if it is only comprehensive reorganization that threatens to change this. But, as anyone familiar with the education system knows, neighbourhood schools have always been the norm for all primary schools and for the majority of secondary-age pupils in Britain, including many grammar-school pupils.*

It is only the very selective (or independent) schools that have been traditionally non-neighbourhood. But debates on comprehensive reorganization have nevertheless been influenced by these arguments. For example, the 1964 and 1965 debates about reorganization in the House of Lords frequently aired worries on this subject. Labour peeress, Dora Gaitskell, spoke of the danger of 'creaming by location' in a comprehensive system, and of schools containing 'one social group' only. David Eccles, former Conservative Minister, disapproved of neighbourhood schools because, he said, they would create 'tension' between 'pupils' background and the school'. Eric James, former High Master of Manchester grammar school, was so concerned about the problem of neighbourhood schools that he felt a special 'committee' should be set up to investigate them.† As can be

* Many chief education officers would agree that although selective, a good proportion of grammar schools were always neighbourhood schools. See, for example, Redbridge CEO, 'Second report of reorganization', p. 5, 1967. Ninety per cent of pupils, he estimates, were in neighbourhood schools before reorganization.

† These debates took place on 3 July 1964 and 10 February 1965.

seen, fears about neighbourhood are not confined to one political party. Nor to politicians, since parents also frequently worry about one-class schools.* Of course, selective schools themselves – both public and state – constantly denigrate the idea of a school that draws all its pupils from, and serves, its own immediate area.[1]

So too do the conservative fringe groups who still support 11-plus selection in principle, for the essence of a selective school is that it must have the right to select from a wide area and must not be tied to a neighbourhood. The non-selective secondary modern in a bipartite system, however, was – and is – left to serve its area as a neighbourhood school to accommodate the majority not selected to the grammar, but this is not often argued against by these same groups. Thus the question of 'neighbourhood' is not discussed obectively, being so intimately bound up as it is with the whole campaign to retain 11-plus or 13-plus selection; and very often used purely emotively to reinforce the rights of the selective school to remain selective. Lately, 'neighbourhood' fears have been joined by 'size' fears, conjured up by a mass media concentration on 'monstrous' schools with several thousand pupils and their problems – often irresponsibly over-sensationalized. It it rarely pointed out that less than half of 1 per cent of comprehensives are over 2000 in size, and less than 7 per cent even over 1500. If a truly objective look were taken at a few of the most disadvantaged schools in some of our inner cities, we would see that in certain cases they are the ones with the least neighbourhood connection and often the smallest in size. A document from Inner London (on its Education Committee agenda 17 May 1972) thus said of London's comprehensives that 'the most popular have the smaller catchment areas. The least popular, in order to fill their vacancies . . . have . . . recruited from nearly as far afield as grammar schools, though for vastly different reasons.' That is, they are partly filled by pupils who have had to be sent to them from quite far away (locally, they are not 'chosen'), and are not 'neighbourhood' schools at all in the sense that they consist mainly of pupils from their own immediate areas. The question of 'neighbourhood schools' in reality, therefore, is very much more complex than crude campaigns for selection present it.

The other difficulty about some discussions on this subject is that they read as though opponents thought all neighbourhood schools were *ipso facto* wrong. In fact, most would not object to a comprehensive school serving all the pupils in a pleasant market town in Oxfordshire or in a Scottish burgh. Nor do most of those who oppose neighbourhood schools object to comprehensive schools that serve a single council estate or a new

* See, for example, the news sheets of many of the Associations for the Advancement of State Education.

town, since many of these same men and women (for example, most Conservative Ministers of Education in the 1950s and 1960s) just as strenuously insisted that comprehensive schools were best suited to – indeed should be confined to – just these 'one-class' areas. Equally, many of those denigrating 'large' schools are not to be found campaigning in the pleasant rural areas where most of the few really big comprehensive schools exist.

What it really comes down to is that it is only certain schools in certain neighbourhoods that are thought to be difficult. These are likely to be schools in crowded premises, in areas where the crime rate and poverty level is high or where 'good' selective schools still coexist nearby: what circular 10/65 somewhat euphemistically referred to as schools that lack 'stimulus and vitality'. Other documents are less discreet. One said that the neighbourhood school worried us because it raised the 'spectre of swarms of socially deprived children'.[2] It is the problem-area schools that worry us rather than the concept of neighbourhood itself.

Problem-area schools are not exclusive to secondary education. Nor are they new. Michael Young put the problem well in describing primary schools that were in bad buildings in districts of 'high delinquency' where teacher turnover was high and there was much poverty. Schools get caught in a vicious circle: the worse things are, the more difficult they find it to attract and keep good staff, and then the worse things get.[3] He was talking of areas in which schools should be given the priority-area treatment recommended by the Plowden Council on Primary Education: special extra expenditure.

Problems of poverty have now become entangled with an even more complicated problem in some areas: immigrants. Government policy about immigrants in schools has vacillated. Under circular 7/65 in 1966 it was proposed that no more than 30 per cent immigrant population be allowed per school, but some LEAs ignored this and more recently another Secretary of State, when opening a school with a 90 per cent immigrant population, said: 'If a school is a neighbourhood school, it must take in children from the neighbourhood it serves.'[4]

American experience about neighbourhood schools is often cited by those who argue against comprehensive education. Once again it is not most schools or neighbourhoods that are singled out as cause for alarm, but only certain ones. There is no doubt that in the centres of 'dying' cities educational opportunity for all races is lower than in the suburbs and most country districts. But there is nothing to suggest it is the schools that have produced poverty, dying towns or race hatred. Or that under another system of schooling these evils would disappear. Certainly the tradition of segregating academic pupils, common in Northern Europe, has not prevented racial disaster or slum secondary schools here.

Once again, in dealing with this problem, we meet the dilemma we discussed in the previous chapter: is it better to manipulate a comprehensive school's intake of pupils in what may have to be a non-neighbourhood and artificial manner for the sake of mixing – either for social, or racial, or ability purposes – or should schools in general serve their own areas? Immigrant and other opinion on this subject in Britain is divided, as is negro opinion divided in America on the question of artificial desegregation – e.g. 'bussing' of pupils – as against leaving schools to reflect local population patterns. Part of the difficulty in leaving schools to reflect local population patterns is that so often in the past – in both the USA and Britain – this has simply resulted in their being literally 'left behind'. For this reason, many are wary of a solution that ties a school to its area. They feel that if only energetic measures could be taken to bring white pupils to a black school or to put middle-class pupils into a mostly working-class school – or vice versa in both cases – attention would at last be paid to those children many feel the system previously had forgotten.

This whole problem is one that individual communities must decide about for themselves. Given maximum goodwill and community agreement on racial mixing or social mixing or balanced-ability policies, allocation schemes of an engineered nature will sometimes work. There has been some success with 'bussing' of pupils in certain American communities, for example. But in most areas, enforced mixing or schemes involving elaborate uprooting and direction have not been successful. As we know, most parents and pupils prefer a local school. In addition, in the case of black or immigrant minorities, prevailing opinion more and more rejects the idea of artificial mixing because it rests on the premises that somehow it is 'bad' to be black. They argue that instead of uprooting populations or devising elaborate or artificial changes in the role of schools, these schools should be given extra support where they are, so that they may be radically improved within the context of their own communities: basically, the priority-area principle.

This solution of improvement-in-situ naturally has drawbacks – especially for those who think that all comprehensive schools must have a hypothetical social or racial mix – for it accepts that a few schools will be largely working-class schools, or middle-class, or, perhaps, largely immigrant. How one views this depends to what extent it is felt that social mixing is essential to education and to a certain extent on the practicability – locally – of possible alternative arrangements for allocation to schools.

As we saw in the last chapter, a very great deal can be done by intelligent drawing of catchment areas and arrangements of feeder schools to give most comprehensive schools a natural and varied mixture of pupils without elaborate or artificial community controls or denial of all choice. Of course, a *sine qua non* is an end to selection itself, which prevails in almost all big cities, and which has traditionally left so many schools 'behind' as abler pupils and highly qualified staff went off to grammar schools. As one head has written, so many old secondary modern schools were depressing and unpleasant 'not because they were neighbourhood schools but (because) there was nothing left for them after local authorities had staffed and equipped grammar schools'.[5] It is this past neglect which has aroused the neighbourhood bogey. One sociologist has written that what society is really worrying about is not disadvantaged areas but that

> some pupils who had formerly gone to grammar schools would have to share the comparative deprivations of the secondary modern schools. The few bright working-class children whom the state now 'rescues' from such conditions would be 'contaminated' by the education it provides for the residue. . . . Yet instead of seeing the moral that the comprehensive school must be part of a wider attack on inequality, the debate turned to give the impression that the comprehensive school would *create* inequality.[6]

The argument here is that ending selection is the only way to get resources redistributed to those areas which really need them.

But there will be a few schools that cannot be helped merely by ending 11-plus selection, schools often in deepest pockets of poverty and decay. They can best be helped by direct assistance – in the form of financial help on the education priority area principle, by extra staff or by concerted community action. But it is also recognized now that mere allocations of 'extra allowances' or additional expenditure on facilities, however necessary and welcome, cannot in themselves improve the quality of education or the morale of a school beyond a certain point. Over and above this, a definite commitment on the part of the staff, parents and pupils towards definite educational objectives and a belief in the ability of the school to meet them is required. Those who have worked and taught in 'disadvantaged'-area comprehensive schools have now built up a considerable fund of experience about the type of strategy required, and the innovations which have been found to be successful in practice. Albert Rowe in Hull, Anthony Bullivant in Sheffield, and Eric Midwinter in Liverpool – to name only three – have all given the comprehensive-school movement thorough-going and definite leads of a positive kind.[7] On several important points they differ in their views about what is required, but on many they are agreed: particularly on the importance of local-community involvement in the comprehensive on a neighbourhood basis.

While recognizing that the problem of difficult schools must be tackled, there is an accompanying danger that we might get into the habit of thinking that a school that is largely immigrant or working-class is a 'bad' school. We as authors have seen and visited far too many excellent comprehensive schools where racial and social mixing is at a minimum to accept this kind of judgement. Others who have examined the relation-. ship between schools and neighbourhoods have come to similar conclusions. Alec Clegg, the Chief Education Officer of the West Riding, undertook a survey some time ago of a number of West Riding schools, rating them on a list from 'best' to 'worst' according to the opinion of local school inspectors, police and welfare officers who knew the schools well. He then looked to see if the schools rated as 'bad' were always those in the areas everyone knew to be most depressed or deprived. He found there was little correlation.[8]

Any neighbourhood can have a good school – provided we know the pupils' and area's real needs and support the school well. But one of the problems is that up to now we have known very little about the neighbourhoods from which our existing comprehensive schools draw their pupils. The NFER Reports of 1965 and 1968 asked head teachers to estimate the parental occupations of pupils.[9] The information received was not unexpected: semi-skilled and unskilled workers' children were over-represented in comprehensive schools, while professional and clerical workers' children were under-represented. This was of interest, but it did not tell us much about the neighbourhoods from which the schools draw.

Our first questionnaire therefore asked schools to describe the *neighbourhoods* from which their pupils came. These neighbourhoods were defined in terms of the type of housing in the area. Housing patterns give a very crude, but at the same time a very definite, indication of the kind of neighbourhood served by a school. Moreover, it is a pattern those teaching in a school are quite sure about – while knowledge of parental occupations for all pupils may be less precise. Lastly, since the whole question of schools' catchment-area policy is so very intricately connected to an authority's housing policy, it seemed a sensible way to approach the definition of neighbourhood.

We listed five types of neighbourhood, as can be seen in Table 21.1: schools drawing *mainly* (1) from council estates; (2) from private housing or residential area; (3) from a mixture of private housing and council estate; (4) from a mixture of private, council estate, and substandard housing; and (5) from substandard housing, with or without some council housing in addition.

Broadly speaking – for the purpose of measuring how many comprehensive schools are 'one class' – categories (1), (2) and (5) could be called 'one-class' schools. This is very crude indeed and assumes a council estate is entirely working-class, and in addition, that there is little distinction between one kind of working-class occupation and another. It also

Table 21.1 Neighbourhood areas from which British comprehensive schools drew their pupils, 1968

Type of housing drawn from	Number and % of all schools		% of schools England and Wales	% of Scottish schools	% of Roman Catholic schools	% intake of top 20% ability	% staying on after leaving age	% staying on after leaving age, Scotland	Average no. O-level and O-grade subject groups	Average sixth form size	Average no. A-level and H-grade subject groups	% of schools in each area competing with grammar schools
	No.	%										
1. Mostly from council estate(s)	103	14	13	28	21·5	11	42	29	12	71	7	65
2. Mostly from private and residential area	28	4	4	0	0	19	63	54	14	131	7	53
3. From a mixture of council housing and private housing	308	42	41	51	34	16	54	54	12	83	8	41
4. From a mixture of council, private-residential and substandard	252	34·5	37	15	43	16	52	39	12	83		55
5. Mostly from sub-standard housing, with or without some council housing	29	4	4	4	1·5	5	39	20	8	55		86
Other	6	1										
Unknown	2	0·5		1								
Total number of schools	(728)	100	100 (661)	100 (67)	100 (65)	(728)	(621)	(52)	(621)	(436)	(436)	(378)

Table 21.2 Neighbourhood areas from which British comprehensive schools drew their pupils, 1958–67

Type of housing drawn from	Percentages of schools receiving first comprehensive intakes									
	1958	1959	1960	1961	1962	1963	1964	1965	1966	1967
1. Mostly from council estate(s)	29	24	10	21	11	26	8	21	13	9
2. Mostly from private and residential area	4	0	0	0	0	21	3	4	0	6
3. From a mixture of council housing and private housing	29	48	40	0	50	26	46	47	47	47
4. From a mixture of council, private-residential and substandard housing	33	19	40	71	28	26	47	26	39	33
5. Mostly from substandard housing, with or without some council housing	0	10	10	0	5·5	0	2	1	1	4
Other / Unknown }	4	0	0	7	5·5	0	0	2	0	0·5
	(100)	(100)	(100)	(100)	(100)	(100)	(100)	(100)	(100)	(100)
Total number of schools founded in each year	24	21	10	14	18	19	62	82	92	201

assumes that working-class families do not live in private housing estates. All these assumptions are wide open to argument, but for the purposes of testing how many 'one-class' schools exist, we will let them remain.

Even though we undoubtedly exaggerate one-class schools by these definitions, we can see that these three 'one-class' categories contain only a small minority of schools: about one-fifth of the total. This is much lower than many of the propaganda pieces about one-class comprehensive schools have suggested. The 'socially mixed' categories – (3) and (4) – contain the vast majority of schools: 77 per cent overall. Moreover, when looking at the year columns in Table 21.2 we see that although there are year-to-year fluctuations, the prevailing pattern of neighbourhood schools over the past ten years has been fairly steady. There is no evidence that, as reorganization proceeds, any one type of neighbourhood school, including those crudely called 'one class', becomes more likely. If anything, the table shows that the socially mixed categories (3) and (4) get more likely as reorganization proceeds.

Scotland's distribution of neighbourhoods is different from that in England and Wales in a few important ways, as we see. It has more council estate schools (28 per cent against 13 per cent overall for England and Wales); and it has no schools at all drawing from the neighbourhood with only private or residential housing. What is most significant in our findings, however, is not only that the number with 'one-class' comprehensive schools is small but that the number of the *real* problem – substandard-area schools – is extremely small indeed: only 4 per cent of all comprehensive schools in the survey. This is important to emphasize, for it means that the real so-called neighbourhood school problem is to date a limited one in the comprehensive movement and not anything like as widespread as assumed. It also means that priority-area assistance for these schools (only twenty-six of our respondents in England and Wales in 1968) should be a manageable and realistic proposition in terms of the money likely to be available.

What do we see in Table 21.1 of differences between neighbourhoods overall? Firstly, the two 'socially mixed' categories (3) and (4) are very much alike. They each have a slightly higher than overall average intake of ability (16 per cent of the top 20 per cent) and a slightly higher percentage of pupils staying on beyond leaving age (54 per cent and 52 per cent respectively) than is average for all schools in the survey, and an about average number of subject-groups offered at O-level and O-grade. At A-level and H-grade, in fact, (3), council-and-private neighbourhood, has the highest average offering of subject-groups of any of the five neighbourhood areas.

What about the other categories? The council-estate schools 'score' a little below the mixed-area schools in all these respects, except for GCE O- and A-level, when they score the same as category (4). The figures for staying on are perhaps more than just a little lower, however. For Scotland they are a great deal lower: 29 per cent.*

The most marked differences in the neighbourhoods came between areas (2) and (5): private- and residential-area schools on the one hand and schools drawing from substandard housing on the other. Each category had about the same number of schools: as we said, a very small proportion of the total. The ability intake in the private-housing-area schools is just about 'comprehensive' at 19 per cent of the top 20 per cent – and highest for any area; while that of the substandard area schools is very much the lowest for any of the areas at only 5 per cent. The staying-on rate for private-housing area schools is the highest for any neighbourhood at 63 per cent, but for substandard-area schools it is much the lowest: 39 per cent, and in Scotland down to 20 per cent. Although the size of the average sixth form in private-housing category is almost three times as large as that in the substandard, the average subject-groups taken at A-level is perhaps not particularly significant in difference: six for substandard schools rather than the average of seven. But the difference at O-level is very marked. For substandard schools it is down to eight, whereas no other area falls below the average for all schools in the survey of twelve. This illustrated what we have found more than once in this survey: that where schools of varying types or circumstances differ in GCE and SCE subject-groups offered, the difference is always more marked at O-level than at A-level.

These figures show that – as most of us would expect – very extreme neighbourhood situations do make a difference to a comprehensive school, and that affluent neighbourhoods tend to produce higher 'scores' all the way around, while the very depressed produce lower ones. Most who have studied these problems know that pupils from better-off homes are likely to be rated as more able at eleven years of age, and that these same pupils are more likely to want, and to be able, to stay on longer after leaving age. But this was not the end of the story, for it was not just the poor housing factor that characterized the category of substandard schools. We found further that almost half (48 per cent) of these schools were associated with the 'guided parental choice' method of allocation, compared to only 18 per cent for all schools overall in our survey.† Undoubtedly this meant that substandard schools were the schools *not* chosen in guided schemes, the abler pupils being 'guided' elsewhere. Even more significant, as

---

* Scotland's 'mixed area' schools in category (3), on the other hand, had the highest staying-on percentage by far for any Scottish neighbourhood: 54 per cent.

† See Appendix 1, Note 3.

Table 21.1 shows, substandard schools were the category with by far the highest percentage of competing grammar schools: 86 per cent. This compares to only 41 per cent of private/council schools (category 3) and 53 per cent private-residential (category 2) schools, for example. Substandard category schools therefore do not merely suffer from pupils' home conditions – although this is a big factor. They are also obviously schools likely to be weakly supported by education authorities and committees.

By contrast, schools that are strongly supported can do a great deal for pupils from disadvantaged areas. This can be seen in schools in areas where all pupils come from rehoused slum families. When these pupils are given genuine comprehensive education in fully staffed comprehensive schools that serve all pupils in a neighbourhood – as in some of the council estates with no competing grammar schools – the story is very different.

One comprehensive school of this kind – in the North of England – has given us figures of an 11-plus intake that went all the way through the school. In 1959 out of 320 pupils, *none* were from professional or managerial families and only eight were designated of 'grammar' ability. Yet this same intake went through the comprehensive school to gain ten university places, twelve places at training colleges, and with sixty-six and twenty-one gaining some passes at O-level and A-level respectively. The head of another such school on an overspill estate told us that at age eleven he had very few high-ability pupils, but by the time they had been through the school – and come into the sixth form – he found there were many more. His problem was that he could not have identified these pupils at eleven. What had 'happened' to these 'disadvantaged' intakes between eleven and eighteen years of age, what had produced academic achievement where high ability had not been there at eleven, was simply genuine comprehensive education in fully staffed and fully equipped uncreamed albeit 'one-class' neighbourhood comprehensive schools. Nowhere has criticism of the comprehensive reform been more thoroughly prejudiced than in its uncritical assumption that able pupils from poor backgrounds always 'suffer' in a comprehensive or that the bright working-class pupil must be completely surrounded by selective or middle-class pupils to succeed academically. We have seen at first hand that a well-supported neighbourhood comprehensive school with an entirely working-class intake can succeed dramatically with pupils of this calibre. In addition, comprehensive school literature and research has now provided endless examples of pupils who were assumed to have 'no grammar-school ability' at eleven plus, but who have succeeded academically in the comprehensive school. In Guy Neave's 1968 study of comprehensive pupils entering university 13 per cent of the total sample had failed their 11-plus.[10] Individual schools have recorded the careers of specific pupils – many of them quite remarkable – such as the boy who entered a new town comprehensive with a VRQ of 79 (educationally subnormal) and yet who obtained five O-levels and three A-levels and then continued at a Polytechnic.[11] At the other end of the scale several national newspapers carried the story of a local council worker's son who went to a large neighbourhood comprehensive school in London, was mathematically gifted, finished his A-level course in five years and entered Oriel College, Oxford, while still aged fifteen, to read mathematics.[12] This case is cited because the argument is so often given that the *really* brilliant child is bound to be held back by the ordinary neighbourhood comprehensive, an argument everywhere expounded in theory but nowhere supported in fact.

The fact that most comprehensive schools draw from mixed housing areas, that substandard-area schools are so relatively few in number, and that genuinely comprehensive neighbourhood schools have produced such a remarkable raising of educational standards, may help us to stop over-concentration on the negative aspects of neighbourhood that have been such a marked feature of recent discussion on comprehensive schools, and to explore instead the many positive features.

For, as we discussed earlier, we know that reorganization is itself a neighbourhood-reinforcing process. The act of making a school a comprehensive school is the act of creating a school to serve its own immediate community. As many LEA documents say,[13] reorganization means 'provision for pupils to be absorbed in their appropriate areas'. Schools formerly grammar or secondary modern served only some of the pupils in their area; when they are enlarged to comprehensive status, or amalgamated, they serve all the pupils. Moreover, as one area reorganizes, it affects neighbouring areas. Pupils formerly sent by LEAs 'across the border' to another area's grammar schools, cease to need to go and this in turn forces the second authority to look again at its own system.[14] Sometimes it is a large percentage of an area's intake that will be withdrawn because of reorganization: ninety pupils out of 270 in one northern authority.[15] For many this provision of full facilities for each area is a great relief, especially where pupils have had to travel long distances and large sums were required for fares for a school with the appropriate course. Pupils could be spared what one area called the 'mass daily exodus' – in this case to attend a selective school.[16] But more important, reorganization will lead to increased interest in and support for local schools and will, as one authority put it, 'strengthen community feeling'.[17]

But even though the effects of reorganization are to keep some pupils nearer home, for most secondary-age pupils the actual school or unit in which they will receive their education will in fact be drawing pupils from a far wider area than before reorganization. This is obvious, for schools will be much larger. They will draw from two or three times as wide an area. The higher the age range of the school, the wider the area in most cases. A sixth-form college will draw pupils from a far wider neighbourhood than most grammar schools in the past. Thus, for the great majority of secondary-school pupils reorganization means a widening, not a narrowing, of horizons.

When most of the ways of organizing comprehensive schools are explored, it can be seen that the only possible way that a comprehensive-school system can function is on the community principle. All early definitions of comprehensive schools included reference to their position as the school for a neighbourhood. As we have seen, in the 1947 Ministry of Education definition a comprehensive school was a secondary school for 'all the pupils in a given area'.[18] In the same year in Scotland, a comprehensive school was defined as: 'the natural way for a democracy to order the post-primary schooling of a given area . . . better than any other . . . to . . . promote the success of the school as a community'.[19]

In 1958 the introduction to the National Union of Teachers' publication *Inside the Comprehensive School* said very clearly: 'The schools should belong to the neighbourhood and the neighbourhood to the school.'[20]

It was only in the 1960s that persistent campaigns against comprehensive schools, by public and grammar schools in particular, began to include a campaign against the idea of 'neighbourhood'. The fact that so many comprehensive schools have had to struggle for recognition side by side with grammar schools has tended to reinforce the idea that academic prestige accompanied non-neighbourhood status. In the ILEA's 1969 brochure for parents whose children were transferring to secondary school, parents thinking of a comprehensive school were advised to choose 'the nearest . . . such school to your home'. For those 'advised' to choose a grammar school, however, there was no such directive. As the brochure states: 'Grammar schools traditionally draw from a wider area and nearness to the school is not such an important factor.' Here the 'difference' between grammar schools and other secondary schools was made specifically one of neighbourhood. There was no mention in the brochure about 'traditional' 11-plus ability selection which is the real conditioning factor for entry to grammar schools – in London or anywhere else.

The campaign of agitation about 'neighbourhood' has also resulted in the 'neighbourhood' connection being dropped from definitions of the comprehensive school's objectives. One important example is the set of objectives drawn up by the working party set up in 1965 to advise the government on research into reorganization carried out by the NFER.

This working party – from which, significantly, representatives of comprehensive schools themselves were almost totally absent (only one out of fifteen members)[21] – laid down three 'objectives' for comprehensive schools: (1) to gather pupils of the whole ability range in one school, (2) to collect pupils representing a cross-section of society in one school, and (3) to concentrate teachers and facilities to use scarce resources economically. What is remarkable here is the absence of any reference whatsoever to the long-standing 'object' of providing education for all the pupils in a given area. This appears to have been jettisoned altogether – with the working party committing itself firmly to a definition of a comprehensive as a school for which the community must *engineer* a mix. Not unnaturally, none of the three NFER Reports contained much about the operation of comprehensive schools in the communities in which they actually existed.

The Second Report of 1970, however, included a short chapter on 'contacts' between the school and the community, although much of what it identified as 'community' activity (non-teaching staff employed, school-magazine work and PTA organizations) would not be regarded as necessarily neighbourhood-directed activities. We have dealt with these subjects elsewhere in this book. There were some interesting findings, however, about such activities as visits made by pupils outside the school, visitors invited into the school, events put on at the school open to the community and courses which involved studying local problems. In general it was found that Southern and Midland schools were more 'open' than Northern and Welsh ones, that more Southern and urban schools went on visits than Northern ones and received more visits from local workers like the police or doctors. But this was not always invariable. What was most interesting, however, was that schools did not divide up into those who did a lot of community work for the old people as against those who encouraged visitors, or between those who had their schools used a lot in the evening as against those who did not but who on the other hand made up for this by sending pupils out to visit local organizations or industries. It turned out that if a school was community minded, it was community minded in all its activities; and if it was not community minded, it was fairly closed and self-contained in everything. Or, as the Report put it

schools which showed the greatest activity in some fields tended also to show high levels of activity in most others, while those organizing little ... in the way of school functions were also relatively isolated from the community in other ways.[22]

Relationship to the community is thus a conscious policy, not a result of haphazard circumstances no one in the school can change. What was also interesting was that the ex-secondary-modern comprehensives tended to go out into the community more and invite more visitors in while the new and the ex-grammars tended to make their connection with the community through mounting events parents could come to see. This suggests an interesting difference in community relationship between those schools who want the community to come *in*, and those who feel they want their pupils to go *out*.

That the bias in some emerging comprehensive schools could be against the idea of neighbourhood – simply because isolation was the mark of prestige in the old grammar school world – is obviously a factor to be considered in some cases. It may be that this is part of the ultra-conservative phase most comprehensives go through in early development, as we have noticed. If it were to be permanent, however, it could be backward looking. A Hertfordshire document, for example, purports to argue for comprehensive developments throughout the authority, but at the same time it argues against secondary schools serving a 'particular neighbourhood exclusively' and against any attempt to 'identify an educational unit with the area it serves' to such an extent that pupils come from the same home backgrounds.[23] The possible implications of this view – that comprehensive schools should not be identified with their own areas, or not serve the areas with which they are naturally identified – are obviously profound. These implications and developments are at total variance with the experience of most of those who are working and teaching in most existing comprehensive schools. Among the head-teachers and staff and parents of the schools we visited and questioned, there was probably more agreement on this point than upon any other: comprehensive schools are neighbourhood schools. Once they are working as genuine comprehensive schools, they cannot be anything else.

The many schools we questioned and visited in our smaller sample were by no means similar, as can be seen by looking at the list in Appendix 1 (p. 517). They represented all age ranges of schools in every kind of area and situation. Nine said their neighbourhoods were 'working class' (six were in cities, one in a small seaport, one in a docks area, one in a mining town). Two drew from mainly middle-class homes. One school said it drew from a 'socially comprehensive' new town, another from a good 'artisan/managerial' area. Five used estate agents' language: a mixture of old residential and new council estate. One was most precise: 'Registrar General's 3B and below'. Another was very subjective: the area was 'depressed'. Other schools answered this question in geographical terms. Three said they were in dormitory suburbs or rural areas just outside large towns. Five were in small towns with some light industry. Two were in scattered rural areas; two in overspill estates outside large cities; two in residential and semi-rural areas. One was in a small village. Another, in a small town, said his community was 'ideal' for a comprehensive school.

All but three were certain about the neighbourhood nature of the comprehensive school. One school, in the middle of a big city, said:

Involvement in community affairs is not a matter of option, as the question suggests. . . . Such a school is . . . a focus for community activities. . . . A comprehensive school is almost of necessity dedicated to changes, or at least modifications, in the community.

Several schools had already spoken of the question of neighbourhood when commenting upon allocation methods. Trying for 'an artificial synthesis' was purposeless, thought one, a school's job was to 'serve the immediate area'. Yet another said: 'Neighbourhood first, then balance of ability and parental choice.' Only three heads were worried that some neighbourhood schools might not have a balanced ability intake. The spirit in which this problem was approached is probably best put by this head:

If a school is to serve its area, it must accept that its area will have a certain nature and certain potentials – and certain drawbacks. All of these will have to be accepted.

But quite a large number of schools seemed to feel that the school's job was to go beyond accepting; it should be an active agent.

'It should create the community.' Another said it must be 'the focus of educational life in the community'; another said that it must not only be the focus of pupil life, but of adult life as well. A third said the school should be 'extended to become a neighbourhood college' and remain open all the time and all the year. And another: 'In an area like this . . . in which cultural standards are generally low, we have a glorious opportunity to make the school a cultural centre for the community.'

Nor is it just that the school should hope to draw in and gain support from the community, but that the school should encourage pupils to take an interest in, and a pride in, and to discover, their own communities.

Most of the schools we visited and questioned have already – some quite unconsciously – begun to play a very big part in local life. Those who work in these schools see that to do otherwise would be to impoverish the school and undermine its work. One of the heads wished a headmaster's house could be built on the school grounds, and many felt staff should live in the community served by the school. Although the comprehensive is only a quarter-century old in Britain, there are signs from those actually involved in the day-to-day life of these schools, that they hope these schools will develop as far more important institutions than even their pioneers thought possible: 'The comprehensive school may take the place of the Church, which has left a gap in community life.'

This is not to say that being a neighbourhood school is problem-free, for it is not. But the real problems are very different from the ones cast up by traditional or elitist fears of neighbourhood. The real problems concern the difficulties involved in actually fulfilling the new and extended community role: serving both its own pupils and the wider community at one and the same time. Only two schools in our smaller sample were not open after school hours (they were country schools). Thirty-three were open after school for two or three hours and thirty-one were open in the evenings. Twelve, about a third of those answering this question, were open in the holidays in addition. Half the schools said they stayed open for school pupils to hold club meetings, rehearsals, use the library and hold extra sports fixtures. One school in the sample (and several others we also visited) used the extended day for extra classes for pupils needing additional help, and for homework supervision. In some cases staff were paid extra for undertaking this work. Half the schools (eighteen) also had evening classes – adult or further education – usually organized by the authority. Half also let the school be used by the community for meetings, film shows, amateur dramatics and sports. Four schools had sports fields and swimming pools in use the entire year round by their community. Two also let the schools be used as play centres in the holidays. The NFER's Second Report showed only seven out of the forty-seven schools studied where the school buildings were left unused after school hours.[24]

Nor are these practices unusual. The wider comprehensive-school movement is full of examples of school/community links. The libraries of both Hartcliffe School and Lawrence Weston School, Bristol, are also the libraries used by the housing estates in which they are situated. Wyndham School in Cumberland is on the high street of its town, Egremont, with the school's library and pool and canteens available for town use.[25] In Nottinghamshire a comprehensive school has been built, with additional funds given by a local recreation group, so that the school's sports facilities can be used by the whole community. Yet another Nottinghamshire school has a special wing for use by teachers for weekend courses. The prototype comprehensive school designed for Inner London (but as yet unbuilt), Thomas Calton, bases itself very closely on identification with its own area and its needs. The examples of school/community cooperation are many and they are only just beginning. The stone upon which they all stand is the assumption that Ounsdale School prints in its prospectus: 'The school is the centre of life of its neighbourhood.'

But how to apportion the time and the parts of the school that will belong to the community and those that belong to the school, staff, pupils and parents? Several staff we met were anxious because they wished to run extra-help classes for pupils needing special work in the after-school and evening hours or to mount ambitious extended-day programmes for their schools – but found they could not do so because the school had to be given up for evening classes. They did not object to the classes but only to the fact that they were not left one small 'part' of the school. Several schools we questioned spoke of the wear and tear involved in community use of a school. The school is 'so heavily over-used that it is impossible to keep clean'. Our chapter on architecture cited some of the failures to build schools for increased use, and our section on administration mentions the additional load put on those who must run the comprehensive complex. In problems of community use, schools often spoke to us of the extra burdens placed on caretaking staff and the need for more assistance for them. One spoke of the diplomatic problem of strained relations owing to 'two sets of users' of a school, although he added that double use 'was well worth the effort'.

There is the additional problem of the isolation of some schools, especially in the countryside – what some call the problem of 'buses at the gates at four'. This raises the whole question of the siting of a school and brings up another dilemma: should the comprehensive school be situated on the outskirts amid acres of playing fields or should it be right inside the community from which its pupils come? There are protagonists for both views. Those who are stuck in old schools in big cities – with long coach rides to playing fields – obviously dream of a school in a pleasanter setting. But there are those who feel they would then be missing something. They believe comprehensive schools should not be banished among playing fields, but be proudly the centrepiece of the locality they actually serve.[26] Several writers have commented on the sad practice of 'hiding' even purpose-built schools in a community rather than making them the centre of local life. Leila Berg, for example, said this of Risinghill.[27] Several heads in our smaller sample spoke of the necessity to design schools that are accessible to parents, and that encouraged them to come in and out.

But although there is agreement on much within the comprehensive movement, we must not think that there is anything like full agreement about either objectives or methods when it comes to serving a community – or wider society. On the one hand there are those who see the comprehensive school as an addition to the hierarchy of schools already in existence, whose prime function is to succeed within the presently accepted system of values and educational practices on behalf of a wider group of pupils. On the other, there are those who reject this philosophy as meritocratic or overly-competitive, one in which basically 'classes and classifications are still accepted . . . all concepts (which) make schools external to the local community'.[28] Again, on the one hand, there are those who argue that comprehensive schools can only reflect social values and operate within social systems as they exist, while others would say that it is the job of comprehensive schools to actively seek to change society – and redistribute resources more equally – through their organization, activity and teaching. On the one hand there are those who think the present school and educational structure needs only modifications of a minor nature in order to become more 'democratic', while others would say that truly democratic schools 'need a different administrative structure and philosophy' altogether so that education can become less isolated and more internally democratic, changing society 'in and through the learning process rather than around but in isolation from it'.[29] And between those two ends of the spectrum are many who take a middle position on the relationship of comprehensives to society. But whatever disagreements there may be about the extent to which education should seek to shape society, there is agreement widely that comprehensives should seek a far closer relation with their own immediate community.

The real problem is not, therefore, whether comprehensive schools should or should not be neighbourhood-based but how they can best and most effectively carry out what they see to be their inevitable community role. The first job of the comprehensive school is to educate all pupils in the disciplines of learning, enabling them to acquire the skills and knowledge necessary both to advance learning and to meet the needs of society. But comprehensive schools will also aim to extend and develop the perceptions and potential of pupils individually, encouraging self-growth and fostering awareness of their own unique personality, of their relationship to others and of their potential contribution to the wider community. In all these tasks the support and cooperation of the home and of many community agencies, officers and institutions are essential. In return, comprehensive schools themselves, both in pupil work and in facilities, can help their own communities. Many staff and many of the secondary pupils now cannot conceive of 'education' as a process that does not include discussion of, or work for and in, the local community. Comprehensive schools also have equipment and amenities that can serve the community: theatres, restaurants, swimming pools, libraries and gymnasia. There are many who feel these schools should be conceived of from the first as more than just a complex of buildings for 1000 pupils to use for only eight hours a day for only thirty-eight weeks in a year.

Since most successful comprehensives develop as community schools from the first, it is only natural that in both function and design comprehensive schools are now being thought of more and more as involved in serving the wider community. Even more natural that the wider community, having invested so much money in these new public buildings – a large new comprehensive can cost one million pounds – should want to have the use of them too. Henry Swain, the Nottinghamshire County Architect, has said that this is the 'right historical moment' to raise the question of the community use of secondary schools. It is also the right historical moment to begin serious discussion about the positive role of the comprehensive secondary school itself in its own community, necessarily involving, as it does, a unique relationship in each case, since each community will have different needs, problems, disadvantages and advantages.

Those who argue against neighbourhood schools are arguing for the old order in education, when schools were entirely closed authoritarian institutions, often educating pupils in isolation – both from other social groups in the community and from the immediate community surrounding the school. The one thing we can be sure about is that this old order is slowly disappearing – in schools, in universities, in Britain and all over the world. Educational institutions everywhere are not only seeking wider intakes, new patterns of self-government and curriculum reform, but seeking them in the context of the local and wider community need. Secondary schools are no exception. Comprehensive schools in particular understand the changes taking place and feel the need, as one head has called it, for 'a new corpus of values'.[30] As the head of Wyndham School wrote in a report of his own community-based and integrated comprehensive school, it has 'abandoned altogether the idea, ingrained since the monastic origins of English education, that a school should train children in isolation from the world'.[31] A Sheffield head adds: 'What I want is to build up a school which is intimately bound up with a local community ... based on neighbourhood units and on the people who live in its streets. It must be a school which belongs to them and to which they belong.'[32] And from Liverpool: 'The true lesson to be learned from all the home and school research is that education is at its most stable when the school and the home are in cahoots ... schools should vary substantially to meet the needs of the neighbourhoods they serve.'[33] Perhaps one of the heads from our smaller survey put it at its simplest and most poetic: 'a comprehensive school is a comprehensive school is a comprehensive school. ...'

Notes

1. For example, see Governing Bodies Association Headmasters' Conference Document 135, January 1969; and also 'In defence of grammar schools', Association of Governing Bodies of Greater London Aided Schools, March 1966.
2. Quoted in Society of Friends, *Education Bulletin*, no. 9, p. 4.
3. Michael Young, speech at a Teach-in, 21 January 1967.
4. Edward Short, quoted in the *Guardian*, 11 December 1968.
5. Anthony Bullivant, 'Neighbourhood comprehensive schools', *Comprehensive Education*, Summer 1971.
6. Denis Marsden, 'Politicians, equality and comprehensives', op. cit., p. 18.
7. These can be found set out in their writings and speeches, and in many of the issues of *Forum* and *Where*. Eric Midwinter's and Anthony Bullivant's speeches to the Conference on the Neighbourhood Comprehensive School are printed in the Summer 1971 issue of *Comprehensive Education*. Albert Rowe's views are given in his book, *The School as a Guidance Community*, 1971.
8. Investigation conducted in Yorkshire, West Riding, 1961.
9. NFER Report, p. 30 and Appendix 1, Table 8.
10. *How They Fared, Impact of Comprehensive Schools on Universities*, in press, Guy Neave kindly gave us permission to quote before publication.
11. From Burnt Mill School, Harlow, reported in 'Academic results from fifteen comprehensive schools in 1970', *Comprehensive Education*, Autumn 1970.
12. The local newspaper cutting is reprinted in *Comprehensive Education*, Autumn 1970. The story was also reprinted in the *Daily Telegraph*, where the fact that the school was a comprehensive – and a neighbourhood comprehensive – was not mentioned. The *Daily Telegraph*, of course, has long been associated with a campaign against the neighbourhood comprehensive.
13. This is said in both counties and boroughs.
14. See, for example, North West Kent, document dated 21 June 1967.
15. See also Derbyshire reorganization document, 1966, p. 20.
16. Sevenoaks, Kent, AASE Bulletin, no. 16, 1968.
17. Herefordshire reorganization document, p. 9, 1967.
18. Circular 144, 1947.
19. Scottish Report on Secondary Education, 1947.
20. *Inside the Comprehensive School*, p. 22, 1958.
21. First NFER Report, p. xi.
22. Second NFER Report, p. 174.
23. Hertfordshire Paper I, 19 October 1965.
24. Second NFER Report, p. 173.
25. See *Building*, 18 March 1966.
26. Henry Swain, Nottinghamshire County Architect, address to RIBA Conference, June 1968, *Forum*, vol. 12, no. 1.
27. Leila Berg, *Death of a Comprehensive*, p. 50, 1968.
28. Anthony Bullivant, op. cit., p. 30.

29. Denis Marsden, op. cit., p. 35.
30. Albert Rowe, then head of David Lister Comprehensive, Hull, quoted in *Observer*, 15 September 1968.
31. John Sharp, quoted in Gordon C. Bessey (Chief Education Officer Cumberland), address to RIBA, 1968.
32. Anthony Bullivant, op. cit.
33. Eric Midwinter, op. cit.

Conclusions and Recommendations*

As we have seen, comprehensive education is now securely established in Britain – and none too soon in view of the urgent requirements of social, scientific and technological advance that make the raising of educational standards and the widening of opportunities for all so imperative. Although the comprehensive reform has been supported by many educationists and ordinary people, it is the comprehensive schools themselves that have really pioneered it and comprehensive staff whose hard and careful work has consolidated it.

As comprehensive schools continue to widen educational horizons, enabling more pupils to stay longer in school and to obtain qualifications, and helping all pupils to participate more meaningfully in the total educational process provided through a community-supported and community-based school, the movement inevitably continues to gain support. It has been accepted by the great majority of the teaching profession, parents, and students themselves, and by all political parties. Historically, the concept of two types of school for two types of pupil is now dead. The only real outstanding argument is that of pace.

It would be wrong to assume, however, that a last-ditch stand will not be made to retain selective schools – both state and fee-paying – for the benefit of the very 'gifted', however variously this may be defined, and for the very wealthy. Once a sound and universal comprehensive system has been established for everyone from eleven to eighteen, a fractional percentage of selective schools or a hangover sector for the rich is not necessarily alarming. What is alarming, however, is the prospect of continued systematic support by governments, the Department of Education and Science, and many local education authorities for 'two sectors' of secondary education.

Many of our findings reveal the harmful and undermining effects that a policy of systematic 'coexistence' of selective schools has upon comprehensive schools. This effect is the same whether the 'coexisting' sector schools are maintained, direct grant or voluntary-aided grammar schools, selective 'interim' comprehensive schools, or fee-paying schools with

* Our main recommendations are numbered and printed in italics.

selective places paid for by an authority. The impossibility of state support for both selective and comprehensive systems side by side is clearly understood both by many of those who support, and oppose, reorganization: where systematic coexistence remains there are no genuine comprehensive schools. A decision – one way or the other – must be taken. Failure to do this to date has resulted in piecemeal reorganization, prolonged retention of selection, including substitution of one kind of 11-plus for another, and a sterile deadlock in many weary education committees and editorial columns – long after the real decision has been taken for Britain by world conditions necessitating an open secondary system to permit the raising of educational standards, and maximization of skill and talent, and a more equitable redistribution of resources to meet the needs and problems existing and arising. A decision is also necessary to meet the growing demands of parents for full opportunity for their children and the demands of young people for a chance to understand themselves, their environment and their world through access to the mainstream of education.

(1) Our first recommendation, therefore, is that *a clear and positive national decision be taken in favour of a comprehensive system up to the age of eighteen years and that legislation to implement this decision be introduced.* Not until this decision has been taken and its consequences underwritten can the full reform be completed.

Circular 10/65 was a national statement of the lines upon which it was hoped comprehensive secondary schools would develop. But it had two major faults. Firstly, it did not specifically envisage a comprehensive system, but only the *ad hoc* introduction of comprehensive schools when, as, and if the 160 or so individual authorities and their committees could make up their minds, and keep them made up, to introduce such schools. Second, it was only a request. No authority was required in law to end selection or to introduce a single comprehensive school. Circular 10/70 did not even request comprehensive schools. It was merely a national re-statement of the 1944 Act's belief in different types of school to cater for different types of secondary-age pupils: both selective and non-selective. It underwrote a policy of coexistence for comprehensives, ensuring they would not develop as truly comprehensive in many areas but would be expected to exist side by side with grammar schools indefinitely. Some comprehensive schools can continue to exist while a two-sector system remains, but a comprehensive system of schools cannot be properly developed. The object of a comprehensive reform is not the introduction of more and more comprehensive schools, it is a changeover from a two-sector system where selection by ability must be retained in some form, to a comprehensive system of schools where selection by ability is no longer necessary, since all schools will be able to take in, and provide for, pupils of all abilities.

To be effective, legislation for a comprehensive reform must do three things – ensure (i) that every authority plans ahead in respect of every single one of the secondary schools in that authority; (ii) that these plans are compatible with a non-selective comprehensive system of secondary education throughout that authority and throughout the age range of 11–18; and (iii) that plans are worked out to be operable within a named and definite period of time. None of these expectations is unreasonable. On the contrary, what is unreasonable is that almost thirty years after comprehensive schools were first introduced, and seven years after circular 10/65 and the whole reorientation of secondary education, dozens of areas are without plans of any kind for the future of many of their secondary schools, dozens more have only the vaguest undated intentions, and the 11-plus itself or its substitutes are continuing for the majority of pupils in the country.

(2) Our second recommendation, therefore, is that *entry to schools should not be based on any form of social or academic selection*. To those who say this is impossible, we would commend present experience in the primary sector. Entry to primary schools, although not without problems, is not based on academic or social selection. Secondary-school and middle-school and sixth-form-college entrance should be the same. Selective divides at any age should be ended for good.

To those who say 'resources' do not permit reorganization, or that there is not enough money to make all schools in a given area equally comprehensive in provision so that selection at eleven or twelve or thirteen may be ended, we would say: look carefully at all the areas that have done just this. They did not do it overnight, but they show that once a clear decision in favour of a comprehensive system itself is taken, reorganization – within the limits of financial reality – has been perfectly possible within a reasonable period of time. At the same time, and as we argue presently, extra funds for certain aspects of the reform are essential.

Once a national decision has been taken in favour of a comprehensive system (abandoning the present policy of merely introducing a limited number of comprehensive schools into the bipartite system), it then becomes possible to work towards the setting of guidelines within which schools can develop. Obviously local tradition and decisions shape the pattern of schools. A comprehensive system is not uniform, as we have seen all too clearly. In fact, the very multiplicity of different age ranges in different types of comprehensive schools, and in further education from 16 to 18, makes it essential that certain definite policy decisions be taken and rules laid down to guide the reform.

(3) Our third recommendation is that *steps be taken to ensure parity of provision between all schools in the school system – from five through eighteen.* With the wide variety of school types developing (there are twenty-two different age ranges for schools at the time of writing), it is essential that within each age range there should be clearly defined regulations governing staffing, class size, general curriculum provision, buildings, equipment, laboratories and play space. Most crucial of all perhaps is the present inequality of the allowance structure which gives such advantages to schools with older age pupils. A re-examination of this whole field – possibly based on the NFER's suggestion that size of school and not age of pupils should be the determining factor – is urgently needed.

Meanwhile, it is wholly illogical and totally unsatisfactory that a comprehensive school, which must deal with the full-ability range and teach the whole complex of subjects available for every age range in the one school, should have a higher staffing ratio (in terms of more pupils per staff) than a school which is only required, as is a grammar school, to deal with a much smaller sector of ability and a far narrower range of subjects.

(4) *The staffing ratio of comprehensive schools must be redefined, therefore, on a realistic basis. This must include a review of allocations of posts of special responsibility and graded posts, and a re-examination of the whole points system at present in operation in respect of secondary schools.* Such restructuring is necessary not only to meet the true needs of the developing system of secondary education, but of specific schools particularly. One such group of schools urgently requiring special attention is schools in areas of special difficulty, for which provision of more posts of special responsibility and, perhaps, a range of special services and support, is needed. As we have shown, the extent of severely deprived

(5) comprehensive schools is not wide, but it may well be deep. *The principle of extra support for certain schools in certain circumstances – educational priority area schools – must be continuous throughout education and not arbitrarily confined to the years below eleven.*

Decisions such as these must be taken nationally, but they require close local-authority cooperation. Some problems require local-authority initiative in even greater measure. One is more local-authority attention to the problem of the administrative needs of comprehensive schools. Help here is urgently required by comprehensive schools and

(6)*local authorities must have clear national guidelines in order to help schools with their clerical, administrative, caretaking and secretarial tasks.* As we have shown, the need is most urgent in the large comprehensive which inevitably has become a community centre as well as a school. The special needs of schools above a certain size – different in kind and not just degree – also need to be recognized. That comprehensive schools can be administered and staffed efficiently and effectively and provide full opportunity for all pupils is evident in the few schools that already receive generous support from their authorities. This kind of support is essential for all comprehensive schools.

As selection is abolished, it becomes necessary to ensure that all comprehensive schools are equitably provided for, efficiently administered and realistically staffed, with each age range assured of parity of provision regardless of the age span covered by the schools. Because this will be difficult and costly, the temptation to semi-reorganize and to fall back on two 'types' of comprehensive is very great. One of the tasks facing parents throughout the 1970s, therefore, will be to discern the true nature of the transfer procedure in their areas and to regularly compare the education inside all their local comprehensive schools. For if guidance between schools on the basis of the 'different type' of education provided in each is maintained – even if the authority names both types 'comprehensive' – this is still selection. So long as the issue of a comprehensive system is dodged, and gross inequalities persist between schools, so long will 'two kinds' of school be maintained, and so long will parents understandably press for entry to one kind rather than another. So long too will the whole question of parental choice in education remain confined within the old and narrow eleven-plus limits of a 'choice' of one type of school for the few, but guidance to the other (7)type for the many. *In a fully comprehensive system all parents must have choice and the choice that is obviously crucial is the one that will be available inside each comprehensive school.* If communities press for fully comprehensive systems, where each school is equally well provided for, staffed and equipped, if they make certain that education committees do not retain two 'types' of comprehensive, and if, in addition, they press for a full range of subjects, options and facilities within all the authority's schools, then the possibility of parental choice for all will become real for the first time in secondary education in Britain.

None of this can be achieved without actively planning and re-distributing resources on a more equitable basis both nationally and locally. As we have said, the law must require each local authority to draw up, date and make public its plans for the future of each school in each area. For it is this planning that is so urgently required. The failure to plan is at the heart of much national difficulty in education, and particularly in the secondary sector. The *laissez-faire* attitude is gradually changing, however, and many educationists now criticize the traditional 'muddling through'.[1] Planning and priorities are needed, they say, and 'if priorities mean anything, they must mean ranking objectives in order'.[2] A first objective, we would suggest, is a firm national decision to commit the country to a system of comprehensive schools.

Failure to commit the nation to systematic reorganization has meant a failure to allocate that share of available resources necessary to implement a comprehensive reorganization policy at the required level and (8)in the required time. *A national policy decision is therefore required to ensure that the principle of special funds for special aspects of the comprehensive reform (e.g. for major buildings) is revived and that these funds are adequate.*

When the country finally makes its decision to introduce a comprehensive reform, it will be necessary to have some body at the centre – perhaps based in the Department of Education and Science – with the staff and expert assistance available to help local authorities in the many problems which will arise as they reorganize to meet the statutory requirements Parliament will lay down. The situations prevailing under both Labour and Conservative governments in the 1960s and 1970s, when long delays were experienced by local authorities waiting for plans to be 'passed', need not arise if a large and efficient staff of advisers is operating within the department. Moreover, any Secretary of State will need advice about the way in which to make grants available to local authorities needing special extra assistance to complete their reorganization or to rationalize their local resources in order to provide for its needs within a comprehensive system of education.

A national policy decision backed by legislation is necessary in respect of the DES, for governments come and go; the department's politicians are permanent. The policy pursued from the 1960s and still with us – of merely introducing more and more comprehensives into a bipartite system as and when local authorities wish (and reverse when they wish) – with no national coordination, no central direction, or national decision-making, and inadequate information, will not achieve a meaningful comprehensive reform. A firm commitment to reorganize in law is required to get a firm commitment from the department itself – in terms of redeployment of departmental time and staff and resources to man the machinery which will be required to carry out the decision and to coordinate reorganization's final phase, (9)particularly for the 16–19 age group. *It also requires that the department of education, together with the local authorities – both such important power centres in educational decision-making – must be open to much more public scrutiny.* We have a right to know the reasoning behind the decisions taken by the permanent politicians no less than by the temporary ones.

Failure to plan on a national scale for the transition to comprehensive education is particularly apparent in the training and education of (10) teachers. *Commitment to a comprehensive system requires a complete reconstruction of the content and methods of teacher education.* Yet the James Committee, which reported early in 1972, made no mention of comprehensive schools; nor, indeed, were its proposals related in any way to developments in the school system. Comprehensive schools pose quite new problems for teachers, not only in relation to teaching itself, but also to their role in terms of guidance, pastoral care, counselling and the neighbourhood function of the comprehensive school. In the reorientation of teacher education the key task is to break down rigid divisions between teachers, resulting from different lengths of education and training and the primary/secondary and grammar/modern differentiation. Comprehensive education provides a means to do this.

In-service training also needs to be viewed as a whole and within the context of a clear and definite commitment to schools containing the full range of ability. Courses are called for to equip staff with the techniques required to pace reorganization as it develops, to master problems of curriculum change and mixed-ability teaching, and to cover special training in such matters as guidance, counselling and remedial teaching. The main proposal of the James Committee for one term's leave every five years for all teachers must be implemented.

It is said that an adequate supply of 'good' teachers, and thus a full range of subjects in all comprehensive schools, is problematical because of the scarcity of qualified staff, particularly in mathematics and science. We would not deny national shortages in many fields, nor the continuing difficulty of maintaining expenditure on education nationally at the level required to ensure adequate staffing. We have already urged appropriation of the funds necessary to complete the comprehensive reform within a reasonable period of time. But finance is only part of the problem. Planning is just as crucial. The Department of Education and Science now has a planning branch and once a national decision is taken to plan a fully comprehensive system targets must be set for a teaching force at all levels and in all subjects – as well as for the necessary overall expenditure – adequate to realize the reform.
(11) *A national campaign to meet this target must be launched, linked with expansion of in-service training, the salaries and conditions appropriate*

to a reconstructed teaching force, and provision of a full range of technical resources and aids.

The resumption of national direction of this reform from the centre requires the staffing and equipping of an effective research organization, perhaps even the setting up of an Education Research Council as (12) an independent funding organization. *There must be regular and full information on the progress of reorganization, including the monitoring of all research into comprehensive education itself and the popularization of results.* Since comprehensive education requires interdisciplinary research – particularly in the fields of sociology, psychology and social psychology, using techniques that can be found in fields as apparently far apart as anthropology and operational research – an effective network for research should involve universities and colleges of education in addition to other research bodies. A plurality of research centres properly coordinated may well be the best way to provide the feedback and guidance that this reform, among others, urgently requires.

Although the reorientation of the DES to monitor and guide reorganization is essential, in addition certain other reforms are required. Many would have been necessary in any case; reorganization (13) merely makes them more urgent. The first is that *the GCE O-level examination must be abolished and an end put to the absurdity of a double examination at sixteen.* The CSE examination is now securely established, is suitable for the whole ability range, is widely thought to be a better examination for any ability level than the GCE, and in its mode III form, the one we would recommend, is suitable for use by all types of comprehensive schools in all stages of development in all areas. This reform would consolidate present academic achievement in the comprehensive school, revitalize and make relevant subject and interdisciplinary teaching, and open the possibility of educational qualifications for the whole range of pupils, since CSE in at least one subject should be a possibility for all pupils in Britain. Most pupils would pursue an examination course in most subjects eventually – as many already do in comprehensive schools. Any attempt to make a new first external examination available to a limited percentage of pupils – as the Schools Council has suggested in its *Examining at 16 plus* – would seriously distort the curriculum in comprehensive schools and create new divisions just at the moment when old ones were being ended. So too would any attempt to make this first examination 'optional' – that is, able to be taken early by some pupils or by-passed by others – so that it becomes a second-class examination for the majority. It is essential for the success of comprehensive education that a unified five-year secondary course, leading to a single examination at the same point in time for all – albeit subject to individual subject choices in part – should be provided for all pupils, not just for some pupils.

GCE at A-level is also an examination clearly in need of reform, not only because of the narrowness of its syllabus in individual subjects, which in turn restricts post-sixteen study to a small minority, but because its effect is to force premature specialization upon pupils and the preparation for it upon schools. It is now evident that the universities themselves want pupils to have a secondary education that will cover the main fields of knowledge up to eighteen: basic requirements, perhaps, being mathematics, English, a foreign language, a science, and social science – with all of which could go, **(14)** perhaps, linked electives. Eventually *a new examination will be required to promote this development, an examination that initially 50 per cent of the population at least should be capable of taking since it will not be a specialist's examination.* Specialization should not be the schools' prime concern: theirs is to provide a broad-based education for all – both for those who will end education at eighteen, as well as for those who will continue. Specialization is a matter for higher education, whose requirements should no longer reach down into and distort so unduly the all-important process of raising educational standards for the majority of pupils in the secondary stage. At the present time the sixth forms of many comprehensive schools are artificially divided between two or more A-level students taking the orthodox course and the others (pursuing a variety of work including GCE courses). The newly proposed Certificate of Extended Education seeks to regularize – and widen – this new division by formally setting a second-level course to students not 'capable' of ordinary A-level work. While these divisions may be necessary in a transition situation, the time will come when not only has A-level work been broadened but the voluntary staying on in full-time education will be so high for the 16–19 age group that the distinctions between those who are on a 'high' academic course and those on a 'low' one will become increasingly artificial and unacceptable just as they are now at 14–16. For this reason a single examination goal at eighteen, as at sixteen – far more flexible and wider than the present A-level – is desirable in the long run.

(15) In this respect we would draw attention again to the need to *drop the requirement of Latin for many of the university courses for which it is now required.* Latin was the international language of the middle ages and hence of great importance at one time, but its continuance in today's curriculum cannot be justified as any more important than any other of the dead languages, e.g. Greek. Since the first edition of this book Oxford University, for example, has dropped Latin as a language qualification for University entrance requirements joining most other universities in this, of course, although many still retain Latin for individual course requirements. It could be retained in schools for those who opt for it, but it should be a requirement only for those who intend to pursue the subject itself in higher education or to pursue special disciplines – like ancient history – requiring direct knowledge of Latin texts. The international language of today is mathematics, and it is this subject in which greater proficiency should be required to far higher levels for all university and college entrants. It is because of the importance of mathematics that we have made one of the (16)conditions of our complete comprehensive school that it *teach mathematics (which includes arithmetic) to all pupils in every year in the school.* Only by realistic and relevant requirements of this kind – rather than by unnaturally prolonging the life of dying disciplines – can educational standards be meaningfully raised.

Meanwhile, resources – both of plant and of people – can be rationalized. One of the further urgent needs that will be met by a national decision to reorganize and by the subsequent requirement to local authorities to plan in respect of all their secondary schools is the need to use all available resources to the fullest advantage. This is crucial throughout education, but particularly so in secondary education. In many places in this book we have given examples of the ways in which individual communities and comprehensive schools share resources and pupils and cooperate with each other and with local further education and technical colleges in the provision of a wide range of subjects and courses for a community. These developments should be encouraged, and successful rationalization methods and use of resources and aids made more widely known. But although rationalization is urgent, the temptation to remove sixth forms from existing comprehensive schools or to fail to agree to their being built up in certain areas because present 'numbers' do not immediately justify their provision, would be short-sighted. More than short-sighted are, and would be, decisions to 'concentrate' sixth forms in existing grammar schools, for this is a barely disguised retention of the bipartite system and of eleven-plus selection, as we have clearly seen.

If the last twenty-five years has taught us anything about planning or about the rise in demand for education, it is that the former has never anticipated, nor been able to meet, the latter. We need not inevitably make these same mistakes again, but if it means that certain schools must be overstaffed temporarily until pupil numbers increase, then this must be accepted as part of a reasoned plan towards the ultimate objective of full-time education for all pupils in the country up to the age of eighteen. The comprehensive sixth form, as it is now developing in many schools, is the ideal base upon which to organize an extension of comprehensive opportunity beyond the age of sixteen. But there is a danger that, with a school-leaving age of sixteen coinciding with the first national external examinations, and so many separate-sixth schemes planned, some authorities will try to make sixteen a cut-off point and to have education selective thereafter. This must be firmly resisted. The eleven plus should have taught us the lesson that any barrier put up, however reasonable at the time, ends up (17)a barricade. To avoid a fight at sixteen-plus *we must plan now to make full-time education until the age of eighteen available for all*. The battle for it beyond eighteen is about to begin in any case. We can get away with no less.

The reforms we have been discussing have been national, requiring for the most part national decisions and allocation of resources. Those we come to now are local, requiring local support and initiative and, for reforms inside the schools, dependent upon the particular policy pursued by head teachers and staff. We have already seen how comprehensive schools are developing as community schools, serving a neighbourhood and identifying with it. This is a significant development, for it means that local participation in secondary education will for the first time become a possibility on a nation-wide scale. To meet this demand for effective participation the government of schools must be ready to change. Governing bodies are in many respects outmoded. It is not just that their political composition is no longer accepted as representative of the community interest in education, but that many of their overseeing functions have been usurped by the inspectorate on the one hand and the local authority on the other. In addition, many governors are remote from schools. Effective governorship of community schools requires men and women who closely reflect the immediate interests of the school and the community it serves. They should be able to act as a court of appeal for staff, student and parent committees and in this connection, their duties and powers may well need redefining in the context of their relationship to the school's own elected bodies: staff councils, student councils and parents' associations. Their relationship to the education committees may also need redefining, for it is probably the case that the governing bodies of the future will not have the same kind of contact with the new large local government units as they had with local education authorities. It may well be that the whole process of contact needs revising – the governing bodies no longer the arms of the Education Committees, but the arms of the local community instead. They could well be given more discretion in the use of resources within the school, within the total budget allocated. This is why governors should be free to act as the schools' representatives, secure that they enjoy the confidence of the staff and parents and (18)pupils. To do this effectively requires that *parents, staff and senior pupils must be represented on governing bodies – elected there by the groups they represent, and making up at least half the body.*

Secondly, fully effective governorship of a comprehensive school in most cases cannot be carried out in isolation, school-by-school. (19)*Representatives from all governing bodies in an area must themselves meet together regularly for discussion of mutual problems affecting all schools in the area.* The problem of liaison, of allocation procedures between schools and colleges, and of sharing facilities and resources are examples of subjects that require community decision-making and discussion by joint bodies of this kind. Governing bodies must also cease to operate entirely in secret, giving a wholly unnecessary air of remoteness and conspiracy to their activities. In addition to their regular meetings and meetings with neighbouring schools governing bodies they should certainly have public meetings in which they, and their decisions in respect of the schools – and more important, the education committee decisions – are open to question and discussion by the school and the wider community. It is in this way that governing bodies can themselves act as representatives of their local communities when it comes to raising matters with the elected education committees and the local authority. When authorities are enlarged to twice their present size, neighbourhood democratic 'committees' of the kind that reformed governing bodies would represent, will in fact be essential to preserve the grass roots connection to education at the local level.

While schools individually can be given more say in the way they run their school and in the disposition of available resources, it is obvious that the needs of the schools must be kept in balance in each (20)area. *Allocation of pupils to schools should be under the control of the wider community and its elected representatives* who will have the task of devising and supervising – and periodically reviewing – entry policy and transfer systems between schools within their areas – with the object of ascertaining a fair and workable and community-agreed system of allocation.

Since the comprehensive school is developing as a community school in the great majority of areas, we recommend that whatever method of allocation of pupils be chosen in respect of each authority or individual school, it should be based upon a recognition of the immense value of the neighbourhood nature of the comprehensive school. While all schools and authorities will seek to minimize and overcome any disadvantages any individual school may have, experience so far has shown that successful comprehensive schools seek to build upon the positive advantages and special nature of their own particular communities and that only in so building can they hope to raise educational standards for *all* pupils in the area, and, at the same time, to engage the support of all parents in their task.

Nevertheless, one of the problems that will loom very large in the next decade is the precise method of allocation between comprehensive schools that will best meet the needs of schools in each area. Should allocation be by zoning, by choice, by ability banding, by feeder schools, or by some combination of two or more of these? Each of these methods has distinct advantages and disadvantages. Communities need to know much more about the long-term operation of these various methods, however, so that agreement on the method adopted can be made with a full knowledge of the consequences and (21)effects on schools of each. *We recommend, therefore, as a matter of urgency, that a continuing research programme be undertaken into different methods of allocation.* This should be extended over several years, and should aim both to monitor methods already in operation and to evaluate the effects of each method in relation to specific educational criteria. We regard research of this kind, undertaken on a national basis and examining different local systems operating in a variety of socio-economic conditions, as research of the first importance for the future of the comprehensive reform, far more valuable than continuing attempts to discover the 'best way' to pick 'grammar' pupils, which, nationally, we still continue to support.

Although we profoundly believe in the value of a close connection between the individual comprehensive school and its own local community, we also recognize that for many children at a certain stage in their education, and for a few children for the whole of their education, boarding education is necessary and may be of value. As we know, many comprehensive schools already have successful boarding houses and wings attached, which already meet the boarding needs, both termly and weekly, of pupils from a particular region. To meet (22)any national boarding need that develops in the future, *we recommend that the present practice of boarding wings and houses attached to ordinary comprehensive day schools be extended to selected comprehensive schools throughout the country, so that all regions are covered.* Although we are not necessarily against experiments of a different nature, we feel that, in the interests of the majority of pupils in the country with boarding needs, it is best to avoid becoming dependent on, or in any way involved in a prolonged argument over, the future of a handful of prestige fee-paying schools whose ethos, circumstances and philosophy of education differ so markedly from the experience of the majority of boys and girls in Britain.

We have stressed the need for democratic participation inside the (23)schools as well as in the neighbourhood community. *Elected student councils, already encouraged in so many comprehensive schools, must eventually be established in every school with senior pupils.* These will take over more and more responsibility for certain well-defined activities and matters within the school and foreshadow the participation young people will be demanding, or asked to enter into, as adults. Pupils will then be in a position to help solve their own problems, and to be consulted about wider decisions, in a way that those in the old closed or selective institutions were neither allowed, nor encouraged, to do.

Staff councils, too, are of very great importance in a comprehensive school, especially a large one. The assistant teacher needs to be involved in decision-making as well as the head of each department. All staff should have a 'voice' in policy and know exactly what is going on throughout the school, if education as a cooperative effort is to become a reality. Achievement of the necessary reforms in teaching and in curricula that reorganization has both responded to and encouraged, depends on effective, flexible and democratic staff organization in (24)each school: *a staff council must be made a statutory requirement just as academic boards now are at colleges of education and polytechnics.*

Contact with all parents at least once in each school year might also be made statutory. Not only would this maintain links between home and school but help to ensure that pupils and parents have advice and guidance upon the important decisions made throughout the school career. The method of organizing counselling may differ from school (25)to school, but whatever the one adopted, *pastoral care and guidance must be systematically organized in respect of each individual pupil for each year of school life.* Guidance cannot be left to the 'high' points, age thirteen or age fifteen, nor pastoral care to an emergency. Both must be conceived of as continuing and integral parts of day-to-day education. In this connection all teachers need some preparation for the counselling role, but especially those who have charge of pastoral (26)units or who have received special training in counselling. *It is essential that all staff with pastoral responsibility be given the time in which to discharge it*. This is another urgent reason for improving the staffing ratio of the comprehensive school. At present most pastoral staff do not get anything like adequate time off teaching.

This brings us to the evolution of the comprehensive school itself, its policy and goals, the most important matter. Here responsibility rests with each school. Whatever the political decisions taken nationally or locally, the truly comprehensive evolution of the re-organized school depends on the individual school itself.

One prerequisite for a comprehensive school is a common course in the first year. This should cover experience in the main areas of knowledge and skills required by all citizens today: the humanities (history, geography, English), the social sciences, science, mathematics, a foreign language, together with aesthetic, technical and physical education. Already many schools carry such a course through (27) three years. *With the abolition of O-level and the institution of a single examination for all at the leaving age of sixteen, the common course, or common core, of studies should be extended to five years. In Scotland where the parallelism between O- and H-grades should be eliminated, a four-year course will be possible, and vital as a mark of genuine re-organization.*

The type of curriculum organization for the years thirteen to sixteen which seems most suited to the eventual introduction of a single examination and extension of a common course to sixteen, is that already adopted in the majority of comprehensive schools: part required subjects (or areas of study) for all pupils, part individual (28) options. *In this connection we recommend that no options be closed to any pupils on grounds of sex.* This extension of opportunity could be realized at once in all mixed comprehensive schools, and planned for elsewhere.

The adding of options to required parts of the course should start on a limited basis at the age of thirteen or fourteen. The question as to which subject areas should be 'required', and the number and rate of introduction of options, are matters calling for research on the basis of experience to date. What seems less desirable, and where now operating restrictive of choice, is the practice of total package courses, among which pupils must choose at fourteen or fifteen. The isolated 'leavers'' course seems especially undesirable, and is more so now that the leaving age is sixteen; to categorize a fourteen or fifteen year old as a 'leaver' is likely to preordain this outcome. Equally the segregation from the mainstream of the school of both remedial pupils and 'express streams' (intended to take examinations early) seems undesirable. Schools have successfully incorporated pupils needing extra help in normal classes, either withdrawing them at stated periods for special attention or involving remedial teachers in the ongoing work of the class (or adopting both measures). To engage all pupils in a common course from the outset, without isolating any special groups, is to work realistically towards raising and consolidating educational standards; moreover schools that have done this have also (29) avoided a number of problems of discipline. *Schools should be encouraged to review at regular intervals all practices involving segregation of groups of pupils, taking account of available research findings, experience elsewhere, and the effect of special grouping on the pupils concerned and the school community.*

The practice of strict streaming, inevitably carried over from a bipartite system incorporating selection at eleven and differentiation after that age, is clearly incompatible with the development of fully comprehensive education. Most comprehensive schools are now exploring one or another of the many alternative ways of grouping pupils. While unstreaming is almost universally recognized as educationally desirable it is often seen as very difficult to accomplish. An important aid would be a planned programme of courses to prepare teachers to work in the unstreamed class situation, organized by professional centres, colleges, university education departments. But the remarkable improvement resulting from unstreaming in many subject disciplines in so many comprehensive schools, and the continually accelerating swing in this direction, is proof that schools can success- (30) fully introduce this reform. In our view, *schools must be encouraged to abolish streaming and similar methods of grouping. Research must be undertaken, exchange of experience about the teaching of unstreamed classes arranged, the necessary resource-centre aids and materials provided, to assist schools to develop the new forms of individual and group work essential to unstreaming.*

A number of the recommendations we have made – for a common course, for internally set and externally moderated national examinations, for unstreamed grouping of pupils throughout the secondary age range – will have repercussions on education after the age of sixteen. The demand for this is bound to grow rapidly. Inevitably the post-sixteen group in school or junior college will to some extent be self-selected, those who have chosen to stay on. But much can be (31) done to encourage the choice. *All comprehensive schools and colleges should operate an entirely open sixth year. All pupils should be permitted to continue their education to the 'next year' as a matter of right – regardless of qualifications already gained and the programme of study for which they have opted.* This is a policy that many authorities can introduce at once. The proposed Certificate of Extended Education (CEE) specifically for the 'new' ('non-academic'?) sixth-former, to be taken at seventeen, is retrograde. Instead A-level should give way to a far more broadly based examination, suitable for *all* staying on to eighteen. Meanwhile sixth forms or their equivalent in colleges will, besides providing A-level courses, encourage and enable pupils to take, or retake, subjects at O-level and for CSE, and provide general or vocational courses for those who have not chosen to work for examinations. Where necessary, institutions can cooperate to provide a range of full- and part-time education for the post-sixteen age group; just as, in some areas, this will be covered by the single 'junior college'. When there is such cooperation, each pupil should be attached to one school or college which he can regard as his main base.

Consideration of sixth-form planning underlines how essential it is for the comprehensive school or college to be flexible, to regard no decision as absolutely final, to seek continually to align administration, curriculum, teaching methods, relations between school and community, with educational objectives. While firm forward planning is necessary nationally and locally to provide a secure framework for comprehensive reform, it rests with individual schools regularly to review their practice so that they can progressively profit from experience. That they should be able to do this requires both a firm educational purpose and a flexibility which allows for easy adaptation and readiness for innovation.

Quite obviously the lines upon which many feel genuine comprehensive schools should develop, and towards which many are already working, will take time to achieve. What we have set out are long-term goals, not measures of current achievement. But at the same time we have shown that a remarkable number of comprehensive schools have already attained many of these goals. That so many comprehensive schools should have already progressed this far is most remarkable. It makes the failure of so many authorities even to experiment with a single comprehensive school seem all the more retrograde. It also underlines dramatically the severe inequalities that still exist in Britain – with students in some authorities guaranteed access to full educational opportunity right up to eighteen while students in other authorities are still being labelled a 'success' or a 'failure' at the age of eleven or twelve and shunted into schools with limited courses and a narrow range of subjects.

This half and half system cannot be allowed to continue indefinitely. No community or government can justify it as long-term policy. A national commitment to a completely comprehensive system of educa-

tion is more urgent than ever so that access to full educational opportunity up to the age of eighteen – so obviously a possibility in all areas
and so clearly a reality in many already – may the more quickly
become the *right* of every girl and boy in Britain.

Notes

1. Stuart Maclure, now editor of *The Times Educational Supplement*,
writing in *Education*, 16 May 1969.
2. ibid.

Appendices

Appendix 1
Notes

1. NFER reports

In 1965 a government working party, set up to advise on comprehensive education, recommended a large-scale research project be undertaken on comprehensive schools. In 1966 the National Foundation for Educational Research (NFER) was commissioned to undertake the main programme over a period of eight years.

In 1968 the first-stage Report, an objective factual description of comprehensiveness in 331 schools in 1965–6, was published: *Comprehensive Education in England and Wales*, edited by T. G. Monks. It is to this publication that we refer as the First NFER Report.*

Our present inquiry covered just over twice as many schools as the NFER's did and was made two and a half years after. Since many of the questions we asked were the same as those asked by the NFER, we were able to measure 'progress' during the two- to three-year period in some important areas of reorganization.

In 1970, a report covering the second phase of the NFER inquiry was published. This was *Comprehensive Education in Action*, edited by T. G. Monks. It surveyed fifty-nine schools about their administration, curriculum, attainment and extra-curricular activities. We refer to this as the Second NFER Report. A final 'evaluative' report based on a study of twelve schools, *A Critical Appraisal of Comprehensive Education*, by J. M. Ross, W. J. Burton, P. Evison and T. S. Robertson was published in 1972.

2. Note on the questionnaires

For the first edition of this survey two questionnaires were sent in 1968. For the second edition two follow-up questionnaires were sent in the school year 1971–2.

The first questionnaire (printed in Appendix 3) was sent to all comprehensive schools in England, Wales and Scotland in June 1968. The second questionnaire in 1968 was sent to a smaller sample of forty-four schools. Those schools assisting in answering the second set of questions

* As with our own data, we have rounded all percentages used from this report.

are listed immediately following (pp. 517–19), together with the names of further schools that helped us by permitting visits or by answering specific questions about their schools. As will be seen, these schools are representative of mixed and single-sex schools, denominations, regions, age range (or type) of school and year of foundation as a comprehensive school. The information on procedure and policy obtained from them can probably be said to be fairly representative of current practice.

The first questionnaire was sent to 958 schools in June 1968. The problem of deciding which schools to include was not easy, as anyone investigating comprehensive schools will know. Whose definition of 'comprehensive' was to be used? Was it to be the definition of circular 144, 1947: a school 'which is intended to cater for all the secondary education of all the children in a given area, without an organization into three sides'? Or was it to be one of the definitions used in the NFER Report: a school 'making a substantial effort to cater for the whole ability range'? Or that of the DES in their evidence to the Royal Commission on Local Government: a school which is 'socially and intellectually comprehensive, catering to pupils over the whole ability range, and with different interests and backgrounds'? Or perhaps, just to the schools on the DES provisional list of comprehensive schools for 1967–8?

If any one definition was taken – say the first – the comprehensive schools coexisting with grammar schools would not be able to be counted. But even if we excluded them, we would still be faced with a problem: how can comprehensive schools established for many years be judged in the same way as those just started? The NFER tried to solve this by dividing schools up into 'fully developed' and 'not developed'. But even this had snags. For example, what about schools that might be fully developed but nevertheless in such close competition with existing grammar schools that they never really became comprehensive? The same applies to the NFER division of schools into competing-with and not-competing-with grammar schools. This kind of alteration in the definition, according to the data being analysed, made it hard for the ordinary reader of the NFER Report to see what the statistics revealed about comprehensive schools in general.

In view of all these difficulties we did not therefore attempt to define a comprehensive school for our questionnaire. Or rather, our definition was all-inclusive. A school qualified for our list of comprehensive schools if it fell into one of four categories: first, if it was on the provisional list of comprehensive schools prepared each year by the Department of Education and Science; second, if it was listed as comprehensive in the annual Yearbooks of the Association of Education Committees; third, if it was named as comprehensive in local authority publications or by education officers in their correspondence;* and fourth, if the school itself claimed to be comprehensive or to be the only school providing secondary education to all the pupils in its area.

There were very few schools in the fourth category, and the third category added only a few more to the largest categories, which were the first and second. Nevertheless, the third and the fourth categories were important. For example, they enabled us to include a number of bilateral schools, for certain authorities class their bilateral schools as comprehensive[1] and many other comprehensive schools – especially in Wales – told us they are still really bilateral. The demarcation line between the comprehensive and the bilateral school did not seem sufficiently clear to justify our being rigid in this matter, especially in view of the fact that so many bilateral schools will develop eventually as comprehensive schools.

Another area where the demarcation line seemed blurred was in the matter of ex-grammar schools now operating as upper schools in 10/65 3 schemes. We sent questionnaires to all those which were on the Department's list. Some answered saying they were comprehensive, some answered saying they were not. Others said they would be unable to answer, since they were not sure. This was very largely a reflection of being in transition and of the selective nature of the reorganization scheme. And, as is shown below, transition uncertainty means that the schools actually used in this survey are probably less representative of the very newly established comprehensive schools than of those established for some time.

But it was not merely the ex-selective schools which sometimes could not make up their minds about their own classification. In one Home County authority there is a reorganization scheme of four schools: three lower schools that receive local pupils on an area basis at eleven and an upper school that receives pupils from all three lower schools at a later age. The three lower schools were exactly alike: all are formerly non-selective schools, all about the same size, and in their present schemes, all operating in the same way. Yet when called to answer our first question: 'Are you officially classed as a comprehensive school?', one answered 'Yes', one answered 'No', and the third, though answering the questionnaire itself, left this particular question unanswered.

It was this kind of uncertainty in definition that not only confirmed us in the wisdom of having made our own definition an inclusive one, but that also led us to decide that although 14 per cent of all the schools in our survey answered 'No' to the question: 'Are you officially classed as a

* The correspondence in this case was from the chief officers and directors to the Comprehensive Schools Committee in answer to that committee's annual request for information about existing and planned comprehensive schools.

comprehensive?', we would nevertheless make no distinction between these schools and those answering 'Yes' when analysing replies. Furthermore, when we analysed the nature of the 14 per cent of schools answering 'No', we found a very high percentage of them – 81 per cent – were from categories other than the 11–18 schools and were either rather recently reorganized or of the opinion that the use of the word 'comprehensive' was not one applicable to a 'lower' or an 'upper' school, but only to be reserved for an 11–18 school. In the case of these 11–18 schools, moreover, there were several schools replying who wrote that although they were classed as comprehensive by the DES or their authority, they would nevertheless answer 'No' to this question because they were not, in the head teacher's opinion, 'genuinely' comprehensive. These answers were a gesture of protest at the continued eleven-plus selection in their own authorities that, as they reported, denied them a genuinely non-selective entry.

In Scotland the position was even more complicated. Many Scottish schools claim they have always been 'comprehensive' – which, in terms of intake of all pupils in an area, may be true, but educationists have warned against using the term 'comprehensive' to apply merely to a Scottish school that included both certificate and non-certificate courses.[2]

Certificate and non-certificate courses inside the same school were not always the same as a comprehensive educational provision, especially where direction to courses had taken place prior to entry. This confusion is reflected in official documents in Scotland. For example, when listing the number of comprehensive schools in existence in Scotland in 1967 the 1967 *Scottish Education Statistics* disagrees with *Education in Scotland, Report of the Secretary of State for Scotland* 1967. In the first document, the number of comprehensive schools is put at 149. In the second it is put at 226. The total number of secondary schools in 1967 was 633 and thus the difference – in terms of the progress to reorganization – is very important. It is due almost entirely to a difference in definition. In the first document, the *Statistics*, only schools with non-certificate and O- and H-grade certificate courses are included. In the second, the *Report*, the list of comprehensive schools includes some schools comprehensive in years I and II only, but non-certificate thereafter.

For our survey we relied on two sources for Scotland: the Yearbooks, and information received from directors and chief officers.* Our total of Scottish schools was thus rather less inclusive than would seem to have been possible: ninety-six in all. But the fact that only 9 per cent of all Scottish schools answered 'No' to the question: 'Are you officially classed as a comprehensive?' (against 14 per cent for all schools) suggests that at

* This information was again in respect of CSC's annual surveys.

least the schools that have replied from Scotland show rather less un-certainty about their status than do schools in England and Wales.

Our overall response rate was 81 per cent. The response from Scotland was 73 per cent, from Wales 82 per cent. But although 780 replies were received to the 958 schools sent questionnaires, only 728 schools were able to be included in the final survey. Fifty-two schools had to be excluded. There were three main reasons: either their questionnaires were very incomplete; or their school had in fact amalgamated with another school also on the list and the first school had answered in respect of the whole 'new' school; or their replies were received too late, after the tape had already been prepared for computer analysis. The analysis was made on an ICL 4130 computer, in the Computing Centre of the University College of North Wales, Bangor. The 728 schools programmed represented 76 per cent of the total number. This involved a total of 568,726 pupils.

It is important to look at the schools that could not be included or that did not reply, to see if their exclusion could in any way bias the results.

In all, forty-five authorities had 100 per cent response rates. Twenty authorities had an initial response rate below 75 per cent. Omitting those with bilateral schools only and with less than five schools overall, these – and their response rates – were as follows: Cumberland (73 per cent), Enfield (73 per cent), Haringey (66 per cent), Staffordshire (72 per cent), Manchester (68 per cent), Oldham (66 per cent), Denbighshire (70 per cent), Pembrokeshire (50 per cent), Banffshire (50 per cent), Edinburgh (57 per cent), Glasgow (72 per cent), Southampton (73 per cent), Mid-lothian (62 per cent), Westlothian (71 per cent). These figures reveal that the schools included in our survey are probably less representative of comprehensive schools that are relatively newly established than of those long established. They also show they might be less representative of all-through schools, since the majority of schools in these low-responding areas are 11–18 and 12–18. In Scotland it is obvious that the major lower-responding areas were the two big cities and lowland areas, making the Scottish schools in our survey probably more representative of the smaller towns and outlying areas than of the urban or highly populated parts.

We should also add that 16 per cent of non-responding schools were girls' comprehensive schools and 10 per cent were boys'. This suggests that girls' schools too may be less well represented in the survey than boys' or mixed, as was also the case in the NFER Report.

It should be added that due to a delay in clearing permission from the ILEA for schools to take part, a larger proportion of responding ILEA schools than others were too late for inclusion in the computer program. The ILEA response rate was 80 per cent, but the number of comprehensives that could be included in the survey was only fifty-six out of eighty-one (69 per cent).

It is also important to note that the overall average size of schools in our survey is 789 in England and Wales. This is slightly smaller than the average size of comprehensive schools based on the DES statistics for England and Wales for 1968: 811. This suggests that the smaller schools may be over-represented, perhaps because the larger schools' administrative problems afforded them less time to answer questionnaires!

A follow-up sample survey was carried out in December 1971 (in respect of the school year 1971–2) specifically on grouping in the first (and subsequent) years in comprehensive schools, and on entry conditions for sixth forms. Selection of the sample was made from the 728 schools whose responses were included in the final 1968 survey. A one in five sample was drawn from 11/12–18 (type 1), 11/12–16, and 11/12–14/15 schools; and a one in three sample from 11/12–18 (type II), 11–13, 13–18 and 14–18 schools. The two sixth-form colleges in the original survey were also included.

The schools were grouped by region (p. 570), and randomly selected by type of school within each region. 146 questionnaires were circulated, and 128 replies received. Four schools had been merged with others or (in one case) become primary, thus giving a response rate of 90·1 per cent (128 out of 142).

In the same month in the 1971–2 school year a further follow-up study – on sixth-form size and growth since 1968 – was made. Seventy-one schools which had answered our 1968 survey from the local authorities of Flintshire, Bradford, the West Riding of Yorkshire, Bristol, Swindon, Haringey and Oxfordshire were asked about their present sixth forms. These seventy-one schools represented the total number of comprehensives in our survey from all these areas in 1968. These were chosen because they gave a reasonable variety of urban and rural areas, of regions, and of types of comprehensive school. In fact, comprehensive school 'types' in existence in 1968 were represented fairly exactly by the sample – with the exception of sixth-form colleges. But the most important factor was that the seventy-one schools' sixth forms in 1968 had averaged eighty-three, the exact average size for all the sixth forms of England and Wales in our 1968 survey of comprehensive schools with sixth forms (see p. 197). Of the seventy-one schools re-surveyed sixty replied (a response rate of 84·5 per cent). Four schools replied too late for inclusion.

3. Statistics and tables

As with the NFER Report, our own inquiry produced a large number of statistics and tables. We have not included tables of all results in this book because there was not the space. Occasionally we have therefore quoted statistics without reproducing the complete table.

4. Percentage figures

In all our tables – both here and in the text – most percentage figures have been rounded. For this reason a few columns may not add up to 100 per cent.

5. School totals

Slight inconsistencies in the totals of schools in different categories in different tables are due to the fact that schools were not always sure into which categories they should place themselves. For instance, a school may have pupils staying on to take GCE O-levels in a sixth year, and would therefore appear in statistics dealing with numbers in the sixth form, but might not be included in statistics dealing with schools claiming to have a sixth form, since the head might not have placed the school in the latter category.

Notes

1. Birmingham's 1968 reorganization document, p. 1, and correspondence from the Chief Education Officer of Cambridgeshire who wrote that the Department of Education and Science had agreed that bilateral schools there 'meet the demands of 10/65'.
2. G. S. Osborne, *Scottish and English Schools*, p. 2, 1966.

Schools answering second questionnaire

Alva Academy, Alva, Clackmannanshire, Scotland
Allerton Grange School, Leeds
Aston Woodhouse High School, Swallownest, W. Riding, Yorkshire
Banff Academy, Banffshire, Scotland
Bicester School, Bicester, Oxfordshire
Brockholes County School, Preston
Calder High School, Mytholmroyd, W. Riding, Yorkshire
Cardigan County Secondary School, Cardiganshire, Wales
Chaucer Comprehensive School, Sheffield
Cirencester School, Cirencester, Gloucestershire
Croxteth Comprehensive School, Liverpool
Duffryn High School, Newport, Monmouthshire, Wales
Dyffryn Ogwen County Secondary School, Bethesda, Caerns, Wales
Felixstowe High School, Felixstowe, Suffolk
Ferneley High School, Melton Mowbray, Leicestershire
Halyard High School, Luton, Bedfordshire
Henry Fanshawe Grammar School, Dronfield, Derbyshire

Holloway School, London
King Edward VI School, Totnes, Devon
Kinning Park Secondary School, Glasgow, Scotland
Lawrence Weston School, Bristol
Longsands School, St Neots, Huntingdonshire
Mayfield School, London
Mellow Lane School, Hayes, Middlesex
Nailsea School, Somerset
Netherall School, Maryport, Cumberland
Ounsdale Comprehensive School, Wombourne, Staffordshire
Peckham Girls' School, London
Rhodesway High School, Bradford, Yorkshire
Ruffwood Comprehensive School, Kirkby, Lancashire
St Illtyd's College, Cardiff, Wales
St Kevin's RC Comprehensive School for Boys, Kirkby, Lancashire
St Teilo's High School, Cardiff, Wales
Saltash County School, Cornwall
Sandfields Comprehensive School, Port Talbot, Glamorgan, Wales
Speke Comprehensive School, Liverpool
Stewards School, Harlow, Essex
Stonehill High School, Leicestershire
The Hereford School, Grimsby, Lincolnshire
Vauxhall Manor School, London
Walworth School, London
Westbourne High School, Swindon
William Penn School, London
Wright Robinson Comprehensive School, Manchester

Additional schools visited or answering specific questions, 1963

Banbury Comprehensive School, Banbury
Bedminster Down Comprehensive School, Bristol
Blessed John Southworth RC School, Preston
Brislington Comprehensive School, Bristol
Brynhyfryd County Secondary School, Ruthin, Denbighshire, Wales
Bushloe High School, Leicestershire
David Hughes Comprehensive School, Anglesey
Dixie Grammar School, Leicestershire
Highbury Grove School, London
Levenshulme High School, Manchester
Myers Grove Comprehensive School, Sheffield
St Bernadette R.C. Comprehensive School, Bristol
Swinton Comprehensive School, Swinton, Yorkshire

The High School, Machyulleth, Montgomeryshire, Wales
Thomas Bennett School, Crawley, Sussex
Towyn School, Towyn, Merionethshire, Wales
West Brideford Comprehensive School, Nottinghamshire

Additional schools visited and supplying information, 1971–2

Belvoir High School, Leicestershire
Exeter College of Further Education
Countesthorpe College, Leicestershire
City of Stoke on Trent Sixth-Form College
The Sixth-Form College, Luton
John Leggott College, Scunthorpe
The Sixth-Form College, Preston
North Devon Technical College and College of Further Education,
 Barnstaple
Wombwell High School, Yorkshire
The Park School, Swindon, Wilts
Elliott School, London

Appendix 2
Tables

Table A.1 Types of comprehensive schools in England and Wales, 1968

Age range of school	Number of schools	Percentage of total schools	Number of pupils	Percentage of total pupils	Average size of school	Percentage of pupils staying on beyond statutory leaving age
11 (or 12)–18 Type I	345	52·1	334,939	64·2	970	56
11 (or 12)–18 Type II*	27	4·1	30,716	5·9	1137	60
11 (or 12)–16	139	21·0	81,715	15·7	587	39
11–13	26	3·9	8887	1·7	341	
11–14/15	69	10·4	34,721	6·7	503	
13–18	34	5·1	18,295	3·5	538	63
14–18	16	2·4	9397	1·8	587	76
16–18 or sixth-form college	2	0·3	1164	0·2	582	
Unknown	3	0·5	1810	0·3		
Totals	661	100	521,644	100		

* With regular transfer of pupils for sixth-form work.

Table A.2 Average school sizes and percentages staying on beyond leaving age in British comprehensive schools, 1968

| Type of school | Geographical areas from which 1968 survey schools drew pupils | | | | | | | | | |
| | City | | Town | | Suburb | | Village and countryside | | Town and country* | |
	Average size	Percentage staying on	Average size	Percentage staying on	Average size	Percentage staying on	Average size	Percentage staying on	Average size	Percentage staying on
11(12)–18(1)	1034	54	1008	54	1056	57	632	52	801	52
11(12)–18(2)	737	49	1207	57	1164	59	906	62	1079	66
11(12)–16	581	27	594	33	618	37	461	43	452	52
11–13	314		485		316		318		—	
11–14/15	355		484		616		380		541	
13–18	483	53	636	64	535	76	—		—	
14–18	—		628	76	433	64	340	50	700	82
16–18	—		582		—		—		—	

* Town and Country – See Table 17.3 for explanation of this category.

Table A.3 **Comprehensive schools, 1968, England and Wales Schools with sixth forms (371* schools)**

Percentage of pupils staying on beyond leaving age	Average size of sixth form	Number of schools
16–20	18	6
21–25	26	6
26–30	31	10
31–35	47	16
36–40	43	20
41–45	58	21
46–50	70	32
51–55	74	25
56–60	63	46
61–65	71	31
66–70	87	64
71–75	113	26
76–80	114	16
81–85	98	13
86–90	135	5
91–95	148	10
96–100	152	24

* Twenty schools with 15 per cent or fewer staying on or without any pupils as yet in the sixth form omitted.

Table A.4 **Percentage of 11/12-plus comprehensive schools with and without a common course or curriculum in the first year, 1968**

England and Wales	*Percentage of each type of school (total numbers in brackets)*					*Total number of schools*	*% of total*
	11/12—18(1)	11/12—18(2)	11/12—16	11/13	11—14/15		
With common course	81	93	82	88	65	488	80·5
Without common course	17	7	17	12	30·5	108	18
Unknown	2		1		4·5	10	1·5
Total number of schools	100 (345)	100 (27)	100 (139)	100 (26)	100 (69)	606	100·0
Scotland							
With common course	82	100	80	33		53	79
Without common course	18		20	67	1	14	21
Unknown							
Total number of schools	100 (44)	100 (4)	100 (15)	100 (3)	100 (1)	67	100

Table A.5 Percentage of 11/12-plus schools with common course: how long continued, 1968

Percentage of each type of school (total numbers in brackets)

England and Wales	11–18(1)	11–18(2)	11–16	11–13	11–14/15	Total	%
Only through first year	23	20	10·5	9	4·5	87	18
Through second year	21	20	41	91	31	145	30
Through third year	54	44	43		53·5	235	48
Through fourth year	0·5	4	2·5		9	9	2
Through fifth year	1·0	4	1			5	1
Unknown	0·5	8	2		2	7	1
Total	100 (281)	100 (25)	100 (114)	100 (23)	100 (45)	488	100

Scotland	12–18(1)	12–18(2)	12–16	12–13	12–14/15	Total	%
Only through first year	69	25	33	100		30	56·5
Through second year	31	50	67			22	41·5
Through third year							
Through fourth year							
Through fifth year							
Unknown		25				1	2
Total	100 (36)	100 (4)	100 (12)	100 (1)		53	100

Table A.6 Percentage of 11/12-plus comprehensive schools beginning a foreign language in each year, 1968, England, Wales and Scotland

	Percentage of each type of school (total numbers in brackets)							
Year begun	*11/12–18(1)*	*11/12–18(2)*	*11/12–16*	*11/12–13*	*11/12–14/15*	*Total*	*%*
In the first year	97	97	97·5	100	91·5	650	97
In second year	2					9	1
In third year	0·5					1	
In fourth year			0·5			1	
In fifth year			0·5		1·5	2	
Not until sixth year							
No foreign language taught			0·5		7	6	1
Unknown	0·5	3	1			4	1
Total	100 (389)	100 (31)	100 (154)	100 (29)	100 (70)	673	100·0

Table A.7 **Percentage of pupils doing a foreign language in 11/12-plus comprehensive schools claiming to provide a common course in first year, 1968, England, Wales and Scotland**

Percentage of each type of school (total numbers in brackets)

Percentage of pupils doing foreign language	11/12–18(1)	11/12–18(2)	11/12–16	11/12–13	11/12–14/15	Total	%
0–25	2	—	5	—	—	13	2·5
25–50	10	7	11	4	2	50	9
50–75	12	10	19	42	31	88	16
75–90	30	24	25	37	27	154	28·5
100	45·5	59	38	17	31	227	42
Unknown	0·5	—	2	—	9	9	2
Total	100 (317)	100 (29)	100 (126)	100 (24)	100 (45)	541	100·0

Table A.8 **First-year grouping by type of school in 11/12-plus comprehensive schools in Britain, 1968**

England and Wales	Percentage of each type of school (total numbers in brackets)					Total number of schools	%
	11–18(1)	11–18(2)	11–16	11–13	11–14/15		
1. In streams	16	15	18·5	38	22	112	18·5
2. In broad-ability bands	37	37	29	19	26	202	33·5
3. In sets	4		8·5	4	10	34	5·5
4. Combination of streams and sets	12	15	19	15·5	17·5	88	14·5
5. Mixed ability (1) (no more than 2 subjects setted)	6	11	9	15·5	1	39	6·5
6. Mixed ability (2) (remedial pupils separated)	12	7	7	8	7	60	10
7. Mixed ability (3) (for all subjects and pupils)	4	7·5	2		6	24	4
8. Other method	8	7·5	6		6	41	6·5
Unknown	1		1		4·5	6	1
Total number of schools	100 (345)	100 (27)	100 (139)	100 (26)	100 (69)	606	100·0

Table A.8 – continued

Scotland	12–18(1)	12–18(2)	12–16	11–13	12–14/15	Total number of schools	%
1. In streams	25		40		100	18	27
2. In broad-ability bands	11·5		13	33·3		8	12
3. In sets	2			33·3		2	3
4. Combination of streams and sets	16	25				8	12
5. Mixed ability (1) (no more than 2 subjects setted)	5		7			3	4·5
6. Mixed ability (2) (remedial pupils separated)	27	50	33	33·3		20	30
7. Mixed ability (3) (for all subjects and pupils)	11·5	25				5	7·5
8. Other method		25	7			2	3
Unknown	2					1	1
Total number of schools	100 (44)	100 (4)	100 (15)	100 (3)	100 (1)	67	100·0

Table A.9 England and Wales

| | First-year grouping in 11-plus schools not doing a common course in first year | | | | | | | First-year groupings in 11-plus schools doing a common course in first year | | | | | | |
| | Percentage of each type of school (total numbers in brackets) | | | | | | | Percentage of each type of school (total numbers in brackets) | | | | | | |
	11–18 (1)	11–18 (2)	11–16	11–13	11–14/15	Total	%	11–18 (1)	11–18 (2)	11–16	11–13	11–14/15	Total	%
1. In streams	38	50	46	33	28·5	41	38	12	12	13	39	18	69	14
2. In broad-ability bands	34		21	67	28·5	33	30·5	38	40	31	13	26·5	167	34
3. In sets	2		4		9·5	4	4	5		9·5	4	11	30	6
4. Combination of streams and sets	7	50	21		19	14	13	13	12	19	17·5	18	74	15
5. Mixed ability (1) (no more than 2 subjects setted)	2					1	1	6	12	10·5	17·5	2	38	8
6. Mixed ability (2) (remedial pupils separated)			4		4·5	6	5·5	13	8	8	9	9	53	11
7. Mixed ability (3) (for all subjects and pupils)						0	0	5	8	3		9	24	5
8. Other method	10		4		5	8	7	7	8	6		6·5	33	7
Unknown					5	1	1						0	
Total	100 (58)	100 (2)	100 (24)	100 (3)	100 (21)	108	100·0	100 (281)	100 (25)	100 (114)	100 (23)	100 (45)	488	100·0

Table A.10 Scotland, first-year grouping in 12-plus schools doing a common course in first year

	Percentage of each type of school (total numbers in brackets)					Total number of schools	%
	12–18(1)	12–18(2)	12–16	11–13	12–14/15		
1. In streams	19		33			11	20·5
2. In broad-ability bands	11		17	100		7	13
3. In sets	3					1	2
4. Combination of streams and sets	11	25				5	9·5
5. Mixed ability (1) (no more than 2 subjects setted)	6		8·5			3	5·5
6. Mixed ability (2) (remedial pupils separated)	33	50	33			18	34
7. Mixed ability (3) (for all subjects and pupils)	14	25	8·5			5	9·5
8. Other method						2	4
Unknown	3					1	2
Total number of schools	100 (36)	100 (4)	100 (12)	100 (1)	—	53	100·0

Table A.11 Length of common course in 11/12-plus schools using one of the three forms of mixed-ability grouping in the first year (percentages of schools)

England and Wales

Length of common course	Percentage of each type of school (total numbers in brackets)					Total number of schools	%
	11–18(1)	11–18(2)	11–16	11–13	11–14/15		
Only through first year	25	29	21			24	21
Through 2nd year	26	14	50	100	56	42	36·5
Through 3rd year	45	43	25		22	42	36·5
Through 4th year	1				22	3	3
Through 5th year	3					2	1·5
Unknown		14	4			2	1·5
Total number of schools	100 (69)	100 (7)	100 (24)	100 (6)	100 (9)	115	100·0

Scotland

Length of common course	11–18(1)	11–18(2)	11–16	11–13	11–14/15	Total number of schools	%
Only through first year	63	50	80			17	65
Through 2nd year	37	50	20			9	35
Through 3rd year							
Through 4th year							
Through 5th year							
Unknown							
Total number of schools	100 (19)	100 (2)	100 (5)			26	100·0

Table A.11 – continued

Wales

	100 (9)	100 (2)	100 (2)	100 (1)	14	100·0
Only through first year	56		50		6	43
Through 2nd year	33	100	50	100	7	50
Through 3rd year	11				1	7
Through 4th year					0	
Through 5th year					0	
Unknown					0	
Total number of schools	100 (9)	100 (2)	100 (2)	100 (1)	14	100·0

Table A.12 Curriculum arrangements by type of comprehensive school (13/14 to 15/16 age group), 1968, England, Wales and Scotland*

	Percentage of each type of school (total numbers in brackets)							Total number of schools	%
	11/12–18(1)	11/12–18(2)	11/12–16	11/12–14/15	13–18	14–18	16–18		
1. Required subjects plus options	71	77	60	36·5	67	93	100	420	68·5
2. Complete course choices	12·5	13	19	9	15			84	13·5
3. Free choice from option groups	7	3	13·5	36·5	3	7		53	8·5
4. Combination of 1 and 2	3·5	7	2·0		6			20	3·5
5. Combination of 1 and 3	0·5		1·5		3			5	1
6. Combination of 2 and 3	0·5		0·5		3			4	0·5
7. Another system	4		2·5	9				19	3
8. Unknown	1		1	9	3			8	1·5
Total number of schools	100 (373)	100 (30)	100 (150)	100 (11)	100 (33)	100 (15)	100 (1)	613	100·0

* Five 11–13 schools which answered this question (perhaps because they were still 'fading out' their older pupils) and three schools which could not be identified by type are omitted.

Table A. 13 Curriculum arrangements by type of comprehensive school (13/14 to 15/16 age group), 1968, England and Wales*

	Percentage of each type of school (total numbers in brackets)							Total number of schools	%
	11–18(1)	11–18(2)	11–16	11–14/15	13–18	14–18	16–18		
1. Required subjects plus options	72	77	57	36·5	67	93	100	377	68·5
2. Complete course choice	12·5	15	21	9	15	7		80	14·5
3. Free choice from option groups	5·5	8	14	36·5	3			43	8
4. Combination of 1 and 2	3·5	8	2		6			19	3·5
5. Combination of 1 and 3	1		1		3			5	1
6. Combination of 2 and 3	1		1	3				4	0·5
7. Another system	3·5		3	9				17	3
8. Unknown	1		1	9	3			7.	1
Total no. of schools	100 (330)	100 (26)	100 (136)	100 (11)	100 (33)	100 (15)	100 (1)	552	100

* Four 11–13 schools and three schools which could not be identified by type are omitted.

Table A.14. Curriculum arrangements by type of school (13/14 to 15/16 age group), 1968, Scotland*

	Percentage of each type of school (total numbers in brackets)			Total number of schools	%
	12–18(1)	12–18(2)	12–16		
1. Required subjects plus options	65	75	86	43	70·5
2. Complete course choices	9			4	6·5
3. Free choice from option groups	19	25	7	10	16·5
4. Combination of 1 and 2	2			1	1·5
5. Combination of 1 and 3					
6. Combination of 2 and 3					
7. Another system	5			2	3·5
8. Unknown			7	1	1·5
Total number of schools	100 (43)	100 (4)	100 (14)	61	100

* There were no 13–18 or 14–18 schools in our Scottish respondents.

Table A.15 **Percentage of schools teaching, or not teaching, mathematics to all pupils in each year of the school, 1968**

England, Wales, and Scotland	*Percentage of each type of school (total numbers in brackets)*									Total number of schools	%
	11/12–18(1)	11/12–18(2)	11/12–16	11/12–13	11/12–14/15	13–18	14–18	16–18	Unknown		
Teaching maths to all in each year	49	64·5	86	97	94	59	37·5	50	33	463	63·5
Not teaching maths to all in each year	50	35·5	13	3	3	35	62·5	50	67	254	35
Unknown	1		1	3	3	6				11	1·5
Total number of schools	100 (389)	100 (31)	100 (154)	100 (29)	100 (70)	100 (34)	100 (16)	100 (2)	100 (3)	728	100

Table A.15 – continued

England and Wales

										Total number of schools	%
Teaching maths to all in each year	52	67	91	100	94	59	37·5	50	33	441	66·5
Not teaching maths to all in each year	47	33	8		3	35	62·5	50	67	209	31·5
Unknown	1		1		3	6				11	2
Total number of schools	100 (345)	100 (27)	100 (139)	100 (26)	100 (69)	100 (34)	100 (16)	100 (2)	100 (3)	661	100

Scotland

	12–18(1)	12–18(2)	12–16	11–13	12–14/15	Unknown	Total number of schools	%
Teaching maths to all in each year	25	50	40	67	100		22	33
Not teaching maths to all in each year	75	50	60	33			45	67
Unknown								
Total number of schools	100 (44)	100 (4)	100 (15)	100 (3)	100 (1)		67	100

Table A.16 Schools not teaching mathematics to all in each year; year mathematics ceases to be compulsory: 1968, England, Wales and Scotland*

Year mathematics ceases to be compulsory	Percentage of each type of school (total numbers in brackets)						Total number of schools	%
	11/12–18(1)	11/12–18(2)	11/12–16	13–18	14–18	Unknown		
In first year	1·5					100	6	2
In second year			10				2	1
In third year	11	9	30	8			30	12
In fourth year	20	9	45		10		50	20
In fifth year	3·5	9	10	17	10		13	5
No pupils excused until sixth year	63	73		75	80		147	59
Unknown	1						2	1
Total number of schools	100 (195)	100 (11)	100 (20)	100 (12)	100 (12)	100 (2)	250	100

* Two 11–14/15 schools, one 11–13 school, and one sixth-form college omitted.

Table A.17 Schools not teaching mathematics to all in each year; year mathematics ceases to be compulsory: 1968, England and Wales

Year mathematics ceases to be compulsory	Percentage of each type of school (total numbers in brackets)						Total number of schools	%
	11–18(1)	11–18(2)	11–16	13–18	14–18	Unknown		
In first year						100	2	1
In second year							0	
In third year	1			8			2	1
In fourth year	21·5	11	82		10		46	22·5
In fifth year	2·5		18	17	10		9	4
No pupils excused until sixth year	74·5	89		75	80		146	71
Unknown	0·5						1	0·5
Total number of schools	100 (162)	100 (9)	100 (11)	100 (12)	100 (10)	100 (2)	206*	100

* Two 11–14/15 schools and one sixth-form college omitted.

Table A.18 **Schools not teaching mathematics to all in each year; year mathematics ceases to be compulsory: 1968, Scotland**

Year mathematics ceases to be compulsory	Percentage of each type of school (total number in brackets)			Total number of schools	%
	12–18(1)	12–18(2)	12–16		
In first year	9		11	4	9
In second year			22	2	5
In third year	64	50	67	28	64
In fourth year	12			4	9
In fifth year	9	50		4	9
No pupils excused until sixth year	3			1	2
Unknown	3			1	2
Total number of schools	100 (33)	100 (2)	100 (9)	44*	100

* One 11–13 school omitted.

Table A.19 Comprehensive schools teaching foreign languages to 100 per cent of pupils in first year. Also teaching mathematics to all in each year of the school in Britain, 1968

England, Wales and Scotland	11/12–18(1)	11/12–18(2)	11/12–16	11/12–13	11/12–14/15	13–18	14–18	Unknown	Total number of schools
Number of schools	75	11	41	4	15	8	0	1	155
% of type*	19	36	27	14	21	24	0	33	21
England and Wales									
Number of schools	70	10	39	4	15	8	0	1	147
% of type	20	37	28	15	22	24	0	33	22
Scotland									
Number of schools	5	1	2	0	0	0	0	0	8
% of type	11	25	13	0	0	0	0	0	12

* Calculated from the total number of schools of each type given in Table 6.2, p. 72.

Table A.20 Intake of the top 20 per cent of the ability range in all-through (11/12–18) schools (type 1) in Britain, 1968

Percentage of first year intake in the top 20% of ability range	Number of schools	Average size of schools	Average % staying on	Average size of sixth forms	With competing grammar schools	Without competing grammar schools
None (0%)	1	1060	50	70	0·5	0
1% to 5%	96	1021	57	70	32	11
6% to 10%	61	953	55	65	20	10
11% to 15%	73	978	52	64	18	21
16% to 20%	97	895	54	68	18	37
21% to 25%	29	949	58	83	7	8
26% to 30%	14	876	60	98	2·5	4
					2†	8†
Total number of schools* 371	371	355	338		100 (236)‡	100 (145)‡

* Excluding eighteen schools having over 30 per cent of the top 20 per cent of ability range.
† Percentages represented by the eighteen excluded schools.
‡ Eight 11–18 schools did not answer this question.

Table A.21 **Numbers and percentages of British comprehensive schools with sixth forms having twenty pupils or less in the sixth in 1968 – related to the year in which the school received its first comprehensive intake**★

Year of first intake	No. of schools	Percentage of schools established in each year with less than 20 pupils in the sixth form in 1968	Number of schools with sixth forms established in each year
1946	0	0	6
1947	0	0	1
1948	0	0	2
1949	0	0	3
1950	0	0	3
1951	0	0	1
1952	0	0	4
1953	1	17	6
1954	0	0	8
1955	0	0	17
1956	1	7	14
1957	1	5	19
1958	3	14	21
1959	0	0	18
1960	1	11	9
1961	0	0	13
1962	1	6	17
1963	5	50	10
1964	9	24	37
1965	10	31	32
1966	9	20	44
1967	32	31	102
Total	73		387

★ Excluding forty-nine schools founded in other years or 'unknown'.

Appendix 3
Documents

1. The main survey questionnaire.
2. The second questionnaire.
3. Certificate of Secondary Education.
4. Option groups in fifth year of an upper school.
5. Social organization in two 11–18 all-through schools.
6. Analysis of the eight regions of Britain.
7. Administrative assistants' duties.

1. The Main Survey Questionnaire
British Comprehensive Schools Inquiry

1. All schools please answer Section A. Sections B and C to be answered only as indicated.

2. Unless otherwise stated all questions refer to present academic year.

3. Where a question requires a numerical answer please WRITE the figure itself in box in answer column at right of question.

4. In all other questions please RING the number of the answer that applies to your school in the answer column at right of the question.

When completed, please post this questionnaire in the envelope provided or send to British Comprehensive Schools Inquiry, 123 Portland Road, London, W11.

Case number

Section A | Mark answers in column below

---

1. Is your school classified as a comprehensive school? | Yes.......... 1
(*Ring appropriate number at right*) | No 2

---

2. What was your school's form entry last September?
(*Please write numeral in box at right*)

---

3. What is the number at present on your school's overall roll?

---

4. What age range does your school cover?
11 (or 12)–18 | 1
11 (or 12)–18 but with regular transfer of pupils from other school(s) for sixth-form or Higher Certificate work | 2
11 (or 12)–16 | 3
11–13 | 4
11–14/15 | 5
9–13 | 6
13–18 | 7
14–18 | 8
16–18 or sixth-form college | 9

---

5. From what kind of population area does your school draw the majority of its pupils?
From the middle of a large city (pop. 200,000 plus) | 1
From a town (pop. 5000 to 200,000) | 2
From a suburban area (on outskirts of town or city) | 3
From a village (pop. under 5000) or from surrounding countryside | 4

	Mark answers in column below

6. From what kind of housing does your school draw the majority of its pupils?

Mostly from council estate(s) 1

Mostly from private housing and residential area 2

From a mixture of council housing and private housing 3

From a mixture of council housing, private/residential housing and substandard housing 4

Mostly from an area of substandard housing (with or without some council housing) 5

From other (*Describe below*) 6

7. Is your school:

Non-denominational 1

Roman Catholic 2

Church of England 3

Other (*state below, if you wish*) 4

8. In what year was your school's first comprehensive intake accepted?   19 ☐

9. Is your school completely purpose built as a comprehensive school?   Yes........... 1   No........... 2

10. Is your school on two or more sites?   Yes........... 1   No........... 2

11. In what way are pupils admitted to your school?

From specific feeder schools (primary or junior secondary) 1

From a specific catchment area, defined by natural geography 2

From a specific catchment area, defined by local authority zoning arrangement 3

By a system of guided parental choice (with or without reference to catchment area or previous school attended) 4

Mark answers
in column
below

By method 1 or 2 described above for some pupils
but others admitted on basis of IQ/examination/
recommendation (i.e. because coming from outside
catchment area or because the local authority wish to
operate a policy of balanced ability intake to its
schools) 5

By other method. (*Please describe below*) 6

12. In addition to a comprehensive school, do some
pupils in your school's catchment area also have the   Yes.......... 1
choice of attending a local grammar school?   No.......... 2
(maintained, direct grant, or independent-with-
LEA-financed-places)

13. What percentage of your first-year intake do you
estimate to be in the top 20 per cent of the ability   %
range?

14. Is your school's internal organization by:
Houses 1
Lower and upper school (or lower/middle/upper) 2
By years 3
By a combination of 1 and 2 above 4
By another method (*Describe below, if you wish*) 5

15. Does the first year in your school have a common   Yes.......... 1
course or curriculum? (i.e. all pupils pursuing the
same basic subjects even if at a different pace or   No.......... 2
depth)

A. If yes, for how many years is this common
course/curriculum continued?
Only through first year 1
Through second year 2
Through third year 3
Through fourth year 4
Through fifth year 5

	Mark answers in column below

16. In what year in your school is a foreign language begun?

In the first year	 1
In the second year	 2
In the third year	 3
In the fourth year	 4
In the fifth year	 5
Not until sixth year	 6
No foreign language taught in the school	 7

17. In the year in which a foreign language is first begun, approximately what percentage of pupils in that year study a foreign language?

0–25 %	 1
25–50 %	 2
50–75 %	 3
75–90 %	 4
100 %	 5

18. Is mathematics taught to all pupils in each year in the school?

Yes........... 1
No........... 2

A. If no, at what stage does mathematics cease to be compulsory for all pupils?

Some pupils excused in first year	 1
Some pupils excused in second year	 2
Some pupils drop subject in third year	 3
Some pupils drop subject in fourth year	 4
Some pupils drop subject in fifth year	 5
No pupils excused until sixth year	 6

19. How is your first year grouped for teaching purposes?

In streams according to ability	 1
In two (or three) broad-ability bands with parallel forms	 2
In sets for most individual subjects	 3
In a combination of streams and sets	 4

In mixed-ability classes (with no more than two
subjects taught in subject ability sets) 5
In mixed-ability classes (but with remedial or very
slow pupils still taught separately) 6
In mixed-ability classes for all subjects and all pupils 7
Other method (*Please describe below*) 8

---

20. For how many years is the grouping described in
question 19 continued?
Only through first year 1
Through second year 2
Through third year 3
Through fourth year 4
Through fifth year 5
Through sixth form 6

---

21. Is your school:
Mixed sex 1
Girls only 2
Boys only 3

A. If your school is mixed sex, are there any subjects
or options open only to boys? (*Not including sports*)
Yes 1
No 2

B. If your school is mixed sex, are there any subjects
or options open only to girls? (*Not including sports*)
Yes 1
No 2

C. If yes to either A or B above, could you state
subjects below.
Open only to boys   Open only to girls

If your school does not sit for external examinations, you have completed
the questionnaire. (Thank you very much.)

Section B

22. Does your school include pupils in the 13/14–15/16   Yes.......... 1
    age group?   No.......... 2

23. What percentage of the leaving year in your school
    stayed on beyond the statutory leaving age this year?   % [   ]

24. In which of the following ways is your curriculum
    arranged for the 13/14 to 15/16 year age group?
    By a system of required subjects, plus options
    (e.g. maths and English required of all pupils, with
    five subject options to be chosen from five groups of
    subjects.)   1
    By a system of complete course choices
    (e.g. commercial, general, academic/GCE/CSE,
    pre-nursing, certificate, etc.)   2
    By a system of completely free choice of subjects from
    a number of different option groups   3
    By another system (*Describe below*)   4

25. Please put a ring around the number next to each of
    the following subjects in which at least one pupil in
    your school's O-level year was entered for GCE or
    Scottish Certificate O-level examination this year.
    (*Do not include O-levels taken in the sixth form.*)

Art.............................. 1	English literature................. 10
Technical drawing........... 2	French 11
Typing/Commerce........... 3	Chemistry.......................... 12
Latin............................. 4	Mathematics 13
Physics 5	Religious knowledge............. 14
Geography...................... 6	History.............................. 15
Woodwork/Metalwork 7	Biology............................. 16
Cooking/Domestic science 8	Music................................ 17
Needlework..................... 9	Language other than French,
	English, or Latin................. 18

26. Does your school also sit pupils for the Certificate of
    Secondary Education (CSE)?

    Yes.......... 1

    No.......... 2

A. If yes, are there any subjects in which all pupils
hoping to sit for an external examination in these
subjects now (or will from the next school year
onwards) sit for the CSE examination rather than
the GCE?

Yes.......... 1

No.......... 2

If yes again, could you write the subject(s) in this space?

If your school age range ends at O-level or CSE examination work, then
you have completed this questionnaire. (Thank you very much.)

Mark answers
in column
below

Section C

27. Has your school a sixth-form; is it a sixth-form college; or does it teach to Higher Certificate level in Scotland?

Yes.......... 1

No.......... 2

28. How many pupils are there in your sixth form (or Higher Certificate classes)?

29. Are pupils able to enter your sixth form or Higher Certificate classes without any passes at O-level? (This question to include pupils who transfer for sixth-form work from other schools.)

Yes.......... 1

No.......... 2

30. Are there pupils in your sixth form or Higher classes who are working for O-level examinations only?

Yes.......... 1

No.......... 2

31. Are there any pupils in your sixth form taking a general course only? (i.e. not studying for any external examinations.)

Yes.......... 1

No.......... 2

32. Please put a ring around the number next to each of the following subjects in which at least one pupil from your sixth form or Higher Certificate Classes was entered for a GCE A-level or Higher Certificate examination in this subject (or one of the subjects in the group named) this year.

Physics........................... 1

English literature 2

Chemistry...................... 3

Art............................... 4

Mathematics (single or double subjects) 5

Zoology, biology, or botany 6

History or geography.............. 7

A language other than English............................. 8

Technical or geometrical or engineering drawing.............. 9

Metalwork or woodwork 10

Needlework, cooking, or domestic science................. 11

Thank you very much for having completed this questionnaire.

If you have any additional comments you would like to make, please use the space below and on the back.

If your comments are continuations of answers to questions in this questionnaire, could you please put the number of the question next to your comments.

2. The Second Questionnaire
British Comprehensive Schools Inquiry

Name of school ....

Address ....

....

Name and position of person giving information can be added here:

....

A. *Foundation of the school*

1. Could you tick the method of foundation that applies to your school?
   ....Founded as a purpose-built comprehensive school.
   ....Founded as a comprehensive school in new, but not purpose-
   built, school.
   ....Founded from a school previously a grammar school.
   ....Founded from a school previously a secondary modern school.
   ....Founded from a school previously a technical school.
   ....Founded from a combination of two or more schools
   (if a combination, could you describe the schools involved?)

2. Do you have any views about the advantages or disadvantages of this particular method of educational foundation?

3. *If your school was, or is being, developed from an already existing school,* do you have any views about the major problems involved in making the transition to comprehensive status?

B. Denomination
If your school is a denominational school, do you feel there are any special problems connected with being a denominational comprehensive school in your area? Do you ever accept pupils not of your school's denomination?

C. Sex
If yours is a single-sex comprehensive school, do you feel there are any particular disadvantages (or advantages) in not being mixed? Do you feel very strongly that some comprehensive schools should always be single sex?

D. Intake and admission
1. Do you feel your school's intake reflects the distribution of ability in the pupil population in your area?............Yes............No.
   If *No*, do you think this is because your school
   ....is creamed by selective schools in the area?
   ....draws its pupils from a catchment area that is itself unrepresent-
   ative of the distribution of ability in the pupil population?
   ....finds its intake affected adversely by the operation of a particular
   LEA policy (e.g. 'free' parental choice of schools)?
   ....Another reason. (Please explain below)

2. If your school is oversubscribed, how do you decide which pupils to admit to it or which to reject?

3. What are your own views about the way pupils should be admitted to comprehensive schools in your area? For example, do you believe 'free' choice should be given to all parents or do you think some form of zoning is necessary? Would you favour regular local reviews of the boundaries of catchment areas in order to maintain as balanced an intake as possible into each comprehensive school in an area?

4. Have you or your local authority altered the admissions policy to your school since it became comprehensive – in the light of experience? If so, could you say how and why?

5. Do you have any views about the problem of top-ability pupils being 'creamed off' from comprehensive schools? What percentage of top ability do you think could be permanently creamed to selective schools and still leave comprehensive schools functioning as true comprehensives? None should be? 1? 2? 3? 4? 5? 6? 10? 20? per cent.
Does not matter how many are?

E. *The community*

1. How would you describe the neighbourhood your school serves?

2. Is your school open.........after school hours?.........in the
   evenings?.........in school holidays?
   If you have ticked any of the above, could you describe for what
   purpose the school stays open? What groups in the community use the
   school (pupils, parents, wider community)? And for what activities?

3. Do you have any views about the part a comprehensive school should
   play in its own community? Or opinions about the advantages (or
   disadvantages) of being a neighbourhood school?

4. Does your school have a.........Parent–Teachers Association,
   ....a Parents Association, ...Neither?
   If it has either a PTA or a PA, could you state briefly what percentage
   of parents belong to it.........
   How representative do you feel these parents are of the school's
   parents as a whole?.........
   What have been some of the contributions parents have made to the
   school?

5. If a parent wished to discuss his child's problem in mathematics (perhaps the parent wished to ask about changing the child from a GCE to a CSE course), to whom at the school would the parent go for discussion about this?

6. If a parent suspected his child might be truanting, to whom at the school would he go for advice on this matter?

7. Do you have any views about the part parents can play in their children's education in your school?

F. *Social organization*

1. Underline the social unit(s) into which your school is broken down: Houses   Years   Upper/Lower and/or Middle Schools. Could you describe briefly the number and size of each unit and the general way in which it is organized.

2. Please tick whether each social unit has its own:
.........separate block or house.........dining room.........assemblies
.........prefects.........own head.........PTA.........teams
.........academic lessons.........social activities
Any other individual features?

3. Do the masters or mistresses or head in charge of each social unit have fewer teaching periods than their colleagues per week?.........
   If so, how many fewer?

4. Do you also have tutor groups or form groups?.........
   If yes, could you say how they are organized (what age range, etc.)?
   Could you say what the function and activities of these groups are?
   Could you also say how long one teacher or leader stays with each group? (one year, all school life, etc.)

5. Have you made any major changes in your school's social organization or are you contemplating any? If so, could you describe these and say why you are making them.

6. Who is in charge of discipline in the school? How is this organized?

7. Do you have any special discipline problems (e.g. many pupils coming before the courts each year); or difficulty in enforcing the wearing of uniform?

8. Have you introduced, or are you thinking of introducing, any form of pupil participation in the running of the school?

G. *Architecture and accommodation*

1. What was the approximate date when your school was originally built?.........

2. Have you had any structural additions to the school since it opened as a comprehensive school (or are you planning any)?

3. *If your school is purpose built*, do you find the accommodation to be generally well planned? (Assembly hall large enough, playing fields, labs, staff accommodation and classrooms adequate, enough parking space, durable fittings, etc). Any general comments on your school's physical accommodation?

4. *If your school is not purpose built*, do you find the accommodation adequate all the same? If not, in what way not? Has the experience of starting up in a school not designed for the purpose proved to be difficult in terms of physical accommodation? Or have certain advantages emerged? Do you have very definite ideas about what you would ask for should you ever be able to move to a purpose-built school?

H. *Liaison between schools*

1. What arrangements does your school have for liaison with primary schools (or with 'lower' schools if you are part of a tiered system) for familiarizing pupils with your school before they arrive? For coordinating teaching method or curriculum? Or for passing on information about the pupils?

2. *If you are part of a tiered system (lower schools of* 11–13 *or* 11–14 *or* 11–16, *with all pupils moving on to upper schools):*
Could you describe briefly the way your system is organized, and say what you feel to be the main problems involved in this kind of scheme? How do you feel you have met these problems in your school?

3. *If you are part of a parallel system (where only some pupils transfer to the upper school, while the rest remain behind):*
Could you state what method is used to decide which pupils will transfer and which will stay? Have you any general comments on this system? Do you feel it will evolve easily into a fully comprehensive system?

4. *If your school is on two or more sites:*
Could you describe briefly how the division between the sites is made? That is, are all younger pupils on one site, older on another? Or is the division conditioned by the facilities? Could you describe how you have arranged your timetable and say how often and approximately what proportion of pupils and staff move between sites each day?

Are the disadvantages of a split-site as numerous as all the critics suggest? Or are there some advantages?

I. Staffing
1. What is your school's staff ratio?.........

2. How many department heads has your school?.........
Could you tick those subjects below which have department heads?

......English   ......History   ......Mathematics
......French   ......Geography   ......Domestic science
......Commerce   ......Chemistry   ......Foreign languages
......German   ......Welsh   ......Classics
......Other language   ......Art   ......Music
......Technical   ......Engineering   ......Science
......Religious education   ......Physical education
......Physics   ......Newsom   ......Biology
......Remedial

Any other not named above?

3. What arrangements are made in the school in respect of graded posts? (Advertised in advance for specific jobs, or given to retain good staff?)

4. Do subject department heads have regular meetings with all their departmental staff?.........
   If so, could you say how often these are held?.........
   Could you say what the purpose and function of the meetings are?

5. Does your school have staff committees?.........
   If so, could you describe their membership and the function of each committee?

6. Does your school have a staff council?.........
   If so, could you state how often it meets and what its activities are?

7. How often does the whole staff meet together?.........
   For what purpose is this?

J. Administration

1. What are the administrative functions of the deputy head?
   Of the senior master/mistress?

2. Have any members of your staff been on any administrative course
   specially designed for comprehensive schools? If so, what was felt to be
   the value? If not, would you feel it would be valuable?

3. Could you *tick* which of the following your school employs or has
   attached to it: (If more than one, *give number*. If member of staff,
   write S).
   ....Secretary   ....Librarian   ....Laboratory technician
   ....Workshop technician   ....Clerk   ....Bursar
   ....Careers master   ....Guidance counsellor
   ....Welfare officer   ....Adult education officer
   Any other?

   If you could employ one more administrative aid, or one you do not
   have, which would you feel would be most valuable to your school?

4. Who is in charge of preparing the school timetable?
   What are the problems, if any, connected with this?

5. Upon what basis is the capitation grant money allocated to different sections of the school?

6. Have you any views about the problems of administration in the comprehensive school as distinct from other secondary schools? Have you any suggestions for improving it? (e.g. appointment of an administrative officer as in some schools)

7. *If you are the head teacher*, could you estimate what percentage of your working week at school is spent in each of these three ways:

.... % of time at your desk doing necessary paper work.

.... % of time spent in teaching.

.... % of time seeing people (staff, pupils, parents, visitors).

Have you any special views about the task of a head teacher in a comprehensive school? How do you see your own role?

K. *Curriculum up to 16 years*

1. *If your school has pupils staying on until at least sixteen years of age*, could you describe how pupils are assisted in making their choice of courses or subject options in their thirteenth or fourteenth years?

2. How are these courses or options grouped on the timetable? (If you give out any descriptive or explanatory sheets to pupils, could you attach copies?)

Could you estimate what percentage of pupils in these years opt for each course or for each major group of options?

3. Do higher-ability groups have different options from lower-ability groups?......... Why is this?

4. What department is in charge of the course for those who will be leaving at the statutory leaving age? What is involved in this course?

5. Do you know offhand what percentage of all the pupils in your O-level year passed in O-level GCE in five or more subjects. Or do you have comments on your school's examination performance?

6. Do you have any views about external examinations and their place in the comprehensive school? (e.g. whether CSE should replace GCE in some subjects)

7. Do you follow up with heads of evening institutes, employers or youth employment bureaux the progress of pupils in their post-leaving years? If so, is this helpful in planning future arrangements for pupils?

8. Does your school have any special course or any unusual subject option chance for pupils up to sixteen years of age that you would like to describe?

L. *Curriculum over sixteen years*

If your school has a sixth form or teaches to Higher Certificate level:
1. Could you describe your policy for admitting pupils to the sixth form?

2. Could you describe how your sixth form is organized? And say approximately how many pupils are involved in each division, if you have divisions? (e.g. how many pupils in O-level sixth, how many in A-level work, vocational courses, etc.)

3. Could you say how pupils are assisted in choosing their sixth-form courses before they enter the sixth form? If you give written advice or information, could you attach a copy of this?

4. Is your sixth form in separate premises or does it have separate teaching rooms reserved for it? Does it have any special privileges? Or its own social council? Do you think it should be treated differently from the lower school?

5. Can pupils pursue vocationally oriented courses in your sixth form? If so, could you describe these?

6. Are any A-level courses taught by non-graduates?.........If so, which ones?

7. Have you any informal arrangements with other schools for sharing sixth-form work in any subject? If so, could you describe these arrangements?

8. In the last academic year (or two years) have you sent pupils on to university or training college or professional courses in technical college?.........If so, how many?

9. Do you keep a record of former pupils' careers in higher and further education?
   If so, what is your impression of their progress there?

10. Are you satisfied that pupils from comprehensive schools who are equally qualified as pupils from selective schools have an equal chance of being accepted by institutions of further and higher education?
    If not, why not?

11. Do you feel the comprehensive-school sixth form is in any way different from a selective-school sixth form?
    If so, what views do you have about the future development of comprehensive sixth forms in view of this difference?

M. *Teaching*

1. Has your school introduced any of the following:

   ....team teaching ....integrated curricula
   ....mixed-ability groups ....programmed learning
   ....instruction by TV ....any other experiments

   If you have ticked any of the above, could you describe briefly the nature of the experiment, the staff who have carried it out, in what subjects it has been tried, and with what result, if any?

2. One of the purposes of our book will be to help schools destined to become comprehensive during the 1970s. Have you any comments based on your experience in a comprehensive school that would be helpful for those about to undertake teaching within a comprehensive context? Have you any views on how teacher training should be conducted in future to prepare staff for working in a comprehensive school?

If you have any other views about reorganization policy locally or nationally, or if there are any special features of your own school you would like to describe, please add them here and on the other side.

3. Certificate of Secondary Education

199 schools in England and Wales in the larger survey (661 schools) stated that, in certain subjects, *all* pupils hoping to sit for an external examination in these subjects in 1968, or from 1969 onwards, sit the CSE examination rather than GCE (Questions 26, 26A).

The percentage of these 199 schools stating this to be the case for each subject listed is given below. Subjects taken by less than 5 per cent of these schools are omitted.

Subject	Percentage of the 199 schools taking it
Music	42
Secretarial/Typing	40
Woodwork	35
Metalwork	34
Needlework	34
Art	33
English	32
Domestic science	32
Technical drawing	28
Geography	27
Mathematics	27
Religious studies	26
History	24
Shorthand	22
Biology	21
French	20
Physics and chemistry	18
General science	11
Cookery	9
Social studies	6
Accounts	5

4. Option groups and number of pupils studying each subject in fifth year of Saltash School, Cornwall, 1968–9*

Option A

French (CSE)	15	German (GCE only)	12
History (Mixed)	29	Biology (GCE)	30
Biology (CSE)	21	Technical drawing (Mixed)	24
Cookery (Mixed)	17	Music (Mixed)	4

= 152

Option B

Physics (GCE)	24	Chemistry (CSE)	25
French (GCE)	17	French (CSE)	17
History (Mixed)	30	Geography (Mixed)	32
Practical science	7		

= 152

Option C

Chemistry (GCE)	14	Needlework (Mixed)	20
History (Mixed)	27	Physics (CSE)	21
Civics and Economics and Public affairs (Mixed)	23	Cookery (Mixed)	17
Technical drawing (Mixed)	22	Religious knowledge (Mixed)	8

= 152

Option D

Human biology (Mixed)	23	Rural studies (CSE)	17
Geography (Mixed)	29	Art (Mixed)	34
General science (CSE)	13	French (GCE)	16
Metalwork (Mixed)	20		

= 152

Option E

Latin (GCE)	10	Geography (Mixed)	31
Geography (Mixed)	26	Woodwork (Mixed)	16
Metalwork (Mixed)	10	General science (Mixed)	13
Cookery (Mixed)	21	Art (Mixed)	25

= 152

Mixed = Mixed ability.

* See pages 265–6.

5. Examples of social organization in large all-through schools using a 'mixture' of basic methods of social organization

(1) *Bicester School*

Lower School:	Years 1–3, about 750–800 in all. Overall responsibility vested in head of lower school.
Upper School:	Years 4–7 (8), about 500 in all. Overall responsibility vested in head of upper school, who from September 1968 has also been deputy head.
Year Groups:	About 250–300 in each year, except fifth (c. 160) and sixth form (100–200 in all). Year tutors (all men) responsible to head of school for discipline and welfare in each year group, assisted by women as deputies. Each year broken into nine or ten forms. In lower school these are also teaching units; in upper school, arbitrary groups.

(2) *Cirencester: a school in three buildings*

Houses:	Eight in number, mixed, with eight tutor-groups in each year.
Junior School:	First and second years under a Director of Junior Studies
Intermediate School:	Third, fourth, fifth years under a Director of Intermediate Studies.
Senior School:	Sixth form under a Director of Sixth Form Studies.
Building 1:	Specializing in two top years in academic courses.
Building 2:	Specializing in commercial and business courses.
Building 3:	Technical, engineering, crafts, etc.

6. Regions of Britain

Table 17.1 (p. 390) analyses the eight regions of Britain. Below is a more detailed description of the areas included in each of these regions.

The regions are (1) Scotland, (2) North of England (Cumberland, Durham, Northumberland, Westmorland, Yorkshire, Cheshire, Lancashire and Isle of Man), (3) Midlands (Derbyshire, Leicestershire, Lincolnshire, Northamptonshire, Nottinghamshire, Rutland, Herefordshire, Shropshire, Staffordshire, Warwickshire and Worcestershire), (4) Eastern (Bedfordshire, Cambridgeshire, Essex, Hertfordshire, Huntingdonshire, Norfolk, Suffolk), (5) Greater London (ILEA plus the Outer Boroughs of London), (6) South (Kent, Surrey, Sussex, Berkshire, Buckinghamshire, Hampshire, Isle of Wight, Oxfordshire), (7) South-west (Cornwall, Devon, Dorset, Gloucestershire, Somerset, Wiltshire and Scilly Isles, (8) Wales.

7. Partial list of duties that the Edinburgh 'O. and M. Review of the Administrative and Clerical Work in Secondary Schools' named for each of the three categories of administrative assistant in a large secondary school (see pp. 359–61).

Clerical:
   (a) Typing, copying, duplicating of exams, assignments, etc.
   (b) Registration and records
   (c) Careers work
   (d) Stationery and textbook supply
   (e) Publications, typing and distributing
   (f) General typing, clubs, camps, prize lists, etc., notices

Secretarial:
   (a) Mail and correspondence
   (b) Preparations of lists, schedules
   (c) Examinations, returns and schedules
   (d) Activities (visits, school events)
   (e) Organization (school meals, attendance, class lists)
   (f) Visitors, public and official, i.e., medical
   (g) Filing, record-keeping
   (h) Supplies
   (i) Finances, accounts, allowances, etc.
   (j) Janitorial overseeing

Administrative:
   (a) Supervision of clerical staff
   (b) Overseeing of domestic staff
   (c) Planning (holidays, exams, reports, school functions)
   (d) Building (repairs, installations)
   (e) Correspondence (screen all mail)
   (f) Finance
   (g) Timetable construction
   (h) Staff and pupil records
   (i) Parents, deal with in first instance and in routine matters
   (j) Pupils, deal with in first instance and in routine matters
   (k) Staff, duty rosters, absentees
   (l) Visitors to school
   (m) Functions
   (n) Supplies
   (o) Meals
   (p) Prizes and certificates
   (q) Distinguishing between executive decisions requiring guidance on educational policy and other decisions, referring former to Head, dealing with latter

Index